D0396867

Just My Soul Responding

Just My Soul Responding

*Rhythm and Blues, Black Consciousness,
and Race Relations*

Brian Ward

University of California Press

Berkeley   Los Angeles   London

University of California Press
Berkeley and Los Angeles, California

University of California Press, Ltd.
London, England

Published by arrangement with UCL Press Limited.

Library of Congress Cataloging-in-Publication Data
Ward, Brian, 1961 –
    Just my soul responding : rhythm and blues, Black consciousness,
and race relations / Brian Ward.
        p.   cm.
    Includes bibliographical references (p.   ) and index.
    ISBN 0–520–21297–5 (alk. paper). – ISBN 0–520–21298–3 (pbk. :
alk. paper)
    1. Rhythm and blues music—History and criticism.   2. Afro-
Americans—Music—History and criticism.   3. Popular music—United
States—History and criticism.   4. Afro-Americans—Civil rights.
5. Music and race.   I. Title.
ML3479.W37   1998
781.643′0973—dc21   97–39138
                                                              CIP

Printed in the United Kingdom by T.J. International Ltd, Padstow.

9   8   7   6   5   4   3   2   1

For Mum and Dad, family and friends

Contents

CONTENTS

Acknowledgements

Over the course of too many years, my work on this book has been generously supported by many institutions and individuals. The British Academy initially awarded me a Major Postgraduate Studentship for my doctoral studies, and subsequently provided a Small Personal Research Grant for further research. Other financial support came in the form of an Archie K. Davis Fellowship from the North Caroliniana Society of Chapel Hill, and a Research Grant from the Small Grants Panel of the University of Newcastle upon Tyne.

Most of the writing was done during the academic year 1995–6, when I was fortunate to hold a postdoctoral fellowship at the Carter G. Woodson Institute for Afro-American and African Studies at the University of Virginia in Charlottesville. I would like to thank all the Woodson staff (Bill Jackson, Mary Farrer, Mary Rose, Lisa Severson and Gail Shirley-Warren), and my fellow fellows (especially Scot French, Michele Mitchell, Kara Skora and Harry West) for helping to make it such an enjoyable and productive year, notwithstanding the untimely death of the Institute's founder and director, Armstead Robinson, in the autumn of 1995. It was intimidating enough to follow so many distinguished scholars into a Woodson fellowship, but I felt an added sense of responsibility knowing that I was the last to be appointed under Armstead. I hope the book justifies his faith in the project, and I will always be grateful for the opportunity he, and the Institute, gave me to complete it.

Special thanks are also due to the Department of History at the University of Newcastle upon Tyne, and to Alison Rowlands, both of whom – with a slightly worrying degree of enthusiasm – granted me leave of absence to spend the year in Virginia. Nobody suffered more for this book than Rowley and, while she may or may not consider it worth the sacrifices, it simply could not have been completed without her support and encouragement.

I should also mention those whose friendship and hospitality over the past several years have made research trips in England and the United States easier and even more enjoyable than they might otherwise have been. Julie Braithwaite, David and Jean Chalmers, Mike Daneker and Amy Kwak, Brian and Alison Dooley, Joe Hanley, Cindy Hoehler-Fatton, Ed, Jo, Steve and Karen Klinge, Steven Lawson and Nancy Hewitt, Will Kemp, Andy Lewis, Stuart Newman, Jo Peacock, Sean Schwinn, Garry and Margaret Smith and Jacob Thiessen were all splendid host(esse)s or travel companions at one – and often more than one – time and place.

In the course of my researches, I was lucky to be able to call on the services of a number of fine archivists and librarians. I am especially grateful to Andy Lineghan at the National Sound Archives in London; Clark Center of the Special Collections Department of the W.S. Hoole Library at the University of Alabama at Tuscaloosa; Cynthia Lewis, who struggles gamely against all the odds in the archives of the Martin Luther King Center for Nonviolent Social Change in Atlanta; Jim Murray and Jim Baggett at the Birmingham Public Library Archives; Randy Penninger in the Special Collections Department of the J. Murray Atkins Library at the University of North Carolina at Charlotte; Kim Meyer of the Bentley Historical Library at the University of Michigan; Jim Neal at the Albert Gore Collection at Middle Tennessee State University; and last, but not least, the Tulane twosome, Bruce Raeburn at the Hogan Jazz Archives and Rebecca Hankins at the Amistad Research Center.

Bruce and Rebecca were not only extremely helpful when I was in New Orleans, but they later also secured the photograph of Harold Battiste and the All For One executives which appears in this book. In addition to Professor Battiste, I would like to thank Ed Roseberry, Harry Belafonte and James Bond for kindly making photographs available. I am also grateful to all those individuals who consented to being interviewed for the University of Newcastle upon Tyne Oral History Collection and this project.

There are many other personal debts which I should acknowledge here. John White has encouraged my work on black music and the civil rights movement from the outset. In the earliest phase of my research, Cliff White in London was a source of much wisdom on matters pertaining to James Brown and Rhythm and Blues in general. Later, in New York, Mark Zucker introduced me to the rich delights of black vocal group culture, took me to some fine oldies record shops, and sung me the songs I could not find on disk. Richard Brewiss and Alastair McKay at Lloyds Bank kept me more or less solvent during some bruising encounters with indebtedness, tax-men, and bureaucracy in America and at home.

Ed Ayers, Brian Dooley and Steve Klinge all read more of the draft manuscript of this book than can possibly have been healthy. Tony Badger has been a good friend to me and this project for many years, and with Steven Lawson dutifully waded through an earlier incarnation when examining my

PhD dissertation. Despite his horror at my lamentable lack of attention to the Shirelles, Steven actually came back for more and has been a careful, caring and constructive critic of the entire book. Adam Fairclough also provided some very useful suggestions and observations as the manuscript neared completion. Although I did not always follow their advice – still no separate chapter on the Shirelles – I am deeply grateful to all of them for contributions which have improved the final book in countless respects.

At various times, and in various ways, Julian Bond, Dan Carter, E. Culpepper Clark, Janice Cummin, Eleanor Cunningham, Pete Daniel, Bob Friedman, Tom Hanchett, Greg Horn, Jenny Hutchinson, Richard King, John Kirk, Ludmilla Jordanova, George Lewis, Peter Ling, John Mason, Andy Nicol, Dawn Parkes, Jim Ralph, the late Anne Romaine, Alison Rowlands, Mike Sewell, Graham Taylor, Fawzia Topan, Tim Tyson and Steve Walsh also offered help, advice, ideas and information – or when that failed, shared revitalizing beers. Not for the first time I find myself acknowledging in print a special debt to Jenny Walker. Having escaped Newcastle for the United States, Jenny had the unexpected misfortune to find herself in Charlottesville while I was desparately trying to finish the book. Remarkably, she still speaks to me. At many crucial moments Jenny took time out from her own work to offer advice and assistance which have not only made the book better, but also helped to ensure that it first appeared during the twentieth century.

Finally, I should thank my commissioning editor, Steven Gerrard – who believed in the project early and treated it with professionalism, and me with much patience and understanding – and Aisling Ryan and Mina Gera-Price, who saw the book over its final hurdles and into print.

BW
Newcastle upon Tyne, January 1998

Introduction

Because we have so often chosen to reduce the extraordinary democratic explosion of the post-World War Two Black freedom movement into a manageable category called civil rights, it has been difficult, usually impossible, to know what to do in our classrooms with the powerful release of creative energy which was so central to that era of transformation. . . . A narrow "civil rights" approach may have led many persons of every age group to miss the possibility that the study of artists and their work can be enjoyable, exciting, *and* fundamental to the creation of a more just and democratic society. (Vincent Harding)[1]

Synchronicity

In the middle of March 1954, the Chords, a black six-man r&b vocal group from the Morrisania district of the Bronx, recorded their reworking of an old jailhouse song called "Sh-boom". A month later "Sh-boom" was the fourth release on the Cat label, a short-lived subsidiary of Atlantic Records. On 3 July, having climbed to number eight on *Billboard*'s national Rhythm and Blues singles chart, "Sh-boom" suddenly appeared on that journal's traditionally white best-seller list.[2]

On 17 May 1954, while "Sh-boom" was beginning to pick up the radio play and white record sales which eventually enabled it to cross over from the black market into the mainstream pop charts, the United States Supreme Court delivered its own blow to segregation in American life, declaring in the case of *Brown* vs *the Topeka Board of Education* that separate public school facilities for black and white children were inherently unequal. This landmark decision undermined the constitutional and intellectual foundations

1

upon which the system of Jim Crow apartheid in the American South had been constructed for more than half a century. While the tradition of black protest and resistance to racial oppression stretched back through the Jim Crow era into the dark heart of slavery, *Brown* marked the dawn of the modern civil rights movement and a new phase of mass black struggle in the southern states and beyond.

These two contemporaneous events provide convenient twin starting points for this book, which employs Rhythm and Blues – used here (capitalized) as a generic term encompassing most forms of post-war black popular music outside the sacred and jazz traditions: namely r&b, black rock and roll, black pop, soul, funk and disco – to illuminate changes in mass black consciousness during the peak years of civil rights and black power activities. Although conceived primarily as a contribution to the historical literature on the black freedom struggle, the book also reinterprets many of the conventional wisdoms about the history of Rhythm and Blues by setting it firmly within the context of changes in American race relations during this period.

At the very least, there was a striking historical parallel between the evolution of the black freedom struggle and the various transformations of Rhythm and Blues, as art and industry, process and product. In the decade after the Second World War, a time when blacks were still routinely, and in the South legally, excluded from equal participation in many aspects of American society and politics, r&b music was also a segregated phenomenon. Honking saxophonists like Big Jay McNeely vied for black attention with electric bluesmen like T-Bone Walker and Elmore James. Vocal groups like the Five Royales, mistresses of rhythm like Ruth Brown, and mighty shouters like Wynonie Harris were hugely popular with black audiences but had only a tiny white following. The diverse sounds and sentiments of r&b were produced by black musicians for consumption on record, or in concert, or on black-oriented radio stations, by overwhelmingly black audiences.

Although it was not the first r&b record to penetrate the white pop charts, the crossover of "Sh-boom" nonetheless signalled the start of a new era in American popular music in which young whites increasingly turned to black music and its derivatives for their entertainment. Black rock and roll, as exemplified by artists like Little Richard and Chuck Berry, emerged as a distinctive sub-category of Rhythm and Blues while the white rock and roll of Elvis Presley and Buddy Holly flourished alongside it. Both forms were bitterly attacked by white adults, who saw them as nothing less than part of a systematic assault on core, essentially white middle-class American social, sexual and racial values. In the heart of the Cold War, hostility to rock and roll thus formed part of a broader conservative and censorious cultural mesh, constructed to preserve the hegemony of these putatively all-American values from a variety of perceived "alien" threats; threats which emanated, not just from beyond the iron curtain, but also from a range of marginalized and mistrusted ethnic, racial and class groupings within America. In the South, the campaign against rock and roll became inextricably linked to the rise of organized white resistance to desegregation and black insurgency in the region.

Rock and roll, like the nascent civil rights movement, survived these challenges but was not unchanged by them. Black rock and roll was quickly supplemented, and then largely supplanted, by a "sweeter", less musically and lyrically earthy black pop style personified by the Platters, Brook Benton, and a whole host of girl groups. This black pop made calculated concessions to nominally white musical and lyrical preferences in order to maintain and extend a major black presence in the pop market which had been unimaginable half a decade earlier. As a result, these black pop stylings have usually been dismissed as an aberrant interlude between the supposedly more "authentic" black sounds of 1950s r&b and the equally "authentic" sounds of mid-1960s soul.

Here, however, the mass black preference for black pop between roughly 1956 and 1963 is treated seriously, since this pattern of creation and consumption – alongside a hitherto neglected black admiration for some of the white pop of the period – reflected a mood of rising optimism about the possibility of black integration into a genuinely equalitarian, pluralistic America. Fashioned by the early promise of the civil rights movement, this was an era in which all symbols of black access to, and acceptance in, mainstream culture were seized upon as portents of a coming new day of racial amity and black opportunity.

When this initial black optimism began to disintegrate amid persistent southern white resistance to black advance and habitual racism and systemic discrimination throughout the nation, a new pattern of black music-making and consumption emerged, grouped around the more nationalistic sounds of soul. Whereas black pop had deliberately muted some of its "blackest" musical and lyrical elements, soul was characterized by its reliance upon musical and presentational devices drawn from a gospel tradition to which blacks had an intensely proprietorial relationship. By the mid 1960s, blacks rarely bought white records anymore, although the white market for black music remained buoyant and, in the South at least, there was a good deal of interracial co-operation in the production of soul. As the decade wore on, however, blacks increasingly consumed soul and funk as a self-conscious assertion of the racial pride which was one of the most important legacies of the Movement, and a defining characteristic of the black power era.

This sort of psychological empowerment was apparent even among the majority of blacks in America who never marched, sat-in, joined voter registration drives, rioted, or took part in any of the myriad political actions which historians have usually recognized as the outward manifestations of

3

inner transformations in black consciousness during the two decades after *Brown*. This book contends that changes in black musical style and mass consumer preferences offer a useful insight into the changing sense of self, community and destiny among those blacks who rarely left the sorts of evidence, or undertook the sorts of activities, to which historians are generally most responsive. Like Lawrence Levine's groundbreaking work on black culture and consciousness during slavery and its aftermath, it is driven by the belief that "historians have tended to spend too much of their time in the company of the 'movers' and 'shakers' and too little in the universe of the mass of mankind".[3]

The book is also guided by the belief that the popular cultures of oppressed groups usually contain within them – explicitly or implicitly – a critique of the system by which those groups are oppressed, and thus actually constitute a mode of psychological resistance to their predicament. Yet this is a complicated and elusive business. As we shall see, black Rhythm and Blues, as art and commerce, politics and entertainment, was also deeply inscribed with many of the social, sexual, moral, economic and even racial values of the dominant culture. Ultimately, the story of Rhythm and Blues reveals the inadequacy of both excessive romanticizations of the counter-hegemonic power of black popular culture, and of Frankfurt School-style critiques of mass culture which reduce it to little more than a succession of profitable commodities whose main function is to reinforce and perpetuate existing configurations of social, sexual, political and economic power. In fact, Rhythm and Blues was a complex, often deeply paradoxical phenomenon which managed both to challenge and affirm the core values and assumptions of mainstream America.[4]

Three premises

In writing this study of the relationship between black protest and consciousness, race relations, and Rhythm and Blues music, I have clung to the belief that, even in this postmodern, thoroughly deconstructed world, it is still possible to write a sensible book about popular culture which is not so heavily freighted with jargon that it becomes inpenetrable to all but a cabal of cultural theorists. As part of this concern for plain speaking, the major theoretical premises which underpin the project will – mercifully – seldom intrude upon, let alone dominate, the pages which follow. It may, however, be useful to mention them briefly here.[5]

The first key assumption is that the social or political meanings of any given piece or style of commercially produced popular music are located at the intersection of a number of different, sometimes antithetical, musical, economic, legal, racial, gender, class, generational and other forces. These factors can be crudely divided into forces of production and consumption. Regarding the former, the diverse agendas of songwriters, musicians, engineers, producers, label owners, lawyers, accountants, music publishers, marketing executives, deejays, and radio programmers have all affected the writing, performance, production and distribution of Rhythm and Blues, and thus contributed to its social functions and cultural meanings.

Yet these factors of production were never the sole determinants of the multiple meanings of Rhythm and Blues. Those meanings were also constructed by individual and collective listeners, sometimes in ways which defied the initial intentions of the artists involved and transcended the economic priorities and racial conventions of the industry within which they worked. Black and white audiences could not only shape the social and political meanings of musical products by the manner of their consumption, but in choosing to consume some styles in great quantities while ignoring others, they could even encourage the industry to move Rhythm and Blues in new directions which reflected the changing moods and needs of its customers. Thus, while it would be foolish to underestimate the potential of the entertainment industry to influence consumer preferences, this book actually illustrates just how ineffectual it has generally been in initiating trends, or even sustaining existing ones, which have not had some kind of genuine social, political, or psychological relevance for their audiences.

The crucial point here, and the second major theoretical plank for the book, is that black consumers have never been passive in their consumption – not even, whisper it gently, when some of them bought white pop records and adored Elvis Presley in the late 1950s and early 1960s. Black consumers were not the perpetual victims of commercial forces, any more than were those black musicians who worked within the exploitative and often racist confines of a capitalist industry to create music which was frequently humbling in its sheer beauty and emotional power. Just as black performers often found room for personal expression and communal celebration in their music, so black fans made conscious, if never entirely "free", choices about what they wanted to buy on record, hear in concert, dance to in clubs, or listen to on the radio. Of course, it is ultimately impossible to isolate all the factors which motivated individual blacks to buy or request individual records. Yet, insofar as those choices were made in conjunction with hundreds of thousands of other blacks and conformed to broadly identifiable shifts in mass black preferences over time, they deserve to be interrogated for what they might reveal about the changing state of mass black consciousness in an era of great racial ferment and struggle.

The third key proposition in this book is that in America there exists a conventionally recognized spectrum of musical techniques and devices which ranges from nominally "black" to nominally "white" poles. The analytical perils of this sort of "black" versus "white" schema have been fully exposed by Philip Tagg, who has pointed out that none of the musical characteristics traditionally associated with black American music are actually unique to the music of black Americans, any more than the techniques considered typically "western" or "white" are unknown in African, or Asian, or African-American musics.[6]

To summarize, as befits a music which has always been inextricably linked to dance, black American styles have tended to be more rhythmically complex and forceful than most, although not all, white American music forms, some of which have also been geared to the needs of the dance. European art music has tended to be slightly more harmonically rooted than most, but not all, black American and African musical forms. There is little to choose between Africa, Asia, Europe, or any admixture of the three continents, as regards the emphasis on melody. The quest by black musicians for a distinctive, individualistic performance style, and the prioritization of emotional honesty and personal expressiveness over classical ideas of *bel canto* precision, all have their equivalents in musics around the globe, including the folk musics of the West. Certainly, in the American context, the long historical process of musical borrowings, theft, parody, influence and counter-influence across racial lines has been so complex that musicologists have frequently struggled to discern the exact provenance of particular musical techniques and sensibilities. In the main, they have struggled even less successfully to explain their conclusions to anyone not also trained as a musicologist.[7]

Despite its shortcomings, however, the idea of a black-white musical spectrum remains a useful conceptual framework simply because both black and white audiences have cognitively accepted its existence. Indeed, to a large extent black and white responses to successive popular music styles were determined by where those styles appeared to fit along this black-white spectrum. Adult white resistance to rock and roll in the 1950s depended crucially on the fact that it sounded "black", even when sung by some whites. Similarly, the special relationship between the black masses and the soul of the 1960s, or between rap and the black b-boys of the 1980s and 1990s, derived from those musics' dependence on devices which were deemed quintessentially "black".

While it can hardly be an exact science, this book plots the changing position of successive and overlapping Rhythm and Blues styles along this notional black-white musical – and lyrical – spectrum. Locating where, at any historical moment, the black masses allowed their most popular musics to settle between two musical poles which were redolent of the "nationalistic" and "assimilationist" strains within black thought, politics and culture, offers a glimpse into the state of black consciousness and the struggle for freedom and equality at that moment.

A word on sources

In order to establish which musical styles the mass of black Americans have listened to most frequently on the radio and bought most heavily on disk since the 1950s, this study relies on the black-oriented charts printed weekly since the late 1940s under various titles in the trade journal *Billboard*. The *Billboard* black singles charts indicated the relative national sales perform- ances of top Rhythm and Blues records in "black" retail outlets, while its deejay charts listed the records most frequently played by black-oriented broadcasters throughout the nation. In addition to these national black charts, *Billboard* also published regional record and deejay charts for many major black urban markets. These local charts suggest that, although import- ant regional and urban-rural variations persisted, Rhythm and Blues was a genuinely national phenomenon. All of the major stylistic transitions with which this book deals were broadly accepted by black audiences across the nation, even if they sometimes proceeded at a different pace, and with a different intensity, according to location.

This idea of a truly national, if regionally differentiated, Rhythm and Blues culture is important. Black popular culture, especially the music dis- tributed by an increasingly sophisticated recording industry and a deeply penetrative broadcast media, was a crucial factor in (re)creating some of the black unity, that incipient black nationhood, which the various mass migra- tions from the South in first half of the century had strained and sometimes ruptured. Indeed, at one level, this book tells the story of what happened after the Second World War to historically southern, often rural, forms of black music when they migrated to the cities of the North and West – and South – and were transformed, just like the people who made those same journeys, by their encounters with a multitude of new urbane, cosmopolitan influences. Perhaps most importantly, this urbanization went hand-in-hand with the steady secularization of much black culture and the transference of many social and cultural functions once associated with the church into the realm of popular culture. That process was more or less completed with the triumph of soul music and style in the 1960s.[8]

Problems and inconsistencies with the ways in which the various *Billboard* black charts have been compiled, coupled with periodic scandals about chart-rigging and payola payments to deejays and retailers in order to get particular records on the air or into store racks, inevitably raise doubts about the reliability of these listings as indices of mass black tastes. By the early 1970s, album sales were outstripping those of singles – even in the black market, which was traditionally singles-based. The widespread avail- ability of cassette recorders and the unquantifiable home-taping of official commercial releases further compromised the reliability of the black sales and airplay charts as an accurate guide to black tastes.[9]

Certainly, the presence of numerous maverick hits on the black singles charts encourages caution when claiming direct links between black consciousness, black protest and patterns of mass black record buying. There is something rather disconcerting about finding that white prankster Ray Stevens' "Harry the hairy ape" was just ending a successful run in the Rhythm and Blues charts at the moment when the 1963 March on Washington was marking the symbolic high point of the early civil rights movement. Nonetheless, even such anomalies can be instructive: in this case by calling into question the sort of racial stereotyping which routinely depicts the black audience as an unimpeachable bastion of cool style and good taste, and denies it the freedom to indulge in whimsical purchases or enjoy the occasional novelty hit.

There are other limitations on the usefulness and accuracy of the black record charts. They are not sensitive to generational differences in black tastes; they do not reveal how many blacks bought these hit records, how often they listened to them, or how frequently they tuned in to the black-oriented radio shows which played them. They do not describe which other records were also available for the black consumer to buy, or request on the radio, or programme on the jukebox – a crucial consideration if one wishes to read political and racial significances into the exercise of consumer choice. The charts themselves do not tell us anything about the actual sound or lyrical content of the records, or about the lives and concerns of those who wrote, recorded and aired them, or about the workings of the industry from which they emerged. Despite these problems, however, the black record and deejay charts remain the best available guide to shifting mass black musical tastes and, fortunately, there are other sources for much of the biographical, musical and statistical information which the charts themselves do not reveal.

Ultimately, of course, there is no substitute for hearing these recordings – the hits and the misses, the released and the canned. And if there are places in what follows where the prose turns a little more purple than might be seemly, it is only in a doomed attempt to convey just a little of the music's enormous emotional and sensual power; its bright wit, intelligence and integrity. It is not necessary to be moved by, or even to know, this music in order to understand the argument and analysis in this book. But it is important to recognize that, although rooted deep in the particularities of the African-American experience, Rhythm and Blues has demonstrated a phenomenal capacity to move hearts, minds, feet and sundry other extremities, irrespective of boundaries of race, class, gender, religion or nationality.

If the recordings themselves comprise the major primary source for understanding the development of the music, there are also some excellent journalistic accounts of Rhythm and Blues in its many incarnations, including those by Arnold Shaw, Gerri Hirshey, Peter Guralnick, and Barney Hoskyns which are essentially oral histories of aspects of Rhythm and Blues. Even better for unearthing the fascinating minutiae of Rhythm and Blues history are specialist magazines like *Yesterday's Memories, Bim Bam Boom* and *Goldmine*, which combined interviews with thoroughly researched accounts of particular styles, artists, writers and labels. Far from being superficial or unrefereed, these popular magazines have enjoyed a sort of instant peer review by experts who seldom allow an erroneous matrix number, or a case of mistaken identity among members of the horn section on a particularly obscure recording session, to pass uncorrected beyond the next issue.[10]

In addition to these secondary sources on the history of Rhythm and Blues, discographical guides to important labels and artists have made it possible to determine what records were actually being cut and issued by whom at any given time. Moreover, the fact that Rhythm and Blues was a lucrative commercial product meant that the record, radio and advertising industries were forever probing the popular music market to see who was buying and listening to what. Consequently, it is possible to place recorded and broadcast Rhythm and Blues somewhere near the heart of a contemporary black culture in which "Statistics show that on a per capita basis, blacks regardless of income buy more records and record playing equipment and spend more money for entertainment than anyone else in the major markets". Although blacks in their late teens and early twenties were usually the heaviest purchasers of records, until the mid-to-late 1970s generational and even class differences in musical tastes appear to have been much less pronounced in the black community than they were among whites.[11]

Away from the music, the vast and expanding literature on the black freedom struggle, together with the many sociological studies dealing with American race relations and the black experience, comprised another major building block for this book. It is astonishing that there has been so little real dialogue between these two adjacent fields of enquiry into the contemporary black experience – the musical and the historical/sociological. Certainly, Movement historians have generally paid scant attention to the cultural dimensions of their subject beyond a perfunctory mention of, typically, the freedom songs or, less typically, the Black Arts movement and cultural nationalism of the late 1960s and early 1970s. The notion persists that, at best, the world of popular culture somehow reflected deeper, more significant, racial struggles going on elsewhere in American society – in the schools, courtrooms and jails, on the buses, and at the polls. In fact, popular culture was one of the most important arenas in which the struggle for black equality was being waged. Popular music and popular entertainment more generally have always constituted major fields of social activity in which black and white racial identities, values and interests have been defined and tested, attacked and defended in America.

Finally, I confess that this book also resorts to the sort of traditional primary sources central to more conventional histories. The black and white press, records of congressional hearings, manuscript collections of private and public papers, the records of leading civil rights organizations, together with a wide range of oral history interviews, were all used to explore extensive, but hitherto undocumented, financial, administrative and cultural links – as well as many fissures and tensions – between formal black protest activities and the world of Rhythm and Blues during the quarter-century after *Brown*. They also made it possible to trace the evolution of contemporary black and white, official and private responses to successive Rhythm and Blues styles against the backdrop of the black freedom struggle.

Authenticity

Although they are by no means mutually exclusive, it is proven commercial success with a mass black audience, not artistic merit, which provides the main criterion for including a particular style or performer in this book. As a result, while disco gets its due, there is not much discussion of the blues, which had already declined in mass black popularity by the mid-to-late 1950s. Nor is there much discussion of modern jazz, which many fans, some activists, and even a few artists hailed as the quintessential musical expression of heightened black racial consciousness during the civil rights and black power eras. Jazz, however, had not been the leading popular music of the black masses since at least the swing of the 1930s, and even some of its foremost advocates recognized that, as Lawrence Nahs put it, it had generally failed to "extend itself into the black community" in the same way as Rhythm and Blues.[12]

It is, however, rather ironic that this book should rest on the idea that sustained commercial success offers one of the best guarantees that a particular musical style, or lyrical perspective, or performance technique, had some real social, political or psychological relevance to the black masses. The historiography of slavery is full of attempts to reconstruct antebellum black consciousness from what we know of the popular culture of the slaves, and there have been numerous attempts to use blues, jazz and gospel to illuminate the black mental and material experience in the twentieth century. Yet Rhythm and Blues, the most pervasive and demonstrably popular form of black cultural production in post-Second World War America, has rarely been used by historians of the contemporary black experience and race relations in similar ways.

There is a sense that these other, earlier black styles were somehow purer, more authentic, less haunted by the spectre of an all-powerful commercial apparatus controlling the production and consumption of the music, than Rhythm and Blues. As a result they seemed to offer clearer insights into the collective black mind. This book offers an extended critique of such views, not least on the grounds that jazz, blues and gospel were themselves cultural commodities and inextricably bound to a commercially oriented and often exploitative entertainment industry. Indeed, as Ted Vincent's pioneering account of black politics, commerce and culture in the 1920s has revealed, energetic black artists and entrepreneurs like W.C. Handy, Lester Walton and Clarence Williams were at the forefront of efforts to create a recognizably modern, national entertainment industry founded on black jazz and blues talents. Any attempt to use twentieth-century black popular music forms to probe mass black consciousness which fails to view them as simultaneously cultural commodities and creative forms of individual and communal expression is deeply suspect.[13]

Even more critically, this book takes issue with the spurious notions of "purity" and "authenticity" which pervade much of the popular and scholarly literature on black music. As black poet, journalist and jazz critic Frank Marshall Davis once explained, "Both culturally and ideologically we are a goulash of Europeans, Africans, and American Indians – with African dominant". As Davis was well aware, African-American music has always been characterized by its willingness and seemingly endless capacity to fuse many varied, often apparently incompatible, influences into a succession of styles which have reflected and articulated the changing circumstances, consciousness and aspirations of black Americans; black Americans who have themselves been differentiated by class, gender and geography, and doubly defined by their immanent American, as well as by their more distant African, heritages.[14]

Indeed, within an American culture which is, as Albert Murray neatly put it, "incontestably mulatto", black American music has been the classic dynamic hybrid. Rich, complex, restless, ceaselessly reinventing itself in the context of multiple overlapping influences and needs, black music has always been, to borrow from Imamu Amiri Baraka, a constantly "changing same".[15]

And yet the earnest quest for some sort of mythical, hermetically sealed, "real" black American music, unadulterated by white influences and untarnished by commercial considerations, continues. This is most apparent in a rather crude form of Afrocentrism which is unable to acknowledge any kind of cross-racial cultural exchange which cannot safely be reduced to simple white exploitation or expropriation of black style and creativity – of which, of course, there have been no shortage of examples. Ironically, however, this sort of racial essentialism actually undervalues the dazzling complexity and syncretic brilliance which have characterized black American musical forms in favour of a desperate search for African roots and retentions, as if these comprised the only criteria for evaluating the worth and relevance of contemporary African-American music. As black writer Eddy Harris has noted, some champions of black identity and heritage appear to "have so little pride that they will look to find their roots generations behind them in a land they never knew and in a people they are not now". "Rather than mourning the loss of some putative ancestral purity", Henry Louis Gates, Jr, has wisely counselled that some of these critics would do better to "recognize what's valuable, resilient, even cohesive in the hybrid and variegated nature of our modernity".[16]

The white audience for Rhythm and Blues and race relations

Unfortunately, many of the notions of what constitutes "real" black American music advanced by some of its more precious black and white guardians have conformed to, and inadvertently helped to perpetuate, hoary old racial stereotypes about blacks and their culture. This has important implications for another of the major themes of this book which concerns the relationship between white responses to Rhythm and Blues and changing patterns of race relations in America. At least until the late 1960s, many blacks genuinely believed that the unprecedented white enthusiasm for Rhythm and Blues reflected important changes in white racial attitudes more generally. In fact, this genuine admiration for black music did not necessarily challenge basic white racial beliefs and assumptions at all, but frequently served to reinforce them.

White enthusiasts routinely reduced the diverse sounds and lyrical perspectives of Rhythm and Blues to a set of stock characteristics which they had always – sometimes correctly, sometimes incorrectly, but invariably in deep ignorance of the realities of black life – associated with the unremittingly physical, passionate, ecstatic, emotional and, above all, sexually liberated black world of their imaginations. Paradoxically, in so doing, white fans of black music neatly fitted black music, style and culture into much the same normative categories so dear to the most bigoted opponents of black music and black equality. Of course, one must be careful not to apply a sort of racial double standard here. Blacks also enjoyed the sweet sensuality and raunchy ribaldry of much Rhythm and Blues music, and revelled in its powerful corporeal drives. Yet black audiences were less likely than their white counterparts to mistake these qualities for the totality of the black experience, or to reify them as the defining characteristics of a diverse and complex black existence.

The Rhythm and Blues industry

If some blacks hoped that a shared love of Rhythm and Blues might offer a much needed means of communication with white America, many also believed that the expansion of black-oriented radio would "bring the races closer", as one black magazine optimistically put it in 1955. While it had a mixed record in this regard, black-oriented radio nonetheless provided the main means of exposure for Rhythm and Blues recordings, which in turn comprised the major portion of its broadcast fare. Indeed, black-oriented radio and its black announcers emerged as important social institutions with considerable power and potential influence within the black community.[17]

Ultimately, however, black-oriented radio struggled to provide black Americans with much in the way of political or economic leadership, or even on occasions with accurate news coverage of their own community and its travails. In part, this was a consequence of the basic racial configuration of economic and managerial power within the industry. Whites historically owned and managed the vast majority of the radio stations and record labels which serviced the black market. Few of these individuals or corporations showed much inclination to use their power and influence to spearhead, or even assist, the black struggle for freedom and equality of opportunity.

Blacks, meanwhile, remained woefully under-represented as owners and executives within both the record and radio industries. For a while in the late 1960s and early 1970s, a concerted effort to improve the number of blacks in positions of financial power and executive influence within the world of black-oriented entertainment formed an important part of the broader black power impulse. Although those efforts, led by the National Association of Television and Radio Announcers (NATRA), met with little success, they revealed much about the complexities and ambiguities of the black power era, and permanently changed the tenor of race relations within the music and broadcasting industries.

Black capitalists, celebrities and the Movement

These efforts at black empowerment in the entertainment and media industries were undertaken in the belief that greater black representation at executive and proprietorial levels would automatically create more responsive and socially responsible services for the black community. In fact, successive generations of wealthy and relatively powerful black entrepreneurs and performers like Jesse Blayton, Sam Cooke, Berry Gordy, Kenneth Gamble and Leon Huff, were remarkably consistent in subordinating, if never eradicating, specifically racial concerns to their personal economic interests. American dreamers to the core, black capitalists and professionals invariably pursued the rewards of the mainstream, rather than settle for success in some segregated racial enclave.

While the black entrepreneurs of Rhythm and Blues were generally conservative in matters of black politics and protest, most Rhythm and Blues singers were equally cautious about publicly associating themselves with formal Movement activities – at least until the black power era, when conspicuous gestures of solidarity with the black struggle became almost obligatory for any artist hoping to maintain credibility and sales. Yet if Rhythm and Blues artists and entrepreneurs were poorly represented among the artists and celebrities who supported the Movement most vigorously in the decade or so after *Brown*, this was not entirely their fault. For reasons which revealed much about the class co-ordinates, strategic concerns, and funding arrangements of the early Movement, the major civil rights organizations failed to produce a coherent strategy for deploying Rhythm and Blues and its artists as fundraisers, morale-boosters, or publicists until the late 1960s, by which time the Movement was already rapidly disintegrating.

If, contrary to the conventional wisdom and sometimes their own retrospective assertions, few Rhythm and Blues artists actually did much to help the organized black freedom struggle before the black power era, they also – again with some notable exceptions like Nina Simone – generally eschewed explicit discussion of the black struggle in their songs until around 1967. Thereafter, soul and funk were filled with graphic descriptions of the black experience and bold celebrations of black pride and style which have much to offer anyone wishing to map the mass black mood during this era. Nevertheless, it is worth looking beyond the more obvious references to black pride, predicament and politics in black music for clues to the changing configuration of black consciousness. In particular, this book focuses on the sexual politics of Rhythm and Blues since the 1950s and the ways in which the level of sexual spite and suspicion, violence and vitriol in black music has been directly related to the changing state of black protest, and the prospects for black equality and justice.

While these lyrical matters are important, often it has not been the things which Rhythm and Blues has said, but the ways in which it has said them, which have carried the burden of its message. Certainly, there are many songs which only made sense and revealed their racial or sexual politics on the dance floor, or through their bass lines, or in the gospel grain of their towering vocals. In other words, Rhythm and Blues absorbed changes in mass black consciousness and reflected them primarily by means of certain musical devices and performance techniques, rather than in the form of neat narrative expositions.

The relative lack of artistic or political engagement with the early civil rights movement by most Rhythm and Blues singers makes rather a nonsense of casual claims that they were the philosophers or messengers of the Movement, community leaders who helped to create, shape and direct black protest in concrete ways. Harlemite Bob Moses, the mercurial organizational genius of the Student Nonviolent Coordinating Committee (SNCC) may have served as a travelling maths tutor for the juvenile black star Frankie Lymon – and as a result received his first introduction to the Jim Crow South – but there is no reason to believe that the lyrics of "Goody, goody" left more of an imprint on Moses' political philosophy than Gandhi and Camus. Even when Rhythm and Blues did deal explicitly with issues of race and the black struggle, there is nothing much to refute R. Serge Denisoff's assertion that "there is very little, if any, concrete or empirical evidence to indicate that songs *do* in fact have an independent impact upon attitudes in the political arena". Nor is there anything much in the pages that follow to challenge Denisoff's insistence that simply hearing, enjoying, or even buying a protest song about a particular cause did not necessarily make one an active supporter or participant in that cause.[18]

And yet, there was another level at which popular music did shape people's views of the world, their sense of selfhood and community, even their perceptions of right and wrong. Popular music did contribute to the ways in which ordinary people arranged their beliefs, values and priorities. As Simon Frith has written, "Pop tastes do not just derive from our socially constructed identities; they also help to define them". Ultimately, the most popular black musical styles and artists of the past 40 years have achieved their popularity precisely because they have dramatized and expressed, but also helped to shape and define, a succession of black consciousnesses. This book is about the relationship between those consciousnesses, Rhythm and Blues, and the ongoing black struggle for justice and equality in America since *Brown*, or rather, since "Sh-boom".[19]

PART ONE

Deliver me from the days of old

CHAPTER ONE

"I hear you knocking . . .": from r&b to rock and roll

I heard Bing Crosby and the Andrews Sisters and the Mills Brothers. The Charioteers, Red Foley, Hank Williams, Glenn Miller, Tex Beneke . . . I heard Sonny Til and the Orioles . . . But then on Sunday I heard *Wings Over Jordan* and the Southernaires, and the Golden Gate Quartet . . . A lot of different influences. (Ruth Brown)[1]

"Sh-boom"

When the Chords' "Sh-boom" crossed over from the Rhythm and Blues charts into the predominantly white pop charts in July 1954, it was not the first r&b record to leap that racial and commercial divide. "Gee" by the Crows – the latest in a flock of "bird" vocal groups descended from the Ravens and Orioles – had pecked at the lower reaches of the pop chart earlier that year. The Dominoes' "Sixty-minute man", Lloyd Price's "Lawdy Miss Clawdy", and Faye Adams' "Shake a hand" were among the other r&b records which had appeared on that chart earlier still. Nevertheless, LeRoi Jones (Imamu Amiri Baraka) was essentially right to claim that r&b in the early 1950s "was still an exclusive music". It was "performed almost exclusively for, and had to satisfy, a negro audience". In 1950, for example, only three of the records which made the national Rhythm and Blues charts also crossed over into the pop field: and all three – saxophonist Lynn Hope's "Tenderly", Nat King Cole's "Mona Lisa", and Billy Eckstine's "Sitting by the window" – were markedly from the slicker end of the broad r&b spectrum.[2]

Before "Sh-boom", r&b forays into the pop record charts were relatively isolated phenomena: musical mavericks which implied no major realignment of white consumer preferences. Accordingly, they elicited little response from the major record companies which were primarily geared to serving

19

the tastes of the mainstream market as they perceived and helped to define it. Capitol, Columbia, Decca, MGM, RCA and the newcomer Mercury showed little interest in leaping onto bandwagons not of their own making, especially ones they believed were of doubtful moral roadworthiness and limited commercial mileage.

After "Sh-boom", however, there was a sustained surge of r&b into the pop charts, with more than twice as many records crossing over in 1954 as in the previous year. In the months that followed "Sh-boom", Joe Turner's "Shake, rattle and roll", LaVern Baker's "Tweedlee dee", the Charms' "Hearts of stone", Five Keys' "Ling ting tong", and Spaniels' "Goodnite sweetheart goodnite" all appeared on the pop record sales lists. By the end of 1954, income from r&b records and tours constituted a $25 million branch of the industry. A growing, if still relatively small, contingent of young white fans had combined with the black audience to double the market share claimed by r&b from 5 per cent to 10 per cent of the total industry gross.[3]

And this was just the beginning. By the end of 1955, rock and roll, as performed and consumed by both blacks and whites, had emerged as a distinct musical style, rather than simply a euphemism for the black r&b which spawned it and with which it continued to overlap. In late 1956, *Billboard* reported that 25 of 125 pop chart entries during the first 50 weeks of the year had been black r&b/rock and roll records. Many others were either white cover versions of black songs or by white artists performing in styles obviously derived from black music. In 1957, the independent record companies responsible for recording much of this material accounted for an astonishing 76 per cent of the year's hit singles. In 1958 more than 90 per cent of the 155 records appearing on the national Rhythm and Blues charts during the year also appeared on the pop charts.[4]

Taken together, the rise of these Independents and the unprecedented popularity of black and black-derived styles with young white audiences threatened the traditional distribution of power and influence within the music industry. According to Charles Hamm, "At no other point in the two-hundred year history of popular song in America had there been such a drastic and dramatic change in such a brief period of time". The powerful alliance of Tin Pan Alley music publishing houses, professional songwriters, network radio stations and major recording labels, which had long dominated the popular music business, was challenged and for a while bested by a new breed of song publishers, black-oriented radio stations, distributors, and record labels.[5]

The reactions of the recording and broadcasting industries to the initial breakthrough of r&b and the hostile responses of sections of adult white America to that phenomenon were closely linked. Together, these reactions reflected the dominant racial assumptions and beliefs of the mid-to-late 1950s, just as they were coming under pressure from the same political, economic, demographic and cultural forces which shaped the modern civil rights movement. Coupled with important developments taking place within the black community, these interlocking commercial and public reactions helped to account for many of the key musical and lyrical changes in r&b as sustained success in the mainstream became a realistic possibility for some of its black practitioners.

Majors and Independents

In *The sound of the city*, Charlie Gillett explained the breakthrough of r&b primarily in terms of a consumer revolution on the part of an increasingly affluent white teen audience and a successful, guerilla-type action waged by small, often under-financed, but endlessly resourceful independent record labels against the major recording companies and established song publishing firms. In most subsequent accounts, Independents have also appeared as the heroes of the piece: feisty outsiders who challenged vested interests within the industry, nobly championed the neglected music of black America, and finally made it available to the mainstream market. For many commentators, this amounted to nothing less than a spirited assault on the hegemony of the middle-class white values enshrined in the popular music of Perry Como and June Valli. This conventional wisdom requires finessing, however, both in order to appreciate important differences among the Independents, and to contextualize them within – albeit often at the margins of – the American entertainment industry, where they were caught in much the same web of social expectations, racial assumptions and commercial aspirations as the Majors.[6]

Most of the Independents involved in the production of r&b had emerged in the mid 1940s, after the Majors, responding to the enforced economies of the Depression and then war, had curtailed minority ranges like black music and concentrated on the more lucrative mass market for white popular music. After the Second World War, however, a disparate group of entrepreneurs moved into the market niches created by these cutbacks, encouraged by the fact that the cost of entry into the business of record production remained relatively low. A thousand dollars was enough to hire a studio (typically at $50 an hour), book musicians, pay American Federation of Musicians (AFM) dues, have a master tape prepared, and press 500 singles at 11 cents a shot.[7]

Although routinely depicted as outsiders, at the heart of the new Independents were men and a few women – like the black ladies Lillian Claiborne, who founded the DC label in Washington, Deborah Chessler, who mistress-minded the Orioles' flight from a Baltimore street corner to national celebrity, and Vivian Carter, co-owner of Vee Jay in Chicago – who had been in and around the music business for years. Genuine industry newcomers, like Ahmet Ertegun, the wealthy, jazz-loving son of a Turkish diplomat who founded Atlantic Records, were rare. And even Ertegun had some experience of booking black acts to perform at the Turkish Embassy in Washington and at the city's Jewish Center, which provided a rare opportunity for integrated entertainment at a time of widespread segregation in the nation's capital. When Ertegun formed Atlantic in 1947, he did so in partnership with Herb Abramson, a talent scout and producer for National Records who had already run his own label, Jubilee, before selling his share to partner Jerry Blaine. Moreover, when Abramson was drafted into the military in 1953, Ertegun brought in another music business insider, ex-*Billboard* staff-writer Jerry Wexler.[8]

Like Abramson and Wexler, most of the key figures in the Independents had industry backgrounds in record retailing, nightclub ownership, music journalism, broadcasting, songwriting, arranging, and record manufacturing. A good many began their careers as jukebox operators. The half-million jukeboxes in place in the mid 1950s devoured between a quarter and a third of all the disks produced in America, but they also acted as "free" advertising for individual records, thereby stimulating further domestic sales. Moreover, as the number of plays each jukebox selection received was regularly checked, they provided operators and record companies with a peculiarly accurate insight into changing consumer preferences in different locations and among different sections of American society.[9]

Thus it was as industry veterans, as insiders, that these Independent impresarios were able to spot the potentially lucrative gaps in the services provided by the Majors. Art Rupe, who founded Specialty in Los Angeles in 1945, having initially dubbed his label Jukebox, recognized the symbiotic relationship between the Independents and the rest of the industry. "I looked for an area neglected by the majors and in essence took the crumbs off the table of the record industry".[10]

Prior to setting up Specialty – later home to r&b stars like Jimmy Liggins and Little Richard – Rupe had worked for Thomas Robinson's tiny black-owned Atlas label in Los Angeles. Nevertheless, relatively few of the more than 2,000 labels in operation by the late 1950s, as many as 600 of which had some involvement in r&b, were black-owned. Of those which were, fewer still – Class, Dootone, Fortune, Peacock and Vee Jay – were really national, or particularly durable, operations.[11]

Black music, whether r&b, gospel or jazz, was actually only one of many minority markets explored by the Independents in the decade after the Second World War. While some of the white entrepreneurs, writers and producers involved, like Ertegun, Wexler and Ralph Bass at King-Federal in Cincinnati, had a genuine interest in, admiration for, and understanding of black music, most cared little if the product was r&b or rhumba, as long as it sold. And even Atlantic in its early days was happy enough to release all manner of product, from poetry and children's stories to Shakespeare plays, to try to turn a dollar. Many Independents issued a similarly eclectic mixture of minority styles and novelty records in their search for an untapped market niche. Ike and Bess Besman's Apollo label grew out of their New York record shop and cut some fine r&b by the likes of the Four Vagabonds and Larks. But Apollo also released calypso, Jewish, Hawaiian, gypsy, polka and country records, while ex-record manufacturer Lew Chudd initially aimed his Los Angeles-based Imperial label, whose r&b catalogue subsequently included Amos Milburn and Fats Domino, at the Mexican market.[12]

Such opportunism was not restricted to white-owned companies. Dootsie Williams' Dootone label, responsible for many of the finest west coast vocal group recordings of the mid-to-late 1950s, made much of its early profit from comedy albums and party singalong records. Jack and Devora Brown's Fortune label, which set up its studio in the garage behind the Browns' Detroit record shop, was one of several "r&b" Independents, including King-Federal, Imperial, Super Disc, Gilt-Edge and National, which maintained hillbilly or country music lines.

Another consequence of the simplistic Majors/Independents distinction in writings on r&b has been a tendency to use the collective term "Independents" to describe a diverse range of recording companies, from relatively stable, nationally distributed labels like Atlantic, Chess, Imperial and King, to tiny, economically vulnerable, and often short-lived, community-based labels like Angeltone in Los Angeles or Celeste in New York. Such casual usage suggests an entirely spurious homogeneity regarding both the sound and business operations of these labels.

Large Independents tended to develop discernible house styles and exert a more consistent musical influence on their performers than small labels, which often recorded local solo or group heroes in a more or less documentary style. To develop and maintain a distinctive label style required a fixed team of writers and arrangers with a broadly shared musical vision and, ideally, a resident house band. At the very least, it required the financial wherewithal to send artists to record with musicians, arrangers and producers who worked together regularly. Imperial and Specialty, for example, hired Cosimo Matassa's New Orleans studio and let Fats Domino and Little Richard record there with the cream of the Crescent City's session players, usually under the musical direction of Dave Bartholomew and Bumps Blackwell respectively.

At Atlantic, an in-house writing-arranging production team of Jesse Stone, Rudolph Toombs, Jerry Wexler, Ahmet Ertegun and later Ray Ellis concocted "something like the authentic blues, but cleaner, less rough and perforce more sophisticated", while a semi-permanent studio band built around the formidable talents of ex-jazzmen Mickey Baker, Willis Jackson, Panama Francis, Sam Taylor and Van Walls provided the complementary instrumental touch. The extraordinary engineering skills of Tom Dowd ensured that the music produced by the likes of the Drifters, Joe Turner and Ruth Brown was committed to disk with astonishing clarity. Moreover, while many Independents preferred to pursue hit songs, racking up a succession of one-off hits with transient artists signed to short-term contracts, Atlantic preferred to recruit performers it felt could sustain long-term careers. Many Atlantic artists stayed with the label for years, which again promoted a certain aural consistency when contrasted with the revolving-door policy of other labels.[13]

Although the Brooklyn-based Onyx label, established in 1956 by Jerry Winston – a typical white r&b entrepreneur who had previously tried his luck with a specialist mambo label called Mardi Gras – regularly featured Sammy Lowe and his Orchestra, such neighbourhood companies rarely enjoyed the luxury of a resident band. Often they simply recruited available local musicians on an *ad hoc* basis to make a session in a hired studio. Moreover, the material they recorded was rarely conceived in terms of a full orchestration. For all their undoubted charm and emotional integrity, many of the vocal group recordings of the 1950s simply sounded like the work of street-corner groups who were used to performing a cappella, or with a single guitarist or pianist, onto which a full instrumental arrangement was sometimes crudely grafted.[14]

By the early 1950s, the seven largest r&b Independents (Aladdin, Atlantic, Chess, King, Modern, Savoy and Specialty) accounted for almost two-thirds of the best selling black singles, and regularly notched up sales of over 100,000, and sometimes many more, to what remained principally a black market. By contrast, the biggest seller in the history of a typical local label like Celeste in the Williamsburg district of Brooklyn was the Mellows' "Sweet Lorraine" which sold barely 2,000 copies. The label's usual expectations can be better gauged by the fact that it pressed only 200 copies of the Minors' "Jerry", half of those as free promotional copies for deejays. Some locally oriented labels did enjoy sporadic national success. "Stranded in the jungle" by the Jayhawks on Flash sold over 120,000 copies in 1956, but sales were usually much more modest. The Jayhawks' previous release, "Counting my teardrops", sold just 987 copies and the label's day-to-day operations were primarily geared to servicing black Los Angeles.[15]

Throughout the decade, most of the national hits on neighbourhood labels were the result of distribution deals with bigger labels, or of selling the rights to a recording outright. In 1958, Al Silver – the owner of the Herald-Ember labels – bought the Silhouettes' hugely popular crossover hit "Get a job" from black deejay Kae Williams' nascent Junior label. Williams simply could not exploit the full potential of a record which was selling rapidly in the group's native Philadelphia. Silver also bought the Five Satins' million-selling "In the still of the night" from Marty Cougle's Hartford-based Standord, because Cougle "was going to lose the hit value of the record because he didn't have the money to press thousands of copies". Indeed, for many under-financed local Independents, success in the form of an unexpectedly large regional or national hit could be fatal, since they usually had to empty the company coffers to pay in advance for mass pressings and then endure an agonizing wait until – hopefully – the revenue from sales came in.[16]

Clearly, then, the r&b recording scene had its own centres of power and influence and some Independents were rather more independent than others. Small companies were often dependent on the production facilities provided either by the Majors, who sometimes hired out their excess pressing capacity, or by the larger Independents, some of whom had their own plants. By the early 1950s, however, a new range of specialized firms had emerged, sometimes from the ranks of the Independents themselves, to handle the production and distribution needs of r&b labels.

One of the first of these independent record-pressing facilities was run by Bob Geddins, a black record store owner and aspiring record producer-songwriter based in Oakland, California. For about a decade after 1946, the bulk of the Bay Area's r&b disks were pressed at Geddins' plant. Together with other new manufacturing firms, like Allied and RGR, Geddins helped free west coast labels like Swingtime, Modern, Aladdin and Imperial from their dependence on the Majors' pressing plants. This proved important as the mass market for r&b and its rock and roll derivative expanded, since the Majors often withheld access to their facilities, or charged extortionate rates, in what was but one of many efforts to undermine their upstart competitors.[17]

In Cincinnati, King-Federal boss Syd Nathan also set up a pressing company, Royal Plastics, as part of an eager quest for genuine organizational independence which also prompted him to create his own recording studio, publishing company and even a photographic laboratory to produce record labels and album covers. Nathan also established an independent distribution network for the marketing and placement of King-Federal products throughout the nation. Other independent distribution firms, such as Jerry Blaine's Cosnat, George and Ernest Leaner's black-owned United in Chicago, Pan-American in Detroit, Davis Sales in Denver and a similar operation run by Jack Gutshall and Leon and Googie René on the west coast, were also crucial in the formation of a truly national r&b scene. By 1954, many Independents had abandoned the crude "trunk of a car and Pullman porter" distribution methods of their early days to become a sophisticated division of the industry, with a small army of legendary sales and promotional men, like Morty Craft, Hy Weiss, Irving Katz and Dickie Kline, scouring the country, using means both fair and foul to get their products onto the airwaves, into the jukeboxes and right to the front of retailers' record racks.[18]

Perhaps the most important of these distributors was the Chicago-based Central Record Sales Company, which handled recordings by Atlantic, Imperial, Specialty and many other Independents. In 1954, Central introduced a daring 100 per cent exchange deal which allowed retailers to order disks without having to forfeit the usual 5 per cent privilege fee if they could not sell them. This was of considerable importance in encouraging the breakout of r&b, since it persuaded cautious white retailers to stock what they considered risky novelty or minority lines like r&b, for which there appeared to be an increasing, if still puzzling, demand among young whites.[19]

While the crude distinction between Majors and Independents exaggerates the nature of the latters' "independence" from the dominant forces in the record industry and obscures differences among them, it also underestimates the steady interest of the Majors in the black market. Nelson George, for example, has voiced the conventional wisdom about the Majors' reaction to the black r&b singers, shouters, vocal groups and honking saxophonists who flourished after the Second World War: "[Louis] Jordan, [Nat King] Cole, and the big bands recorded for large, nationally distributed companies such as Decca, Victor, and Capitol. However, all the new artists were signed to independent labels that began appearing during the war and would proliferate in the next seven years".[20]

George's "all" is simply incorrect and most commentators have ignored, or grossly underestimated, the amount of r&b recorded for the major labels and their subsidiaries in the decade after the Second World War. It is true that racial prejudices and simple market considerations combined to make the Majors' presence far less pronounced in r&b than in pop, or in the country field, where they accounted for around 95 per cent of the best selling disks in the early 1950s. Nevertheless, as Table 1.1 shows, many r&b acts did record on major labels for an overwhelmingly black audience, long before the crossover of r&b and the advent of rock and roll. In 1947, four of the five most successful labels in terms of r&b sales were Majors, while as late as 1951 RCA and Decca were still among the top ten purveyors of black music. For the period 1955 to 1959, Mercury, Capitol, Decca and the recently formed ABC-Paramount were all among the ten most successful producers of black chart hits.[21]

With the dollar value of the black consumer market rising from around $3,000 million in 1940 to $11,000 million a decade later and $20,000 million by 1961, it would have been surprising if the market-conscious Majors had entirely neglected black popular music. Although the annual median income of non-white families was still only 55 per cent that of white families at the end of the 1950s, it was actually rising more rapidly, increasing more than fourfold between 1940 and 1957, and nearly doubling during the 1950s. Moreover, while reliable figures on black teen income during the decade are scarce, it appears to have been broadly comparable with white teen income, and occasionally in excess of it. Paradoxically, widespread poverty and cruelly limited educational opportunities meant that black teens were more likely than their white counterparts to seek paid work, while the traditionally low wages foisted on all black workers made them attractive propositions for menial jobs. Partly as a consequence of this greater level of employment, by the late 1950s median black teen income in New York State was actually 131 per cent that of the equivalent white cohort. Of course, much of this income was dedicated to buying the bare necessities of life, but estimates suggest that blacks spent much the same proportion of their earnings (3.5 per cent) on recreation as more affluent whites (4.1 per cent).[22]

Table 1.1 Black r&b acts recording for major labels and their subsidiaries before 1956

Capitol:
Annisteen Allen, Joe Alexander, Blue Lu Barker, Tiny Brown, Esquerita, Five Keys, Julia Lee, Nellie Lutcher, Nuggets, Sugar Chile Robinson, T-Bone Walker.

Columbia (includes the Okeh and Epic subsidiaries):
LaVern Baker (as Bea Baker), Joyce Bryant, Charioteers, Arnett Cobb, Paul Gayten, Roy Hamilton, Screamin' Jay Hawkins, Annie Laurie, Big Maybelle, Chris Powell, Red Saunders, Shufflers, Sugartones, Treniers, Titus Turner, Velvetones, Chuck Willis.

Decca:
Barons, Dave Bartholomew, Blenders, Cabineers, Chorals, Four Knights (also recorded for Capitol), Jackson Sisters, Louis Jordan, Marie Knight, Mello-Tones, Tommy Ridgley, Shadows, Singing Wanderers, Skylarks, Tangiers.

Mercury (includes the 8000 series and Wing subsidiary):
Wini Brown and her Boyfriends, Empires, Four Blue Jackets, Four Plaid Throats, Steve Gibson and the Red Caps, Helen Humes, Joe Huston, Ivories, Buddy Johnson (also recorded for Decca), Penguins, Platters, Ravens (also recorded for Columbia and Okeh), Bill Samuels and the Cats 'n' Jammer 3, Eddie "Cleanhead" Vinson, Dinah Washington.

MGM (includes the 5500 series and the Orbit subsidiary):
Blentones, Carter Rays, Crickets, Five Satins, Bill Gaither, Harptones, Hide-A-Ways, Ivory Joe Hunter, Marie and the Decors, Normanaires, Preludes, Ramblers, Sam "The man" Taylor, Twilighters.

RCA (includes the Bluebird, X and Groove subsidiaries):
Avalons, LaVern Baker (as Little Miss Sharecropper), Blow Top Lynn, Billy Bunn and his Buddies, Arthur Crudup, Deep River Boys, Du-Droppers, El Vinos, Four Tunes, Four Vagabonds, Erskine Hawkins, Heartbreakers, Illinois Jacquet, Etta Jones, Little Richard (1951–2), Mickey and Sylvia, Mr Sad Head, Nitecaps, Robins, Sycamores, Tampa Red, Sonny Boy Williamson.

In short, there was a relatively buoyant black consumer market, with particular areas of strength and growth among the teens and young adults most likely to buy records. The Majors, just like the Independents, sought to exploit this market. The crucial point, in terms of the configuration of racial consciousness in mid-century America, is that it never occurred to any of those companies that – the odd maverick hit notwithstanding – they could consistently sell anything resembling r&b to more than a tiny, fleeting, and economically inconsequential audience of whites.

The marginalization and oppression of peoples of African descent in America has always been more than a purely legal, political, economic and social phenomenon. It has involved an integrated system of thought, categorization and action which constitutes the fundamental grammar of American racism. As part of that system, the recording and broadcasting industries did not merely reflect the prevailing racial assumptions of the 1950s, they internalized them, functioned according to their dictates and, in so doing, helped to perpetuate them. Racial conventions permeated the organization and structure of the music industry at every level. The very existence of separate "Race" and, from 17 June 1949, "Rhythm and Blues" charts for black popular music, symbolized the routine segregation of blacks in American society as much as the segregated schools and separate drinking fountains of the South, or the restrictive housing covenants and discriminatory hiring practices of the North.

In accordance with these racial customs, the Majors carefully kept r&b off their white popular music labels. They set up special series or subsidiaries, like Mercury's Wing and 8000 series, Columbia's Okeh label, and RCA's Groove, to cater to the segregated black market, distributing the disks to a different range of retailers and radio broadcasters from those handling white pop. Racial assumptions even shaped the actual sound and content of the material deemed appropriate for the Majors' black-oriented subsidiaries. Black artists recording for the black market were usually expected to conform to preconceptions about black style which held that r&b should never be anything other than raw, relentlessly uptempo, sexually risqué or riotously funny. Indeed, in the early 1950s, RCA actually rejected the black vocal group the Four Fellows for sounding too polished, professional and therefore too "white" to attract a black audience. This reductionist view denied the diversity of both r&b and black consumer preferences, and instead substituted the sort of racial stereotypes which continue to haunt and stultify discussions of black music nearly half a century later.[23]

Whenever artists of either race challenged these aural and, by extension, social conventions, special arrangements were made to alert the public. For example, when a Major recorded more pop-oriented black performers, hoping to emulate the exceptional crossover success of black pop acts like Nat King Cole and the Ink Spots, they often appeared on the company's popular label and not its r&b imprint. Thus, pop-oriented black vocal groups like the Charioteers and Velvetones appeared on Columbia, rather than its r&b subsidiary Okeh. In 1955, the Platters' "Only you" was originally released on Mercury's "purple" race label; only after mounting interest beyond the traditional black market was this melodramatic masterpiece transferred to the company's "black" pop label.[24]

Conversely, when white Frankie Laine fused a country-pop sensibility with the bellow of black shouters like Amos Milburn, he found his first home at the r&b label Exclusive, before moving on to Mercury and a succession of major hits like "That's my desire" which charted on both sides of the racial divide. Similarly, when the theatrically lachrymose white crooner, Johnny Ray, "the prince of wails", borrowed some of the raw emotionalism of black music, his records, which included the number one Rhythm and Blues hit "Cry", were released on Okeh rather than Columbia.[25]

The Independents, with their more extensive and intimate links to the core black market through local black performers, deejays, club owners,

28

record retailers and jukebox operators, were generally more responsive and sensitive than the Majors to the diverse tastes of their primary black audience. Nevertheless, it is clear that the Independents, large and small alike, were hardly immune from the racial assumptions which circumscribed the Majors' policy towards the categorization, production and marketing of black music.

This was certainly true of Atlantic. Just as RCA had rejected the Four Fellows for sounding too white for the black market, so Atlantic felt obliged to transform the Clovers from the smooth, pop-oriented balladeers who cut "Yes, sir, that's my baby" for Eddie Heller's Rainbow Records, to the streetwise roisterers of "Your cash ain't nothin' but trash", in an attempt to target the national black audience more effectively. A similar, if less dramatic, process was inflicted on the Mellotones, a slick black group from East Baltimore whose idols included staid white harmonizers like the Ames Brothers. The Mellotones duly emerged, slightly rougher and bluesier around the vocal edges, as the Cardinals.[26]

Like the Majors, Atlantic and the other Independents were party to the segregated mentality which characterized American racial consciousness in the early 1950s. This mentality continued to structure the operation of the music business even after sales ledgers and account books offered powerful evidence that the old compartmentalization of musical tastes along racial lines was vanishing fast. "We were making black records, with black musicians and black singers for black buyers. It never occurred to us in the beginning that there were crossover possibilities", Jerry Wexler admitted. He did, however, notice that some young white southerners had picked up on the music. "Many people believe that rhythm and blues records sold exclusively to a Negro market up until that time (1953–4). This is not true. 'Drinkin' wine spo-dee-o-dee', for example, 'went white' throughout the South, as did many Ruth Brown and Clovers records in both North and South prior to this", Wexler recalled.[27]

Black-oriented radio and black consciousness

Most young southern whites first heard black music on jukeboxes or on one of the growing number of black-oriented radio stations in the region. In Lubbock, Texas, Niki Sullivan, Buddy Holly's third cousin and later a member of the Crickets, noted how the music defied the routine segregation of southern culture. "I started listening to rhythm and blues in high school. I can remember in my junior year, the Midnighters were very popular – where I ate lunch they had those records on the jukebox, like 'Work with me, Annie'. And we listened to KWKH in Shreveport, Louisiana, and XERF in Del Rio and by 1954 or so, there were radio shows on KSEL".[28]

Black-oriented radio was a vital cog in the commercial machinery and creative process which enabled r&b to establish itself at the heart of a national black popular music culture and then cut across customary and, in the South, legal barriers between the races to make that music available to young whites. In the decade or so after the Second World War, the broadcasts of black deejays like Spider Burks on KXLW-St Louis, Vernon Chambers on KCOH-Houston, Bill Spence on WNLA-Indianola, Mississippi, and Chuck Richards on WBAL-Baltimore, together with those of their white counterparts, Dewey Phillips on WHBQ-Memphis, Jay Perry on WEAM-Washington DC, and Alan Freed on WERE-Cleveland and later WINS-New York, made possible the chaotic black-white collisions, fusions, thefts and homages which characterized the new musical hybrid: rock and roll. Consequently, these deejays have justly been hailed as the midwives of the whole rock and roll tradition, although in the course of such celebrations they have frequently been credited with an unrealistic degree of economic independence, artistic freedom and political power.[29]

The development of black-oriented radio after the Second World War closely paralleled and frequently intersected with the rise of the r&b Independents. By the late 1940s, when white-owned WDIA in Memphis and WOOK in Washington DC adopted the first all-black programming formats, the three main characteristics of black radio – aside from the preponderance of black records on air – were already apparent. The first was the flamboyance and vernacular virtuosity of those at the microphone. Black-oriented radio was dominated by men and women, black and white, whose personalities were as vital to their success as the records they spun. The second characteristic was the brokerage system of broadcast financing, whereby deejays bought airtime from station management and were then personally responsible for re-selling portions of that time to sponsors and advertisers to make money. Variations on this brokerage system, which left deejays with considerable latitude in what they chose to play and say on air, remained the mainstay of black radio until the early 1960s.

The third key characteristic of black-oriented radio was that few of the station owners, managers, or even technical staff, were black. "We had heap paleface men", recalled the pioneering black Chicago deejay Al Benson. In 1949, Jesse Blayton, a wealthy Atlanta accountant and financier, became the first black to own a station in the United States when he purchased WERD from some white business associates for $50,000. Yet by 1960 there were still only four black-owned radio stations in the nation (WEUP-Birmingham, WCHB-Inkster, KPRS-Kansas City and WERD) and at most 14 a decade later.[30]

Three major factors shaped the dramatic growth of black-oriented radio during the decade after the Second World War. One was the decline of network radio, which had dominated American broadcasting since the 1920s. Between 1947 and 1955 the proportion of America's AM radio stations which were network affiliates fell from 97 per cent to just 30 per cent. Moreover, by the early 1950s drama shows, not their increasingly jaded musical offerings, were the networks' most successful fare.[31]

The second factor was the rapid growth of television, which lured away much of the traditional adult white radio audience. In 1945 there were six commercial television stations in the United States; a decade later there were 411. By turns desperate and daring, radio programmers in the late 1940s and early 1950s began to explore the minority markets which television, with its overwhelming emphasis on middle-class adult white audiences, did not serve at all and mainstream radio served poorly. Just as the independent recording companies of the era exploited the gaps in the services provided by the Majors, so a new breed of radio stations emerged in concert with those Independents, often heavily dependent on their disks for cheap programming, to cater to the more than 90 per cent of American blacks who owned radios by the late 1950s. Again like their Independent record label cousins, these ambitious radio entrepreneurs were not only concerned with targeting black audiences: they also sought out other neglected sections of the market. KOWL-Santa Monica, jointly owned by cowboy singing star Gene Autry and an Irish impresario named Arthur Kroghan, targeted black listeners but also "had programs beamed toward the large Mexican American segment of the Southern California populace, and foreign language shows in Jewish (sic), in Japanese, Serbian, and half a dozen other tongues".[32]

The third major factor in the growth of black-oriented radio was the discovery of an expanding and increasingly concentrated black consumer market. The greater urbanization of the black community after the War meant that even small wattage stations in key locations could reach vast numbers of black listeners. Moreover, the average income of those blacks rose by 192 per cent between 1940 and 1953, when 90 per cent of blacks were in some form of paid employment, and the total value of the black consumer market was $15,000 million. Local and national, often white, advertisers increased their support of black-oriented stations in line with this burgeoning purchasing power and by 1961 were spending $9 million annually on black-oriented radio advertisements. Whereas in 1954 corporate advertisers accounted for barely 5 per cent of the revenue on a major urban black-oriented station like WLIB-New York, by 1964 the proportion was 85 per cent.[33]

The history of WDIA-Memphis revealed how these essentially economic motivations on the part of white businessmen could provide a showcase for black music, limited employment for blacks, and a cultural institution which resonated to the changing moods of the black community. The station opened on 7 June 1947 and endured a disastrous year trying to penetrate the white Memphis pop radio market. In response, white co-owners John Pepper, who in the 1930s had successfully utilized black programming on his Mississippi station, WJPR-Greenville, and Bert Ferguson, who had witnessed

31

the success of black-oriented shows during a stint as programme director at WHBQ-Memphis, gradually switched WDIA to an all-black format. On 25 October 1948, Nat D. Williams, an educator, journalist and Beale Street nightclub compere who had previously served as an announcer on WHBQ, became the first black deejay on WDIA, which in turn became the first radio station in the country to be programmed entirely for the black community.[34]

Blacks bought an estimated 40 per cent of the merchandise sold in Memphis. The success of WDIA depended on its ability to attract a large and prosperous enough proportion of those 150,000 blacks to convince Memphis businesses to advertise on the station. As *Variety* pointed out, the use of black deejays and the programming of r&b immediately helped to rally this segregated black audience into a solid block of potential customers.

> The Negro disk jockey has a much stronger standing in the colored community, particularly in the South, than the ofay platter pilots have generally due to the social situation. This influence over their listeners is proportionately stronger and that explains why their shows are solid commercial stanzas . . . Their accent on R and B platters stems from that music's widespread and almost unique acceptance by Negro audiences.[35]

Ferguson and Pepper recognized and shrewdly exploited black listeners' identification with black announcers by hiring almost exclusively black on-air staff at WDIA. They also orchestrated a 40,000-flyer mailshot to the black Memphis community to encourage a lucrative racial pride in this black-oriented, black-staffed operation. But while black deejays like Williams, Maurice "Hot Rod" Hulbert, Martha Jean "The Queen" Steinberg, and Rufus Thomas provided the creative flair and commercial appeal, executive and managerial power at WDIA remained firmly in white hands.

By 1956, when it had become part of the Sonderling chain of stations, WDIA was broadcasting 50,000 watts westwards into Arkansas, east to Atlanta, north to Cairo, Illinois, and south to Jackson, Mississippi, reaching more than 500,000 blacks. In Memphis, it was heard regularly in seven out of ten black homes. Of course, its r&b and gospel shows were also heard by many southern whites, not least Elvis Presley and Sam Phillips at nearby Sun Records.[36]

WDIA's success heralded the major expansion of black-oriented programming in the South and beyond. Hordes of other charismatic black deejays emerged, including Ernie "The Whip" Brigier in New Orleans, Bruce "Sugar Throat" Miller in Winston-Salem, Andrew "Sugar Daddy" Dawkins in Bessemer, and half a dozen Dr Daddy-Os scattered around the South under the tutelage of the original, Vernon Winslow in New Orleans. By 1956 there were 28 radio stations with all-black programming and another 36 which broadcast over 30 hours a week specifically for blacks. Many more stations offered at least some regular black programming.[37]

Few of those who owned or managed these black-oriented stations consciously sought to use them to promote or even facilitate the gathering black struggle for equality. Nat Williams explained that Bert Ferguson and John R. Pepper were not driven by any sense of racial enlightenment or philanthropy in switching WDIA to the service of the black community in Memphis. "They are businessmen. They don't necessarily love Negroes. They make that clear. But they do love progress and they are willing to pay the price to make progress". Even when white owners and executives did permit the airing of news programmes, discussion forums, history features and public service announcements which inevitably touched upon the racial situation, it was the commercial wisdom of doing so which was usually uppermost in their minds. Ferguson warned those who neglected these "community" aspects of black programming that it would "cause the weakness or failure of many an operator who thinks that the key to the mint in the negro market is a few blues and gospel records, and a negro face at the mike". For the most part, the white – and even the handful of black – owners, managers and technicians in black-oriented radio in the 1950s, especially in the South, were extremely cautious about airing any material relating to race relations or black protest because of the hostility it might arouse from precious advertisers and other whites.[38]

For Mort Silverman, the station manager at WMRY-New Orleans, commercial considerations, rather than any affinity with blacks, their culture or their struggle for equality, certainly lay at the heart of his interest in r&b. "Before 1950 we were featuring good music and failing. May twenty-eighth of that year we switched to a solid Negro format. In a month we paid our way, and revenue has increased steadily ever since". Silverman's casual distinction between "good music" and "Negro format" suggests the pejorative white value judgements routinely applied to black culture and music in the 1950s, even by those who made a living from it.[39]

In the late 1940s, Shelley Stewart was a resourceful, self-educated young black man who had spent considerably more time on the streets of Birmingham, Alabama, than in its segregated public school system. In August 1949, Stewart parlayed boundless enthusiasm for black music and a rare rhetorical gift into a job at WEDR, which had just opened with its white owner, J. Edward Reynolds, carefully announcing his black-oriented station's intention to "stay completely out of politics". Stewart knew the bottom line for such men. "It was about dollars and cents. It was not about supporting racial justice . . . for some of the white station owners you could not do a PSA [public service announcement] for the NAACP [National Association for the Advancement of Colored People] . . . They didn't want you to do an announcement on voter registration . . . 'cause that would empower coloreds".[40]

For Shelley "The Playboy", as Stewart became known, there was no mistaking where the power in black radio resided. Although some resisted the yoke, black announcers were usually expected to bite their talented and persuasive tongues on matters of racial politics and even fair remuneration for their efforts. According to Stewart, many WEDR deejays "would talk one thing in the control room as blacks and show our dissatisfaction. But if there was a meeting called with . . . whomever was in charge, when they get before the white ownership or the white management, most of the blacks would say, 'oh, everything is fine'".[41]

All of which makes rather a nonsense of Nelson George's nostalgic depiction of the 1950s as a golden age of black-oriented radio, during which independent r&b jockeys established a "self-sufficient" black radio industry, exalted the beauties of an "autonomous" black culture, and provided the black community with grassroots economic and political leadership:

> black radio grew through the war and in the ten or so years after to become institutions and examples of "natural integration" – that is, the mix of whites and blacks it created shared genuine interests economically and musically. Moreover, if you consider the deejay as entrepreneurs – as I do – and not merely as employees, then in the midst of this integration (but not assimilation) it is clear the era produced a wealth of Washingtonian figures.[42]

It is true that blacks and whites in the business of radio and recording did share broad economic interests upon which musical kinships were sometimes built – which is to say, both wanted to reach the widest possible black audience and appreciated that r&b was the best way to do it. Yet, to collapse completely the tensions and contradictions present in the unequal relationship between black announcers and the overwhelmingly white-controlled financial, legal and managerial framework within which they operated is misleading. The multiple restraints on the black deejays' economic power, their political influence, and even their artistic freedom were always far greater than George allows.

Even in the early 1950s, when a combination of the brokerage system and general white indifference to the content of shows they assumed only reached black ears gave black deejays unprecedented freedom in what they said and played on air, they were still bound by the Federal Communications Commission (FCC) rules and guided by a code of conduct prepared by the National Association of Radio and T.V. Broadcasters known as the "Broadcasters' creed". Both these august bodies were white – the FCC did not have a single black member until the appointment of Ben Hooks in 1972 – and their charters enshrined the values of the dominant culture. The "Broadcasters' creed", for instance, demanded that broadcasters "observe the proprieties and customs of civilized society . . . honor the sanctity of marriage and the home".[43]

R&b was initially well stocked with vibrant songs explicitly about sex, infidelity, alcohol, gambling and crime which potentially contravened these codes. Thus station owners usually set broad guidelines on "good taste" within which r&b deejays had to operate, even before the crossover successes of the mid 1950s. In 1951, King, a company hardly prudish in its attitude to the raunchier side of r&b, felt it necessary to record a special "radio version" of the Dominoes' carnal classic "Sixty minute man", while Atlantic later shelved the Drifters' sublime tale of bought sex, "Three thirty three". These were acts of pre-emptive censorship by Independents who recognized that certain disks might not get airplay, even on black-oriented stations.[44]

While some of the leading black titans of the turntable did diversify into related businesses, such as promotion, nightclubs, recording and publishing, which were more convincing examples of the black petty-capitalism George exalts, most remained in financial thrall to white station owners and sponsors. Tommy Smalls, one of George's entrepreneurial "Original 13" of "Washingtonian" black deejays, did not even own his radio name, "Dr Jive", which had been copyrighted by WWRL-NY station manager Fred Barr in 1950. Similarly, Vernon Winslow's Dr Daddy-O persona was owned and franchised by the Jackson Brewing Company. When his kids asked him what he did for a living, the Dillard University graduate, teacher and radio pioneer ruefully replied, "I sell beer".[45]

Few black-oriented deejays or stations could survive without white advertising revenue: not even in Harlem, where WWRL flourished with major sponsorship from corporate giants like Coca Cola, Arrid, Budweiser, Vaseline and Wrigleys, as well as the odd large black firm like Parks Sausage and spot announcements for local, often white-owned, neighbourhood retailers. The pressing need to court such sponsors was certainly evident in WWRL's sales pitch for Tommy Smalls, which boasted that "Commercials are delivered by Dr Jive in his easy free-flowing conversational style, that will deliver sales for you . . . This is the same Dr Jive who broke 25 yr. attendance record at the Apollo 3 times . . . who can sell YOUR PRODUCT for you to over 1 million Negro people in New York and get the same following and brand loyalty to your product".[46]

Black deejays were hardly culpable for finding themselves caught between their personal ambitions and the political economy of American race relations. Most were only too grateful for the opportunity to sell their sponsors' goods and services to the black community. "Genial" Gene Potts of WGIV-Charlotte, another of the celebrated "Original 13", offered a jive analysis of the economics which allowed him to air both r&b and the community announcements which made him the *Charlotte Post*'s "Man of the Year" in

1953: "Most of my commercials are done in rhyme but I am sincere all the time . . . I love my sponsors and hold them in the highest esteem. They can always count on their job being well done by 'Ye Olde Swingmaster Genial Gene'". Most black deejays found themselves using their status within the black community in this way, promoting national and local white-owned businesses in addition to a few, invariably under-financed, black enterprises. This was not the result of any "natural integration", but a pragmatic response to the harsh realities of black economic underdevelopment and restricted opportunity which inadvertently strengthened the grip of corporate white America on the black economy.[47]

Ultimately, this racial and economic configuration of power in the broadcasting industry meant that black-oriented radio struggled to meet the challenges of a new age of mass black protest, both in terms of the quantity and quality of its news and public affairs broadcasting, and in the extent of its public commitment to the struggle. Nevertheless, the medium's contribution to the emerging Movement and its attendant black consciousness in the 1950s should not be underestimated. The multiple meanings of black radio cannot simply be reduced to the base racial politics and economics of its production, since those meanings were also dependent on the specific content of the programming, and the manner in which those programmes were consumed by black listeners. As blacks became part of an interactive radio community, that interaction took place primarily with deejays and the records they played, not with the whole paraphernalia of the thoroughly exploitative and generally racist industries which lurked behind them.

Simply by airing black music, speaking in the distinctive argot of the black streets and fields, promoting black concerts and dances, and, in so far as it was allowed, reporting on the achievements of black leaders, athletes and celebrities, and announcing the latest black community and national news, black radio helped to define what was distinctive about black American culture and to legitimize it as something unique and valuable. Throughout the country, black-oriented radio helped to codify and promote new patterns of increasingly urbane black conduct and consciousness.

As a result, black radio, together with the emergence of a genuinely national, if regionally distinct, r&b scene, helped to revitalize and reshape a sense of common identity which had been severely strained by the successive black migrations of the first half of the century. Of course, this revived black consciousness was also critically linked to the shared experience of a long struggle against the diverse effects of racism. But it was also arranged culturally around distinctively black styles of leisure, pleasure, humour, sport, worship, fashion and dance. Above all, a rejuvenated black consciousness was expressed and validated through the various forms of Rhythm and Blues music which, not coincidentally, also comprised the major portion of programming on black-oriented radio.[48]

Reaching a white audience, keeping a black one

Barely less significant in terms of the construction of this new black consciousness was the success of black-oriented broadcasts in breaching the
walls of habitual and legal segregation to reach eavesdropping young whites.
Throughout America these black-oriented broadcasts, coupled with increasingly effective methods of marketing and distribution, steadily undermined
the traditional racial boundaries of musical production and consumption.
This was a commercial and cultural development which many hoped and
some believed heralded a new era of race relations.[49]

The precise composition, motivations, and even geographic locations, of
this original white r&b audience remain elusive. In the absence of much
systematic research, the literature is strewn with plausible, but usually unsub-
stantiated, generalizations which tend to homogenize what was clearly a
rather disparate group of early white fans. Certainly, while contemporary
critics routinely associated any enthusiasm for black style with lower-class,
usually "delinquent", white youths, early r&b fans were actually drawn from
all classes and could be found in most regions of the country – after all,
Johnny Ray was from Oregon; Eddie Cochran from Oklahoma.[50]

These diverse white fans consumed the music in rather different ways.
Discographer Al Pavlow recalled that his early enthusiasm for r&b did not
necessarily entail a rebellious rejection of the white pop of the day, but sometimes merely supplemented it with admiration for a "'new' kind of music
that we liked even more". For others, however, a love of r&b and early
rock and roll did seem to symbolize some kind of revolt against the social
norms and expectations of middle-class adult white America as encoded
and disseminated through church, school, the workplace, and Tin Pan Alley
pop. Jonathan Kamin felt that in the early 1950s, "becoming an R & B fan
required a certain amount of enterprise and individualism, and generally,
rebelliousness as well". In La Canada, California, he discovered that some
white youths had even "developed an entire deviant lifestyle around rhythm-
and-blues", while others, from Minneapolis to New Orleans, were doing
much the same.[51]

Yet this relationship between r&b and social revolt was complex and
highly ambiguous. Although one should never underestimate the genuinely
subversive and counter-hegemonic potential of radical stylistic gestures, or
of support for alternative forms of popular culture derived from sources
marked "taboo" by the dominant culture, relatively little of that potential
was actually realized among white r&b fans. In the early-to-mid 1950s,
southern working-class white male youths managed to make the r&b they
found on the radio, in jukeboxes, and in black clubs on the wrong side of
town into an integral part of lives which – haircuts and lurid suits notwithstanding – generally conformed to the social, religious, sexual and racial

orthodoxies of the contemporary white South. There was really nothing particularly "unorthodox", or novel, or intrinsically counter-cultural, about southern whites like Elvis Presley and Jerry Lee Lewis enjoying and imitating black music, even in a time of legal segregation. In the decade after the Second World War, the steady, sometimes brutal and largely unchallenged assertion of white supremacy in the South made jumping Jim Crow's cultural barriers relatively safe for whites and virtually suicidal for blacks.

Perhaps the only group of early fans whose interest in black r&b posed a major challenge to prevailing racial and sexual orthodoxies were young white women, especially insofar as admiration of black male performers was concerned, and even more especially in the South. Yet white women do not appear to have been quite so central to this early white r&b vanguard as men. Indeed, Martha Bayles has speculated that at live r&b shows, white women were sometimes reduced to the status of troubled, if fascinated, bystanders while their male companions cut loose and fully immersed themselves in the experience. On one hand, black male r&b singers never seemed to pitch their passionate songs of love and lust directly at the white women in their audience, since such gestures were fraught with dangers in a culture tormented by the spectre of miscegenation. On the other hand, exuberant emotional or physical responses to the music of black male performers seemed somehow unseemly for decent white girls.[52]

In this context, Bayles suggests that one of the greatest contributions made by Presley, Lewis and their white rockabilly brethren, and the main basis for any claim rock and roll might have had to being "revolutionary", was that these artists made it acceptable for white women to participate more fully in the passion and frenzy, the "alien ecstacy" and sexual energy, which white men had always been free to enjoy in black r&b. Thus, Bayles suggests, early white rock and roll struck "a blow not against sexual morality per se, but against the moral hypocrisies of a color-coded double standard".[53]

While some of these original young white fans were zealots, with an intense romantic infatuation with all things black and therefore indubitably hip, many others enjoyed the music far more casually. High-school kids often saw it as a slightly risqué, eminently danceable, soundtrack to parties or trips to the local diner, where jukeboxes first began to register a growing white fondness for the music. Then they went home to their parents and school books and whatever passed for racial orthodoxy in their particular social world. For many older college kids, r&b was also part of an escapist leisure world of Greek dances, nightclub sorties and spring-break trysts at coastal resorts like Daytona and Myrtle Beach, where the private sexual cravings of young whites could be simultaneously sublimated and publicly expressed by dancing to the sinewy sounds of the Clovers' "Good lovin'". It was here, Jerry Wexler noted, that "The southern market opened with kids at the University of Virginia and young people all through the Carolinas on the sea-coast".[54]

Ultimately, however, what is striking about this white r&b consumption and imitation, irrespective of class, gender or geography, is that it all took place within a thoroughly conventional set of white stereotypes about blacks and their culture. Whites habitually reduced r&b, a richly diverse musical genre which embraced every aspect of human experience, to the hypersexual, sensual and instinctual characteristics they had associated with and projected onto blacks for centuries. Consequently, any counter-cultural potential which support for post-war r&b may have had among whites was inseparable from the highly racialized way in which that music was perceived, consumed and redeployed by white fans. For some whites, r&b undoubtedly did offer a good rocking critique of mainstream America and its prevailing social, gender and class order. Yet it was a critique they only glimpsed through the lens of race and racism. It depended on the operation of a white racial logic which had long reified black culture as the perpetually fascinating but feral, alluring but alarming, sensual but sordid antithesis to the dominant white one.[55]

Whatever its precise motivations and composition, Charlie Gillett has suggested that by 1953 Atlantic was already consciously seeking this furtive white audience for r&b. Gillett offers as evidence the abandonment of documentary style recordings and the advent of carefully conceived "commercial R&B arrangements" by Jesse Stone. Stone, who had cut his musical teeth playing with the queen of double-entendre, Julia Lee, and his own Blue Serenaders in St Louis and Kansas City in the late 1920s, had made a reputation as a fine swing writer-arranger for the bands of Duke Ellington, Chick Webb and Benny Goodman. At Atlantic, Stone added a lyrical gift for droll social and sexual commentary ("Money honey", "Shake, rattle and roll") and pinned his sophisticated arrangements to a robust dance beat plucked straight from southern dancehall blues. As Gillett put it, "While the other indies seemed to get pop hits by accident, Atlantic's records sounded as if they were deliberately intended to sound commercial. The customary rasps of black singers had been softened. The songs included sing-along choruses, and the beats were easy to dance to".[56]

As a description of Atlantic's sound after 1953 this is perfectly accurate. But, allowing for improvements in recording technology, it seems just as accurate for Ruth Brown's "Teardrops from my eyes" or the Clovers' "Don't you know I love you", both recorded for an overwhelmingly black audience in 1950. Thus, it hardly indicates a deliberate attempt to change Atlantic's style to break into a mass white market which the label, trapped within the conventional racial and commercial wisdoms of the time, was not even sure existed.

Nevertheless, it is certainly true that, after a brief flirtation with downhome blues and jump bands in the late 1940s, and alongside an abiding interest in modern jazz, Atlantic consciously cultivated a cleaner, more mannered r&b style which fused blues elements with some of the musical conventions of white pop. Moreover, as Ertegun recognized, "We certainly were not the only firm which had succeeded with this formula". Yet, this initially had little to do with courting a tiny white teen market; rather it was a response to the changing demands of black audiences who remained the key consumers of mid-1950s r&b.[57]

In the 1940s, the non-white population of the American South declined by 16 per cent; during the following decade it fell again by a further 14 per cent. By 1960, some 3 million blacks had moved out of the region, mostly to the cities of the North, Midwest and far West. Many of those who remained in the South also made their way to cities and larger towns as mechanization and the consolidation of land holdings brought to an end age-old patterns of rural life and labour in the region.[58] After the Second World War it was this increasingly urbanized, increasingly non-southern black audience – especially its youth – which first began to reject the gritty, rural, downhome sounds of the old blues in favour of the eclectic mixture of ineffable dance beats, sweet harmonies, bustling good humour, romance and ribaldry, which characterized r&b. While the traditional Delta blues and its electrified offspring continued to enjoy considerable popularity among southern and older migrant black communities – especially in San Francisco, Chicago and Detroit – and an urban black vanguard joined white beats and intellectuals in their love of modern jazz, the *Billboard* regional black record charts for the period show a definite national trend away from such styles towards the various new r&b forms. "As a kid in the fifties", Tennessean Isaac Hayes recalled, "I was taught to be *ashamed* of the blues. We thought of it as plantation darkie stuff. And that was miles from where *we* wanted to be".[59]

Black writer Woodie King also viewed the rise of r&b in terms of an escape from the relentless intensity and realism of the blues. It was an escape which often paralleled the move to the urban North, where a certain optimism flourished even in the grim ghettos:

> When we added rhythm to our blues, we did it so that our existence would be less of a burden than could be detected by the casual observer . . . And our blues singers kept telling us in no uncertain terms that we were blue . . . But we did not have to deal with those things if we could create an alternate. The rhythm became an alternate.[60]

In accounting for the emergence of a smoother, poppier strain of r&b in the late 1940s and early 1950s, it is also important to recognize that, in an era before the civil rights and black power movements had encouraged a certain healthy black cultural chauvinism, the standards of white popular music often constituted extremely important yardsticks of "quality" and "sophistication" for black performers and audiences alike. Certainly, by 1950 the influential Baltimore vocal group, the Orioles, was already featuring slick, putatively "white", pseudo-classical string arrangements on songs like "Everything they said came true", much to the delight of overwhelmingly black audiences. As deejay Jay Butler of WCHB-Inkster explained in a phrase which connected evolving black musical tastes to the integrationist agenda which characterized black America in the mid 1950s, "Back in 1954, the black community didn't want to be associated with the blues . . . they wanted to be accepted by whites".[61]

Post-war black communities, for all their rural poverty or urban ghettoization, were no more isolated from the influence of the dominant, so-called "white", culture than they were immune to the effects of other mainstream political, social, ideological and economic forces. Many blacks did listen to white pop, country and even European classical music on radio and records. They saw white performers on film and television. Moreover, they clearly enjoyed much of what they heard and incorporated aspects of it into their own idioms to create vital, increasingly urbane new syntheses which reflected and dramatized the changing circumstances of their lives.

New Orleans shouter Roy Brown began his career imitating his hero Bing Crosby, while in St Louis, Chuck Berry "never heard Muddy Waters, never heard Elmore James. I heard Frank Sinatra". In Memphis, in the early 1950s, B.B. King's radio show on WDIA regularly aired records by Sinatra, Tony Bennett and Frankie Laine, simply because his predominantly black audience liked them. Even Imamu Amiri Baraka, by the late 1960s a committed cultural nationalist and eloquent spokesman for a uniquely black aesthetic, admitted he grew up liking "stuff like Rosemary Clooney and Vaughn Monroe and Johnny Ray and Frankie Laine". Baraka also confessed liking "Bing Crosby better than Frank Sinatra", while young Ruth Brown's breakthrough at an "Amateur night" at Harlem's Apollo Theatre came when she sang "It could happen to you" – a song she had learned from a Crosby record. Billy Williams, whose delicate hiccuping tenor worked well on breezy r&b numbers like "Don't let go", similarly claimed Crosby as "the most influential one in the singing portion of me . . . I just sat and listened real carefully to whatever he did and sort of absorbed it . . . As a singer nobody caps him. He's tops".[62]

Even in the small-town South, nominally white musics found their way into black households and synapses by a variety of routes. Bernice Johnson Reagon, a founding member of the SNCC Freedom Singers and later the mainstay of Sweet Honey in the Rock, grew up near Albany, Georgia. Her family subscribed to the mail-order Columbia Records Club, which routinely sent out all manner of unsolicited white disks to its black members. In Ripley, Tennessee, and Clarksdale, Mississippi, respectively, Tina and Ike Turner grew up on a musical regimen which, in the marked absence of much black-oriented radio programming, featured substantial helpings of white country. As Tina recalled, "Like most other blacks in that place and time, Ike's musical diet was mainly white hillbilly music – particularly the

Grand Ole Opry, broadcast out of Nashville". Bobby Bland, a Tennessean from Rosemark, similarly conceded the early, inescapable, influence of Roy Acuff, Eddie Arnold, Hank Williams and Hank Snow, and even of middle-of-the-road crooners like Perry Como, Tony Bennett and his old army colleague, Eddie Fisher, on aspects of his gargling blues style. "I had a country and western, spiritual Baptist background . . . All of them are somewhat alike, it's just a different delivery", Bland explained.[63]

Even before 1954, then, r&b and its practitioners were caught in the midst of stylistic cross-currents which edged some of it away from the blues and closer to the musical and lyrical orthodoxies of post-war "white" popular musics, especially Tin Pan Alley pop and country which was itself undergoing a process of urban gentrification at this time. These transformations derived principally from a combination of technological changes, most obviously the widespread availability of radios and record players, and social, economic and generational factors which were evident, in different degrees, in black communities throughout the nation. They were certainly not foisted upon a reluctant black audience by an all-powerful, determinative music industry consciously looking for crossover hits by diluting "authentic" r&b. In retrospect, however, as Ahmet Ertegun observed, "It was not altogether unpredictable that this combination of polished performance and down-to-earth blues material should produce records which would have an appeal beyond the traditional and limited rhythm and blues market".[64]

Covering all races: the industry and the birth of rock and roll

When r&b first began to infiltrate the white pop charts regularly in 1954, the entire industry believed that there was but a finite and transient white audience for this black music. Eighteen months and countless crossover hits later, it still struggled to accept the fact that rock and roll, as the new biracial style which emerged from r&b was dubbed, marked a major realignment of American popular music tastes and markets along new generational and racial lines. Among other things, that tardiness reflected the pervasiveness and tenacity of racism within the industry, as in the country at large.

In March 1955, Hugo Peretti and Luigi Creatore, who were at the time A&R (Artists and Repertoire) men at Mercury, voiced the common view among the Majors that "the current r&b trend has just about hit its peak and is on its way down". Certainly, although Bill Haley and the Comets' pathbreaking 1955 success "Rock around the clock" – a hit with both races – was recorded for Decca, it was only during the course of 1956, following RCA's unprecedented triumph with Elvis Presley, that the Majors really made a concerted move into the field. Even then, many continued to devote considerable time and resources to trying to undermine a genuinely biracial musical phenomenon which actually promised to revitalize a moribund singles market in which sales had still to regain immediate post-war levels and retail income had actually slumped from $205 million in 1953 to $195 million in 1954.[65]

The Independents proved no more able than the Majors to abandon the powerful racial categorizations according to which they had operated for so long, even when the market potential of r&b had been clearly demonstrated and expanded economic opportunity beckoned. James McGowan of the Four Fellows recalled, "We mistakenly judged it to be a fad. We believed that the white teenager would soon lose interest and that Rhythm and Blues would return as music enjoyed almost exclusively by Blacks". Deejay and Earl Records owner Tommy Smalls was still sceptical about the fad's durability in early 1956, suggesting that "Rock 'n' Roll will fade away, it has to".[66]

While some Independents enjoyed the unexpected bonus of mainstream chart success, established interests within the industry responded in a variety of ways. Many simply tried to ignore the trend and wait for its inevitable demise. In February 1955, *Variety* expressed the views of the great music publishing houses, which stood to lose much from the popularity of r&b since few fans wanted the sheet music to "Maybelline" – they wanted Chuck Berry's Chess record, the specific performance. "Top publishing firms' execs have assumed a 'this too shall pass attitude' while the major disk companies, which are riding along with the r&b fad, figure it's due for a pop fade out before the summer".[67]

Some elements within the industry naïvely hoped to defuse growing adult white concerns about the racial origins and propriety of the new styles by semantics. They followed the lead of deejay Alan Freed, who since 1951 had been calling the black r&b he played initially on WJW-Cleveland and later on WINS-New York "rock and roll". Yet, if this was a deliberate attempt to obscure the black origins of r&b and its derivatives, it was singularly unsuccessful. Nelson George, while accusing Freed of a cynical attempt "to disguise the blackness of the music", concedes that "calling it rock & roll didn't fool everybody". In fact, it hardly fooled anybody. The whole tenor of popular opposition to the style depended on public awareness of its racial origins, while, paradoxically, much of its support among young whites hinged on its association with the hip, alluring but forbidden, world of black culture.[68]

If the mainstream success of r&b was indeed but a passing fad, some within the industry reasoned that it might easily be replaced by another. There were concerted efforts to promote alternative dance crazes, most conspicuously the mambo, a Latin dance which had first found favour in late 1953. In 1954 and 1955, the mambo was vigorously promoted via radio and the trade journals in direct competition to the r&b boom. At the end of 1954, mambo overkill prompted *Variety* to ask if "Papa had enough mambo?", before cheerfully predicting that hot on the clicking heels of recent samba, rhumba and mambo crazes, the bambuco was about to sweep the nation off its dancing feet. In fact, the mambo continued to be a force on the charts and dance floors until 1956, when it was joined by the calypso boomlet. The bambuco craze, meanwhile, never materialized, illustrating the industry's inability to impose styles upon the market simply according to its own economic agenda.[69]

Interestingly, the mambo also swept across black America in the form of, among many others, Ruth Brown's "Mambo baby", Ivory Joe Hunter's "I've got to learn to do the mambo", the Charms' "Mambo sh-mambo", and – best of all – the Treniers' wild and woolly "Who put the 'ongh' in the mambo". For the opportunistic Independents any potentially lucrative craze was worth exploring, while for black artists, the new trend offered a possible source of both musical inspiration and profit. As for black listeners, notwithstanding subsequent critical attempts to reify the unimpeachable cool and flawless taste of black audiences, they were just as susceptible to passing fads as any other section of the market. The proliferation of r&b-mambo melds may also have reflected widespread doubts about the longevity of the new r&b craze with white record buyers: mixing r&b with the latest national craze seemed to offer r&b labels the best chance of crossing over.[70]

By far the most important industry response to the growing popularity of r&b was the practice of covering, or copying, black hit records with white artists, which was especially prevalent between 1954 and mid 1956. This was not a simple case of the Majors exploiting the creativity of the Independents. Although Mercury was heavily involved in the cover trade with the Crew Cuts, Georgia Gibbs, Patti Page, and the Diamonds, and other Majors dabbled (RCA with Perry Como; Capitol with the Cheers; Columbia with Mindy Carson), much of the covering was actually done by other Independents. The most successful were Randy Wood's Dot, out of Gallatin, Tennessee, which recorded Pat Boone, Gale Storm, and the Fontane Sisters alongside creditable black r&b by the Cap-Tans, Chanteclairs and Counts, and Coral, which had Teresa Brewer and the McGuire Sisters.

Most commentators have viewed the cover phenomenon, with its careful "whitening" of black style, as a deliberate affront to black dignity and a glaring example of the systematic economic and cultural exploitation of black America. From the heart of the black consciousness movement of the 1960s, Baraka wrote angrily of "the harnessing of Black energy for dollars by white folks". More recently, black musicologist Portia Maultsby has described the cover syndrome, together with the success of white singers like Bill Haley and Elvis Presley in obviously black-influenced styles, as "the most wide-spread, systematic rape and uncompensated cultural exploitation the entertainment industry has ever seen".[71]

There is much historical truth and even more moral force in these assessments. Yet, paradoxically, nothing did more than the cover phenomenon to facilitate a mass market for r&b and extend the opportunities for black artists, writers and entrepreneurs – except, perhaps, the success of Elvis

Presley. As so often in the past, resourceful blacks refused to become mere victims and strove to transform an oppressive and exploitative situation into an opportunity for personal and collective advancement.

Foremost among the putative victims of the cover trade were r&b songwriters and singers. Yet, in purely economic terms, black songwriters often profited from covers, either by selling the publishing rights of their songs outright or simply by reaping the rewards of having them promoted by white artists far beyond the "natural" boundaries of the black market. For Winfield Scott, a justifiable sense of racial outrage was partially assuaged by the thrill of previously unimagined economic opportunity. When Scott saw Georgia Gibbs' cover of his "Tweedle dee" eclipse LaVern Baker's original, he

> was torn. I had to think two ways . . . As a writer you think, "Gee, I have another record", so here's a chance to secure a bigger income. And again, I had to feel, "Wow, this must be devastating to LaVern", because her record came out first, now here comes the cover and all of a sudden she fades into obscurity. And I didn't know how to deal with that.[72]

Although such decisions did not necessarily come easily, most black songwriters subordinated genuine concerns about the racial implications of the cover phenomenon to their more immediate personal ambition. Otis Blackwell, composer of songs like "Fever", "Great balls of fire" and Elvis Presley's hits "All shook up" and "Don't be cruel", was required by Presley's manager, Colonel Tom Parker, to share specious songwriting credits with the singer in order to generate additional publishing royalties. While the claim of some critics that Elvis based his performances on note-for-note renditions of Blackwell's demos are nonsense, since Presley had woven together the black and white threads of his essential style at Sun Records in Memphis during 1954 and 1955, long before Blackwell entered the picture, the songwriter certainly had cause to feel exploited.

> Then I realized that songwriters who'd been in the business much longer than I had, and who were much better off financially, were going along with this. Some people would even have paid to have a song done by Elvis. So I figured what the hell. And I can't complain about how I made out.[73]

For many black writers, this expanded market for r&b represented something of a Pyrrhic victory: it simply meant that the rewards they were still routinely being denied were bigger than before. And yet, while exploitation of unwitting composers – white as well as black – surely continued, one aspect of the growing organizational sophistication of the r&b scene was the increased diligence of many writers in securing better legal protection of copyrights and proper royalty payments. One factor here was the rise of Broadcast Music Incorporated (BMI), a copyright protection organization which, unlike the older, New York-centred, American Society of Composers and Performers (ASCAP), welcomed composers in minority styles, and "recognized the fact that the United States does not end at the banks of the Hudson River". Another factor was the emergence of independent publishing companies like Atlantic's Progressive Music, the René brothers' Leon René Publications and Recordo Music Publishers, Bobby and Dan Robinson's Bob-Dan Music, Harry and Gene Goodman's Arc and Regent Publishing, and the Bihari brothers' Modern Music Company.[74]

Not that all of these companies were necessarily havens of fair treatment for songwriters. Henry Glover, who wrote many King-Federal hits, resented the fact that Syd Nathan's Lois Publishing only grudgingly paid him one cent – half the statutory rate – per recorded side in the early 1950s. Glover fought to secure a better publishing deal and by mid-decade was a 50 per cent partner with Nathan in the profitable Jay & Cee Music publishing company.[75]

While the economic consequences of the cover phenomenon for black writers were ambiguous, black performers undoubtedly did lose potential sales and income as the result of white cover versions. Yet the continued fragmentation of the record-buying market meant that the impact on the sales of black r&b was limited. Black audiences invariably favoured the black originals, while the sort of early white devotee who risked parental wrath and peer incredulity to seek out the Marigolds' "Rollin' stone" in a record store on the wrong side of a town's racial divide was unlikely to be caught dead buying the Fontane Sisters' anodyne cover. Conversely, whites who happily accepted Georgia Gibbs' jaunty cover of Etta James' "The wallflower" (renamed "Dance with me Henry"), would seldom contemplate buying the earthy original.

The American record-buying market was not divided by race alone, but also by region, gender, class, generation and simple predilection. Consequently, any song was likely to appear in a variety of formats aimed at different sections of that market. Covering certainly was not restricted to white exploitation of black music. Between 1951 and 1953, for example, Hank Williams' country songs were routinely covered for the pop audience ("Cold cold heart" by Tony Bennett, "Hey good lookin'" and "Jambalaya" by Jo Stafford, "Half as much" by Rosemary Clooney, "Your cheatin' heart" by Joni James) as part of an industry initiative, literally, to "pop"-ularize southern country music for a national audience.[76]

The practice of covering hit records was even rife within black music. Thus, while writers have routinely referred to "Sh-boom" being covered by Mercury's white Canadians, the Crew Cuts, this was merely the most successful of a host of competing cover versions, including at least three by black artists: Billy Williams, Sy Oliver and Leon McAuliffe. Similarly, black artists on larger Independents regularly covered black recordings made for smaller Independents. The Cadets on Modern (who also recorded as the Jacks on Modern's RPM subsidiary) were particularly adept at this, covering Nappy Brown's "Don't be angry", the Willows' "Church bells may ring", Jayhawks' "Stranded in the jungle", and Velours' "Hands across the table".[77]

Black acts also regularly covered white hits for the r&b market. The Chords' "Sh-boom" began life as the flip-side of a cover of Patti Page's pop hit "Cross over the bridge" and only became the A-side in response to public demand. This was nothing new. In 1950, the veteran Birmingham bandleader Erskine Hawkins successfully covered Page's "Tennessee waltz", which was one of six black covers of white pop hits to make the Rhythm and Blues record charts that year. In 1952, country singer Sonny Gale's "Wheel of fortune" – itself a big hit with black fans – was covered by both Dinah Washington and the Cardinals, while the Orioles' hugely popular "Crying in the chapel", which even made the pop charts in 1953, was a cover of a country hymn by Darrell Glenn. This practice even survived the advent of rock and roll. In 1956, for example, the Cadets covered Presley's first RCA hit, "Heartbreak Hotel", on the B-side of "Church bells may ring".[78]

At King, black versions of white country material had been common from the start. Indeed, in 1943, Syd Nathan had originally conceived of his enterprise as a country label and he continued to record artists like the Delmore Brothers and Cowboy Copas long after assembling his formidable r&b roster. Shouter Wynonie Harris cut Hank Penny's "Bloodshot eyes", while Bullmoose Jackson recorded both Wayne Raney's "Why don't you haul off and love me", and Aubrey "Moon" Mullican's "Cherokee boogie". In the maelstrom of biracial influence and counter-influence which energized the Cincinnati label, this pattern was sometimes reversed. Under Henry Glover's guidance and with King's black musicians regularly guesting on drums, bass, and even horns, Mullican – a powerhouse boogie pianist from Texas with an impressive barnyard yelp and competing fondnesses for r&b and moonshine whiskey – cut exhilarating hybrid covers of many black songs from "Goodnight Irene" to Todd Rhodes' "Rocket 69" (re-christened "Rocket to the moon").[79]

Setting the cover phenomenon in this broader context of a routine commercial strategy should not detract from the specifically racial dimensions of the practice, or of the media's response to that practice, especially in the period between 1954 and mid 1956. In the late 1940s and early 1950s, it was usually songs, rather than records, which were copied. The versions cut for the separate r&b, pop and country markets often had relatively little in common in terms of sound or arrangement. By contrast, as those musical streams converged around r&b in the mid 1950s, white covers tended to lift entire arrangements from black records, hoping to reproduce their power and passion through acts of artistic theft against which there was little legal protection. "I wasn't so upset about other singers copying my songs because that was their privilege, and they had to pay the writers of the song", Ruth Brown explained. "But what did hurt me was the fact that I had originated the song, and I never got the opportunities to be in the top television shows and the talk shows. I didn't get the exposure. And other people were copying the style, the whole idea".[80]

What made this situation worse was the fact that many black artists were locked into extraordinarily exploitative contracts which substantially reduced their capacity to profit from even the records they did sell. When lawyer Howell Begle investigated claims by a number of r&b veterans that they had routinely been deprived of proper payment by their record companies, he discovered that in the 1940s and 1950s most had contracts which paid royalties at a meagre rate of between 1 and 4 per cent of the retail price of recordings sold, or else provided one-off payments of around $200 in return for performances which sometimes made millions of dollars. Such practices retarded black capital accumulation within the music industry and ultimately had a chilling effect on the extension of black ownership and economic power.[81]

None of this was of much concern to the producers of white covers. They groped uncertainly for some of the musical magic which had initially made r&b popular with whites, but also sought to deepen their penetration of that white market by paring the music to its bare, functional, rhythmic bones and fleshing it out again according to "white" musical and lyrical specifications. These agendas were clearly audible in the differences between Otis Williams and the Charms' "Hearts of stone" on King, and the Fontane Sisters' cover on Dot. While the basic arrangements had much in common, the King record showcased Otis Williams' expressive lead tenor, which peeled away from the strict melody line and toyed with the basic rhythm. The vocal accompaniment and the bass-drum-saxophone instrumentation provided a molten, contrapuntal, rhythmic and harmonic backdrop, while in the middle-eight section the saxophone took off on a typically rubato, or free, solo. By contrast, the Fontane Sisters abandoned the vocal and rhythmic fluidity of the original in favour of a rigid adherence to the melody and a more explicit statement of the dominant beat. A stolid male chorus sang in unison, anchoring the song to its melodic and rhythmic foundations, rather than providing the harmonic shadings offered by the Charms.

Most covers followed this basic pattern. As Jonathan Kamin has put it, r&b originals "were systematically changed in the direction of Euro-American patterns, or expectations relevant to pop music". Thus, "Cover versions could be seen as an 'improvement' over the originals, for any approach closer to the unquestioned European standards would be regarded as an improvement". This dramatized not only that there were significant differences in the conventions of nominally white and black popular musics, but that there were moral as well as aesthetic values attached to those differences.[82]

The media's response to the cover phenomenon also betrayed a clear racial bias. Pop radio, by definition, was supposed to play the most popular songs and records in the country. Between 1954 and mid 1956, however, the persistence and intensity of certain racial attitudes and assumptions appear to have impinged upon the economic agendas of many broadcasters. Pop radio simply did not always play the most popular records in the nation if they were by black artists.

Some details illuminate this general pattern, whereby black records were consistently denied the airplay their popularity and sales warranted, while white cover versions were frequently played more than their chart position merited. In 1955, "Earth angel" by the Los Angeles black vocal group the Penguins, occupied a top ten position on the *Billboard* pop best-sellers chart between 5 February and 5 March. During that period, however, the Penguins' record was never placed higher than thirteenth on the list of the most played pop records in the nation. The Crew Cuts' cover version, however, was already in the top ten most played records on 19 February, when it stood at just number 14 in the best-seller lists; that same week, the Penguins had the eighth best-selling disk in the United States, but only the fifteenth most played.

In March 1955, Johnny Ace's "Pledging my love" climbed to number 17 on the best seller lists. It received roughly commensurate pop airplay until Teresa Brewer's cover was released. On 26 March, Johnny Ace's record suddenly disappeared from the airplay lists, while Brewer's cover appeared as the nation's seventeenth most played disk – this despite the fact that Ace's record was still a full ten places higher in the best-sellers chart. Almost exactly one year later, Frankie Lymon and the Teenagers' "Why do fools fall in love" had already spent four weeks in the national best-sellers list, rising to number nine, before it made its first appearance on the most played list on 10 March 1956. By contrast, a cover version by Gale Storm was the ninth most played record in America while it was still only at number 19 in the sales charts. Another white cover of the same song, by the Diamonds, also received immediate and extensive airplay.

The Penguins, with their sweet harmonies and devotional love song, the tragic Johnny Ace – who blew his brains out losing a game of Russian roulette – with his plaintive pop-blues ballad, and the 13-year-old Frankie Lymon and his lovestruck Teenagers, were hardly the most threatening manifestations of black music and manhood to confront white pop stations between 1954 and 1956. And yet they suffered obvious discrimination. Other, more lubricious black artists like Bo Diddley, Chuck Berry and Little Richard initially stood even less chance of a fair airing. In February 1956, Richard's "Tutti frutti" made number 18 on the pop best-seller lists with virtually no pop airplay, unlike Pat Boone's hilariously clinical cover, which threatened to deafen listeners with the whip-crack of perfectly articulated consonants. Richard's follow-up, "Long Tall Sally", peaked at number six on the best-seller charts in May 1956, yet at the time was only twenty-first on the most played record lists.

By the time "Long Tall Sally" was issued, however, the situation concerning covers was changing. Pat Boone's unlikely version this time failed to make the Top Twenty best-sellers list and *Billboard* reported that "it certainly looks as tho (sic) the public is beginning to show a decided preference for the originals – regardless of their origin", by which it meant, regardless of the race of the performer. From around this date, black records competed so successfully for sales with white covers that, while some pop stations redoubled their efforts to repel the rock and roll nightmare, most could simply no longer afford to ignore it. In late 1955, *Billboard* had already noted that there was "barely a die-hard pop jockey left who has not felt compelled to program the big r&b or rock and roll hits", however reluctantly. Bob DeBardelaben of WLEE-Richmond put the commercial case for rock and roll programming on pop radio plainly: "We use much of it on our music shows because surveys here and all across the nation indicate a heavy rock 'n' roll schedule also invites heavy sponsorship".[83]

While such economic considerations eventually compelled many pop stations to play the new music, the selective way in which they did so revealed how racial concerns continued to intersect with and shape commercial agendas. Having first championed white cover versions of r&b hits, pop radio then began to give preferential treatment to those black artists – like the Platters, Clyde McPhatter and Sam Cooke – who appeared to be easing r&b in the direction of more acceptable pop norms. It was ironic that while black-oriented radio had broken r&b out of the segregated market into the mainstream, it was pop radio, with its racially circumscribed preferences and access to a larger, more lucrative mass audience, which most critically influenced its development once it was there.

Two principal factors accounted for the growing popularity of the original black recordings in the white market place. The first was what Jonathan Kamin has described as a process of "perceptual learning" and "musical acculturation" by the white audience. According to this thesis, Little Richard, Bo Diddley and the rest initially represented such an assault on mainstream white musical values that the covers, with their "Europeanization" of the blackest, most alien elements of r&b, were a necessary intermediate step between traditional white popular music and black r&b. The covers prepared cautious sections of the white audience to appreciate and enjoy the sounds of the black originators.[84]

The second factor was that in late 1955, black r&b had itself, really for the first time, deliberately and systematically begun to court the crossover market. Crucial to this process was the conspicuous crossover success, both in terms of sales to whites and of media exposure, of certain types of black artists. The Platters, for example, were one of the few black acts to escape the full effects of racist pop programming and were enormously significant

With the enormous crossover success of their melodramatic romantic ballads, the Platters were an important influence on the development of r&b and black rock and roll in the late 1950s.

in shaping the subsequent development of r&b. Having started as a rather generic vocal group at Federal, they were remodelled by manager Buck Ram at Mercury into a highly slick ensemble, bridging the gap between r&b and Tin Pan Alley pop almost entirely by means of Tony Williams' stratospheric lead vocals. With their melodramatic, highly orchestrated ballads, many of which were old standards like "Smoke gets in your eyes", the Platters indicated precisely the nature of the transformations black r&b needed to undergo in order to get coverage on pop radio and attract a wider white market.

This was a matter of image as well as sound. The Platters with their neat tuxedos and pretty girl singer (Zola Taylor) seemed reassuringly safe when contrasted with Hank Ballard and the Midnighters and their odes to "Annie" and her sexual adventures. After initially treating the Platters with the same disdain as other black artists – in October 1955, their first hit, "Only you", was in the national best-sellers chart for five weeks, rising to number nine, before it made the airplay lists for the first time – white pop radio became more enthusiastic about the group. In February 1956, "The great pretender" made number one on the airplay chart, although it never rose higher than number three in the best-seller lists. Almost until the end of the decade the group continued to receive airplay commensurate with, and sometimes in excess of, that warranted by the sales of their records.

Other black artists who seemed closer to traditional white musical tastes and moral values also received preferential pop programming and sub-sequently enjoyed greater white sales. A conspicuous example was New Orleans' Antoine "Fats" Domino, who was an Imperial recording star of several years' standing before he started an unmatched string of crossover successes in 1955 with songs like "Ain't that a shame" and "I'm so in love". Domino had to change little in his rollicking piano style and slightly coun-trified vocal cadences to become the most successful of all black rock and rollers. "That's just what he did", recalled his New Orleans neighbour, the multi-talented musician-composer-arranger-producer and entrepreneur, Harold Battiste. "And he was a hell of a piano player too . . . That cat could play some boogie woogie, man!", which serves as a reminder that rock and roll was not necessarily a dilution of r&b: sometimes what was dubbed rock and roll simply *was* r&b; at other times, it was an innovative hybrid which fused r&b with other influences to make a new sub-genre which, like all forms of popular music, could be good, bad or indifferent.[85]

Domino's essentially romantic songs, genial persona and rotund appear-ance simply defused much of the sexual threat which whites routinely asso-ciated with other black male rock and rollers. According to Battiste, "He was just a happy jolly guy. He wasn't a sexual threat. He might have been, but he didn't *appear* to be. He was more like Santa Claus". This allowed Domino to cross into the mainstream with relatively few problems. Vocal groups like the Coasters, Huey Smith and the Clowns, and the Olympics, who – the Coasters' hymen-popping "Young blood" notwithstanding – tended to offer a humorous rather than raunchy brand of rock and roll, also broke through onto pop radio and into the best-seller lists, outflanking white temerity in the face of black male sexuality through comedy. There was also a marked white media and market preference for juvenile or high tenor male lead vocalists, like Frankie Lymon and Tony Williams; for black girl groups, like the Bobbettes and Chantels; and for female soloists like Ruth Brown and LaVern Baker. Again, these artists generally avoided projecting the sort of dark disturbing sexuality which alarmed white adults and often excluded them from pop radio playlists.[86]

Intriguingly, even the androgynous Georgia peach, Little Richard, whose glitter-splashed suits, steepling pompadour and lusty lyrics actually presented a potent challenge to cherished sartorial and heterosexual norms, claimed that it was his high-camp appearance – "eyelashes longer than Josephine Baker's" – which secured him at least some access to the mainstream media and white audiences. "By wearing this make-up I could work and play white clubs and the white people didn't mind the white girls screaming over me. I wasn't a threat when they saw the eyelashes and the make-up. They was willing to accept me too, 'cause they figured I wouldn't be no harm".[87]

The Independents noted this pattern of white preferences and from late 1955 began to tailor their products accordingly. The white covers and the highly successful black mixture of novelty, romance and big beat balladry served as their musical templates. *Billboard* recognized this new turn of events in October 1955:

> Originally, Broadway publishers and record companies fought the trend [towards r&b]. Yet it overwhelmed them, forcing an attempt to understand it and latch on to it. Now many popular writers are writing r&b material. The most remarkable turn of events, however, is relatively new. It is the attempt of r&b writers to write for the pop field, and r&b singers to sing pop.
>
> In the last couple of months, this reverse twist – r&b making a studied attempt to go pop – has reached very sizeable proportions. One publisher termed the development "ironic" pointing out that r&b went pop because it was r&b, and also pointing out that as r&b tried to go pop, popular publishers are trying to go r&b.[88]

At Atlantic, it was Clyde McPhatter's "Seven days", recorded in August 1955, which marked the start of this calculated bid for a truly mass market. "We went much further to the straight pop side with 'Seven days'", recalled Ahmet Ertegun. "This retained only vestigial touches of r&b. It was the first date on which we used arranger Ray Ellis". Ellis' brand of "pop (but swinging)" writing and arranging increasingly dominated the Atlantic sound. McPhatter's beautiful high gospel tenor, which had stretched out across the shifting rhythms and perky harmonies of the Dominoes' and Drifters' hits in the early 1950s, was increasingly reined-in to the basic melody, which in turn was tethered to simple backings and driven by a forceful, but less supple, rhythm section. For proof, just compare McPhatter's exhilarating vocals and the instrumental and vocal accompaniments on the Dominoes' "That's what you're doing to me" (1952) or the Drifters' "Money honey" (1953), with his charming but more mannered solo recordings "Treasure of love" (1956) or "A lover's question" (1958).[89]

McPhatter's tremendously expressive voice salvaged many of his later recordings from their increasingly glutinous productions. Other acts were less fortunate. In 1956, the Clovers were re-converted, this time into an unconvincing rock and roll group who recorded tawdry teen material like "Love love love" and "So young" for the new biracial youth market. The group abandoned much of the clever vocal interplay of "Good lovin'" and "In the morning time" along with their adult tales of sex and insobriety. In their stead appeared a functional 4/4 beat and an increasing emphasis on linear harmonies which moved the songs along their rather predictable rhythmic and melodic lines. Finally, on "Your tender lips" the group's once vital harmonies were swamped by a shrill female chorus – a technique which, along with the gratuitous (mis)use of slick string arrangements, came to symbolize r&b's self-conscious bid for the mainstream market.[90]

By the end of the decade, Atlantic's crossover ambitions had compelled it to inflict the same sort of bowdlerization on its more "risqué" material that had characterized the sanitized white r&b covers of the mid 1950s. Just as Bill Haley had muted the sexual content of Joe Turner's "Shake, rattle and roll", so when Clyde McPhatter re-recorded the old Clovers' hit "Lovey Dovey" in 1959 the deliciously evocative poetry of "I really love your peaches, wanna shake your tree" was changed to the platitudinous "I really love you, baby, won't you come with me".

Atlantic's efforts to attract a mass white audience by sweetening the sound and sense of black r&b were matched by most of the Independents. At Aladdin, the Shirley and Lee of 1956's boisterous crossover success "Let the good times roll", with its almost child-like vocals, were not quite the same as the rapt Shirley and Lee of the 1952 r&b hit "I'm gone". Lloyd Price, the ABC rock and roll star who belted out "Stagger Lee" and "Personality" in front of a massed brass section and female chorus was barely recognizable as the passionate wailing bluesman who had cried "Lawdy Miss Clawdy" for Specialty in 1952.[91]

The smaller, neighbourhood Independents generally followed a similar policy, emphasizing the dominant beat, streamlining the harmonies, and cultivating "novelty" vocal techniques like the booming bass parts popularized by Sherman Garnes' introduction to "Why do fools fall in love", and culminating in the riveting vocal nonsense of the Marcels' "Blue moon". A comparison of the a cappella, "street" versions of the Mellows' songs for Celeste with the final released versions reveals repeated attempts to wrap the group's complex harmonies and flowing lead vocals in a variety of voguish commercial formulas. "I'm yours", for example, a lush mid-tempo ballad in its a cappella form, was given a rather incongruous mambo accompaniment. The swinging "Lucky guy" was transformed into an archetypal rock and roll work-out, complete with an off-beat piano derived from Johnny Johnson's work with Chuck Berry, an obligatory roaring saxophone, and a genuinely propulsive drum attack which drove the whole performance irresistibly forward – straight past the subtle rhythmic changes and rich harmonic blends of the vocal group. Sometimes, however, the new priorities worked to produce a sound which, while different from the r&b which preceded it, was in no respect its artistic or emotional inferior. The Mellows' soulful rock and roll ballad "My darling" was as poignant as anything in the whole wide world of Rhythm and Blues.[92]

"Down in the alley": sex, success and sociology among black vocal groups and shouters

Never trust a woman,
unless you know what's going down.
She'll hype you for your gold,
and cut out for another town. (T-Bone Walker, "Wise man blues")

It came not only from Memphis

The entwined commercial and racial agendas of the recording and radio industries, and the responses of adult whites to the sudden mass popularity of black and black-derived musics, profoundly affected the development of Rhythm and Blues in the mid-to-late 1950s. Yet irresistible forces at work within and upon the black community were also crucial in shaping those developments. Certainly, the evolution of black male vocal group style during the 1950s indicated that important social and demographic changes had already coalesced to produce widespread black approval for a "sweeter" strain of r&b, long before the industry began to pursue a similar strategy in its quest for a broader white audience. Indeed, in the late 1940s and early 1950s, these "sweet" musical and lyrical stylings had occasionally allowed a handful of romantic black harmonizers – including the Orioles ("It's too soon to know"), Five Keys ("Glory of love"), Vocaleers ("Be true"), and Harptones ("Sunday kind of love") – to infiltrate the white pop charts.[1]

In the mid 1950s, those same sweet qualities – in particular, an idealized vision of relations between the sexes which increasingly eclipsed the lusty adventurism, misogyny and fatalism at the heart of the male blues tradition – also enabled a new breed of young groups to spearhead the crossover of r&b. The Crows, Chords, Charms, Penguins, Spaniels and Moonglows had all enjoyed major pop hits before mid 1955 when Fats Domino and Bo

Diddley became the first r&b soloists of the rock and roll era to make the same transition.

While there were some notable southern exceptions, the secular vocal group scene was primarily a northern and an urban phenomenon. Consequently, placing these groups in the vanguard of r&b's breakthrough into the mainstream challenges traditional accounts of the origins of rock and roll in which the South, often Memphis, and sometimes just Sun Records, have routinely been hailed as *the*, rather than *a*, birthplace of the music. Certainly, it was in the South that *white* rock and roll had first appeared in the potent brew of country, r&b and pop influences known as rockabilly. The region boasted virtually all the key white figures in the early years of the music – Elvis Presley, Buddy Holly, Carl Perkins, Bobby Charles, Gene Vincent, and Jerry Lee Lewis.

By contrast, neither black r&b, nor black rock and roll, were so exclusively linked to the South. This is not to deny that Rhythm and Blues continued to flourish in the region. Memphis and New Orleans remained crucial centres of r&b activity throughout the 1950s, while black southerners like Fats Domino, Little Richard, Larry Williams and Shirley and Lee crossed over to become important early rock and roll hitmakers. Nevertheless, in the mid 1950s there were actually many more black acts based outside the South who made the same leap. Throughout the decade there was always as much black Rhythm and Blues of various stripe being cut in Cincinnati, New York, Chicago, Detroit and Los Angeles as below the Mason-Dixon line.

A remarkable amount of that non-southern r&b was made by black vocal groups. During the 1950s around 15,000 of them recorded for the first, and in many cases the only, time. By 1954 these groups accounted for more hit records in the black market than blues singers, shouters, jazz vocalists or instrumentalists combined. Untold numbers of groups never made a record, yet they all contributed to a remarkable flowering of organized r&b "musicking" in urban black America, where there flourished a vibrant, participatory vocal group culture, analogous in its social function to other black urban institutions like the churches and the street gangs. Some of these groups eventually led r&b's assault on the white charts and thus helped to define what the diverse phenomenon called rock and roll was all about. Moreover, because of their enormous popularity throughout black America in the 1950s they offer a fascinating insight into mass black culture and consciousness, just as the modern civil rights movement was emerging.[2]

Street culture, street sounds

When a small army of cultural anthropologists and sociologists invaded black urban America after the Second World War, they reported on a distinctive sub-culture with its own elaborate system of values, standards of excellence and codes of behaviour. The urban black masses, as a consequence of their unique historical experience and continuing marginalization within American society, had evolved their own ways of viewing the world and created distinctive cultural institutions and popular art forms in order to express and validate that perspective. Among the institutions which synthesized and dramatized the post-war black urban experience most effectively and effusively were the vocal groups.[3]

Although distinctive, black urban culture was crucially shaped by its relationship to a white-dominated mainstream culture which constantly affected both the material existence and the changing consciousness of black Americans. Black vocal groups of the 1950s, like other black performers and artists – indeed, like most black Americans – existed in a sort of cloven experiential, psychological and musical environment. They operated at the intersection of several overlapping heritages, exemplifying in their ambitions and reflecting in their music a vocalized version of the "double-consciousness" which W.E.B. Du Bois located as the central feature of the black American experience. On one hand there was something which both races conventionally recognized as "white" American popular music – although, historically, Tin Pan Alley pop was greatly indebted to African-American influences, most obviously ragtime, jazz and blues. On the other hand was the syncretic African-American musical tradition, with its own repertoire of favoured devices and performance practices, some of which were traceable back to Africa, but all of which had been recast to meet the needs of blacks in America. Where, between those shifting, notional, yet conventionally understood, black and white musical poles the mass black audience has allowed its most popular music to settle at a particular historical moment offers an imperfect but suggestive index of black racial consciousness at that moment.[4]

Black urban culture was no more monolithic than it was autonomous. Gender, generational and status differences were important within the community, even if broadly shared race and usually class characteristics produced a core of common experience and values. Certainly, ghetto culture was not, as some argued, a "pathological" response to the black predicament; a futile attempt to imitate the mores of the white world in much reduced circumstances. Rather, it represented a creative attempt by the black masses to establish a viable cultural arena for personal achievement and communal solidarity, while venting the accumulated frustrations of centuries of discrimination.[5]

Perhaps most crucially, the black world view and the culture which it generated, and by which it was in turn sustained, was not static. World views change as worlds change, or rather as they appear to change. Consequently the dominant modes of cultural adaptation to, and representation of, the black experience have changed with every perceived oscillation of black fortunes. The development and remarkable popularity of vocal groups in the 1950s revealed just such a process of adaptation to what many blacks perceived to be the dawning of a new era of expanded black opportunity.[6]

Among the social institutions which delineated black urban associational life, the one most closely related to the vocal group was the street gang. Sometimes the groups and the gangs even shared the same membership. In Baltimore, Johnny Page of the Marylanders doubled as a member of the Dungaree Boys gang, while Julius Williams had dual affiliations as a battling member of the Shakers and as a balladeer with the Royal Jokers in Detroit. "Julius Williams was the terror of the school", recalled his classmate Woodie King. "He was sixteen. He enjoyed fighting teachers and singing in class". When Claude Brown returned from a juvenile detention centre in upstate New York in the early 1950s, he noticed that many of the old gangs from his Harlem neighbourhood had turned to doowopping in the wake of the Orioles' inspirational rise from a Baltimore street corner, via an appearance on Arthur Godfrey's CBS radio show *Talent Scouts*, to national celebrity.[7]

Like the gangs, groups were comprised primarily of teenage or slightly older black male youths. Many were formed in the schools of black residential neighbourhoods, which even in the North were effectively segregated by a combination of racial custom, widespread black poverty and discriminatory real estate practices. In Los Angeles, Dootsie Williams harnessed talent from the Fremont High School for his Dootone and Dooto labels, including the Penguins, Medallions, Hollywood Flames and Dootones. Jefferson High in the same city schooled the Poets and Jayhawks, as well as other key figures in the local harmony scene like Richard Berry (Flairs, Pharoahs, Crowns), Cornelius Gunter (Flairs, Platters and Coasters), Curtiss Williams (Penguins) and Alex Hodge (Platters).[8]

Although the penetration of the mass media meant that young blacks were constantly exposed to the influence of white musical styles, the *de facto* residential segregation of their community and its educational facilities provided a relatively secluded racial environment within which they could cultivate their own forms of musical expression, drawing from an eclectic range of proximate and distant influences. Other "closed", predominantly or exclusively black institutions like athletics clubs, social and fraternal organizations, even prisons and detention centres, also provided the camaraderie and, in some cases literally, the captive audiences conducive to vocal group culture, where instant peer appraisal was an integral part of the doowop dynamic. The Prisonaires, for instance, were formed in the Tennessee State Penitentiary and relied on the beneficence of the state's country-loving Governor Frank Clement to allow them trips to Memphis to record for Sun. Similarly, James Brown began singing with Johnny Terry – later of Brown's Famous Flames vocal group – while serving three years in the Georgia Juvenile Training Institute for petty theft.

Reflecting the generational as well as demographic and socio-economic factors which gradually eroded the power of the black pulpit after the Second

World War, churches do not appear to have been particularly important as training grounds for northern secular vocal groups. Stuart Goosman's study of Baltimore and Washington revealed that even in those regionally schizo-phrenic border cities, few members of vocal groups had actually sung in sacred quartets. Certainly, many of the groups with deeper southern roots who did begin life in gospel, like the Five Royales or the Five Keys, marked their secularization with a move north, anxious to escape the spectre of profanity which still haunted any Dixie doowoppers not harmonizing in the service of the Lord.[9]

While there were sometimes differences in priorities between the gangs and the groups – "some teens grouped, whether in a social club or as harmony groups, and singing was the *purpose*, whereas some teens ran as a gang, and singing was the *consequence*" – they shared important functional characteristics. Both were essentially transient, adolescent affiliations: who else had the time to practice the harmonies or fight in the rumbles? Both were inherently unstable aggregations: members regularly came and went, their departure often related to the assumption of adult responsibilities, like marriage, parenthood, the draft or a job. Those who stuck at singing longer might form any number of associations. Jesse Belvin, the honey-voiced Texas-born singer-songwriter, who grew up in Los Angeles idolizing Frankie Laine and later wrote the Penguins' "Earth angel", recorded with the Gassers, Feathers, Cliques, Sheiks, Sharptones, Shields, Big Jay McNeeley's Orchestra, Red Callender's Orchestra and as half of the duo Jesse and Marvin, before pursuing a tragically brief solo career as a slick beat-balladeer for RCA which ended in 1959 when he was killed in an Arkansas car crash.[10]

At the local level, the group scene was remarkably incestuous. Everyone knew everyone else's songs, swapped members and copied ideas merci-lessly. This was community music and only if songs were recorded did legal questions of ownership and copyright become truly relevant. Then street composers were often robbed of, or persuaded to share, the legal title to songs they had worked out without formal notation by label owners and arrangers whose creative contributions were minimal. At Gee, George Goldner convinced Frankie Lymon, still a minor at the time, to share the copyright to "Why do fools fall in love". Goldner subsequently sold that share to Morris Levy, one of the more shadowy figures in the Independent scene with fairly undisguised links to organized crime. It was only in 1992 that two middle-aged Teenagers, Herman Santiago and Jimmy Merchant, finally persuaded a jury that they, not Levy or Goldner, had co-written the song with Lymon and were owed literally millions of dollars in unpaid royalties.[11]

This was not simply a case of white entrepreneurs exploiting black artists, but of those with some measure of money, power and expertise exploiting those without any of those things. Black deejay John Dolphin owned the Hollywood Records store in South Central Los Angeles. The shop also housed a rough and ready studio where he recorded and, by general consensus, regularly ripped-off local black talent for a succession of his own labels, the names of which, Cash and Money, said something about Dolphin's entrepreneurial agenda.

Gaynel Hodge, who recorded with and wrote for Jesse Belvin, the Turks and the Hollywood Flames, recalled that Dolphin "could put a record on the air the same day you recorded it, so you wanted to cut for him, even though you knew he'd screw you . . . he treated everyone like a fool". Dolphin hung around young black groups, plundering ideas, sometimes stealing songwriting credits outright. This happened with Jesse Belvin's self-penned "Dream girl", which was originally released in 1951 on the Dolphins of Hollywood label with one of its owner's many pseudonyms, Jacques, cited as composer. According to Hodge, this exploitation all became too much for one disgruntled young black songwriter called Percy Ivey, who finally got credit for a hit of sorts when he shot Dolphin to death.[12]

The black New York label owner Paul Winley also claimed co-credit for some of his young artists' songs. On the streets, however, it was simply known that "Hey little schoolgirl" really belonged to the Paragons, although this did not preclude outright plagiarism or creative reinterpretation by other groups. Sometimes the true origins of a street song were simply impossible to determine since so many people had contributed to its evolution. "Lily Maebelle", for example, was formalized and recorded by Richard Barrett and Raymond Briggs of the Valentines, but on the Harlem streets it was also associated with the Velvets and Keynotes.[13]

There were numerous examples of this sort of in-group expertise. "We bought the records by label colours", recalled Arlene Smith of the Chantels. Such arcane knowledge of the latest releases, dances, sartorial styles, and shifting group personnel contributed to the budding sense of, and pride in, a distinctive black sub-culture which would later flower in the black consciousness movement of the 1960s. Vocal groups were part of a homological black urban world with its own values and symbols, its own pantheon of heroes and indices of achievement, which functioned according to codes and rules sometimes only dimly apprehended by mainstream society.[14]

In his canonical text, *Urban blues*, Charles Keil broadly defined black "entertainment" to include most forms of non-literary performance like athletics, talking, preaching, hustling, sartorial style, dancing and music. This entertainment, he argued, constituted a "special domain of Negro culture wherein black men have proved and preserved their humanity". Notwithstanding Keil's casual disregard for the place of black women in this cultural project, he was correct in that entertainment was a critical arena for the formation and celebration of individual and communal black identities; for the winning of personal prestige and dignity within a sub-culture, whose members – with the partial and ambiguous exceptions of a Joe Louis, Jackie Robinson or Nat King Cole – were routinely denied the chance to earn that kudos in the wider social and economic sphere.[15]

The street, with its bars, laundromats, pool halls, liquor stores, corner stores, shoe-shine stands, barbershops, pawn shops, record stores and store-front churches, formed a distinctive lower-class milieu in which this black entertainment culture operated. Black vocal groups inhabited and helped to define this vibrant, if far from untroubled, environment. Imamu Amiri Baraka recalled that the sound of their music was "everywhere in that space, in the air, on the walls, in the halls, in the laundromats, whistled and sung and stomped to". Vocal groups were conspicuous features in the landscape and soundscape of post-war urban black life.[16]

Aspiring groups besieged neighbourhood clubs and theatres, waiting back-stage to impress their visiting idols or else performing in the many talent shows which provided a rich recruiting ground for record companies. In West Baltimore, the Plants, heroes for about a block around Schroeder Street, signed with J&S Records in New York after they were heard singing backstage at the Royal Theater prior to a Five Keys and Moonglows show.[17]

Some hopefuls swarmed around the offices of local labels hoping to give impromptu auditions. The Valentines cornered Hy Weiss of Old Town records in his Triboro Theater office cum cloakroom in East Harlem, while the Cleftones toured Old Town, Baton, Hull, Apollo and Red Robin before finally convincing George Goldner to hear them and offer them a contract with Gee.[18]

Other groups congregated at local record stores, learning the latest hits, hoping that the store owner's contacts with the record companies or their distributers might secure an opportunity to try out. The Swallows were discovered by a King representative as they rehearsed in Goldstick's record store in Baltimore. The Cardinals were auditioned by Jerry Wexler and Ahmet Ertegun in Sam Azrael's Super Music Store, another favourite hang-out for Baltimore groups, as was Shaw's shoe-shine parlour. Some groups, like the Five Blue Notes, recorded demos at local studios – US Recording Studios in Washington, D.C. charged just $1.25 a side in 1953 – and played them to label executives in the hope of securing a deal.[19]

Sometimes groups were discovered by chance, singing in and for their neighbourhood. Legend has it that the Charms were spotted by Syd Nathan at a park softball game in Cincinnati. The El Dorados were taken to Vee Jay by their school custodian who had heard them practising in the hallways of Chicago's Englewood High School. Black Harlem impresario Bobby Robinson found the Mellomoods "singing on a stoop up in the Harlem River Projects", and discovered the Channels in a Lenox Avenue rehearsal room. Ben E. King originally sang with the Five Crowns, and was subsequently the first in a long line of lead vocalists with the post-Clyde McPhatter Drifters. As King recalled, "They found you where you lived. And they didn't have a whole lot of selling to do. That was taken care of by the guys who had already made it, got a contract and all that garbage. News travelled fast. And those guys were instant heroes".[20]

Success stories quickly became part of black urban folklore and dreams of a recording contract and national stardom probably lurked somewhere in the minds of most group members. However, such conspicuous success was rare and invariably brief. Many groups never cut a disk; thousands released fewer than three. Every city had groups like the Chessmen in Washington, D.C., who cut one single ("I believe"/"Lola") at a local studio (Rodel) for a local label (PAC) as the culmination of a short career spent in neighbourhood clubs, theatres and bars. For the majority it was this local success, the quest for approval from a peer audience within their own neighbourhood or city, which was the primary goal. As Richard Berry, the Pharoah who would later carve himself a permanent niche in rock and roll history by cutting the original version of "Louie Louie", put it: "Our whole thing was singing, that was how we gained respect in our community". Vocal groups were thus part of a competitive world, in which contention for the available esteem was especially fierce and the quest for performative excellence also a struggle for self-respect, expression and status.[21]

This was nothing new to the 1950s. Between the wars, Harlem's secret gangs like the Meteors, Jolly Fellows, True Pals and Bullaloes had often danced, as well as fought, against each other. A victory on the dance floor of the Savoy Ballroom was as significant for gang prestige as one on the street. As Dan Burley recognized, the vocal group scene was just as competitive and territorial, sparking fierce loyalties from practitioners and fans. Most of the teen gangs had "their own singing quintets in which they take great pride very much the same as neighborhood gangs and clubs in the old days had their Charleston and Lindy Hop dance teams which they supported to the hilt".[22]

Because of this territoriality, distinct, sometimes antagonistic, vocal group scenes developed in most major cities, rooted in an intense commitment to a particular geographic locale and socio-psychological community. Thanks to Stuart Goosman, we know most about the demographics of the Baltimore and Washington, D.C. street corner group scenes which between them generated more than 60 recorded groups from the late 1940s to the early 1960s. In Baltimore, for example, there were fierce rivalries between East Baltimore groups like the Swallows, Cardinals, Honey Boys, Sonnets, Magictones, Jolly Jacks and Blentones, and groups like the Twilighters, Four Buddies and Plants who followed the Orioles out of the Old Town-West Baltimore area, with the bustling entertainment strip alongside Pennsylvania Avenue serving as both boundary and neutral zone between the two sections.[23]

Territorial loyalties could also create local celebrities who loomed larger than national stars within their own neighbourhoods, cities and regions.

Billboard's Rhythm and Blues record charts, while listing 231 black male vocal group entries between 1954 and 1963, merely hinted at the enormous popularity of such recordings, which often sold to purely local or regional markets and, therefore, did not make national lists. For example, despite failing to have a single national Rhythm and Blues chart hit, Nolan Strong's Diablos were probably the most consistently popular and influential group in mid-1950s Detroit. Similarly, while a record like the Five Blue Notes' "My gal is gone", recorded for the Chicago label Sabre, failed to make an impact elsewhere, in the group's hometown of Washington, D.C. it was a best-seller.[24]

Some recording companies and promoters capitalized on this balkanization of the black vocal group scene by packaging "confrontation" albums and sponsoring shows as "Battles of the Bands". Jubilee, for instance, released *The Cadillacs Meet The Orioles* and *The Paragons Meet The Jesters*. The last featured both groups' Winley singles and capitalized on the Brooklyn rivalry between them. The liner notes made the gang analogy explicit: "Gangway! It's the Paragons! Gangway! It's the Jesters! Relax! This is no *rumble*". The iconography of the sleeve was also revealing. It featured two brooding, leather-clad white teenagers. One, drawing on a cigarette, had "Jesters" emblazoned on his studded motorcycle jacket. Confronting them was an ominous, shadowy figure, presumably a rival "Paragon" gang member. Such artwork and copy did little to allay popular fears that black music and white juvenile delinquency were inextricably linked.[25]

Within the vocal group scene, the meld of a harmony, the daring of a particular vocal curlicue and the strict maintenance of, or smooth transition to, a difficult tempo, assumed a cultural currency peculiar to the ghetto. The channel, in particular, became the focus of intense scrutiny. The channel was the bridge, or middle-eight, section in a 32-bar song, usually coming around two-thirds of the way through the lyric. It was often characterized by a marked shift in the tempo, a remoulding of the melody, and a dramatic change in the vocal texture, sometimes with a new lead temporarily taking over, or a new combination of voices coming together, or the harmony parts disappearing to leave a single confessional voice. Often it was exhilarating, as on songs like the Dominoes' "I'd be satisfied", where the measures were seemingly spontaneously cut in half so that the song suddenly shifted up a gear. As Clyde McPhatter's lead vocal soared away from the strict melody, the rest of the group responded to the ecstatic new mood with excited shouts and get-happy handclaps drawn straight from the black gospel tradition. In retrospect, the seeds of soul were sown in such joyous, passionate outbursts.

The stylized channels on r&b ballads were just as critical. In the 1940s Hoppy Jones of the Ink Spots and Jimmy Ricks of the Ravens had popularized the spoken bridge with its specially heightened romantic lyrics. In the following decade most groups had at least one such spoken, "confessional", channel in their repertoire, as in the Marylanders' "Sittin' by the river", the Flamingos' "I'll be home" and the Velours' "Hands across the table". Even when it was not actually spoken, the channel still sounded the emotional heartbeat of many songs. It was also communally acknowledged as the moment when a group showcased its talents. Tiny nuances and manipulations of harmony, timbre and rhythm, often undetected by outsiders, carried great import for black cognoscenti. At the Apollo in Harlem, the channel was considered the litmus test of a group's capabilities and one group was even named in its honour. The Channels' magnificent "The closer you are" employed one of the most common channel change-ups – the switch to a three-part harmony lead *in front of* a bass and tenor vocal accompaniment – but in this case sustained that inverted arrangement throughout the whole song.[26]

Black vocal groups were not just concerned with the complexities of harmony, phrasing, rhythm and pitch. They also worked hard to project their material effectively. Success at local talent shows, club bookings, or the simple admiration of friends and rivals gathered in a school hall or tenement yard, often depended on an arresting presentation. An extra spin, split or shuffle or an especially lurid set of suits could set a group apart in the scramble for recognition and status. Inspiration for their stage acts came variously from touring gospel groups, like the Five Blind Boys of Alabama with their frenetic, possessed performances, or from older secular groups like the Five Royales and the Treniers who had already tapped into the drama and theatre of gospel shows. There were also masterly black Vaudeville dancers to emulate, like Honi Coles, Bill Robinson and, in particular, Cholly Atkins who mentored several vocal groups and later choreographed the early Motown revues. While many groups, including the Swallows, Nutmegs and Harptones, developed reputations for especially exhilarating live performances, the Cadillacs, coached by Atkins, seem to have been the most inspirational. "Oh, they were so sharp it hurt", recalled Ben E. King, "the Cadillacs had the best clothes, the best steps". "All the quartets sang louder when the Cadillacs cruised Brook Avenue", wrote poet David Henderson.[27]

Careers in harmony

With so much social prestige at stake, doowop was rarely just a hobby. Yet it seldom provided its many practitioners with a livelihood. "Think of all the money you're making", quipped an anonymous Vita engineer as he persuaded the exhausted Squires to attempt a thirteenth take of their song, "S'Cadillac". The spontaneous peals of laughter which broke around the Los Angeles studio suggested the paltry financial rewards actually available for most street-corner groups. According to Anthony Gourdine, variously of the Duponts, Chesters and, more famously, leader of the Imperials, "A hit record

Little Anthony and the Imperials typified the growing vogue for fresh-faced teen groups in the late 1950s.

to me was always when your friends heard you in your neighborhood, or heard your record on Doctor Jive . . . That's all that interested me, that the guys in my little world in Brooklyn heard it". As Bill Millar explained, "success in financial terms was statistically rare, but the gratification achieved by way of self-fulfillment, idle pleasure or fleeting recognition was no less important".[28]

With few groups enjoying the sort of sustained success required to make careers from their music, most fluctuated between amateur and temporary professional status depending on the existence or promise of a recording contract and the performance of their most recent release. Lillian Leach and the Mellows, for example, recorded four singles for Joe Davis' Jay Dee label in 1954 and 1955, the same number for Celeste, and one for Candlelight in 1957. Compared with many of their Brooklyn contemporaries, this made them virtually industry veterans. Yet the Mellows always remained essentially a local, street-oriented group. Their recordings sold primarily in New York and they never played a bigger concert date than the Baby Grand up on 125th Street. At a Celeste rehearsal on 12 October 1956, the talkback prior to the tenth rehearsal take of "Ain't she got a nerve" betrayed the group's continued connection with the street. One member can be heard complaining that he still could not get used to singing in front of a microphone. In general, doowop was an integral, if transient, part of many young black lives, rather than a career option.[29]

Because of this "amateurism" there was a tendency to dismiss the doowop groups as crude and unpolished, not least within the industry itself. Paradoxically, at Atlantic, where the Clovers and Drifters were an immense influence on young groups, Jerry Wexler, and to a lesser extent Ahmet Ertegun, harboured an almost congenital dislike of their impecunious street-corner imitators. Wexler felt that their style was invariably too raw, their harmonies too shabby and unsophisticated for the carefully manicured r&b material which Atlantic initially aimed at an increasingly urbane black audience. Furthermore, Atlantic was interested in cultivating durable star performers, not one-off hit records, and few of the doowop groups appeared to have the ability or flexibility to sustain successful careers.[30]

Certainly, Atlantic recruited relatively few street-corner groups directly from the neighbourhood talent shows, record stores, and schoolyards which provided such rich pickings for other labels. And when it did gamble on raw talent, like the Chords or Cardinals, the concern for harmonic precision and vocal clarity persisted. "Sh-boom", for instance, took 22 takes to get right, while Jesse Stone used to go to Baltimore prior to the Cardinals' recording sessions in order to rehearse them to Atlantic's rigorous musical standards. "They couldn't read music, which made it very difficult, and it took them six or eight months before we started getting hits", he recalled. Little wonder, then, that Atlantic, with its concern for many of the musical values which underpinned traditional white popular music, became the most consistently successful of the independent labels in the early years of crossover.[31]

In truth, the range of talent and commitment among vocal groups was enormous. Paul Winley was driven to despair by the erratic performances of some of his Brooklyn youngsters. Commenting on his first session with the Paragons, which produced unusable versions of subsequent doowop anthems "Florence" and "Hey little schoolgirl", Winley said, "It was murder! . . . the guy who sang lead for the group, Julius McMichael, could never sing the same thing twice and if he could he couldn't remember what he was saying. The people could never understand what he was saying".[32]

Other groups, however, were both conscientious and highly proficient. For groups invariably lacking a formal musical education, learning the intricacies of vocal harmony required long hours of patient practice. "Getting the perfect mix of voices and personalities was difficult", recalled Herbie Cox of the Cleftones. James McGowan of the Four Fellows remembered,

> Harmony. It became a magic word to us. We were totally captivated by it . . . we vowed we would learn it. But our first attempts were pathetic. The secret, we knew, was that each of us had to sing a different part. But what were those parts? Our young and untrained minds could hardly tell . . . we were frustrated most of the time.

The groups laboriously learned their trade from disks, radio, concerts and other more accomplished groups in their neighbourhoods. "For us", continued McGowan, "it was an extremely long and difficult process . . . we had nothing more than the sound of other groups to go on."[33]

Many groups were remarkably successful in mastering the mysteries of well-honed harmony. Recordings of the Mellows' audition and subsequent a cappella rehearsals at Celeste reveal a disciplined group with a sophisticated harmonic and rhythmic conception and two magnificently controlled lead vocalists in Howard Johnson and the incomparable Lillian Leach, whose voice somehow contrived to blend the world-weary ache of Billie Holiday with the upbeat exuberance of a Little Esther. Yet the Mellows were formally untutored and relied heavily on Johnson's ability to work out the individual harmony parts and hours of careful practice to perfect them.

The hard work behind these fine harmonies belies easy assumptions of some kind of natural polish and rhythm among black groups, although exposure to the rich black sacred and secular musical traditions undoubtedly helped to encourage and mould any vocal talents. It is also important to recognize that harmony, the elusive quality these black groups so diligently sought to master, was rather more central to the "European" classical and white pop traditions than to the blues tradition. With its refracted echoes of African musical sensibilities and techniques, the blues tradition tended to subordinate harmonic considerations to melodic and rhythmic priorities and emphasize vocal expressiveness over notions of *bel canto* precision.[34]

The vocal groups, however, embraced a rather more "European" conception of close harmony, even as they, like the gospel groups before them, radically subverted it to suit their own needs, and recast it to preserve the primacy of the testifying individual voice in a group context. Without seeking to make the link between musical forms and the societies which produce them too mechanistic, the increased deployment and popularity of "sweet", "Euro-American" harmonies after the Second World War does appear to have been related to the emergence of a new urbane black audience which was heavily exposed to and influenced by nominally "white" musical forms, imbued with deep integrationist aspirations and, at least from the mid 1950s, armed with a guarded faith in the potential of the nascent civil rights movement to realize those dreams.

Just as many vocal groups dissolved the rigid distinction between "amateur" and "professional", they also existed at the intersection of nominally "folk" and "commercial" musical traditions. They invariably learned their songs by rote, their dance steps by observation, and passed them on to their contemporaries by the same process: all mechanisms associated with oral and folk traditions. At the neighbourhood level, instant feedback from those rivals and friends who gathered to hear the latest quartets, quintets and sextets perform enabled audiences to influence the sound, sense and style of the vocal groups directly. This relationship was preserved even as it was commodified in such hotbeds of commercial enterprise as the Apollo Theatre in Harlem, where aspiring black talent was regularly exposed to the hyper-critical attentions of black audiences on Amateur Night. If the Apollo audience did not like an act, a barrage of catcalls summoned a character called Porto Rico from the wings to usher the luckless performers out of the spotlight and into oblivion.[35]

At the Regal in Chicago, the Uptown in Philadelphia, the especially notorious Royal in Baltimore – "there was only one place in the world we wanted to be in less than Korea", explained Herb Cox, "that was the Royal Theater" – and many other far less illustrious locations, from street corner to community hall, groups had their performances vigorously critiqued by their peers. By abandoning or refining songs, styles and dance steps of which their audience disapproved, while retaining those techniques and innovations which were most popular, the groups absorbed the pervasive spirit of their community and, quite literally, re-presented it to them in musical form. With their proximate and participating peer audience, the groups provided urban blacks with precisely the sort of "musicking" described by Christopher Small, in which "the identity and the values of the members of a social group are explored, affirmed and celebrated".[36]

The intrusion of the recording and broadcasting industries inevitably modified, but did not necessarily destroy, this intimacy between the vocal groups and the black community. The neighbourhood location of many of the smaller Independents, and the commercial priorities of them all, helped to guarantee their basic responsiveness to the shifting tastes of their primary black audience. Thus, the growing popularity of the groups reflected more than the simple manipulation of consumer preferences by an exploitative industry. The black community's power of consumption and non-consumption acted as a powerful restraint on industry attempts to impose new styles against its will, or to reorient particular artists in ways which black audiences rejected. After all, there were always other musical choices available, some of which continued to flourish alongside the increasingly popular vocal groups.

Significantly, however, the tiny neighbourhood labels of the North and West which were most heavily dependent on the black "backyard" market often recorded little besides vocal groups. For obvious commercial reasons, these labels concentrated on recording the most popular types of acts for local consumption and, notwithstanding the continued popularity of the blues among older migrant southerners and the limited support for modern jazz among the urban masses, these were invariably vocal groups. Celeste, Flash, Derby, Onyx, Hull and their ilk recorded virtually nothing else. The larger, but still regionally rooted, Fortune label in Detroit included 101 vocal group records in its 177 releases between 1950 and 1961 (57 per cent). In New York, Bobby Robinson's Red Robin released 39 singles between 1952 and 1956, including 23 by groups (59 per cent).[37]

Larger, nationally oriented Independents, with the resources to exploit what were becoming minority tastes even within the black community, included a larger proportion of shouters, blues singers, gospel choirs, jazz vocalists and instrumentalists among their artists, but vocal groups were still heavily represented. Atlantic's 547 single releases between 1947 and 1961 included 155 by vocal groups (28 per cent); Vee-Jay's 289 releases between 1953 and 1961 included 87 vocal group records (30 per cent); Herald's 197 and Ember's 103 releases between 1952 and 1963 included 76 and 47 group recordings respectively (39 per cent and 46 per cent).[38]

Ultimately, participation in vocal group culture, whether as singer or listener, served as a means of socialization for young black men which enabled them to identify and conform to the norms of urban adult male behaviour. This was especially important for those recently arrived in the city from the country. "In the early fifties", recalled Woodie King, "the South was not far behind. It was not far behind any of us." For those young blacks physically and mentally fleeing the rural South, the vocal group scene served alongside other ghetto institutions to ease them into a strange new environment. As King's namesake Ben, a migrant from Henderson, North Carolina, explained, "Singing could help you get it all together. Turn you into a city boy, you know?"[39]

But just as gang membership required the individual to make compromises in the interest of the collective by acknowledging particular rules of conduct and hierarchies of command, so joining a vocal group required young blacks to concede certain personal, musical and social freedoms in the interest of the group. This promoted a degree of discipline and interdependency among the young doowoppers which was common among jazz musicians but somewhat less marked among the solo electric bluesmen, honkers and shouters who had previously dominated black secular music's non-jazz stream. Some of the intense individualism, which an older generation of bluesmen had reified in their songs and personified in their lives, evaporated under the unificatory demands of group rehearsals, tight harmonies, and synchronized dance steps. The reward for this subordination to gang or group discipline was a sense of belonging, community and camaraderie. "It's just real hard to describe now the feeling a quartet gave you", said Ben E. King. "You never felt alone, is all."[40]

At their most resonant, vocal groups not only reflected the material circumstances of black urban life and its key values in their structure and songs, they also articulated the community's deepest aspirations. Traditionally, that is one of popular culture's most important social functions. It offers a creative space in which to dream; an arena in which to play with and test alternative ideas and realities, as well as one in which to explore and express existing ones. Vocal groups symbolized and, as we shall see, increasingly sang of an idealized vision of a united, harmonious black community which was seldom seen in the real world.

The vibrant street-corner group scene of the 1950s declined precipitously during the following decade. The increased sophistication and cost of studio technology rendered the raw, documentary style recordings of most local groups *passé*. The sound of a cappella street-corner singers was far removed from the fulsome productions of Motown and Stax, which increasingly dominated the black charts. There may even have been some sense that whereas it was hip in the 1940s and 1950s to join a group or a gang, it had become just as hip by the early 1960s to join the Movement. David Henderson wrote of the transformation of an old group hang-out into a civil rights headquarters, "1501 Boston Road is Bronx C.O.R.E./(stompers have risen to politics)", while in Oakland, David Hilliard eventually gave up his quartet to join the Black Panthers. It was as if some of the desires, energies and frustrations previously channelled into, and to some extent diffused by, cultural means and intra-communal competition had at last found expression in genuine action against the sources of black oppression.[41]

Early teen groups and politics of black macho

For the sociological reasons already described, teenagers had always dominated the vocal group scene. Yet there were important differences in the musical style and sexual politics of the young male groups which emerged around 1954 when compared with their predecessors. This amounted to something rather more significant than the fact that their mean ages tended to drop a couple of years, or the related fact that their voices tended to be pitched a couple of tones higher. Instead, it represented – in the cultural sphere at least – a new vision of black sexual politics, which itself reflected important changes in black consciousness as a new phase of the black freedom struggle began.

The young groups of the late 1940s and early 1950s had developed a style which was remarkably "adult" and virtually indistinguishable from that of their older mentors – the pioneer r&b vocal groups like the Dominoes, Drifters, Clovers and Five Royales. This was evident in both the sound and sense of their music. In Baltimore, for example, Leon Harrison of the Four Buddies and Eddie Rich of the Swallows were both teenage leads, but their singing represented an attempt to transcend that fact, not to dwell on or celebrate it. They wanted to sound like their adult idols, not like lovesick teenagers. For Harrison that urge manifested itself in a smooth, rather mellow vocal style on songs like "I will wait" and "My summer's gone" which hinted at the elegance of Nat King Cole. Rich, who sang lead on the Swallows' romantic ballads "Eternally" and "Dearest", had a slightly world-weary, blues-tinged delivery which similarly belied his youth.

The subject matter for these early teen groups was also imitative of their older idols, comprising an "adult" mixture of smouldering, sometimes quite bitter, blues ballads, romantic torch songs, lowlife picaresques and joyous jump tunes, often with a heavy helping of male braggadocio and sexual innuendo. The teen groups of the early 1950s sang themselves and their peers into black adulthood. Like their vocal group elders, the electric bluesmen and the shouters, they sang, codified and helped to perpetuate the conventional social, and especially sexual, wisdoms of male black America as embodied in the blues lyrical tradition. As Amiri Baraka recalled:

> The lyrics of the blues instructed me. Explained what the world was and even how men and women related to each other, and the problems inherent in that. Even later so basic a communication as "Work with me Annie", then "Annie had a baby (Annie can't work no more)", could just about sum up some aspects of life in the black ghetto part of the Western Hemisphere.[42]

In the blues tradition, forged in the South just as the false dawns of emancipation and Reconstruction gave way to the long debilitating darkness of Jim Crow and disenfranchisement, the portrayal of relationships between the sexes was often pessimistic, vicious, exploitative and sometimes just plain petrified. This was overwhelmingly the case with male performers, although anger, disillusionment, bitterness and frustration with the opposite sex were also conspicuous elements in many female blues songs. In the male blues tradition, women were paradoxically depicted as both the primary source of disorder and grief in the black man's world and as indispensable to his happiness and self-esteem. Women in the blues were sirens: irresistible yet lethal, they were to be loved, but more importantly, to be tamed and controlled.

The historical roots of this perspective are tangled and complex. Some writers like E. Franklin Frazier and later, with serious repercussions for the black psyche and the struggle for civil rights, Daniel Moynihan, argued that the matriarchal nature of black society and the emasculation of the black male was one source of the black man's hostility towards the black woman and, for Moynihan at least, the key to continued black disadvantage in America.[43]

Black matriarchy was traced to slavery, when the black man was rendered unable to fulfil his "natural" patriarchal function as breadwinner and protector. As the black male was forced to submit to humiliating physical abuse at the hands of a master or overseer, and compelled to watch impotently as his wife and children were similarly brutalized, so his authority, respect and power within his own family were fatally undermined. This emasculation produced a matriarchal society, with the black woman emerging as titular or functional head of the household. This pattern was sustained after emancipation as black women found relatively abundant, if still tightly circumscribed, opportunities in the job market, while black males struggled in vain for the economic opportunities and social status which might restore their patriarchal authority and self-respect.

Subsequent scholarship has both undermined this crude concept of a black matriarchy and refined our understanding of its origins. The extent to which the black male was emasculated under slavery and afterwards has been re-evaluated by historians like Eugene Genovese and Lawrence Levine, who have stressed cultural modes of resistance to that process. In the 1970s, Herbert Gutman began the process of reincorporating the black men of history into a more stable, double-headed family structure than previously imagined. As New South historian Edward Ayers has summarized, despite the powerful disruptive forces which have constantly worked to undermine the black family, North and South – the perpetual discrimination, the forced and voluntary migrations, the endemic poverty – in the main, "two-parent black families had been able to hold together under the buffeting of slavery and war, and most even managed to stand up to the postbellum world as well". Indeed, by 1950, 77.7 per cent of black families in America still had both parents at home and only 17.2 per cent were headed by a female.[44]

The concept of a black matriarchy has also been attacked from other perspectives. Joyce Ladner has decried a distortive "confusion of the terms *dominant* and *strong*", in discussions of the black woman whereby she "has almost become a romantic, legendary figure . . . almost superhuman, capable of assuming all major responsibilities for sustaining herself and her family through harsh economic and social conditions". Historians like Deborah White and Brenda Stevenson, who rightly stress the centrality of black women to the black social and familial experience, prefer to think in terms of a community which has often been "matrifocal", rather than matriarchal. Whatever their status within the confines of the family, black women have enjoyed none of the economic, social and status power advantages associated with a real matriarchy. At best, they have historically experienced a relatively elevated situation according to certain economic indices, most notably employment rates and educational opportunities, within a racial group which has been severely disadvantaged relative to American society as a whole.[45]

And yet, the myth of black matriarchy has remained largely impervious to such empirical refutation and careful analysis, precisely because it has always been such a coherent, flexible and convenient one. The myth of matriarchy and the attendant images of the overpowering, emasculating black woman have helped render black America and its apparent failings easily comprehensible to whites. Black matriarchy explained the reality of black disadvantage without raising awkward doubts about the basic soundness of the socio-economic system in which racial inequality was embedded.[46]

One of the deepest tragedies of black history is that the same matrix of racial and sexual stereotypes also offered many black males an easy rationale for their, and their community's, plight. Frustrated at their continued exclusion from full social, economic and political participation in American society, convinced that black women enjoyed special privileges and power in that world, and jealous of the white man's patriarchal authority, many black men turned to the myth of matriarchy to explain their distress.

The two poles of the negative female categorizations enshrined in the myth of black matriarchy were personified by the Aunt Jemima and Sapphire stereotypes: one compliant, deferential and domesticated; the other, increasingly dominant during the twentieth century, manipulative and sensual. These stereotypes, with their capacity for endless refinement, formed part of a discursive regime, the continued strength of which depended upon its ability to explain and legitimize a perceived social reality. Sapphire, especially – demanding, fickle, vengeful, domineering, vain and cunning – lay at the heart of the black man's problems. Consequently, she was also the pivot around which most distinctively black male culture traditionally revolved.[47]

The overwhelming psychological imperative of many black male public rituals and forms of popular expression has been the symbolic destruction of the power and dignity of the black woman and the reification of a powerful, resolutely masculine, compensatory male identity. Many of the jokes, toasts, proverbs, tales and superstitions collected from urban black America by folklorists revealed the deep sexual antagonisms of the ghetto. According to Daryl Cumber Dance, most of the tales black men told about women were "blatantly anti-female . . . most of the jokes are bitter". Indeed, many were terrifying in their conflation of sexual desire, crude sexual objectification and violence towards women. "Frequently the sexual desire for the woman is in itself a longing to violate, to humiliate, to injure and even to kill the woman".[48]

Those tales which did not actually depend for their "humour" on the degradation of women sought to inflate the black male ego in other ways. Male sexual prowess was valorized and exaggerated to become chiefly a mechanism for asserting an often brutal authority over the troublesome, unruly and sexually insatiable black woman. This cultural attempt to resuscitate flagging black manhood by destroying the integrity of black womanhood reached its zenith in the long toasts, or rhymed poems, with their distinctive pantheon of macho heroes. These "Bad Niggers", like John Henry, Dolomite, Stack O'Lee, Jody The Grinder and Shine, "are sexual supermen, but their women are enemies to be conquered, humiliated and controlled, rather than partners to be loved".[49]

This celebration of black macho and the systematic denigration of the black female was also a central feature of the male blues tradition, where, according to Matthew White, bluesmen "were able to exert power and control . . . exercise the prerogatives and privileges of a man in a patriarchal society through song . . . The very act of singing the blues . . . is an unconscious exercise in the assertion of male control." While bluesmen readily conceded the black woman's sexual allure – a pretty woman could, as Sonny Boy Williamson put it, bring "eyesight to the blind" – they usually did so with a mixture of awe and trepidation, since this sexual magnetism robbed men of agency and empowered women.[50]

Bluesmen routinely blamed the black woman for the breakdown of personal relationships, citing her congenital avarice and promiscuity. Her insatiable quest for greater riches and better sex may have been "natural" from the bluesman's perspective, but it was also an unacceptable affront to male pride and authority. Bluesmen frequently resorted to terror to try to bring their women to heel, as in Robert Johnson's "32-20" ("If she gets unruly . . . Take my 32-20, now, and cut her half in two"). Sometimes the violence directed against women in the blues was chilling. "I'm gon' get my pistol/ 40 rounds of ball,/ I'm gon' shoot my baby,/ just to see her fall", sang Furry Lewis.

By contrast, male infidelity was presented not just as a natural manly trait, but often as one to be positively encouraged; a source of pride not shame. In the blues, a man's social esteem was frequently measured by the number of sexual conquests he could boast, or the drinks he could down, or the fights he had won. This macho posturing was more than simply a matter of lyrical theme, it was projected and validated in the personae of the tough, hard-drinking, womanizing bluesmen and the legends surrounding their lives. In the 1930s, Robert Johnson had set the standard. His febrile guitar playing, possessed vocals and soul-wrenched lyrics combined with a hedonistic lifestyle to give credence to the legend that he owed his talent and earthly delights to a pact with the devil. When Johnson died, poisoned, it was said, by a lover's jealous husband, his mythic status as the ultimate "Bad Nigger" soared, not least among the white music critics and fans who rediscovered Johnson in the mid 1960s, and who have always preferred their black musical heroes, from Johnson through Charlie Parker to Jimi Hendrix, to fit romantic, libertine stereotypes.[51]

The image of the early bluesman as a sexually prolific "Bad Nigger" struggling to control the alluring, but insubordinate and untrustworthy black woman was carefully tended by the likes of Peetie Wheatstraw, the self-styled "Devil's son-in-law", and endorsed in the work of post-war electric bluesmen like Howlin' Wolf, Muddy Waters, Eddie Boyd, John Lee Hooker and Elmore James. It passed easily enough into the repertoires of the r&b shouters of the 1940s and early 1950s, and into the ribald, "adult" side of the vocal group repertoire of the same era, where the Dominoes' "Lovin' Dan", the inexhaustable "Sixty minute man" and his many imitators – among them the Heartbreakers' "Rockin' Daddy-O", and the Sultans' "Lemon squeezing daddy" – were quintessential macho heroes.[52]

The shouters, in particular, were unremitting in their assertion of black male sexual potency. While a self-deprecating humour frequently crept into their macho celebrations, moderating them in a way which was rare in the blues, the primary thrust of their songs was to exalt black manhood. The superhuman feats they celebrated above the hard-driving sound of Kansas-City-style horns were mostly in bed, with sexual domination the primary mode of subduing the troublesome black woman and asserting male control. Roy Brown and his Mighty-Mighty Men, Bullmoose Jackson and his Bearcats – the names alone revealed much – Wynonie Harris, Joe Turner, Amos Milburn and others, constructed powerful macho mythologies around themselves and their carnal capacities. Brown, for example, was a "Mighty mighty man", a "Midnight lover man", a "Good rockin' man", and an independent "Travelin' man", who offered his women an endless dose of "Good rockin' tonight". Bullmoose Jackson announced "I want a bowlegged woman", and may have got his wish thanks to his "Big ten inch . . . (record)". Amos Milburn trumped them all on "Walking blues" by claiming that a shake of his formidable penis could even raise the dead.

Complementing this celebration of male sexual prowess was the recurring, if often poetically inventive, sexual objectification of women, usually coupled with a claim of male propriety, as in Wynonie Harris' "I like my baby's pudding". This image was chosen from a lengthy menu of culinary tropes, and in the early 1950s most r&b performers spent at least some of their time eating cherry pie, baking jelly roll, squeezing lemons, churning milk until the butter comes, or savouring the delights of dripping honey. Car imagery, in particular the phallic hood, was also very popular, as in Roy Brown's "Cadillac baby", Howlin' Wolf's "Mr Highway Man" ("This here cadillac is a long ragged machine/me and my baby can ride and ev'rything'll be good to me"), and the Hollywood Flames' "Ride Helen ride".

In this lyrical tradition, the imperative to cultivate a strong macho image tended to overwhelm, if never entirely eradicate, themes which implied male tenderness or vulnerability. Peculiarly male faults rarely occasioned feelings of contemplation or guilt, but were instead transformed into symbols of manhood. Thus, the failures of marriages and other relationships, failures which were often rooted in the psychological and economic ravages of poverty and racism, were explained in terms of the black man's impressively rampant libido and the black woman's shameful lust and greed. "You should have seen what a girl of 17 did to me!", exclaimed the Du-Droppers, who as real black men were naturally powerless to resist such advances and therefore conveniently absolved of all responsibility for seizing their chance to do the "Bam-Balaam".

Instead of being viewed as a vice, the prodigious, almost competitive, drinking, through which some black men occasionally sought to escape the grim realities of their everyday lives, also became the subject for a redemptive humour, boasting and celebration. "Came home one night with a spinning in my head/ reached for the pillow, missed the whole darned bed", moaned Jimmy Liggins on "Drunk". Texan Amos Milburn served up many of the best drinking songs, with "Bad bad whiskey", "One scotch, one bourbon, one beer", and "Vicious, vicious vodka" highlights in a well-stocked repertoire. Many of these lushes' lullabies were written by Atlantic songwriter Rudolph Toombs, who mixed tales of drunkenness and sexual adventurism in a heady, often hilarious, r&b cocktail, most famously in the Clovers' "One mint julep" with its classic vow, "I'm through with flirting and drinking whiskey/ I got six extra children from a gettin' frisky".[53]

While black men were often depicted as sexual, if sometimes heroically inebriated, supermen in the male r&b of the early 1950s, black women were inevitably trouble. Paradoxically, their ravenous "unfeminine" sexual appetites placed unfair demands upon even the indefatigable black man, as in Wynonie Harris' "Hard ridin' mama" and the uproarious "All she wants to do is rock". Harris was perhaps the most formidable and gifted of all the shouters. A Nebraskan blessed with lungs like leather, Harris first came to prominence belting out the blues above Lucky Millinder's jump orchestra in the mid 1940s. He fancied himself to be something of an expert on female psychology and assured readers of *Tan* magazine that what black women really hankered after "deep down in their hearts was a hellion, a rascal". Modestly billing himself as the "Hard-drinkin', hard-lovin', hard-shoutin' Mr Blues", Harris was proud to be of service.[54]

Yet even the mighty Harris sometimes despaired of ever being able to exercise the requisite control over the black woman. In "Adam, come and get your rib" he portrayed himself as the innocent victim of female duplicity, slyly linked black women with original sin, and sought nothing less than to reverse the Biblical account of her creation: "She's been cheatin'/she's been lyin'/she's left my poor heart cryin'/So Adam, come and get your bone". As for himself, Harris had already decided that rather than waste his time trying to forge a satisfactory relationship with a flesh and blood black woman, he was better off servicing his not-insubstantial sexual needs with a home-made, mechanical "Lovin' machine" ("put some money in the slot/ you hear some buzzin',/kisses while they're hot/five cents a dozen"). The

Five Royales had even more obviously dehumanized female sexuality in "Laundromat blues" ("Her machine is full of suds . . . / it will cost you 30 cents a pound"), while the Toppers' "Let me bang your box" lacked any of the lyrical ingenuity which ironically characterized some of the most demeaning songs.

Many of Harris' songs, because of, rather than in spite of, their outrageous sexism, were genuinely hilarious. A failure to appreciate the politically incorrect humour in this music risks ripping it from its historical context and reducing the true complexities of what was going on here to hollow platitudes. Harris, like many of his fellow bellowers, was at one level exaggerating and parodying a jaundiced black male view of relations between the sexes. Black audiences recognized, in a way which often eluded white r&b fans, that this broad mockery represented but one possible aspect of black male consciousness and behaviour. The shouters depicted an all-too-common, but in no way all-pervasive, pattern of black domestic relationships and sexual attitudes, rather than their totality.

And yet, at another level, the cumulative effect of drawing almost all their humour from the denigration of women, the aggrandizement of a predatory, irresponsible machismo, and the depiction of preternaturally doomed, exploitative, personal relationships was to help legitimize and routinize such thoughts and attitudes. While Tin Pan Alley pop was hardly without its own sexism, the blues lyrical tradition to which the shouters were heirs had by sheer repetition helped to make a peculiarly intense, aggressive, and often violent form of sexism seem entirely banal. In the blues and much early r&b, a fatalistic resignation to the improbability of stable, mutually respectful domestic relationships was commonplace. These tendencies in black society, and their representation in its popular culture, did not reflect some aberrant pathological trait in black male personalities; it was what happened when the patriarchal and sexist impulses and patterns of American society at large were amplified by the particular pressures of racism and poverty.[55]

Given that pervasive poverty, it was not surprising that another recurring complaint in male r&b was that the scheming black woman frivolously spent the black man's hard-earned cash and rewarded him with nothing but infidelity and demands for more money. This was the message of the Robins' "All night long", Amos Milburn's "Money hustling woman", and Roy Brown's comical "Whose hat is that?". Ray Charles also explored this theme in "It should've been me", a Memphis Curtis composition from 1954 which linked the black hero's lack of money to his failures with the opposite sex. Money, and what it could buy, was one means to get attention and respect from the avaricious black woman, since a real man was one who could provide material well-being as well as sexual satisfaction. "It should've been me with that real fine chick,/ Drivin' that Cadillac", moaned Ray Charles. The ubiquity of the phrase "romance without finance can be a nuisance", and even more so its sentiments, further reflected the extent to which black unemployment and poverty frequently shaped relations between the sexes. The Drifters' "Money honey" opened with a classic image of black tenement life – "My landlord's ringing the front door bell,/ I let it ring for a long, long, spell" – and then described how poverty had moulded the hero's attitude to women: "you need money, honey,/ if you want to get along with me".

Eddie "Cleanhead" Vinson was a bald saxophonist-shouter whose vocals on romps like "Cherry red" incorporated a distinctive sibilant hiccup, a bit like a leaking tyre. When, in 1954, Vinson confessed that he had blown over $100,000 on "whisky and women", even his contrition took on a peculiarly boastful and accusatory tone. "There was a lot of married women mixed up in this spending spree of mine", he revealed. "That's one thing I have yet to understand: why a woman with a home and a good husband liked to sneak around on the side with the payoff a fur jacket, some steak dinners and plenty of scotch". Not that Vinson let this bemusement prevent him from taking his own pleasures as and when they presented themselves. What did make him mad, however, was the craven acquisitiveness of these women. "All she wanted was to get hold of my bankroll", he complained of one woman, incredulous that a spin on the sheets with the dome-headed sax-machine was not reward enough. "The chicks were . . . milking me for every penny I had", he added, clearly seeing himself as the helpless victim of female cunning and a surfeit of manliness in these encounters.[56]

What was at stake in all these macho r&b songs, and in black male culture more generally, was power. Mastery over the black woman could compensate for the black man's lack of social, economic and political power, for his inability to control many of the crucial circumstances of his life. And while it is vitally important to stress that in that reality most black men did not succumb to these extreme macho or misogynistic stereotypes, their pre-eminence in male popular culture served to validate their right, indeed duty, to try to claim and assert a "natural" patriarchal power over the black woman.

Not surprisingly, black women had a rather different take on this whole business. Male r&b always needs to be seen as part of an ongoing, often hilarious, sometimes vicious, and usually highly inventive dialogue with female r&b. It is a dialogue which has dramatized, sometimes caricatured, but in turn helped to shape a genuine debate over sex roles and domestic responsibilities within the black community. Ruth Brown, Dinah Washington, Joyce Bryant, Little Esther, Julia Lee, Big Mama Thornton and their like gave as good as they got in the r&b sex wars of the 1940s and early 1950s. Extending the sexual politics of the classic women's blues canon of Bessie Smith, Ma Rainey, Mamie Smith and Ethel Waters, they offered sharp and witty critiques of black male inadequacies – usually transposed into the sexual and economic spheres – and a measure of female assertiveness and genuine eroticism which had no equal in the white pop canon. In the process, they, like their 1920s predecessors, constructed themselves as sexual subjects, rather than remaining the sexual objects they were reduced to in most male blues songs.[57]

Many female r&b songs, including Little Esther's "Double crossin' blues" and Ruth Brown's "Mama, he treats your daughter mean" roundly denounced faithless and callous men. Others, like Dinah Washington's "Baby, get lost" and Big Mama Thornton's "Hound dog", boldly affirmed women's right to personal space and independence. Julia Lee's ribald "Don't come too soon" and "Can't get enough of that stuff", Etta James' "Good rockin' daddy" and Ruth Brown's "5–10–15 hours" – no paltry 60 minutes for "Miss Rhythm" – proclaimed their own right to sexual fulfilment wherever they might find it.

Nor were these women to be outdone in poetic inventiveness. Even the regal Dinah Washington, whose repertoire ranged from jazzy torch songs to the most salacious r&b, pined for a "Long black shiny thing", which may or may not have been a Cadillac. On the evocatively titled "Long John blues", Washington paid her respects to the dentist who "Thrills me when he drills me." Capitol Records' Julia Lee was the queen of such double-entendre – on a Major label, note – massaging the black man's ego on "My man stands out", and returning to the kitchen for inspiration on "All this meat and big ripe tomatoes".

Much of this material was clearly tongue in someone's cheek. Like its male equivalent, some of it was rather more sexy than sexist. Nevertheless, the dominant ethos regarding relations between the sexes in the female r&b in the early 1950s was profoundly pessimistic. While there were a good many songs of romantic epiphany and foreverness, like Faye Adams' doting "I'll be true", relationships in female r&b were often doomed, exploitative, or personally stultifying. In other words, the women of r&b shared much the same fatalism as their male counterparts when it came to ideas of domestic happiness, peace and harmony.

An alternative vision

What made the pioneer vocal groups of the late 1940s and early 1950s so different from almost anything else within the Rhythm and Blues canon was the fact that they always offered some relief from r&b's dominant vision of opportunistic, predatory, distrustful and often destructive black sexual politics. Their extraordinary popularity in the 1950s may thus have reflected a growing black need and support for this alternative perspective.

All the early vocal groups, but especially the younger ones, featured sentimental, idealistic ballads alongside the more "adult" material they shared with the bluesmen and shouters. Sometimes the romance was just the flip of a 78-rpm disk away from the macho and misogyny. The Swallows, for example, are best remembered by historians of r&b for their salacious celebration of the fleshy charms of "Bicycle Tillie," and a ribald variation on a theme by Masters and Johnson "It ain't the meat it's the motion" – there were actually a few r&b homages to sex study pioneers, notably Stomp Gordon's "What's her whimsy, Dr Kinsey". Yet, their success with their black contemporaries depended at least as much on romantic ballads like "Will you be mine" and "Beside you".

Long before the first stirrings of a crossover market, black groups also regularly recorded white Tin Pan Alley pop, such as the Four Buddies' "Heart and soul", Harptones' "A Sunday kind of love" (also by Bobby Hall and the Kings and at least 25 other groups), Dominoes' "These foolish things", and Castelles' "Somewhere over the rainbow". These supplemented a large repertoire of sweet, romantic and idealistic r&b ballads like the Larks' "Hopefully yours", Marylanders' "I'm a sentimental fool", and the Flamingos' melancholic masterpiece "Golden teardrops". Lyrically, "Golden teardrops" and its like were much closer to the standard white pop fare of the 1950s than was the norm for either the r&b shouters or the electric bluesmen whose ascendency the vocal groups challenged by daring to rhyme "moon" with "June" and "eyes of love" with "stars above".

But what of the music itself? The actual sound of a record or performance the grain of a voice, the tone of an instrument, the manipulation of harmonies and rhythms – contributed at least as much to its meaning as any lyric. The manner in which r&b vocal groups performed their romantic ballads had the potential to modify or subvert any literal meaning.

Examples of this type of subversion can certainly be found, as, for example, in the radical deconstruction of "White Christmas" by the Ravens and, in much the same vein, by the Drifters. While the familiar yuletide lyric remained intact, both versions were quite deliberately disjointed, with an agonizingly slow tempo, heavily exaggerated vocal slurs and a wayward, slightly menacing, bass vocal line which ruptured rather than underpinned the well-known melody. Applied to a song with such a peculiarly suggestive title and precious place in white American popular culture, this calculated distortion brilliantly challenged the song's conventional meaning. It was firmly in the black cultural tradition of "putting on whitey", in this instance producing a broad parody of Bing Crosby's sentimental pop classic and, by extension, a black satire on all things white. It was a defiant gloss not lost on some of those whites, since in the winter of 1954–5 the Drifters' recording was widely banned.[58]

In a rather different vein, the Velours' "Can I come over tonight" featured a burbling, wordless bass vocal which somehow transformed an innocent, rather anodyne lyric into a riveting saga of barely contained lust and sexual expectancy. The Verstones used a similar trick to make the incomprehensible "Bila" much racier than their more explicit and routinely banned "Tight skirt and sweater". At the start of the decade, the honking saxophonist Earl Bostic conjured up similar carnal joys in the absence of any lyric at all, cutting a breathtaking instrumental version of the ballad "Flamingo" which was little short of orgiastic in its bump'n'grind riffing.

Nevertheless, the overwhelming impulse of male vocal groups was to tease out and explore the obvious lyrical sentiments of romantic ballads rather than to subvert or parody them. This was the main function of the channel and the spoken bridge, which served as many a song's centre of emotional gravity. The skill and inventiveness with which genuine emotion could be distilled from even the most saccharine lyric by the adroit manipulation of voices separated the best vocal groups from their rivals. Thus, Nate Nelson's aching lead vocal and the Flamingos' shimmering harmonies combined to highlight the essential qualities of nostalgia and loss in a song like "Golden teardrops".

In sum, then, all the early r&b vocal groups, but especially the younger ones, performed genuinely idealistic love songs, balancing them with more "realistic", frankly cynical and fatalistic material culled from the blues tradition. This would not need such careful emphasis, but for the fact that the romantic strain of vocal group style has seldom been acknowledged as an "authentic" part of the r&b canon. Black groups which unashamedly specialized in such "sweet" stylings – the Sentimentalists, Four Buddies, Sugartones, Velvetones, Embers, Charioteers, Five Bars, Victorians, Four Tunes and Four Knights – have rarely been accorded the artistic status of earthier and therefore nominally "blacker" groups, while the romantic sides cut by groups like the Swallows, who sang with equal conviction on both sides of the romance-ribaldry divide, have often been dismissed as inferior, or even aberrations.

White blues aficionado Chris Strachowitz has expressed this conventional wisdom, discussing "sweet" groups purely in terms of commercialization and sell-out. "In its early period R&B had guts. It had the drive and thrust and excitement of Sanctified Church rhythms. It lost all of this in the rock and roll era. But it actually started losing the blues, real blues feeling, when the schmaltzy vocal groups came in around 1956 – I hated them and still do". This conveniently ignored the "schmaltz" which most r&b groups, not to mention pop-oriented black soloists like Nat King Cole, Ivory Joe Hunter and Lena Horne, had been crooning to appreciative black audiences long before the rock and roll era. Instead, it exposes the persistence of certain conventional, but ultimately untenable, normative categories into which commentators have often expected all "authentic" black music to fit.[59]

A new generation, a new orthodoxy

In striking contrast to their predecessors, who had tried to balance romantic material with raunchier macho boasts and sexist put-downs, the new young groups of the mid-to-late 1950s largely ignored "adult" material and concentrated almost exclusively on evoking a juvenile world of specifically teen trauma and romantic delight. These were the songs – "Gee", "Sh-boom", "Earth angel" – which ushered in the rock and roll era by crossing over into the white pop charts. The Spaniels' "Goodnite sweetheart goodnite", Moonglows' "Sincerely", Flamingos' "I'll be home", and Frankie Lymon and the Teenagers' "Why do fools fall in love", confirmed and extended this trend towards devotional lyrics, setting new idealistic standards for post-pubescent r&b.

Frankie Lymon was just 13 years old in 1956. His colleagues – two Puerto Ricans and the remarkable juvenile bass singer Sherman Garnes – were not much older. Coached and produced by the ubiquitous Richard Barrett, a Philadelphia native who was himself a member of the Valentines, the group followed up "Why do fools fall in love" with several other crossover hits on the Gee label, including "I want you to be my girl" and "Goody goody". In the wake of Lymon's success, other Independents intensified their trawl of black neighbourhoods for likely teen talent. As Lymon later commented, "Kids who sang rock 'n' roll were snatched out of high school because of a hit record. When the success blew over they didn't even have a high school diploma". Even members of Lymon's own family were recruited. Brother Lewis Lymon and the Teenchords responded to Frankie's first big hit with "I'm not too young to fall in love", while another sibling, Timmy Lymon and the Tellers also emerged alongside a veritable crèche of black talent: Little Butchie Saunders and his Buddies, Little Anthony and the Imperials, the Juveniles, Students, Minors, Collegians, Colts, Cubs, Squires and Schoolboys.[60]

Lymon's own career folded after barely 18 months as his relationship with Gee and the other members of his group disintegrated. Although he continued to make solo recordings for several labels into the 1960s, no one much cared once his soaring juvenile falsetto slipped down into adult tenor range. In 1968, he died, alone and impoverished, of a drug overdose.

Although the industry could hardly claim credit for creating the teen group scene, it was not long before the Independent record companies recognized its peculiar market potential. Smiling young blacks sporting neat tuxedos or collegiate sweaters and singing devotional love songs were simply more palatable to many whites and the media than rock and rollers like Bo Diddley, whose fierce masculinity was forged in the forbidding black belt of McComb, Mississippi, and tempered in the blues-soaked South Side of Chicago. They were even preferable to the androgynous Little Richard, who threatened to "Rip it up" and looked like he just might. These adult singers stirred deeply rooted white fears of black sexual and, by extension, political aggression, while perfectly groomed blacks in their early teens could pass more easily as real-life incarnations of the submissive, emasculated black "boy" of white rhetoric and imagination.

Despite dwindling demand for his resolutely macho Rhythm and Blues records in the early 1960s, Bo Diddley remained an extremely popular live act, even on segregated southern campuses like the University of Virginia.

Yet, even if black child-stars could evade some of the worst stereotyping often accorded to adult blacks – Lymon and his group were happily posed for promotional stills with the white movie-star Jane Russell – youth itself did not always guarantee blacks immunity from white racial and sexual paranoia, especially in the South. In August 1955, Emmett Till, a 14-year-old Chicago boy visiting relatives in Mississippi, was savagely beaten and then murdered. Precisely what Till said or did to store worker Caroline Bryant to provoke her husband Roy and J.W. Millam to kill him, will probably never be known. Any one, or any combination of a wolf-whistle, asking for a date, saying "Bye, baby" as he left the shop where Bryant worked, boasting of white girlfriends up North, or simply being black in the wrong place at the wrong time, was sufficient violation of southern racial and sexual etiquette to condemn him to death. Two years later, Frankie Lymon, by then the same age as Till, caused an uproar when he was spotted dancing with a white girl on Alan Freed's short-lived *Rock 'n' Roll Dance Party* television show. Thirteen CBS affiliates, mostly, but not all, in the South, immediately cancelled the show, which the network dropped shortly afterwards.[61]

The promotion of young black vocal groups continued, ironically encouraged by the emergence of a new breed of young white groups whose homages to black vocal style were remarkably faithful, particularly at a time when many black groups were themselves edging closer towards the lyrical and musical norms of white pop. Of course, there had been white barbershop and glee club traditions long before the emergence of rock and roll, but in its wake a flotilla of Italian-American groups began searching for their own high Cs: Dion and the Belmonts, Vito and the Salutations, Dante and the Evergreens, Nino and the Ebb-Tides, Randy and the Rainbows, the Duprees and Crests. There were also a number of Hispanic vocal groups, including the Emerals, José and the Aztecs and Little Julien Herrera and the Tigers.[62]

As memories of the first crude white copycat groups of the cover era faded, it became increasingly difficult to tell white from black vocal groups by sound alone. "In the South, where I grew up", recalled Michael Banc, "the key to doo-wop's success was its racial anonymity. Since it was not clearly identifiable as 'nigger' music, it was acceptable in a time of legal segregation". This racial anonymity greatly expanded the opportunities for black groups on the racially sensitive airwaves and therefore broadened their potential audience: another market advantage not lost on the recording companies.[63]

While the trend in the vocal group music of the mid-to-late 1950s was overwhelmingly towards romance and idealized relationships, it would be wrong to suggest that "adult" themes of one sort or another disappeared completely. In 1958, the Silhouettes' "Get a job" offered a remarkably frank account of the domestic ravages of black unemployment, describing how the black man's inability to find work, despite his best efforts, had poisoned relations with his partner:

> Every mornin' about this time,
> She gets me out of my bed,
> A-cryin' "get a job".
> After breakfast every day,
> She throws the want-ads right my way,

And never fails to say, "get a job" . . .
I go back to the house,
I hear the woman's mouth,
Preachin' and a cryin',
Tells me that I'm lyin',
'Bout a job, that I never could find.

Astonishingly, this prime cut of ghetto sociology, brilliantly concealed from casual listeners beneath layers of "da"s, "yip"s, "sha"s and "mmm"s, was a major pop hit. The group's follow-up, "Headin' for the poorhouse", was an even bleaker trawl through urban deprivation which failed to make either the black or white charts outside the group's native Philadelphia. At a time of rising black optimism about access to the mainstream job market such songs were reminders of a reality which blacks hoped would soon be consigned to history.

The Miracles' "Got a job", co-authored by William "Smokey" Robinson and Berry Gordy, was a sequel to the Silhouettes' song. Not only did "Got a job" highlight the difficulty of actually finding work, but rather like Fats Domino's "Blue Monday", with its evocation of the enervating misery of menial labour ("Blue Monday, I hate blue Monday,/ Got to work, like to sleep all day,/ Here come Tuesday, oh-oh, Tuesday,/ I'm so tired got no time to play"), it also exposed the soul-destroying, exploitative nature of much black employment. "Got a job" ended on a note of barely suppressed rage, contained only because of the black hero's economic entrapment:

He said to me,
"Get the boxes, take them to the basement,
Do the job or I'll get a replacement,
Get that mop and clean the dirty floor,
And when you've finished, wash the windows and the doors" . . .
Well, this old man's gonna drive me insane,
One of these days I'm gonna have a fit,
But though the thought's running through my brain,
I'll never ever quit my brand new job.

Even more remarkable was "Cotton picking hands" by that relatively rare phenomenon, a New Orleans vocal group. The Dukes' song extended the tradition of blues paeans to black workers whose ability to endure the awesome physical demands of unrelenting manual labour had itself become a source of pride and self-respect. Just as John Henry had become a quintessential black hero because of his phenomenal capacity for laying railroad spikes and tunnelling – and, by symbolic extension, sex – so the hero of "Cotton picking hands" was transformed by his labouring prowess from callow youth to sexually potent, self-assured, independent black folk hero: "100 sturdy bales of cotton,/ Can change a very timid man,/ who used to say his prayers,/ but now he's put on hairs,/ that champion cotton picking man".[64]

The paradox here was that this black hero was still trapped within an exploitative, white-controlled, highly regimented labour system. He even had to miss the end-of-season barbecue to continue the prodigious feats which ultimately served the economic interests of his planter boss. His triumph was in creating a space for personal expression and achievement in the midst of these most oppressive and debilitating circumstances. In the Jim Crow South and beyond, pride in performance at work, even on behalf of whitey, co-existed with another tradition of sabotage and dalliance designed to undermine the smooth functioning of a racist and discriminatory system – even if in the process the latter ploys served to reinforce white stereotypes of black ignorance, incompetence and lassitude.[65]

Perhaps the most remarkable feature of "Cotton picking hands", particularly given the Dukes' southern origins, was the suggestion that the hero's new pride and confidence, his manhood, had somehow rendered God less important as an emotional crutch and source of deliverance. Without wishing to over-interpret a single line, this was highly significant in an era which saw many blacks organizing for their own salvation, rather than waiting for divine intervention, and which witnessed the steady secularization of many aspects of black life.

Meanwhile, even some of the youngest new vocal groups emerging in the mid-to-late 1950s found themselves back in the bedroom again and locked into the old macho stereotypes. The Cadillacs' "Speedoo" and the Cadets' "Love bandit" were worthy heirs to the macho mantle of Lovin' Dan. Even Little Butchie Saunders offered pretty explicit instructions about how to handle his "Peppermint stick" when he guested as lead vocalist for the Elchords in 1958. The Penguins' "Let's make some love" was a passable attempt to get down and dirty, while the Jayhawks' "Don't mind dyin'" and the Orbits' "Knock her down" ensured the old blues traditions of misogyny, sexual jealousy and domestic violence survived. "When your baby goes out and roams around, knock her down, knock her down, knock her down to the ground", the Orbits crooned.[66]

Fascinating though these songs are, however, such "adult" material was simply nowhere near as common in the repertoire of young vocal groups after 1954 as previously; nor, with rare exceptions like "Speedoo" and "Get a job", were they as widely popular when they did appear. Instead, there was the youthful, inchoate exuberance of the Dells' "Zing zing zing" and the Pearls' "Ice cream baby". Love itself was carefully solipsized in the Aladdins' "I had a dream last night", and the Kodoks' "Teenager's dream", or else depicted as something celestial as in the Satellites' "Heavenly angel" and, of course, the Penguins' "Earth angel". There were also countless proclamations of undying love to "Mary Lee" (Rainbows), "Tina" (Spaniels) and "Carol" (Schoolboys). And while according to doowop historians Anthony Gribin and Matthew Schiff many of the girls addressed by the early vocal groups "had already 'done it' "– a matter for both censure and celebration according to the double standards of the blues tradition – those celebrated in later songs were more chaste than caught. They were respectable and respected young ladies, waiting, like the Willows, for church bells to ring.[67]

Even when ballads like Little Anthony and the Imperials' "Tears on my pillow", Lee Andrews and the Hearts' "Teardrops", or the Sonics' "This broken heart" did introduce classic blues themes of personal loss, loneliness and pain into the idyllic world of teenage romance, the sheer inescapable youthfulness of the vocals implied a transient, finite, quality to the suffering. The increasingly lush musical arrangements also served to lighten the tone of such songs, while most of the teen angst in them stemmed from a failure to fulfil romantic ideals of a stable, mutually respectful, monogamous relationship. Such a relationship was usually depicted as an attainable, if often elusive goal. These songs were certainly very different in their emotional resonance from the lovelorn laments of the bluesmen or the shouters, who tended to wrap their personal sorrows and romantic disappointments in layers of fatalism and bitter recrimination.

Mary Ellison has written that "the blues are often taken to be synonymous with sadness. The blues are more than that. They are a reflection of life". This is an important corrective, since the blues embraced every aspect of human affairs and, as Albert Murray once pointed out, even when they were at their bluest, they were ultimately "nothing if not a form of diversion", designed to "make people feel good". Nevertheless, the blues certainly articulated some moods better than others and were most comfortable with particular themes and perspectives. As Ellison herself notes, the blues were mostly concerned "with the deepest and most elemental aspects of life". There was an epic quality to them, with their mixture of stoicism, irony, fatalism, self-ridicule, and heroic self-aggrandizement. The blues had pondered the black experience as it stretched from a horrific past into an uncertain future, and found ways to explain and survive that obdurate, oppressive reality.[68]

By contrast, the post-1954 teen groups rarely mined the terrifying seams of despair near the heart of the blues, and tended to steer clear of the raging misogyny and sexual anxieties which coursed through them. And, in any case, their concerns were usually very different. Among the teenage groups the fatalism and historicism of the blues was almost entirely abandoned. The songs either took place in a perpetual present which, although sometimes problematic, was often wondrous, or else they imagined a future bursting with exciting possibilities. They dealt uncondescendingly with the faddism, exuberance and idealism of youth in a way that was largely beyond the repertoire of the blues, except as satire.

Teenage groups were probably at the forefront of this growing trend towards romantic idealism in r&b because their youth allowed them to flaunt some of the more entrenched sexual mores of adult black male culture. Male teenagers were caught in a transitional, liminal phase between the adult world of the toasts and dozens, the macho bluesmen and the shouters – those forms of expression which enshrined the myths of matriarchal oppression and helped to routinize male distrust and hostility towards black women – and their own proximate personal experiences of maternal or sororial love, or even a first romantic infatuation. While they readily affected the machismo, cynicism and fatalism of their adult mentors, they had not yet entirely internalized those attitudes, nor completely buried other, more generous ideals beneath layers of prejudice and sexism. As they learned to deal with the "contradictions between ideal and reality in female behavior", they often allowed their idealism to shine through.[69]

The fact that the idealistic aspect of the teen group repertoire increasingly appealed to black audiences of all ages, classes, sexes and locations in the 1950s suggests that it articulated ideas and emotions which were always present, but often latent, obscured and under-commemorated elsewhere in male black popular culture. Certainly, sociologist Elliot Liebow found that in private men of the Washington ghetto often wrote or spoke to black women in a peculiarly elevated, romantic and stylized language, far removed from that employed in public. Liebow believed this symbolized a desire to replace the "normal" defensive, exploitative and vindictive aspects of black sexual politics with a more compassionate ideal.[70]

It is in this context that black acceptance of the heightened romantic language of songs like "Golden teardrops" and "Earth angel", and even of the sweeter, "whiter", sounds of many vocal group recordings from the mid 1950s, assumes new significance. Without denying the importance of the industry in encouraging these changes as it slowly became aware of a potential mass white audience for r&b, the initial black popularity of idealistic lyrics and lighter sounds derived in part from the fact that they provided a stylized "conventional conversational language for use in dating and courtship", which circumvented the routine macho posturing and hostility of much black sexual politics. Vocal group – and solo – "schmaltz" expressed common ideals concerning relationships between the sexes which other forms of black male popular culture had seldom dared to articulate. By the turn of the decade, this new idealistic, romantic ethos would dominate the black pop styles which were the most popular strain of Rhythm and Blues with black audiences.[71]

CHAPTER THREE

"Too much monkey business": race, rock and resistance

We need less be-bop, less rock and roll, fewer hep-cats, and more of our people who are concerned about the very life of the nation. (Congressman D.R. "Billy" Matthews)[1]

The industry strikes back

During 1956, changes in the sound and sense of much r&b, together with the "musical acculturation" of a substantial section of the white audience, enabled many black artists to cross over into the pop charts with greater regularity and deeper penetration than ever before. But as black rock and roll emerged alongside white rock and roll as a distinct sub-category of Rhythm and Blues, so various forces of resistance to the music intensified their efforts to halt its spread.[2]

This opposition to r&b and its biracial rock and roll derivative has been reasonably well documented. Yet these accounts have often neglected the historical context for that opposition, failing to note how or why it changed, developing new converts and different emphases, over time and across regions. They have also consistently underestimated or simplified the ways in which racism permeated every aspect of a campaign which betrayed deep-seated white fears about black sexuality and the prospect of racial integration just as the civil rights movement was stirring.[3]

Before 1956, criticisms of r&b/rock and roll came largely, if by no means exclusively, from within the industry, from individuals and organizations who saw the rising popularity of the new style as a threat to their own status and denounced it principally for reasons of economic self-interest, although they often couched their objections in terms of morality and aesthetics.

Typical of the early critics was Peter Potter, a pop deejay at KLAC-Hollywood and compere of television's prestigious *Jukebox Jury*. In September 1954, Potter condemned r&b as "obscene and of lewd intonation, and certainly not fit for radio broadcasts". The new music, he declared, was responsible for "inculcating [the] poor listening tastes of today's teenagers". Six months later, Potter sounded a note which became commonplace in subsequent protests against rock and roll, warning that "All Rhythm and Blues records are dirty and as bad for kids as dope". As one of the deejays listed in a *Variety* survey of the nation's top paid performers, Potter was a man for whom any genuine moral concern about the spread of r&b and its derivatives was entwined with a palpable self-interest in preserving the musical status quo.[4]

Elsewhere in the industry, established music publishing firms were especially alarmed by the sudden popularity of a style which generated relatively low sheet music sales. In late 1954, the Music Publishers' Protective Association condemned "dirty songs . . . showing bad taste and a disregard for recognized moral standards and conventions as detrimental to the music publishing industry". Complaints were also registered by the National Ballroom Operators Association, whose business fell by over 50 per cent in the first half of 1954, and the National Piano Tuners' Association, who feared in equal measure the damage which rock and roll pianists were inflicting upon the nation's keyboards and moral well-being. At the piano tuners' 1956 annual convention in Kansas City, New Orleans delegate, O.J. Dodds, told a shocked audience that he had seldom seen the thick bass string on a piano broken before the advent of rock and roll pianists who hit the keys "like a hammer". Since such vamping vandalism would actually have generated more business for the piano tuners, there were clearly important matters of moral decency, as well as economic self-interest, at stake here.[5]

The two major industry journals responded to the breakthrough of r&b in subtly different ways. A succession of *Billboard* editorials in the autumn of 1954 had reminded recording companies and radio stations alike of their responsibilities for promoting "decent" material. "Control the dimwits", demanded *Billboard*, appealing for the industry to weed out the "occasional distasteful disk". In fact, *Billboard* had been pursuing this line for some time prior to r&b's crossover. While it was critical of manufacturers and programmers who ignored "propriety and good taste", it generally welcomed the boost that r&b was providing for an otherwise stagnant singles industry.[6]

Variety adopted a far more critical and aggressive posture towards the new music than its main rival. Its shrill editorial outbursts also called for industry self-regulation, but the conflated moral and racial co-ordinates of its attack on r&b were more overt than at *Billboard*:

We're talking about "rock and roll", about "hug" and "squeeze" and kindred euphemisms which are attempting a total breakdown of all

The Drifters, featuring Clyde McPhatter (centre), were one of the most important r&b vocal groups in the mid 1950s, but frequently fell foul of the censors with songs like "Honey love".

> reticences about sex. In the past such material was common enough but restricted to special places and out-and-out barrel houses. To-day "leer-ics" are offered as standard popular music for general consumption by teen-agers . . .[7]

The *Variety* editorial illustrated how conventional assumptions about the correct place and inherent nature of black music informed industry reactions. R&b ribaldry was acceptable if segregated in "special places": the forbidden, debauched world of black culture. Once in the mainstream, where it threatened both white morality and vested interests within the industry, it certainly was not.

Beyond the industry, there had been a certain public unease about the propriety of r&b from the moment it began to attract young whites and infiltrate previously lily-white radio schedules. In the spring of 1954, the Drifters' "Honey love", a sexy homage to female unctuousness which just failed to make the pop Top Twenty, and the equally erotic "Such a night", both created quite a stir. Public complaints against "Such a night" led to a ban at radio station WXYZ in Detroit, while a year later, in March 1955, Lt. Francis O'Brien's Crime Prevention Committee in the Boston suburb of Somerville included "Honey love" on a list of unacceptable records. That same month also saw some of the first bans on live rock and roll in Bridgeport and New Haven, both in Connecticut.[8]

It was partly in response to this initial, relatively subdued, ripple of public concern, that many labels, spurred on by *Billboard*'s sober promptings and the constant fear of being barred from the airwaves, recommitted themselves to purging r&b of what remained of its alleged lewdness. At King, Ralph Bass was worried that Hank Ballard and the Midnighters' "Sock it to me Annie" might be too strong even for the increasingly conservative r&b airwaves at which he was still aiming in mid 1954 ("we were making records for R&B, weren't thinking in terms of white kids"). Somewhat disingenuously the title was changed to "Work with me Annie" and the number one Rhythm and Blues hit was widely banned on black-oriented stations anyway.[9]

One of the stations which banned "Annie" was Nelson George's vaunted symbol of black economic independence, cultural autonomy and political leadership, WDIA-Memphis. It was Bert Ferguson who reasserted his authority over his black broadcasters to impose this internal censorship, indicating where the real power in black-oriented broadcasting lay. Ferguson wrote to leading r&b labels announcing WDIA's intention to boycott "off-color" songs. He also had a tape prepared, to be aired whenever the station received requests for taboo tracks. The text reflected the essentially conservative broadcasting framework within which the rock and roll explosion took place and sought to defray the sorts of moral concerns typically raised in complaints against the new style: "WDIA, your good-will station, in the interest of good citizenship, for the protection of morals and our American way of life does not consider this record (blank) fit for broadcast on WDIA".[10]

Of course, this process of gentrification was also heavily associated with the white cover phenomenon, whereby the song cycle which began with "Sock it to me Annie" could turn safely to Georgia Gibbs' "Dance with me Henry". Nevertheless, as John Broven and Giacomo Ortizano have both noted, it was also evident in the all-black musical chain which connected Al Collins' unplayable "I got the blues for you" on Ace, through Eddie Bo's "I'm wise" on Apollo, to Little Richard's relatively safe "Slippin' and Slidin'" on Specialty. Indeed, it is important to appreciate that the controversy surrounding what Ortizano describes as a "rash of double-entendre songs in 1954" actually heralded the end, or at least the temporary and relative demise, of such once-commonplace raunchy, adult-oriented r&b material.[11]

But for the pervasive influence of racism and the concatenation of a number of particular trends and events in the mid 1950s, such lyrical adjustments might have spelled the end of white adult opposition to Rhythm and Blues and its rock and roll offspring. Instead, during 1956 the music became a major public obsession. National, state and municipal authorities, private pressure groups, religious organizations and individual citizens joined hostile elements within the industry to denounce the corrupting influence of black and black-derived music on the nation's youth.

Far from being an isolated phenomenon, this outcry constituted part of what James Gilbert has described as a "cycle of outrage". During the 1950s, much of adult white America became concerned that the mass media was destroying traditional American values of family, deference to authority, sobriety, chastity and industry by bombarding teenagers with images of violence, sex and delinquency. Like the virulent anti-communism of the era, to which Gilbert makes legitimate connection, the campaign against the media and new styles of teenage leisure addressed the fear that "society was coming apart, that pernicious outside influences could now breach the walls of community and family institutions". This "cycle of outrage", and the reification during the same period of a set of values and practices which became known simply as "The American way of life", provided a vital generational context for the growing public opposition to rock and roll.[12]

In an age of Cold War anxieties, strange new patterns of teenage leisure emerged which were "centred on high schools, souped-up cars, teen magazines, and a social order of gangs, new dating customs, drive-in theaters, hair cuts and clothes marked 'inaccessible' to unsympathetic adults". Above all, however, youth culture became centred on rock and roll: a music, a style and an attitude drawn from the "deviant" black underworld and the boisterous, rowdy sub-culture of southern country music, which seemed fundamentally opposed to the "American way". Thus it was always likely to face hostility from the mainstream – particularly after the use of Bill Haley's "Rock around the clock" in the film *Blackboard Jungle* and Smiley Lewis' "I hear you knocking" in *Baby Doll* had cemented the relationship between rock, delinquency and promiscuity in the public mind.[13]

Such a contextualization, however, still does not entirely explain why the tidal wave of condemnation against rock and roll did not break across the country until early 1956, more than 18 months after the first sustained surge of r&b crossover successes, and at a time when many black artists had already excised the most risqué elements from their repertoires – the songs explicitly about sex, infidelity, drink and violence which most affronted mainstream white sensibilities. As early as January 1955, *Billboard* was celebrating the triumph of "the drive against smutty disks . . . it is gratifying to report that today most of the r&b disks are comparatively dirt free". Moreover, as has been noted, by the beginning of 1956 much black r&b was already edging in the direction of nominally white musical, as well as lyrical, norms.[14]

In fact, by the spring of 1956, the campaign against rock and roll had assumed a symbolic significance which incorporated, but transcended, simple aesthetics and economic self-interest. Clues to the nature of that significance can be found in the South, where massive resistance to rock and roll first intensified. More particularly, they can be found in Birmingham, Alabama, in the circumstances surrounding the assault on the black balladeer Nat King Cole by a faction of the white citizens' council movement which had dedicated itself to stamping out rock and roll as part of a wider campaign to resist the integration of southern society. While the situation in Alabama and the South was necessarily unique in the midst of the desegregation crisis, the Cole incident nevertheless revealed the complex interplay of racial, psycho-sexual, moral and generational factors which informed much of the hostility to rock and roll throughout America.

Massive resistance to rock and roll in Alabama

Nat King Cole was attacked on 10 April 1956 as he gave a whites-only concert at the Municipal Auditorium in Birmingham. Cole, who was head-lining a "Record Star Parade of 1956" package tour which also featured white acts like June Christy and Ted Heath's "Famous British Orchestra", was midway through his third song, a rendering of the Tin Pan Alley stand-ard "Little girl", when someone shouted "Let's go get that coon". Four men sprinted down the centre aisle towards him. One turned back and was never apprehended, but the other three, Willis Vinson, his older brother, E.R. Vinson, and Kenneth Adams vaulted over the footlights and onto the stage. Cole was hit in the face by a falling microphone and wrenched his back as Adams wrestled him over the piano stool onto the floor.[15]

There was a touch of grim farce amid the confusion as plain-clothes policemen, tipped off about possible trouble, rushed to protect Cole, only to clash briefly with uniformed officers who thought the plain-clothes men were a second wave of attack. Meanwhile, the Ted Heath Orchestra, with whom Cole was sharing the stage, stayed at its post in time-honoured "dance-band on the Titanic" tradition and, at a loss to play anything more appropri-ate, launched into "God save the Queen" as the curtain was brought down and Cole rescued.

Birmingham detectives investigated the attack with a thoroughness and alacrity not always associated with southern police departments in cases of white violence against black citizens. They quickly uncovered the full extent of the plot against Cole. Hatched four days before the attack in Kenneth Adams' Anniston filling station – which proudly sported the sign "We serve white customers only" – the plan called for more than a hundred white men to storm the stage on Adams' command, but the expected mob failed to show.[16]

Six men were arrested in connection with the attack: Jesse Mabry, Mike Fox and Orliss Clevenger, in addition to Adams and the two Vinson brothers. All, except Jesse Mabry, came from Anniston, a city located about 60 miles east of Birmingham which became notorious in May 1961 when local white racists, Kenneth Adams among them, firebombed a Greyhound bus containing an integrated group of freedom riders. Mabry was from Birmingham itself.[17]

Originally, all the men were charged with assault with intent to murder, but ultimately only Kenneth Adams and Willis Vinson were indicted, although never convicted, on that count. On 17 April, Judge Ralph Parker sentenced the four men charged with lesser public order offences to the maximum available custodial sentences of six months each, plus various fines of around $100. In addition, Orliss Clevenger was fined $28 for possession of a concealed weapon. He and Mike Fox had been arrested outside the Auditorium, waiting in Clevenger's car, possibly with a view to abducting Cole. The weaponry found inside the car included brass knuckles, a blackjack and two .22 calibre rifles – equipment for a turkey shoot, according to the two men.[18]

Much white opinion appears to have been generally sympathetic to Cole and condemnatory of the culprits. At a time when white southerners were pleading to be left alone to dictate the pace and nature of racial change in their region, there was a great fear that lawlessness in defence of segregation would bring direct federal intervention. Much of the criticism was directed specifically against the North Alabama Citizens' Council (NACC), led by the rabidly anti-semitic, anti-communist, segregationist Asa "Ace" Carter, to whose statewide co-ordinating organization, the Alabama Citizens' Council (ACC), the assailants belonged. Jesse Mabry was editor of Carter's newspaper *The Southerner* and Kenneth Adams was on the board of directors of the affiliated Anniston Citizens' Council. Even other branches of the Alabama council movement, although like Carter resolutely committed to the defence of segregation, were quick to condemn the use of violence. Carter's great rival within the Alabama resistance movement, state senator Sam Englehardt, stressed that his own organization advocated "peaceful and legal means of settling the segregation question" and pledged that "If we find any members like these in the Citizens' Council of Alabama (CCA), they will be thrown out".[19]

The peculiar factionalism and rivalry within the Alabama council movement, personified by Carter and Englehardt and characterized by one contemporary observer as "part of the old feud between the Bourbon and the Redneck", provided an important context for the attack on Cole. Equally important was the marked intensification of massive resistance in Alabama, as throughout the South, in early 1956. Both factors help explain the timing and tenor of the rising hostility towards rock and roll in the region, and the deeper significance of the attack on the hapless Nat King Cole, who, paradoxically, did not even perform in the style.[20]

When, in May 1954, the Supreme Court declared segregated schools "inherently unequal" and thereby destroyed the intellectual and constitutional foundations of Jim Crow, the white South was naturally alarmed.

Nevertheless, faced by this portentous threat to its peculiar racial arrangements and the whole way of life predicated upon them, reaction was generally calm and restrained. After years of litigation sponsored by the NAACP, the decision was hardly unexpected. As early as December 1952, Georgia's governor, Herman Talmadge, was already reviewing plans for a committee to formulate a response to any Supreme Court ruling against the constitutionality of segregated schools and thus prevent "the inter-mingling and the association which would ensue from white and negro children attending the same school". Like Talmadge, most whites trusted to a variety of local political, economic and legalistic strategies to preserve the racial status quo.[21]

In May 1955, the Supreme Court's second ruling on *Brown*, which called for desegregation with "all deliberate speed", undoubtedly intensified white anxieties. Nevertheless, the timetable was still vague enough to prevent a major southern panic. Moreover, by assigning to local school boards the responsibility for implementing desegregation, the Court, as Aldon Morris recognized, "in effect gave the very groups that adamantly opposed school desegregation the responsibility to desegregate the schools". Consequently, even after May 1955, the South still found the Court's rulings relatively easy to circumvent and, as Francis Wilhoit has noted, "though southern resistance perceptively hardened after *Brown II*, the resistance had not yet taken on the form of overt violence that would be so much a part of the South's backlash in later years".[22]

This pattern was clearly evident in Alabama where, immediately following the first *Brown* decision, Sam Englehardt pledged himself to "keep every brick in our segregation wall intact", and the Birmingham City Commissioners declared themselves "unalterably opposed" to the desegregation of schools in the city. Yet, while there was intense concern about the decision and its implications for the future of race relations, there was no real panic, and little doubt that it would be possible to avoid desegregation for the foreseeable future. The *Birmingham News* editorialized that "some southerners predict a 'century of litigation' before any major admission of Negroes to white schoolrooms". The resounding victory of racial moderate Jim Folsom in the gubernatorial election of 1954 also suggested that Alabama was still some way from making overt opposition to *Brown* and strict racial orthodoxy the only criteria for election to public office.[23]

In Alabama, as throughout the white South, this relative calm disintegrated in late 1955 and early 1956 as southern blacks increasingly took the initiative in the struggle for desegregation, not just in schools, but in a whole range of public amenities. A series of legal actions, protests and boycotts not only began to mobilize the black community in a mass movement for civil and voting rights which reached full tide in the 1960s, it also brought forth the full force of white resistance.

In August 1955, Alabama blacks began to petition local education officers to implement the immediate desegregation of public schools. In December

1955, the year-long Montgomery Bus Boycott began, heralding a new era of effective mass nonviolent direct action by southern blacks and the emergence of an exceptional black leader in Martin Luther King, Jr. In February 1956, Autherine Lucy won her three-year battle to be admitted to the previously segregated University of Alabama at Tuscaloosa and duly sought to attend classes. Southern anxieties were also raised by series of pro-desegregation decisions emanating from the Fourth and Fifth Circuit Appellate Courts based in Richmond and New Orleans respectively. The racially partisan workings of southern justice had once been considered a trusty bulwark against the horrors of desegregation.

By early 1956, then, many white Alabamians felt that the entire edifice of Jim Crow was under immediate threat. In this newly intensified, embattled situation, they responded forcefully as Virginia senator Harry Byrd called for a campaign of massive resistance across the South. It was a campaign which eventually operated at a number of political, economic, legal and extra-legal levels. In January 1956, the Alabama state legislature was one of many during the desegregation crisis to invoke the dubious doctrine of inter-position, declaring the Supreme Court's ruling "null, void and of no effect" and interposing state power between what was perceived as a hostile, un-constitutional edict and the white citizens of Alabama. Also in early 1956, state senator Albert Boutwell introduced a "freedom of choice" school bill, designed to avoid compliance with the Supreme Court's desegregation rul-ings. Similar evasive "pupil placement" and "freedom of choice" strategies were adopted throughout the South.[24]

In March 1956, Alabama senators and representatives signed the South-ern Manifesto, joining the majority of the southern politicians in Washington in a formal declaration of their implacable opposition to federally forced integration. In April 1956, Birmingham's Interracial Council, for many years a major point of contact between the races in a city where racial tensions were notoriously acute, finally collapsed. The Council was no longer able to reconcile the demands of anxious whites with those of an increasingly restless and assertive black community, whose efforts to break segregation in the city were encouraged by the fearless leadership of Reverend Fred Shuttlesworth. The first months of 1956 also saw concerted – and ultimately successful – efforts to destroy the NAACP in the state, led by state attorney-general John Patterson. In 1958, Patterson was rewarded for his efforts to thwart black progress with the governorship of Alabama, replacing Jim Fol-som in a very conspicuous rejection of "Big Jim"'s allegedly soft approach to the preservation of white supremacy.

White Alabama's growing anxiety about integration was also reflected in the escalation of racial demagoguery, violence and intimidation. Autherine Lucy's brave attempt to desegregate the University of Alabama ended after three days of white mob action with her suspension from classes. As E. Culpepper Clark has noted, this was a crucial turning point in the development of white resistance throughout the region. Once violence and mayhem had proved successful in preventing desegregation at Tuscaloosa, other segregationist die-hards turned more readily to the systematic use of terror to supplement the political, economic and legal machinations of massive resistance. The Ku Klux Klan re-emerged to intimidate and brutalize blacks who challenged segregation and their few beleaguered white allies. By 1957 there were at least seven distinct Klan groups operating in Alabama, with at least 530 incidents of racial violence attributed to the organization across the South between 1955 and 1959.[25]

Although publicly disavowing the violence of the Klans, since they liked to boast that they drew support from the respectable "active middle and upper class of businessmen", the white citizens' councils also prospered, waging their own shadowy campaign of organized resistance. Able to attract only scattered support before the end of 1955, the various councils in Alabama alone claimed membership of around 40,000 in February 1956, including an impressive collection of the state's leading white politicians, clergy, businessmen and professionals. That same month, Alabama's council leaders organized their first statewide association, whereby local groups became affiliated to one of four regional bodies, all centrally co-ordinated by the Alabama Association of Citizens' Councils (AACC). Sam Englehardt was chosen as the AACC's executive secretary.[26]

Asa Carter, a former radio commentator, sometime soft-drink salesman and secret member of the savage Ensley Klan Klavern No. 31, dominated the NACC, which quickly became estranged from the statewide organization. While the patrician planter Englehardt tried to preserve an aura of respectability about the Council's legal and political resistance to desegregation, Carter, a rough-hewn product of the north Alabama upcountry, courted the blue-collar workers of Birmingham and its environs with a much more vigorously populistic and occasionally violent approach to the preservation of Jim Crow. While the two men recognized each other's ability to reach different constituencies within white Alabama, their relationship was quickly strained.

Significantly, in terms of the events at the Municipal Auditorium on 10 April and the escalation of the campaign against rock and roll, the rift between Carter and the AACC widened dramatically during the early spring of 1956. It became an unbridgeable chasm over the question of the appropriate response to the Autherine Lucy affair. Carter angrily demanded the dismissal of O.C. Carmichael, president of the University of Alabama, for allowing even temporary desegregation when Lucy had spent her three nightmarish days on campus. When the rest of the AACC refused to support Carter's proposal, thus in Carter's mind sanctioning a treacherous breach in the solid wall of white resistance, Carter left and established his own independent umbrella organization, the ACC, to co-ordinate a less compromising, direct action response to the gathering threats to the southern way of life.[27]

Despite Carter's fiery rhetoric and a series of rallies held during the spring, he struggled to match the popularity of Englehardt's more subtle, though no less determined, brand of council activity. In March 1956, Carter's ambitions were dealt a severe blow when 2,000 members of his ACC defected to Englehardt's group, denouncing both Carter's extremism and his dictatorial running of the organization.[28]

By March 1956, then, Asa Carter desperately needed something – a theme or an event – with which to maintain the credibility of his organization and raise his own personal stock as a leader of Alabama resistance. One of the key issues with which Carter hoped to revive his fortunes and invigorate his campaign was rock and roll. It was Carter who helped to orchestrate the public outcry against that black-derived musical style. In rock and roll, a music which drew on black r&b, white pop, and the South's own beloved country music for its inspiration and techniques, and which boasted black and white performers and fans, Carter located a powerful metaphor for the horrors of integration. He skilfully used rock and roll to tap into all manner of social, political and generational, as well as racial and sexual, anxieties afflicting adult white America at mid-century.

Asa Carter's first formal statement on the evils of rock and roll had appeared in the pages of his newspaper, *The Southerner*, shortly before the Cole incident. This followed a period of relative calm, even indifference, to the spread of the music, which paralleled the initial concerned-but-measured response to *Brown*. When an integrated rock and roll show, featuring Bill Haley and the Comets alongside black acts like Joe Turner, LaVern Baker and Smiley Lewis, had played in Birmingham in January 1956, and when an all black rock and roll show appeared in March, neither had attracted white violence, mainstream press comment or the sort of vehement public condemnations which Asa Carter would help make commonplace by mid-year.[29]

Indeed it is impossible to understand the attack on Nat King Cole, or the subsequent outpouring of hostility towards rock and roll, without reckoning with Carter's new, very public, preoccupation with the perils of the music in the spring of 1956. Local press coverage of the incident certainly depicted Cole as an unfortunate victim of Carter's campaign against rock and roll, while carefully noting that the singer did not actually perform in that style. Not a particularly sophisticated thinker on matters of musical differentiation, Carter himself used the term rock and roll interchangeably with "be-bop", "blues", "congo rhythms", "jungle music" and a whole host of other choice epithets which stressed the style's racial origins. In any case, he explained, it was only "a short step . . . from the sly, night club technique vulgarity of Cole, to the openly animalistic obscenity of the horde of Negro rock 'n' rollers".[30]

Carter, whose personal complicity in the planning of the Cole attack remains unclear, later confirmed that his men had gone to the Auditorium as part of what the press characterized as "the Council studies of be-bop

and rock-and-roll music". There had, Carter insisted, been no planned violence. He blamed the assault on a black man in the rear of the Auditorium
who had "deliberately" knocked a camera held by one of the Council men.
"The incident", Carter explained, "made him mad, and he ran down the
aisle towards Cole, who was just another Negro to him". Quite what this
villainous "Negro" camera-knocker was doing attending a strictly whites-
only performance was never explained.[31]

Thanks largely to Asa Carter's efforts, during the spring of 1956 rock and
roll became part of what Francis Wilhoit has termed the South's "demonology" of massive resistance. Although Wilhoit himself is silent on the southern campaign against rock and roll, his proposition that "Massive resistance
included not only a pantheon of saints and martyrs and verbalized propositions such as white supremacy and states' rights federalism, but also a vast
panoply of symbols, icons, emblems, totems, taboos, scapegoats, and stylized rituals", provides an extremely useful context within which to place the
rise of southern opposition to the music.[32]

By early 1956, the intensification of southern anxieties had manifested
itself, not just in political and violent resistance, but in the widespread
affirmation – one might argue, reaffirmation – of a sectional ideology based
upon the twin doctrines of states' rights and white racial supremacy, with its
correlate of black inferiority. Woven into this southern ideology were fears
about communism, juvenile delinquency and race-mixing which were by
no means unique to the South, and which also informed the campaign
against rock and roll.

Paramount in the white southern mind was the notion that desegregation
would lead directly to the unspeakable horrors of miscegenation and compromise the spurious purity of the white race. A second strand in the web of
ideas which supported resistance was the notion that exposure to Negroes
and their culture would increase the incidence of juvenile delinquency and
sexual immorality among white youth. This linkage was made explicit in
the comments of one white Birmingham parent who explained "some of
the reasons why I will never willingly send my children to a mixed school",
by offering a catalogue of suspect statistics about the higher incidence of
homicides, venereal disease and illegitimate births among the black community. "I would no more expose my children to this condition than I
would deliberately expose them to the bubonic plague or any other dread-
ful disease".[33]

Another thread in the southern demonology of resistance was the dread
of outside interference in the region's racial affairs, which often took the
form of a regional xenophobia and involved the reification of something
which whites recognized and cherished as "the southern way of life". This
defence of the South's peculiarities was often expressed in a language which
revealed the persistence of antebellum racial stereotypes of docile, con-
tented blacks and benevolent, paternalistic whites. Just prior to the attack

on Cole, J. Melancon, a self-professed Birmingham moderate, wrote patron-
izingly that "speaking generally the Southern position is a feeling of friendship and kindly regard for the Negro. He is with us in large numbers, good
natured and carefree, happy-go-lucky and easy to get along with when not
swayed by extraneous influences". Describing the Supreme Court's 1896
Plessy decision, which gave constitutional sanction to segregation, as the
catalyst for "phenomenal progress both in education and the assumption of
civil rights", Melancon argued that "it is in the best interests of both races
that segregation be maintained at least for the foreseeable future". Black
Alabamians differed on this subject, and no longer begged to do so.[34]

Frequently, southern fears of outside intervention and agitation mingled
with the anti-communism so prevalent throughout America in the 1950s.
The Supreme Court, Martin Luther King and the NAACP were routinely
accused of being communist agents or, at best, unwitting dupes of Moscow.
One commentator, Lois Crick from Hueytown, Alabama, insisted that "If the
northerner, the politician and the Communist will let us alone with our way
of life we will handle such situations as we are now confronted with in the
usual diplomatic manner which must be agreeable to all concerned, certainly to the Negro, otherwise we wouldn't have so many of them".[35]

These crucial icons and demons, ideals and fears were not discrete phenomena, but were fused together in a sensational and emotive legitimation
of the southern white way of life and a bold affirmation of the moral rectitude of trying to preserve it against internal and external threats. In a single
speech in January 1956, state senator and council activist Walter Givhan
was able to condemn "outside agitators" like the NAACP ("champions of
mongrelization"), synthesize gnawing fears of communism with terror at the
prospect of miscegenation ("The communists know that if they can mon-
grelize the Anglo-Saxon southern white, they can destroy us"), and warn
against the corruption of white youth, all in a heartfelt plea for organized
resistance to desegregation. "The reason we're here and the reason we've
fought these battles is your little boy and your little girl", explained Givhan.
"That's who we're fighting for. We're going to keep these little white boys
and these little white girls pure".[36]

The fact that ideas of racial purity and the horror of black defilement of
white youth and womanhood were so central to the ideology of massive
resistance may even help to explain the actual timing of the assault on Nat
King Cole. It was only when Cole began to sing "Little girl" – his third song
of the evening – that his assailants rushed the stage. It is conceivable that
the sight of a black singer crooning to his "little girl" conjured up the mythical black rapist of the white psyche and acted as the immediate trigger for
the attack.

Certainly, Cole's attackers were particularly angry at his appearance
on stage with the female white singer June Christy. "More than once", Asa

Carter noted, "Cole has publically degraded that which the white man holds most dear as the protector of his race – white womanhood." *The Southerner*, which frequently featured pictures of interracial couples, often at dances or concerts, accompanied by outraged captions like "THIS IN ALABAMA!", even printed pictures of Cole with various white female fans in photographs bearing the legends "COLE AND HIS WHITE WOMEN" and "COLE AND YOUR DAUGHTER".[37]

Perhaps most revealing of all was the publicity shot featured in the August 1956 edition of *The Southerner*, which showed Cole seated at a piano while June Christy stood close behind with her hands resting on his shoulders. Regardless of the dangerous proximity of a white woman to a black man, this particular pose – the black man seated with a white woman standing behind in dutiful attendance – visually challenged the very core of southern sexual and racial etiquette. "How close are the Cole's (sic) and the innumerable Negro entertainers bringing the white girl to the Negro male?" Carter asked in the article accompanying the photograph. "How many negroes have been encouraged to make advances to white girls and women, by the constant strumming of such propaganda into their minds? . . . You have seen it, the fleeting leer, the look that stays an instant longer . . . the savagery, now, almost to the surface".[38]

Carter and other southern opponents of rock and roll employed precisely the same rhetoric and terms of emotional reference in their condemnations of the music that massive resisters like Walter Givhan used to decry integration. Carter denounced rock and roll as "sensuous Negro music" which, "as the utter beast is brought to the surface", eroded "the entire moral structure of man, Christianity, of spirituality in Holy marriage . . . all the white man has built through his devotion to God: all this, was crumbled and snatched away, as the white girls and boys were turned to the level of the animal".[39]

Resorting to the sort of conspiracy theories so important to southern resisters, Carter also accused the "communistic" NAACP of deliberately seeking to corrupt white teenagers with rock and roll music. This prompted the NAACP's executive secretary Roy Wilkins to comment that "Some people in the South are blaming us for everything from measles to atomic fallout".[40]

Undaunted, in an interview on WNOE-New Orleans, which was later reprinted in the national jazz magazine *Down Beat*, Carter insisted that rock and roll was part of a longstanding NAACP strategy to integrate the nation's youth. Carter claimed that Roy Wilkins' predecessor Walter White had described black music as "the best way to bring young people of both races together". Black New Orleans bandleader, writer and arranger Dave Bartholomew responded by pointing out that whites, rather than blacks, were ultimately responsible for the unprecedented growth of the market for black and black-derived styles. "The record companies are owned 100 percent by white people", he noted with only slight exaggeration. "They are the ones who are responsible for the success of r'n'b by promoting it with their top names to create bigger and better records. To give the NAACP credit for its rise in popularity is laughable".[41]

The widespread press coverage which followed the Cole incident provided exposure for Carter's views far beyond his native Alabama. In late April 1956, he was interviewed in *Newsweek*, where he explained the intimate links between black-derived music and sexual promiscuity for a national audience already anxious about the latest dating rituals associated with youth culture. "[Rock and roll] is the basic heavy beat of Negroes", said Carter. "It appeals to the very base of man, brings out the animalism and vulgarity".[42]

Back in Birmingham, on 20 May 1956, members of Carter's NACC picketed the whites-only performance of a concert at the Municipal Auditorium featuring the Platters, LaVern Baker, Bo Diddley, and Clyde McPhatter, as well as the white rock and roller Bill Haley. The banners held by the demonstrators and the slogans chanted again reflected the congruency between the attack on rock and roll and massive resistance: "NAACP says integration, rock & roll, rock & roll"; "Jungle Music promotes integration"; "be-bop promotes Communism"; "Jungle music aids delinquency"; "Churches must speak out against these anti-Christ forces".[43]

As well as publicizing the immorality of the music, council activists urged local authorities to take formal action against it. On 8 May 1956, Asa Carter and Ralph Edwards, chairman of the Woodlawn Citizens' Council, who just prior to the Cole assault had ominously threatened to "visit" those in Birmingham responsible for playing the sort of music which "promotes integration", had written to Mayor James Morgan protesting the continued use of the Municipal Auditorium "for indecent and vulgar performances by Africans before our white children". Such public auditoria, rather like the buses, bus terminals, lunch counters, parks, swimming pools and beaches of the South, were rapidly becoming key sites in the battle for the future of the region.[44]

Other anxious whites, fearing the creeping integration of southern popular culture, also urged civic authorities to lead resistance by banning all-black performances for all-white audiences. "The City of Birmingham does not need money badly enough to rent the Auditorium to negroes to entertain white people", read one petition. "There is not a negro singer nor a negro musician anywhere who does not at some time during his or her program sing or play 'suggestive' songs or music and become vulgar." Despite these protests, the 20 May shows at the Auditorium – one for whites, one for blacks – were allowed to proceed. This time, however, the organizers were careful to ensure that "the negro stars ... appeared first and were all off stage before the white groups came on", reflecting the widespread view that it had been Nat King Cole's presence on the same stage as white artists which had in part provoked the April assault. By the end of the year, however, the city commissioners had further tightened the regulations, to prevent even this sort of staggered integration on stage. Auditorium manager Fred McCallum was instructed "not to book any shows, basketball games, or any other type of event that had mixed races in the personnel".[45]

Resistance spreads

Throughout the South, opposition to black and black-derived styles of music quickly escalated in the wake of the Cole incident. Beyond Birmingham, many other civic leaders were also convinced by the sheer zealotry of the massive resistance campaign that the vast majority of southern whites were already irredeemably committed to fighting desegregation to the last ditch. In fact, bolder leadership from white moderates, not to mention unequivocal support for desegregation from President Eisenhower in the wake of *Brown*, might still have convinced the majority of vexed, but basically law-abiding, white southerners to comply, however reluctantly, with the law of the land. In the absence of such leadership, massive resisters were allowed a virtually free hand to define the race-based agenda of southern politics for the next decade, and they made a fierce commitment to segregation the litmus test of electability and satisfactory public service in the region. In this climate, civic authorities often bowed to pressure to hold the line against the desegregation of southern culture and that sometimes included opposing rock and roll.[46]

In the summer of 1956, for example, Louisiana passed a package of state law revisions designed to preserve segregation in every aspect of life from dining to education. The revisions not only prohibited "all interracial dancing, social functions, entertainments, athletic training, games, sport or contests", but were framed in such broad language that one authority claimed they extended to "the personal affairs of private citizens", and thus made it illegal for the races to play music together even behind closed doors.[47]

In Little Rock, in mid 1957, as the forces of white resistance pushed the school board and Arkansas governor Orval Faubus towards open defiance of court orders to desegregate the city's public schools, the spectre of integrated rock and roll dances lurked somewhere in the background. When Arkansas citizens' council leaders asked if in an integrated system black students would be allowed to attend the same dances as whites, a horrified school board responded that "social functions which involve race mixing will not be held".[48]

In October of the same year, singer Larry Williams, of "Bony Maronie" and "Dizzy Miss Lizzy" fame, was arrested during his segregated show at the Municipal Auditorium in Norfolk, Virginia, when he broke local Jim Crow ordinances by jumping off stage to dance with his white fans. Williams' offence may have been compounded in white minds by the fact that he had wantonly discarded his shirt before his leap across the race line and was, therefore, clearly bent on a spot of forestage miscegenation. The singer claimed he had already suffered the same fate at the hands of authorities in Augusta, Georgia, and Alexandria, Louisiana.[49]

In Jacksonville, Florida, Judge Marion Gooding of the Duval County Juvenile Court attended Elvis Presley's 10 August 1956 performance in the city, waiting in the wings of the Florida State Theater to serve an arrest warrant "if there is a vulgar performance". In Texas, where in July 1956 the San Antonio Parks Department banned rock and roll from the jukeboxes at the city's swimming pools, the Houston Juvenile Delinquency and Crime Commission issued a list of objectionable records to be banned from the air-waves and threatened to bring in the FCC if local stations did not comply.[50]

The Houston Commission was headed at this time, not by a typical white guardian of moral rectitude and racial purity, but by Dr H.A. Bullock, a black sociology professor from Texas Southern University. In this context, it is worth noting that radio historian John A. Jackson found evidence that, even before r&b had crossed over and – in more ways than one – cleaned up, middle-class blacks in Cleveland had protested r&b songs which they felt perpetuated debilitating racial stereotypes by depicting blacks as disso-lute, over-sexed hedonists. Moreover, many black adults were just as alarmed as their white counterparts by incessant media warnings of rampant teenage delinquency and immorality. The *Carolina Times* was not the only black newspaper to carry some kind of "Youth page", dedicated to giving young blacks a thorough grounding in middle-class values and respectability, which included a cautionary "Date data" column signed by "The Chaperone".[51]

Nevertheless, there is little evidence to suggest that black adults of any class supported what was fundamentally a racist campaign against rock and roll. Even when *Tan* ran a lurid confessional story entitled "Rock'n'roll ruined my life", which described an infatuated female fan's impregnation by an unscrupulous rock and roller, this was a morality tale about the need for chastity and eternal vigilance against predatory black males, not an attack on the music.[52]

Beyond the South, the sheer vehemence and drama of southern resist-ance to rock and roll helped to sharpen national white anxieties about the relationship between rock and roll, communist infiltration, juvenile delin-quency and sexual impropriety by adding the terrible tinctures of misce-genation and black sexual degeneracy. These basic ingredients may have been mixed in different proportions in the North and West, but they were all to be found in the cocktail of public disapproval and abuse poured upon the style after the spring of 1956. Taking a leaf out of Asa Carter's photo album, a white supremacist group based in Inglewood, California, even included its own pictures of young black men and white women dancing together rock and roll-style in its hate sheet, adding the captions, "Boy meets girl . . . 'be-bop' style", and "Total mongrelization".[53]

In the summer and fall of 1956, city councils as far apart as Santa Cruz and Jersey City joined their southern counterparts in banning rock and roll performances. In a widely publicized statement which betrayed the racial stereotyping at the heart of the opposition to rock and roll, Hartford psychiatrist Dr Francis J. Braceland branded rock and roll a "tribalistic and cannibalistic" style of music and declared it a "communicable disease". Another critic, the Very Reverend John Carroll, similarly warned the Teachers' Institute of the Archdiocese of Boston that "Rock and roll inflames and excites youth like jungle tom-toms . . . The suggestive lyrics are, of course, a matter for law enforcement agencies".[54]

As the controversy escalated, some radio stations – among them WAMP-Pittsburgh, WCFL-Chicago, KDEN-Denver, KSEL-Lubbock and WZIP-Cincinnati – dropped rock and roll from their playlists. Others became more hysterical, not to say environmentally hazardous, in their resistance. At WISN-Milwaukee, deejay Charlie Hanson publicly burned 200 rock and roll records. KWK-St Louis jettisoned rock and roll in January 1958; "Simply weeding out undesirable music", said station president Robert T. Convey.[55]

The embattled networks, ABC, CBS, Mutual and NBC, were also highly censorious, banning scores of records. There was, however, a curious twist in March 1956 when the NBC censor declined to rule Little Richard's "Long Tall Sally" obscene, arguing that as he could not understand the words he would not risk a judgement as to their propriety. In August 1958, the Mutual Broadcasting Network changed its Top 50 format to a Pop 50 format so as to excise "that which is, distorted, monotonous and/or has suggestive or borderline salacious lyrics".[56]

Most of the rock and roll programming in the United States after 1956 took place on radio stations which also carried other programmes beamed at adult white pop audiences. Consequently, many complaints were directed against deejays working in this mixed broadcasting environment, or against the contamination of previously lily-white Top 40 shows which now felt compelled to feature successful black and white rock and roll. In the spring of 1958, John L. Greendack filed a law suit against WSIX in Nashville on behalf of "the people of Tennessee", aiming to get a traditional popular music programme, *LP Showcase*, reinstated in place of the rock and roll-riddled chart show which had replaced it. Greendack cited the FCC regulations which declared that "on matters of controversy which are in the interest of the public, equal air time for each is granted". He argued that rock and roll was most definitely a matter of controversy and public interest and that, since rock and roll music could be found on numerous other stations, the case for the opposition, namely good music and decent values, was not being given equitable coverage. Perhaps not surprisingly given the racial connotations of rock and roll and the rise of Massive Resistance, Judge Henry F. Todd upheld the cause of decency and issued a "mandatory and permanent" injunction to WSIX to return *LP Showcase* to its original time slot.[57]

While John Greendack took the legalistic route to rock and roll radio resistance, others in the South were less subtle. On the fourth anniversary of the first *Brown* decision, the switchboard at WEDR's downtown studio in Birmingham was suddenly jammed with complaints about a fading signal. Deejay Shelley "The Playboy" Stewart called Charles Kirkpatrick, the white engineer at the transmitter site up on nearby Red Mountain, to find out what was going on:

> "Mr Kirkpatrick, we're losing the signal, Sir".
> "I know".
> "Mr Kirkpatrick, what are you doing about it?"
> "We're not going to do anything".
> "Mr Kirkpatrick, why aren't you going to do anything?"
> "Well, you're losing the signal because the tower is being cut down
> – the guide wires".
> "Mr Kirkpatrick, who's cutting the guide wires?"
> "The Ku Klux Klan".
> "Mr Kirkpatrick, well why don't you go out and stop the Ku Klux
> Klan from cutting the tower down?"
> "'Cause I'm one of 'em!"[58]

A month after this vivid demonstration of the racial views of some of the whites running black-oriented radio, Stewart arrived for work to find "KKK-Negger" daubed in blood on the walls of the WEDR studio. Edwin Estes, a radio entrepreneur who had acquired the station from J. Edward Reynolds – and who Stewart believed may also have once had links with the "Invisible Empire" in Etowah County, Alabama – publicly denied that dyslexic Klansmen were responsible for the vandalism. Disturbed by "at least 25 calls demanding that we go off air", including one the day before the attack which threatened "to level the building", Estes assured Birmingham whites that WEDR still represented no threat to the racial status quo. "We stay completely out of controversial issues", he said, "and we do not accept political announcements under any circumstances".[59]

The point is that, whatever the restrictions on what black announcers could say, play, or do on air in the early 1950s, these were undoubtedly tightened in the decade after *Brown* and Montgomery. Even in the North, the first stirrings of a Chicago campaign to secure better schools in black neighbourhoods and end discrimination in real estate practices drew an agreement among broadcasters to control the timing and content of news reports which might inflame racial tensions. These measures remained in force until at least 1966. Pressure on southern black-oriented stations to remain neutral on racial matters was even more intense. Bert Ferguson insisted that WDIA was "doing enough, and we'd rather move ahead as we've been moving in race relations than get involved in that". KOKY-Little Rock was typical, with manager Eddie Phelan justifying the station's reluctance to offer conspicuous support for the civil rights struggles of his listeners on the grounds that "When you choose one side you alienate people". More specifically, he noted, you alienate important – white – advertisers.[60]

Just as the political and racial content of news and public service programming on black-oriented radio came under greater scrutiny during massive resistance so, in a related development, did the music played on such stations. Ralph Bass recalled that "Censorship at that time was very tough . . . All the people who were on the radio stations were tough because they valued their licenses. If you had a black station you figured you gotta be twice as cool as the other cats, so they were screening everything". By the late 1950s, the airwaves, like the public spaces in which rock and roll was played and heard, indeed, like the sound and sense of the music itself, had become a fiercely contested cultural terrain in which biracial forces of youth, progress, racial tolerance and moral enlightenment appeared to face off against ageing, but powerful, white armies of reaction, racial paranoia and [moral absolutism].[61]

Sex, race, delinquency and rock and roll

While the particular racial sensitivities of the adult white South played a major role in encouraging a national outcry against rock and roll, several other factors also contributed to the intensification of opposition during 1956. One was the improved chart performance of original black recordings against white covers. The growing acceptance of black artists by young whites suggested that, far from disappearing, the rock and roll aberration was actually gaining momentum while at the same time reiterating the racial origins of the music.

A second factor was the enormous commercial success of Elvis Presley. Indeed, although much of the criticism of rock and roll had an overt or covert racial impulse, the two individuals who suffered the most vicious public attacks were white: deejay Alan Freed, who was ultimately hounded to his grave, and Elvis Presley, whose unprecedented celebrity made him the epicentre of the rock and roll controversy.

After his first national pop hit with "Heartbreak Hotel" in January 1956, Presley secured eleven more, including five number ones, before the end of the year. He also appeared, amidst much controversy, on a succession of nationally networked television shows, arousing adult anger and disgust with every primetime swivel of his hips. One television critic described

Presley as "an unspeakably untalented and vulgar young entertainer", while *Look* magazine called Presley "mostly nightmare. On stage his gyrations, his nose wiping, his leers are vulgar". *Life* magazine, which had been able to report the new rock and roll craze with relative calm and equanimity in April 1955, had by the following summer branded Elvis "a disturbing kind of idol".[62]

Roger Thames, whose entertainment columns in the *Birmingham News* offered a useful barometer of rising hostility to rock and roll in Alabama, underwent a similar hardening of heart. In January 1956, he felt able to give Presley's "I forgot to remember to forget" a favourable review, confessing he "was pleasantly surprised; he's got a good voice". Certainly, there was no hint of moral outrage in Thames' admission that "I don't Dig that type of music, which is not to say I don't think he's good". By the spring of 1956, however, Thames' column regularly featured readers' laments that "the air is filled with be-bop, blues, congo rhythms – all disgusting".[63]

Thames himself dismissed rock and roll as "an abomination", describing Presley's singing voice as "unintelligible – which is all right because the words he sings don't make sense". As massive resistance reduced the scope for moderation on any issue tinctured by the race issue, Thames did his bit for the preservation of civilized white values by virtually deifying Perry Como – whose version of "The Lord's prayer" made Thames "wonder what moves people to listen to rock and roll" – and by championing Doris Day's "Whatever will be will be" against the cacophony of Presley's "Hound dog" and "Don't be cruel". The Day song, he insisted, was "a mighty pretty tune, and it's heartening to see such a rose in a virtual field of thorns".[64]

For many adults, the flagrant sexuality of Presley's style seemed to confirm the debasing effects on a decent, God-fearing, mother-loving, country boy of over-exposure to black culture. His phenomenal rise also coincided with Tennessee Senator Estes Kefauver's energetic chairmanship of the Senate Sub-committee on Juvenile Delinquency which excited public concerns about youth, media and morality to still new heights. One troubled parent even wrote to the Kefauver Committee, "His [Presley's] strip-tease antics threaten to 'rock 'n' roll' the juvenile world into open revolt against society. The gangster of tomorrow is the Elvis Presley type of today".[65]

Many commentators recognized that such fears were greatly exaggerated. Jonathan Daniels' *Raleigh News and Observer* calmly editorialized that "there seems to be little or no reason to believe the music is an impetus to juvenile delinquency", while Bill Randle, the influential white r&b deejay at WERE-Cleveland, argued, perhaps somewhat less reassuringly for concerned parents, that "R&B may not cause delinquency, but reflects it". Nevertheless, there really was more than enough genuine scandal and violence surrounding rock and roll in the late 1950s to keep much of adult white America in a state of funk.[66]

It certainly did not help ease those anxieties when Ferriday's finest rocker, Jerry Lee Lewis, took his 14-year-old cousin Myra as his third bride. Even more damning were those scandals involving black artists which offered fresh grist to an already overstocked racist mill. In May 1956, Ardra Woods of the Midnighters was arrested after a show at the Madison Ballroom in Detroit for desertion and non-support of his wife and children. In August 1959, the same month that the Flamingos were busted in Colorado for drug offences, came confirmation of the irredeemably venal nature of all black men when the four male members of the supposedly wholesome Platters were discovered, conspicuously without their tuxedos on this occasion, "entertaining" one black and three white women in a Cincinnati hotel room. Although the men were actually acquitted of charges of aiding and abetting prostitution, lewdness and assignation, Judge Gilbert Bettman still took the opportunity to deliver a lengthy rebuke, encapsulating white fears of rampant black sexuality: "You have taken that which can be the core of reproductive life and turned it into a socially abhorrent, tawdry indulgence in lust".[67]

The same explosive mix of white racial and sexual paranoia also blew apart Chuck Berry's career. Berry had developed a distinctive guitar style which boogied somewhere between T-Bone Walker's elegant arpeggios and Bo Diddley's choppy dance rhythms, and recorded some of the most incisive and witty music of the period. He was also one of the sexiest performers around. On stage and on disk Berry exuded a lean and hungry sexual power. "Brown-eyed handsome man" proudly celebrated the historical potency and allure of black men and mocked white racial and sexual taboos by explaining how the Venus de Milo – the quintessence of white female beauty – had "lost both her arms in a wrestling match,/ to win a brown-eyed handsome man".

None of this augured well for Berry's chances of a fair trial when he was arrested in his hometown of St Louis, Missouri for violating the Mann Act, which prohibited the transportation of minors across state lines for immoral purposes. Berry claimed that he had brought Janice Escalanti, the 14-year-old Mexican-Indian prostitute in question, from Juarez to St Louis simply to work in his nightclub. Whatever the veracity of Berry's explanation, it is clear that Judge Gilbert Moore saw before him just another uppity nigger indulging his base sexual predilections and handled the case accordingly. In March 1959, a jury found the singer guilty and Moore revelled in the chance to sentence Berry to five years' imprisonment and a $5,000 fine. An appellate court later nullified the trial, noting that Judge Moore had deliberately "intended to disparage the defendent by repeated questions about race".[68]

Another Mann Act charge dating from 1958 was pursued mainly to discredit Berry before the pool of jurors who would adjudicate in the Escalanti trial. The case was dropped when it became clear that the alleged victim, Joan Martin, did not feel like a victim at all and was still besotted with the singer. However, a re-trial on the Escalanti charges in the spring of 1961 finally resulted in Berry's conviction and incarceration, first in Leavenworth and then in the Federal Medical Center in Springfield, Illinois. In the interim, while the dubious legal process was taking its course, Berry was also briefly imprisoned in Meridian, Mississippi, in August 1959. Berry had allegedly tried to date a white girl who asked for his autograph. Initial reports suggested that Berry was held without bond in Lauderdale County Jail, but he was actually released on a $750 bond and was only temporarily detained by police for his own safety.[69]

There was a chilling irony here, since Mississippi jails rarely offered black men security from whites seeking vengeance for alleged sexual transgressions with white women. Just four months earlier, a white mob had abducted Mack Charles Parker from his cell in Poplarville, where he was awaiting trial on a highly questionable rape charge. Parker was shot twice and his corpse thrown in the Pearl River. Despite investigations which revealed the identity of some of the lynch mob, the courts of Mississippi, which had never convicted a white person for the murder of a black, issued no indictments for Parker's murder.[70]

Mississippi, the archetypal racially closed society, was a notoriously extreme case. Nevertheless, with black life so cheap and, in the absence of political or economic power, legal protection of black rights so elusive, the whole of the Deep South was fraught with dangers, especially for touring black artists who did not live daily with the peculiar folkways of Jim Crow. It was certainly perilous for artists like Berry, who perfectly evoked the terrible thrill of adolescent sexual awakenings in songs like "Sweet little sixteen", much to the delight of, among many others, young white women.[71]

Indigenous southern r&b performers, like New Orleans pianist and bandleader Tommy Ridgley, certainly appreciated that appealing to southern whites in the 1950s was a decidedly mixed blessing if it meant attracting female fans. Ridgley, a stalwart of Louisiana's vibrant club scene for decades, often preferred working for white audiences at clubs like Jimmy Mulano's and the Sands, finding them less cynical and more eager to be pleased than some black audiences. "With a white audience, as soon as you're on, you're ON!" he enthused. Yet, while Ridgley and his contemporaries welcomed the opportunity to play for appreciative and generous whites, they also feared the lure of "forbidden fruit" which drew some black musicians and white women to each other, knowing that this was a highly dangerous proposition. When it was rumoured that local stars Danny White and the Cavaliers were spending rather too much time with their white female fans, local police placed bullets on the stage before they performed in a not-too-subtle warning to stay away.[72]

There's a riot going on

Notwithstanding a tendency to describe every minor fracas as a "riot" – itself indicative of the hysteria surrounding rock and roll – there was actually serious violence at several rock and roll concerts which further fuelled adult white concerns about the music. In November 1955, for example, two dozen black teenagers fought in the streets around the Apollo Theatre on Harlem's 125th Street where bandleader Willis Jackson and the Heartbeats vocal group were performing. In June 1956, a series of fights and knifings at the National Guard Armory in Washington, D.C., prompted police captain Thomas Edwards to ban rock and roll at the venue. Similar actions were taken in Richmond, Virginia, after disturbances at the municipally owned Mosque Auditorium in the summer of 1956 and, more seriously, in March 1958.[73]

While most histories of early rock and roll stress the ways in which a shared passion for the music brought fans of both races closer together, this celebratory tone has obscured the fact that some of the worst rock and roll violence was explicitly racial in nature. In February 1956, for example, a black boy was shot in the ankle by a white fan at a rock and roll dance in New York, suggesting that there was no simple or necessary correlation between love for the same music and deeper racial amity.[74]

Less than three months later, on 4 May 1956, there was a major racial incident at the American Legion Auditorium in Roanoke, Virginia, where a revue featuring the Cadillacs, Ruth Brown, Little Richard and Fats Domino was playing. As was the custom for "black" entertainments which attracted white customers to the Legion, segregation laws were observed by allocating the balcony to white patrons while blacks occupied the main floor below. Such was the popularity of r&b, however, that more than 2,000 whites at first tried to cram into an allotted honky heaven which barely had space for half that number. Some sought to escape the crush by moving down to the less densely packed main floor, where they were not only spotted sharing some of the bleachers, but "actually dancing" along with black fans, as one paper noted incredulously.[75]

As the three-hour show concluded, some whites – perhaps incensed by the flagrant violation of Jim Crow laws they had just witnessed, perhaps just drunk – began to hurl bottles down onto the mainly black audience below. With "whisky bottles . . . flying through the air as thick as hailstones", about three-dozen on- and off-duty policemen broke up the fighting in the auditorium, although in the aftermath violence also erupted between black and white motorists, and at the Dumas Hotel where the acts were staying. Six people, including two black patrons, were eventually charged and convicted of disorder offences and resisting arrest.[76]

As elsewhere in the South in the spring of 1956, the riot had suddenly made rock and roll a major, racially charged public issue in Roanoke: a city where both white authorities and a cautious black leadership insisted race relations had previously been devoid of "tenseness". City councilman Walter Young immediately promised to introduce a resolution to prohibit the mixing of races at public dances in the city. In fact, the city council, under the leadership of Arthur Owens, declined to support such a resolution, preferring to let individual venues make their own arrangements within existing state segregation laws. This touching faith in the willingness of Roanoke's white venue-owners to prevent dancehall integration was instantly rewarded when the American Legion summarily banned the use of its facility for such events. It was a decision which the local press noted was announced "without reference to race, although it was clear what its intent was". Just to be sure, however, after discussions which City-Attorney Ran Whittle admitted were coloured by "racial sentiment over the [Supreme] court decision", the Council set up a special committee to study the disturbance and recommend action to prevent further rock and roll trouble.[77]

Fats Domino was the headliner at the ill-fated Roanoke show. Before the year was over the cuddly Cajun had starred in two more shows which ended in violence. Both these later incidents involved interracial groups of military personnel and, although in neither case was a clear racial motivation for the fighting ever established, it was heavily insinuated by the press coverage. In September 1956, about a dozen black and white servicemen were hospitalized after fighting in the enlisted men's club at a Newport, Rhode Island, naval base. The base commander, Rear Admiral Ralph Earle, Jr, immediately imposed a moratorium on rock and roll. He also ruled that in the future beer at the club would be served in paper cups, not the glass bottles which, as Fats Domino – who, as a seasoned veteran of such brawls, had taken refuge under his piano during the chaos – pointed out, made frighteningly effective missiles. Two months later, another Domino concert in Fayetteville, North Carolina, ended with police deploying tear gas to break up fights involving black and white civilians and servicemen from nearby Fort Bragg.[78]

Rock and roll-related racial violence continued the following year. In April 1957, there was a pitched battle between black and white fans after a concert at the Boston Gardens, during which a 15-year-old white youth from Medford, Kenneth Myers, was stabbed and thrown onto a subway line. "The fight was senseless. There was no good reason for it, but we expect difficulty every time a rock 'n' roll show comes in", explained Police Lieutenant Francis Gannon, assuring the white public that "The Negro youths were responsible for it". Just in case Boston parents had missed the connection between rock and roll and juvenile delinquency, the *Boston Globe* thoughtfully reported the incident next to a story about the bloody battles raging between rival teen gangs in the suburbs of Waltham and Newton. In Dallas, in July 1957, six people were stabbed or beaten when "knife-fights and gunfire erupted from a mass of interracial rock 'n' roll fans".[79]

Not all rock and roll "riots" had this racial dimension, not least because interracial concerts in the South, where such racial explosions were most likely to occur, were still something of a rarity. Indeed, the situation became so tense after the Cole incident that white artists frequently skipped the southern legs of the integrated package tours which criss-crossed the country, many of them organized by Irving Feld's GAC theatre booking agency. Bill Haley, who was on the road with the Flamingos, Platters, Frankie Lymon and the Teenagers and Clyde McPhatter at the time of the Cole attack, played the 20 May date in Birmingham, but then quickly withdrew in the face of further Klan pickets and various bomb threats.[80]

In 1957, Buddy Holly and the Crickets were also booked onto an otherwise all-black tour. This was not, as legend would have it, because they were mistaken for the black vocal group Dean Barlow and the Crickets, but because songs like "That'll be the day" were selling well to blacks and shrewd theatre managers like Frank Schiffman at the Apollo reasoned they would go down well with black audiences. Although the initial reception was lukewarm, after some personal tuition from their black co-stars to bring them up to the level of musicianship and stagecraft expected by black audiences, the Crickets did manage to win a measure of approval for their countrified pop'n'roll. Certainly, there was no obvious black resentment about these young Texans sharing the bill with black artists. When his mother asked him what it was like to be around blacks so much, Holly replied with the earnest, if painfully naive, comment, "Oh, we're Negroes too! We get to feeling like that's what we are". In the South, however, the Crickets were invariably unable to perform in integrated shows, even before segregated audiences, and they eventually left the tour.[81]

Northern black performers, hardly unaware of racism and discrimination at home, found the whole experience of touring the South especially disturbing. In 1957, Willis Jackson reckoned he lost 50 pounds during a three-week tour of southern one-nighters, playing the "empty stomach blues" as he struggled to find restaurants which would serve him. When the New York girl group, the Bobbettes, headed South on an integrated tour with Elvis and Paul Anka in the wake of their success with "Mr Lee", they found their exposure to southern-style race relations deeply traumatic. "We even saw a guy hanging from a tree once", recalled Reather Turner. Her colleague Emma Patron remembered:

> We used to get our allowance, which was $50 a week. We went into a Woolworths in Georgia to get toiletries and things we needed. The woman didn't want to take our money. Everybody in the group had a $50 bill, and the lady said, "You all must have picked a hell of a lot of cotton". We didn't know what she was talking about, because we were raised in New York. We wanted to buy a hot dog, and we sat there for about half an hour and nobody waited on us.

115

Finally, some old lady came and told us real nicely, "I'm sorry we can't serve colored people over here. You have to go round the back". We had to endure that. We couldn't do anything about it, but we hated it . . . people that paid to see you sing but couldn't sell you food because this color was such a terrible thing. And we had a lot of white followers. They would come to see the show, but they couldn't serve you.[82]

Alongside such humiliation and insult were still more sinister signs that, while many southern white youths may have embraced r&b, others in the region were still dedicated to preventing any such biracial intercourse. When the Heartbeats, B.B. King, Bobby Bland, and Little Junior Parker took an all-black package tour to an all-white date in Chattanooga, they found a noose drawn on the dance floor.[83]

ASCAP versus BMI

The most famous of all the rock and roll "riots" occurred on 3 May 1958, not in the South, but at an Alan Freed show in the Boston Arena. A young sailor, Albert Raggiani, was stabbed and 14 others were "slugged, beaten or robbed by a satin-jacketed pack of teen-agers who attended the show". Originally described in the press as a "brawl", this incident quickly escalated, via a "wild melee", into a fully fledged "riot". Mayor John B. Hynes promptly banned similar rock and roll dances in the city, singling out Freed for special vilification. "I am not against rock 'n' roll as such", he said. "However, I am against rock 'n' roll dances when they are put on by a promoter such as the performance at the Arena. This sort of performance attracts the troublemakers and the irresponsible". Other bans and cancellations for Freed followed in New Haven, Newark, New Britain, Connecticut, and Troy, New York, while his employer, radio station WINS-NY, quickly distanced itself from the deejay, prompting him to move to WABC. Freed's culpability extended to the fact that he allegedly said "It looks like the police in Boston don't want you to have any fun" when, in the middle of the show, the house lights at the Arena were turned on to help authorities prevent fans from dancing on the seats. For this, he was indicted for "inciting the unlawful destruction of property", and later for "unlawfully, wickedly and maliciously" inciting a riot. Eighteen months and much expensive legal wrangling later, Judge Lewis Goldberg placed the flimsy riot charge "on file", leaving Freed free, but bankrupt.[84]

Of all the major northern cities, Boston, a traditional centre of Roman Catholic conservatism and working-class ethnic rivalries, had always exhibited a peculiarly intense hostility to rock and roll. In March 1955, Lieutenant O'Brien's Crime Prevention Committee had produced its list of unacceptable records; in May, Alan Freed's first attempt to bring an all-black revue to Loew's State Theater had aroused opposition from the local Boston Diocese newspaper; a year later, the Very Reverend John Carroll launched his famous broadside against rock and roll. The city also seemed to suffer more than its fair share of rock and roll-related violence, what with the Kenneth Myers incident, the Freed "riot", and an earlier disturbance at a Massachusetts Institute of Technology dance.[85]

Perhaps it was in response to growing public unease about rock and roll in Massachusetts' biggest city that, in August 1957, the state's junior senator, John F. Kennedy, asked for a hostile *Newsday* article on the music to be read into the *Congressional Record*. The piece condemned rock and roll and denounced the improper links between radio broadcasters, record companies and music publishers which had brought it to the airwaves. Less than a week later, at the behest of the senior music publishers' association, ASCAP, Florida senator George Smathers called for an investigation into BMI, the rival music licensing organization which administered the rights and royalties to many r&b/rock and roll songs. Smathers introduced a bill to amend the Communications Act of 1934 so as to prohibit broadcasters from owning recording companies or music publishing firms.[86]

Nothing illustrated more vividly the ways in which concern over the new music had brought together diverse sections of American opinion than that both John Kennedy and conservative Arizona Republican Barry Goldwater spoke from the floor of the Senate in support of the Florida segregationist's proposals. For Kennedy, support for his after-hours carousing partner was part of an eager courting of those southern Democrats whose support would be vital for his presidential chances in 1960. Kennedy dutifully endorsed Smathers' bill as a "matter which involves importantly the public interest". Barry Goldwater, also testing the depths of southern support for his brand of states' rights Republicanism, graciously fed Smathers a loaded question, asking if he felt that "the airwaves of this country have been flooded with inferior music ever since BMI was formed?" Smathers did, of course, and the subsequent hearings revealed just how often "inferior" actually meant "black".[87]

The Smathers bill hearings began in March 1958. They marked the culmination of a series of law suits and congressional investigations in which the various strands of opposition to rock and roll, popular and professional, moral and aesthetic, economic and racial, fused. They were also an expression of a longstanding conflict between ASCAP and BMI. From its inception in 1914 until the foundation of BMI in October 1939, ASCAP had monopolized the publishing, recording and performing rights aspects of the entertainment industry. However, by championing the sorts of minority music which ASCAP largely ignored, BMI had gradually come to challenge the domination of ASCAP songs, especially in the singles market and on radio. This shift of economic power within the industry – although less dramatic and sinister than ASCAP propaganda claimed – provided the background to ASCAP's campaign against its rival.[88]

The rock and roll explosion, with its singles orientation and reliance on songwriters from musical streams which ASCAP rarely trawled, gave ASCAP particular cause for concern. With so many composers of the new r&b/rock and roll styles in the BMI camp, even *Variety* conceded that the boom had given its songs an edge over those of ASCAP, commenting rather snootily that "ASCAP usually dominates the hit lists when the song fads fade and straight pop takes over". Paradoxically, however, the success of rock and roll had also provided ASCAP with an opportunity to inject a new moral and racial urgency into its campaign against BMI.[89]

Arthur Schwartz, veteran songwriter and public relations man for an ASCAP front organization, the Songwriters' Association of America, stated ASCAP's case very plainly in a lengthy letter and memorandum to Smathers:

> It is just plain wrong for . . . broadcasters to own music publishing and recording firms, because [they] own the only means by which music becomes popular . . . Station owners, disk jockeys, program directors, recording companies, and the directors of BMI itself have all been guilty of keeping off the air music not owned by the broadcasters. The concern of the Senate is that the public has suffered seriously from these suppressive devices . . .

ASCAP charged that the nation's broadcasters had conspired to foist BMI-registered musical outrages like rock and roll onto the public by denying airtime to "good music", which is to say ASCAP-registered songs. This was a matter of creeping monopoly which Schwartz was sure senators like Smathers and Kennedy, to whom Schwartz wrote in gushing gratitude for his support in the "unequal battle against one of the strongest power-combines in our country", would wish to crush.[90]

There was nothing new in these accusations. In 1953, 33 writer members of ASCAP, led by Schwartz, had initiated an unsuccessful $150 million federal anti-trust suit in the New York courts, accusing BMI of seeking to monopolize the airwaves for its own products. In June 1957, an anti-trust sub-committee of the House Judiciary Committee chaired by New York congressman, Emanuel Celler, having spent over a year investigating ASCAP's allegations, declined to rule that broadcasters must divest themselves of their interests in BMI, as ASCAP had hoped. In his published report, however, Celler called for an extensive Justice Department investigation of the entire music publishing and broadcasting field to check any abuse of anti-trust laws.[91]

This phase of ASCAP's attack on BMI had floundered largely because of the basic implausibility and inaccuracy of its accusations. While ASCAP claimed that BMI "owned" some 2,000 publishing firms, it actually owned just two. Conversely, while ASCAP described BMI as being owned by America's broadcasters, only 624 of the nation's nearly 4,000 stations held any stock in the company – which had not actually issued any new stock since January 1942, had never declared a dividend, and licensed music to non-stockholders on exactly the same basis as stockholders. Moreover, most stations had "blanket licenses" with both ASCAP and BMI, whereby they paid as much for a single performance of a song as for a million plays, giving stations little incentive to favour songs administered through one organization rather than the other.[92]

Even more damning was the fact that ASCAP had clearly prospered since the formation of BMI. Its total annual income had risen from $6.5 million in 1939 to $25 million in 1956, when its rival's income was still just $1.4 million. In the same period, ASCAP had expanded its list of affiliated publishing companies from 137 to 974, and its active songwriting membership from 1,100 to 3,732. By contrast, in 1956 BMI claimed only 300 publishing firms and 1,600 songwriters as active affiliates. Moreover, as the rock and roll boom gathered momentum, ASCAP's turnover actually increased by 5 per cent, helped by the fact that some rock and rollers had re-recorded old ASCAP material, like Fats Domino's "Blueberry Hill". A few of the writers at the heart of the r&b scene had even registered songs with ASCAP as well as BMI. Jesse Stone, for example, used the pseudonym Charles Calhoun for songs like "Your cash ain't nothing but trash", which was published by the BMI affiliate Carlin Music, and his own name for songs such as "Money honey", which appeared through an ASCAP company, Walden Music. At the start of the Smathers hearings ASCAP licensed about 85 per cent of radio performances of copyrighted works and 75 per cent of the music which appeared on albums – a sector of the industry which still accounted for 60 per cent of total record sales in America.[93]

Clearly, then, the emergence of rock and roll had at worst marginally eroded rather than destroyed ASCAP's ascendancy, and then only in the singles market and on certain types of radio and television shows. Indeed, less than a year after the Celler committee report, a House Select Committee on Small Businesses was actually investigating allegations that certain large publishing houses were exerting an improper influence within ASCAP, and that it was ASCAP's notoriously exclusive policies and resistance to minority styles which constituted an illegal restraint on free trade.[94]

As the economic and legal grounds for its complaints against BMI crumbled under the weight of its own commercial success and restrictive practices, ASCAP shifted the focus of its attack to include ever more vehement condemnations of the quality and character of the music which it claimed BMI sponsored. In what was at heart a bitter struggle over market shares and economic spoils, ASCAP increasingly invoked and manipulated the rising moral and racial fears of white adult America concerning rock and roll in order to garner public and legislative support. Again, this was not an entirely new tactic. Appearing before the Celler committee, former ASCAP president Stanley Adams had vilified rock and roll songs as "musical monstrosities". In the Smathers hearings, however, morality, aesthetics and economics merged and, mediated by the racial stereotypes of the day, became much more prominent.[95]

Certain key propositions dominated the hearings. Rock and roll was a musical travesty, wantonly deviant from idealized notions of what American popular music should sound like, and successful only because of BMI's illegal control of the airwaves. Frank Sinatra, who like most crooners of his generation felt intensely threatened by rock and roll, cabled Smathers to offer support for his bill. Sinatra sarcastically noted that unless broadcasters were prohibited from owning publishing firms and record companies, "THE AMERICAN PUBLIC WILL HAVE TO PUT UP WITH THE SONGS WHICH THE BROADCASTERS ALLOW TO BE HEARD; MASTERPIECES LIKE 'HOUND DOG', 'BEBOP-A-LULA' AND 'ALL SHOOK UP'". Such material, Sinatra implied, was totally contrary to the sort of music he, as "A SINGER OF SONGS", recorded.[96]

Professor Arlan Coolidge of Brown University told the hearings that he did not expect "to replace popular music with the symphonies of Beethoven . . . but I do believe that we owe it to our children and our families to limit the consumption of cheap and questionable music on the air and at least provide light music of the best grade at our disposal". BMI was preventing such quality music from being heard. Clearly for Coolidge, the ultimate standard of musical quality was the "European" classical tradition. As a music educator and an academic, Coolidge was more explicit in his invocation of that tradition than other ASCAP supporters. Most, however, retained some notion of a mainstream white American musical tradition, in which they recognized familiar social and moral values. This they compared to a black tradition which they barely recognized as music at all and associated with all manner of backwardness, sin and dissolution. It mattered less that there had been a long, reciprocal, process of theft, borrowing and synthesis between these nominally "black" and "white" musical streams than that these categorical divisions had assumed a notional validity in American minds and race-conscious ears. After all, everyone knew that Elvis and Jerry Lee sounded black, while the Mills Brothers and Lena Horne sang white.[97]

In *Hidden persuaders*, one of the best selling conspiratorial exposés of the era, the prominent social critic Vance Packard had found the advertising executives of Madison Avenue in league with corporate industry to manipulate American consumer preferences. Packard also saw the broadcasters of "cheap" – a moral as well as economic term in Packard's vocabulary – music in cahoots with BMI to manipulate public tastes. Packard appeared at the hearings as an ASCAP witness.[98]

The BMI conspiracy, according to Packard, had generated an unnatural demand for rock and roll by saturating the airwaves with the music and suppressing the alternatives. What made this so alarming, aside from its basic conspiratorial aspect, was the "gross degradation in the quality of the music supplied to the public over the airwaves". Packard elaborated on his objections. "Our airwaves have been flooded in recent years with whining guitarists, musical riots put to a switchblade beat, obscene lyrics about hugging, squeezing and rocking all night long". Whatever the exact rhythmic character of a "switchblade beat", the link with sex, violence and delinquency was clear, and Packard was in no doubt as to the principal source of this sonic unpleasantness. Rock and roll "was inspired by what had been called race music". And its pernicious effects were to "stir the animal instinct in modern teenagers". Apparently, those southern resisters had been right all along: it was the corrupting influence of lyrically lascivious and musically barbaric black music which lay at the heart of the teenage problem.[99]

In an era which idealized, if rarely realized, some kind of all-American middle-class conformity, many minority and regional sub-cultures were viewed with suspicion. Accordingly, Packard also expressed reservations about the propriety and social effects of rock and roll's other great influence, country or hillbilly music, much of which was also licensed by BMI. Packard's derogatory remarks included an ill-informed attack on Hank Williams and a claim that country, like r&b, enjoyed its contemporary vogue only because of self-interested favouritism towards such material by the radio stations which "owned" BMI.[100]

Packard's comments drew particular hostility from Tennessee, where Nashville was the centre of the nation's country music business. Tennessee senator Albert Gore, himself a mean country fiddler, appeared before the hearings to make a personal statement defending country music. Gore also read out a cable from Governor Frank Clement which described Packard's remarks as "a gratuitous insult to thousands of our fellow Tennesseans both in and out of the field of country music". There was, however, no equivalent attempt during the hearings to defend the good name of r&b, certainly not from southern white politicians for whom any perceived "softness" on the race issue had become potentially fatal. BMI was certainly sensitive to the racial co-ordinates of the campaign against it, presenting friendly testimony almost exclusively from whites, although supportive written statements from acceptable, non-r&b, black artists like Lena Horne, Count Basie and Nat King Cole were also read into the record.[101]

The Smathers bill was finally axed in July 1958. The thousands of pages of oral and written testimony revealed no evidence of conspiracy or legal impropriety on the part of BMI. Rather, the vast majority of testimony delivered to the hearings and presented to George Smathers personally held that BMI had curtailed an existing monopoly and greatly expanded opportunities within the industry.[102]

John Pastore, the Rhode Island senator who patiently chaired the hearings, and confessed in the course of them that his own daughter owned a copy of the Coasters' "Yakety yak", concluded that what ASCAP and its supporters really wanted was for Congress to legislate "taste", which it would not do.

> I don't like rock and roll too much as a personal taste, but there are a lot of people who do. And I don't think it is within the province of Congress to tell people whether they should listen to *South Pacific*, or listen to some rock and roll, provided of course we don't get into the field . . . of being obscene and objectionable to the public.[103]

In a sense, of course, the whole point was that much of mainstream white America had found rock and roll decidedly obscene, if for no other reason than that it was so obviously rooted in black culture. Nevertheless, resistance to rock and roll ultimately proved no more able to prevent the spread of the music than massive resistance was able to quash the burgeoning black struggle for civil rights.

CHAPTER FOUR

"Our day will come": black pop, white pop and the sounds of integration

It broke down a lot of stereotyped barriers. I credit the music with opening a lot of eyes, ears and doors to a better understanding. (Harry Weinger of the Platters)[1]

An integrated market

Any attempt to herd together artists as diverse as the Shirelles, Sam Cooke, Brook Benton, Chubby Checker, Mary Wells, Jimmy Soul, Garnet Mimms, Dee Clark, Barbara Lewis and Sammy Turner into a single category risks doing great injustice to the distinctive qualities of each. Nevertheless, in the late 1950s and early 1960s, these and many of the other black artists who dominated the black record charts and airwaves made black pop recordings which shared important characteristics.

Stylistically, these recordings consolidated and extended many of the lyrical and musical trends which were initially the special preserve of vocal groups. Indeed, one such group, the reconstituted Drifters, recorded a string of immaculate crossover hits during this period, including "There goes my baby", "Up on the roof", and "On Broadway", which exemplified the stylized emotion of the best black pop. Moreover, with their reliance upon the carefully crafted songs and inventive productions of young whites like Jerry Leiber and Mike Stoller, Gerry Goffin and Carole King, Barry Mann and Cynthia Weil, and Phil Spector, the Drifters typified the *modus operandi* of the era, in which a new breed of writers, arrangers and producers appeared to dominate the production of the most successful black and white popular music.[2]

In commercial terms, as traditional pop themes and arrangements fused with the basic beat of rock and roll and black vocal style, black pop was directed at the new biracial youth market with great success. Between 1957 and 1964, recordings by black artists accounted for 204 of the 730 Top Ten hits on the *Billboard* best-seller chart, while the same period also saw the unprecedented growth of a young black audience for white pop. This was arguably the most racially integrated popular music scene in American history. Young audiences of both races bought records by artists of both races, performing in styles which were often broadly interchangeable. As late as March 1964, by which time the high tide of pop biracialism had already passed, the student newspaper at the black Greensboro A&T college gently mocked both the new wave of outlandish "animal" dances ("dog, monkey, fly and bird") which were a conspicuous element of the new pop, and the national hysteria over the Beatles. Yet it made absolutely no distinction in its ridicule of the black and white musics which were popular on campus. "One walks down the corridors in the dormitory and is met on all sides by a steady drone of 'yeah, yeah, yeah', and", referring to Tommy Tucker's recent black dance-floor filler, "'put on your high heel sneakers'".[3]

Of course, there were some styles whose popularity remained racially specific. Not all r&b artists were interested in, or capable of, making the stylistic transformations necessary to appeal to the crossover, or even the new young black, market. During these years, however generational, gender, class and geographical differences were often as significant as racial ones in accounting for popular music tastes.

This black pop era has seldom been considered a particularly important phase in the history of black music. Instead, it has been viewed as something of a hiatus between two more significant eras: as the end of a golden age, when the original energy and vitality of "undiluted" r&b was compromised in the quest for the mainstream market, or as the tentative beginnings of the soul phenomenon, when the gospelesque vocals of singers like Jackie Wilson struggled to escape the elaborate strings and shrill choral accompaniments which adorned much black pop.[4]

The underlying assumption has been that the earlier r&b and the later soul styles constituted more "authentic" or "legitimate" expressions of black culture and consciousness than the dance-floor stomps of Bobby Freeman, the smooth, romantic balladry-with-a-beat of Adam Wade, or the carefully manufactured girl group pop of the Crystals. In fact, the popularity of black pop and its white counterpart with black audiences represented just as important an expression of mass black consciousness as r&b before it and soul a few years later: it was just a profoundly different consciousness, linked to a particular historical moment.

The birth of the Movement

The early history of the modern civil rights movement has been the subject of a vast and expanding literature and needs only brief rehearsal here.

That literature tells the story of how the black struggle for equality spread beyond the courtrooms where the NAACP had initially waged its campaign against Jim Crow and disenfranchisement, into the streets, schools, lunch counters, highways and bus terminals of the South, where mobilized southern blacks and their allies directly challenged the racial status quo.

Mass black actions and legal battles against segregation in Montgomery, Tallahassee, Albany, Birmingham, Atlanta, Danville and elsewhere; dramatic challenges to educational segregation at Little Rock and the Universities of Alabama, Georgia and Mississippi; the sit-in movement, which spread across the South from Nashville and Greensboro in early 1960; the freedom rides which began in the spring of 1961; the blossoming of important, nationally prominent, activist organizations like the Congress of Racial Equality (CORE), Southern Christian Leadership Conference (SCLC) and SNCC, and countless local and regional projects staffed by the extraordinary ordinary people who ultimately made the Movement happen; the emergence of charismatic black leaders and effective organizers drawn from all stratas and sections of black America – all of these events contributed to a genuine, if guarded, belief that meaningful challenges to the pattern of racism and discrimination were underway which would lead to full and equitable participation in American society for blacks. As Diane Nash, organizer of the Nashville Student Movement and subsequent SNCC stalwart, commented, "I think we started feeling the power of an idea whose time had come".[5]

The nonviolent direct action campaigns of the early Movement promoted a new sense of black pride and potential far beyond the southern communities most directly involved. Northern blacks were also encouraged to believe that the southern struggle for civil and voting rights presaged a national change in black fortunes. In Detroit, black union organizer Charles Denby joined a huge March for Freedom in June 1963, at which Martin Luther King delivered an early version of his "I have a dream" speech, and marvelled that "the feeling and morale was so high that I felt as though I could almost touch freedom, and that nothing could stop this powerful force from winning". Ivanhoe Donaldson, who became involved with SNCC while a student at Michigan State University, recalled the same burgeoning black pride and optimism which culminated around the time of the August 1963 March on Washington: "I think a lot of people felt, because of the drama and the vast greatness of it all, that somehow we had turned the mystical corner, that a new era of humanity and social consciousness and social justice was now on the table".[6]

Because of the fundamentally unequal power relationship between blacks and whites, black mobilization alone was not sufficient to effect meaningful changes in the social, economic and political situation of black Americans. Historically, such changes have always depended upon the support, or at least acquiescence, of critical elements within white society. But here too, there appeared to be cause for black hope. There were signs that the civil rights movement was variously coercing, coaxing and shaming much of white America into support for basic civil and voting rights.

Beyond government and juridical circles, northern white support for black civil rights grew steadily during the decade after *Brown*. A Gallup Poll in February 1956 showed 71 per cent of non-southern whites approved of the Supreme Court's desegregation edict. Five years later, even a majority of white southerners recognized the inevitability, if by no means the desirability, of fundamental changes in their region's racial arrangements: 76 per cent acknowledged that the day would come when whites and blacks would share the same public accommodations. In the early 1960s, white support was stimulated by the stream of media images of stoic, nonviolent black demonstrators confronted by vicious white supremacist mobs and racist southern law officers. Such images appalled and embarrassed many ordinary Americans.[7]

Even in Dixie, where post-war economic and demographic factors had conspired to produce a new breed of white business progressives, there were signs of vulnerability and change. These progressives rarely led the call for racial change and were more often to be found at the forefront of resistance. Yet they ultimately proved unwilling to sacrifice their economic stake in a modernizing South simply in order to preserve a system of racial segregation which was expensive, inefficient and increasingly the source of unwelcome publicity, censure and civil disorder. In many key civil rights campaigns, such as those in Birmingham and Selma, the moderates who eventually emerged as reluctant intermediaries between die-hard segregationists and black and white activists were largely drawn from the ranks of these businessmen.[8]

The *Brown* decision itself had seemed to continue a post-war trend towards federal recognition of black grievances which had begun with the creation of Harry Truman's Committee on Civil Rights in 1946, and the publication of its sympathetic 1947 report "To secure these rights". It was furthered by President Truman's executive orders outlawing discrimination in the armed forces and federal employment. Although Truman's successor, Eisenhower, was far less sympathetic to racial initiatives, and was extremely lethargic in actually enforcing the Supreme Court's school desegregation orders, even the dilatory Ike finally used federal power at Little Rock's Central High School in 1957 to uphold the law and protect black children attending the school. Taken together, the *Brown* decision and the complementary rulings which emerged from southern appellate courts, Little Rock and, for all their shortcomings, the Civil Rights Acts of 1957 and 1960 – the first for more than 80 years – suggested that powerful federal forces were at last moving towards the recognition and protection of black rights.

In the 1960 presidential campaign, both Richard Nixon and John Kennedy sought to skirt the sensitive issue of race and civil rights reform wherever possible. Nevertheless, a well-judged phone call to Coretta Scott King, offering assistance when her husband was jailed in Georgia, and a celebrated – if undischarged – promise to end housing discrimination with the "stroke

of a pen", meant that many blacks greeted Kennedy's election enthusiastically.
As James Meredith, whose efforts to integrate the University of Mississippi
in 1962 later compelled Kennedy to use federal troops to secure his safe
admittance, remarked of the period between Kennedy's election and inaug-
uration, "the new spirit that had swept Mississippi . . . cannot be overrated".[9]

In an era when integration was the dominant black goal – the separatist
and still numerically insignificant Black Muslims excepted – co-operation
with liberal whites was acknowledged as indispensable to black progress
and as a symbol of future racial harmony. James Farmer of CORE, for instance, believed blacks should occupy the major positions of authority in
the organization, but argued that "it is only realistic to maintain touch with
white people, for we cannot live in our dreams nor carve a nation for
ourselves in our mind's eye alone. We must dwell in this land of ours –
America". Although their presence sometimes caused tensions within the
Movement, many young whites joined the Struggle. Northerners like Dorothy
Miller and Bruce Payne, and southerners like Casey Hayden and Bob Zellner,
provided further evidence that the tide of opinion and events was turning,
often slowly and painfully, but nonetheless inexorably, in the direction of
black freedom and equality.[10]

The early struggle, then, seemed refreshingly clear and simple. "The
beautiful truth warred against the ugly lie. Right against might. Peaceful
blacks against violent white segregationists". Even the physical suffering,
during the voter registration drives and boycotts, on marches and at sit-ins,
seemed to have meaning in the pursuit of clear and attainable objectives.
John Lewis, later chairman of SNCC, recalled his experiences at a Nashville
sit-in in 1960, and noted the profound sense of purpose and psychological
empowerment. "I will never forget it", Lewis remembered. "You had the
fear, but you had to go on in spite of that because you were doing something that *had* to be done, and in the process maybe you would make a
contribution towards ending the system of segregation".[11]

As Martin Luther King had warned the racists and massive resisters in his
account of the Montgomery bus boycott, confidently entitled *Stride toward
freedom*, "We will soon wear you down by our capacity to suffer. And in
winning our freedom we will so appeal to your heart and conscience that
we will win you in the process". Black enthusiasm for black pop and its
white counterpart was in many ways the cultural expression of a similar
faith in the eventual triumph of the freedom struggle and the possibilities of
an integrated, equalitarian America.[12]

Crossover, civil rights and black consciousness

Blacks imbued the breakthrough of r&b into the mainstream of American
popular culture with much the same sort of symbolic significance which

127

had accompanied Jackie Robinson's 1947 breakthrough into major league baseball, and which continued to surround the arrival of other success-ful black athletes in traditionally "white" sports, such as Althea Gibson in tennis. They viewed the success of black artists with white audiences as a portent of, maybe even a vehicle for, eagerly anticipated changes in the broader pattern of American race relations. They saw the world of entertain-ment as one arena where the war against prejudice and discrimination might be waged effectively. It was ironic that when bigots like Asa Carter denounced black music and dance because it threatened to erode barriers between the races, they were actually echoing the best hopes of many blacks, although with rather different views on the desirability and conse-quences of such cultural interaction.

This black perspective was already clear in 1954. The *Baltimore Afro-American* eagerly reported Faye Adams' crossover success with her rocking ode to brotherly love, "Shake a hand", as redolent of crumbling racial bar-riers. "Not too long ago, 'rhythm and blues' discs were even referred to in the trade as 'race' records and were beamed primarily to colored audiences. With 'Shake a hand', however, the results have been different".[13]

In 1956, the Platters argued that rock and roll was "doing a lot for race relations. It's giving the kids a chance to meet rock and roll artists, and this is helping them find out that so many of the stories that they hear are not true." Over 30 years later Harry Weinger, the group's bass singer, still insisted that the music had helped to undermine venerable white racial stereotypes. "Because of our music, white kids ventured into black areas. They had a sense of fair play long before the civil rights movement. We were invited into a lot of homes by kids whose fathers looked at us like we were going to steal the goddamned refrigerator". After playing to mixed audiences on the South Carolina shore in the 1950s, Chairman Johnson of the group Chairman of the Board also maintained that young white enthu-siasm for black music had heralded a real, if generationally circumscribed, change in racial beliefs and practices. "It was at the beach that racial segrega-tion began to break down, white kids could listen to R&B behind their folks' backs". In the late 1950s, Herbie Cox of the Cleftones really believed that "disk-jockeys and record distributors were doing more for integration than *Brown versus the Topeka Board of Education*".[14]

That was certainly how Shelley Stewart viewed matters at the turn of the decade. Aware of a growing white audience for his WEDR shows from the early 1950s, Stewart believed "Music really started breaking the barriers long before the politics in America began to deal with it. [The races] began to communicate . . . because of the music . . . and the black radio in the black community being accepted and enjoyed . . . by the white community."[15]

One incident, in particular, convinced Stewart that music might help turn the tide in southern race relations, or at least be the occasion of such a revolution. On 14 July 1960, Stewart turned up to play his lucrative weekly, segregated, record hop for white fans at Don's Teen Town in Bessemer, not far from Birmingham. Just before he was due to go on, club manager Ray Mahony warned him that about 80 klansmen had surrounded the building and were preparing to jump him. Nearby, an Alabama state trooper sat in his car, calmly observing the scene. Mahony announced to the young white audience that the show could not proceed because the klan did not think Shelley "The Playboy" was good enough to play for them. At that point, as Stewart recalled events, "Those 800 white kids . . . burst out those doors and jumped on the klan . . . fighting for me". While white rock and roll fans fought their klanish elders on behalf of their black hero, Stewart and his three black colleagues were smuggled out to his '59 Impala. Eventually, they made it to safety, although only after shaking off the pursuing state trooper, who evidently considered a black man speeding in fear of his life more worthy of his attentions than a white mob gathering for a lynching. Stewart also survived a roadblock in Lipscomb, half-way back to Birmingham, where police looking for "that nigger, Shelley 'The Playboy' . . . out there trying to dance with white girls" failed to recognize their man.[16]

Shortly after this incident, Stewart reflected on what had happened and pondered its significance for the future of southern race relations. "It was a surprising thing to see that the white teenagers were the ones to actually save my life", he explained. "If it were not for the white teenagers, I doubt if I would have made it out of the club that night. I may not be able to play for these kids again soon, but someday I'll be able to give them the entertainment that they want without any trouble". Over the next few years, such optimism was to be sorely tested by the sheer tenacity of racism in the South and beyond. There lay ahead a long, heroic and often bloody struggle to overthrow statutory segregation and secure some measure of black political power, not least in Birmingham itself. It was not until the early 1970s that Shelley Stewart finally got to spin records before an integrated audience in his hometown for the first time.[17]

Shelley Stewart interpreted the Teen Town incident in a thoroughly positive manner. Yet, at another level, it actually revealed one of several ironies which compromised the capacity of shared musical and dance tastes to promote greater racial understanding among American youths. Most of the locations where whites, or for that matter blacks, heard their favourite musics in the late 1950s and early 1960s were still segregated. School proms, diners, bars, soda fountains, youth clubs, cars and homes were often racially exclusive, whether by custom, preference, economics, residential patterns or, in the South, law. Paradoxically, while the technologies involved – jukeboxes, radio and record players – had largely dismantled the racial barriers between artists and audiences, those same technologies had also made it possible to preserve an enormous level of racial segregation among fans enjoying the same music. Technology allowed white and black audiences to listen to white and black musics, in public and private, in groups and

individually, without ever actually having to mix with fellow fans of a different race.

Obviously there were important exceptions to this pattern and whenever
black and white fans did attend the same record hops or live performances
they frequently did mingle, even in the South. And if events like the 1956
Roanoke "riot" suggest that those interracial meetings were not always harmonious, most were the sort of joyous celebrations in which many, including Ralph Bass, detected the roots of greater racial amity:

> . . . they'd put a rope across the middle of the floor. The blacks on
> one side, whites on the other, digging how the blacks were danc-
> ing and copying them. Then, hell, the rope would come down, and
> they'd all be dancing together. And you know it was a revolution.
> Music did it. We did it as much with our music as the civil rights
> acts and all of the marches, for breaking the race thing down.[18]

In the autumn of 1963, Dion was wandering the South with Sam Cooke,
Bobby Bland and Little Willie John on one of the many integrated tours which
cautiously traversed the region in the early 1960s. When the tour reached
the New Orleans Municipal Auditorium, the black *Louisiana Weekly* gushed
over the welcome sight of "white girls and Negro girls, white boys and
Negro boys seated side by side and together whooping it up". It was almost
as if the "beloved community", that radical democratic vision which guided
SNCC in its early years, had been conjured up by nothing more than a good
beat and some of the finest singing ever to grace that city's storied stages.
Almost. This concert's progressive symbolism was heightened because it
came shortly after a US District Court had pronounced the 1956 Louisiana
Act prohibiting interracial performances unconstitutional. Yet it was another
nine years before the offending Act was finally removed from the Louisiana
statutes.[19]

While black and white fans sometimes spontaneously desegregated clubs
and concert halls, there were also signs that some now felt black performers
should wage open war on segregation and discrimination within the entertainment industry. Certainly, the black response towards Nat King Cole after
his 1956 attack bespoke such rising expectations. Once the immediate condemnations of racist violence had abated, the black reaction was largely
one of anger towards the singer, whose response to the whole incident had
been entirely conciliatory. "I can't understand it", Cole said, carefully dis-
tancing himself from black activism, "I have not taken part in any protests.
I haven't said anything about civil rights. Nor have I joined an organization
fighting segregation. Why should they attack me?"[20]

Cole appeared eager to forgive and forget the whole affair, assuring the
white South that he bore no grudges and denouncing those trouble-makers
who sought to make political mileage out of the incident. "There will be a

few who will keep it going a while but I'd just like to forget about the whole thing". He defended his decision to play segregated dates, insisting that he "was not intending to become a politician", but was "crusading in my own way . . . I don't condone segregation. But I can't change the situation in a day".[21]

Perhaps, then, it was not surprising that Cole was generally applauded for his conduct by white southerners who recognized a black man who knew his place; one who had little intention of challenging the South's racial norms and who even echoed its deep concerns about outside agitators. Blacks like Cole were not the problem and, in an era of burgeoning black militancy, were to be encouraged and protected. Judge Ralph Parker, in sentencing Cole's attackers, had portrayed Cole as a model black southerner. "He has displayed an understanding of our customs and traditions. He was born in Alabama. And he has conducted himself in a manner so as to win the respect of his white friends in the South. He didn't violate any of our customs and our traditions, or any of our laws".[22]

By contrast, Cole's self-professed political indifference, and his continued willingness to play segregated shows, were denounced from all points on the black political spectrum as treasonous in the midst of the struggle against Jim Crow. The *Chicago Defender* called Cole's appearance at a Jim Crow date "an insult to his race . . . if he couldn't have played to a group of American citizens on an integrated basis, he just should have stayed out of Birmingham". Black columnist Abner Berry, of the communist *Daily Worker*, felt a similar sense of betrayal. "For nearly five months now the 100,000 marching feet of Montgomery Negroes (two feet to a citizen) have been tapping a message to the world; 'no compromise with the evil of segregation' . . . But the famous Negro singer Nat 'King' Cole, a native of Montgomery, seems not to have got the message".[23]

While Thurgood Marshall, the NAACP's chief legal counsel, reputedly commented that all Cole needed to complete his Uncle Tom performance was a banjo, executive secretary Roy Wilkins telegrammed the singer, urging him to publicly pledge his support for the civil rights movement:

YOU HAVE NOT BEEN A CRUSADER OR ENGAGED IN AN EFFORT TO CHANGE THE CUSTOMS OR LAWS OF THE SOUTH. THAT RESPONSIBILITY, NEWSPAPERS QUOTE YOU AS SAYING, YOU "LEAVE TO THE OTHER GUYS". THAT ATTACK UPON YOU CLEARLY INDICATES THAT ORGANIZED BIGOTRY MAKES NO DISTINCTION BETWEEN THOSE WHO DO NOT ACTIVELY CHALLENGE RACIAL DISCRIMINATION AND THOSE WHO DO. THIS IS A FIGHT WHICH NONE OF US CAN ESCAPE. WE INVITE YOU TO JOIN US IN THE CRUSADE AGAINST RACISM IN ORDER TO CREATE A SOCIETY IN WHICH THE BIRMINGHAM INCIDENT WOULD BE IMPOSSIBLE.[24]

Cole tried to defend his record on civil rights issues against this on-slaught. In an open response to Wilkins, and in a public statement delivered to the Detroit branch of the NAACP, and again in an open letter to *Down Beat*, Cole noted his regular contributions to several chapters of the NAACP, and his financial support for the Montgomery bus boycott. He was espe-cially proud of his successful battle to desegregate the ritzy Hancock Park section of Los Angeles, and of his various law suits against northern hotels which had hired, but would not serve, him.[25]

Significantly, however, Cole's acts of conspicuous defiance to racial dis-crimination had all taken place outside the South. It was as if he was willing to challenge Jim Crow when he confronted it beyond its "natural" bound-aries, but was able to tolerate it, however reluctantly, as a peculiar feature of southern life. In the spring of 1956, as the nascent civil rights movement began to challenge the evils of segregation in Jim Crow's own backyard, it was hardly surprising that Cole's moderation was interpreted as cowardice or indifference by the black masses. "Overnight, he has practically lost his audience", claimed Abner Berry, while the *Amsterdam News* reported that "thousands of Harlem blacks who have worshipped at the shrine of singer Nat King Cole turned their backs on him this week as the noted crooner turned his back on the NAACP and said that he will continue to play to Jim Crow audiences". As black boycotts of his records and shows were arranged, one black magazine hailed the ritual smashing of "Uncle" Nat's disks as "a new sport", and reported that some Harlem restauranteurs had pulled Cole's records from their jukeboxes. To keep them, said one, "would be supporting his 'traitor' ideas and narrow way of thinking".[26]

Less well-known than the bus boycott in Montgomery, this particular flexing of black economic muscle was equally effective. At the end of April, Cole succumbed to the new combative mood of the black community and paid the Detroit branch of the NAACP $500 to become a life member of the Association. Thereafter, until his death from cancer in 1965, Cole emerged as a rather steadfast and conspicuous supporter of the mainstream civil rights movement.

Harry Belafonte, who stood handsome head and broad shoulders above all other black entertainers in the level of his public commitment and private contribution to the struggle at this time, believed that it was Cole's chastening experiences with his pathbreaking television show which prompted his cautious politicization. Debuting on NBC in October 1956, Cole's show was the first networked television programme to be hosted by a black performer. It survived barely a year, not because ratings were poor, but because the network could not find sufficient sponsorship for a show with a black headliner. Advertisers were petrified that association with a black artist would undermine their sales to whites. As Cole himself angrily noted, sponsors "scramble all over each other to sign a Negro guest star to help boost the ratings of white stars, but they won't put money on a Negro with his own show". According to Belafonte, after this Cole "really began to understand things about America which were very, very harsh. And then he found that he could no longer stay silent . . . and he got on board. It was still quite muted . . . but the fact is that he began to stand up and be counted".[27]

One example of this new commitment came in early 1960. When Martin Luther King faced trumped-up charges of tax fraud in Alabama, Bayard Rustin, Stanley Levison and Belafonte hastily organized a Committee to Defend Martin Luther King Jr (CDMLK). Nat King Cole served as treasurer for this fundraising and publicity vehicle.[28]

Another example of Cole's engagement with the struggle came during the initial planning of the 1963 March on Washington. When bitter arguments arose within the civil rights coalition over the precise purpose of the demonstration, a concerned Cole wrote to the NAACP, CORE, SNCC and SCLC, stressing "the utmost importance that there not appear to be dissension and disagreement among the leaders of our top Civil Rights organizations . . . We must not be divided. As Negroes on the verge of attaining true equality, we are fighting for a common cause". In order to further that cause, Cole announced a "giant benefit performance for Los Angeles on August 8, 1963". This "Salute to freedom concert" drew Roy Wilkins, James Farmer, James Forman and, once Cole had telegrammed him to say that the others had accepted, Martin Luther King, all at Cole's expense. When the final accounting was complete, Cole had raised nearly $4,000 for each of the organizations. Cole's lawyer, Leo Branton – himself a civil rights activist and brother of Voter Education Project (VEP) director Wiley Branton – explained to Christopher Taylor, the president of the Los Angeles NAACP branch, that "Mr Cole . . . wanted to assure that the NAACP netted at least $5,000.00 as its share of the proceeds and, accordingly, is making an additional out-of-pocket contribution of his own".[29]

Cole's public engagement with the Movement in the early 1960s, limited though it may appear, was actually far more exceptional than his earlier refusal to associate himself publicly with civil rights insurgency. Due to a mixture of economic self-interest, fear and contractual constraints, most successful black entertainers proved extremely reluctant to make much public commitment to the struggle until the mid-to-late 1960s. Indeed, the black *Carolina Times* identified precisely this combination of factors behind Nat Cole's initial refusal to become either totem or visible ally of the southern Movement.

Less shrill and judgemental than many other black voices in 1956, the *Carolina Times* appreciated that Cole was a wealthy black entertainer with a huge white following at a time when the accumulation of wealth and fair access to mainstream markets and economic opportunities were key goals of the Movement. Yet Cole's position remained precarious. He "is NOT in a position to fight back . . . he walks a tightrope . . . He has worked long and hard to get this kind of money ($83,000 a week). And the slightest wrong move could set everything in motion against him. Let's face it, it's money plus position as the top in his field that's making Nat Cole say the things he's saying", the paper editorialized. It may not have been a particularly noble or heroic agenda at a time when nobility and heroism were becoming almost commonplace among ordinary southern blacks and their allies in the Movement. Nevertheless, it typified the priorities of most successful black performers and entrepreneurs for the next decade.[30]

A forgotten interlude: Elvis and reverse crossover

Despite continued strictures on mixed-race shows and audiences in the South, the sheer popularity of black music with a mass white record-buying, radio-listening and movie-going audience continued to erode the traditional segregation of American popular culture throughout the nation. Just as significant in that process, however, was the widespread black acceptance of white performers in styles which were ultimately derived from r&b. This reverse crossover had actually begun with the first white rock and rollers. In April 1956, *Billboard* noted with some surprise the unusual success of Carl Perkins' "Blue suede shoes" and Elvis Presley's "Heartbreak Hotel" with black audiences.[31]

Notwithstanding their obvious popularity with black consumers, Presley, Perkins, Jerry Lee Lewis and the rest have routinely been cast as cynical exploiters and defilers of black musical style, for whom the black community had only contempt. Commenting on the popularization of black idioms by these white artists, Carl Belz typically asserted that "commercial exploitation made the Negro people who had grown up with the blues feel that their fundamental heritage had been wrenched from them".[32]

Such sentiments were not unknown in the 1950s, particularly before mid 1956, whereafter black artists began to compete more successfully for the biracial mass market. But the key issue usually seems to have been economic exploitation, not cultural expropriation. In an era before the heightened black consciousness of the mid-to-late 1960s, it was black entrepreneurs, artists and deejays – rather than the black masses – who expressed the greatest resentment against whites "trying to get the beat and cash in on the loot", as the black magazine *Our World* put it. There was widespread condemnation of both the unfair treatment afforded black artists on the airwaves, and the discriminatory pay scales for black acts whereby Bill Haley could command $1,500 for an appearance while "the numerous Negro quartets lead a precarious life and make only $300 to $700 at the height of popularity".[33]

Such legitimate grievances aside, however, the black reaction to the success of white stars in obviously black-derived styles in the decade after

Brown was far more complex and ambiguous than commentators like Belz have allowed. Even many of the black artists who did cross over to the mainstream market clearly recognized the importance of white artists and deejays in making that transition possible. "Thank God for Elvis Presley!", commented Little Richard, while Screaming Jay Hawkins acknowledged Alan Freed's crucial role in the careers of his black contemporaries: "We *all* had to thank that man."[34]

Black journalist Dan Burley was certainly happy to acknowledge that the new rock and roll style drew on white, as well as black, musical traditions. "Rock and Roll, then, is a combination of gospel songs, blues, the 'oo bop shee bam' of bebop, the sentimentality of the love ballad, the folksy material of the hillbilly or western type song, and things based on personal experiences", he explained. "Rock and Roll today has no color line in listening appreciation or in its development".[35]

Mass black reaction to Elvis Presley was especially revealing, and by no means universally hostile. Between "Heartbreak Hotel" and the cessation of a separate black singles chart at the end of November 1963, Presley had 24 Rhythm and Blues hits, including four number ones. In 1956, when Presley was unexpectedly introduced to 9,000 black Memphians gathered in the Ellis Auditorium to see B.B. King and Ray Charles perform a Goodwill Revue concert for WDIA, the crowd went wild, requiring police intervention to rescue the besieged singer from over-enthusiastic black fans. Before this incident, only Rufus Thomas of the WDIA staff had fully appreciated the extent of Presley's black popularity and played Elvis' disks regularly. Thereafter, Presley was a fixture on WDIA's playlists.[36]

Nat Williams, the dean of black announcers on WDIA, had an interesting spin on Presley's black appeal – especially to women. Duly noting that Elvis had a stylistic debt to some of Beale Street's famed black bluesmen, Williams cleverly inverted white anxieties about miscegenation to ask:

> How come cullud girls would take on so over a Memphis white boy . . . when they hardly let out a squeak over B.B. King, a Memphis cullud boy . . . Beale Streeters are wondering if these teenage girls' demonstration over Presley don't reflect a basic integration in attitude and aspiration which has been festering in the minds of your women-folk all along. Hunh??[37]

The following year, *Tan* and *Jet* published companion articles on Presley, based on an interview with the singer by *Jet* associate editor, Louie Robinson. Both pieces were highly positive, noting Presley's early exposure to black sacred and secular musics in Tupelo and Memphis, and listing among his favourite artists and influences Bill Kenny of the Ink Spots, Arthur "Big boy" Crudup, Roy Hamilton, Josh White, Nat King Cole and Fats Domino. This was all part of an evenhanded effort to explain Presley's style in terms of his

southern roots and impeccable good taste in (black) singers, not to condemn him for his craven filching of black style. Indeed, the articles were
at great pains to scotch the rumour that Presley had once said "The only
thing that Negroes can do for me is shine my shoes and buy my records",
and pictured him consorting with black stars like Billy Ward and B.B. King.
Tan stressed that "Presley makes no secret of his respect for the work of
Negroes, nor of their influence on his singing. Furthermore, he does not
shun them, either in public or private". Presley insisted that "A lot of people
seem to think I started this business. But rock 'n' roll was here a long time
before I came along. Nobody can sing that kind of music like colored
people. Let's face it: I can't sing it like Fats Domino can. I know that".
Revealingly, even when *Tan* contemplated the discrepancy between Presley's
annual earnings of $2 million and the $700,000 earned by Domino, "his No.
1 Negro counterpart", it skirted the full racial implications and explained the
difference – inadvertently punning on Domino's weight – in terms of the
fact that "Domino does not draw fat movie and consumer product fees".[38]

In a similar vein, far from attacking Bill Haley for bowdlerizing Joe
Turner's "Shake, rattle and roll" and reaping the major economic rewards
for his puritanical plunder, both the *Birmingham World* and the *Chicago
Defender* reported his success without censure or rebuke. Instead, they welcomed Haley's enthusiasm for r&b, and appreciated his contribution to its
wider popularization. Indeed, Haley shared the belief of many blacks that
"rock and roll does help to combat racial discrimination. We have performed to mixed groups all over the country and have watched the kids sit
side by side just enjoying the music while being entertained by white and
Negro performers on the same stage".[39]

Even the cover phenomenon did not always arouse the same intense
outrage among contemporary black audiences as among slighted black artists and subsequent critics. The arch-villain of the cover scene, Pat Boone,
enjoyed a couple of hits on the black charts, including his version of the El
Dorados' "At my front door". In the late 1950s, Mary Wilson of the Supremes
was a black teenager growing up in Detroit's Brewster Projects. She "Loved
Little Richard, Chuck Berry and Sam Cooke", but confessed her "personal
favorites included the McGuire Sisters, Doris Day and Patti Page".[40]

Julian Bond was SNCC's communications director and subsequently the
longest serving state representative in Georgia's history. He and his brother
James, another SNCC worker and later an Atlanta city councilman, hardly
had the sort of upbringings which are taken as typical in the literature on
black music, but which actually illustrate the diversity of black experiences
and the dangers of homogenization. Sons of the eminent black scholar and
educator Horace Mann Bond, both attended predominantly white, northern, high schools – Julian, a Quaker school near Philadelphia; James, a
boarding school in Massachussetts. They grew up in the mid-to-late 1950s,
listening, as James succinctly put it, to "*American* popular music".[41]

In Pennsylvania, although he had an early interest in jazz and what little r&b he heard, Julian "got comparatively little of the black originators . . . I heard probably what a white teenager would have heard". The first record he bought was the Chords' "Sh-boom". "I remember not disliking the cover version, but being aware that the Chords were first and the Chords were better. Although I wouldn't have called it this at the time, it was more soulful". In 1957, when Horace Mann Bond took up a post at Atlanta University, the family relocated. Julian enrolled at the prestigious all-black Morehouse College and became immersed in a musical and social world which was much "blacker" than his northern experience. WERD and WAOK were beaming out all manner of black musical fare; the Royal Peacock Club on bustling Auburn Avenue was one of black America's foremost entertainment venues; Herndon Stadium was just a few blocks away from the family home. Both brothers remember sitting on the porch when Ray Charles played a date which WAOK's owner-deejay, Zenas Sears, recorded for a celebrated live album.[42]

Yet even in this black milieu, as Julian developed his knowledge and love of r&b, there was still no dramatic rejection of white music. At an "ice-breaker" event organized by a Morehouse professor, Bond and his fellow students were all required to recite or perform something:

> Three friends of mine and I sang . . . "Teddy bear" . . . And I remember thinking it not at all remarkable that we would sing this Elvis Presley song. So here's these four black young men singing, "Just wanna be, your teddy bear, put your arms around my neck and lead me anywhere". And looking back on it now, it seems remarkable to me . . . We just said, "this is ok . . . this guy is alright". I think my peers thought Elvis Presley, at least in that early stage, was ok.[43]

Jerry Lee Lewis hit the top of the black charts with "Great balls of fire" and had another three Rhythm and Blues hits before the controversy over his marriage derailed his career in 1958. The Louisiana piano-pumper also earned respect for his music from young blacks like Julian Bond, despite a lingering suspicion that he was probably more a part of the racial problem in the South than its solution. "On the one hand Jerry Lee Lewis is the typical cracker and the kind of guy if you saw coming down the street, you'd cross the street to get away from him. But sitting down at that piano and singing . . . he was just another persona, another personality". This black appreciation of Lewis' exhilarating music, despite some of the more odious aspects of his redneck credentials, was a telling counterpoint to the ways in which young whites were actually able to be passionate about black music without necessarily changing their racial prejudices. Clearly, when whites could cut the musical mustard and deliver whatever it was that blacks wanted in their music, they were simply accepted alongside black artists who did the same.[44]

The response of the black community to white r&b deejays like Alan Freed, rather like its attitude towards the first wave of white rock and rollers and teen idols, has also been much distorted. The desire to expose the greed and rapaciousness of cynical white deejays ("To Freed, it [rock and roll] purely and simply meant money", asserted Nelson George), has obscured a much more complex reality.[45]

Certainly, white deejays were among the most important early boosters of black r&b to audiences of both races. While at one level the presence of so many whites playing r&b reflected systemic and habitual impediments to blacks within the industry, at another, these deejays were initially appreciated, not vilified, by black listeners simply because they played black records at a time when precious few did. Shelley Stewart remembered the *Atomic Boogie Hour* which Bob Umbach ran between 1946 and 1953 on WJLD-Birmingham with a typical mix of gratitude and frustration. For some time Umbach's show "was the only place that you could hear black music on the radio", Stewart recalled, but he resented the fact that here was a white man whose success came from trying "to act black" on air. This was not uncommon. Vernon Winslow created the "Poppa Stoppa" character for WMJR-New Orleans, but was not allowed to go on air because of the station's lily-white announcer policy. Instead, Winslow was required to teach white announcers to "talk black".[46]

The motivations of white r&b deejays were often an elusive mixture of personal ambition, keen entrepreneurial instincts, and genuine admiration for the music they played – in other words, much the same as their black colleagues. Many attracted a fiercely loyal black following, although adulation for these white r&b deejays was inseparable from love of the mostly black records they played. In 1949, Dewey Phillips, a white ex-serviceman with a "Southern drawl . . . as thick as a stack of Aunt Jemima's pancakes", took over the *Red Hot and Blue* show on WHBQ-Memphis. By the following year his catch-phrase, "Phillips sent me", was "on the lips of practically every Negro in Town", and his night-time show rivalled anything which the dawn-to-dusk WDIA had to offer. Like many of his contemporaries, black and white, Phillips soon extended his core black audience to include young whites.[47]

Brother Esmond Patterson, a "born salesman" and indefatigable gospel deejay from Atlanta, first went on air at WERD in 1956 and could still be heard greeting the dawn on the city's WAOK 40 years later. Patterson acknowledged Zenas Sears' enormous popularity and prestige among black Atlantans in the 1950s and early 1960s. According to Patterson, Sears "could come down and shake hands with you, fellowship with you and . . . you'd think, 'he's one of us'". Sears was so much a part of black life in the city that Julian Bond had no idea that he was white until he met him in the early 1960s.[48]

Even more significant in the future development of black and white southern music was mighty WLAC in Nashville. The Station had switched to all-black programming in 1949 with 50,000 watts of 24-hour power and a Holy Trinity of rocking white deejays: Bill "Hoss" Allen, "Daddy" Gene Nobles and John "John R" Richbourg. "Everybody listened to WLAC at night. Everybody", recalled Tommy Ridgley. Certainly, when WGIV-Charlotte went off the air at dusk, young Stanley Wise, later one of SNCC's most effective campus organizers, habitually retuned to the station. "WLAC was all we ever listened to", vouched singer James Brown. "You could hear the station all over the eastern half of the United States". Moreover, as Ridgley noted, whites were listening too: "This is when the whites started coming into rhythm and blues, through the WLAC". One of those young white listeners was John Egerton, the future historian of Dixie's embattled liberals. Egerton, like most black listeners, could scarcely believe that the deejays spinning r&b records "were white guys who just sounded black".[49]

Black admiration for white deejays was not restricted to the South. Photographs of Alan Freed's early appearances in Cleveland show a mass of black fans with barely a white face in evidence. In 1954, *Billboard* noted with some surprise that the audience for a June show in New York had risen to nearly one-third white, while his Newark Coronation Ball later the same summer also attracted mostly black fans. From late 1954, Freed's New York audience may have been rather whiter than that of, say, Tommy Smalls, but substantial sections of the black audience stayed tuned and turned up for his personal appearances, simply because Freed played the music they wanted to hear. Certainly, in early 1960, when Freed brought his show to the Apollo, the *Amsterdam News* welcomed him as someone "responsible for many a Negro rock'n'roll artist finding success", and for "carrying his war on racial bigotry over the airwaves when he integrated his *Dance Party* over a local TV station. He then insisted that Negro teenage couples share the cameras with whites".[50]

There were other signs of a new interracialism on the airwaves. The conventional wisdom that black deejays, with more than enough prime black musical product to choose from, simply did not programme white rock and roll or the big beat pop artists, is highly suspect. For example, on *Billboard*'s first national Rhythm and Blues deejay chart in January 1955, Bill Haley's "Dim dim the lights" was ranked fourteenth. Later, Haley's "Rock around the clock" reached number four in the black record chart and number three in the corresponding deejay list. Overall, "Rock around the clock" was the twenty-first most played record by r&b deejays during the year. Elvis Presley's airplay on r&b radio was even more impressive. In 1956, he was the fourth most programmed artist – only Little Richard, Fats Domino and the Platters were played more.[51]

Unfortunately, the *Billboard* charts did not distinguish between what was played by white r&b deejays and what by black "platter pilots". There is, however, more than enough circumstantial and anecdotal evidence to suggest that black deejays extensively programmed white artists. Given their commercial aspirations, it would have been difficult to ignore the records which their primary audience was obviously buying in substantial amounts. Since sensitivity to changing audience tastes was a deejay's professional lifeblood, it would have been strange if Tommy Smalls had disregarded the evidence from his own Harlem nightclub that "Even in the music box in my cafe I find patrons spinning more white artists than Negro", and not programmed white records on his show.[52]

Shelley Stewart had always had an eclectic playlist. "My position was that you could take it all. It took onions, it took potatoes, it took carrots, it took beans, and peas, and all of these things to make a soup. And I like great soup. I would mix the blues with anything". In the late 1950s, Stewart responded to the shift in young black preferences. "I played Bobby Darin. Blacks did like Bobby Darin . . . I played Elvis Presley". Similarly, at WCIN-Cincinnati in 1959, when "Jockey" Jack Gibson actually managed to squeeze in some records between campanological pitches for his chief sponsor, Bell Furniture – Gibson rang a bell every minute – Bobby Darin was there alongside Ray Charles, Brook Benton and James Brown.[53]

Certainly, there is little evidence of any pedagogical desire among black deejays to play what they thought, for reasons of political, economic or racial advancement, black audiences *should* have listened to. Deejays always preferred to programme what they knew their audiences wanted to hear; knowledge gleaned from their personal contacts with local promoters, record shop proprietors and the fans who attended their personal appearances, or phoned and wrote to the stations. Factor into this scenario the overwhelming power of white station owners, programme managers and sponsors, who lacked any racial incentive to privilege black artists, and it becomes even harder to imagine black deejays being allowed to ignore popular white artists.

Paradoxically, as the raw sound of early white rock and roll gave way to the smoother sound of white big beat pop, and thus grew further away from its black influences, the white presence on the black charts and airwaves became even more marked. Harold Battiste clearly recognized this trend. In the mid 1950s, the advent of an Elvis Presley, or even a Pat Boone, had offered black artists, songwriters, musicians and entrepreneurs a necessary "white vehicle . . . so that black music began to reach a bigger market". Thereafter, however, Battiste "found that rather than white kids being able to come and accept the real thing, more black kids began to go for the imitation".[54]

Only five of twelve Rhythm and Blues chart toppers in 1957 were by black artists. In 1958, 45 of 86 top-ten black chart hits were by white artists. Between 1956 and November 1963 there were 175 top-ten hits on the Rhythm and Blues charts by white artists, while more than 120 white acts had black chart entries. Some of these hits, like "Tie me kangaroo down, sport" by

Table 4.1   White artists with three or more hits on the *Billboard* Rhythm and Blues chart, 1956 to 1963

Paul Anka (6)	Lesley Gore (3)
Frankie Avalon (5)	Brenda Lee (6)
Beach Boys (4)	Jerry Lee Lewis (5)
Bill Black Combo (4)	Rick Nelson (9)
Freddie Cannon (3)	Roy Orbison (5)[b]
Jimmy Clanton (3)	Elvis Presley (24)
Crickets (4)[a]	Jimmy Rodgers (4)
Bobby Darin (7)	Bobby Rydell (3)
Dion (7)	Neil Sedaka (7)
Everly Brothers (8)	Ray Stevens (3)
Four Seasons (4)	Conway Twitty (3)
Connie Francis (8)	Andy Williams (3)

Notes:

[a] Three entries listed as the Crickets, one as Buddy Holly.

[b] Includes one double A-side, where both "Mean woman blues" and "Blue bayou" charted.

Australia's doyen of the didgeridoo, Rolf Harris, were one-off novelties but, as Table 4.1 shows, there were 24 white artists who enjoyed three or more black hits; there were a further 20 who had two. Significantly, aside from Elvis, the most successful white artists with blacks – Paul Anka, Frankie Avalon, Connie Francis and Neil Sedaka – were actually the same sort of clean-cut teen idols who increasingly dominated the national pop charts with their smooth beat balladry.

Those writers who have not simply ignored this mass black consumption of white pop have struggled to interpret it in ways which maintain a dubious autonomy for black culture and, in so doing, have helped perpetuate venerable, but ultimately debilitating stereotypes of what constitutes "authentic" black popular music. Nelson George, for example, ignores the historical context for the biracial pop era and obscures its real significance by arguing that while black teens might listen to white pop "their heads were in different places". The argument is that for about seven years large numbers of blacks consistently spent a considerable proportion of their sorely limited income on records they did not actually like or really relate to, in preference to other available and nominally "blacker" options such as blues, gospel, jazz and nascent soul, which, according to George, really reflected their racial consciousness.[55]

How, then, is one to reconcile the contention that young blacks bought white rock and roll and pop recordings extensively between 1956 and 1964, although in rapidly diminishing amounts towards the end of that period, while black deejays happily played those popular white disks on black-oriented shows, with the orthodoxy encapsulated in the recollections of a

Chicago deejay, who told Norman Spaulding that "my listeners just don't dig many white artists. Presley was the biggest thing in the country, but he didn't sell that well in the Black areas"?[56]

The problem here is one of writers like Spaulding and Nelson George, and their informants, projecting backwards into the late 1950s and early 1960s an intense racial consciousness, a robust pride in things distinctively black, and a determination to isolate, protect and valorize those cultural traits, which did not fully emerge among the mass of black Americans until the mid-to-late 1960s. SNCC's Stanley Wise appreciated the way in which hindsight and the experience of raised and dashed expectations have patterned black memories of the black and white pop era. In the early 1960s, "There were a tremendous number of blacks buying the music of white artists", Wise recalled. But later, in the wake of the cultural nationalism which informed all strains of the amorphous black power impulse, "it went out of style to listen", or even "to let people know" that you ever had.[57]

The piebald black charts and playlists of black-oriented radio in the late 1950s and early 1960s reflected the pervasive, if guarded, optimism of a very different moment in black America's struggle for freedom. It may have been an unintended consequence of much baser economic forces, but thanks largely to radio and the record industry, an entire generation of blacks and whites came of age in America at this time listening to much the same popular musics. Such a development could only seem hugely portentous as the civil rights movement attracted first the attention and then the bodies of thousands of young whites. In this atmosphere of burgeoning black hopes for meaningful changes in the pattern of racial relations throughout the nation, integrated airwaves, like integrated charts, integrated concert halls, integrated cinemas, sports facilities, restaurants, stores, universities and schools, seemed to promise much for a genuinely integrated, egalitarian America.

In the shadow of black pop

While black and white pop flourished, the decidedly patchy commercial performance of other, nominally "blacker", musical styles in the late 1950s and early 1960s is striking. The prodigious avant-garde jazz explorations of John Coltrane, Cecil Taylor and Ornette Coleman never attracted a mass black following, while even the most popular jazz style of the era – the funky hard-bop of Horace Silver, Charles Mingus and Milt Jackson – failed to match the mass popularity with black audiences of a Chubby Checker or, for that matter, a Bobby Darin.

"Rock 'n' roll", reported the *Amsterdam News*, "has rolled in more youngsters into rhythm and blues shows and dance halls in one year than bop has ever rolled in during all its years of fame". Even Dizzy Gillespie rather condescendingly conceded that "Jazz never attracted a real big audience, like rock 'n' roll or the singers that came along . . . because jazz is strictly an art form". Jerry Wexler at Atlantic, which remained a bastion of modern jazz recordings into the 1960s, understood that the music, breathtaking in its verve and artistry as it frequently was, remained a minority interest for both races: "In spite of a noble attempt to represent a broad spectrum of jazz and jazz-tinged music", he knew that "it was rhythm and blues and rhythm and blues alone that paid the rent".[58]

In the late 1950s and early 1960s, more traditional electric bluesmen, like Muddy Waters and B.B. King, retained the loyalty of their older south- ern and migrant black audiences, but they, too, found themselves isolated within a dwindling and ageing black market for their music. In the first half of the 1950s, Waters had helped keep the macho blues tradition alive with testosterone-fuelled hits like "I'm your hootchie coochie man" and "Man- nish boy". Yet Waters managed only three hits with black audiences after 1955 and none at all after 1958. Similarly, when B.B. King opened shows for new black pop heroes like Sam Cooke and Lloyd Price, he sometimes found himself heckled by black teenagers, "a fact he attributed to the blues being associated with black Americans' poor origins in this country", accord- ing to his biographer Charles Sawyer. The only new blues talent to enjoy any sustained national commercial success during the black pop era was Jimmy Reed with gentle shuffle boogies like "I'm gonna get my baby" and the immaculate "Bright lights, big city".[59]

Like the majority of professional black musicians, B.B. King was rather more concerned with earning a living and staying alive than preserving any sort of spurious purity for the benefit of subsequent critics. As he told Lawrence Redd:

> Whatever trend of music come out, I sing my same old blues but try to use just a little bit of some of that background. You know, for instance, like when calypso was big, I did things like, "Woke up this morning, my baby was gone", things of that sort. Same thing with rock and roll. When rock and roll came out, I did several things with rock type background. Like soul, since soul has been out, I do a few things with just a little bit of soul touch to it.

Encouraged by his record label, Kent, in the early 1960s King leapt uncer- tainly on board several of the passing dance craze bandwagons with songs like "Hully gully (twist)", "Mashed potato twist", "Mashing the popeye", and an album called *Twist with B.B. King*.[60]

By the turn of the 1950s, many of the seminal black r&b/rock and roll artists were also struggling. Some, like the Clovers, Five Keys, Lloyd Price and Ruth Brown, tried to revamp their styles to accommodate the tastes of the new integrated audience. Those, like most of the macho shouters, who could not, or would not, adjust, simply slipped out of favour with black

Sam Cooke was one of the biggest stars of the biracial pop era, and a major entrepreneuria
presence within the industry.

audiences and lost all hope of crossing over to white fans. "Rock and roll as we've recently known it is somewhat on the wane", observed the black keyboard star Bill Doggett in the spring of 1958. "You hear an awful lot of Sam Cooke and Johnny Mathis, however, and that's not rock and roll".[61]

Bo Diddley and Little Richard both felt this shift in tastes. Diddley had only two black chart entries between 1960 and 1963 and, although his popularity as a live act and jukebox pick continued, he felt obliged to recast his distinctive "shave and a haircut" riffing style in an effort to meet the demands of the new biracial pop audience. He released an album called *Bo Diddley's a Twister* and, after the Beach Boys and Jan and Dean had ridden the quintessentially white surf craze into the black charts in a good illustration of the way in which conventional racial categorizations broke down at this time, released *Surfin' with Bo Diddley*. When Little Richard returned to music in the early 1960s after a brief religious sabbatical, he also discovered that the black audience had largely rejected the raw excitement of his rock and roll for something smoother. "Blacks didn't want my sound, you know".[62]

Aside from the romantically inclined Fats Domino, the one original black rock and roller who appeared to confront the new biracial pop era without any discernible change in style was Chuck Berry. This was the result of both musical and circumstantial factors. First, while Berry could affect a range of vocal styles from sub-T-Bone Walker flyblown blues ("Wee wee hours"), through ersatz calypso ("Havana moon"), to rockabilly ("Oh baby doll"), he always had a relatively raceless voice, characterized less by an r&b roar than a mid-western twang. Second, his major compositions had invariably focused on the classic themes of the new pop: the music itself ("Rock and roll music"); adolescence ("Almost grown"); cars ("The Jaguar and the Thunderbird"); parents and authority ("Thirty days"); and girls ("Carol"). Third, since Berry spent much of the period around the turn of the decade in a series of trials and subsequently behind bars, he was unable to record much new material. His fidelity to his original rock and roll sound and apparent indifference to the slicker new pop styles was hardly optional and most of the material released under his name between 1960 and 1963 had been recorded several years earlier. Generally speaking it was not as successful with audiences of either race as in the 1950s.[63]

The domination of the black-white pop ethos not only made life difficult for black artists in older styles in the early 1960s, it also accounted for the mixed fortunes of those who were laying the foundations of soul by intro-ducing more generous helpings of a distinctively black influence – gospel – into their music. Georgia baritone Roy Hamilton, for instance, hit big with songs like "You'll never walk alone" and "If I loved you" in the mid 1950s, but then sang against the tide of mass black taste to give his smooth bal-ladry an ever more gritty, sanctified feel on songs like "I need your lovin'". In the early 1960s, Hamilton lost much of his audience.

James Brown, meanwhile, recorded a succession of gutsy, raw-edged, nascent soul cuts like "Just won't do right" and "That dood it" in the late 1950s to the general indifference of black audiences beyond his adopted Georgia. Although his relentless touring reflected his popularity as a live act, in the four years following his national breakthrough with the awesome primal plea, "Please please please" in 1956, Brown managed just two more Rhythm and Blues chart entries. These included the melodramatic "Try me", which made a considerable concession to the vogue for big beat balladry. Thirty years later, far from crowing over the way in which he had preserved some kind of authenticity during an era of compromise, Brown simply bemoaned the fact that he had been unable to cross over into the mainstream: "['Just won't do right'] should have crossed over, but my musicians held me back. They could only think in terms of R&B and didn't understand what I thought about. They were singing R&B, but their voices were too heavy; I should have had girls singing with me".[64]

Of course, there were many other recordings in the late 1950s and early 1960s which did presage the sound of soul and were also enormously successful with a national black – and sometimes white – audience: Ray Charles' "What d'I say", the Impressions' "For your precious love", Falcons' "You're so fine", Isley Brothers' "Twist and shout", and Sam Cooke's "Bring it on home to me". Moreover, towards the end of the black pop era, such gospel-influenced records undoubtedly became more popular with black audiences. Nevertheless, it does appear that between 1956 and 1963 black audiences throughout the nation were supportive of black and white pop styles which had been quite deliberately shorn of some of their "blackest" musical and lyrical characteristics.

Sam Cooke, black balladeers and the dreams of an era

One of the defining features of the black pop era was the emergence and biracial success of a large number of male r&b-pop balladeers, including Brook Benton, Gene McDaniels, Sammy Turner, Dee Clark, Mel Carter, Ed Townsend, Tommy Hunt, Wade Flemons, and Garnet Mimms. Clyde McPhatter was a big influence on these smooth black stylists, some of whom would later record in a much more soulful vein. So, too, were the first wave of crossover vocal groups with their resolutely romantic visions. But the key figure was Sam Cooke. "They all had to come by Sam Cooke after he hit the scene", recalled Harold Battiste, who worked with Cooke regularly. "He was the model".[65]

Cooke was born in 1931, in Clarksdale, Mississippi, son of a Baptist preacher. He moved to Chicago as an infant and after singing with various little league gospel groups joined the majors in 1951 as a replacement for the legendary R.H. Harris in the Soul Stirrers. Notwithstanding his contemporary standing as one of the most charismatic, sensual and emotive gospel stylists of his generation, and his posthumous deification as the father of soul, Cooke's earliest secular forays were firmly in the teen pop vein. Indeed, in 1957, the enormous popularity of Cooke's "You send me", along with "Diana" by Canada's teen crooner Paul Anka, did much to consolidate the trend towards romantic beat balladry initiated by teen vocal groups like the Penguins and Spaniels.

While the glutinous strings and perfunctory female choruses on records like "Lonely island" and "Cupid" could never entirely swamp the grace of Cooke's mellifluous vocals, he was not, as Bernice Johnson Reagon charitably put it, particularly "challenged as a singer" on these early secular recordings. Aside from his trademark note-bending glissandi "woah and oh and woah oh ohs" and immaculate timing, they offered only fleeting glimpses of either Cooke's gospel roots or his subsequent pop-soul explorations.[66]

Nelson George has attributed the saccharine quality of some of Cooke's early secular sides to "the obnoxious studio input of white producers, Hugo Peretti and Luigi Creatore", although he insists elsewhere that "Cooke always remained his own man". The last is much nearer the mark. Peretti and Creatore did not even work with Cooke until his move from Keen to RCA in 1960, by which time his wistfully romantic pop style had already been perfected in collaboration with black arranger-producer Bumps Blackwell. Even at RCA, with the exception of his first outing for the label, "Teenage sonata", Hugo and Luigi generally left Cooke, manager J.W. Alexander and arranger René Hall in charge of studio production. Moreover, the slushy "Teenage sonata", with its "obnoxious studio input", was actually one of only a handful of Cooke recordings which, thanks to Cooke's loyal black fans, made the Rhythm and Blues charts, but not the pop listings.[67]

In reality, Sam Cooke probably had more control of his career, both artistically and commercially, than any of his black or white pop contemporaries. In conjunction with Alexander and his road manager, the former Soul Stirrer S.R. Crain, he founded his own song publishing company (KAGS), two record labels (SAR and Derby), and later his own production company (Tracey). From the fall of 1963, Tracey supplied Cooke's recordings to RCA for marketing and distribution. "Control was very important to Sam", recalled Hugo Peretti, who even interpreted Cooke's songwriting primarily as a means to maximize both his artistic freedom and the financial rewards from his recordings. "He saw what had happened to a lot of other black artists, and he didn't want to get ten percented to death".[68]

It was symptomatic of the mood of the times that Cooke chose to exercise this rare artistic license and relative economic power to court a biracial market for his singles and an overwhelmingly white audience for his albums of, mostly, Tin Pan Alley standards – a notable exception being the low-key, midnight-blues songs of the *Nightbeat* album. Just as significantly, his core black audience appears to have generally accepted the stylistic gestures which initially cropped his gospel roots and made such a crossover possible.

In the period between his 1962 recording of "Bring it on home to me", on which Cooke traded exhortations with fellow gospel refugee Lou Rawls against the backdrop of a churchy organ, booming blues guitar and muted strings, and his death in 1964, Cooke allowed his gospel influences to come more to the fore – as on the ecstatic horn-led dance stomp "Shake", or on the gorgeous, long-lined, pop-spiritual "A change is gonna come". Yet even during this period, Cooke remained extremely concerned not to alienate the less musically adventurous sections of his white audience by offering up too generous a dose of gospel fervour. Many of his most powerful and influential secular performances were never actually released during his lifetime. Instead, they could be found on demos of his own compositions like "Soothe me", "Lookin' for a love", and "Meet me at Mary's place", which he cut to illustrate to the likes of the Sims Twins and Johnnie Morrissette precisely the sort of gospel-pop fusions he had in mind for the more exclusively black-oriented artists he signed to SAR and Derby.

Cooke's desire to reach and maintain a mass white market was also reflected in his live performances, which were vastly different according to the racial and generational composition of his audience. At the Harlem Square Club in Miami, he was vocally and emotionally unfettered, alternately cooing and roaring his way through blistering reinterpretations of many of his pop ballads and transforming the concert hall into a revival meeting. At the Copacabana, where he bombed in 1958 but triumphed in 1964, he offered fans who were generally white, wealthy and well beyond their teens a smooth blend of showtunes, soaring strings and carefully prepared arrangements and choreography. In his 1964 club appearances, however, Cooke insisted on including a galloping version of Bob Dylan's "Blowing in the wind". This appears to have been simultaneously a reflection of his own growing political sensibility and a simple acknowledgement of folk's enormous popularity with whites at the time. The black pop era was full of such complicated negotiations between the demands of rising racial consciousness and commercial considerations.[69]

The only other two r&b artists with anything like comparable control over their careers in the early 1960s were Ray Charles and Lloyd Price. Like Cooke, they both chose to bid boldly for the crossover market and did so without alienating their core black audiences. In 1956, in Washington, D.C., ex-Louisiana bluesman Lloyd Price set up his own KRC Records with two white partners, Harold Logan and William Boskent. Price, however, preferred to record for ABC, and directed his brassy pop'n'roll ("Just because", "Personality") straight at the crossover market. Black teenagers loved it, too.

In 1960, Ray Charles, the good ol' Georgia country boy whose first professional gigs had been with a white Jacksonville jug and fiddle band called the Florida Playboys, signed a lucrative deal with ABC and honed the country-pop-blues stylings ("Unchain my heart", "I can't stop loving you") which made him a huge national star with both races. In so doing he deliberately moved beyond the more racially circumscribed, r&b-gospel furrow he had ploughed so innovatively at Atlantic – although even there he had given notice of his country predilections with an impossibly poignant version of Hank Snow's "I'm movin' on". Nobody held a Colt to Brother Ray's head to make him sing this seminal r&b-country mix. The decision was born of an elusive blend of commercial considerations and the same restless musical genius which also led him to collaborate on jazz albums with vibraphonist Milt Jackson and the elastic larynx of Betty Carter, and which also enabled him to transform sentimental staples like "Georgia on my mind" into mighty affirmations of his own black, American and southern identities. As Sid Feller, an A&R man at ABC, confirmed, all Charles' records were cut "exactly as he wanted them, right down to the last note of the arrangements".[70]

If Ray Charles' diverse output in the early 1960s was a function of his diverse ambitions, interests and influences, many new young black stars of the early 1960s found themselves lurching rather less certainly between a number of musical styles and perceived markets. James Ray's eponymous first album on Caprice stands as a bizarre monument to the era's tendency towards musical schizophrenia. Ray bravely battled against producer Hutch Davie's unwieldy brass and string arrangements to do a passable imitation of Charles on "Lazy bones". He veered towards the classics on the ludicrously overblown, but weirdly compelling, three-part suite "Got my mind set on you", which featured an operatic chorus and burbling banjo riffs. Elsewhere, with more appropriate settings, Ray sounded more assured, especially on "If you gotta make a fool of somebody" – his only national hit – where he offered the sort of bittersweet pop-soul for which Dee Clark before him and Deon Jackson afterwards were better known.

A much bigger star of the black pop era, Detroit-born Jackie Wilson, also showed visible and audible signs of the difficulties of trying to reconcile these multiple musical, commercial, and, by extension, racial agendas. Wilson, a spellbinding live performer who in the mid 1950s had replaced Clyde McPhatter with Billy Ward and his Dominoes, produced a janus-faced music which looked back to the black gospel and blues tradition while keeping its eyes firmly on the prize of success in the white mainstream and observing many of its musical and showbusiness preferences. His vocal gymnastics were well-served on material like "Reet-petite" and "You better know it". But often, as he unleashed his remarkable gospel-blues vocals on unlikely material which ranged from banal teen ballads ("The tear of the year"), through reworked folk songs ("Danny boy"), to ersatz opera ("Night"), it was as if he was trying to obliterate the stifling overproductions with which he was frequently saddled by the sheer, irreducible power of his voice.

With the predictability of a stuck record, Nelson George has interpreted Wilson's inability to rid himself of inappropriate material and kitsch showbiz trappings almost entirely in terms of the manipulation of his white manager Nat Tarnopal and the plantation mentality of Brunswick, his white-owned and white-oriented record label. Although such forces undoubtedly played their part in accounting for Wilson's sometimes strained musical mergers, it hardly helps to explain how, or why, this "Uncle Toming" secured 20 black hits between 1958 and the cessation of a separate chart at the end of 1963.[71]

Instead of simply ignoring the tens of thousands of black consumers who bought records or attended concerts by Wilson and other stars of the black pop era, or reducing them to mindless victims of shrewd marketing ploys, it is rather more useful to consider what Wilson's style and this pattern of mass consumption may reveal about black consciousness in the late 1950s and early 1960s. Wilson's dogged efforts to assert his own personality and honour traditional black musical priorities through the sheer emotive power of his vocal performances, while still retaining the commitment to success in the mainstream symbolized by slick arrangements and sentimental material, reflected precisely the position of many black Americans in the early-to-mid 1960s. It was because, not in spite, of its stylistic turmoil, its frenetic and often unfocused experimentation, its refusal to adhere only to the epic, self-consciously "black" subject matter associated with the blues, and its juggling of multiple musical traditions, that black pop was the perfect soundtrack to black America's attempts to work out the relationship between its own overlapping black and American identities.

A vision shared: the sexual politics of black pop

Sam Cooke and his fellow black pop-r&b balladeers evoked relatively little of the sexual threat associated with male r&b or early rock and roll. Continuing and extending the trend which had begun with the vocal groups, these singers largely eschewed the brazen machismo and misogyny of much male blues and r&b. Insecurity, compassion, fidelity, trust and a sense of personal responsibility for the success or failure of relationships were staples of black male pop. Chuck Jackson, for example, admitted "I wake up crying"; Sammy Turner expected love to last for "Always"; loyal Dee Clark wanted "Nobody but you"; Ben E. King pleaded for a woman to "Stand by me". In "He will break your heart", Jerry Butler described – but in a significant departure from the blues orthodoxy, did not glorify or excuse – male infidelity, while in the magnificent "Man's temptation" Gene Chandler grappled with his conscience and resolved "to be strong", which in the new world order now meant faithful.

Traditional male attitudes did not disappear completely, of course, and neither did the songs of male sexual braggadocio, hostility and suspicion towards the opposite sex. Jackie Wilson's "Doggin' around", Gene Chandler's "Duke of Earl", Eugene Church's "Pretty girls everywhere", and Marvin

Gaye's "Hitch hike" kept the tradition alive. Smokey Robinson, whose clever love songs, sweetly sensual voice and image of coy vulnerability encapsulated key values in male black pop, faced hostility from black men who objected to his "soft" approach and reproached him for singing like a woman. Well-versed in the sexual orthodoxies of black Chicago and Detroit, Robinson himself was initially uneasy at exhibiting the kind of sensitivity he so admired in black female jazz singers like Sarah Vaughan: "I loved the way she [Sarah Vaughan] cried with her voice; I was awestruck by her subtlety and sensitivity . . . it was a woman who shaped my style. But I wondered: Should a cat like me be singing like a chick?"[72]

Nevertheless, the songs of Robinson, Cooke, Curtis Mayfield, Florence Greenberg and Luther Dixon, and the many white writers – Bert Bacharach and Hal David, Goffin-King, Mann-Weil, Doc Pomus and Mort Schuman, Bert Berns and Jerry Ragavoy – who also provided the raw material for black pop artists, expressed and, to some extent, legitimized, romantic ideals which had always been present in the black male psyche, but which had been routinely eclipsed by macho and misogyny in most forms of black male popular culture. It was, however, no coincidence that both should lose favour with black audiences at this particular historic moment.

Black macho and black matriarchy were essentially elaborate myths: cultural constructions which served to explain black disadvantage and compensate for the awful sense of powerlessness which afflicted black males. They symbolically displaced black male frustration at the whole matrix of racial discrimination, social marginality and economic distress into the world of sexual politics where victories of a sort could be won, "heroic" deeds performed, and "evil" destroyed.

Historically, the potency of these myths reflected the absence of viable political or economic strategies to alleviate black oppression or promote black male self-esteem. In Mississippi, "a black man was not able to protect his family . . . it was shameful, dehumanizing and degrading to his manhood", recalled June Johnson, who by the end of 1963 was already a teenage veteran of Greenwood's civil rights activities and, along with Annelle Ponder and Fannie Lou Hamer, victim of a particularly horrific beating in a Winona jail. "It created a lot of tensions. There may have been killings within families that were swept under the rug". From a very different corner of black America, singer-actress Lena Horne felt that black women often needed to be " 'spiritual sponges' to absorb the racially inflicted hurts of their men".[73]

In the late 1950s and early 1960s, many of the resentments which had previously fuelled such sexual demonologies and domestic violence within the black community, North and South, were rechannelled towards the system which actually accounted for black disadvantage. Vicarious or direct engagement in the struggle gave black men, just as it gave black women, a glimpse of a possible better future and a sense of empowerment and self-respect they had previously sought in sexual warfare and internecine competition. The rise of the civil rights movement, and the cautious optimism which initially attended it, rendered black matriarchy less compelling as an explanation for the black predicament and an aggressive black macho less necessary as an outlet for black male frustrations.[74]

Jo Ann Robinson, president of the Montgomery Women's Political Council and a crucial figure in the Montgomery bus boycott, clearly understood this connection:

> Grown men frequently came home on particular evenings angry from humiliating experiences on buses, to pick fights with their wives or children. They needed a target somewhere, a way to relieve internal conflict. These quarrels often ended in cuttings or killings, divorce or separation. . . .
>
> After December 5, 1955, the people were able to release their suppressed emotions through the boycott movement, which allowed them to retaliate directly for the pain, humiliation, and embarrassment they had endured over the years at the hands of drivers and policemen while riding on the buses. There was no need for family fights and weekend brawls.[75]

It is even possible that the conspicuous commitment and courage of women of all ages, from all sections of the black community, who played such a critical role at the grassroots level of the burgeoning freedom struggle, may have encouraged some kind of partial thawing in black male attitudes and conduct. Black men may have begun to see black women more as allies in a common struggle against racism and political and economic powerlessness, and less as the principal source of their distress, or as a focus for their anger and frustrations.[76]

And yet, Stokely Carmichael's celebrated 1964 quip that "the position for women in SNCC is prone" hardly bespoke a new era of sexual enlightenment among black men, not even in the very heart of what was in other ways the most progressive mass movement in American history. In fairness to Carmichael, this remark has been used altogether too casually by historians to locate his views, and perhaps even more unfairly those of other black males in SNCC, on the role of women in the Movement. Nevertheless, even if Carmichael's position in 1964 was prone to misrepresentation, and scholars and veterans continue to debate whether, in what manner, and to what degree, women in the Movement were variously empowered or exploited, liberated or oppressed, June Johnson certainly had no doubts that in the grand scheme of things, "Men ran the Movement . . . they made many of the decisions". Moreover, the way in which SNCC's first chairman, Marion Barry, tried to exercise some kind of crude *droit de seigneur* over some of his female associates, leaving a paper trail of betrayals and sexual misadventures in the SNCC papers, suggests that some men in the Movement were still struggling to shake off old stereotypes. "He was abusive", recalled John Lewis. "He knocked women around".[77]

With hard evidence scarce, any conclusions about the relationship between the new romantic ethos in Rhythm and Blues' black pop strain and changes in black sexism and domestic violence are necessarily tentative. It seems unlikely that the romantic idealism which characterized so much black male pop, and briefly eclipsed the misogynistic and macho tendencies of the blues tradition, corresponded to a similarly rapid and radical reorientation of male prejudices and practices within the black community. Rather the sound, sense and image of male black pop dramatized and symbolized a fleeting vision of *possible* changes in those patterns of behaviour. It represented alternative modes of male thought, being and action which were not necessarily accurate reflections of what was happening in the "real" world, but which were, nonetheless, linked to it, since events in, and changing ways of seeing, that "real" world largely determined what earthly dreams it was permissible to dream in black culture. Thus black pop admirably fulfilled John Street's dictum that "pop's inability to change the world is compensated for by its ability to articulate and alter our perceptions of that world and, perhaps more importantly, to give a glimpse of other, better worlds".[78]

Much of what has been said already about the changing sexual politics of black male Rhythm and Blues applies equally well to its female counterpart. Among black female artists in the black pop era there was a similar truce in the more vicious sexual hostilities of Rhythm and Blues, which, while inextricably linked to the industry's quest for a crossover market after 1956, can only be fully explained in the context of black responses to the early promise of the civil rights movement.

"Black women", according to historian Evelyn Brooks Higginbotham, "have historically lived in a community whose collective behavior derived not only from Afro-American traditions, but also from the values and social behavior of the dominant American society." Indeed, the black woman has been simultaneously female, black, American and, usually, poor. Each of these factors has made its distinctive, but overlapping, claims on her consciousness and helped to define her social being.[79]

After the Second World War, with the valorization and dissemination of white middle-class codes of behaviour by a powerful mass media, black women increasingly internalized mainstream models of domesticity and womanhood alongside more independent, assertive traits derived from their own unique heritage and experiences. Many sought to escape the matriarchal stereotype which had often blighted black sexual politics and their own personal relationships, even at the expense of conforming to conventional sexist notions of femininity and deference to patriarchal authority, including the Western male's trusty sexual double-standard.

Tan magazine, with its black working-class and lower-middle-class female readership, articulated this agenda perfectly, commending its readers to preserve their virginity until entering into an idyllic marriage, where they could raise children, dote on their husbands and generally keep house in the time-honoured manner. Should a husband stray from this shangri-la, it was probably the woman's own fault for reverting to her domineering, hectoring Sapphire mode. *Tan* advised her to "make an honest examination of [herself] . . . Do you nag and complain?" "I can remember the conversations we had at college about what our ideals were", recalled Bernice Johnson Reagon. "We were all going to have this really nice house . . . and the guys were talking, 'my wife is not going to work'. And that had nothing to do with anything which comes out of the black community, that really comes straight off TV".[80]

Racism and poverty often combined to undermine the possibility of conforming to such ideals and by 1960 22 per cent of black families, as opposed to 9 per cent of white ones, were headed by a female. Consequently, black women led the way in fashioning alternative social and domestic arrangements, more suited to the realities of black life – most notably extended kin and fictive kinship networks and the whole ethos of matrifocality in many black communities.[81]

Nevertheless, these creative survival strategies did not, as some have argued, represent a total rejection of "larger societal expectations" by black women. Between 1950 and 1970 most black families remained "traditional" dual-headed nuclear arrangements, although the percentage of such families declined from 78 per cent to 67 per cent during the period and they sometimes functioned rather differently to white nuclear families. Just as importantly, the *ideal* of a traditional family unit retained its psychological appeal and lustre for black women, even when the realities of the black situation demanded alternative arrangements. "Even the masses, held down by poverty and racial oppression, deemed certain mainstream values and behavior as proper and correct, despite their inability to manifest them in practice", explained Higginbotham. Moreover, "many blacks increasingly linked the new values with upward social mobility and the old with backwardness".[82]

According to bell hooks, black women traditionally "measured black men against a standard set by white males. Since whites defined 'achieving manhood' as the ability of a man to be a sole economic provider in a family, many black families tended to regard the black male as a 'failed' man". The full and equitable participation of black men in the educational, social, political and economic life of America thus promised not only to make the most virulent male hostility towards black women a relic of a frustrated, segregated and discriminatory past, but also to provide the material and mental environment in which black women could finally assume the mainstream standards of femininity and domesticity which they associated with

racial equality. Consequently, the optimism of the early civil rights movement was inextricably bound up with the prospect of "normalizing" black
family and gender relations according to conventional middle-class white
codes.[83]

The complexity of these female attitudes towards black men and the
black woman's own role within black and American society provides an
important context for understanding the changing styles of female r&b performers. Just as the male shouters and r&b artists of the 1940s and early
1950s had adhered to the blues lyrical tradition, proclaiming their machismo
and denigrating black women, so the most typical black female r&b singers
of the post-war decade had responded in kind, ridiculing the black man's
inability to provide the economic, emotional or even physical security to
allow them to become "good" women according to mainstream ideals.

As with male r&b, however, in the mid-to-late 1950s those songs which
dwelt on destructive carnal hungers, perennially doomed relationships and
vicious domestic warfare declined in relative importance in the repertoires
of the most successful female performers. Moreover, this trend, again as in
male r&b, appears to have been underway before black artists or their
recording companies fully appreciated the possibility of a mass white audience for black music and began to tailor their songs accordingly. In January
1954, *Tan* reported that "voluptuous nightclub chanteuse" Joyce Bryant,
whose early 1950s recordings for Okeh had rarely made it past the censors
onto black-oriented radio, had "bridled her usual sex intonations", and the
"uninhibited presentation of sex" on her recent releases.[84]

More established stars like Ruth Brown similarly adjusted to the new
ethos by blessing her "Lucky lips" and, in a semantic sidestep common to
rock and roll, expressed her creativity and independence on the dance floor
rather than in bed on "This little girl's gone rockin'". LaVern Baker, the
Chicago-born Atlantic star who was the most popular of the black female
rock and rollers, preserved a suggestive growl in her voice but rarely handled
particularly raunchy material after mid-decade. Her rock and roll hero "Jim
Dandy" was more a portent of the idealized black hero eulogized by the girl
groups of the black pop era than a throwback to the predatory backdoor
loverman of earlier generations. In the follow-up record, "Jim Dandy got
married", he even made it down the aisle. As the biracial market for rock
and roll and then big beat pop prospered, a generation of smooth female
rhythm crooners emerged, including Nancy Wilson, Ketty Lester, Damita Jo
and Dionne Warwick. Like their male counterparts, these women appealed
to both races and sexes with their lush romantic ballads.

Long before the crossover market had fully materialized, a new breed of
very young girl groups, or mixed-sex groups with a dominant female lead
singer, had also flourished. These groups were female counterparts of the
male doowoppers. Invariably drawn from the same urban culture, they
shared the same predilection for romantic idealism, although from a female

Emerging from Passaic, New Jersey, the Shirelles pioneered the classic girl group sound of the early 1960s.

perspective. The first girl group crossover hits were in this female doowop tradition: the Teen Queens' "Eddie my love" in 1956, the Bobbettes' "Mr Lee" in 1957, and the Chantels with a string of hits, beginning with "Maybe" in 1958.

That same year, the Shirelles emerged from Passaic, New Jersey. Fronted by young Shirley Alston's guileless vocals, the four teenagers cut "I met him on a Sunday" for Tiara, a local label run by Florence Greenberg, whose daughter was a classmate of the girls. The disk was picked up by Decca and became a minor national hit, whereafter the Shirelles recorded a couple of flops for the label and then rejoined Florence Greenberg at her newly formed Scepter Records. There, under the direction of Luther Dixon, a stylish, pop-oriented producer and former singer with the Four Buddies vocal group, the Shirelles cut timeless teen anthems like "Dedicated to the one I love", "Will you love me tomorrow" and "Mama said", all dominated by the sound of Alston's plaintive voice.[85]

The Shirelles ushered in the distinctive sound, subject matter, and image of the classic girl groups of the biracial pop era. Yet one of Alan Betrock's many useful insights on the girl group phenomenon is that it was not actually restricted to groups, or girls, or either race. Records by black soloists like Dee Dee Sharp, Little Eva, and Claudine Clark; by white soloists like Lesley Gore, Shelly Fabares and Little Peggy March; by white groups like the Shangri-Las, Angels and Murmaids; by black groups like the Cookies, Chiffons and Dixie-Cups, and even by certain mixed-sex groups like the Orlons, Exciters, and Ad-Libs, shared similar production values, musical arrangements and lyrical themes. They all concentrated on the traumas and delights of young love, the vagaries of fashion, and the intricacies of the latest dance crazes.[86]

Girl groups, whatever their exact composition, provided flexible singing vehicles for the carefully crafted songs of the producers and songwriters at the heart of the new pop. Ellie Greenwich and Jeff Barry, Cynthia Weil and Barry Mann, Gerry Goffin and Carole King, Florence Greenberg and Luther Dixon, and, above all, the manic, self-obsessed genius Phil Spector, wrote and produced many of the quintessential girl group recordings. Certain labels specialized in the style: Philles, Red Bird, Dimension, Scepter, and Colpix. At the fledgling Motown corporation, Smokey Robinson, Ivy Hunter, William Stevenson, Brian and Eddie Holland and Lamont Dozier forged a gospel-tinged variant on the girl group sound with Mary Wells, the Marvelettes, and, ultimately, the Supremes.[87]

Because of the enormous creative input by these producers and writers, Betrock emphasized the essentially "manufactured" nature of the girl group phenomenon: "In an attempt to fuse the urgency, creativity and honesty of rock 'n' roll's roots into a style that could be widely accepted on . . . [the] newly emerging national Top Forty Network, a handful of writers, producers, singers and businessmen soon created what would come to be known as the girl-group sound". Certainly, the lyrical bias towards the experiences and dreams of young women specifically targeted an underexploited market niche. Early rock and roll had been sung about girls and to girls, but less often from the perspective of girls.[88]

Moreover, the girl groups also served the industry's desire to deracialize and tame the sexual urgency of early rock and roll, transforming it into a new, safe, biracial pop form. Like the male vocal groups, they were essentially raceless, particularly on the radio. Indeed, until the emergence of the black Ronnettes in 1963, and the white Shangri-Las a year later, girl groups, with the partial exception of the Shirelles, were all rather faceless. This was largely a function of the fluid – sometimes fictional – membership of the groups themselves, which were often simply assembled in the studio from available session singers.

Charlotte Greig has made an interesting attempt to locate a burgeoning sense of female consciousness and solidarity in girl group culture, detecting a sort of proto-feminist élan in the depiction of ideals and experiences, and especially of the moments when ideals and experiences collided, which were shared by performers and their female fans. Recordings like the Marvelettes' "Playboy", with its warning of male infidelity, and the Ronnettes'

"Be my baby", where Ronnie Spector's mighty vocal scaled husband Phil's celebrated wall of sound to transform what might have been a plea into an urgent demand, could be interpreted in this way. Songs like Betty Everett's "You're no good", coming from the gospel fringes of the black girl sound, certainly displayed the sort of pride and assertiveness which would later characterize the soul of Aretha Franklin and Candi Staton. Many songs even contained an internal dialogue, often between the lead singer and her choral confidantes, in which the merits of individual boys and the incomprehension of parents were discussed, and where the entire range of social expectations surrounding dating and, of course, sex and marriage were vigorously debated.[89]

Too easily dismissed as a dilution, or "feminization", of rock and roll's initial, putatively "masculine" energies, girl groups actually captured the fundamental dramas and concerns of teen life with a bracing, unaffected honesty. Moreover, the songs, composed by writers of both sexes and races, rarely reduced women to the passive objects of male whims and expectations. The girls were usually subjects and actors in these songs. They articulated their own agendas, made choices and took action in order to try to fulfil their ideals. What is striking, however, is how those choices, actions and ideals invariably revolved around thoroughly conventional notions of a sublime, thrilling, monogomous romance which would be solemnized within the emotional and material security of a traditional marriage.

Cocooned in ultra-feminine outfits of swirling chiffon and satin, black girl groups, like their white counterparts, usually expressed, indeed enthusiastically endorsed and pursued, mainstream notions of a woman's role, responsibilities and needs in a patriarchal world. Man, usually the epicentre of the girl groups' universe, was venerated in songs like the Essex's "A walking miracle", while even the feisty Betty Everett admitted "It's in his kiss" – "It" being the true happiness that only a man's love could bring. The Chiffons hoped that "One fine day" they too would find a faithful, strong, protective man and commemorated that unsurpassable joy in "I have a boyfriend". For most girl groups heaven was at the end of a marital walk down the aisle of the Dixie Cups' "Chapel of love".

If such sentiments seem staid by the standards of contemporary feminism, they had a rather different resonance in the black community of the early 1960s. The mere fact that young blacks dared to identify with the girl groups' vision of a conventional domesticity, which poverty and racism had so frequently placed beyond their grasp, reflected the hope that fundamental changes in the pattern of racial oppression were at hand. As Ruby and the Romantics put it, in a title which captured the essence of the black pop era, and, indeed, the early years of the civil rights movement, there was a profound belief that "Our day will come".

Building on the notion that "gender is the modality through which race is experienced", Paul Gilroy has suggested that in black life, "An amplified and exaggerated masculinity . . . and its relational feminine counterpart become special symbols of the difference race makes". In the blues tradition, Sapphire and the black stud were traditional representations of these peculiarly intense, often bitterly antagonistic black sexual identities. Within the broader American context, these sexual stereotypes had also served as critical markers of black racial identity. Consequently, by generally refusing to embrace or project these conventional "symbols of the difference race makes", black pop functioned as a mildly rocking metaphor for the integrationist aspirations of a new generation of blacks.[90]

Yet if the racially defined – and defining – Sapphire and stud stereotypes were generally absent from the most popular music of the black pop era, there was a price to pay for this progress. In black pop some of the sexual frankness, the genuine humour and eroticism of r&b disappeared along with its more odious sexism. Furthermore, black pop traded the "traditional" aggressive black macho of male r&b for the more insidious, if no less oppressive patterns of sexism and patriarchy practised by much of mainstream male society; it swapped the empowering wit, cynicism and sexual power of black female r&b for white female pop's quieter accommodation to the patriarchal status quo.

A Major resurgence; an Independent influence

The principal aim of this chapter has been to reconsider the popularity of black and white pop among black consumers in terms of a particular historical moment and its attendant consciousness; to emphasize the element of conscious choice in black consumerism and interpret some of the most conspicuous elements of black pop in those terms, rather than ascribe them purely to the machinations of the industry. Nevertheless, the industry's enthusiasm for the biracial pop synthesis was important in shaping both the sound and presentation of the music, while its historical and social meanings were also, in part, derived from those production factors. As ever with mass produced cultural forms, the multiple meanings of black pop were contested and not determined exclusively by either the forces of production or consumption.

The Majors embraced the new pop as a means to regain some of the ground they had lost to the Independents between 1954 and 1957, when r&b and its derivatives had helped to boost revenue from record sales from $213 million to $460 million. Independents, in breaking the grip of the Majors and the old publishing interests, had encouraged competition, innovation and diversity. Three times as many companies had hits between 1956 and 1959 as in the previous seven years, while the number of Top Ten pop records per year increased by 74 per cent between 1955 and 1959. During that period, 59 of the 89 Top Ten hits were on Independent labels.[91]

The actual shift in economic power was less than suggested by the Independents' success in the singles market. Long-playing albums were more important for "good quality" popular, classical and jazz music, and were bought by an older, "whiter", audience. By 1960 these albums still accounted for 80 per cent of the $400 million record market in the United States and this lucrative sector of the market was still dominated by the Majors and ASCAP-registered publishers.[92]

Nevertheless, established publishing and recording interests remained fearful of further challenges by a new breed of labels and publishers who had already snatched away much of the singles trade and occupied valuable airtime with their products. The ASCAP suits against BMI were one expression of this anxiety. When these failed, the Majors – eager for an increased share of the vibrant youth market for singles, yet anxious to preserve their traditional adult audience for "quality" popular music – began to sign artists of both races who might bridge the gap between these two markets. RCA had Sam Cooke, Jessie Belvin and Neil Sedaka; Decca added Brenda Lee and the black country-tinged crooner Bobby Helms to its list; ABC boasted Ray Charles and Lloyd Price alongside Paul Anka and Danny and the Juniors; Mercury had Leslie Gore and Johnny Preston as well as black stars like the Platters, Phil Phillips and later Clyde McPhatter; Capitol signed the Beach Boys and Nancy Wilson; Columbia picked up Johnny Mathis and Dion; MGM had Connie Francis, Jimmy Jones and the veteran black balladeer Tommy Edwards.

In pursuing this new biracial market with artists of both races, the Majors' economic muscle helped to give the trend towards greater lyrical idealism, a slicker big beat sound, and relative racial anonymity – at least on radio and disk – an important boost. In the main, this strategy was a resounding success. By April 1958, *Billboard* was already reporting that the "majors – for some time knocked off balance by indie competition – are now meeting it more successfully", and had secured a bigger percentage of single sales than in the previous two years.[93]

During the black-white pop era, Major and Independent labels appeared to be heading in much the same musical direction. The Independents, however, were still often transitory phenomena, coming and going with a rapidity which made a dance craze like the hooka-tooka look like a venerable national institution. But while some Independents disappeared in the black pop era many new ones emerged. These newcomers were frequently geared to serving the new biracial market with artists of both races performing in styles which were broadly interchangeable. The Cameo-Parkway label in Philadelphia, for example, had black artists like Chubby Checker, the Rays and Dovells, and white acts like Bobby Rydell and Charlie Gracie. The label promoted all its acts in much the same way, often using television's *American Bandstand* as a shop window. Checker and Rydell were even teamed up for an album. In New York, Kapp boasted white teen stars Jerry Keller and

Johnny Cymbal alongside black popsters Shirley Ellis and Ruby and the Romantics. Big Top featured black pop balladeers Sammy Turner and Don and Juan, as well as white singers Del Shannon and Curtis Lee. Laurie, Red Bird, Dimension, Colpix and most of the other classic pop labels founded in the late 1950s and early 1960s also featured artists of both races and sent them out on integrated tours to all but the most impenetrable bastions of southern resistance.

In order to compete in a commercial environment very different from the rigidly segregated one in which they had been founded, some of the older, more durable Rhythm and Blues Independents also signed white acts to perform the new pop alongside their black stalwarts. Atlantic's subsidiary Atco, for example, enjoyed huge interracial success with Bobby Darin. Ace Records, the Jackson, Mississippi, label once associated with downhome bluesmen like Lightnin' Hopkins and Sonny Boy Williamson, scaled the pop and Rhythm and Blues charts with southern white pop'n'rollers Frankie Ford ("Sea cruise"), and Jimmy Clanton, whose "Just a dream" was also a black number one in 1958. In Chicago, Vivian and James Bracken's black-owned Vee Jay was equally committed to reaching a biracial market with a biracial roster. While maintaining its black stars (Gene Chandler, Betty Everett, Dee Clark, and the Impressions), the label also signed the hugely popular white vocal group the Four Seasons, and was the first in America to take up an option on the Beatles.

Of the all the new labels to emerge in the black pop era, none would pursue the integrated market with more energy, skill and success than Berry Gordy's Detroit-based Motown Corporation. With his roster of young black hopefuls, all eager to succeed in the American mainstream, not marginalized in some segregated racial enclave, Gordy intended his label to become "The sound of young America", and not just of young black America. Nothing better symbolized the optimism, the sense of expanding possibilities and the integrationist agenda of the period, than Gordy's belief that such a feat was possible, even for a music which was unmistakeably energized by the sound and spirit of black gospel. Just five years earlier, such aspirations would have been unthinkable, but the civil rights movement had already changed the scope and nature of the dreams it seemed safe for black Americans to dream.

Not really rockin' on *Bandstand*: race and payola

One final dimension of the biracial pop era and the economic revival of the major players in the recording and broadcasting industries warrants attention. These were the congressional payola investigations of 1960 which undermined the position of the Independents by denying them an import-ant, if illegal, means of securing access to the airwaves for their products.

The Majors were simply better able to wage legitimate promotional campaigns to push their wares than their smaller competitors, who often relied on payola – an unearned songwriting credit here, a free holiday there, sex, booze and cash everywhere – to induce deejays to play their records on the overcrowded airwaves.

Much like the ASCAP/BMI hearings, the payola investigations were at root a battle over market spoils between powerful corporate interests and dynamic upstart competitors. Both sets of investigations raised the spectre of conspiracy and had ostensibly moral overtones. Moreover, even in the absence of the sort of explicitly racist condemnations of rock and roll which had punctuated the ASCAP/BMI battles, there remained an underlying racial agenda to the payola proceedings; a set of cultural assumptions which still routinely equated "good" music and moral decency with traditional "white" pop forms.

Payola took two main forms. The first was a simple pay-for-play policy, whereby record companies or distributors provided individual deejays with gifts and in return they gave certain records preferential treatment. The second ploy was to hire deejays as consultants, paying them for their expert opinion on which of a batch of recordings stood the best chance of selection for airplay, and planning single releases accordingly. Many of these consultants and their benefactors viewed consultancy fees as bribes, and the deejays simply played to death whatever records they had selected for release.

Such practices were hardly unique to Independents or Rhythm and Blues. As Paul Ackerman of *Billboard* testified before the House sub-committee which investigated the practice, "historically, payola is an outgrowth of a music-business tradition – song plugging". It was already evident around the turn of the century, as the first wave of Tin Pan Alley publishing companies consolidated New York's position at the centre of the music publishing world. By the 1930s, payola was rampant, usually taking the form of payments from music publishers to swing era bandleaders and singers, but also passing from artists and record companies to deejays.[94]

Significantly, there was relatively little public concern about the payola of the swing era, since the music being promoted was generally considered respectable. But when r&b and rock and roll reached the mass airwaves, accusations of payola began almost immediately in order to explain the pollution of radio by these dark disturbing sounds. In February 1955, *Variety*, for example, approvingly reported that a group of Detroit deejays had banned all Coral, Jubilee, X and Kapp recordings because these labels were paying two local deejays for preferential treatment.[95]

The immediate catalyst for the congressional investigation into payola in the recording industry was the revelation that a popular television quiz show, *Twenty-One*, had been rigged and the FCC's subsequent demands that all undisclosed payments made to or by licensed broadcasters should be made public. In May 1959, a government probe of the music business became inevitable when several prominent newspapers carried news of a "Babes, booze and bribes" convention organized in Miami by the record industry's favourite mobster, Morris Levy. Levy hoped such junkets would foster friendly business relations between Independent record men and the deejays who might air their products.[96]

When the hearings on such practices began, under the chairmanship of Arkansas congressman Oren Harris, few in the music business bothered to deny that payola was a key component in the relationship between record labels, their distributors and deejays. Some, however, did try to draw a distinction between different types of gifts and their significance. Morty Craft was a colourful, no-nonsense record salesman who had once owned his own label (Sitting-In-With). He subsequently worked as an A&R man for MGM, where he handled white singer Connie Francis – rather too literally for Francis' father, who withdrew his daughter from the label after he found Craft chasing her around his office. Craft proposed a sliding scale for measuring payola's corrupting influence. "You might buy somebody a five dollar meal. I can't see anything corrupt about a five dollar meal. But if you buy them a hundred dollar meal and give them cocaine – that's corrupt". Craft made the same distinction between providing $25 and $100 prostitutes for friendly deejays.[97]

From the other side of the bargain, black deejay Greg Harris of WFMQ-Chicago argued that, while "cash is a bribe and there is no other way of viewing it . . . no jockey worth his airtime is . . . in a position to refuse accepting an occasional gift". Payola, Harris contended, was only reprehensible when it induced deejays to programme poor quality or distasteful music. Of course, the whole point was that middle America and elements in the music business had found much black-derived music thoroughly distasteful.[98]

In any case, to deny the existence of payola would have been pointless: the evidence was overwhelming. Music Suppliers Inc. of Boston, one of the most heavily implicated distributors, paid out over $27,000 to 19 different deejays in 1958 and 1959. George Goldner, owner of the classic doowop labels Gee, Rama, Gone and End, admitted paying Philadelphia deejay Joe Niagara $500 a month to play records in which Goldner's companies had an interest. Tom Clay and Harry Dixon in Detroit and Tommy Smalls in New York were also recipients of Goldner's largesse. Joe Smith, another seminal r&b deejay at WILD in Boston, was reckoned to have accepted about $9,000 in bribes from, among others, Morris Levy and Goldner – not to mention a free theme song courtesy of Goldner's signings, the Valentines. As veteran deejay Norman Prescott explained without intentional irony, payola "is the only way that you can honestly exist today . . . because of the tremendous output of records, and the fierce competition that exists within the industry, it is a matter of who can play what, when there is a limited amount of play on the air".[99]

If the pervasiveness of payola was a given, its efficacy in securing hits was a moot point. Crusty Syd Nathan of King Records, who admittedly rarely felt he was getting a fair deal from anyone, told the hearings that he had stopped the company's regular $1,800 a month payola payments because his records did not seem to be played any more frequently as a result. Moreover, Nathan argued, airplay alone could not guarantee a hit record.[100]

George Goldner admitted assigning copyrights for a number of songs to *American Bandstand* host Dick Clark, or companies in which Clark had an interest, hoping to gain favourable treatment. Having given away the copyright, Goldner's profits depended entirely on record sales. Among the songs involved were the Dubs' "Could this be magic", and Little Anthony and the Imperials' "So much". Goldner's "gift" seems to have worked on one level, since late in 1957 "Could this be magic" was played on Clark's show 25 times before it saw any chart action. Despite this constant exposure, however, it reached only number 23 on the *Billboard* pop charts, and failed to make the national Rhythm and Blues listings at all. "So much" was even more favoured, gaining 27 plays from Clark, yet it never made the pop Top Forty and barely penetrated the black charts. Payola, then, was always a necessary gamble: consumer preference meant that airplay alone could not guarantee a hit record, yet lack of airplay could certainly ruin the chance of one.[101]

George Goldner's testimony was by no means the only evidence presented against the genial host of ABC's *American Bandstand*. It took four pages of testimony and several flow charts just to itemize the 33 companies in which Clark had an interest and describe their labyrinthine interrelationships. It was also revealed that in the early days of *American Bandstand* the artists who appeared were not actually paid. To comply with industry regulations, Clark went through the motions, but any payments were later reimbursed by the artist's record company, or distributor, who in turn deducted them from the artist's earnings. In effect, artists were often paying Clark to appear on his show, hoping that the exposure would generate enough sales to make it worthwhile. Moreover, Clark had clearly used his position to advance his own financial interests. Over half of the recordings made available by manufacturing companies in which Clark had an interest were played on *Bandstand*, 65.4 per cent of these *before* they had appeared on any *Billboard* chart.[102]

The evidence that Clark was up to his brilliantined hair in dubious practice was hard to ignore. But the Harris Committee was up to the job, happily accepting Clark's claim that he had done absolutely nothing to earn a $7,000 cheque given to him by Bernie Lowe of Maryland Music and mysteriously made out to his mother-in-law.[103]

Certainly, Clark's defence of simple naiveté modestly belittled the considerable skill with which he created his empire and maximized the rewards of his position. Yet, the most powerful broadcaster in American popular music, the idol of legions of impressionable white teenagers, escaped with a gentle reprimand and an undertaking to divest himself of financial commitments in music publishing and record manufacturing firms which might constitute a conflict of interest. Meanwhile, many veteran black and white r&b/rock and roll deejays – including Tommy Smalls, Hal Jackson, "Jumpin'" George Oxford, Jack Walker, Tom Clay, Joe Smith and Alan Freed – were vilified as moral degenerates who had engaged in the worst kind of cynical profiteering as they foisted the jungle cacophony of rock and roll on the American public. Many were dismissed and some prosecuted.[104]

Nothing revealed more clearly the underlying moral and implicitly racial agenda of the hearings than the uneven treatment meted out to Clark and the older r&b deejays of both races. Clark escaped because *American Bandstand* was the flagship of the new pop styles, in which the lyrical themes, musical techniques, and even the dance steps which had made early rock and roll seem so sexually threatening, were invariably muted. After a fairly adventurous start in 1957, when Gene Vincent, Buddy Holly, Jerry Lee Lewis, Chuck Berry, Jackie Wilson and Thurston Harris had all appeared, *Bandstand* was increasingly dominated by a host of white teen idols, invariably sporting tidy quiffs and Latinate good looks (Fabian, Bobby Rydell, Bobby Vinton and Frankie Avalon), wholesome girl-next-door vocalists (Connie Francis, Joni Jones and Jodi Sands), benign beach-bimbos of both sexes (Annette Funicello and Ed "Kookie" Burns), girl groups of both races, and the cream of the new, sophisticated "inoffensive" black pop stars (Jesse Belvin, Sam Cooke and Brook Benton).[105]

Clark himself added to the sense of conservatism and decency. He had written a thoroughly conventional guide to correct teenage behaviour and responsibilities, explaining that "Good manners are good sense", reminding those with access to a car – always a potential vehicle for delinquency and promiscuity – that "a license is a responsibility", counselling restraint in dating, and concluding that "Teenagers and parents *can* be friends".[106]

American Bandstand was also responsible for popularizing many of the dance crazes of the early 1960s, of which the twist was the most famous. Based upon a sanitized reworking of the Hank Ballard and the Midnighters' song of the same name, the twist made Philadelphian Ernest Jones, otherwise known as Chubby Checker, the most famous ex-chicken-plucker on the planet. Where Checker led, many other black artists, from erstwhile bluesmen like Jimmy McCracklin to girl groups like the Crystals, eagerly followed.[107]

Checker also introduced a host of other dances, among them the pony, fly, limbo rock, popeye, birdland, loddy-lo and Freddie. By 1964, the madison, wah-watusi, Bristol stomp, mashed potato, swim, dog, monkey, matador and bird had all enjoyed their moments of dance-floor glory. The direction of terpsichorean innovation was definitely from black kids to white, but like so much else in this era the dance crazes of the early 1960s were genuinely

The fact that Bobby Freeman could demonstrate the Swim in close proximity to so much naked white female flesh suggests that by the early 1960s some of the intensity of the campaign against black music and its alleged sexual impropriety had diminished.

biracial phenomena, derived from and selling to a commercially integrated youth culture. Checker himself was eventually even more popular with whites than blacks, enjoying only 12 black chart entries compared with 16 pop hits before the suspension of separate listings in late 1963.

Whereas early rock and roll dancing had been denounced as lewd and offensive because of the intimate contact between partners and the fact that the dips, lifts, straddles and splits associated with the style had seemed like a choreographed Kama Sutra, the new styles involved relatively little body contact. Thus, they furthered efforts to defuse the explicit sexuality of rock and roll, which both blacks and whites saw as one of the major markers of its racial origins. If these dances seemed to represent some kind of retreat from the "blacker" elements of Rhythm and Blues, their racial politics were actually far more complicated in an era when blacks were negotiating new definitions of self and collective identity within what appeared to be a changing American racial environment.

Indeed, even Eldridge Cleaver, writing retrospectively with heavy irony born of deep disillusionment with the integrationist promise of the early

1960s, appreciated the optimism which had attended "Chubby Checker's mission", and the interest of white youth in black music and dance. The twist, he recalled, had been "a guided missile, launched from the ghetto into the very heart of suburbia. The Twist succeeded, as politics, religion, and law could never do, in writing in the heart and soul what the Supreme Court could only write on the books." By the end of the decade, few had exposed more ruthlessly than Cleaver the practical shortcomings of such symbolic breakthroughs, be they cultural or political, in securing real freedom and equality for blacks. Yet even his bitter mocking betrayed just how seriously such symbols of the coming new day had been treated in the decade after *Brown*.[108]

Certainly Cleaver recognized that black, as well as white, teenagers enjoyed much of *Bandstand*. "I would sit and watch programs like the Dick Clark show and just swoon over people like Frankie Avalon", recalled Vera Brooks, who in the early 1960s was a black California schoolgirl from a politically active family with profoundly integrationist aspirations. Only subsequently, in a very different racial climate, did she question the stylistic compromises, imitations and pastiches which characterized much of the programme's pop fare. At the time, however, Brooks, like many of her young black contemporaries, was excited to be part of a national pop scene which promised to unite black and white youth around shared musical tastes.[109]

Others, however, were less sanguine about the programme's racial co-ordinates in the early 1960s. According to Los Angeles r&b bandleader Johnny Otis, *Bandstand* was at heart "an anti-Negro set up". Otis was a truly seminal figure in the development of west coast r&b and one of the most intriguing characters in a world where the unlikely has frequently battled the improbable for pride of place. Born Johnny Veliotes, the son of Greek immigrant parents, he lived and worked, loved and married, in the black communities of Berkeley and Los Angeles. Graduating from a series of minor jump'n'swing bands, Otis began to make a name for himself as an itinerant drummer with Lester Young and Charles Brown in the 1940s. He later put together the Johnny Otis Show, a remarkable revue which in its time mentored Little Esther Phillips, Etta James, Little Willie John and Sugar Pie Desanto, among many others. In the 1950s, Otis recorded such hits as "Cupid's boogie" and "Willie and the hand jive", and produced others like Johnny Ace's "Pledging my love".[110]

In addition to his musical accomplishments, Otis could list deejay, preacher, cartoonist, sculptor, author, television presenter and organic farmer on his CV. Moreover, at a time when relatively few r&b stars were saying or doing very much publicly on the civil rights front, "Reverend Hand-Jive" had a combative weekly column in the *Los Angeles Sentinel* where he wrote "not as an entertainer", but as someone "sincerely concerned with certain conditions that exist in our community". Pre-dating many of the concerns of Black Power, Otis' "Let's talk" column was all about black empowerment and community control. Some of his earliest writings protested police harassment and brutality; others helped mobilize black voters to elect black representatives to the city council and state legislature. On 28 January 1960, however, "Let's talk" carried an angry indictment of *Bandstand*'s – and Dick Clark's – racial policy.[111] "Our 'All-American boy', Dick Clark, who waxes so moral and ethical in his 'advice' to teen-agers, should be ASHAMED OF HIMSELF! . . . and I'm not talking about 'payola'", Otis railed. "Dick Clark had the golden opportunity to advance the cause of democracy in a wonderful way. But, instead he and/or the TV network he works with chose to travel the lily-white Jim Crow route!" Otis, who had refused to appear on Clark's show, was furious at the "obvious and apparently deliberate discrimination against Negro people on his programs. I've never seen a colored face in his studio audience and Negro youngsters are rejected as dancers on stage".[112]

At one level, this attack was puzzling. Clark had officially integrated the show in 1957. A quarter of a century later he acknowledged that "rock 'n' roll – and by extension *Bandstand* – owed its very existence to black people, their culture and their music. It would have been ridiculous, embarrassing *not* to integrate the show". Otis was, however, right that in the early 1960s this integration was rarely extended to the show's prestigious on-stage dancers, and was carefully regulated out on the dance floor. Julian Bond, who had followed *Bandstand* since the early days when Bob Horne hosted it on a local Philadelphia station, remembered that "you always had a black couple. Usually 'A' black couple, never more than one. A couple, because they always had to have someone to dance with. Each other". No doubt memories of the way in which Alan Freed's networked television show was summarily axed after Frankie Lymon was seen dancing with white girls, were fresh in everyone's mind.[113]

In fairness to Clark, other popular local dance and music shows, like Buddy Deane's in Baltimore and WWL-TV's *Saturday Hop* in New Orleans, were equally unwilling to test the boundaries of acceptable interracial fraternization on primetime television. Instead, they offered special, segregated shows for black fans and dancers. As with *Bandstand*, whatever on-air integration took place – at least until the NAACP led protests to desegregate Deane's show – was usually a matter of carefully selected black artists performing before appreciative, often entranced, white kids.[114]

American Bandstand stood both as a testament to rock and roll's rapprochement with white middle-class values, and as an example of the dominant culture's capacity to absorb, transform and ultimately commodify "threatening" sub-cultural styles in accordance with its own core values. It positively reeked of WASPish sensibilities. The payola investigations meanwhile revealed a deep wellspring of racially charged hypocrisy when it came to American business ethics. Just a few years before the payola scandals, political scientist Daniel Bell had commented on the historically "schizoid character" of American moralism, which "would be imposed with vehemence in areas of culture and conduct – in the censorship of books, the attacks on 'immoral art', etc., and in the realm of private habits; yet it was heard only sporadically regarding the depredations of business or the corruption of politics".[115]

Bell was right. Corruption and graft, *per se*, have rarely been potent issues in American history unless public opinion has disapproved of the results of these malpractices. It was certainly ironic that Oren Harris should chair the payola investigations. Under Harris' enlightened leadership the FCC in 1957 had pressured the four major television and radio networks into restoring the use of the word "Darkies" in the songs of Stephen Foster and their ilk, rather than offend southern white sensibilities. Some years previously, while heading a committee to probe the sometimes dubious ways in which television licences were granted, the Arkansas congressman had mysteriously become a 25 per cent partner in KRBB-TV in El Dorado, Arkansas. Interestingly, KRBB's request for a power increase, which had earlier been rejected, was happily accepted just as $500 and an unpaid promissory note for $4,500 bought Harris his share of the station. In the wake of Harris' involvement, the once beleagured station also managed to secure a bank loan of $400,000, and a further $200,000 from RCA.[116]

This sort of everyday wheeling and dealing attracted relatively little official censure or public outrage. Even when Bernard Schwartz, a staff counsel for the Legislative Oversight Committee, leaked the story to the press, Harris was still able to sell off his interest in KRBB at a healthy profit. By contrast, payola in the music industry was deemed a public outrage: it had supposedly contaminated white popular music culture, challenged the traditional configuration of power within the recording, publishing and radio industries, and brought forth the dark horrors of rock and roll. This had little to do with its intrinsic immorality or statutory illegality. Consequently, Dick Clark might possibly have been every bit as guilty as Alan Freed or Tommy Smalls, but since the former was seen as a saviour, not a defiler, of white youth, his business and accounting "oversights" could be excused in respect of the greater social good they encouraged. Here, then, was American moral pragmatism triumphant. It was another example of the "extraordinary talent for compromise in politics [and business] and extremism in morality", which Daniel Bell had noted. Moreover, for all the optimism of the early civil rights movement, it was clear that there remained a distinctly racial cast to mainstream definitions of morality.[117]

PART TWO

People get ready

CHAPTER FIVE

"Can I get a witness?": civil rights, soul and secularization

The profound sacred and spiritual meaning of the great music of the church must never be mixed with the transitory quality of rock and roll music. (Martin Luther King, Jr)[1]

The end of an era

On 16 September 1964 a new youth music show called *Shindig* premiered on the ABC television network. Produced by Jack Good and hosted by Jim O'Neal, the first show opened with a view of a darkened studio. Suddenly a single spotlight speared through the gloom and illuminated two young white women, Jackie and Gayle, who gently eased themselves into a folksy version of the black gospel song "Up above my head, I see music in the air". After a verse, the duo was joined by a white male trio, the Wellingtons. By the second chorus the Blossoms, a black female vocal quartet who anonymously furnished the vocals for many Phil Spector girl group hits, were on board too. Before the song was over, the Righteous Brothers and Everly Brothers had also added their blue-eyed soul and country-pop harmonies to the mix and this unlikely biracial choir began to rock the studio like some kind of southern revival meeting.[2]

Perhaps it was even just a little like some of the mass meetings held in southern communities where civil rights activists worked with local blacks to register voters and desegregate public facilities, meetings which invariably concluded with the stirring singing of freedom songs. As white SNCC staffer Mary King recalled, "the freedom songs uplifted us, bound us together, exalted us, and pointed the way, and, in a real sense, freed us from the shackles of psychological bondage". One of the most popular of those freedom songs was "Up above my head, I see *freedom* in the air". Like so many other free-dom songs it was forged in the very heart of the struggle from an amalgam of old tunes and new consciousness – in this case by Bernice Johnson Reagon in Albany in 1962.[3]

The headline act on the first *Shindig* was Sam Cooke, yet the ex-Soul Stirrer remained conspicuously absent from the show's gospelesque open-ing. Instead, Cooke served up a decidedly unfunky version of "Tennessee waltz" – his current single – and breezed unenthusiastically through Bob Dylan's "Blowing in the wind", although the choice of material was again interesting in those a-changing times. Cooke only really came to the boil when he picked up a guitar and joined the Everly Brothers for a boisterous rendition of Little Richard's "Lucille". Until that point, the most arresting performance had been the Righteous Brothers' full-throttle version of Ray Charles' "This little girl of mine"; the worst was when white teen idol Bobby Sherman joined the Blossoms for an ill-conceived showtune duet. As the final credits rolled, however, Sam, Don and Phil recaptured the mood of the show's opening and whipped a docile audience into something not too far from frenzy.

With the studied interracialism of its audiences, artists and material – awkward and strained as those fusions sometimes were – *Shindig* was both a product and a reflection of the black and white pop era. Yet, ironically, by the time the show premiered, that era was drawing rapidly to a close and new patterns of white and especially black musical preferences were becom-ing clearer. About a year before *Shindig* debuted, on 23 November 1963, *Billboard* had published what it believed would be its final Rhythm and Blues singles chart. Such a racially segregated index of consumer prefer-ences seemed an anachronism with white artists regularly making the black listings and black singles routinely appearing in the pop charts. Just 14 months later, however, on 30 January 1965, *Billboard* had to revive its Rhythm and Blues chart on the grounds that black tastes had once more become suffi-ciently distinct from white tastes to demand separate registers.[4]

The restoration of a separate black chart did not indicate a return to the days before 1954 when white consumption of Rhythm and Blues had been a relatively minor, often rather surreptitious affair. The white audience for black music remained largely intact, while both the folk boom of the early 1960s and the "British invasion" of 1964–5 served to stimulate and extend white American interest in black musics far beyond the black pop and emer-ging soul styles which dominated the black market. Bob Dylan's eponymous first album, for example, included versions of Bukka White's "Fixin' to die", Willie Johnson's "In my time of dyin'", and Blind Lemon Jefferson's "See that my grave is kept clean". By recording such material, Dylan and other folkies helped to acquaint their white audiences with a venerable country-blues tradition of which they, and many of their young black contemporaries, were only dimly aware.

In a similar way British groups like the Beatles and Rolling Stones encouraged, rather than retarded, white American exploration and patronage of black music by initially recording a diverse range of r&b. Although they later suffered the bitter barbs of black nationalists like Imamu Amiri Baraka for expropriating black musical culture and reaping far greater financial rewards than their mentors, *Billboard* noted that these groups were, in fact, "the first to tell their audiences which Soul artists they were imitating – which led to the wider recognition of such greats as Chuck Berry, Muddy Waters, Little Richard, Don Covay, etc.".[5]

Most of the other British beat groups successful in the mid 1960s – the Animals, Them and the Spencer Davis Group among them – had also cut their musical teeth on Rhythm and Blues. As black artists and activists appreciated, their public acknowledgement of black influence and inspiration contrasted with the silence of many white American performers on the subject. When Nina Simone arrived in London in the summer of 1965, she "found all the kids playing and singing Negro rhythm and blues", and pointedly remarked that "the nice thing is that they give credit and respect where it is due, something they don't do too much at home". Julian Bond, who with his brother James attended a 1964 Beatles press conference in Atlanta, recalled "reading some Beatle comment about [their black influences] and just being taken aback and saying, 'Hey, way to go!'. And while Martha Bayles is right that sometimes these British enthusiasms had the unfortunate effect of reducing black creators to perpetual "forerunners" in the minds of white rock fans – a tendency accentuated when bands like the Stones let their blues heroes open concerts for them in the States – "forerunners" was precisely what those artists were in this context of intercontinental, cross racial hybridity: r&b was simply the most important of several influences which collided and merged in these white anglo-pop-blues.[6]

In the mid-to-late 1960s aftermath of these early British acts came a whole slate of earnest white British and American "blues" bands, like the Yardbirds, John Mayall's Bluesbreakers, and the Paul Butterfield Blues Band. A few years later "progressive" blues leviathans like Canned Heat, Ten Years After and Big Brother and the Holding Company lumbered into the spotlight. At the same time, venerable bluesmen like Muddy Waters, Mississippi John Hurt, John Lee Hooker and Howlin' Wolf, who had been largely ignored by young, increasingly urbane, black audiences, were suddenly in demand again. By the end of the decade B.B. King, a major beneficiary of this white-led blues revival, was one of many bluesmen playing mostly to young white, often college, audiences, although a sizeable black contingent, eager for a therapeutic and indubitably chic shot of rootsiness in an era of heightened black consciousness, had also joined his loyal core audience of older southern and migrant blacks.[7]

Clearly, then, young white American interest in black musics continued to flourish alongside enthusiasms for folk, British pop and the mid-1960s

American folk-rock syntheses of the Byrds and Lovin' Spoonful. Black artists featured extensively in the first pop Top Forty of 1965 and for the remainder of the decade rarely accounted for less than a quarter, and often for closer to half, of the nation's pop singles chart entries. In 1966, even *Time* magazine noted that James Brown ranked third behind only the Beatles and Dylan in a national campus popularity poll. Its finger fumbling uncertainly for the pulse of youth pop culture, *Time* rather belatedly ventured that Brown's "rise in the mass market gives a sign that 'race music' is perhaps at last becoming interracial".[8]

Given that many whites continued to consume music by black artists alongside white ones, the principal reasons for the revival of a racially specific chart in January 1965 are to be found within the black community and its changing musical preferences. Whereas a third of the records on the "last" Rhythm and Blues Top Thirty in November 1963 were by white acts, including Elvis, Dion, Lesley Gore and the Beach Boys, only three made the first revived chart. One of those, the Kingsmen's "The jolly green giant", was clearly a novelty hit and only the Righteous Brothers' Spector-produced epic "You've lost that lovin' feeling" made the top ten. While individual songs by white artists still found occasional success on the *Billboard* Rhythm and Blues and, following a name change in August 1969, Soul charts, in the second half of the 1960s the black masses simply no longer bought such records regularly, or in great quantities. Instead, they overwhelmingly bought the diverse sounds of black soul, while black-oriented radio stations often programmed little else.

By mid-decade, then, the marked biracialism of black tastes evident in the late 1950s and early 1960s had already given way to more racially discreet musical preferences. This shift in mass black tastes reflected important political and psychological developments within black America, North and South, as the Movement entered a crucial phase of triumph and disappointment, continued progress and rising frustration.

The zenith of the Movement

Looking back at the development of the civil rights struggle, James Farmer of CORE suggested that the March on Washington in August 1963 marked "the zenith of the Southern Movement". The Southern Regional Council estimated that "930 individual public protest demonstrations took place in at least 115 cities" in the South during that year – more than in any other year, before or since. The most widely publicized campaign took place in Birmingham, where peaceful black protesters, including young schoolchildren, were dramatically pitted against the racist brutality of Eugene "Bull" Connor's police force with its high-pressure, flesh-peeling firehoses and snarling dogs. The national outcry provoked by Connor's ruthless methods of law enforcement and the cumulative effects of sustained protest and petitioning throughout the country finally compelled the Kennedy administration to seek comprehensive civil rights legislation. On national television on 11 June 1963, the president denounced the continued denial of black civil rights as both a legal and moral issue. The following summer, Kennedy's successor, Lyndon Johnson, presided over the passage of the 1964 Civil Rights Act, designed to end discrimination in public accommodations, housing and employment throughout the nation.[9]

At one level, then, it appeared as if a united and resourceful civil rights movement was still making inexorable progress towards the attainment of black equality by simultaneously transforming white racial attitudes and pressurizing recalcitrant federal authorities into making the Constitution "a charter of equality", and the law an instrument of protection against those people and institutions whose racial attitudes proved slower to change.[10]

Yet, beneath the surface of such soothing legislative balms much deeper racial sores continued to fester untreated. Although integration remained the dream of the vast majority of blacks, they were confronted by a bewildering array of contradictory signals about the imminence, or even likelihood, of ever being allowed to enter the mainstream of American life as a respected part of a truly equalitarian plurality. For almost every advance made by the southern Movement in the early-to-mid 1960s it appeared as if there was a set-back which highlighted the sheer tenacity of racism and frustrated rising black aspirations throughout the nation.

This was graphically illustrated by the assassination of Medgar Evers, the NAACP's energetic and courageous Mississippi field secretary, on the very night in June 1963 when John Kennedy first publicly advocated civil rights legislation. Evers' murder, which went unpunished for almost three decades despite the open secret that a white supremacist named Byron De La Beckwith was responsible, was just one of at least ten deaths resulting from participation in Movement activities that year. There were also some 35 racially motivated bombings in the South, including the slaughter of four black children attending Sunday school at Birmingham's 16th Street Baptist Church in September. More than 20,000 of the blacks and whites who determinedly protested Jim Crow and disenfranchisement in 1963 were jailed by southern authorities equally determined to preserve white supremacy.[11]

There was a similarly high price to pay for the achievements of the young blacks and their white colleagues who undertook the painstaking and highly dangerous work of registering black voters in the Deep South. The 1964 Mississippi Freedom Summer saw many more jailings, beatings and murders of civil rights workers, coupled with the steady application of economic pressure and psychological terror by those who hoped to discourage local blacks from registering or casting votes. By the end of 1964, white resistance meant that the proportion of eligible Mississippi blacks on the electoral roll had crept up to just 6.7 per cent. As ever, Mississippi was a particularly extreme case and in the South as a whole similar voting rights efforts had more than doubled black registration since the early 1950s. Nevertheless, by the end of the year still only 43 per cent of the region's eligible blacks were registered.[12]

The Freedom Summer of 1964 ended with perhaps the biggest single blow to the pervasive optimism of the early 1960s, when a delegation from the Mississippi Freedom Democratic Party (MFDP) failed to win accreditation at the national Democratic Party convention in Atlantic City. The MFDP maintained that the Magnolia State's official, whites-only, delegation could not claim to be truly representative of the people of Mississippi while there were still manifold procedural, economic and terroristic restraints upon the rights of blacks to register and vote. The MFDP waited in vain for the party's national leadership to recognize its claim to be the only democratically chosen state delegation. Despite the urgings of some established civil rights leaders, the MFDP proudly refused to accept a shabby compromise which would have assigned it just two token at-large seats while allowing the segregated delegation to assume its traditional place.[13]

It was this "betrayal" of the MFDP by white liberals, the Democratic Party, and some of the established civil rights leadership which began to prise open the cracks in the Movement coalition which public displays of interracial and inter-organizational unity had largely, if by no means always, concealed. For many younger members of the Movement such as Stokely Carmichael and Cleveland Sellers of SNCC, and even for some older apostles of nonviolence and interracialism like Bob Moses and Jim Forman, the disappointments of Atlantic City permanently altered their attitude towards working with whites and their perception of the potential for equitable black treatment in America. It also radicalized their approach to the goals and tactics of the freedom struggle. "The MFDP challenge", wrote H. Rap Brown, one of the young SNCC workers most affected by the affair and a future chairman of the organization, "not only pointed up the total lack of power Black people had, but it also showed that even when you're right you lose . . . When people cannot find a redress of their grievances within a system, they have no choice but to destroy the system which is responsible in the first place for their grievances". Although relatively rare in 1964, such sentiments increasingly characterized the black power rhetoric and politics of the later 1960s.[14]

In the meantime, however, the Movement continued to present a public image of solidarity and common purpose wherever possible. Despite bitter tactical and jurisdictional disagreements between SNCC and SCLC, this front was just about maintained in Selma, Alabama in 1965, during the last great set-piece confrontation of the southern Movement. On 7 March, much of America watched in shame as Sheriff Jim Clark, Al Lingo and their posse of policemen and state troopers trampled and clubbed peaceful marchers making their way across Selma's Pettus Bridge, hoping to go on to the state capitol in Montgomery to petition Governor George Wallace in support of black voting rights.

The scenes of "Bloody Sunday" hastened the passage of a comprehensive Voting Rights Act later that summer. In Dallas County, where Selma was situated, the impact of this Act was immediate and dramatic with the number of registered black voters increasing more than eightfold in the months following its enactment. By 1968, even in Mississippi more than 59 per cent of eligible blacks were registered, while by the following year almost 65 per cent of southern blacks were on the rolls. The number of black elected officials in the region expanded in tandem with this increased political power. From around 100 in 1964 the number had risen to 1,185 in 1968, although most of these gains were made at the lower echelons of municipal politics.[15]

Despite the Herculean efforts of the Movement and its significant legislative and political successes, however, material advances for black Americans in the South and beyond were frequently slow, sometimes non-existent, and invariably equivocal. Massive resistance and federal lassitude meant that by the end of 1964, more than a decade after *Brown*, only 2 per cent of southern black children attended integrated schools. Nationally, black adult unemployment declined steadily throughout the decade from 10.2 per cent in 1960 to 6.4 per cent in 1969, yet this continued to represent around twice the level for whites. Similarly, although in constant dollars the median black family income rose from $3,230 to $3,393 between 1960 and 1965, that actually represented a decline in its strength relative to median white family income from 55.4 per cent to 55.1 per cent. This gap closed slightly during the next decade, but by 1975 the black median family income of $8,779 was still only 61.5 per cent that of white families.[16]

Moreover, while southern blacks could draw strength from the recent experience of mass mobilization and political action, and look forward to exploring the possibilities of the new world they had created without Jim Crow laws and with the vote, by the mid 1960s northern blacks were already disillusioned with the absence of any major changes in the patterns of their usually poor and marginalized lives as a consequence of the victories of the southern campaign. In the summers of 1964 and 1965 these smouldering black frustrations, sometimes exacerbated by callous or ill-considered programmes of urban redevelopment which variously devastated or quarantined black inner-city neighbourhoods, exploded in a series of major racial disturbances. Often fuelled by specific incidences of white police brutality and harassment, in 1964 there were riots in Harlem, Rochester, Chicago, Philadelphia and several other northern cities. The following year there was a still more serious black uprising in the Watts district of Los Angeles, which left at least 34 people – one of them Charles Fizer of the Olympics vocal group – dead, 1,000 injured and 4,000 under arrest. Damages were estimated at $200 million. Watts served dramatic notice that the struggle for black control over black lives, and for the recognition and redress of black grievances, was far from over. Instead, it was entering a new and highly volatile era of long hot summers.[17]

In 1966, Martin Luther King conducted his first major campaign outside the South, directed primarily against housing discrimination in Chicago. The failures of that campaign, and the terrifying violence of the white suburban reaction to it, confirmed political commentator Samuel Lubell's warning that, despite a general "readiness to concede the Negro political and economic rights . . . opposition mounted quickly on anything that touched social life". Growing white support for basic black civil and voting rights was not indicative of an end to prejudice and discrimination closer to home, when daughters, jobs and neighbourhoods were held to be under threat. While Lubell reported that only 10 per cent of northern whites opposed the idea of blacks working in any job for which they were qualified, more than 90 per cent still opposed allowing blacks to buy houses in white neighbourhoods.[18]

In the aftermath of Atlantic City and Watts, there was another important change in the temper and tactics of the black struggle. The nonviolent direct action strategies which had characterized the southern protests of SCLC, CORE and SNCC came under intense scrutiny from those who now saw such methods as inappropriate for the national struggle against black economic powerlessness and systemic, institutionalized discrimination. In 1965, the Deacons for Defense and Justice and the original Black Panther Party emerged in Jonesboro and Bogalusa, Louisiana, and Lowndes County, Alabama, respectively, embracing ideas of armed self-defence in place of nonviolence. In late 1966, another more famous Black Panther Party emerged in Oakland, California, and quickly garnered support for its unique and turbulent mix of street theatre, class politics, black nationalism and armed self-defence. Although King's SCLC retained its commitment to nonviolence, by the end of 1966 key elements within CORE and SNCC had disavowed the tactic. Soon afterwards they would also reject the interracialism which was such a hallmark of their early efforts.

In sum, then, the period between the March on Washington and the Meredith March through Mississippi in the summer of 1966, on which Stokely Carmichael first popularized the Black Power slogan, was deeply paradoxical. The Movement continued to make significant progress and succeeded in having its demands addressed in two important pieces of legislation. Yet it was also a period which fostered a much deeper appreciation of the limits of white popular and federal support for the black cause. Important doubts were raised about the functional effectiveness of the legislation which had been won in securing real black equality of economic, social and political opportunity, let alone condition, within the existing socio-economic structure. As blacks confronted the obdurate forces of systemic and habitual racism throughout the nation, the Movement not only began to lose some of its internal cohesion, but also some of the confidence, that sense of focused, unshakeable purpose which had sustained its initial efforts.

The Movement and black consciousness

If significant improvements in the material circumstances of black life often seemed elusive, there were other important consequences of the early freedom struggle which were less easy to quantify in terms of registered voters, economic opportunities and equitable access to public facilities, housing and education. In the South, in the course of participating in the Movement, the black sense of self and community, of rights, destiny and potential had been completely transformed. Doug McAdam has described a process of "cognitive liberation", whereby southern blacks moved from widespread accommodation to oppressive conditions to a much greater willingness to challenge those conditions. Even in campaigns like Albany and St Augustine, which were relative failures in terms of securing actual changes in local discriminatory practices, there emerged what Richard King has described as "a new sense of individual and collective self among southern black people through political mobilization and participation".[19]

This feeling of personal empowerment through political action was vividly evoked by Franklin McCain, recalling the first day of the Greensboro sit-ins in February 1960. "I probably felt better on that day than I've ever felt in my life. Seems like a lot of feelings of guilt or what-have-you suddenly left me, and I felt as though I had gained my manhood, so to speak, and not only gained it, but had developed quite a lot of respect for it".[20]

Even in the absence of a mass movement on the southern scale – except, perhaps, in Chicago – northern blacks were also inspired by the very existence of the southern campaign to form "Friends of SNCC" groups, to partake in sympathy demonstrations organized by CORE, NAACP and SCLC, and to undertake a variety of independent local initiatives designed to improve and extend black control over the crucial circumstances of their lives. As James Farmer – whose CORE not only initiated the freedom rides but also led direct action attacks on discriminatory employment and housing practices in the North – noted, the larger Movement "provided literally millions of Negroes with their first taste of self-determination and political self-expression".[21]

Nevertheless, no matter how massive a mass movement the freedom struggle was, even at its zenith the majority of blacks, even in the insurgent South, did not actively participate in its boycotts, sit-ins, marches, voter registration drives, and political campaigns. Yet few, North or South, remained psychologically untouched by its early promise and triumphs, or unmoved by its tragedies, stallings and reversals. It is significant that Franklin

McCain believed that his activism had not only liberated himself, but that by association or identification with the struggle in which he was so conspicuously engaged it had also psychologically empowered and liberated other blacks. It was, he said, "not Franklin McCain only as an individual, but I felt as though the manhood of a number of other black persons had been restored and had gotten some respect". Thus, while scholars like McAdam and King are undoubtedly right to emphasize the special sense of personal and collective empowerment experienced by those participating on the frontline of the Movement, their actions and utterances also resonated in the hearts and minds of many other black Americans, even in the cities of the North and West, where they helped to stimulate a new era of roused black consciousness and self-respect.[22]

It was precisely this nationwide revitalization of black pride which made the disappointments of the mid-to-late 1960s so intense, and continued white resistance, prejudice and discrimination so difficult to stomach. A combination of new black assertiveness, raised expectations and mounting disillusionment with the rate and nature of racial change prompted a realignment within the nationalistic-integrationist spectrum of black political thought and consciousness with the nationalistic components acquiring greater prominence. Yet, although the balance between them may have changed, these nationalistic and integrationist strains in black consciousness continued, less as clearly defined alternatives than as messily and mutably interlocking impulses which expressed the black desire for both self-determination and equitable access to the rewards and respect of mainstream America. After mid-decade, however, it no longer appeared so certain to many blacks that they would ever be accepted into America on equal terms, with dignity and pride intact. Moreover, as Anne Moody, a young black Mississippi CORE activist, noted at the conclusion of her autobiography, it was no longer clear that blacks should even want to integrate into a society which now seemed so fundamentally and irredeemably rotten.[23]

It was in this atmosphere that many blacks sought an antidote to white assumptions of cultural superiority by self-consciously valorizing their own culture and celebrating peculiarly African-American experiences and practices as the critical repositories of identity and worth. It was also in this social, political and psychological climate that the soul phenomenon emerged, eventually encompassing most aspects of black life to become almost synonymous with "negritude". Soul style, as manifested in distinctively black ways of walking, talking, eating, dressing, joking, thinking, working, playing, dancing and making music, defied easy analysis or imitation by outsiders. Blacks themselves rarely felt the need to offer concrete definitions. "Something is felt to be soul", discovered sociologist Ulf Hannerz, who, like most other observers, believed that the lack of a formal definition indicated that it was recognized intuitively as "the exclusive property of blacks".[24]

It was in this assertion and celebration, rather than denial or evasion, of cultural and racial differences, that the self-respect and pride engendered by the early civil rights movement was most forcibly registered, even among non-activists. Thus black consumers gradually, but inexorably, began to reject white pop and some of the more obviously "whitened" Rhythm and Blues of the black pop era: instead, they increasingly embraced the "blacker" sounds of soul music. And while John Szwed's shrill 1966 assertion that soul was "overtly anti-white in function" rings false, the popularity of the style did indicate that Rhythm and Blues' new musical mean had moved in concert with shifts in mass black consciousness towards the black end of the conventional black-white musical spectrum.[25]

And yet, there was a curious and telling irony embedded in the black embrace of this "blacker", more nationalistic style of Rhythm and Blues. From the early 1960s into the heart of the black power era some of the best and most popular soul was produced, not in racially exclusive black environments, but by integrated groups of southern musicians, writers and producers who relied heavily on white country music for both form and inspiration.

At the risk of over-schematizing a complex reality, the fact is that the soul music of the 1960s was not simply – and certainly not only – a product of the upsurge in black nationalism born of mid-1960s disillusionment. Rather, it was doubly anchored in each of the two major ideological streams which have traditionally coursed through and mingled in black consciousness. The first, nationalistic current was powerfully expressed by soul's reliance on gospel techniques which were unmistakeably black in origin and resonance. As will be discussed in the next chapter, the second, integrationist current was reflected most obviously in southern soul's debt to country music and the vital contribution of white musicians to that regional variant, although it also found expression in the ways that black-owned soul labels like Motown eagerly pursued the white market. Perhaps the broader significance here is that soul, like all major black cultural forms, ultimately embodied the diversity, ambiguities and paradoxes of the black experience in America, as well as its common features, certainties and essences.

Brother Ray and the gospel roots of soul

By the mid 1960s, soul was already a rich and variegated bloom in the Rhythm and Blues garden. Classic examples were recorded in cities and small towns throughout the nation: in Detroit and Shreveport, Chicago and Muscle Shoals, New York and Miami. And yet, from the southern country-soul fusions of Jimmy Hughes and Percy Sledge to the horn-laced blues-soul of Bobby Bland and Howard Tate, from the full-throated gospel roars of Wilson Pickett and Aretha Franklin to the seductive purrs of Major Lance and the Supremes, from the sweltering funk of James Brown to the sweet flowing harmonies of the Impressions, these diverse soul styles were united by the pervasive influence of gospel and the black sacred music tradition. "The Memphis sound started in a church", commented Booker T. Jones, keyboardist with Booker T. and the MGs, a group which, in addition to having many hits of its own ("Green onions", "Soul limbo"), performed on most of the Stax recordings of the 1960s. In Chicago, Mike McGill, of the veteran vocal group the Dells, echoed this belief in the centrality of gospel to soul: "It's got a gospel flair to it . . . It stems from the church".[26]

It was the ubiquity of certain musical and presentational devices drawn from a gospel idiom to which blacks had an intensely proprietorial relationship, which gave soul music its nationalistic credentials and enabled it to fulfil its major psychological and social functions – functions which had once been largely the province of the black church. Indeed, while it has become commonplace to note the constellation of soul stars who started their careers in the gospel universe (Sam Cooke, Bobby Womack, Johnnie Taylor, Curtis Mayfield, Candi Staton, etc., etc.) it is only really possible to understand soul's significance by placing it within the twin historical contexts of changes in mass black consciousness generated by an evolving black freedom struggle, and the steady secularization of black culture which culminated in the late 1950s and 1960s.

In musical terms, the black sacred tradition's influence on soul was most evident in the style's tumbling gospel triplets, its call and response instrumental and vocal patterns, the regular rustle of sanctified tambourines, and the energizing slap of get-happy handclaps. At its best, soul presented a remarkable blend of melodic and harmonic fluidity, and rhythmic certainty and drive, all built upon the solid rock of repetitive, yet inventive, bass, drum, piano, guitar and horn figures. Above all, however, soul borrowed from gospel a breathtaking expressive freedom for its finest individual and collective vocalists. As soul singer-songwriter Don Covay – himself a veteran of both the Cherry Keys gospel quartet in Orangeburg, South Carolina and, like Marvin Gaye, of the Rainbows vocal group in Washington, D.C. – explained, "soul is total vocal freedom".[27]

In soul, as with all black musical forms, individual performers searched for, and the best of them found, a unique voice through which they made public private emotions and experiences with which their black audiences closely identified. For the performer, a profound sense of selfhood emerged from the full, forceful and, when appropriate, ecstatic expression of these personal truths or emotions. In this context, Ray Charles' comments on the fusion of sacred and secular styles he pioneered at Atlantic in the mid-to-late 1950s are revealing.

Brother Ray redeployed the ecstatic sound of gospel music to underwrite his pulsating tales of sexual ardour. "This little girl of mine", for example, was a reworking of "This little light of mine", while "What d'I say" sounded like a raunchy revival meeting with Charles as the preacher cum gospel singer, driving his congregation of possessed Raelettes – his female backing group – ever closer to some kind of heavenly release with urgent pleas to "shake that thing", and a series of wordless moans which were every bit as expressive. "I'd always thought that the blues and spirituals were close – close musically, close emotionally – and I was happy to hook 'em up", he explained. "I was determined to go out and just be natural . . . My first concern was seeing whether Ray Charles as Ray Charles – not as Nat Cole or as Charles Brown – was going to work". For Charles, then, the incorporation of gospel elements into his blues was a means to emerge from the shadow of his musical mentors and assert his own voice and individuality. This was what soul, like gospel music, black religion, and for that matter the civil rights struggle, was largely about: affirming individual worth within the context of black collective identity and pride.[28]

Ray Charles' artistic triumph was to make his personal history live and breathe through his music, making it available to other blacks as a commentary on their own experiences and as a dramatization of their deepest feelings. Charles was the hero of the young Julian Bond's poems "Ray Charles – the bishop of Atlanta", and "I, too, hear America singing". "He just seemed to me to be such a compelling personality. The voice, the music, the whole package taken together pulled me in, as it pulled in many, many others", recalled Bond. Bernice Johnson Reagon was even more specific, linking Charles' appeal both to the new black consciousness associated with the young civil rights movement, and to the new secularism in black society. "Ray Charles does the church has gone into the street . . . People are walking out of churches into the street, going to jail and that sound is Ray Charles".[29]

In Mississippi, Anne Moody was not initially a big fan of Charles' music. Then the double shock of Medgar Evers' murder and the Birmingham 16th Street Church bombing in 1963 shook her faith in the prospects for a successful nonviolent revolution in the South. At that point of acute frustration, despair and exhaustion, it was Ray Charles' blues, on this occasion nibbling at overt social commentary, which articulated her mood best:

I put a Ray Charles record on the box and he was saying, "feeling sad all the time, that's because I got a worried mind. The world is in an uproar, the danger zone is everywhere. Read your paper, and you'll see just exactly what keep worryin' me". It seemed as though I had never listened to Ray before. For the first time he said something to me.[30]

Ray Charles was one of the first artists to reject Jim Crow dates in the mid 1950s. Indeed, in March 1962, when he was successfully sued and fined for refusing to play a scheduled date in Augusta because he learned it was to

Ray Charles boldly mixed sacred and secular styles in the 1950s to lay the foundations of soul.

be segregated, even the separatist Black Muslims grudgingly applauded his stand. *Muhammad Speaks* conceded that although Charles "is wealthy and will probably lose no sleep over the $757 pittance, [he] seemed to have been willing to sacrifice it in his fight against racial segregation".[31]

Such gestures demonstrated Charles' support for Movement goals and no doubt added to his special status within the black community. However, like most of his Rhythm and Blues contemporaries, Charles' involvement in formal Movement-related activities was minimal. He performed in a few benefit concerts, but generally avoided overtly "political" or racial themes in his songs. He rarely aligned himself publicly with any civil rights organizations, or participated in any protest campaigns – although Stanley Wise recalled that when Charles played towns where SNCC had projects, the singer would acknowledge the presence of civil rights workers in the audience and say a few precious words of support and encouragement, perhaps even "have you come back stage and they'd feed you or something like that".[32]

The point is that blacks, activists or not, located the political and cultural meanings of Rhythm and Blues in many places other than in lyrical discussions of the struggle, or in the personal participation of its artists. Brother Ray's entire career was inspirational and pregnant with political and racial significance. Rather like James Brown, whose South Carolina roots and Georgia upbringing were similarly mean and uncompromising, Charles' struggle against crushing poverty and discrimination, compounded by the fact of his blindness and his personal wrestling with the demons of drugs and alcohol, was the black community's struggle against disadvantage and prejudice writ large. His see-saw story of travail and triumph served as a potent symbol of how to overcome, achieve enormous commercial and material success, with personal dignity and racial pride intact. His music expressed every emotional nuance of that story by blending the worldly wisdom of the blues with the transcendent ecstacy and visionary promise of gospel.

Soul and the secularization of black America

The fusion of sacred and secular idioms at the heart of soul music had not always been wholly acceptable in black American culture. Faced with a proscription against "unholy" dancing during their religious worship, antebellum slaves had developed the ring-shout, a form of dancing by any other name, which avoided the worldly crossing of feet and thereby official censure. Although these slaves were desperate to preserve dancing in their religious rituals, feeling that the freeing of the Holy Spirit demanded some kind of physical celebration, they were careful to preserve a notional distinction, imbibed from their white religious mentors, between sacred and profane terpsichore.[33]

Historian Lawrence Levine has suggested that with emancipation and the decline of the "sacred world view" which dominated the mental lives of the slaves, previously fuzzy distinctions between black sacred and secular realms of thought and practice actually became more precise. Levine noted, for example, the frequent reluctance of church-going blacks, particularly in the South, to perform secular material for the folklorists who roamed the region between the wars. A Texas cotton-picker, for instance, refused to sing a boll-weevil ballad, explaining, "Boss, dat a reel. If you wants to get dat song sung, you'll have to git one of dese worl'ly niggers to sing it. I belong to de church".[34]

Big Bill Broonzy, an Arkansas-born bluesman who, with Leroy Carr, Sonny Boy Williamson and Lonnie Johnson, was one of the most important figures in the development of a new, urbane, jazz-inflected blues style in the 1930s, was certainly wary of compromising the distinction between sacred and secular spheres. Broonzy had begun his musical career around the First World War playing fiddle in Mississippi. For a number of years he supplemented his income with a little jackleg preaching, but abandoned that sideline, partly because he calculated that the blues were more lucrative, but mostly because of disquiet about combining sacred and secular careers:

> One day I was sitting astride on a fence and my uncle came up to me and said: "That's the way you's living: straddle the fence", he said. "Get on one side or the other of the fence". That's what he said and he meant preach or play the fiddle, one at a time. Don't try to be both at the same time.

Forty years after opting for the life of a bluesman and heading North, Big Bill Broonzy was still troubled by the relationship between sacred and profane practices, not least in the music of Ray Charles. "He's got the blues, he's crying sanctified. He's mixing the blues with the spirituals. I know that's wrong. He should be singing in a church", Big Bill complained.[35]

In truth, the division between the sort of dance and music deemed legitimate for the worship of God and that which often smacked of carnal, rather than spiritual, pleasures was always rather stricter in pious theory than in popular practice. "The two musics – religious and secular – have always cross fertilized each other", noted Imamu Amiri Baraka. Bernice Johnson Reagon also recognized this interpenetration of sacred and secular musical influences, but warned against homogenizing, or simplifying, the various black responses to that alchemy, which differed according to class, generational and regional factors, and changed over time.

Reagon's father was Rev. J.J. Johnson, the pastor of Mt Early Baptist Church, located in Worthy County, just outside Albany, Georgia. She grew up in the 1950s in a "conservative family in terms of what was expected of you if you were a real upstanding member of the church". Certainly, she recalled there was "a line that said, 'over there is the street and that's where the blues and the rhythm and blues are'". Yet, she also appreciated that this line was more permeable than in the past or, for that matter, than it still was in other "more rigid churches . . . where if you sang the blues, you were sort of worshipping the devil almost". In Reagon's case, her parents' reaction to her interest in secular music was more bound up with typical concerns about a teenage daughter's first outings to parties, dances and proms, than any sense that r&b was inherently evil. With whatever reservations, the Johnsons simply "decided, it was not sinful for me to be in a doo-wop group in high school".[36]

Nevertheless, it is clear that some sort of notional distinction between the music of God and that of the Devil remained a feature of black culture and consciousness for many blacks in the mid-to-late 1950s. In Elisabeth City, North Carolina, Yasmeen Williams, another daughter of a baptist minister who later joined Bernice Johnson Reagon in Sweet Honey in the Rock, "had to sneak listening to popular music growing up". In retrospect, however, Williams too saw signs that the power of the old taboos was waning. She was sure that her "mother was tapping her feet in the kitchen and I don't remember her ever telling us to turn it off". In June 1958, 14-year-old Alleasie Titus wrote to Martin Luther King, confessing her interest in "Rock 'n' roll" – although, in an echo of the old slave proscriptions, she thoughtfully reassured him that "I do not dance". Deeply troubled by the prospect of spending eternity amid great balls of infernal fire, Titus asked King, "Can a person be a Christian and interested in those things? I am a church worker. Would listening to those things be considered as devil-work? I know I can't combine the work of the devil and the Lord. Should I quit listening to them?" In his regular *Ebony* "Advice for living" column, King had already warned a 17 year old reader who played both gospel and rock and roll that "the two are totally incompatible". Echoing the concerns of middle America, the eminently respectable King argued that rock and roll "often plunges men's minds into degrading and immoral depths".[37]

Certainly, for black singers contemplating a move from gospel to r&b in the late 1950s, the decision was still not one to be taken lightly. In early 1957, for example, when Sam Cooke released his first secular side, "Loveable", it was felt prudent to do so under the pseudonym Dale Cooke. Cooke had been agonizing about recording Rhythm and Blues for several months before finally taking the plunge. He even considered the possibility of pursuing simultaneous secular and sacred careers and continued to sing with the Soul Stirrers into the spring of 1957. Cooke realized, however, that he could not juggle these two agendas and maintain either peace of mind or an audience. While some blacks still viewed all secular styles with suspicion, special opprobrium was reserved for those performers who tried to fuse sacred and profane styles, or to sing on both sides of the gospel-r&b divide.[38]

At a 1957 Easter gospel programme in Detroit, Cooke admitted to Roscoe Shelton, who was then singing with the Nashville-based Fairfield Four gospel group, but also hearing the rising call of the secular world, " 'Man, if I ever decide, I'm gone. I'm not gonna play around with it' ". Shelton "had the same feeling" that it was still wrong to "straddle the fence". By the end of the year Shelton was singing r&b for Ernie Young's Excello label and Cooke was a household name. Meanwhile, another God-fearing young black southerner had crossed over in the opposite direction. In late 1957, Little Richard interpreted the sight of an orbiting Sputnik satellite as a message from God to abandon secular music and enter the ministry. Richard was unable to reconcile his deep religious zeal with r&b and a hedonistic lifestyle which set standards for sheer physical excess and toxic tolerance which generations of wasted rock stars have struggled to match. "If you want to live for the Lord, you can't rock 'n' roll. God doesn't like it", Richard explained as he dumped all his jewellery into Sydney's Hunter River, and headed back to Huntsville, Alabama to enrol at the Seventh Day Adventists' Oakwood College.[39]

While Sam Cooke's father, a Mississippi Holiness Church minister transplanted to Chicago, blessed his son's decision to cross over, and most of his black business and musical associates, like producer Bumps Blackwell, J.W. Alexander and S.R. Crain, were quick to point out the financial benefits which might help to assuage any spiritual misgivings, Art Rupe, Cooke's white boss at Specialty, was deeply disturbed. According to Harold Battiste, who played in some of Cooke's sessions and later worked as an A&R man for Specialty in New Orleans, Rupe had two distinct, but related, reservations about Cooke's secular excursions. The first was that Rupe genuinely feared offending, and thereby losing, his black gospel customers if he put out r&b sides by one of his most successful sacred stars.[40]

Rupe's second reservation concerned the style rather than the simple existence of Cooke's secular recordings. Rupe was hardly opposed to r&b, having had enormous success with artists like Joe Liggins ("Honey dripper"), Guitar Slim ("The things that I used to do") and, most notably, Little Richard. But he had very clear views about how black r&b should sound. According to Battiste, during the "You send me" sessions to which Rupe had reluctantly assented, the boss "came in the studio and really got upset that we were doing this salty music with these white girls singing". Rupe, who in most reminiscences comes across as one of the more principled, intelligent and honest figures in the murky world of the r&b industry ("I really admired him", confessed Battiste) was nonetheless one of those white label owners who, according to Battiste, "sincerely felt, 'well, we understand you people and this is what you do best'". In fact, Rupe had a very narrow, stereotypical conception of what music blacks liked or were capable of performing. "He had this notion that everything had to be loud", recalled Battiste with wry amusement. If Cooke had to sing secular at all Rupe expected him to sound more like Little Richard and less like a mildly sanctified Frank Sinatra. Unable to fathom Cooke's smooth poppy style, or imagine a viable market for it among either race, Rupe freed Cooke from his contract and let him and Bumps Blackwell take their newly recorded masters to Keen Records. Keen promptly put out "You send me" and the rest, as they say. . . .[41]

Art Rupe was not entirely mistaken to fear a backlash to Cooke's secularization. In the early 1960s, Cooke was given a rough time when he appeared at a Soul Stirrers reunion concert in Chicago. That audience, however, consisted of the sort of pietistic gospel fans who had felt particularly betrayed when Cooke descended into the secular world. They were the spiritual – sometimes, no doubt, the actual – cousins of the "older people, deacons and the sisters in the church" in Tennessee, who also never accepted Roscoe Shelton's move into r&b.[42]

There were always people who would never come around, like Atlanta's venerable gospel deejay Brother Esmond Patterson. Patterson, who had met Cooke a number of times when the Soul Stirrers were in town, was proud to be "a gospel man. Exclusively". He refused to play secular music, even when his job appeared to depend on it. When Cooke defected to r&b his "relationship with him was over then". Patterson called it "playing with God . It was dangerous to make that change". And he meant this quite literally. Patterson saw Cooke's shooting, by the manageress of a shabby Los Angeles motel he was using for an adulterous fling with a local prostitute, as proof of what could happen to those who left the gospel fold in search of fame and Lucifer's lucre. And there was "another fella, named Jimmy Butler", Patterson remembered, "they bought out of the Soul Stirrers too . . . His own brother killed him with an axe".[43]

Despite the persistence of such sentiments, however, the real significance of Cooke's crossover, coming hot on the heels of Ray Charles' sinewy and highly successful explorations of the nether regions where physical and spiritual sanctification met, was not the outpouring of black criticism, but its widespread acceptance. As Nina Simone recalled, the emergence of the soul styles pioneered by Charles, Cooke, Little Willie John and James Brown, coincided with the maturing of a generation of blacks who were simply much more relaxed about such sacred-secular distinctions than their elders. Simone, herself a preacher's daughter from Tryon, North Carolina, explained, "my parents have a way of looking at it – I always give them a hard time about it because I have never believed in the separation of gospel music and the blues . . . Negro music has *always* crossed all those lines and I'm kind of glad of it. Now they're just calling it soul music".[44]

This general acceptance of gospel-influenced r&b both reflected and helped to consolidate the lowering of traditional barriers between secular and sacred realms in black culture. Although generational, denominational and demographic factors affected the rate and precise nature of this process, it does appear to have quickened and reached maturity throughout black America in the late 1950s and early 1960s, as many of the social and psychological functions of organized black religion were transferred to a variety of secular practices and institutions, most notably commercial entertainment and black popular culture. There was also a related phenomenon, which saw the increased commodification of black religion, particularly in urban centres, which brought much of it within the orbit of the secular world of black entertainment and commerce. These twin developments coalesced to provide the historical and social context for the emergence of the soul phenomenon as a mass black secular faith, with soul music as its principal liturgy.[45]

It is important to stress that during the 1960s, this process of secularization enveloped not just music, but most areas of black life. The only religious group in the ascendant was the Black Muslims, whose nationalistic social and economic programmes, and bold championing of black pride and self-reliance, were often of more importance to followers than the specifics of their eschatology. Elsewhere, organized black religion was in "distinct decline", even in the South, where sociologist Daniel Thompson discovered that "very few adults or youth ever become meaningfully involved in the church's interests and programmes". Throughout the nation, there was a precipitous decline in the number of black clergy which cannot simply be explained by increased urbanization and the resulting concentration of blacks into fewer, but larger, congregations. By the end of the decade this trend prompted Wilbur Bock to comment that "Negroes are becoming less involved in the religious institution as they have lost faith in its function for social change".[46]

Indeed, despite the critical importance of the black church as a source of leadership, organization and finance in some civil rights campaigns, and the centrality of Christian precepts to the tactics and goals of many activists, new organizations and institutions had emerged to fight for black rights and social change. One young black man actually interpreted Martin Luther King's appeal to his own generation as being in spite of, not because of, King's church background: "it was great to see a black person who could get up and move an audience the way he did without talking out of the bible". Even at the apparent height of its influence in the South, in the 1963 Birmingham campaign, for example, 90 per cent of the city's black clergy spurned the protests. Historians John Dittmer and Adam Fairclough both found that cautious black churches in Mississippi and Louisiana respectively were often as much an impediment to Movement activities as a help.[47]

Such widespread, if by no means universal, clerical conservatism, North and South, necessitated the creation of alternative protest vehicles and political institutions to meet the needs of rising black aspirations. Thus, the centre of black political gravity during the course of the 1960s moved inexorably away from church-based institutions towards secular, or rapidly secularizing, organizations like SNCC, CORE and the Black Panther Party; away from moral arguments and strategies for the redemption of American society informed by Christian ethics, to the pursuit of black economic power and the exercise of black interest group politics.[48]

Enterprise and ecstacy: the gospel business

If the process of secularization in black life and culture hastened and hardened in the 1950s and 1960s, its roots went back at least to the time of "The great migration" around the First World War when 1.5 million blacks left the South, while many of those who stayed behind moved to the region's cities. In this urban environment, black preachers and religious charismatics found themselves in fierce competition for black souls and dollars, not only with each other but also with secular institutions which offered many of the services once the preserve of the church. Whereas the rural and small-town church had once been virtually unchallenged as the focus of black community affairs, politics, education and recreation, in the city there were alternative associational possibilities, new political organizations and expanded, if still severely restricted, educational and economic opportunities. There was also a vibrant and variegated entertainment network, including movies, theatres, bars and dancehalls, which threatened to lure away from the pews new generations of blacks less imbued with the trenchant religiosity of their parents.

In response to this secular competition, urban churches deliberately accentuated the spectacular, participatory, ecstatic elements which had always been a feature of black religious worship. "To hold their people", black poet Claude McKay noted in 1940, "the preachers are partial to the excessive demonstration of primitive emotionalism in the pews . . . The improvised shaking and shuffling of the angels' feet on the floor of a Harlem Heaven was often more highly entertaining than the floor show of a Harlem cabaret".[49]

For many young blacks, this "entertainment" element in black churches came to exercise an appeal quite independent of any strictly religious dimension. Consequently, as sociologists St Clair Drake and Horace Cayton noted, after the Second World War the line between the sacred and secular realms in black culture became increasingly blurred once more, especially in the cities of the North.

> In order to meet the competition of Chicago's night life, [some churches] have evolved the custom of giving "special programs" in addition to, or instead of, preaching. These take the form of dramas, musical extravaganzas, or occasional movies. These Sunday night services are usually entertaining enough to appeal to a circle far wider than the membership of the church. In fact, a great deal of inter-church visiting takes place without regard to denominational lines and many persons will attend services of this type who make no claim to being religious . . . They attend church, they say, because they "like good singing" and "good speaking", or because the services are "restful and beautiful".[50]

Claude Brown's memories of post-war Harlem churches similarly stressed their extra-religious appeal. He attended one simply because he lusted after the preacher's daughter and fondly recalled Father Divine's 155th Street Mission, not for its spiritual nourishment, but because he could get all the food he could eat there for 15 cents. Brown also appreciated that the black churches of Harlem were commercial, as well as religious, enterprises. At Mrs Rogers' storefront church, he recalled, "people jumped up and down until they got knocked down by the spirit, and Mrs Rogers put bowls of money on a kitchen table and kept pointing to it and asking for more".[51]

As preachers did whatever was necessary to attract and retain patrons, and swell the church – and sometimes their personal – coffers, the emergence of gospel music was, frankly, a God-send, often helping to keep young blacks in the churches regardless of their formal denominational affiliations or beliefs. Building on the musical experiments of Philadelphia Methodist minister C.A. Tindley in the early twentieth century, the principal architect of the modern black gospel tradition was Thomas A. Dorsey.

Dorsey was a "saved" blues pianist, formerly known as Georgia Tom. After his religious conversion in 1929, Dorsey abandoned the salacious themes in his blues, which had included choice cuts like "It's tight like that", to write such devotional staples as "Precious Lord, take my hand" and "Peace in the valley". Yet the gospel style he pioneered remained heavily influenced by the sounds of jazz and blues and the showmanship of vaudeville. These were elements of a secular entertainment culture which was under constant attack from black pulpits for its alleged depravity and sinfulness. In his recorded sermon "After the ball is over", Rev. A.W. Nix had typically linked the evils of booze, sex and dance music with the prospect of eternal damnation: "A great many people are livin' in hell today, that started on the ballroom floor." As a result of such attitudes, when Dorsey first tried to rouse support for his gospel-blues, he "got thrown out of some of the best churches".[52]

Despite initial resistance, however, gospel proved well-suited to the emotional and social needs of an increasingly urbanized black community. Although the majority of the newcomers to the North were accommodated within the Baptist and Methodist churches, many were unimpressed by the large congregations and relatively impersonal style of worship. Searching for a more fulfilling, participatory form of religion, more in keeping with the southern tradition, they often turned to the storefront churches and various sects which proliferated in the city. In these churches, physical and emotional engagement was central. "The chief religious activity of the members of the Holiness cults is that form of ecstatic worship which is known as 'getting happy' or 'shouting'", remarked sociologist E. Franklin Frazier. As Arthur Fauset recognized in his own study of black urban sects, gospel music provided the catalyst for much of this emotional fervour: "music is employed not merely to preface or conclude or even to relieve the programme: it is the backbone of the service itself, even including the performance of the preacher or chief speaker".[53]

While the esoteric and holiness churches were first to embrace the new gospel sound, in the competitive world of black urban religion, gospel's growing popularity meant that mainstream denominations were not far behind. Gospel's first major breakthrough came in 1932, when Dorsey performed "If you see my saviour" at the National Baptist Convention in Chicago and began selling the sheet music for his compositions in the foyer of the convention hall. With Sallie Martin, a shrill-voiced singer and shrewd businesswoman, Dorsey immediately set about hawking his gospel songs to the churches, music publishers and record companies of America.

From its inception, then, modern gospel music was a holy hybrid of spirituals, hymns, jazz, blues and sentimental balladry which quickly became inseparable from the world of professional black secular entertainment. In the 1930s, the Stamps-Baxter Music and Printing Company of Dallas began publishing gospel songs, promoting them initially on KRLD-Dallas and later nationally by means of the Stamps Quartet gospel group. By 1940, Sallie Martin and Kenneth Morris had established another nationwide gospel publisher: the Martin and Morris Publishing Company. In 1957, this gospel market was lucrative enough to warrant a BMI versus ASCAP-style court battle over alleged monopolistic practices. It even had its own little payola scandal, when Clara Ward of the Ward Sisters confessed to "kicking back" half her television appearance fee to NBC, describing it as "common practice".[54]

Such controversies did little to halt the spread of gospel, although the pace of its acceptance varied according to the location and resources of individual churches, and the predilections of particular pastors and their congregations. In the rural South, for example, it was often a struggle for small black country churches with limited revenue to buy the piano or organ which usually accompanied gospel performances. Some preachers and their congregations also felt that the very act of deploying a gospel choir to offer a "performance" within the service was an unwelcome departure from traditional, participatory forms of congregational, usually a cappella, hymn and spiritual singing.

"In south west Georgia, inside the city limits of Albany, the bigger black churches would probably have gospel choirs", recalled Bernice Johnson Reagon. "But out in the counties those churches would not have gospel choirs . . . until the 1950s. So we are 20 years behind, say, Chicago, in terms of gospel. What is really happening though, is that we are hearing gospel on the radio." Reagon's own church did not get its first piano until around 1953, whereafter it established a gospel choir with members spanning several generations. As in most southern churches, Mt Early's new gospel choir supplemented, rather than replaced, the older forms of communal singing. Certainly, although there were still those who would not countenance any contamination of their services by gospel, concerns about the propriety of this jazzier, more worldly style of musical worship had largely evaporated by the mid-to-late 1950s. Reagon's own parents "were as taken with the gospel music as we were. I grew up in a church where you didn't have to choose between the gospel music and other forms".[55]

While initially rooted in black churches, gospel music quickly found its way into the concert halls and theatres of black America, although this too provoked some initial pangs of conscience. In 1955, Thurman Ruth of the Selah Jubilee Singers organized the first Gospel Caravan – a pulsating package of touring gospel talent modelled on the r&b revues – and took it to the Apollo Theatre. There was still some opposition from the clergy, and a few doubts among the artists themselves, about the propriety of performing the Lord's music at that shrine of black secular entertainment. Nevertheless, the show went on and gospel tours have been wailing their way around America ever since.[56]

By the mid 1950s, gospel was also an important force in both the recording and broadcasting industries, where it retained an overwhelmingly, if by no means exclusively, black listenership at a time when r&b was beginning to attract a substantial biracial audience. Later, when soul borrowed from gospel, it was the latter's relative racial exclusivity which helped to establish the former's racial credentials. "What you have to understand", singer Cissy Houston told Gerri Hirshey,

> is that it was no accident. You started to hear gospel in black popular music in the mid-fifties because that's what was going on in black life. Everybody was getting crazy that R & B was making it big, crossing over for whites and all. But gospel stations were just as exciting to listen to. Gospel was making folks jump in a big, big way.[57]

The thrilling gospel records which graced black turntables and the black-oriented airwaves were usually produced by the same enterprising Independent labels who recorded r&b. Savoy featured James Cleveland, the Ward Sisters, Bessie Griffen and the great gospel showman Alex Bradford; Specialty had the Soul Stirrers and the Pilgrim Travellers; Apollo recorded Mahalia Jackson, and Atlantic was home to the Silver Leaf Quartette, Gospel Pilgrims and Essie Mae Thomas. Two black-owned labels were especially strong in the field. The Five Blind Boys of Mississippi, Sensational Nightingales and Dixie Hummingbirds recorded for Don Robey's Peacock, one of a stable of influential Robey labels around which black musical life in Houston largely revolved in the 1940s and 1950s. Vee Jay boasted the Swan Silvertones, Maceo Woods Singers and Staple Singers.

Once signed to these labels, gospel artists were just as susceptible as their secular counterparts to the influence of producers and executives.

Their records were designed to sell as broadly as possible and, since by mid-century few blacks lived wholly in the realm of sacred entertainment, gospel record companies, writers and performers were acutely sensitive to changes in secular black tastes. In the mid 1950s, for example, Don Robey insisted that his gospel artists should record with a drummer and, where possible, a full r&b band, so as to approximate the sound of groups like the Drifters. There was an intriguing circularity here, since the Drifters were themselves seasoned in church and steeped in gospel style. Clyde McPhatter was the son of a Baptist minister in Durham, North Carolina, who, like the four singers he recruited for the first coming of the Drifters, had once sung with the Mt Lebanon Singers in Harlem. When this prototype Drifters collapsed, the second coming featured McPhatter and four members of the Thrasher Brothers gospel group. By the mid 1950s stylistic barriers which had once required careful circumvention were beginning to prove highly porous.[58]

Despite the obvious commercial co-ordinates of gospel, much of the writing on the music has been characterized by preciousness and elitism. As with the many hagiographies of jazz and the blues, gospel has frequently been depicted as some kind of pure, unmediated, expression of black "folk" mentality. In such accounts, its cultural integrity and emotional veracity usually depend entirely on its alleged immunity to the crass and distortive business considerations which have made other forms of black popular music, like black rock and roll, pop and soul, somehow less "authentic", less truly representative of mass black consciousness. Charles Hobson's view was typical in acknowledging the musical affinity between soul and gospel while pouring contempt on the former's artistic qualities and denouncing its commercialism. "Nothing in soul can match the best in Gospel", Hobson opined, sanctimoniously protesting that although the brilliant gospel diva Dorothy Love Coates seemed well-suited for a bid at soul stardom, there was "some money so dirty you hate to touch it".[59]

In fact, while gospel's emotive power and artistic merits were indisputable, the music was forged by writers, singers, musicians and, in the case of recorded gospel, producers, working within the context of powerful commercial, as well as spiritual, forces. Publishing, recording, broadcasting and touring interests shaped gospel's sound and presentation for professional groups. Their recordings, radio shows and concert appearances in turn influenced the music of local congregations. As with any modern mass popular music form, a great gospel record, song or live performance was often one which had to transcend the more prosaic and sometimes craven forces which circumscribed its production. Genuinely fired with the Holy Spirit, gospel performers, from the Five Blind Boys of Alabama to Mahalia Jackson, and from the Sensational Nightingales to Inez Andrews, have been more transcendent than most. Their artistry and passion have often allowed the exploitative paraphernalia of the industry to recede into the background at the moments of musical creation and individual or collective consumption. Their musical and lyrical messages, and the manner in which black audiences responded to them, were the critical determinants of gospel's "meanings". Together, they ensured that gospel's basic social and psychological functions could be maintained, regardless of the economics of its production.

In 1964, however, the complexities of this relationship were clearly lost on black theologian Joseph R. Washington, as he launched a withering attack on the commercialism, divisiveness and apoliticism of much contemporary black religion. Washington charged that black churches had become little more than "amusement centers for the disengaged", concerned with internal politics, status and profit in default of the pursuit of black liberation which was the traditional role of what he called black "folk religion" – a peculiar spirit which transcended denominational allegiances and cut across geographical, gender, generational and class divisions to unite black Americans in a commitment to freedom, equality, individual pride and collective dignity.[60]

At the heart of Washington's critique was a deep mistrust of the ecstatic core of much black religious practice and, more specifically, the gospel music which frequently promoted it. Gospel, he argued, was

> the most degenerate form of negro religion . . . Shorn from the roots of the folk religion, gospel music has turned the freedom theme in Negro spirituals into licentiousness. The African rhythm detracts from the almost unintelligible "sacred" texts. It is commonplace now; it is sheer entertainment by commercial opportunists . . . Ministers who urge their people to seek their amusement in gospel music and the hordes of singers who profit from it lead the masses down the road of religious frenzy and escapism.[61]

By the early 1960s, Washington's description of many black churches as "amusement centers", if overstated, had a certain legitimacy. There is certainly no doubt that blacks continued to encourage and celebrate the descent of the Holy Spirit with joyous music and dance. Yet such emotionalism – what Cornel West has described as the "passionate physicality" of black religion – was rarely frivolous or peripheral. Washington's principal error was to assume that a combination of ecstacy, entertainment and enterprise *inevitably* encouraged purely escapist and, therefore, vacuous rituals. In fact, it was the participatory fervour which the best gospel artists and preachers inspired among their audiences which accounted for the effectiveness of many black religious meetings. Perhaps even more than any specifically numinous element, it was the emotionally charged, participatory dimension of black worship which enabled individuals, saved and Godless alike, to express themselves freely, and to share in a common, essentially democratic experience with other blacks. Amid the passion of many black religious services, conventional gender, generational, status and class hierarchies were often, at least temporarily, dismantled.[62]

Cornel West has recognized this phenomenon by suggesting that in the second half of the twentieth century, blacks "do not attend church, for the most part, to find God, but rather to share and expand together the rich heritage they have inherited". In fact, in an age of declining formal religious affiliation and faith, it was not so much in church, but rather in the secular world of black popular culture, of soul concerts, dances, recordings and broadcasts, that this exploration and celebration of black heritage and community largely took place. This transference, as opposed to loss, of function and meaning from sacred to secular forms of black culture was what Amiri Baraka had in mind when he wrote that "The Jordans, the Promised Lands, now be cars and women – flesh and especially dough. The older religiosity falls away from the music, but the deepest feel of spirit worship always remains as the music's emotional patterns continue to make reference to".[63]

Perhaps more than any other artist, the ample figure of Solomon Burke symbolized the ways in which spirituality and commerce, ecstasy and entertainment, sex and salvation, individualism and brotherhood, could blend in the world of 1960s soul music. Apparently as a result of a vision seen by his grandmother, Burke was groomed from his birth in 1935 to lead a Philadelphia mission called The House of God for All People. By the age of 12 he had his own radio ministry· Solomon's Temple. Burke came of age listening to "all types of music . . . I loved Gene Autry and Roy Rogers", just as the secularization of the urban North was taking firm and irreversible hold. Of course, even in the Godless urban North there were still many deeply religious blacks, not all of whom had formal denominational affiliations, and Burke was one such true believer. When he started his secular singing career as a sort of sub-Belafonte balladeer at Apollo in the mid 1950s, he still felt the tug of old pieties and rejected the label of an r&b singer. Even in his 1960s pomp, Burke preferred the more dignified, if not more modest, title of "King of rock 'n' soul".[64]

"I was always of the church and once in grace, always in grace", he explained. "I don't smoke, I don't drink and I believe very strongly in my religious beliefs, so I refused to be classified as a Rhythm & Blues singer. In those days that was a stigma of profanity". Semantics aside, however, it is clear that as Burke racked up a long run of hit records, beginning with the seminal country-soul ballad "Just out of reach (Of my two open arms)" in 1961, he saw no real conflict between his secular singing career, sacred ministry, and financial ambitions. As far as Burke was concerned, church and soul both enabled him to cope with life's fundamental concerns of "God, money, and women . . . truth, love and get it on".[65]

Nobody could accuse Solomon Burke of not practising what he preached. Not only were songs like "Cry to me", "If you need me", and "The price"

Solomon Burke fused gospel, r&b and country influences to create a distinctive brand of soul music which would, he believed, help bring the races closer.

classic soul fare, drenched in gospel passion and often slipping into fully fledged sermons, but stories of Burke's entrepreneurial ingenuity were legion. In 1964, he invested in a popcorn factory and, having secured a written agreement from the Apollo Theatre for all the merchandising rights when he played there, arrived in Harlem with a truckload of "Soul popcorn" and other foodstuffs to sell to hungry punters. Bob Schiffman, the Apollo manager, had assumed Burke would only want to sell personal merchandise like records and posters. Schiffman eventually bought all the popcorn just to get rid of him and placate the traders who had already signed for the food and drinks concessions.[66]

On soul package tours, while other artists squabbled over who should headline and therefore close the show, Burke was happy to go on first. This left him ample time to sneak off to a local grocery store, where he would buy food to sell to the exhausted and famished musicians and crew who staggered onto the tour bus at the end of the concert. His zest for life, in all its forms, continued unabated after his career waned in the 1970s. By the mid 1990s the "Bishop of soul" had sired 21 children, expanded his bishopric to embrace an association of some 168 churches, and established a chain of lucrative west coast mortuaries which enabled him to live in some luxury in Beverly Hills.[67]

"Really saying something": Rhythm and Blues and community building

It was no coincidence that the musical devices and performance techniques which soul borrowed most conspicuously from gospel were those which promoted corporeal responses and audience participation, and which, in emphasizing the individual's "testifying" voice, put a premium on the integrity of personal experience. With its towering lead vocals framed by supporting call and response instrumental and vocal structures, soul was the sound of a radical democratic vision of individual identities realized and proudly asserted within the context of a sustaining collective culture.

In soul, again as in gospel performances and church services, it was in the "live" setting that these individual and communal agendas were often most dramatically integrated. The soul concert was a public ritual in which the ecstatic responses provoked by the artists, like those excited by the preacher or the gospel singer, simultaneously assumed a unificatory and an individuating function. Anyone moved by the sheer excitement of the music to dance or holler could find personal release and expression in the midst of a communal celebration, with their own "performances" becoming an intrinsic part of the show, triggering the fervour of others.

Few soul artists were more adept at inspiring this sort of response than James Brown. Indeed, in the 1960s, few artists appeared live before more black Americans than "the hardest-working man in showbusiness", whose touring schedule frequently took in more than 300 shows a year. On 24 October 1962, "Butane James" arranged for his midnight performance at the Apollo to be recorded. In January 1963, King Records reluctantly released the resulting album with little publicity and an initial pressing of just 5,000 copies. In a market where album sales were notoriously low, *Live at the Apollo* was a phenomenal commercial success with both races.[68]

Quite rightly, *Live at the Apollo* has long been considered one of the essential recorded documents of soul. Peter Guralnick has eloquently and sensitively evoked the emotional power of the album, noting the "dramatic artifice" and "intentional artistry" with which Brown worked the Apollo audience, by turns provoking, seducing and surprising it, until it surrendered itself to the compelling drama of the performance. Like the great gospel showmen, Brown was relentless in his pursuit of ecstasy. He would never let up, always coming back for one more scream, one more chorus, one more spin and split, one more exhausted collapse to the floor from where, time after time, he was lifted, fanned, draped in a crimson cape and ushered away by concerned attendants, only to reappear, possessed of new energies, dancing and singing until he and his audience were utterly spent. "I have to say he would give a performance that would exhaust you, just wear you out emotionally", enthused Michael Jackson. "His whole physical presence, the fire coming out of his pores, would be phenomenal". As Greensboro A&T student Reginald Defour said after witnessing a Brown show, "James Brown can make an audience do anything he wants".[69]

Repetition was as crucial to live soul as the powerful ostinato rhythmic and melodic patterns were to recorded soul. Technically, repetition served a communalizing function, reinforcing phatic contact between performer and audience. It built up a suspense which could be manipulated, delayed, renewed and then either resolved "pleasurably" or shattered "euphorically" by the sudden interruption of a genuinely ecstatic scream or note – as in the innumerable "ooh-wee"s Brown himself unleashed in his songs. Both *plaisir* and *jouissance* had their place in soul, which like most black music was a potent mixture of musical formula and inspired spontaneity.[70]

Soul singers like Brown, Solomon Burke, Wilson Pickett and Aretha Franklin recast the "house-wrecking" tactics of black preachers and gospel acts into an exhilarating showbiz ritual. Even devoid of any numinous dimension and often driven by a desire to replace spiritual with sexual gratification, such shows still fulfilled the basic social and psychological function of black religion. As performer and performing audience immersed themselves in the music and the compelling drama of the spectacle, they succumbed to an ecstatic state in which they could "experience intensely the human condition" and, more specifically, their blackness, which was at the celebratory core of many soul songs. A soul concert enabled each member of the audience to bear witness to the formidable strength and daedal qualities of black culture and affirm their own place within it.[71]

Soul music ultimately served as a sort of cultural cement for the mass of black Americans in much the same way that the freedom songs served to unite and fortify those at the forefront of civil rights activities in the South. Indeed, there were even examples of exchanges between the two idioms.

Civil rights activists cheerfully plundered r&b and soul, along with gospel, hymns, spirituals, union songs, folk, country and any other musics they could lay their larynxes on, to create new material fitted for a particular incident, moment or theme in the Movement. Once Cordell Reagon got hold of Little Willie John's "Leave my kitten alone" during the 1960 Nashville sit-ins it could be heard throughout the southern movement as "Leave my desegregation alone". Ray Charles was an especially rich source of material. Brenda Gibson, a student at Spelman College, fused the Five Keys' "Ling ting tong" and Charles' "What d'I say" to create "Sit-in showdown: the A & P song" during the Atlanta sit-ins of 1960. In Nashville, Bernard LaFayette and James Bevel adapted Charles' version of Hank Snow's country ballad, "I'm movin' on", while "Hit the road Jack" resurfaced as "Get your rights Jack".[72]

When they were not mining r&b for lyrical inspiration, young activists sometimes customized existing freedom songs by grafting r&b-style arrangements onto them, rather than using the more usual gospel-spiritual-folk musical settings. This happened with Guy Carawan's "Ballad of the sit-ins", which SNCC students not only hooked to an r&b riff, but from which they later excised a verse about Martin Luther King as if to emphasize the organization's independence from the older civil rights leadership.[73]

CORE volunteer James Van Matre recalled working on a voter registration project in Plaquemine, a small Louisiana town just south of Baton Rouge, where "Almost invariably, every time a group gets together, waiting for dinner or resting afterwards, we sing freedom songs. They range from old Negro spirituals to modified rock and roll. When a group breaks up, the final songs sometimes drives the people into a thoughtful silence: 'May be the last time, may be the last time I don't know'". As these young black and white workers remodelled "The last time" to suit their immediate emotional needs, it really did not matter whether they knew it from the Staple Singers and the black gospel tradition, or from the Rolling Stones' anglo-pop-blues.[74]

The analogy between soul and the freedom songs was not exact, of course. In the freedom songs, medium, message and messengers were always intimately and overtly linked to the organized struggle, whereas in Rhythm and Blues that connection was often coded, ambiguous, and sometimes tenuous. With relatively few soul songs and even fewer soul singers openly embracing the organized struggle during the decade after Montgomery, black audiences sometimes found themselves bestowing political meanings and Movement messages on ostensibly apolitical songs. These acts of creative consumption reflected changes in black consciousness as the civil rights movement developed, and sometimes involved popular readings of songs which were far removed from the original intentions of those who made the music.

In the spring of 1965, for example, the Chicago-based soul-bluesman Little Milton had a chart-topping black hit with "We're gonna make it". This uplifting ode to true love's power to see a couple through hard times was seized upon as a soundtrack to the black struggle in much the same way as the Impressions' more obviously engaged "Keep on pushing" was adopted the previous summer. Nobody was more surprised by this public response than Milton. Although in retrospect he could see how the positive sentiments of "We're gonna make it", with its evocation of triumph over adversity, might have struck a chord with a newly mobilized black community, his intentions were more mundane – if quite typical of soul's commercial priorities. "Now when we did this we had no thoughts, none at all, concerning the great Reverend Martin Luther King's movement which at that time was really beginning to pick up oodles of momentum. We were just trying to get a hit record . . .".[75]

In a similar vein, Marvin Gaye and Imamu Amiri Baraka both detected political messages in the records of Martha and the Vandellas, despite the absence of any explicit social commentary in their Holland-Dozier-Holland songs, or anything much in the way of personal commitment to the struggle from the group. "Funny, but of all the acts back then, I thought Martha and The Vandellas came closest to really saying something", remarked Gaye. "It wasn't a conscious thing, but when they sang numbers like 'Quicksand' or 'Wild one' or 'Nowhere to run' or 'Dancing in the street' they captured a spirit that felt political to me. I liked that." Baraka agreed. "The Impressions' 'Keep on pushing' or Martha and The Vandellas' 'Dancing in the street' (especially re: summer riots, i.e., 'Summer's here . . .') provided a core of legitimate social feeling, though mainly metaphorical and allegorical for Black people".[76]

This growing black thirst for more engaged social commentary in soul eventually resulted in a proliferation of such songs in the late 1960s. But even prior to this shift, soul – and Rhythm and Blues more generally – displayed a distinctive set of lyrical concerns and perspectives, deployed a set of stock motifs and phrases, and expressed itself in unmistakeably black musical voices which had a peculiar currency in the black community. Rhythm and Blues often worked to express the black experience in ways only dimly understood by white fans and subsequent commentators, thereby encouraging the national sense of black pride and identity which bloomed in the 1960s.

In the decade or so after Montgomery, the essential realism of Rhythm and Blues, its musical and lyrical affinity to the material circumstances of black lives, dictated that economic factors often loomed large in its songs, just as they did in black life. Black unemployment continued to run at about 10 per cent – twice the level for whites – but became endemic in the inner cities during this period, with over 35 per cent of the urban black population out of regular work by 1967. For those in work, jobs were frequently repetitive, degrading and poorly-paid. Indeed, for all the statutory successes of the early Movement, a third of black Americans still lived in poverty in

1966 and the median income of black men was only 55 per cent that of white males, having been 50 per cent in 1954. Perhaps significantly, in terms of the revival of matriarchal stereotyping and compensatory macho posturing in the black power era, black women narrowed the gap rather more successfully, with a median income which was 76 per cent of white female income in 1966.[77]

The durability of the "romance without finance can be a nuisance" sentiment in Rhythm and Blues lyrics was testament to the fact that widespread black poverty continued to shape relations between the sexes. In 1961, Curtis Mayfield had provided his old colleague from the Impressions, Jerry Butler, with "I'm a telling you", a poignant pop-soul ballad which offered a compelling account of working-class life on the breadline:

I'm a telling you,
my days get longer,
and my nights get shorter,
and my way gets darker,
and my work gets harder.

When I get home,
the wife is mad,
the little girl is feeling bad.
The little boy, he's got the blues,
says he needs a pair of baseball shoes.

Allen Toussaint was a multi-talented lynchpin of New Orleans Rhythm and Blues, who wrote a number of pithily humorous studies of black work and its absence for Lee Dorsey in the mid 1960s. "Gotta get a job" echoed the Silhouettes' "Get a job", and portrayed unemployment as an occasion for male shame and domestic unrest: "The roof is leaking and the rent ain't paid,/ need a new pair of shoes and I'm underfed,/ Old lady fussin' about the bills she made,/ I have to get me out and find a job". Recorded in late 1965, just before doubts regarding the Movement's ultimate capacity to overcome became pervasive, Dorsey's weary vocals nonetheless sounded an ominous note of resignation. He even turned, somewhat uncertainly, back to the Lord as the only source of comfort and respite: "Never made enough to put nothing on the side,/ Problems, problems, Lord, I'm so tired . . . I don't know how I'm gonna live,/ Something gotta break, Lord,/ Something gotta give".

Dorsey's "Working in a coalmine", also written by Allen Toussaint, suggested how little the heroic struggles of the Movement had changed the workaday experiences of ordinary southern blacks during the decade since Fats Domino's "Blue Monday" had similarly chronicled the enervating drudgery of much black labour:

5 o'clock in the morning,
I'm already up and gone.
Lord, I'm so tired,
How long can this go on?

'Course, I make a little money,
Hauling coal by the ton.
But when Saturday rolls around,
I'm too tired for having fun.

And yet, despite no hours, long hours, low wages, and often dreary and dangerous work, blacks had always sought and found that fun. Moreover, precisely because of their debilitating social and economic circumstances, it was often a mighty, passionate, irresistible fun which was by turns desperate and gaudy, cool and sublime. Rather like those poor white southerners with whom southern blacks often appeared simultaneously locked in mortal racial combat and an uncertain cultural embrace, blacks invested enormous emotional and physical energy in their Friday and Saturday night rituals. Throughout America blacks used their leisure time and entertainment as a focus for an intense, joyous celebration of self and community. As the absolute centrality of the church in many black lives declined, it was through their popular cultures that blacks – especially younger blacks – expressed their individual and collective identities; their histories: those distinctive aspects of the black experience in America that in the 1960s they came to talk and sing about as their soul.[78]

"Well, it's Saturday night and I just got paid./ Fool about my money, don't try to save./ My heart says go, let's have a time./ It's Saturday night and I feel fine . . . Gonna rip it up . . . and ball tonight", roared Little Richard, just as Bobby Bland celebrated his own payday on his remake of "Stormy Monday blues": "The eagle flies on Friday and I go out to play". The whole weekend was an almost sacred quest for adventure and thrills. "There's a thrill up on the hill, let's go, let's go, let's go!", panted Hank Ballard and the Midnighters. These were precious moments away from the weekday routine in which to "Let the good times roll", enjoy black companionship and sample distinctively black pleasures.

In the 1950s shouter Roy Brown had proclaimed "Saturday night" as the time when he most felt himself, relaxed deep in the cultural and geographical heart of the black community. "Saturday night, that's my night", he half-sang, half-whooped with unbridled delight. It was the peculiar intensity of weekends in the black community which gave Sam Cooke's "Another Saturday night" much of its exquisite melancholia. "Another Saturday night, and I ain't got nobody./ I got some money, 'cause I just got paid./ How I wish I had someone to talk to,/ I'm in an awful way". Saturday night, of all nights, was not a time to feel alone.

Long before the soul of the 1960s, Rhythm and Blues lyrics had repeatedly evoked, invoked and comemmorated the crucial features of black style, leisure, pleasure and place. Chuck Berry was a pivotal figure here. He foreshadowed many of soul's lyrical concerns to encourage black communal pride and identity by focusing on the beauties and redemptive possibilities of black music itself, even as he universalized this theme for a young biracial audience.

Over the decades Chuck Berry has become almost as notorious for the red herrings he has encouraged gullible journalists to fillet, as for the red Gibson with which he helped to define rock and roll. Nevertheless, his 1988 account of the composition of "Johnny B. Goode" adds credence to the notion that he deliberately crafted his songs to work at multiple levels of meaning, with a more racially specific sub-text lurking beneath the more general celebrations of rock and roll's energy and excitement. " 'Johnny' in the song is more less myself", Berry explained, while the "Goode" derived from the St Louis Street in which he was born and raised. The "little country boy" had originally been a "little colored boy", but the ambitious Berry changed it because he "thought it would seem biased to white fans". "Johnny B. Goode" began with the unlettered hero living in rural poverty, "Deep down in Louisiana,/ across from New Orleans", which to Berry represented "the gateway from freedom . . . where most Africans were sorted through and sold". The song described Johnny's dream of wealth and fame; a dream which, as in so many of Berry's songs, was conceived as an actual journey from oppression to freedom. In "Johnny B. Goode" Chuck Berry offered a mythical representation of the sort of rise which he and some of his contemporaries had actually achieved, and which the vast majority of blacks hoped the success of the civil rights movement would enable them to emulate in their own fields of endeavour.[9]

Johnny B. Goode merits a place alongside the folk heroes of earlier black tales and blues ballads, like John Henry, Shine, Stack O'Lee – or, for that matter, Joshua and Moses – since like these men, he embodied the hopes and aspirations of the black community. There were, however, important differences which reflected the changed mood of black America in the late 1950s and early 1960s. Typical black heroes from slavery and the heart of the Jim Crow era were usually depicted in some act of cunning defiance or violent rebellion against white society and its institutions. They symbolically waged battles which in reality blacks had often been unable to wage effectively. After Montgomery, however, with a diverse and dynamic civil rights movement orchestrating a concerted and apparently successful campaign against discrimination, there was less pressing need for mythical heroes who would martyr themselves in epic battle with an oppressive system: such heroes were now available in real life.

Johnny B. Goode, then, was a black hero for the promised new age of integration, respect and equal opportunity in America. He was a hero because, much like Berry himself, or Ray Charles, or Berry Gordy, he achieved conspicuous success, not just in his own black Louisiana backwoods, but in the mainstream, where he secured recognition of both his talent and his humanity. "I imagine most black people naturally realize but I feel safe in stating that NO white person can conceive the feeling of obtaining Caucasian respect in the wake of a world of dark denial, simply because it is impossible to view the dark side when faced with brilliance", Berry explained. For him, white appreciation of black genius, in this case Johnny's guitar prowess, should have made continued white denial of black humanity and equality impossible. This may have been naive, but Berry was undoubtedly articulating the prevailing optimism of the early civil rights years.[80]

While Chuck Berry and Johnny B. Goode pursued the black American dream of mainstream acceptance and success, Berry also gave early notice that this should not be achieved at the expense of the distinctive qualities of black culture – after all, even Goode's success derived from his mastery of black musical style. Berry subtly expanded upon this theme in "School days", where he sang "Hail! Hail! Rock and Roll,/ Deliver me from the days of old/ The feeling is there, body and soul".

Lines like these may have expressed the feelings of earnest white fans, and provided easy platitudes for others, but for blacks they had a much deeper resonance. Sung by a black performer, lines like "Deliver me from the days of old" tapped into a black theological tradition, enshrined in the spirituals and gospel, which stressed ultimate black deliverance from oppression. Historically, a vibrant, distinctive, participatory musical culture had always provided one mechanism whereby the black community prevented physical and social oppression becoming mental and spiritual bondage. Music was a cultural space in which "feeling", "body and soul" – in other words, black humanity and identity – had been preserved in the face of repeated attempts to deny it.

As Berry nearly sang in "Rock and roll music", black culture had a back beat it could not afford to lose if it was to survive. As the Movement unfolded, such testimonials to the sustaining and defining power of black music became ever more common. Berry's work and Arthur Alexander's "A shot of rhythm and blues" were proud progenitors of numerous soul celebrations such as Gene Chandler's "A song called soul" and a triumvirate of classic tracks released by the Atlantic subsidiary Atco in 1967: Ben E. King's "What is soul?", King Curtis' "Memphis soul stew", and Arthur Conley's "Sweet soul music".

Conley's "Sweet soul music", with its roll-call of distinguished soulmen, typified a trend among black singers to refer approvingly to other black artists in their songs. Sometimes, as in "Sweet soul music", or Warren Lee's "Star revue", this simply involved providing lists of the cream of black talent, their hit songs, and favourite dances. Thus, Lee attempted to impress his girl by offering to take her to see an unmissable alignment of black soul stars:

208

Now when the show gets real hot,
Joe Tex holds on to what he got.
So hurry get your ticket,
If you want to see Wilson Pickett.
Tell the world where we're headin',
That you're going to see Otis Redding.

Warren Lee – an obscure Louisiana soulman who recorded for Allen Toussaint and Marshall Sehorn's Deesu label – proudly added his own name to this list of soul luminaries. In much the same way Edwin Starr boasted in "Soul master" that he was "the guy that they named soul after", while James Brown and Gene Chandler presented their own soul credentials at the end of their respective versions of Brown's "There was a time". Brown concluded his funky catalogue of black dance styles with a bold assertion of his own creativity and identity: "You should see me do the James Brown", he urged. Chandler's brassier version, replete with a breathtaking barrage of Chicago-style cresting horns, also ended with a boast of personal prowess: "You ain't seen nothing yet,/ until you see me do the Gene Chandler". In all of these songs, as in soul culture more generally, there was an assumption that personal respect and identity could, indeed must be, founded on individual expression and action within the sustaining framework of the black community and its distinctive cultural forms.

While rather too much has been made of soul's tendency to replace the "I" of the blues with a stated or implied "we", it was nonetheless a self-consciously inclusive musical form. While soul's musical structure was dependent on repetition and call and response devices which established phatic and empathetic contact between performers and listeners, the lyrics often worked in the same communalizing way. For example, black singers often referred to other soulmen, not just as musical idols, but as trusted friends and confidantes, suggesting a mutually supportive black world in which personal success and failure, happiness and heartache, were experiences to be shared, weathered or celebrated by the whole community. Don Covay's rap at the end of "Temptation was too strong" was typical, namechecking some of the artists he would later join in an ill-conceived, but tellingly titled group called the Soul Clan, as if they were a team of personal advisers:

You know, a friend of mine called me the other day, by the name of Joe Tex. He said, "Don, try to hold on to what you got". And "Ninety-nine and a half won't do", like Wilson Pickett said. I tried a "Lover's prayer", like Otis Redding said. It just didn't work, I'm gonna follow Solomon Burke's advice, "Tonight's the night" . . . I need someone to "Stand by me", like Ben E. King said. . . .

Rhythm and Blues lyrics further encouraged this sense of inclusiveness by deploying a distinctive lexicon of "black" words and expressions. The songs were brimful of exhortations to "walk that walk, talk that talk", "move on up", "get down", "feel it, don't fight it", and "tell it like it is", and variations on stock phrases like "just a little bit higher", "love come tumbling down", and "so high I can't get over it, so low I can't get under it, so wide I can't get around it".[81]

Although many of these phrases, like the be-bop-derived "cat", "man" and "crazy" before them, quickly passed into the mainstream of hip white clichés, and even suffered from some glib over-use in the soul of the late 1960s, they initially represented black vernacular speech in song. Moreover, while white writers and singers could and did use these idioms, there was something unimpeachably black about the way in which a Wilson Pickett or an Aretha Franklin exclaimed "Lord have mercy", "great God almighty" or "can I get a witness" in mid-song, drawing on the vocabulary, as well as the vocal techniques of gospel to lend absolute veracity to their secular tales. In all Rhythm and Blues, the ultimate test of quality was a song's emotional honesty. It was, as the Five Royales and Ray Charles agreed, the singer's duty to "Tell the truth".

Another way in which soul helped to foster a growing, national, sense of black community and shared culture in the 1960s was through its depictions of, and invitations to, dance. In the early 1960s there was a whole sub-genre of Rhythm and Blues songs which provided instructions on the latest dance steps, from Hank Ballard and the Midnighters' "Coffee grind", through the Dovells' "Bristol stomp" to Rufus Thomas' "Dog". This was no trivial matter for young blacks, for whom social prestige, not to mention success with the opposite sex, could depend on mastery of the latest moves. "Do you love me, now that I can dance?", begged the Contours, who further emphasized the need to grasp the nuances of black dance style in "Can you do it?". Don Covay advised his lovelorn brothers, "If you do the Boomerang right,/ she'll come back and say you're out of sight", while the *Baltimore Afro-American* even carried diagrams of the Madison to enable its black readers to follow a dance which some claimed had its origins in the Charm City.[82]

At one level, this emphasis on dance was, as the Miracles put it, still an attempt to "dance to keep from crying". But it was also part of the intense creativity which characterized black leisure time. Dancing represented action and initiative, and as such it counteracted the passivity and sense of being acted upon which still frequently blighted black lives. Moreover, in the mid 1960s a new breed of dance songs emerged, which, like "I gotta dance to keep from crying", Art Neville's "House on the hill", James Brown's "Papa's got a brand new bag", the Sapphires' "Slow-fizz", and countless others, did not offer instruction, but instead listed a range of dances which it was assumed all blacks would know. Chris Kenner's oft-copied "Land of a 1000 dances" was the prototype, namechecking, among others, the twist, mashed potato, alligator, yo-yo, go-go, sweetpea, watusi, slop and chicken. Like the sung lists of soulmen and women, these recordings were for the black cognoscenti; danceable directories of critical components in contemporary black culture.

Through this process of listing and participation, black dances became highly politicized, recognized by black leaders and the black masses alike as touchstones of black identity and solidarity. Stokely Carmichael, for example, proudly affirmed the strength and beauties of black music and dance, in the midst of a 1966 attack on white and black cultural elitism:

> We are not culturally deprived. We are the only people who have a culture in America. We don't have to be ashamed of James Brown. We don't have to wait for the Beatles to legitimize our culture. Black intellectuals ought to come back to the community and let the community define what an intellectual is and what art is. Nothing is more artful to me than seeing a fine black woman doing the Dog.[83]

Similarly, black poet Larry Neal believed that James Brown's "There was a time" did nothing less than "trace . . . the history of a people through their dances". Indeed, there was arguably as much racial politics in the list of dances on the fade-out of James Brown's 1968 anthem, "Say it loud – I'm black and I'm proud" as in the main body of the lyrics, with their obvious, if effective, "we'd rather die on our feet,/ than keep livin' on our knees" sloganeering.[84]

The very act of claiming, naming and evaluating distinctive elements of a shared black world according to black standards in a uniquely black musical and lyrical form was enormously empowering for the black community in a psychological sense. It reflected the acknowledgement and valorization of black cultural forms which the white mainstream had habitually ignored, denigrated or consumed as exotic novelties. Aside from dance steps, this inventory of black cultural predilections could extend to earnest discussion of sartorial style wars, as in Tommy Tucker's "Hi-heeled sneakers", Sugar Pie DeSanto's "Slip-in mules", and James Brown's compendium of ghetto chic "Out of sight". It also included honourable mentions for favourite black dishes, sometimes in the titles of instrumental cuts like Andre Williams' "Bacon fat" and Jr Walker's "Home cookin'", but also in vocal tracks like the Soul Runners' "Grits 'n corn bread" and James Brown's "Make it funky", where he drools over "neckbone, candied yams, grits and gravy, cracklin' bread", or even Little Willie John's "All around the world", with its matchless declaration of streetwise affection: "If I don't love you, baby,/ then grits ain't groceries,/ eggs ain't poultry,/ and Mona Lisa was a man".

There were also many variations on the "Mashed potato", most notably by Dee Dee Sharp – whose well-balanced diet of soul hits also included "Gravy" – and James Brown, whose "Mashed potato, USA" offered a remarkable terpsichorean tour around most of the major black communities in the nation. "I'm gonna start by going to New York City", Brown announced, before dancing on into Boston, Buffalo, Cleveland, Detroit, Chicago, St Louis, Memphis, Nashville, Charlotte, Dallas, Houston, Miami, Jacksonville, Columbia, Norfolk, San Francisco, Seattle, Los Angeles and Richmond. Brown's marathon ended back in his adopted hometown of Augusta, Georgia, but he was concerned lest he might have missed some of his black brothers and sisters on his travels. "Now if any of these places I called,/ and I missed your turn,/ I just want you to know I'm coming". Nowhere, it seemed, was to be denied a visit from "Soul brother no. 1", again reflecting the strong communalizing imperatives in soul music.

"Mashed potato, USA" was part of a much broader lyrical vogue for black travelogues which also included Brown's "Shout and shimmy" and his reworking of Bill Doggett's "Night train". Marvin Gaye's "Hitch-hike", Lee Dorsey's "Ride your pony", Cliff Nobles' "The horse", and, perhaps most compelling of all, Martha and the Vandellas' "Dancing in the street", worked in much the same way, listing major black cities around the country, often in conjunction with lists of black dance styles, to create an impression of black cultural nationhood long before the Black Panthers declared "It's nation time".

These travelogues also presented vivid images of black mobility, thereby tapping into one of the central themes in black history, culture and consciousness. According to Keith Miller, the Exodus story, in which salvation for the Israelites was attained by means of an epic journey out of the land of oppression, has occupied a privileged position in the religion and popular consciousness of black America, since "no other story proved more sublimely expressive of the themes of deliverance". Moreover, in addition to the many other constraints upon their liberty, blacks were often denied freedom or ease of movement, first by slavery, then by peonage entrapment laws, Jim Crow transportation, whites-only bus terminals and segregated interstate motels, and always by insufficient funds. Consequently, the ability to move to a better life, as in the countless "Chicago bound blues", or even just to a better love life, as in Wilbert Harrison's "Kansas City", was much prized in black society:

Going to Kansas City,
Kansas City, here I come.
They got some crazy women there,
and I'm gonna get me one.

Well, I might take the plane,
I might take the train.
But if I have to walk,
I'm going just the same.[85]

212

It was in this context that Chuck Berry's fetishistic delight in cars, jet-liners, trains and the thrill of sheer motion assumed particular significance. Berry tapped into the Exodus story most explicitly in 1964's "The promised land", which operated in a similar way to those black sermons analyzed by Miller, where historical and Biblical figures are introduced as actors in – and archetypal stories presented as explanations for – contemporary events.[86]

"Swing low chariot, come down easy, taxi to the terminal zone", sang Berry, in a demonstration of what Miller has termed "sacred time". Even more remarkable was the way in which Berry weaved his own Exodus story in and out of the story of the 1961 freedom rides. Described by James Farmer as an attempt, literally, to put "the movement on wheels", the free-dom rides were designed to test the South's compliance with the Supreme Court's 1960 *Boynton* decision outlawing racial segregation in interstate bus terminals, and its earlier *Morgan* decision prohibiting segregation on inter-state transport. CORE's plan was to travel in an integrated group through the South and arrive in New Orleans in time for the anniversary of the first *Brown* decision on 17 May 1961.[87]

In "The promised land" Berry's journey began on a Greyhound bus in Norfolk, Virginia, whereas the freedom riders left from Washington, D.C. on both Trailways and Greyhound buses. Berry also ended up in Los Angeles, rather than New Orleans. In between, however, there were some striking parallels in the two tales. Berry, for example, "stopped in Charlotte, but by-passed Rock Hill" – a wise move as Rock Hill was where the freedom riders first encountered violent white resistance. It was in Alabama, however, that they had really come to grief. White racists bombed one bus just outside Anniston, while in Birmingham Bull Connor allowed a mob of klansmen 15 minutes in which to beat up the riders at the bus terminal before his police arrived.

Following these events, the freedom riders were stalled in Birmingham, not least because it was impossible to find a driver willing to continue the increasingly hazardous journey through the Deep South. Many of the battered CORE workers chose to abandon the ride and fly down to New Orleans. They were replaced by SNCC activists from Nashville, who resumed the bus journey to Montgomery, where mob violence again broke out, and eventually on to Mississippi. A secret deal between the Kennedy administra-tion, Mississippi senator James Eastland, and governor Ross Barnett ensured that the riders were protected from vigilante violence and, at least before the eyes of the media, politely arrested by police on their arrival in Jackson.[88]

It is hard to imagine that Berry's black audience did not hear echoes of these incidents in the verse: "We had most trouble,/ it turned into a struggle,/ half-way across Alabam'./ And that 'hound broke down,/ and left us all stranded,/ in downtown Birmingham." Nor would they have been sur-prised that after his, and the freedom riders', experiences in Alabama, Berry abandoned his bus for the journey through Mississippi to New Orleans: "Right away I bought me a through train ticket,/ right across Mississippi clean,/ by sundown I was half-way 'cross Louisiana,/ smokin' into New Orleans."

Despite his trials and travelling tribulations, at the end of the song Berry phoned back to Norfolk, Virginia, triumphantly announcing his deliverance into "The promised land" of California. Berry was clearly relieved to have escaped the oppressive South. Yet unlike some of his Rhythm and Blues contemporaries in the decade or so after *Brown*, he refrained from ridiculing southern or country lifestyles, as had been the case in songs like the Showmen's "Country fool", or in the Coasters' disdain for hominy grits in "What about us". Indeed, around the mid 1960s there was a marked change in the treatment of the South in Rhythm and Blues as soul began to reclaim and celebrate the distinctive features of the black experience. In 1965 the Carter Brothers released "Southern country boy", a rough-edged blues-soul stomp on Stan Lewis' Shreveport-based Jewel label, which proudly boasted the band's regional allegiances. James Brown was forever going back to Georgia in his songs to recharge his soul batteries, while Otis Redding, performing *In Person at the Whiskey*, interjected into "These arms of mine" word that he was "Going down to Georgia to get some soul", as if that was where the essence of the black American experience could be found.

This soulful re-evaluation of the South's place in the black experience was but one aspect of a growing concern with notions of roots and place. That concern even extended to a new pride in the black urban environment which was frequently eulogized as the site of a vibrant black community and culture, and a place of psychological refuge from the pressures and hostility of the outside world.

One of the most powerful early celebrations of the ghetto was the Crystals' "Uptown". "Uptown" told the story of a black worker who works downtown, "where everyone's his boss,/ and he's lost in an angry land,/ he's a little man . . . Downtown, he's just one of a million guys,/ he don't get no breaks,/ and he takes all they got to give,/ 'cause he's got to live". Back uptown after work, however, back in the heart of the black community, "he's tall, he's not poor, he's a king . . . he can hold his head up high". Partly, of course, it was the singer's devotion to her man, for whom she dutifully waited in her tenement each night, which generated this self-respect. Nevertheless, it was also explicitly linked to a sense of place and community.

"Uptown" was written by the white songwriters, Cynthia Weil and Barry Mann, just as many of the Coasters' wry observations of black street life were penned by Jerry Leiber and Mike Stoller. Indeed, in the first half of the 1960s, when most black writers, singers and label executives were still very cautious about cutting songs with racially specific settings or subjects lest they might jeopardize their chances of crossover success, white lyricists were among the most forthright in their portrayals of black, especially urban, life and its social, domestic and economic travails. The Drifters' "Up on the roof" (Goffin-King), Ben E. King's "Spanish Harlem" (Leiber and Phil Spector), Garnet Mimms' "A quiet place" (Jerry Ragavoy) were also penned by whites. In collaboration with the black artists who performed and thus helped to legitimize their observations for black audiences, these writers sensitively evoked key aspects of the black mental and physical world.

Another immaculate Mann-Weil-Leiber-Stoller "message" song was the Drifters' "On Broadway", which brilliantly used Broadway as a neon-lit symbol of the wealth and opportunity routinely denied to most blacks.

> They say the neon lights are bright,
> On Broadway.
> They say there's always magic in the air,
> On Broadway.
> But when you're walking down that street,
> and you ain't got enough to eat,
> that glitter all rubs off,
> and you're nowhere,
> On Broadway.

In 1965, Edwin Starr's "Back Street" amplified and extended some of the themes of "Uptown" and "On Broadway". Written by Charles Hatcher and Bill Sharpley, "Back Street" represented a careful mythologization of the ghetto, emphasizing the black camaraderie and soul style which thrived there. Even a black man who had managed to move up and move out appreciated that the Back Street offered him some kind of spiritual home, a place of transcendent soul brotherhood, "where people stick together, one for all and all for one".

> I've been along Main Street,
> where society is the thing.
> People that live on Main Street,
> they don't know how to swing.
> But the people on Back Street,
> they swing all night long.
> Although I live on Main Street,
> the Back Street is where I belong.

Not all soul offered such positive images of ghetto life. Garnet Mimms, on Jerry Ragavoy's "A quiet place", complained "I can't get no sleep,/ in this noisy street", but despaired of escaping to the "quiet place" of his dreams: "Tell me, where do you go,/ when you got no dough,/ there must be a way out of here?" The Drifters were luckier, finding respite from the hassles of street life "Up on the roof". As the decade wore on, and it became clearer that inner-city problems were proving unresponsive to federal War on

Poverty or Model City initiatives, some songs, like Jackie Wilson's melodramatic "No pity (In the naked city)" and Walter Jackson's "Deep in the heart of Harlem", began to offer much bleaker images of ghetto life. Echoing the sentiments of "Uptown", Jackson sang "I push and kick,/ and get my feelings hurt./ Downtown, I'm just a little spoke that helps the wheel go round". For Jackson, however, there was no sense of solace uptown in Harlem, just a desire to escape. "If I was rich,/ maybe I'd move away,/ out to the country,/ where my kids could play", he mused, though with little of the optimism which had characterized the early years of the civil rights struggle. "We got to stay, can't get away", he wearily sang. In the late 1960s and early 1970s, this lyrical trend would find full expression in songs like Marvin Gaye's "Inner city blues (Make me wanna holler)" and Aaron Neville's "Hercules", which stressed the intensely competitive, individualistic, often brutally exploitative society which poverty and racism had generated, rather than rhapsodizing about ghetto harmony and soul brotherhood. In its early years, however, soul's perspective on black culture and community was generally far more optimistic. This was only natural in a music which was suffused with the pride and passion of a people newly roused in concerted action to secure black opportunity and respect within a redeemed America.

CHAPTER SIX

"Everybody needs somebody to love": southern soul, southern dreams, national stereotypes

We hated Blacks in the abstract, but our greatest heroes were the Black stars of the great St Louis Cardinals baseball teams of the sixties. We listened to Chuck Berry and Tina Turner . . . A few of us became firm fans of Motown music, especially Smokey Robinson. These tastes did not supplant racism. (David R Roediger)[1]

A southern soul paradox

That whites continued to own most of the record companies which produced soul music in the 1960s was not surprising given that the triumphs of the early civil rights movement had done little to alter the iniquitous racial distribution of economic opportunity and power in America. Yet the contribution of whites to the development of soul, especially in the South, was critical in artistic, as well as purely economic terms. At one level this musical miscegenation reflected the "freedom high" which touched many parts of the black South, and even some parts of the young white South, in the early 1960s as the civil rights movement began to dismantle Jim Crow. Significantly, even when black nationalism became more prominent within black consciousness and liberation politics in the mid-to-late 1960s, the widespread interracialism in southern soul endured, only finally crumbling in the face of a particularly reactionary brand of black power militancy around the turn of the decade.[2]

Perhaps, in retrospect, it was only in the South that such interracialism could have persisted for so long at the heart of a musical form which was in many respects the quintessential expression of a distinctive, self-consciously black identity. While the concrete achievements of the southern civil rights movement were frequently less than blacks had hoped and struggled for, they nonetheless constituted quite remarkable progress against a racial system which had seemed entirely unassailable a decade or so earlier. The galvanizing experience of mass black mobilization and the psychological fillip of major legislative and practical victories meant that some measure of cautious optimism about the possibility of securing genuine black freedom, equality and respect within an integrated and redeemed America may have lingered longer and stronger in the South than elsewhere.

Certainly, the popularity of southern soul, with its tangled roots in Rhythm and Blues, country and gospel, stood as symbolic testament to the durability of integrationist sentiments within the broad spectrum of black political and cultural consciousness. This chapter begins by describing some of those interracial entanglements; it ends by confronting the complex question of how white enthusiasms for black and black-derived popular music and dance actually connected to the operation of white racial attitudes more generally.

A southern soul stew with biracial sides

Most of the owners of southern soul labels and recording studios were white. Most of those whites were musicians, songwriters and producers deeply involved in the practicalities of making Rhythm and Blues music. Rick Hall, for example, was a country fiddler from Mississippi with a penchant for the r&b put out by Chess and Atlantic and a band called the Fairlanes which toured a frothy r&b-pop-country cocktail around the southern university campus circuit. Having written a few successful country songs for Brenda Lee and Roy Orbison, in 1961 Hall set up the Fame studio, and subsequently the Fame record label, in Florence, Alabama. There he hooked up with Dan Penn – a white songwriter, guitarist, engineer, producer and occasional, but glorious, singer from Vernon, in rural west Alabama. Together, they helped to forge what became known as the Muscle Shoals sound, named in honour of the airport nearest to Florence.

The Muscle Shoals sound was characterized by magnificent black vocalists weaving their gospel magic over fluid, relaxed, vaguely blues-tinged country music backdrops provided by a succession of brilliant white studio musicians. The first Fame studio band comprised David Briggs (piano), Norbert Putnam (bass), Jerry Carrigan (drums), Terry Thompson (guitar) and Dan Penn. After 1964, when Briggs, Putnam and Carrigan headed to Nashville, a second white studio band was assembled with Roger Hawkins (drums), Tommy Cogbill (bass), Jimmy Johnson (guitar) and Spooner Oldham (piano). Often their sound was punctuated by the keen blasts of the Memphis Horns, resurrected from the ashes of the Mar-Keys group which had racked up one of Stax's first hits with "Last night" in 1961. With a salt and pepper core of black saxophonist Andrew Love and white trumpeter Wayne Jackson, the Memphis Horns seasoned innumerable southern soul stews with their crisply percussive brass riffs.[3]

Early successes for material recorded at Fame included Arthur Alexander's "You better move on" and Jimmy Hughes' countrified sermon "Steal away". Alongside Solomon Burke's "Just out of reach (Of my two open arms)", Esther Phillip's "Release me", William Bell's "You don't miss your water", and Ray Charles' country trilogy, "I'm movin' on", "I can't stop loving you", and "Take these chains from my heart", these songs mapped out the borders of the r&b-gospel-country territory subsequently explored by some of soul's finest, usually southern, practitioners.

After the breakthrough with Alexander and Hughes, many Rhythm and Blues labels began to send their singers to work in the Fame studios. Among the first customers were the Tams, an Atlanta-based vocal group who cut a diverse range of soft soul material, most successfully "What kind of fool do you think I am" and "Hey girl don't bother me", which were largely written and played by southern white boys, Joe South and Ray Whitely. "Hold what you've got", Joe Tex's first major hit – and the first southern soul record to make the pop Top Ten – was also cut at Fame in late 1964 and released on the Dial label run by Tex's mentor, the white Nashville country producer Buddy Killen.

Perhaps the most famous visitors to Fame came from Atlantic, which had previously used the Stax studio and its integrated musicians to get a funkier groove on songs like Wilson Pickett's "In the midnight hour". It was symptomatic of changing tastes within the core black market for Rhythm and Blues that whereas in the 1950s Atlantic had often hauled southern artists north to apply an urbane gloss to their earthy blues, by the mid 1960s it was regularly sending them down river to immerse themselves in the gutbucket sounds of the South, or else shipping southern white studio musicians north to its own studios. When Stax closed its doors to outside producers in 1966, Atlantic turned to Fame, where Pickett and Aretha Franklin cut classic soul like "Land of a 1000 dances" and "I never loved a man (The way I love you)", again with white producers and predominantly white musicians.

Like Dan Penn and Rick Hall, Chips Moman was another pivotal white figure in southern soul. Georgian by birth, Moman had once played alongside Booker T. Jones of the MGs in one of the first integrated bands in Memphis: the Triumphs, which had also included Wayne Jackson. It was Moman who persuaded Memphis bank manager cum fiddle player Jim Stewart to locate his fledgling Stax label in the black section of town and try his hand at r&b. It was Moman who brought William Bell into Stax's McLemore Avenue studio and produced Bell's seminal "You don't miss your water" – a self-penned ballad with aching, gospel-tinged vocals, understated churchy piano-organ accompaniment, and filigree guitar work which set the template for much southern country-soul.

After leaving Stax in 1961, Moman spent a couple of years freelancing as a producer and writer at Fame and Dial, slipped in and out of sobriety, and tried to muster enough cash to run a studio of his own by painting buildings and playing pool. In 1964, with financial support from Arkansas farmer Don Crews, Moman regained control over both his personal habits and the American Studios he had set up in a black neighbourhood in northwest Memphis. At American, Moman recruited mainly white musicians, including guitarist Reggie Young, drummer Gene Chrisman, pianists Bobby Emmons and Bobby Wood, bass players Mike Leech and Tommy Cogbill. Together they established a distinctive house style which was a bit more polished and poppy than at some other southern studios, but still firmly rooted in the soils of r&b and country. Like Fame, American attracted custom from a wide range of labels (Atlantic, Bell, Ward, Minit, Dial) who sent an equally diverse range of singers, at first mostly black, to record there. Bobby Womack, who stayed on as a session guitarist, James and Bobby Purify, Oscar Toney, King Curtis, Joe Simon, Joe Tex and Wilson Pickett were among those who cut some of the finest southern soul of the decade at American.[4]

Moman himself also wrote some of the classic songs of southern soul, like the much covered "The dark end of the street" and "Do right woman – Do right man", a song recorded first by William Bell and subsequently immortalized by Aretha Franklin. Both of these songs were composed in collaboration with the ubiquitous Dan Penn, but Penn's favourite writing partner was Muscle Shoals pianist Spooner Oldham. Together, they wrote some of country-soul's most moving ballads, including Joe Simon's "Let's do it over", James and Bobby Purify's "I'm your puppet", and Percy Sledge's "Out of left field".

Another Penn-Oldham composition was "Take me (As I am)", originally recorded by Spencer Wiggins on yet another white-staffed Memphis soul label, Goldwax. The brainchild of former honky-tonk guitarist Quinton Claunch, Goldwax recorded sublime country-soul with O.B. McClinton – who was very country indeed on songs like "The day the world cried" – and James Carr, a deeply troubled spirit who seemed to capture effortlessly on his recordings the moods of utter desolation and rapture which Otis Redding sweated buckets to evoke. Carr's hits included Claunch's own upbeat "Love attack" and arguably the most spine-tingling and guilt-ridden of all soul's many visits to "The dark end of the street".

There were many other white musicians and songwriters who lent their talents to the making of southern soul, among them Marlin Green, Charlie Freeman, Eddie Hinton and Donnie Fritts. There were also several other important white producers who helped to frame the performances of soul's vocalists and showcase their formidable emotional power. Louisianan Shelby Singleton, for example, was an ex-promotion man for Mercury Records with a background in country music. Singleton owned the Nashville-based SSS

International and its multiple affiliates, most notably Silver Fox, which was run by white Texan Lelan Rogers and was home to the highly countrified soul of Big Al Downing and Reuben Bell. Singleton himself produced some of the greatest of all country-soul sides for New Orleans' Johnny Adams, "the tan canary", whose soaring vocal technique was well served on cuts like "Reconsider me" and "In a moment of weakness".

Then there was Quin Ivy, a white sharecropper's son from Oxford, Mississippi who produced Percy Sledge's definitive southern country-soul record "When a man loves a woman", again with an all-white band, at his Norala studio in Muscle Shoals. And finally, for this list at least, there was John R. Richbourg, the revered veteran white r&b deejay from WLAC-Nashville. In the 1950s, Richbourg had briefly owned his own label, Rich. In the early 1960s, he had produced a couple of successful soul sides by Roscoe Shelton, most memorably the tortured "Strain on my heart", for the Sims label. In 1965, however, John R. began to produce black acts regularly for Sound Stage 7 (SS7), a new country-soul label founded by white North Carolinian Fred Foster, who had once worked for ABC-Paramount before founding the pop-oriented independent Monument.

Roscoe Shelton remained one of Richbourg's star turns on SS7. The Nashville-born gospel refugee had grown up listening to Uncle Dave Macon and the Grand Old Opry on his grandfather's crystal radio set, as well as to John R. and WLAC's gospel and r&b fare. "I've had a country flavor all my life, although it wasn't because I tried to", Shelton conceded, recognizing the inevitable interplay of multiple secular and sacred, black and white, musical influences in his own dramatic, but at its best strangely intimate and tender, singing style.[5]

Until 1970, when Richbourg assembled an all-white studio band for SS7, most of the label's output was recorded at Stax or Fame. Richbourg and Shelton worked with Dan Penn at Muscle Shoals on the grandiose "There's a heartbreak somewhere". "That was all white musicians", Shelton remembered. "There wasn't a black musician in the studio". Aside from Shelton, some of John R.'s finest work was with the highly successful Joe Simon and the lesser known Sam Baker, whose "Sometimes you have to cry" was one of those angst-ridden country-soul songs which shredded nerve ends and seared itself forever into the memory. Recorded at Stax, "Sometimes you have to cry", as Barney Hoskyns has pointed out, "exemplifies the country-soul cross breed: written by the black Allen Orange from New Orleans, arranged by white country veteran Cliff Parman from Nashville, played by blacks and whites from Memphis".[6]

Aside from some of William Bell's early work and Otis Redding's occasional expeditions into country-soul borderlands on songs like "These arms of mine", the sound at Stax in the 1960s was generally fatter, funkier, and, notwithstanding black songwriter-producer David Porter's admiration for

Hank Williams, less obviously country-influenced than elsewhere in the South. Nevertheless, whites still played major roles in the writing and performing of Stax soul until the late 1960s.

Booker T. and the MGs, the organ-bass-drums-guitar group which laid the musical foundations for most Stax recordings, was an integrated group. Roscoe Shelton, who recorded his SS7 release "I know your heart has been broken" in Memphis, recalled: "One thing I liked about Stax, it was totally integrated". This referred not just to the race of the musicians, but also to the dynamic combination and collisions of black and white styles and sensibilities. "There was always that little something that they always put in there . . . I found it was the mixture between the horns and the guitar. Steve Cropper had the guitar". That guitar, never entirely purged of the country inflections Cropper picked up as a farm boy in Missouri, helped to define every song he ever picked on. Like Chips Moman and Dan Penn, Cropper also emerged as a fine producer of both blistering uptempo soul struts and melancholic ballads, and as an excellent soul songwriter, collaborating on material for the likes of Carla Thomas and Otis Redding.[7]

The crucial point in all of this is that southern whites, and the musical traditions of which they were the notional custodians, were indispensable, rather than incidental, to the development of distinctively southern soul styles which were often genuinely, proudly biracial in conception and execution. "Our rhythm'n'blues", Dan Penn told Barney Hoskyns, "was about black and white people intermingled". In a suggestive symbolic inversion of the region's traditional racial hierarchy, the white Alabamian also noted that "blacks did the foreground and the whites did the background. I mean you got your country in there, you can't turn it, but the black singer made it go rhythm'n'blues". This was a blend Joe Tex credited for his own success: "I used the same formula every time – half soul musicians, half country musicians". David Porter emphasized the same combination of influences when describing his work at Stax with collaborator Isaac Hayes. "It's a mixture of people giving their ideas . . . and moulding them into an individuality. Hayes and I even study country-and-western tunes because we have discovered some of the greatest lyrics in the world come from there".[8]

It is important to take time to consider the precise implications of recasting 1960s country-soul as a biracial phenomenon. First, it is worth stressing that not all soul, not even in the South, flowed from such an integrated community of musicians, writers and producers, or utilized country components in the way that recordings by Joe Tex, Percy Sledge, Bettye Swann and their ilk so obviously did. Second, none of what has been said about the interracialism of personnel and techniques at certain southern labels should obscure the fact that power relationships within the recording and broadcasting industries in the South were still defined along essentially racial lines. Moreover, apart from Jim Stewart's sister Estelle Axton, who was an early partner at Stax, there does not appear to have been a single woman of

Joe Tex and his manager/producer Buddy Killen made many fine country-soul records in the 1960s and 1970s.

either race in a position of executive power in southern soul. In the main, black musicians, like many of their white colleagues, worked for – albeit more often *alongside* than in previous generations – white male bosses as salaried employees, often paid at meagre hourly union rates for performances which sometimes earned millions of dollars.

Certainly, the intention here is not to arouse misplaced nostalgia for some lost "golden age" of southern racial harmony, built four square beats to the bar upon musical miscegenation. As Tony Russell has rightly noted, the black and white curators of historically fluid and promiscuous southern musical traditions – from Jimmie Rodgers, Bob Wills and Hank Williams on the white side, to DeFord Bailey, Tommy Johnson and Ray Charles on the black – were "not purists, but eclectics". They had been stealing and trading ideas and techniques across racial lines for centuries without ever seriously challenging the established racial order of their region, even as they deepened and enriched its, and ultimately America's, cultural complexity.[9]

Above all, this emphasis on country-soul's mulatto credentials should not detract from its unique relationship to those sections of the black community, North as well as South, who enjoyed it. As Paul Gilroy has warned, the urge to challenge the claim that all "authentic" black music has some kind of immutable, "fixed" black essence – usually held to be undetectable by non-blacks – which has somehow been transmitted across the centuries from the heart of an idealized African past, miraculously unaffected by its multiple encounters with other historical and cultural currents, can too easily lead "towards a casual and arrogant deconstruction of blackness".[10]

Instead of operating within the restrictive boundaries of a sterile debate about "authenticity" and "inauthenticity", Gilroy has urged critics to explore the terrain between, on one hand, crude racial essentialism and, on the other hand, the "anti-essentialism" which would reduce the particularities of black experience and culture to a wholly contingent aspect of America's wider multi-culturalism. Southern country-soul provides an excellent opportunity to slipstream Gilroy into those contested waters, with their raging cross-cultural currents, where black life and consciousness in America have always been situated. Country-soul exhibited in particularly dramatic form the essential hybridity of all black American musical culture, which has constantly transformed and reinvigorated itself in the context of multiple external, as in notionally "non-black", influences, while retaining deep roots in its own distinctive traditions.[11]

These deep roots obviously need to be accorded the same respect as the bright new shoots of syncretic innovation. If many southern soul songs were lyrically and musically structured like country ballads and were written and played by white, as well as black, musicians, the style was nonetheless suffused with the rhythmic urgency and compelling call and response strategies of gospel, and always dominated by the interpretive flexibility and emotional integrity of black sacred music. Moreover, the ways in which black audiences heard and interpreted the music were different from the ways in which white fans enjoyed it. The racial politics and social meanings of all soul music, southern or northern, country or urban, Stax or Motown, depended not just on the circumstances of its production but also on the manner of its consumption by its various audiences. Black listeners certainly brought racially specific agendas, memories and sensibilities to the music, along with various gender, class and purely personal ones. They invested their music with special significances appropriate to their individual and collective circumstances at a particular historical moment.

Nevertheless, the fact remains that southern country-soul brought together black and white musicians and combined three great musical traditions – country, gospel, and Rhythm and Blues – in a sound which at the point of production was as *southern* as it was black or white. This confluence of musical streams offered a potent symbol for the erosion of barriers which had traditionally worked to try to keep those musics and their practitioners apart. And that was a cultural cognate of what the freedom struggle, in its broadest and most radical sense, was primarily about. It was about erasing, legally and mentally – and for both races – the stigma and discrimination associated with being black in America. This was not to be achieved by abandoning a distinctively African-American identity and culture, but by trying to create an America which finally respected all, and even openly, rather than covertly or guiltily, embraced some of those distinctively "black" characteristics as crucial to the construction of its own multivalent identity.

Rhythm and Blues: a bridge over troubled racial waters?

During the 1960s, many blacks within the industry and beyond it continued to see southern soul as both an occasion and a mechanism for promoting greater racial tolerance, respect and understanding. Al Bell, the black Stax songwriter, executive and later president, clearly believed that the label's biracialism carried great symbolic significance, even into the heart of the black power era:

> when you look at our company, you see a combine which has been integrated, basically, since its inception – *this in Memphis*. I'm very proud of this and think that because of this we should be considered a model for other businesses – not just the record business, but *any* businesses that doubt that black and white people can work together . . .

Solomon Burke had earlier offered a more danceable version of the same sentiments on "Everybody needs somebody to love". "There's a song that I sing, and I believe if everybody was to sing this song, it would save the whole world", Burke preached. In particular, Burke believed that his own brand of country-soul, which got him "a lot of bookings in the Deep South" including an unwelcome one before an audience of enthusiastic Alabama klansmen – "bridged a lot of waters".[12]

To a certain extent, such optimism appeared justified by the absence of the sort of explicitly racist hostility towards soul which had characterized white opposition to black r&b and rock and roll in the late 1950s. By 1966, those, like Rev. David Noebel of Tulsa, who still fulminated against the communist plot to destroy America through black and black-derived musics, cut rather absurd and lonely figures. Noebel sounded as if he had stumbled across an old Ace Carter speech when he declared that the roots of rock were in the "heart of Africa, where it was used to incite warriors to such frenzy that by night fall neighbours were cooked in carnage pots! The music is a designed reversion to savagery!"[13]

This is not to deny that soul singers were often still snubbed, exploited, denounced or victimized purely on account of their colour. There are numerous horror stories of encounters with racism on the road, particularly in the South where the *de facto* segregation of motels, restaurants and service stations continued to make touring a logistical and psychological nightmare long after the 1964 Civil Rights Act had supposedly outlawed such practices. Gladys Knight recalled that "when we played the South, we had to get used to the fact that sometimes we'd have to give one show for white audiences and another for black. And we were good enough to perform in some club, but not good enough to stay there for the night, or even shower there". Marvin Gaye remembered how "sometimes there weren't even segregated accommodations for us. We had nothing except the back seat of the car or the cold, hard ground".[14]

To discomfort and indignity were sometimes added terror and violence. If whites saw "a car going down the street with out-of-state tags, they'd assume that you were a freedom rider, or something of that nature", recalled Roscoe Shelton, who once had to hide under his car to escape klansmen just north of Sardis in Mississippi. Shelton was forever "being harassed and stopped and things of that nature. Getting speeding tickets unnecessarily". Mary Wilson of the Supremes and Martha Reeves of the Vandellas both remembered whites shooting at the Motown tour bus as it pulled out of Birmingham after an interracial concert in late 1962 had desegregated the local ballpark. Solomon Burke was with Sam Cooke in Shreveport, Louisiana when local white police picked them up for seeking service in a segregated restaurant next to their motel. The policemen took the singers to the local fire station, forced them to strip naked and made them perform their greatest hits before letting them go.[15]

Unlike in the 1950s, however, such incidents, although indicative of the persistence of racism among elements of the southern white community, did not form part of a concerted effort to rid American stages, jukeboxes, record shops and airwaves of black music. Indeed, by the mid 1960s the permanent place of black artists among young America's favourite performers was generally accepted, even in the heart of Dixie. It was eventually even accepted at the University of Alabama at Tuscaloosa where, in the summer of 1963, segregationist icon Governor George Wallace made his celebrated stand at the schoolhouse door in a failed bid to prevent the court-ordered admission of two black students, Vivian Malone and James Hood. The story of the University of Alabama's belated and grudging acceptance of its students' interest in Rhythm and Blues provides a fascinating glimpse into generational cleavages and cultural tensions in the South during the tortuous transition from uneven but powerful resistance to reluctant and prevaricating compliance with desegregation.[16]

In May 1962, while the university's administration was processing – a euphemism for stalling – Hood's and Malone's applications, the campus Cotillion Club polled the all-white student body to see which entertainers it would most like to have perform at Tuscaloosa. The questionnaire listed a selection of possible candidates under five headings: big bands, comedians, female vocalists, male vocalists, and vocal groups. No black entertainers were posted as options, but the questionnaire did include two final questions which hinted at a growing student interest in having black artists visit Tuscaloosa: "Would you favor Negro entertainers on this campus?", and "Would you favor a complete Rock and Roll show?"[17]

On 17 May, the eighth anniversary of *Brown*, the results of the poll were reported in the university newspaper, the *Crimson-White*. In the male vocalist category, the un-nominated Ray Charles had won by an "overwhelming majority with a write-in vote". James Brooks, the president of the Cotillion Club, also revealed that "of 1789 students who voted . . . a surprising number were in favor of Negro entertainers". Surprised he may have been, but bound by the verdict of campus democracy Brooks wrote to Charles, then visited him in Chicago, and apparently secured the singer's agreement to play the date – segregated though it was certain to be. In late September, however, the scheduled performance was abruptly cancelled, officially due to the "excessive costs in arranging the show".[18]

In fact, the executive committee of the university's Board of Trustees had decided at a meeting on 16 August that to bring Charles onto campus was "unwise at present time", just as Governor Wallace and the state government, which controlled much of the university's funding, were preparing for a final stand against federally imposed integration. One of the governor's chief advisors during the Tuscaloosa crisis, and on much else relating to the preservation of white supremacy in the state, was the lawyer Seymore Trammell, who managed to win the hotly contested title of "meanest son of a bitch in the Wallace administration" while still doing a decent job as manager of the black Harmony Jubilee Quartet gospel group. The university's administrative vice-president J. Jefferson Bennett was charged with explaining the executive committee's reasoning to Brooks. Although Brooks insisted on discussing the issue with university president Frank Rose – himself under intense pressure from state officials to hold the line on desegregation – he was persuaded that there would be no reconsideration. "Fine and reasonable fellow" that he was according to Bennett, Brooks dutifully backed the official story.[19]

A little over two years later, in December 1964, with a token handful of black students now precariously installed, the university administration again stymied the Cotillion Club's plans to bring black entertainers to Tuscaloosa. It cancelled a show by Louis Armstrong scheduled for the following February, and made it clear that Ray Charles, again the students' first choice, was still not welcome. Dean of Men John Blackburn gamely tried to insist that this was "not a decision against Negro entertainment, but taking in consideration all problems relative to this performance we thought it unwise at this time". With the South squirming to evade the full consequences of the recent Civil Rights Act, the administration was reluctant to sanction black performers on a campus which many still saw as a symbol of white supremacy, to be redeemed from the horrors of integration, not abandoned to black students and entertainers.[20]

One of the ironies of this situation was that Louis Armstrong had actually played the university with no problems in 1955, prior to Montgomery, the Autherine Lucy riots, and the subsequent mobilization of Alabama white resistance. Another irony was that while the administration tried desperately to stem the flow of black music onto the campus by barring Armstrong and Charles, the *Crimson-White* noted that "Most fraternities sponsor between 8 and 10 parties each year with Negro bands", and had been doing so for years. The fact is that the desegregation of the university's popular music had taken place long before black students were admitted, and long before the administration finally felt it safe to welcome black entertainers officially onto campus.[21]

Indeed, while the Tuscaloosa student body undoubtedly contained its share of committed segregationists, and campus racism hardly died with the admission of Malone and Hood, a majority of white students appeared to accept the inevitability of integration much more readily than their elders. In February 1965, with the nearby Selma campaign rising in intensity, Gene Guerrero, chairman of the Southern Student Organizing Committee (SSOC), visited students and even a few faculty with a view to organizing a local branch. Although the initiative failed to produce a Tuscaloosa SSOC chapter at this time, Guerrero reported that he was surprised to find "many who are concerned about Alabama and anxious to make some effort". By the end of 1965, even the Tuscaloosa administration had begun to move, like most of its white students slowly and none-too-surely, to deal with the realities of a new post-Jim Crow South. Late that year the Cotillion Club successfully brought Johnny Mathis and trumpeter Al Hirt to Tuscaloosa. In 1966, students and administrators alike officially welcomed James Brown and the sounds of black soul to the campus.[22]

The slow administrative thaw at Tuscaloosa was by no means unique, but during the decade or so after *Brown* there was quite a range of official and informal, administrative and student, responses to the appearance of black performers on white southern campuses, and to the growing popularity of various black and black-derived musics on student turntables and radios. At the somewhat elitist University of Virginia, for example, there was strong support for jazz and initially signs of a rather disdainful attitude towards the more proletarian rock and roll on Grounds. In April 1956, the student newspaper, the *Cavalier Daily*, incorporated a hostile, racially inscribed piece from the *Connecticut Campus Daily* into an editorial mocking the new music, "once known by the somber title of 'rhythm and blues'", as "a form of tribal chanting" characterized by "mystic lyrics mumbled in howling fashion by groups of aborigine-inspired singers".[23]

In general, however, black musicians of every stripe were welcome at Virginia, where the political and racial climate was palpably different from that at Tuscaloosa. At Virginia there was a thin but tenacious strain of progressive racial politics, traceable to Palmer Weber's efforts to rally students, faculty and Charlottesville's black community behind an unsuccessful campaign to win Alice Jackson entry to the university's graduate school in the mid 1930s. Although it was not until 1968 that the first black undergraduates were admitted to the College proper, Mr Jefferson's university had technically desegregated in 1950, when Gregory Swanson enrolled in the law school. By the early 1960s there was already a handful of black students enrolled in Virginia's professional, engineering and graduate schools.[24]

Meagre and tentative though they were, these progressive tendencies gave Virginia its relatively moderate, if still paternalistic racial cast. This was reflected in the official tolerance of black performers on Grounds, even at the height of Massive Resistance when black jazzmen like Dizzy Gillespie, Erroll Garner, Bud Powell and Count Basie, and folk stars like Josh White, Odetta and Miriam Makeba visited freely. Indeed, despite Virginia senator Harry Byrd's pre-eminence in the Massive Resistance movement he had named, and the fact that Prince Edward County and even Charlottesville itself actually closed their public schools rather than see them desegregated, the state's flagship university had not even balked when an integrated show featuring Sonny Rollins, Dave Brubeck and Maynard Ferguson came to the Grounds in October 1958. Such tolerance was highly unusual after 1956, since, even where black performers were officially allowed onto segregated southern campuses to perform, such on-stage integration usually remained taboo. The University of Georgia, for example, cancelled a Brubeck show in March 1959 because his bass player, Eugene Wright, was black, while in New Orleans in 1961, Tulane banned Dizzy Gillespie because his Argentinian pianist, Lalo Schiffren, was white.[25]

At Virginia, however, even the terror of Tuscaloosa, Ray Charles, was allowed to appear without a problem in November 1964, followed a few days later by Bo Diddley. By the time Chuck Berry, Martha and the Vandellas, Shirley Ellis and Jimmy Reed performed in Charlottesville in 1965 there was already a strong Students for Social Action group on campus, which organized anti-Vietnam protests and a rain-soaked march across Jefferson's manicured lawn in support of the Selma protests. Shortly afterwards an important chapter of SSOC appeared to co-ordinate growing student activism. Throughout the decade Rhythm and Blues artists were a regular attraction at both official university functions and fraternity parties.[26]

Elsewhere, at Vanderbilt, Fats Domino, Clyde McPhatter, Count Basie and Bo Diddley were among the black acts who had "performed without restriction or incident" for all-white student audiences in the late 1950s. Perhaps influenced by the nearby black colleges and seminaries which spawned Nashville's prototype sit-in movement and which later provided some of SNCC's most influential early members, Vanderbilt students, some of whom participated in those sit-ins, were beginning to contemplate the possible relationship between white responses to black music and broader white racial attitudes. A *Vanderbilt Hustler* editorial in February 1958, for

Despite segregation, in the 1950s and early 1960s black artists like Ike Turner
were regular performers on southern white campuses. Here he is shown
(far right) with fellow musicians at a fraternity party at the University of
Virginia in April 1962.

instance, drew an explicit comparison between deejays who burned rock
and roll records and the plight "of the bus boycotters vs. the lynchers, et
al.". A year later, the *Hustler*, noting that black political leaders were never
invited to Vanderbilt, pondered whether the administration's "liberal policy
toward Negro entertainers is, at best, a stop gap method". A means to
present an acceptable, progressive front on racial matters, without confronting the deeper issues of wholesale desegregation or the lack of equal
black opportunities, not least in being unable to attend prestigious private
colleges like Vanderbilt.[27]

The editorials in the *Vanderbilt Hustler* raised questions about the nature
of white responses to black music and musicians which are at the very heart
of this book. Did the widespread white acceptance and often stone-crazed

passion for Rhythm and Blues musics in the 1950s and 1960s really reflect, or even to some extent shape, new racial attitudes and thus help to facilitate the successes of the early civil rights movement? Or did, perhaps, this enthusiasm for black music actually reflect, reinforce and extend traditional white responses to blacks and their culture, thereby helping to define the limits of racial communication, progress and reform? Since history seldom operates in accordance with such neat, binary oppositions, it should come as no surprise to find that there were elements of truth in both these formulations.

What has been stressed so far is the fact that many blacks, their white allies, and even their white opponents, genuinely believed that the desegregation of popular music culture was terminally eroding traditional barriers between the races. For those who welcomed such developments, shared tastes in music and dance were simultaneously a cause and a symptom of racial enlightenment and progress. This is an important point to make since hindsight, usually such a boon to historians, has largely obscured it. Because we "know" that white racism and black disadvantage have persisted despite the fact that whites continue to consume and enjoy large quantities of black music, it is easy to deny there was ever a time when such patterns of consumption were held to reflect or herald real improvements in white racial attitudes and black circumstances. Yet, to ignore this dimension – and it was but one dimension – of black thought, is to root black consciousness for all time in the disillusionment of the post-civil rights era and neglect its development and rather different configuration before the later 1960s.

So what, precisely, did blacks and their allies invest in their defiantly optimistic take on white admiration for black music in the decade or so after *Brown*? Richard King has argued that at the heart of the philosophy of nonviolent direct action and the faith in *satyagraha*, or soul-force, central to the early Movement was the belief in a common bond of humanity which united all God's children and gave them "the potential to transcend boundaries of race, class, gender and culture in speaking to and understanding others". The key to racial progress was to find a way to make whites recognize this basic human bond with blacks. Once this was done, whites would surely rally to end further inhumane treatment of their fellow – black – men and women. Like the nonviolent direct action protests which dramatized the plight of southern blacks and the obscenity of racial oppression, the mass popular appeal of black music and dance appeared to offer a means to establish "mutual recognition", even empathy, across racial lines.[28]

Although hard evidence is scarce, there were doubtless genuine examples of this sort of conversion experience; of racial enlightenment wrought by the sheer power of black music. In the early 1960s, journalist Dave Marsh had Smokey Robinson to thank for just such a miraculous experience. Marsh grew up in Pontiac, Michigan. He accepted as natural local white resistance to attempts by upwardly mobile blacks to move into all-white neighbourhoods and the racial fears which motivated it. Then, in 1964, he heard "You really got a hold on me" for the first time. Marsh recalled that "The depth of feeling in that Miracles record, which could have been purchased for 69c at any K-Mart, overthrew the premise of racism, which was that blacks were not as human as we, that they could not feel – much less express their feelings – as deeply as we did".[29]

This recognition of a shared humanity was precisely what Martin Luther King and others hoped would compel whites to recognize the legitimacy of the black freedom struggle. Indeed, as late as 1967, by which time black faith in such interracial communication and the basic receptiveness of whites to any form of moral-suasion was fading fast, King still maintained that soul music and dance could prepare the ground for improved race relations. "In a real sense", he told the black deejays gathered in Atlanta for the annual NATRA convention, "you have paved the way for social and political change by creating a powerful, cultural bridge between black and white. School integration is much easier now that they share a common music, a common language, and enjoy the same dances. You introduced youth to that music and created a language of soul and promoted the dances which now sweep across race, class and nation".[30]

Entertaining racism: a brief history of racial stereotyping

Despite Martin Luther King's optimism, however, there was no simple or necessary congruency between white passion for black music and dance, and positive changes in white racial attitudes more generally. Historically, whites had always been capable of admiring black culture and acknowledging the skill, even genius, of individual blacks in certain areas of endeavour – most notably "entertainment" and "performance" in their broadest sense – without necessarily conceding the full humanity of blacks as a race, let alone supporting their bid for genuine equality of opportunity in America.

"Even the diehard segregationalists loved the black music", recalled Wolf Stephenson, a student at the University of Mississippi who later worked for another Ole Miss alumnus, Tommy Crouch, at the Malaco label responsible for light funk classics like Jean Knight's "Mr Big Stuff", King Floyd's "Groove me", and Dorothy Moore's magisterial country-soul "Misty blue". Stephenson was adamant that for most of his peers enthusiasm for Rhythm and Blues did not necessarily reflect any deeper changes of racial attitude. "It was like two worlds – the students danced to the music but the moment the musicians left the stage they would have nothing to do with them".[31]

Roscoe Shelton, who also played Ole Miss on his rounds of the segregated white college circuit in the early-to-mid 1960s, was rather more positive about the significance of his reception by young white students. Shelton felt that, removed from the immediate influence of their more intractable parents, the youngsters "really loved it . . . I think music played a big part in pulling the races together". Yet even Shelton, a remarkably placid man without apparent malice towards anyone, has bitter tales to tell of whites who played in bands with him, but who would not fraternize off-stage because of his race. Drawn together across racial lines by love of the same music, "the moment the show was over, they'd disappear".[32]

This sort of bifurcation within white racial consciousness has a long and complex lineage. The simultaneous lure and loathing of blacks and their culture – or at least of white imaginings of black culture – represented a not-so-simple paradox central to the operation of white racism as a colour-coded system of thought and action in America. Indeed, it was not only crucial to the construction of white concepts of racial "otherness", but was also central to the related historical process of defining "whiteness" as a discrete racial category to which many social, economic, psychological and status privileges adhered.[33]

It is worth taking a moment to consider, albeit with indecent haste, the origins and development of these white conceptions of what blackness and whiteness were all about. Historically, white racial attitudes had their roots in antiquity. In their modern form, however, they were linked to the European experience of expansion and colonialization which gathered momentum in the sixteenth and seventeenth centuries. For the most part, Africans were seen as barbaric heathens by these adventurers and their private and imperial sponsors. They were somehow less than human and thus ripe for various forms of exploitation which included plundering the natural resources of their homelands, subjegating them to colonial or client rule, and inducting millions into New World slavery. Many of those transplanted Africans laboured in North America, where most Euro-American settlers viewed them at a dubious best as exotic novelties, and at worst as an inferior sub-species, doomed to perpetual servitude and ignorance, if not extinction.[34]

And yet, from their first encounters with peoples of African descent, there was a certain ambiguity in the responses of white Americans. For example, whites often guiltily admired blacks for their supposed proximity to a shamefully enticing state of nature and condescendingly conceded to them a childlike innocence and deep spirituality. Even if such perceptions were often just a roll of the eyeballs away from images of blacks as superstitious savages, they betrayed a white capacity to view blacks as attractive, even enviable, humankind. Moreover, some whites, particularly from the lower orders, acknowledged common social and economic interests with both free and slave blacks, joining with them in activities as diverse as slave uprisings in Virginia and New York, and a wide array of popular festivals throughout the colonies and the young republic. In sum, although generally hostile to blacks, white racial ideas before 1800 were still somewhat fluid, spilling messily in many different, sometimes quite contradictory directions.

233

Certainly the full social implications of racial differences were yet to be fixed firmly in either American law or lore.[35]

As historians Reginald Horsman, David Roediger and Alexander Saxton have explained, white attitudes towards blacks, and prevailing ideas of what racial distinctions actually meant in American life, became much more sharply defined with the rapid industrialization and territorial expansion of the United States in the first half of the nineteenth century. As white workers, particularly in the North, increasingly came under the purview of industrial labour discipline, many felt robbed of whatever autonomy they had once enjoyed as relatively independent farmers, craftsmen and artisans. They dreaded a slide into wage dependency which not only reduced their control over the conditions of their working lives and denied them a certain degree of economic power, but which was also an affront to the powerful republican ideals of an independent, propertied male citizenry that had taken root in the revolutionary period.[36]

To compensate for this loss of status, autonomy and power, white workers strove to attach ever more social, psychological and economic significance to the distinction between their position as free white wage labourers, and the position of most blacks as unfree slave labourers. This heightened self-consciousness of what it meant to be white and free was largely shaped in negative opposition to congealing ideas of what it meant to be black and enslaved. In fact, it required whites to construct much more fully realized, relatively fixed but still complex, images of blacks and their characteristics against which to posit the distinctive qualities of whiteness and ultimately their own superiority.

Under these pressures, whites increasingly imagined and invoked blacks as, in Roediger's evocative phrase, "'other' – as embodying the preindustrial, erotic, careless style of life the white worker hated and longed for". Indeed, as white male workers proudly – if by no means always accurately – presented themselves as reliable, hard-working, thrifty, family-oriented bread-winners, they helped to propagate powerful countervailing visions of blacks as indolent, over-sexed, profligate and unreliable. They were actively assisted in this project by America's economic, social and political elites, who, irre-spective of their own links to older strains of Euro-American racial prejudice, stood to gain much from exacerbating racial divisions within the ranks of labour. After all, it was a lot cheaper to pay off white workers in the scrip of racial solidarity, pride and privilege than to provide them with higher wages, better conditions, or more control over their productive lives. It was also a means to minimize any possibility of working-class solidarity coalescing across racial lines.[37]

The grim irony in all of this celebration of whiteness and white labour was that most black workers, in freedom as in slavery, actually worked longer and more gruelling hours than their white counterparts and were invariably less well-rewarded. But, then, perhaps one of the crucial points in this brief historical digression is that white racial beliefs have seldom had much to do with the realities of black character, culture or experience. Rather, they have revolved around two major, overlapping white imperatives which have transcended distinctions of class, gender, region and era. The first has been the need to assert and protect the social, psychological and economic privileges associated with whiteness in America. The second has been what Jolande Jacobi has described as the white tendency "to project onto the Negro the primitive drives, the archaic powers, the uncontrolled instincts that they do not want to admit in themselves". Paradoxically, this last impulse virtually ensured that wide-eyed admiration and green-eyed envy of blacks and their imagined lifestyles became as much features of white racial thought as the most vicious hatred and bigotry.[38]

American popular culture has always provided an important arena in which white ideas about race and racial identities have been explored, tested and verified. The minstrel shows which began in the 1830s and endured to the turn of the century were a good example. With their broad blackface burlesques of black life, the shows proudly affirmed the social, moral and cultural superiority of whiteness; indeed, they helped to define its key social and cultural components for the American masses by opposing them to the crude, uncivilized antics of the "blacks" on stage. At the same time, however, the shows also allowed whites to partake vicariously in some of the forbidden pleasures they routinely projected onto the uninhibited, sensual and perpetually preindustrial world of blacks.[39]

The post-Civil War "coon-songs" of Stephen Foster and other white songwriters operated in a similar way, becoming a beloved staple of vaudeville, latterday minstrel shows, and even early talking pictures like Al Jolson's *The Jazz Singer*. Usually these songs presented broad caricatures of docile, lazy, simple and sometimes shiftless blacks which accorded easily with what had become deeply entrenched white stereotypes. Yet they also incorporated more ambiguous images of black expressivity and stylishness which betrayed a genuine, if still clichéd, white admiration for black talents in matters leisured and sensual. In these "coon-songs", such "typical" black traits could again be simultaneously enjoyed, ridiculed and condemned by whites.[40]

Some successful "coon-songs" were actually composed by black songwriters. Bob Cole and J. Rosamund Johnson's hits like "Chicken, you can't roost too high for me" formed part of a long tradition in which blacks have taken white racial stereotypes – in this case of the insatiable black appetite for chicken – and deployed them for their own economic advantage, and even for the enjoyment of other blacks who have been perfectly able to distinguish between accurate characterizations and broad lampoons of black lives. A somewhat similar phenomenon occurred with the widespread black enthusiasm for the radio show *Amos 'n' Andy*. The show, which began in the 1920s, featured two black-voiced white comedians, Charles Correll and Freeman Gosden, as credulous southern black innocents abroad in Chicago.

Although its peak years were between the World Wars, *Amos'n'Andy* remained on the radio in some form until the dawn of the 1960s, and even spawned a short-lived television series with a black cast in the early 1950s.[41]

From the sly double-dealing and pomposity of Kingfish, leader of the local black lodge (The Mystic Knights of the Sea), to the avarice and shrewishness of his domineering wife Sapphire; and from Andy's sloth, selfishness and misplaced sense of self-importance, to Amos' almost supernatural stoicism, humility and honesty, *Amos'n'Andy* was always at one level an assemblage of stock black stereotypes. However, as the show's historian Melvin Patrick Ely has noted, *Amos'n'Andy* also harboured more generous and positive images of blacks which won the sympathy of its white and many black listeners. Perhaps even more telling, Ely explains how blacks themselves were often able to enjoy even the most exaggerated and racist caricatures of archetypal figures they recognized only too well from black life. Again, it was a black laughter which depended on a clear understanding of where reality and fabrication, truth and comic distortion began and ended. It was also a laughter which sparked lively debate among blacks about whether they should be enjoying such portrayals at all, lest they encourage whites in the mistaken belief that these were accurate, unproblematic depictions of the black community, its values and aspirations.[42]

The powerful and influential racist renderings of black characters in Thomas Dixon's hugely successful novels, and later in D.W. Griffith's 1915 film version of Dixon's *The Clansman* (retitled *Birth of a Nation*) raised no such dilemmas and were roundly condemned by most blacks. As eugenics and various forms of quasi-scientific racism exerted an increasingly pernicious influence on much American racial thought, these entertainments helped to popularize the white idea that without the benevolent control of slavery blacks were rapidly degenerating into a state of barbarism and rapine lust. Just as America was picking up the white man's burden by flexing its imperial muscles against non-white peoples in the Pacific and Caribbean, as well as debating and enacting anti-immigration laws directed against non-WASPs, Dixon and Griffith encouraged whites to mobilize against the darkest of all domestic threats to white civilization by joining the Ku Klux Klan. More particularly, white men were called upon to defend the idealized white woman, in whom virtue, purity and the future of the race resided, against defilement by the sexually insatiable black beast.[43]

By the late nineteenth and early twentieth centuries, then, most American whites came to "know" blacks, and "understand" their own relationship to them, less through direct observation or the sort of hierarchical but nonetheless personal contacts which had characterized slavery, than through minstrel shows, "coon-songs", popular literature, radio shows like *Amos'n' Andy* and movies. These various forms of popular culture rarely slipped the yoke of stereotype, but helped to encode and perpetuate the conventional range of white responses to blackness: from intrigue and admiration, through paternalism and condescension, to fear and brutal suppression.

Now, patience, gentle reader, all of this might seem one step, two steps, maybe even the whole hully-gully, removed from the immediate matter in hand, but there are a couple of important points here for understanding the relationship between white racial attitudes and white responses to Rhythm and Blues. The first point is that, since popular culture had long been a major conduit through which white Americans came to think they knew about blacks and their culture, the significances of white reactions to Rhythm and Blues need to be contextualized within this broader tradition. Put another way, what many whites learned or had confirmed about blacks through popular culture was pretty much the extent of what many whites thought they really "knew" about blacks.

The second point is that although sound recordings, movies, radio and television ultimately gave whites greater access to genuine black cultural forms – as opposed to black-face travesties and bare-faced lies – than at the turn of the century, whites brought to those encounters much the same racial values and socio-psychological needs they had always brought to the world of entertainment whenever race was involved or invoked. Although reinscribed to meet the demands of a modern, putatively more rational and informed world, many of the core white assumptions about blacks and their culture had changed remarkably little over the nearly four centuries that peoples of African descent had been in North America. Partly this was because the basic configuration of economic and political power which helped to define and sustain modern racism had changed rather more in style than substance during that time. Partly it was because over those centuries racism as a mode of prejudicial thought and discriminatory action had itself assumed a degree of autonomous power, enabling it to function, in the short term at least, in quasi-independence from the capitalist socio-political-economic system which nurtured it. That, to cannibalize Antonio Gramsci, is hegemony for you: it makes particular systems of thoughts, beliefs and values – no matter how grotesque – appear timeless and natural, and thus conceals their connection to the specific arrangements of social, economic and political power whose interests they serve.[44]

Same as it ever was: black music, white stereotypes

Moving rapidly from the cultural general to the musical particular, in the twentieth century Western racial thought has subsumed and permitted a wide range of possible responses to black music. Linking them all, however, has been something not too far from what Martha Bayles has described as "the tendency, in its foes and friends, to reduce Afro-American music to a crude caricature of dehumanized sex". In the 1920s, for example, the forces of moral decency in white America launched a major campaign against the new jazz craze and dance styles, voicing much the same objections as when their heirs denounced rock and roll music and dance 30 years later. Derived from the dark and debauched world of black culture, jazz was condemned for its unseemly passion and the physical frenzy it induced among its listeners, particularly on the dance floor. One critic held that "These moaning saxophones and the rest of the instruments with their broken, jerky rhythm make a purely sensuous appeal . . . jazz is the very foundation and essence of salacious dancing". Lurking behind these criticisms was the belief that jazz celebrated and encouraged the sort of dissolution and sexual licence which whites traditionally associated with blacks.[45]

On the other side of the jazz controversy, those whites who supported the music did so because they located precisely the same characteristics in the style as its critics, but applied a different gloss to them. For enthusiasts, jazz's black origins were also vital to its appeal. Young white devotees reified the dark inscrutable world of black culture and romanticized its alleged "primitivism"; its ease with leisure and apparently effortless style; its sensual, rather than mental priorities; its spontaneity, and, above all, its supposed lack of sexual inhibition. These black jazzy qualities were contrasted favourably with a mainstream culture which many found cold, overly intellectual, mechanistic and sexually repressed.[46]

A similar scenario unfolded after the Second World War with many of Norman Mailer's "White negroes"; those self-styled Beats and hipsters who adopted be-bop and, to a lesser extent, r&b, as a sonic symbol for their general alienation from mainstream, "white", cultural norms and societal expectations. White – and for that matter many black – bebop fans particularly idolized tragic geniuses like Charlie Parker and Bud Powell, who lived messy, self-destructive, but oh-so-wonderfully intense lives, forever dancing on the very edge of human experience and playing an urgent music which faithfully chronicled every monumental high and chasmic low. In the process, however, fans like Mailer tended to reduce black musicians and the complexities of black urban culture to nothing more than the unremittingly cool, hedonistic, darkly passionate stuff of their highly racialized imaginations.[47]

As jazz critic Nat Hentoff noted in a terse riposte to Mailer, those who glibly romanticized black jazz in this way usually remained blissfully unaware of, or were deeply uninterested in, "the depth of anxiety, desperation, and sheer physical discomfort which ghetto living imposes on all the poor, hip and square". Black activist-writer Lorraine Hansberry concurred, stressing that blacks actually did not find it in the least bit romantic to be outsiders, excluded from the main flow of American economic, social and educational opportunities, and denied the benefit of the basic civil rights enjoyed by whites. Blacks wanted an end to such marginalization, no matter that those bitter circumstances had helped to spawn a culture of phenomenal vitality and power. "Misery may be theatrical to the onlooker but it hurts him who is miserable", Hansberry wrote, echoing author Richard Wright's mordant contemplation of "the unconscious irony of those who felt that Negroes live so passionate existence. I saw what had been taken for our emotional strength was our negative confusions, our flights, our fears, our frenzy under pressure".[48]

Same as it ever was, in the early-to-mid 1950s, a new vanguard of young whites had become enthralled by a black music form. These youths self-consciously set themselves apart from their parents and peers through their peculiar musical allegiances. Many sought to escape the stifling workaday discipline of school, office, shop, field and factory by embracing sounds, dance steps and sartorial predilections which were mainly derived from the hip, partially hidden and potentially oppositional world of black culture.

Once more, while blacks continued to enjoy r&b and its dances as a celebration of their own heritage, identity and changing racial conscious-ness, young white fans used it primarily as a means to register dissent from certain aspects of their own, or rather their parents', culture. In the process, of course, they transformed it into a celebration of their own generational identity and sensibility. By 1956, as a whole generation of whites warmed to rock and roll as both symbol and soundtrack for its own leisured and limited social rebellion, white adults once more condemned the music for precisely the reasons their children loved it. It was loud, sexy, fetishistic about the material trappings of young lifestyles – cars, clothes, girls, boys, haircuts, television, music and dance – unmistakeably "black" in origin, and increasingly biracial in production and usage.

Ironically, by the turn of the 1950s, with black pop the ascendent strain in Rhythm and Blues, the unprecedented success of black artists with whites had rather devalued the music's currency as a measure of generational, class or peer independence. "It had gotten to the point where Mom nor Pop, neither one of them, was gonna stop you from listening", recalled Roscoe Shelton. To compensate, some whites began to cultivate an intense purism about precisely which sorts of black popular music were "authentic" and acceptable to them. Again, there was nothing especially new about this sort of purism, which had always offered a way for fargone devotees to distinguish themselves from more casual white fans of black music. In the early 1950s, for instance, Texans Buddy Holly and Bob Montgomery had quite deliberately ignored those r&b artists who were beginning to cross over with southern whites in favour of older blues artists with few white fans, and, for that matter, with declining appeal to most young blacks. "Blues to us was Muddy Waters, Little Walter, and Lightnin' Hopkins, and we didn't really think of the Drifters or the Clovers as being *blues* singers – because they *weren't*. They were pop artists as far as we were concerned", recalled Montgomery with tell-tale disdain.[49]

The blues revival of the 1960s saw an extension of this trend. A hard core of precious white fans and critics on both sides of the Atlantic tended to reject more commercially successful and, therefore, in their eyes inevitably "inauthentic" black pop and soul styles, in favour of artists who seemed suitably steeped in an older, purer, allegedly pre-commercial or sub-commercial Delta blues tradition. In 1965, British bluesologist Paul Oliver observed that even within the ranks of white blues lovers the "myth has developed of a scale of authenticity which relates to a singer's proximity to the country; a fallacious and unworthy argument which can do great harm to the recognition that many city artists rightly deserve". Robert Palmer has noted that many white British blues fans ignored the influential recordings Big Bill Broonzy had made with a small jazz'n'jump combo in Chicago, accepting him only when he adopted the solo "role of the folk-bluesman fresh from the cottonfields". Some aficionados were even horrified when Muddy Waters, in reality the quintessential electric Chicago bluesman, dared to plug in his guitar – a potent symbol of commercial and artistic sell-out among recalcitrant white blues fans, as well as among the folk purists who were distressed when Bob Dylan went electric. Waters was expected to pretend he still lived in backwoods Mississippi, patiently awaiting the arrival of power lines.[50]

Even as the freedom struggle made the plight of black Americans headline news, white love of Rhythm and Blues was still less likely to indicate support for that struggle than for certain practices, priorities and values which it was imagined were more common in black culture than white. Sometimes those imaginings were correct. Often they were not. But they were almost invariably arrived at in ignorance of, and often indifference to, the realities of black life. Moreover, as a diverse range of popular and influential social theorists, from Herbert Marcuse, Wilhelm Reich, and Norman O. Brown, to James Baldwin and Eldridge Cleaver, announced that mainstream "white" adult American culture was becoming ever more one-dimensional, regimented, creatively sterile and grimly impersonal, blacks were again hailed for being more in tune with their bodies and emotions. For many whites, blacks embodied the sensual, spontaneous, creative and sharing side of human nature with which they themselves were rapidly losing contact.

In a celebrated 1963 essay, *Commentary* editor Norman Podhoretz shared with the world the joyous news that he was "capable of aching with all my being when I watch a Negro couple on the dance floor, or a Negro playing baseball or basketball. They are on the kind of terms with their own bodies that I should like to be on with mine, and for that precious quality they seemed blessed to me". Podhoretz himself was clearly on very good terms with a white idealization of black athleticism, rhythm and grace which – without for one moment denying that black America has produced more than its share of sublimely gifted athletes or compelling dance music – was still highly selective and constructed around utterly conventional racial stereo-types. "Where *do* they put the old and the ugly, the fat and the scrawny?", Nat Hentoff mocked, comparing Podhoretz's mythologization of black culture with old MGM musicals crammed full of happy-go-lucky, all-singing, all-dancing, darkies.[51]

Even within the ranks of the Movement in the mid 1960s, black activists sometimes poked gentle, but deadly serious fun at the racial assumptions of the young white volunteers who joined them in the South. For all his deep love of music, Julian Bond was, by his own admission, tone deaf, possessed of a highly irregular – more charitable friends called it distinctive – sense of rhythm, and suddenly cursed with a surfeit of left feet whenever he got onto a dance floor. Bond's memo "How to be SNCCY" was a tongue-in-cheek guide to correct SNCC behaviour which spoofed white notions of universal black rhythm and grace. Having compiled a glossary of use-ful terms ("'What I think is . . .' means that you're about to say something you heard [Bob] Moses and [James] Forman say at lunch yesterday"), Bond described the "auxiliary habits" white volunteers should cultivate in order to become effective allies in the black freedom struggle. "One is dancing – extremely hard for some – and another is hand-clapping. A note to the wise: when in a mass meeting, watch some Negro staff member and try to make your hands come together *at the same time as his do*". Bond warned sternly, however, that "UNDER NO CIRCUMSTANCES SHOULD YOU WATCH JAMES FORMAN OR JULIAN BOND!"[52]

Same as it ever was, black culture in the years after *Brown* was habitually reduced to simple connotations of sexual freedom, sensual pleasure, and a sheer expressiveness which was apparently unmediated by mental process or moral conscience. "The first time I ever saw a guy put his hand down a girl's pants was at the Paramount", recalled one white fan of Chuck Berry when asked to explain his love of r&b. For two University of Virginia stud-ents, dancing to rock and roll music was simply a means for "young men . . . [to] release their excess libidinal energies".[53]

Bonnie Bramlett, a white r&b fan from Granite City, Illinois who later became one of Ike and Tina Turner's Ikettes, recalled sneaking "down to East St Louis to see the Kings of Rhythm at the Harlem Club . . . It was definitely the wrong neighborhood for white girls. But me and my friends were havin' a ball – sneakin' and smokin' and drinkin' and doin' damn near everything". Recognizing the insatiable hunger of whites like Bramlett for dramatic black enactments of sex and sleaze, Ike Turner later took time off from beating his wife with a shoetree to fashion their live revue into the high-stepping, short-skirted, tail-shaking epitome of white ideals of black female hyper-sexuality. While Ike, a marvellously gifted r&b guitarist-arranger, looked on like a proud pimp from the back of the stage, his ladies, Tina and her Ikettes, bumped and ground, sucked and licked their way through moves which sacrificed the genuine eroticism, wit and candour of much Rhythm and Blues on the altar of a crass, demeaning, if undeniably athletic and occasionally pruriently compelling form of sexual exhibitionism.[54]

Many whites struggled to differentiate between eroticism and obscenity in Rhythm and Blues because all black depictions of sexual matters, whether sensual or brutal, erotic or exploitative, seemed to confirm the notion that black lives were essentially governed by mighty, irrepressible sexual passions, or bodily demands of one sort or another. And, of course, what made this tendency to reify black sensuality and sexuality even more pronounced was the fact that black music was indeed often more emotionally charged and sexually frank, and certainly more corporeal, more directly linked to the physical needs of the dance and the body, than just about anything else available in American popular music. As Susan McClary has put it, in twentieth-century American culture, "African-Americans took over the making of images, the shaping of bodies and subjectivities through music".[55]

And so, in the 1950s and 1960s, it was to the sounds of Rhythm and Blues and its derivatives that many young whites began to reclaim, however awkwardly at times, some kind of intimacy and connection to their bodies and their expressive potential. It was a link which the physical and mental demands of modern life, especially the regimentation and monotony of many forms of industrial labour, white-collar office work, and jobs in retail had indeed threatened to erode. McClary oversimplifies the issue somewhat when she suggests that black music enabled white fans to "start experiencing their own bodies in terms of an African-American sensibility". Nevertheless, even Eldridge Cleaver believed that young whites' embrace of the "potent erotic rhythms" of r&b, even in the "diluted" form purveyed by the Beatles, allowed them to enjoy the sort of "communication between the listener's own Mind and Body" which was central to black culture.[56]

The argument here, then, is not that the exquisite sensuality, or forthright sexuality, or emotional intensity, or rhythmic potency of much Rhythm and Blues was any less real than has been traditionally claimed. Indeed, one should not lose sight of the fact that those same qualities attracted blacks to the music, too. Rather, it is to make two interrelated points about the peculiarly racialized ways in which whites responded to the music and those qualities.

The first point is that when whites detected and embraced these "typically" black characteristics in the Rhythm and Blues of the 1950s and 1960s, they rarely considered the huge price blacks paid for that formidable music. Whites seldom appreciated that black music and dance were part of a culture of survival and self-affirmation, the very intensity and brilliance of which was rendered absolutely necessary by the myriad abuses and indignities inflicted by racism and usually poverty. Its musical structure, lyrical preferences, performance practices and ultimate power and meaning all derived from the overwhelming need to preserve community, self-respect and a sense of human dignity in a world which had often conspired to try to deny blacks any of those things. Thus, what Podhoretz and other fans of black music saw only as a blessing, blacks recognized as a cultural means to exorcize the curse of racism, if never race.

The second point is that, while black fans could enjoy the bold sexuality, fierce passion and corporeal energies of Rhythm and Blues without believing that those qualities exhausted the entire range of black emotions, aspiration, or cultural characteristics, whites still tended to locate black artists, their music, and the culture they represented wholly within the boundaries of a few clichéd "typically black" co-ordinates. This meant that many white Rhythm and Blues fans missed, ignored, or dismissed as inauthentic, a whole range of black moods and preoccupations, styles and sensibilities, which did not appear, or were but faintly inscribed, on the ancient mental map by which whites habitually navigated black culture.

Ironically, however, it was there, in the thousands of songs about workaday problems, passing infatuations, frivolous diversions, little happinesses, small disappointments, and romantic dreams that blacks affirmed their full human complexity and refused to become simply the objects of white imaginations, living perpetually at a fever pitch of sexual excitement or epic existential angst. Indeed, most Rhythm and Blues songs were about the ordinary stuff of everyone's everyday life. They were suffused with, but transcended, an ever-present, but not always, at all times, in all conditions, wholly determinitive consciousness of race. This was, after all, the musical expression of real people who were men, women, workers, unemployed, poor, occasionally rich, rural, urban, happy, sad, in love, out of love, pessimistic, optimistic, as well as black.

With most whites still suffering from a sort of racialized tunnel vision whenever they listened to and enjoyed Rhythm and Blues, its capacity to generate deeper racial understanding or any real sense of a shared humanity with blacks was somewhat compromised. No matter how much black artists were genuinely revered and sincerely imitated on white turntables, radios and stages they often still existed as racial archetypes.

Putting on whitey, putting on blackface: Redding, Hendrix and Joplin

As usual, black Rhythm and Blues performers proved unwilling to become mere victims of these white racial stereotypes. Many found ways to manipulate and profit from white expectations, just as the black "coon-song" composers, and black vaudevilleans like Bert Williams and Stepin' Fetchit, had done when they took the sambo stereotype and reworked it to make money – and more quietly fools – out of any whites who believed in it. As Harold Battiste explained, black artists, indeed black people, frequently conformed to white stereotypes in public, simply "because that's the way to get along.

That's what they expect of me, so I get more out of them by acting like they expect me to act". Gary Giddins detected a hint of this venerable black tradition of "putting on whitey" in Jackie Wilson's stage theatrics, while Johnny Otis knew that white audiences responded best to performances which exaggerated the heavily corporeal, rhythmic elements they always expected to find in "real" black music. "We found that if we played a blues or a very bluesy thing, we lost them. But when we played very spirited R and B things, we captured them. And when we did a *caricature* of rhythm and blues, we *really* got to them".[57]

In this context, it is significant that the soul singer most fêted by white fans at the time of his death in 1967 was Otis Redding. A native of Macon, Georgia, for all his undoubted talents Redding was occasionally given to over-emoting, coming perilously close to becoming a parody of the relentlessly dynamic soulman. By turns sexually rampant ("Love man") and emotionally devastated ("Pain in my heart"), Redding could sometimes lack subtlety and nuance. He always appeared to be living, loving, losing and lusting at the very limits of human existence, which is exactly where whites expected their black heroes to live their entire creative public and, ideally, private lives.

White fans were encouraged by the sheer sweaty conviction of Redding's performances to overlook the possibility of any difference between the show and the showman. Since black music was all about honesty and integrity, it rarely occurred to them that Redding was putting on, in the very best sense of the term, a performance; that Redding was assuming a stage persona which was a highly dramatized, lustier than life, representation of certain aspects of his own complex black male identity, but not, as his black audience appreciated, the whole story. Meanwhile white fans appeared to rest happy in the belief that Redding was indeed "Hard to handle", although his finest song, the posthumous hit "Dock of the bay", revealed a quieter, more introspective personality who was fast becoming disillusioned with conforming to the role of tireless soul stud.

In June 1967, Jimi Hendrix had basked with Redding in the glow of white approval at the Monterey International Pop Festival. Before his own death in 1970, however, Hendrix would also feel trapped by the racial expectations of the white rock audience which formed his major constituency. Born in Seattle of Cherokee, black and white lineage, Hendrix produced a sort of space-aged blues-rock amalgam of great technical virtuosity and power which does not fit neatly into any conventional black musical category – which is as good a reason as any to discuss him here.

The slipperiness of his style has made it easy for many critics to exclude Hendrix from the Rhythm and Blues canon. Thus they have largely surrendered him to the not-so-tender mercies of rock critics, who have routinely undervalued his umbilical ties to various black musical traditions while bestowing upon him the dubious honour of inventing hard rock and heavy metal. To some extent, this simply highlights problems inherent in the whole process of musical categorization and canonization, which seeks to impose order, hierarchy and coherence on musical forms which, thankfully, have constantly influenced and energized each other in thoroughly disorderly, often strikingly democratic and refreshingly spontaneous ways.[58]

What makes Hendrix's frequent absence from the Rhythm and Blues canon particularly interesting, however, is the racial politics of that exclusion. It appears to be grounded less in his conspicuous failure to establish a mass black audience for his music than in the awkward fact that it was Hendrix's move to England and contact with white progressive rock musicians which opened up to him a whole new range of sonic possibilities. Just as problematic is the fact that Bob Dylan was the most obvious direct influence on Hendrix's lyrical blend of interior monologue, blues epigram and psychedelic fantasy. For critics like Nelson George and the funk chronicler Rickcy Vincent – who does at least see Hendrix as part of an r&b/funk continuum, but generally disregards possible white influences on the development of his style – this process of interracial synthesis and accretion is viewed principally in terms of contamination, dilution or even denial of a black identity. No matter that Hendrix was a walking cocktail of red, white and black blood, with a guitar style already as creole as gumbo by the time the ex-Animal Chas Chandler brought him to England in 1966.[59]

Hendrix had paid his musical dues as a sideman with Ike Turner and the Isley Brothers and everything he ever played was filtered through a musical sensibility defined by his connections to jazz, blues, gospel and soul. Yet it was the angular, snarling juxtaposition of these black forms with white "psychedelic" rock influences which helped lift Hendrix from the ranks of gifted guitar journeyman to become a true musical innovator. Similarly, his interest in the electronic manipulation of highly amplified guitar sounds and the possibilities unleashed by advances in studio technology were encouraged by the sonic sculpting of innovative white bands like the Beatles of *Revolver* vintage, and Cream. It was this open embrace and creative redeployment of "outside" influences, rather than some turgid adherence to an inviolable blues tradition, which made his best music burn with a bright new incandescence.

On classic Jimi Hendrix Experience recordings, like his cover of the Leaves' "Hey Joe", or Dylan's "All along the watchtower", or his own "Purple haze", "Crosstown traffic" and "Voodoo chile", a white English bassist (Noel Redding) and drummer (Mitch Mitchell) provided Hendrix with a curiously rumbling, slightly dishevelled, yet hypnotic backdrop against which to weave beguiling tapestries of barbed electric sound. On these cuts, Hendrix's playing was focused, urgent, but still somehow expansive and unhurried as he nimbly, two-handedly one might say, dissolved the gap between rhythm and lead guitar. On soulful ballads like "The wind cried Mary", "Little wing" and "One rainy wish" his playing and singing could be sweet and tender, liquid in a way which invoked but transcended the mellow blues of a T-Bone Walker by touching bases with torch-song jazz, even folk and pop melancholy. These recordings permanently changed the way many black and white musicians conceived and played their music. From the jazz-rock fusion of *Bitches Brew*-era Miles Davis to the fuzztoned guitar solos of Isley Brother Ernest on songs like "That lady", and from the baroque'n'roll heavy-metal guitar extravaganzas of Iron Butterfly and Led Zeppelin to the distinctive wah-wah sounds which pedalled so much funk, Hendrix's musical legacy was formidable.

Yet, without denying the quality or influence of the music itself, it is clear that for many of Hendrix's predominantly white fans, the "authenticity" and worth of this high-watt hybrid were inextricably bound to perceptions of their hero's sexuality. Certainly, Hendrix was the prize catch for the Chicago Plastercasters, two terminally sad white groupies who spent much of the late 1960s making plaster moulds of male rock stars' erections. "Everybody and his brother in England still thinks that spades have big dicks", commented Eric Clapton in reference to Hendrix's huge success with British audiences, again illustrating that white Western, rather than simply white American, racial assumptions were at work here. "And Jimi came over and exploited that to the limit . . . and everybody fell for it". As Clapton appreciated, like the "coon-song" composers and Bert Williams before him, Hendrix was perfectly willing and able to "put on whitey" in his art. "He'll do a lot of things, like fool around with his tongue and play his guitar behind his back and rub it down his crotch", Clapton noted. "And he'll look at the audience, and if they're digging it, he won't like the audience. He'll keep on doing it, putting them on. Play less music".[60]

Paradoxically, while many Hendrix songs conformed to the old boastful macho blues formula ("Stone free", "Foxy lady"), he brought a healthy disrespect for white stereotypes of black hyper-sexuality to the stage. He then partially inoculated himself against their worst ravages by exaggerating and manipulating them in a gaudy, sometimes gauche, often compelling phallic farce. Tall, lithe and lean, with a perpetually dishevelled, just-out-of-bed afro, flamboyant sub-Regency garb, conspicuously cunnilingual tongue and a penchant for dry-humping and then immolating his guitar with lighter fluid, Hendrix was the prince of bad-nigger minstrelsy – pun intended, since his Royal Purpleness, the artist frequently known as Prince, later adopted much of Hendrix's stage persona, and not a little of his music, in the construction of his own highly, if ambiguously, sexed, musichameleon identity.

Succumbing to, but playing with, white expectations gave Hendrix some kind of control over the stereotypes routinely affixed to him. But this was ultimately a pyrrhic victory; a temporary mental survival ploy wrapped in a sound commercial strategy which left pervasive white assumptions unchallenged and tacitly endorsed. Psychologically and musically this was an extraordinarily tough route to take and it took a heavy toll on the man, who sought both refuge and release in an ever more voracious appetite for hard drugs. In the last 18 months of his life, Hendrix tried to abandon his stud theatrics and put greater emphasis on his always challenging musicianship. It was not always easy. His white fans had their expectations to be met. In late 1968, against Hendrix's better judgement, Reprise released the double album, *Electric Ladyland*, with a rainbow-hued harem of naked women on the cover.[61]

In September 1970, Jimi Hendrix died in London. He choked on his own vomit after taking too many sleeping pills. Not long before his death he had begun to proselytize on behalf of his Electric Sky Church, which was both a series of loose musical associations and a sort of philosophy of music. Never particularly consistent or coherent about what precisely this meant, Hendrix seemed to have in mind a more calculated effort to use the power of music to alleviate tensions within individuals, and to break down barriers between disparate social groups. Without real programme or substance this was mostly just hippy doggeral; the product of a druggy world of wish-and-make-it-so politics. Yet its naiveté and imprecision did not make it any less sincere. The idea of the Electric Sky Church certainly suggested that Hendrix, like the sisters and brothers of soul, thought that the old communitarian and salving functions of black religion were now to be found in the realm of popular culture.

The broad oecumenical Electric Sky Church concept may also have been another manifestation of Hendrix's desire to reject an imposed "black" racial identity and the expectations it entailed. He had similar motivations in cultivating his Electric Gypsy persona with its symbolic embrace of rootlessness and disregard for national, or other, boundaries. With black militants screaming for the doggedly apolitical Jimi to publicly champion one or another form of black power – mostly in vain, since, as one of his many biographers has noted, his "political sympathies in the late 1960s were more obviously directed toward Native American rights than the black struggle" – and white fans still struggling to see the man and musician beyond the phallic flamboyance, Hendrix styled himself a rock nomad. Thus he honoured all the roots of his music and identity by privileging none. It was a bold declaration of his right to cultural and personal complexity in the face of both black and white efforts to make him conform to stereotype.[62]

Ironically, Hendrix settled into his gypsy persona just as he dismantled the integrated Experience and recruited black drummer Buddy Miles and bassist Billy Cox to serve at the core of his Band of Gypsies. This combination did produce breathtaking musical highs ("Machine gun", "Angel" and "Who knows", for example), but the musical results were actually decidedly uneven. This was a phase of restless, but none-too-certain experimentation in which some of his extended solos lacked the focus, inner logic and essential lyricism which marked his best playing, even when shrouded in yawls of feedback and distortion. Some of his "free" music was simply dull, pretentious and unwieldy. The fact that few of these meanderings were released in his lifetime reflected, at least in part, Hendrix's own dissatisfaction with the results.

Like Redding and Hendrix, Janis Joplin was another great and doomed success with the fans at Monterey. In the late 1960s, the white Texan screamer was hailed by some whites as a great blues talent because she sought to replicate the soul-searching intensity and emotional turbulence of many blues, gospel and soul singers. That Joplin genuinely revered the great black female vocalists was not in doubt; she even paid for the tombstone which finally marked Bessie Smith's unkempt Philadelphia grave. Moreover, she was clearly inspired by the personal strength and sexual confidence she detected in these singers to make her mongrel blues the vehicle for her own efforts to carve out a powerful, independent, assertive female identity.

And yet Joplin's reification of indomitable black womanhood actually rested upon a rather uncritical acceptance of traditional stereotypes about black female stoicism, passion and hyper-sexuality. Similarly, Joplin's borrowings from black music were highly predictable and clichéd. Joplin's vocals showed precious little appreciation of the understatement, the subtle phrasing and manipulation of dramatic tensions which were also central to the emotional potency of black music. In much the same way that nineteenth-century minstrels prided themselves on capturing the authentic flavour of the black experience in shows which were actually enactments of white racial stereotypes, so Joplin desperately sought to capture the essence of the black experience as defined by whites. In so doing, she exaggerated the passion and frenzy of her vocals until many of her performances became little more than extended tantrums. These mostly revolved, as many of her fans no doubt believed all "real" black music did, around the trials and tribulations of getting too much or too little sex. As far as new feminist agendas went, claiming the right to drink, swear and screw like one of the boys was probably not quite as radical as Joplin and her admirers liked to think.

By the time of her death from a drug overdose in 1971, Joplin's whole life had disintegrated into a tragic pastiche of what white fans expected from suffering, tortured black musicians as a guarantee of their artistic integrity. In the main, black audiences found little they recognized and nothing they wanted in Joplin's music. Like many before her, Joplin had put on the mask of musical blackness in order to confront and critique some of the dominant gender and social expectations of her time. Yet she failed to show any real comprehension of the racial stereotypes she was inadvertently helping to perpetuate with her fervent minstrelsy.[63]

Janis Joplin was by no means the only white fan-turned-imitator to isolate and exaggerate the particular elements she found most attractive in black music to meet her own needs. Indeed, the ways in which whites in the 1950s and 1960s typically sought to copy or incorporate elements from black idioms into their own music offers further evidence that they continued to reduce multi-faceted black musical forms to the same narrow set of characteristics and meanings.

Again, this selective appropriation of nominally "black" musical techniques was nothing new. In the 1920s, white jazz acts like the Original Dixieland Jazz Band, Ted Lewis, and the Mound City Blowers usually played much faster than their bluesier black counterparts. They believed that the hot, sexy dance music they so admired depended simply on the speed of musical execution, rather than a mastery of timing and phrasing. Although there have been many exceptions among white jazzmen – Bix Beiderbecke, Gerry Mulligan and Stan Getz all learned to swing gently with melancholy – black musicians themselves recognized a marked tendency among white musicians to equate a fast tempo with high passion. When trumpeter Hot Lips Page heard the young Roy Eldridge ostentatiously reeling off hell-for-leather solos in New York in the early 1930s, he asked simply "Why are you playing like an ofay?". More than 30 years later, the same glorification of exceptional technical facility and sheer speed of execution partially explained the cult status whites afforded to quickfire white blues guitarists like Eric "Slowhand" Clapton of the Yardbirds and Cream and Alvin Lee of Ten Years After.[64]

This white obsession with the pace or tempo of black music was part of a broader concern with its rhythmic potency, wherein resided much of black music's success as dance music, its links to the body, and much of its sexual resonance. Thus, when the southern rockabilly rebels of the mid-to-late 1950s – Dick Busch, Johnny Todd, Carl Perkins, Roy Orbison, Sonny Burgess and Elvis Presley – turned to black music for inspiration, it was not, in the main, to the sweet romantic harmonies and lyrical idealism of much of the black vocal group repertoire, since they could find those qualities in white music. Instead, they were besotted with the sexual frankness of some r&b lyrics and its dance beats, which they honoured in the words of Warren Smith's "Ubangi Stomp":

Well, I rocked over Italy and I rocked over Spain.
I rocked in Memphis, it was all the same.
'Til I rocked into Africa and rolled off the ship,
and seen them niggers doin' an odd lookin' skip.
I parted the reeds and looked over the swamp,
and I see them cats doin' the Ubangi Stomp.

With its tell-tale blend of casual racism and unabashed admiration for the vibrancy of black musical culture, "Ubangi Stomp" vividly captured the basic compatability of racial prejudice with a genuine, if circumscribed, appreciation of black musical prowess.

Perhaps even more indicative of the sheer power and pervasiveness of these reductive racial stereotypes was the way in which they even framed white responses to black music and culture among genuine Movement supporters, like the ones Julian Bond had teased in "How to be SNCCY". In 1965, Alan Wells, a white musical therapist from California, wrote a remarkably telling letter to Martin Luther King in the wake of the Watts riots, suggesting that "In the present struggle to achieve equality among races music can play a much greater dynamic role than it already has in breaking down barriers between peoples through its power as a universal langauge". Wells advocated organizing "groups of negro musicians and entertainers to go about the country as 'goodwill ambassadors' – to offer to the white people the balm (which they are in great need of) of spiritual and emotional healing . . . That way [the negro] will come more quickly into recognition of his rightful status in society and harmony and brotherhood will be established among all men".[65]

This, of course, was not too far removed from the way in which many blacks also hoped that black popular music might function. But what made Wells' manifesto so revealing was the way in which its progressive message was so firmly rooted in old stereotypes. The whole letter was predicated on the assumption that "the negro does himself an injustice by becoming too rational and methodical – his great natural gifts are of the emotions and physical expression, of soul and body as is witnessed by the wealth of riches brought into our American music". While there was little to argue with in the last part of this statement, more troublesome was the implication that blacks need not worry themselves with the alien, mental and cerebral side of life. Instead they should start using the "freedom and joyful abandon of rhythm and hand-clapping which are the negro's heritage", not only to win their own freedom, but also to redeem the lost sensuality of white Americans, who – no doubt preoccupied with all that deep thinking – had become "inhibited and frustrated in expressing themselves emotionally much more than the negro".[66]

Wells seemed oblivious of the fact that black Americans had been clapping in rhythm and singing songs of astonishing power for centuries without winning their freedom, ending discrimination, or eradicating what Wells called "the ugly pictures of [the negro] held in the minds of many white people through misunderstanding and prejudice". The irony was that the romantic images of blacks and their culture which many white devotees of black music carried in their minds were sometimes as much an impediment to genuine racial communication, understanding and co-operation as the ugly racist stereotypes they so earnestly disavowed.[67]

So where did this leave the dream that shared music and dance could foster mutual respect and understanding across racial lines and help generate white support for the black freedom struggle? Were such beliefs entirely fanciful in the decade or so after *Brown?* Certainly, it seems that – Dave Marsh's personal experiences notwithstanding – neither cultish white ardour, nor a far more common casual white enthusiasm for black music, *in themselves* necessarily undermined, let alone destroyed, prevailing racial attitudes concerning blacks, their culture, or their place in American society. Just as antebellum white southerners, slaveholders included, had frequently marvelled at the vibrancy and beauties of black song without feeling that this required a fundamental re-evaluation of white supremacy, let alone emancipation, so a hundred years later there was still no reason to believe that the Alabama klansmen who enthused over a Solomon Burke concert and drawled along with "Everybody needs somebody to love" were prompted to hang up their hoods when they got home.[68]

Nevertheless, white exposure to black music has always contained the potential to put pressure on and test old verities about black inferiority, to compromise notions of black baseness and inhumanity, simply because of its abundant grace, intelligence, wit and vigour and the universal human concerns at its heart. In 1961, civil rights champion and acid wit Harry Golden noted that the University of South Carolina's plan to prohibit the use of black bands for campus-wide dances had roused strong opposition from white students. This was not from any pressing sense of moral urgency or racial progressivism, but because the students felt that "their music is more enjoyable; their price is more reasonable". Golden remarked that this was "A fine way to go about winning equality for our citizens. But then again, every little thing helps". Golden recognized that any exposure to blacks and their culture held the prospect, however slim, of white enlightenment.[69]

Certainly, for those whites whose interest in Rhythm and Blues did lead them beyond its refreshing sexual candour and sheer danceability to appreciate its multiple moods and themes, reductive stereotypes were often undermined. Moreover, in an era when the civil rights movement was openly defying old racial assumptions, and even dismantling some of the most dehumanizing legal and institutional expressions of them, black music worked upon a white racial consciousness already under pressure from a variety of other sources. Historian David Roediger appreciated that a youthful love for black Rhythm and Blues did not necessarily destroy the racism which existed among his peers in Cairo, Illinois. Nonetheless, he felt that those predilections "did open the possibility of antiracism". Put another way, although love of black music did not in itself reflect, let alone create, deep changes in mass white racial attitudes, the new appreciation and growing acceptance of black artists and performers – not just in music, but also in film, theatre, television, literature and sports – intersected with and reinforced the bold demands of the Movement for white America to reappraise its racial beliefs, laws and practices.[70]

In the main, however, white racism and the social and economic structures which helped to sustain it proved powerful and flexible enough to withstand such challenges. Indeed, in the decade or so after *Brown* white America tended to make only those adjustments necessary to preserve domestic civil order and international credibility, and to salve its momentarily ruffled collective conscience. The "wages of whiteness" were still being claimed and paid in full.

Gospel refugee Roscoe Shelton has been a stalwart of a biracial southern Rhythm and Blues scene since the late 1950s.

CHAPTER SEVEN

"All for one, and one for all": black enterprise, racial politics and the business of soul

There's nothing wrong with singing and dancing or running track . . . the only thing that's wrong is that we don't own it. (Harold Battiste)[1]

The AFO experiment

As soul music matured during the early-to-mid 1960s, the racial pattern of record label and radio station ownership changed very little. Whites continued to own all but a handful of black-oriented stations and to control most of the companies producing and distributing black music. There were, however, a number of important black initiatives and enterprises during the first half of the 1960s which appeared to augur well for improved black economic opportunity within the industry. They also revealed that most successful black entrepreneurs behaved suspiciously like their white counterparts when pursuing and protecting their own economic interests.

One partial exception to this generalization was Harold Battiste's All For One Records (AFO), which represented the most self-consciously politicized and imaginative bid for black economic and artistic power within the Rhythm and Blues field in the early 1960s. Born in New Orleans in 1932, Harold Battiste came of musical age around the end of the war listening to an eclectic range of secular and sacred, black and white, musical forms. "It was just music that you either liked or you didn't. It was not separated into categories", he recalled. On radio he heard big band jazz, much of it white swing played on the *Mid-day Serenade* show, and was fascinated by the stirring, but unidentified, theme tunes to programmes like *The Lone Ranger*. Closer to home, he heard blues and even a little gospel, admired and emulated the jump sounds of Eddie "Cleanhead" Vinson and Louis Jordan, and flipped over the dazzling artistry of be-bop. After showing early flair as a drummer, he dabbled in clarinet, played occasional alto sax with the Joe Jones Band, and more regularly contributed baritone sax to local favourites, the Johnson Brothers.[2]

In the late 1940s and early 1950s, Battiste also attended Dillard University, where he earned a degree in music education, finally got to put names to all those anonymous classical theme tunes, and received an invaluable grounding in musical theory which would later serve him well as a writer-arranger. After graduation he worked for several years as an itinerant teacher in Louisiana's black public schools. In 1956, he resigned rather than succumb to the racist expectations of a segregated system. Battiste felt that while white kids were being taught music properly, learning the fundamentals which would enable them to understand, appreciate and play in any style, it was considered more than enough if black children could learn tunes by rote. No great believer in theories of innate, or at least untutored, black musical excellence, Battiste tried to offer his pupils the same thorough grounding in the rudiments of music that white children enjoyed. He was duly censured by the school superintendent for such "uppity" ideas. "I felt that they expected less coming out of the black schools . . . and when I was challenging it, they felt threatened or something by me being aware that there was a descrepancy between black and white".[3]

Disillusioned with teaching in this environment, Battiste headed out to the west coast hoping to pursue a jazz career. He hooked up with Ornette Coleman and cut a demo, "Janie", which he tried to hawk around various companies before ending up at Specialty and running into Bumps Blackwell. Blackwell was not particularly interested in the Coleman side, but asked Battiste to sit in on a session he was doing with a newly secularized Sam Cooke. Battiste helped write the vocal arrangements and played on "You send me". Shortly thereafter, he was back in New Orleans working as pointsman for Specialty in the Crescent City, rather like Dave Bartholomew did for Imperial.

Battiste's broad remit for Specialty gave him an insight into every aspect of the recording business. He was responsible for distribution and promotion – although his attempts to get Specialty's disks in shops and on the radio were impeded by owner Art Rupe's steadfast refusal to pay payola. He also served as a talent scout and a writer-producer, cutting big hits with local white rocker Jerry Byrne ("Lights out"), Little Richard, and his clone, Larry Williams. Battiste was even expected to place the orders for everything from stationery to recording tape, and to keep on top of the office's accounts.

When his formal relationship with Specialty ended in 1959, Battiste rejoined the revitalized Joe Jones band, which was then riding high on the success of its Battiste-produced hit "You talk too much" on Joe Ruffino's Ric Records. Battiste began to work for Ruffino as an A&R-man-arranger-producer, both in New Orleans and in New York. It was around this time that his welling frustrations with the workings of the record industry came to a head. Battiste later described Joe Ruffino as "a scoundrel of a man . . . he didn't pay people and that's why he was my jumping board to AFO". Ruffino's reluctance to pay what was due was hardly uncommon among either white or black record executives, but Battiste now saw it as "an extension of what was bothering me in the school system". More precisely, what was bothering Harold Battiste was the rampant exploitation of black musicians in the industry and a woeful lack of black power to correct such abuses.[4]

Since the mid 1950s, Battiste had been interested in the teachings of Elijah Muhammad and the Nation of Islam. Under the influence of local trumpeter Emory Thompson, Battiste, like Lynn Hope, Chuck Willis and Screaming Jay Hawkins, had joined the Black Muslims. In particular, Battiste was drawn to Muhammad's economic programme, which called for blacks to secure ownership of the businesses which served their community and thereby create black-controlled wealth and opportunity. "I began to go over in my mind what he was saying . . . one of the fundamental problems we are having: we don't own anything". While the mainstream civil rights movement prioritized the ballot and the desegregation of public facilities, Battiste "felt that to have economic independence was more important than to be able to go to the same hotel, or sit-in, or go to a movie, or whatever they wanted, whatever they were fighting for. Y'know, I was with them, but I just thought that we needed to have economic independence first". He felt that the experience of other successful ethnic groups in America proved that, "Once you've got economic independence, then you can *demand* [political and civil rights], you don't have to ask for that, you can buy it".[5]

In November 1959, Battiste drafted a manifesto for a "Musicians' Co-operative", to be "founded on the principle that today's record industry is realizing tremendous success which is largely due to the participation of MUSICIANS". Those musicians, he argued, "have performed millions of dollars worth of music on record", but "rarely shared in the profits that they have contributed their talents to earning". This, Battiste reasoned, was "Because they have performed as *laborers*, thus earning a salary . . . and thereby eliminating any possibility of becoming eligible to share in the profits of the very lucrative record industry". To emphasize his point, Battiste calculated that if saxophonist Lee Allen (suggestively disguised as "Musician X" in the original document) played on one recording date a week, with each session yielding three songs, he would earn an annual income of $2,522 for his contribution to 156 sides, or 78 record releases. If, however, Allen had a 2 per cent royalty deal and just one of those records sold 500,000 copies, he would earn over $10,000 from that disk alone.[6]

As Battiste saw it, blacks were being hired because they were such good and profitable musicians and they needed to capitalize on their special talents. "We sing and dance. We ought to own that", he explained. On 29 May 1961, in conjunction with five like-minded black New Orleans musicians collectively known as the Executives, Battiste successfully incorporated

Harold Battiste and the All For One executives. Left to right, back row: Alvin "Red" Tyler, John Bordreaux, Roy Montrell, Peter "Chuck" Badie; front row: Melvin Lastie, Harold Battiste.

AFO (All For One) Records and At Last Publishing, both designed "to demonstrate to musicians that they could own the product of their creativity and enjoy greater independence".[7]

Much as envisioned in Battiste's 1959 blueprint, AFO was run as a sort of co-operative enterprise in which the musicians who played on the label's sessions waived any payment for their work, but became co-owners of those recordings. They then took an agreed percentage of any money their recordings earned and thus escaped the tyranny of the existing system, where they were usually paid a flat rate union session fee – around $45 in the early 1960s – regardless of the extent of their creative input, or how many millions of copies of their work were later sold.

The biggest problem AFO faced was circumventing the rules of the American Federation of Musicians (AFM), which insisted on designating all musicians as labourers, to be paid no more and no less than the standard fee per session. This lack of co-operation from the union was not unusual in New Orleans, or elsewhere for that matter. In 1960, the AFM had more segregated locals than any other union except the railway clerks. Moreover, while some black AFM officials campaigned vigorously to overthrow a Jim Crow structure which was by no means unique to the South, many others actually supported continued segregation. In 1957, the leaders of 40 out of 47 all-black locals voted against mergers with their white colleagues. The most sincere of these leaders did so out of concern that black demands would go unheeded in integrated locals where there were simply more white members than black. Others more selfishly feared the loss of the personal prestige and power which they had established in their own little black fiefdoms.[8]

Tommy Ridgley, who spent a good part of his career in and out of trouble with the segregated black New Orleans AFM Local 496, felt the whole thing had "always been a racket", and told tales of greed, corruption, and two sets of account books kept by a self-perpetuating black clique. Battiste felt much the same. Local 496 was "more a hindrance than anything else. We had a lot of run-ins with the union. It seemed as though those guys, that was their private club and they ran it the way they wanted, they manipulated the rules to suit them". It was not the last time Battiste was to be disappointed by the attitude of blacks in positions of relative power in the industry.[9]

While AFO was a very self-consciously black enterprise, from its black business cards to its use of black lawyers, it also harboured ambitions to shift as many units as possible to as many buyers as possible, irrespective of race. Consequently, Battiste arranged for the national distribution of AFO products through the New York based Sue label which had already enjoyed major success with Ike and Tina Turner ("A fool in love", "I idolize you"). When the deal was first mooted, Battiste was blissfully unaware of the race of Sue's owner, Henry "Juggy" Murray, and was simply looking for effective, affordable, distribution. However, "When I met him at the airport and he turned out to be black, I said, 'wow, man, this is better than I thought!'" Battiste saw his relationship with Murray as another step towards his dream of building a black "conglomerate entertainment enterprise" which would incorporate recording, theatre bookings, management: "all the facets of entertainment that basically they say niggers can't do".[10]

In its first year of business, AFO produced a number of fine nascent soul records, all with a highly distinctive polyrhythmic echo of New Orleans marching-band and jazz music. The most successful of these were Barbara George's black chart-topping "I know" and Prince La La's vaguely voodun "She put the hurt on me". Unfortunately, however, Battiste's bold experiment began to flounder as narrow economic self-interest began to eclipse any broader sense of racial unity and co-operation. The connection with Sue ended acrimoniously when Juggy Murray, who had begun to describe and treat the fiercely independent AFO as nothing more than a subsidiary of Sue, lured away Battiste's biggest star, Barbara George, with a fur coat and a Cadillac. It was, Battiste noted bitterly, "the same thing we expected some white folks would do".[11]

At the time Battiste was deeply aggrieved that another black man could have treated him this way. "That disillusioned me completely", he recalled.

In retrospect, however, he recognized his own naiveté in assuming that racial solidarity, rather than economic and status considerations, would automatically dominate the agendas of black capitalists like Murray. "I was operating on an ideal; Juggy was operating on the real . . . The blindness I had, of feeling that because he was a black cat he would understand what I was trying to do, made me very vulnerable". Murray, on the other hand, had pursued a perfectly consistent and predictable course in seeking to maximize his economic rewards and leverage. It was Battiste, with his heroic, but perhaps intrinsically flawed vision of a more co-operative, communalist form of black capitalism who was the exception to the black entrepreneurial rule, not Juggy Murray.

Before the falling out with Murray, AFO "wasn't work, it was a mission", Battiste recalled. After the "bubble had been burst", however, he rapidly lost interest. In August 1963, Battiste and most of the AFO executives moved to Los Angeles to work for steady pay at Sar and Derby, the labels co-founded by his old associate Sam Cooke. After Cooke's death, Battiste spent a lengthy period as musical director for Sonny and Cher, and as a producer for Sonny Bono's Progress Records. In 1967, he produced the critically acclaimed *Gris Gris* album for Dr John, a persona he helped to create for Mac Rebbeneck, the gifted, if dissolute, white New Orleans musician who had been playing black clubs and sessions since before anyone could remember – and who was so thoroughly integrated into the black r&b scene that he even joined the black Local 496, for all the good it did him.

Battiste's appetite for black economic and educational empowerment diminished little over the years. As well as keeping AFO and At Last Publishing just about alive – and relaunching them in the 1990s – he founded Marzique Music. In tandem with AFO's cornetist and executive secretary, Mel Lastie, he also ran Adormel Music and the Hal-Mel production company responsible for 1970s hits by Tami Lynn, King Floyd and Alvin "Shine" Robinson. In the 1980s, Battiste fused his educational and musical concerns by founding the National Association of New Orleans Musicians, from which emerged a jazz outfit called Novia and a wild r&b-funk ensemble called the New Orleans Natives. Undaunted by a minor heart attack and stroke, the indomitable Battiste returned from Los Angeles in the late 1980s to take up a teaching position at the University of New Orleans, where he joined a remarkable jazz studies department chaired by Ellis Marsalis, an old jazz buddy from the days when they had chased Ornette Coleman and their dreams over to the west coast.[12]

The Motown miracle

Harold Battiste was always a musician first; then a writer, an arranger, a producer and, finally, almost by default, a record label owner and music publisher. He deeply resented the fact that racism and corruption in the industry meant that he had to devote so much of his time and energies to playing entrepreneur instead of playing music. Nevertheless, when he started AFO and At Last Publishing in the early 1960s Battiste had high hopes that it would serve as a model for other blacks to move into ownership of the means of Rhythm and Blues production and dissemination. Ever the educator, he saw what he was "doing as more of an experiment or demonstration" for others to follow.[13]

It was, of course, pure coincidence that a few years after Battiste founded AFO, Smokey Robinson won Berry Gordy's in-house competition to write a company song for Motown with an anthem called "Hitsville, USA" – sung in unison once a week at Motown's plenary studio meetings – which included the line "we're all for one and one for all". Yet Motown and Gordy's triumph, so redolent of broader black aspirations, struggles and achievements in the 1960s, did represent an ambiguous and partial realization of Battiste's dream "that someone like him would surface". Sometimes, however, Motown also evoked memories of Juggy Murray and the mercurial nature of racial loyalties in the face of economic self-interest.[14]

The basic history of the Motown Corporation has been recounted many times, by insiders, outsiders, mud-slingers and tribute-bringers. Yet, that remarkable story warrants brief rehearsal here since it illuminates both the nature and dilemmas of black entrepreneurial capitalism and the routine misrepresentation of the label's achievements and racial credentials in much of the existing literature.[15]

In 1929, Berry Gordy was born into an ambitious middle-class black family with roots in Georgia farming and retail, which had relocated to Detroit during the 1920s. There, in addition to running a painting and construction firm, his father, Berry Sr, opened the Booker T. Washington Grocery Store, and instilled in his children the virtues of frugality, discipline, family unity and hard work so dear to the "Wizard of Tuskegee". Less committed than some of his siblings to the formal education which Booker T. Washington had also advocated, Gordy left school at the 11th grade to become a professional boxer. In 1953, he indulged his love of modern jazz by opening the 3-D Record Mart. Unfortunately, the masses of black Detroit cared little for the music and in 1955 the venture failed, forcing Gordy into a much-vaunted, but relatively brief, sojourn on the production line at Ford. The failure of 3-D had a profound impact on Gordy: rarely again would he put aesthetic, artistic or, for that matter, racial, considerations ahead of a simple concern for whether and how widely his products would sell.

Gordy's breakthrough in the music business came as a songwriter when he co-authored "To be loved" and "Reet petite" for Jackie Wilson. In early 1958 he produced "Got a job" for the Miracles, with whom he also had a management deal. As the Miracles' career took off, Gordy apparently managed to retain control over their contract only by persuading black deejays to threaten a boycott of several white labels who were trying to poach the group with more generous terms. Apocryphal though this story may be, it illustrates a recurring pattern in Gordy's business dealings whereby he appealed to black solidarity and pride to secure whatever protection and preferential treatment the few blacks with power in the industry could offer. Throughout the 1960s, Gordy would shrewdly use race, so often an impediment to black economic advance, as one of the tools of his entrepreneurial ambitions.[16]

Using family money, Gordy had formed Tamla – his first label – in January 1959, releasing a blues-tinged black pop number called "Come to me" by husky-voiced Marv Johnson. When that disk began to pick up extensive regional airplay on WJLB-Detroit and the black-owned WCHB-Inkster, Tamla simply could not cope with the demands of mass production and national distribution and leased the master to United Artists. UA had both the financial resources to pay for the pressing of tens of thousands of copies before it had recouped any monies from sales, and the distribution network to place those disks on record racks and radio playlists around the nation. Gordy learned more about distribution in 1960 when Tamla acted in that capacity for Barrett Strong's highly successful, and aptly titled, "Money": a song co-written and produced by Gordy and released on the eponymous Anna label run by his sister and her husband, the ex-Moonglow Harvey Fuqua.

By this time Gordy had established various fiefdoms within the Motown empire: the Motown Record Corporation, Hitsville USA, and Berry Gordy Jr Enterprises. He also set up his own publishing firm, Jobete Music, and a management agency, International Talent Management Inc. (ITMI). Around the turn of the decade he supplemented Tamla with a host of subsidiary labels like Motown itself, Miracle (which was renamed Gordy in 1962), Mel-O-Dy, VIP and a gospel experiment, Divinity. This strategy was primarily designed to protect against the possible failure of individual labels, but it proved unnecessary as Gordy began to rack up an impressive run of crossover hits with artists like the Marvelettes, Contours, Marvin Gaye and Mary Wells.

Aside from the astonishing quality of so much of Motown's music, what differentiated the label from most of its rivals was Gordy's extraordinary business acumen and ingenuity, and the single-mindedness, many would later claim ruthlessness, with which he set about realizing his dreams. At the heart of Motown's economics were the classic business strategies of vertical integration and cross-collateralization. Gordy controlled and profited from every aspect of the careers of his artists, writers and musicians, and every dimension of record production and promotion. Put simply, Gordy developed a structure which enabled Motown to offset losses on any unprofitable projects with income from another branch of the total operation. For example, all Motown performer-writers were required to sign with Gordy's Jobete Music publishing company, which not only claimed its own share of the songwriter's income, but also ensured that Gordy could recoup any costs incurred in the preparation of recordings by making deductions from the relevant artist's songwriting royalties.[17]

Similarly, all Motown acts and creative personnel were managed by ITMI, which did relatively little to protect their financial or artistic interests, but made money for the corporation by arranging notoriously mean and restrictive contracts for the young black hopefuls who joined the label. ITMI routinely took a cut of the weekly salaries paid to all the corporation's creative staff, whether they had been productive that week or not. Gordy considered paying non-productive staff a gesture of great generosity, but it has to be measured against the fact that all weekly payments were later reclaimed by the company against the artist's royalties from any recordings. ITMI also controlled the income from live performances, organizing gruelling Motown tours on which the artists were given a daily allowance, again deductable from any future royalties. In return, artists and writers were allowed only periodic access to Motown's accounts, which Gordy refused to allow the Recording Industry Association of America to audit until the 1970s, and had few rights concerning when, what and with whom they recorded.

Motown royalties were usually fixed at a meagre rate of 8 per cent of 90 per cent of the wholesale price of albums and singles. By 1968, bitter disputes over those royalties led the brilliant songwriting and production team of Lamont Dozier and the brothers Eddie and Brian Holland to leave the label, eventually winning a court settlement worth several hundred thousand dollars. Others, like Eddie Kendricks of the Temptations, also began to question if Motown's much vaunted family ethos was really just a front for an exploitative mode of black paternalism, not very different from exploitative white paternalism. Martha Reeves was torn between gratitude and disillusionment with the way Motown treated its artists. "Motown had signed us to ironclad contracts and turned us into international stars. Yet after several years of million-selling records and sold-out concerts, in 1969 I realized that my personal income was but a fraction of what it should have been". When Reeves began to ask questions about her earnings, she "suddenly experienced a lack of personal and professional attention".[18]

There is some evidence that Motown's studio musicians were treated more generously than its name artists and writers, but this was all relative. The going rate for a Motown session in 1962 was $7.50 a side and until 1965 the label routinely paid musicians below union scale. Although by the second half of the decade musicians like pianist Earl Van Dyke, leader of the Funk Brothers studio band, could earn five-figure sums annually, there was still resentment about the lack of artistic credit and adequate financial recompense for musicians who had virtually co-written songs which later earned millions of dollars. Although Gordy later protested that Motown writers and musicians were paid exactly what they were owed according to the letter of their contracts, Motown was in fact perpetrating precisely the kind of exploitation of its artists which had prompted Harold Battiste to form AFO.

James Jamerson, one of Motown's finest bassists, recalled: "there is sometimes a tear because I see how I was treated and cheated. We were doing
more than we thought and we didn't get any songwriting credit".[19]

The Motown sound and the myth of authenticity

Consummate musicians like James Jamerson, Earl Van Dyke, Benny Benjamin
(drums) and James Messina (guitar) were crucial in the development of
what has become instantly recognizable, if analytically elusive, as the "Motown
sound". Yet, given the oceans of print devoted to this "sound", one of the
most striking features of Motown's early output was not its homogeneity,
but its diversity.[20]

Bluesy performers like Mabel Johns, Barrett Strong and Marv Johnson
were initially balanced by coy girl groups like the Marvelettes and soloists
like Mary Wells. Long-forgotten white acts like the Valadiers co-existed with
the Four Tops, who at first found themselves on Gordy's Jazz Workshop
subsidiary where they experimented with big band arrangements of Tin Pan
Alley standards. The Supremes recorded everything from Rodgers and Hart
tunes to country and western, and from a Sam Cooke tribute album to a
collection of Beatles songs, hoping to find a winning formula. Meanwhile
Marvin Gaye was encouraged to indulge his considerable talent for crooning on albums like *Hello Broadway* and *A Tribute to the Great Nat King
Cole*. With such an eclectic mixture of styles, and Gordy's keen eye for any
potentially lucrative market niche, it was easy to credit the 1962 *Detroit Free
Press* article which announced that Motown was about to launch a line of
polka records.[21]

Eventually, however, Motown did more than just produce a diverse range
of records, any one of which might appeal predominantly to a different
market. It forged a flexible house style which appealed across regional,
racial and even generational boundaries. "We were a general-market company. Whether you were black, white, green or blue, you could relate to
our music", Gordy rightly boasted. From the maelstrom of early experimentation, it was Martha Reeves who blazed the gospel-paved, string-lined trail to
the label's mid-1960s crossover triumph. In the summer of 1963, Holland-
Dozier-Holland furnished Reeves with "Heatwave" and then "Quicksand"
on which they enlivened the slightly mannered basics of the girl group
sound with a driving gospel beat, tambourine frenzy and soaring strings.
Above it all, Reeves, who was comfortably the finest female vocalist on
Motown's books until Gladys Knight joined and ran her close in the late
1960s, unleashed her rapt soul vocals.[22]

Following the Top Ten pop success of these recordings, this basic formula was refined and adapted to fit the peculiar talents of individual Motown
acts. The leonine roar of lead singer Levi Stubbs meant that the Four Tops

retained the melodrama of the Vandellas' recordings on songs like "Reach out, I'll be there" and "Bernadette". By contrast, the Temptations harked back to their doowopping origins as the Primes to feature rich harmonies and a generally sweeter sound on Smokey Robinson-penned and produced songs like "Its growing" and "My girl". The most successful of all the Motown acts to work within this basic framework was the Supremes, for whom Holland-Dozier-Holland softened the hard-driving gospel beat with more prominent strings and muted brass. The mix was topped with vocals by Diana Ross which were much lighter and breathier than Martha's on chart-topping songs like "Where did our love go?" and "Baby love". The Supremes proved to be the perfect black crossover act. Between 1964 and Ross' departure from the group in 1969, they secured 25 pop hits, including 12 number ones – only the Beatles could claim more.

If there was a classic "Motown Sound", neither its ubiquity nor its rigidity should be exaggerated; not even for the period between 1964 and 1967 when it was at its zenith. In 1965, Motown released the Miracles' soulful post doowop lament "Ooo baby baby", Jr Walker's saxophone-led blues stomp "Shotgun", Stevie Wonder's grinding rock'n'soul remake of Tommy Tucker's "Hi heel sneakers", and Marvin Gaye's gospel shout, "Ain't that peculiar". All were highly successful, yet all somehow circumvented, or greatly extended, the basic formula.

Even those artists who stuck tight as a Benny Benjamin backbeat to the classic Motown Sound, could, just like that precocious skinsman, actually produce a broad range of moods and shadings within its confines. Thus, 1965 also saw the release of the Temptations' melancholic "Since I lost my baby", the Contours' barnstorming "Can you jerk like me", the Four Tops' distraught "Ask the lonely", and the Vandellas' disturbing, claustrophobic masterpiece "Nowhere to run".

Despite this constrained diversity, however, the idea of a single Motown Sound, clinically designed by a team of songwriters and producers led by Gordy, Robinson, Holland-Dozier-Holland, William Stevenson and Ivy Hunter, and mechanically riveted onto the label's recordings by musical artisans, pervades the literature. Not only is this view inaccurate, but it betrays an insidious form of racial stereotyping, and has become, in Jon Fitzgerald's phrase, a "major impediment to general acknowledgement of Motown's role as a major *innovative* force in 1960s popular music".[23]

The signs adorning the offices of Motown and Stax respectively – "Hitsville, USA" and "Soulsville, USA" – have frequently been taken to symbolize a completely different musical ethos, a different commercial agenda, and even a different degree of artistic and racial integrity between the two labels. Critics have regularly made unfavourable comparisons between the slick Motown soul production line and the more relaxed, spontaneous, atmosphere of southern labels like Stax, with their rootsier feel and country-fried licks. Paradoxically, southern soul, largely recorded on white-owned labels by integrated groups of musicians who drew on black and white musical influences, has been reified as more authentically black than the secularized gospel recordings of black musicians on a black-owned label with virtually no white creative input – at least not until English woman Pam Sawyer made a name for herself as a staff writer in the late 1960s with songs like the Supremes' "Love child".

Even the usually sensible Arnold Shaw fell headlong into this trap, describing Motown in terms which made it sound like a pale imitation of something blacker, something more real, more substantial, lurking in the southlands. Motown songs, Shaw claimed, "are light and fluffy. It is hardly soul food, but rather a dish for which white listeners have acquired a taste". In a similar vein, Mike Jahn derided Motown as "a black-owned version of popular schmaltz", thereby recycling conventional stereotypes about the nature of "real" black music, much as Tony Cummings did when he casually dismissed Marvin Gaye's crooning as "appalling . . . ill-conceived mush-mallow". Cummings was apparently unable to countenance even the possibility that a black American singer could be a magnificent interpreter of Tin Pan Alley Americana.[24]

Critics have tended to privilege the recordings of Stax, Fame and their southern brethren over those of Motown, largely because the musicians who played on those southern sessions have been viewed as genuine artists, not artisans. Southern players, so the legend goes, improvised amazing riffs and spontaneously wove together sublime rhythmic and harmonic patterns from the very warp and weft of their souls. Those protean moments were then instantly committed to tape and transferred, unsullied, onto vinyl.

Contrary to this popular myth, however, southern soul records – with some exceptions – were rarely produced in single, improvised live takes. Overdubbing was common – even at Stax, where Otis Redding's oft-quoted statement that "we cut everything together, horns, rhythms and vocals . . . we didn't even have a four-track tape recorder. You can't over dub on a one-track machine" has been accepted as chapter and verse for all 1960s southern soul. In fact, even at Stax, vocals were frequently added after the instrumental tracks were laid down, and many records were assembled from carefully splicing together the best moments from alternate takes.[25]

This is not to deny that southern studios had marvellously talented musicians whose long hours of practice and laid-back jamming generated moments of great musical invention and almost uncanny understanding. Rather it is to suggest that, just like at Motown, arrangers, producers and engineers were also vital in shaping the recorded, or more accurately, the released sound of southern soul records. A good example was Joe Tex's magnificent soul jeremiad "Hold what you got", which was an unusable mess until Buddy Killen took the tapes from Muscle Shoals to Nashville for remixing and overdubs. The point is that while purists have tended to see post-recording technologies as, by definition, a corrupting influence on

Rhythm and Blues, such interventions have often helped to realize the musical vision of the artist or writer more fully.[26]

An even more telling example of this creative use of studio technology involved James Brown's "Papa's got a brand new bag", which was originally an extended slow-groove jam, recorded in February 1965 in Charlotte, North Carolina, by a dog-tired band dragging its weary way to a gig. In post-production, however, Brown decided to remaster and slightly speed up the recording to create the familiar dance cut. With volcanic bass lines erupting in surprisingly on-beat places, stabbing brass riffs, and the percussive chiming of Jimmy Nolen's guitar, "Papa's got a brand new bag" was a truly seminal moment in the development of soul and funk. It did not, however, emerge fully formed in a single impromptu session, but from a potent combination of inspiration, contemplation and technological manipulation.[27]

And yet, a crude reification of black spontaneity has continued, linked to the enduring belief that all real black music must be visceral rather than cerebral in character, springing from the instinctual needs of the body, rather than the intellectual or meditative workings of the mind. Certainly, when Rickey Vincent wanted to validate the brilliance of the Godfather's 1973 hit, "The payback", he automatically turned to Brown's superfine trombonist Fred Wesley and his recollection that the session had been "a rush job", with James delivering a "completely spontaneous" vocal and rejecting the engineer's offer to remix with an imperious "don't *touch* this". For Vincent this represented the quintessence of Brown's black art and creativity. Yet the fact remains that a month later the basic track was remixed and garnished with the brass overdubs and eerie female vocal embellishments which transformed a fascinating funk fragment into a classic record.[28]

Indeed, it is worth remembering that much of Brown's music, live and in the studio, was actually heavily orchestrated. In some ways Sammy Lowe and Alfred "Pee Wee" Ellis, who wrote many of the charts for Brown's bands, were heirs to jazz arrangers like Duke Ellington and Charles Mingus, who tailored their compositions to the specific talents of their musicians. Lowe and Ellis translated Brown's musical ideas and sketches into flexible, but highly structured arrangements. These allowed his musicians to stretch out and express themselves, but demanded that they maintain the discipline and cohesion necessary to keep the whole thing together. Post-production technology was then applied to turn these slabs of raw funk into a series of sharp, utterly compelling dance records.

Part of the problem in all of this has been a confusion between what it takes to be a great, creative, innovative musician, and what it takes to make great records. Of course, the two are not mutually exclusive, but they are certainly not synonymous. Rock and pop are full of wonderful records made by players of sorely limited musical ability who have barely known which end of a piano to blow, but who have been blessed with a fine ear for the combinations of words, rhythms and sounds which can move minds, bodies and souls. Even in Rhythm and Blues, where the calibre of musicians was generally high, neither technical proficiency nor simple sincerity were necessarily enough to guarantee a great record.

Given, then, that there was considerably more to making southern soul records than simply opening the mikes to pick up the sounds of innate black and/or white musical genius, the differences between the Stax and the Motown studios were rather less marked than the similarities. Motown's Funk Brothers mostly comprised gifted southern jazz exiles. Much like its integrated southern counterparts, it was a tight unit consisting of musicians who were simultaneously skilled craftsmen and trusty production workers, with a maverick streak of inventive genius bubbling to the surface every once in a glorious while. "They'd let me go on and ad-lib", explained James Jamerson, using precisely the term Jerry Wexler applied to the atmosphere in southern studios ("extremely ad lib"). "I created man", Jamerson insisted; "it was repetitious, but had to be funky and have emotion".[29]

Bidding for the mainstream

While there is no evidence that any black-oriented label or Rhythm and Blues artist ever sought anything less than the widest possible commercial success, it is nonetheless true that Berry Gordy went to extraordinary, often hugely creative, lengths to give his performers the opportunity to make it with white audiences. This was a matter of presentation as well as sound. Motown acts were formally schooled by Maxine Powell, the owner of a Detroit finishing and modelling school, in matters of etiquette, deportment, cosmetics and elocution. Gordy felt this might make them more acceptable to white America and an expanding black middle class for whom mainstream notions of respectability remained important.

Veteran dancer Cholly Atkins was hired to supervise the sophisticated stagecraft and slick choreography which was designed to equip Motown acts for the "transition from the chitlin' circuit to Vegas". Touring London in the autumn of 1964, Mary Wilson made no secret of Gordy's and the Supremes' crossover ambitions, and their willingness to adjust to white expectations to achieve them. "We want to get into the night-club field and we know we're going to have to change our style a good bit to get there. We're working on that kind of singing now . . . I know there's a lot of work ahead of us but we really hope to play the Copa some day". The following July, the Supremes became the first of many Motown acts to play that New York shrine of middle American wealth and respectability; in 1967 they were the first Motown artists to play the even ritzier Las Vegas Copa.[30]

Music critics, far more than fans, have frequently struggled with the idea that showmanship, artifice and spectacle can sometimes be the vehicles, as well as adornments – or, worse, replacements – for genuine creativity, expression and artistic endeavour. Certainly, most accounts which focus on Motown's unapologetic pursuit of the mainstream market assume that it was simply impossible to produce a music which was artistically potent, truly expressive of aspects of contemporary mass black consciousness, and at the same time an ambitious showbiz phenomenon hugely popular with a biracial audience. For example, in a particularly pompous and insensitive 1967 article, rock critic Ralph Gleason used the fact that the Supremes and Four Tops were choreographed to support his claim that black soul performers were "almost totally style with very little substance". Gleason denounced them for being "on an Ed Sullivan trip, striving as hard as they can to get on that stage and become part of the American success story". In fact, as Simon Frith has recognized, "if some of Motown's marketing strategies have touched depths of cynicism that just makes its continued musical inspiration even more humbling".[31]

Motown's unparalleled popularity among black consumers suggests that the black masses shared little of the critics' sense of fakery and fraud. The corporation enjoyed 174 black Top Ten entries during the 1960s. Apparently unable to recognize "real" black music without the guidance of critics like Gleason, blacks even bought huge numbers of records by the Supremes, the bewigged flagship of Gordy's race treachery and integrationist aspirations, giving them 23 black hits and 5 number ones between the restoration of a separate black chart in 1965 and 1969. These black consumers were not unthinking, malleable sponges, who, racial loyalties notwithstanding, bought Motown products they did not really much like simply because Berry Gordy told them to, or because they were force-fed them on the radio. They bought Motown records because they could dance to them and relate to their timeless, witty, erudite and passionate messages of love, loss, loneliness, joy and belonging.

Moreover, black acts at Motown and elsewhere had always worn their sharp mohair suits and silk gowns with, as Marvin Gaye might have said, much pride and joy, seeing them as symbols of how far they had come from humble beginnings. Certainly, the spangled pursuit of success carried no stigma among black fans who had routinely been denied equal opportunity to compete for the financial rewards of the mainstream, but who in the 1960s glimpsed the prospect of a real change in their fortunes. While Gleason and other critics may have preferred their black artists poor and marginalized, Motown made the earnest bid for mainstream success and respect a matter of black pride.

Singer Kim Weston believed that it was the voracious black appetite for such conspicuous images of material success which explained much of Motown's extra-musical appeal and cultural resonance. "When I was coming up in Detroit I had no one to look up to who had made it. Through Motown's help and guidance, today's kids have all the Motown stars to emulate. We were from all sorts of backgrounds and we found success right here in our hometown". Fortunately, this fitted perfectly with Gordy's personal ambitions and his own conception of the role and responsibilities of black capitalists. For Gordy, the creation of personal wealth and the spirited pursuit of mainstream success was in itself a form of political, black economic and cultural leadership.[32]

What Motown offered in its 1960s pomp, then, was less a dilution of some authentic black soul than a brash new urbane synthesis of pop, r&b and gospel, derived from, and perfectly fitted for, a particular moment in black and American history. Stylistically, Motown resolved some of the earlier musical and personal dilemmas of the black pop era, when a Jackie Wilson, or even a Sam Cooke, had sometimes struggled to reconcile roused black pride with the enduring dream of making it, the bigger the better, in the mainstream of American entertainment.

Realizing that dream was a large part of what the Movement was all about in the 1960s, and Berry Gordy succeeded better than any black man of his day. Between 1960 and 1969, Motown released 535 singles, of which 357 made either the Rhythm and Blues and/or pop charts. Of those records, 21 reached number one on both the pop and Rhythm and Blues listings; 6 made the top slot in the pop charts alone; 29 reached number one in the Rhythm and Blues charts only. By 1965, Motown had a gross income of around $8 million and was the nation's leading seller of singles. Five years later it was the richest enterprise in African-American history. All this was achieved with a music which was fuelled by gospel and much closer to the "black" end of a notional black-white musical spectrum than any popular style which had previously enjoyed such sustained and massive white appeal.[33]

Recording the Movement

With Berry Gordy viewing his own economic success as a form of progressive racial politics, it was perhaps not surprising that he did not wish to jeopardize his position by becoming too closely associated with a still controversial black Movement for civil and voting rights. Certainly, there is little evidence of any direct financial support for the Movement from Motown until 1966, when CORE received a donation of $3,000 for its Scholarship, Education and Defense Fund. The previous summer, however, the Hitsville Merchandising branch of the Motown Corporation did assist with the production and distribution of the *Americans in Harmony* souvenir book associated with a benefit concert of the same name. The book raised around $4,000, distributed in unequal amounts among the major national civil rights organizations, the United Negro College Fund (the biggest single beneficiary), and various Detroit community projects.[34]

The "Americans in harmony" concert, and a show organized in March 1965 by WDAS-Philadelphia deejay and local NAACP Freedom Fund Committee treasurer, Georgie Woods, to raise funds for the Selma campaign, marked the tentative beginnings of a much greater presence for Motown at Movement-related events. In the early years of the Movement, however, Motown artists performed at relatively few such benefit concerts. This was hardly usual. Junius Griffin – a Pulitzer Prize-nominated black journalist who worked as director of the SCLC's publicity department in the mid 1960s before moving to Motown's public relations office in early 1967 – could not "recall black or white entertainers playing a major visible role in the Movement . . . until the Selma March".[35]

An exception was Stevie Wonder's appearance at a 23 August 1963 Apollo benefit sponsored by the Negro American Labor Council (NALC), which raised $30,000 for the March on Washington. Without wishing to impugn Gordy's motives, allowing Wonder to appear alongside jazz luminaries like Art Blakey, Carman McCrae and Herbie Mann and, especially, white celebrities like Paul Newman, Joanne Woodward and Tony Bennett in a show where ticket prices ran as high as $100 certainly did nothing to harm Motown's bid for recognition as an emerging power in the wider American entertainment business. At the same time, of course, it safely aligned the company with what was to be the Movement's greatest symbolic expression of biracial brotherhood and faith in the ultimate inclusiveness of the American Dream.[36]

This, however, was not Motown's only connection with the March on Washington. In late 1963, the company put out an album featuring Martin Luther King's "I have a dream" oration and other key speeches from the March – although not until King had obtained a court injunction against the label and taken steps to sue it for infringement of copyright. Before describing the details of this particular legal wrangle and its vinyl solution, it is worth pausing to consider the relationship between King, the early civil rights movement and the recording industry, since it represents a fascinating and revealing, if not altogether surprisingly unexplored lacuna in the literature on both the civil rights struggle and the record business.

The first albums to emerge from the Movement captured the sounds of the sit-ins and freedom rides and were released on Folkways, a label which specialized in various types of what it called People's Musics – union songs, rural ballads, field and factory worksongs, immigrant songs, and other historical pieces. 1960's *Nashville Sit-In Story*, for example, offered a collage of interviews with participants in the city's protests, dramatic re-enactments of key events in the campaign, and ten freedom songs, including the ubiquitous "We shall overcome", and "Keep your eyes on the prize, hold on". The collection was linked together by Rev. C.T. Vivian's narration and accompanied by a booklet which described the campaign and the origins of the recording through contributions by Guy Carawan and Nashville's foremost activist minister, Rev. Kelly Miller Smith.[37]

Over the next few years Folkways released several such albums, mostly in collaboration with SNCC and usually produced by the indefatigable Guy Carawan, the music director of Highlander Folk School and a keen advocate of trying to use grassroots music in the Movement's educational work. In 1961, for example, the label released *We Shall Overcome: Songs of the Freedom Riders and the Sit-Ins*, and *The Sit-In Story: The Story of Lunch-Room Sit-Ins*. The following summer, however, the relationship between SNCC and Folkways threatened to sour due to an incident which revealed the difficulties faced by enthusiastic but inexperienced SNCC members when they attempted to take their beg-steal-and-borrow fundraising philosophy into the often cutthroat world of commercial entertainment and record production.

In the summer of 1962, Bernard LaFayette, one of the SNCC activists who had actually sung on both the *Nashville Sit-In* and *We Shall Overcome* albums, tried to beg 1,000 free disks for SNCC to sell and "eliminate some of our financial strain". Folkways production director Moses Asch replied that the tiny company was in no "position to donate 1,000 records on your request" and that he was "sorry that the SNCC places us in the embarrassing situation of having to say 'no' to such a cause, particularly in view of the fact that we have issued this material which no other company dared to do. We feel that this in itself is a donation to the cause". What made Lafayette's request worse in Asch's mind was that SNCC had apparently decided not to release its next record on Folkways.[38]

Executive secretary Jim Forman just about managed to heal the rift with Folkways by immediately writing to Asch, thanking him for his past support and arranging to buy 500 copies of the Nashville album. The sympathetic Asch in turn offered SNCC a special rate of $1.50 each, if payment was enclosed with the order, or else $2.00, in either case leaving a healthy profit on sales at $3.98 per album. Interestingly, Asch explained that the extra fee for an unpaid consignment of disks was necessary because "we have had some sad experiences in this type of situation, as for instance, the $51.00 due us since September by Hosea Williams of the Savannah Crusade for Voters; it seems they have run out of funds". For a commercial record company, albeit one with a conscience and progressive politics like Folkways, the financial unreliability of many civil rights groups was clearly a concern.[39]

Nevertheless, by the end of the year Asch was again bidding, unsuccessfully as it transpired, to take over production and marketing of SNCC's next album, the Carawan-produced *Freedom in the Air – Albany, Georgia*. The album was eventually distributed by the jazz-oriented Vanguard label, but Forman diplomatically sent Asch ten free copies, "in recognition of the services you and Folkways have rendered in the past". Thereafter, Folkways and SNCC continued to do business, co-operating on recordings like *Selma*

Freedom Songs, Songs of the Selma-Montgomery March, and *The Story of Greenwood, Mississippi.*[40]

In purely financial terms, the market for these Movement albums was rather modest. In 1963, for example, record sales accounted for just $2,862 of SNCC's total income of $308,695; in 1965, it provided $1,293 out of a total of $592,078. To put this into perspective, during the same two years, 1963 and 1965, live shows by the SNCC Freedom Singers raised $17,429 and $13,744 respectively.[41]

Somewhat more lucrative were celebrity benefit records, like CORE's *A Jazz Salute to Freedom* double-album. However, the broader appeal of such releases sometimes raised additional problems. Some copies of CORE's first album – a 1962 release on Dauntless Records entitled *Sit-In Songs: Songs of the Freedom Riders* – had mysteriously found their way into the personal collections of civil rights workers and their friends without payment. Assistant community relations director Val Coleman was thus careful to stress to branch workers that, with the *Jazz Salute* album, "No one, but no one, including James Farmer gets the album free. The albums I'm sending you today should be sold, not given away".[42]

A Jazz Salute was released on Roulette, the label owned by Morris Levy. At the time, Levy was also co-proprietor of the storied Birdland club and commonly held to be a pointsman for the mafia's showbiz operations in New York. Not noted as an advocate of nonviolence, the bullish Levy was apparently an admirer of CORE. Certainly, he was a big help in preparing the album for release, advising Val Coleman on which material to include on the compilation, how to obtain copyright clearances from the various publishers and labels involved, and how to promote the album through the trade press, radio and sympathetic deejays.[43]

Levy even underwrote a $25-a-head fundraising party to celebrate and publicize the official release of the album in early October 1963. Although Coleman was bitterly disappointed by the fact that "some 400 telegrams . . . and some 50 direct invitations" to black celebrities urging them to show support for the Movement by attending the launch party had yielded virtually no response, he expressed the organization's gratitude to Levy for "everything you've done" to produce the record. Within four months of its release, *A Jazz Salute* had raised more than $50,000, which represented around 17,000 copies sold. This number was boosted to an indeterminate extent by James Farmer's quixotic campaign to persuade firms to use the album as a Christmas gift for business contacts, employees and friends. Patrick Cudahy Inc., of Cudahy, Wisconsin, purveyors of "meat products smoked with sweet apple wood", was persuaded to buy 40.[44]

If this was all some way short of Val Coleman's hope that "we may sell hundreds of thousands of these records", it was still hugely helpful for an organization which was in permanent financial difficulty. Coleman's superior, Marvin Rich, complained that he was "constantly juggling to bring in a few extra dollars to meet bills as they came due". Ironically, the revenue from *A Jazz Salute* actually coincided with an unusually buoyant phase in CORE's finances, which like those of all the civil rights organizations had improved in the aftermath of the March on Washington. Nevertheless, total revenue from record sales still accounted for around 8 per cent of CORE's total income for the peculiarly flush half-year period ending on 31 January 1964.[45]

Not surprisingly, the most sought-after and potentially lucrative Movement recording star was Martin Luther King Jr. Almost from the beginning of his public career some of the same independent labels which cut the bulk of Rhythm and Blues music saw in King an opportunity to make money and earn some kind of progressive image among the audiences most likely to invest in King on disk. King, meanwhile, saw recordings as yet another useful means to raise funds and spread the Word.[46]

One of the first overtures came from Atlantic, which wanted to record about 40 minutes of King live, preferably at a convention or meeting "rather than in a church where often emotional displays might mar the reproduction of his speech". Apparently, there was just no shaking Atlantic's concern for a clean-cut sound. Although his assistant Maude Ballou reported that King was "quite interested in getting some of his speeches recorded", nothing ever came of the Atlantic connection and it fell to Dootsie Williams, the black baron of Dootone/Dooto Records, to put out King's first solo album.[47]

Unfortunately, however, this pioneering 1962 release was actually an unauthorized bootleg, recorded at the Zion Hill Baptist Church in Los Angeles. SCLC's executive director Wyatt Tee Walker recalled, "As is our custom, I asked a gentleman who was preparing to set up a recorder, for what purpose the tape would be used. He replied it was 'for the church'. Three months later while we were in Albany, the record came out . . . Neither Dr King nor anyone connected with SCLC knew anything about the record until it was being distributed." After some five months of trying to persuade Williams to withdraw the disk, the SCLC finally filed for a court injunction to prevent further sales.[48]

Not only was the sound quality of the *Martin Luther King at Zion Hill* album wretched – Wexler and Ertegun would have had a fit, or at least hauled King back into a studio for overdubs – but King was also upset that it had captured a rather rambling and lacklustre performance. "I would never have considered using an extemporaneous speech for national distribution", he explained. As Walker pointed out, however, there was a still more troubling aspect to the affair. The Movement and black aspirations were being cynically exploited for personal gain by an ambitious black capitalist. It was, he said, "tragic that dishonesty on the part of Dooto Records and Mr Williams has characterized the entire history of the recording. So many people purchase the record believing the proceeds benefit our movement".[49]

As Walker continued, "After the record was on the market, Mr Williams offered SCLC a skimpy 3% on each record. Most artists receive a minimum of 10% and some receive as much as 20% or 25%". Indeed, even Juggy Murray later offered civil rights groups a royalty rate of 5 per cent on 90 per cent of the sales for *Another Step Forward*, an album recorded at a December 1964 "Tribute to Dr Martin Luther King" in New York. Among other speakers, the album featured Ruby Dee, Ossie Davis, John Lewis, James Farmer, Dorothy Height, Roy Wilkins and Whitney Young, all honouring King in the wake of his Nobel Peace Prize award.[50]

The final indignity came in the autumn of 1962, when Dooto presented King with a statement detailing the income from sales of the record against the costs of production, advertising and administration. It indicated a deficit of $98.30. Nevertheless, King and his colleagues could hardly have failed to notice that the gross income from this shoddily produced, poorly marketed bootleg had actually topped $4,750 and contemplated the possibilities of securing a more favourable recording deal.[51]

As the Dooto debacle faded, Berry Gordy's sister and Motown vice-president Esther Edwards took the first steps towards offering just such a deal. In September 1962, Edwards wrote to King about the "possibility of recording some of your literary works, sermons and speeches". After negotiations, King agreed to let Motown record and release his speech at Detroit's Cobo Hall, which followed a major rally in the city on 23 June 1963. All royalties from the recording were to be assigned to the SCLC, a decision which clearly left its mark on Berry Gordy. It says something about Gordy's priorities that 30 years later, when he wrote his autobiography and tried to explain the depths of his personal admiration for King, he could think of no better testament to the civil rights leader's true, almost otherworldly greatness than the fact that he had rejected Gordy's suggestion that "since it was his artistry and his performance, it was only fair that half the royalties go to him and his family".[52]

By late August 1963, no recording of the Detroit oration had been released. Then suddenly, in the wake of the enormous publicity surrounding the 28 August March on Washington for Jobs and Freedom, the Detroit speech appeared on an album cleverly entitled *The Great March to Freedom*. Gordy had also christened a portion of King's untitled Detroit address "I have a dream". According to King, it was only after Motown "saw the widespread public reception accorded said words when used in the text of my address to the March on Washington", that it retrospectively bestowed this title on part of his earlier Detroit speech.[53]

King was clearly piqued at the way Gordy's name games exploited his success at the Washington march to promote Motown's Cobo Hall album. But the real crux of the suit he brought against Motown and two other labels – Mr Maestro and 20th Century Fox – in the fall of 1963 was their intention to use the "real" Washington "I have a dream" speech on albums which were produced in direct competition to the "official" March on Washington record, as sanctioned by the leaders of the Council for United Civil Rights Leadership (CUCRL). King and his lawyer Clarence Jones claimed that the CUCRL – a sort of multi-partisan clearinghouse which divided the income from major joint projects among the different civil rights groups – held exclusive rights to King's Washington speech and non-exclusive rights to those by other participants in the March. Moreover, the CUCRL had already arranged for WRVR, the radio station of New York's Riverside Church, to produce the official record of the events, with all the profits going to the Movement.[54]

Not surprisingly, in addition to WRVR and the three labels which had simply gone ahead and issued records of the event without permission and with no arrangement to pay anything to the CUCRL, there were several other companies which had submitted more courteous formal bids for the contract to record the March. Bobby Robinson's black-owned Enjoy label was one, offering CUCRL a highly respectable 50 per cent share of the anticipated $1.40 per album profits. Another was the non-profit-making Pacifica Foundation's WBAI-New York radio outlet, whose proposal would have netted the CUCRL around $3.00 per disk, assuming they were sold at $4.98 each. In the end, Maele Daniele Dufty, longtime manager of Billie Holiday and wife of William Dufty, the ghostwriter for Holiday's autobiography *Lady sings the blues*, worked with Jack Summerfield of WRVR to put out the unambiguously titled *The Official March on Washington Album* for a bargain $2.98. Although they hoped to attract more sales by keeping the price at rock-bottom, this arrangement still yielded more than $1.80 per sale to the CUCRL.[55]

There was a curious conclusion to Motown's involvement in this episode. On 3 October 1963, New York federal Judge James Bryan granted King a temporary injunction which prevented Motown, 20th Century Fox and Mr Maestro from selling recordings which featured the "I have a dream" speech until further hearings on the matter could be held in November. Shortly after this preliminary decision, King suddenly dropped the suit against Motown while continuing to press those against the other two companies. Clarence Jones claimed that this was because Motown had only intended to use excerpts from King's Washington speech, but by the end of the year the company was promoting its snappily titled *Great March to Washington* album, featuring "I have a dream" in its entirety. It may never be clear precisely what prompted King to relent in his suit against Motown while pursuing the other companies into the courtroom. But it is not too fanciful to suggest that there may simply have been a sense that it was impolitic to assail a black-owned company of increasing financial power and prestige in this way.[56]

As for the remaining suits, the legal position concerning the status of King's speech was pretty murky, and certainly not everyone was as confident as Clarence Jones that King would win. When L. Joseph Overton, secretary of the NALC, one of the original sponsors of the March and part of the CUCRL, discovered the Mr Maestro record he "immediately consulted with my attorneys to inquire as to whether or not we could stop the issuance of this record". Unlike Jones, Overton's lawyers believed that, given the widespread television and radio coverage and the reprinting of the speech in the press, "this would be practically impossible, since this was public property".[57]

With so much legal uncertainty, King and Jones were mightily pleased when, on 13 December 1963, a New York federal court held that King's Washington utterances were still technically "unpublished", not in the public domain, and protected by laws of intellectual property. The earlier temporary injunction to prohibit further reproductions of the speech without King's express consent was made permanent. Then, with the legal case settled, King promptly empowered the CUCRL to negotiate a proper deal with 20th Century Fox, by which it secured a $5,000 advance and a 5 per cent royalty on sales of the *Freedom March to Washington, August 28, 1963* album which appeared complete with "I have a dream". By the end of 1964, even Folkways had a CUCRL-approved album out, called, with a woeful lack of imagination, *We Shall Overcome: Documentary of the March on Washington*. Several other March recordings would follow King's death in April 1968, all generating income for either the SCLC, or the Martin Luther King, Jr Memorial Fund.[58]

Meanwhile, in the wake of the March on Washington, Morris Theorgood of the Philadelphia-based Progress Records wrote to Marvin Rich, hoping to secure the contract for distributing King's next album. Theorgood carefully pointed out that Progress was "the first Negro owned and operated distributor in this territory", and praised CORE for "all you have done in our fight for freedom". Theorgood clearly sought to align himself and his company with the mounting black struggle for equal opportunity. Rich politely advised him to try the SCLC which was, after all, King's organization.[59]

The dilemmas of black-owned record companies

None of the other black-owned labels to emerge in the early-to-mid 1960s could rival the visionary aspect of All For One, or the entrepreneurial verve and commercial triumph of Motown. Nevertheless, there were several others which contributed heavily to the richness of soul music and more modestly to the slow growth of a significant black proprietorial and executive presence within the industry. These included a number of hangovers from the r&b and black pop eras, including Dootsie Williams' Dooto, Sam Cooke's SAR and Derby, Juggy Murray's Sue, Vivian and James Bracken's Vee Jay, and Florence Greenberg and Luther Dixon's Scepter and Wand. Of the newcomers, Kenny Gamble's Gamble records in Philadelphia was perhaps the most significant. In 1966, Gamble began a long run of light soul hits with the Intruders' "(We'll be) united", which eventually led to the mighty Philadelphia International Records empire he created with Leon Huff.

Most black-owned labels remained small, under-capitalized, and intensely vulnerable affairs with tiny rosters, limited independence, and often short lifespans. This was certainly true of most artist-owned labels, like Harvey Fuqua's Anna, Tri-Phi and Harvey, Roscoe Robinson's Gerri, and Syl Johnson's Shama, all based in Chicago. Even Ray Charles' Tangerine, a label distributed by ABC and featuring veterans like Percy Mayfield and Lula Reed, remained a sleeping pygmy in the field. Slightly more successful was Double-L, the latest enterprise by the indefatigable Lloyd Price, whose diverse business dealings also included the acquisition of the Birdland club from Morris Levy in 1964. For a while Double-L was home to both Price, who resurfaced in 1963 with a hit version of "Misty", and Wilson Pickett, who did well with "It's too late" before moving to Atlantic and a string of major hits.[60]

The leader of the Impressions, Curtis Mayfield, got off to a promising entrepreneurial start with his twin Chicago labels, Mayfield and Windy C. Distributed by the New York label Calla, Mayfield had decent national black hits with the soulful girl group, the Fascinations, notably "Girls are out to get you", while Windy C, distributed by Cameo-Parkway of Philadelphia, had major crossover successes with the juvenile soul stars, the Five Stairsteps. Neither label lasted very long, however. Windy C collapsed along with Cameo-Parkway in 1967; Mayfield disintegrated the following year when hits for the Fascinations dried up. Curtom, Mayfield's next enterprise, proved more durable, but the fate of Windy C and Mayfield was probably more typical of small black labels which remained heavily dependent on the success of one or two acts, or the support of a bigger label, for survival.[61]

In Detroit, where Jack and Devora Brown's Fortune was a model of black enterprise until its demise in the mid 1960s, a number of other black-owned labels emerged around the same time as Motown. In various accidental and calculated ways Motown contributed to the collapse of most of these rivals, not least because its very success meant that the best talent gravitated towards it. Ric-Tic and Golden World were both founded by WCHB-Detroit deejay LeBaron Taylor and co-owned with Joanne Jackson and local club proprietor Ed Wingate. Their most successful releases used moonlighting Motown musicians, eager to earn some extra cash, on songs like Edwin Starr's pulsating "Agent double-o-soul". In 1968, Gordy effectively ended such practices and removed Motown's only real local competition by buying the labels for $1 million and recruiting Starr to his own Motown galaxy.[62]

Lu Pine and Flick were just a bit older than Motown. Founded in the late 1950s by an Alabama migrant, Robert West, the labels recorded a rough-and-ready style of gospelized male r&b by Mack Rice, the Falcons (who boasted future soul luminaries Eddie Floyd and Wilson Pickett in their line-up), the Primes (who later became the Temptations), and the Ohio Untouchables, whose lead singer-guitarist, Robert Ward, later found fame and no little fortune with the gelatinous funk of the Ohio Players. West also experimented with a variety of girl groups, among them the Corvells, Kittens, Satin Angels and a sister act to the Primes called the Primettes, who released one histrionic single, "Tears of sorrow", in 1960. Reduced to a trio by the departure of Betty Travis, the Primettes – Diana Ross, Florence Ballard and Mary Wilson – soon made their way to nearby Motown, where Berry Gordy also had a notion that girl groups might be the key to major cross-over success. The Primettes were rechristened the Supremes.[63]

Lu Pine was distributed by an independent black-owned Detroit firm called B & H, and never really recovered when B & H was ruined in the payola scandals of the early 1960s. Payola also had a part to play in the demise of Vee Jay, the vibrant Chicago label founded by James and Vivian Bracken, which was the most successful of all the black-owned independents before the rise of Motown. There was, however, more to Vee Jay's mid 1960s collapse than a taste for extravagant payola which included flying in 12 Norwegian call-girls to entertain a gathering of influential black deejays in Las Vegas. There was more even than the fondness of some of its chief executives and creative forces, Ewart Abner, E. Rodney Jones, Bill "Bunky" Sheppard and Calvin Carter, for the odd flutter on those Las Vegas tables. Vee Jay president Abner, who organized many of the company's legendary junkets, secretly "borrowed" over $170,000 from the company and later admitted to using some of it to fund his own gambling.[64]

The real problem lurking beneath all these high jinks and misdemeanours was that Vee Jay was still being run much like the local family r&b label it had been in 1953. This sort of enthusiastic amateurism proved totally inadequate for the demands of a national label with a multi-million-dollar turnover and eager designs on the biracial market. Management was relaxed to the point of torpor, particularly after the firing of the innovative and energetic, if capricious and profligate, Abner in 1963. There was simply little at the label which passed for financial accounting, forward planning or a coherent sales strategy, let alone a sound administrative structure to co-ordinate these aspects of a large independent label. Cash flow crises were endemic and while the label had excellent relations with black deejays and distributors, it never systematically cultivated links with white distributors, or with the Top Forty deejays and programme managers whose co-operation was vital in securing access to the mainstream market.

In 1964, the Brackens attempted to arrest the company's slide into anarchy by hiring a white executive, Randall Wood, as president. Wood tried gamely to sort out the company's finances, unearthing hundreds of thousands of dollars in undischarged debts and taxes and launching an ambitious effort to expand and diversify operations. That year Vee Jay still did some $15 million of business, but much of it was from its old Beatles records. Amid all the managerial and fiscal chaos it had already lost some of its most successful acts (Gene Chandler, Dee Clark, the Beatles and Four Seasons), while others, like Jerry Butler, were suddenly stone dead in the market place. In this uncertain climate, with a shaky financial base and dwindling artistic assets, what was needed was consolidation and retrenchment, not a speculative leap into new ventures.

What made matters worse was that Wood's initiatives also became associated with the deteriorating racial situation at the label. One of his first moves had been to set up plush new offices in Santa Monica, to where he and most of the label's handful of white officers and sales representatives withdrew. This split left the Brackens and most of Vee Jay's veteran black staff back in their less than palatial Chicago offices, pondering, as the crisis deepened, whether the new white executives were simply creaming off whatever they could before the whole operation went sour.

In February 1965, the Brackens fired the white west coast management team, except for Wood who continued for a while as titular president of the company before James Bracken assumed that role. The prodigal Ewart Abner was recalled as general manager. He promptly dismantled the expensive and unproductive west coast operation and tried once more to charm and hustle the label into solvency. But the rot was set too deep. In May 1966, the label suspended all operations and in August it was officially declared bankrupt with combined debts to the IRS and various creditors of $3.3 million.[65]

The lack of professional expertise and organizational structure at Vee Jay was only too apparent at other ill-fated Independents, which were often started more as a hobby than a business enterprise. That such problems were especially acute at black-owned labels did not indicate a lack of black managerial talent or aptitude, or some preternatural black tendency towards embezzlement and larceny. It reflected the continued absence of professional training and executive experience for blacks in the recording and radio industries. Al Bell, one of a handful of senior black executives in white-owned companies in the 1960s, recognized that "The record business has been just like everything else in America for the black man. He hasn't had exposure. He hasn't had a chance to get in and *learn* the mechanics of the business". This was a widespread problem and many black label owners were forced to turn to white professionals to provide the necessary level of financial and managerial expertise.[66]

Sam Cooke, for example, took a deep pride in his entrepreneurial activities. He wrote in the *Pittsburgh Courier* of how few artists understood "that show business is a business", or prepared themselves "for the inevitable day when . . . record sales take a sudden drop". He, however, had "organized [his] career on a business-like basis", set up his companies and rested comfortably knowing that "If, in the future, I can't find anyone who will pay me to sing, I'll still be in a position of getting paid when others sing".[67]

With blacks still struggling to exert real power and influence within the recording industry, even black power militancy often appeared on white-owned labels. *Seize The Time* by the Black Panther's Elaine Brown was released on Vault.

In fact, although his fledgling empire of SAR, Derby and KAGS did well enough at first, making a small fortune from his own songwriting and putting out sacred and secular records by the likes of the Soul Stirrers, Johnnie Taylor and the Sims Twins, Cooke and his associates actually lacked the business and financial expertise to capitalize on the talent they recruited, or the respectable sales they racked up. In an attempt to sort out his chaotic finances, Cooke hired rock and roll's most legendary ledgerman, Allen Klein, first as an accountant, but subsequently as his manager. Cooke's faith was quickly justified as Klein's financial fine-tooth comb unpicked nearly $150,000 in unpaid royalties from RCA. Klein imposed order on Cooke's scrambled fiscal affairs and added a mob-like muscularity to his business dealings. In September 1963, he negotiated a new contract with RCA, which incorporated a massive four-year advance of $450,000, whereby Cooke's songs were actually cut for a company called Tracey, officially owned by Klein, but with Cooke as president. The recordings were then sold to RCA for marketing and distribution, with Cooke taking his money out of Tracey. Klein's personal stake in this arrangement remains unclear but his relationship with Cooke later soured when the singer became suspicious of some of his dealings. Nevertheless, the 1963 contract apparently gave Cooke total control over his money, with much reduced tax liability, and absolute creative control over his music.[68]

Berry Gordy also experienced difficulties finding suitable black professionals to help him run Motown efficiently and so filled many of Motown's key executive positions with experienced whites. Alan Abrams, who headed the publicity department, was one of his first appointments, while in 1962 Gordy hired Sidney Noveck as the chief accountant for Jobete and Motown. Noveck's brother Harold expertly handled the company's tax affairs for years. Liberal New York attorney, George Schiffer, who was also one of CORE's retinue of volunteer lawyers, was Motown's chief copyright lawyer. Schiffer was instrumental in successfully internationalizing the operation in the mid 1960s. Barney Ales ran the distribution department, along with Phil Jones and Irving Biegel. Legal advisor Ralph Seltzer became Gordy's special assistant and later head of the A&R department. Along with other whites, Michael Roshkind – who succeeded Abrams at the helm of the public relations department – and Ales, Seltzer eventually became a vice-president of the company.[69]

Gordy's attitude towards the hiring of these white executives again illustrated that, for all his appeals to black brotherhood when it came to selling records, or placing them on black playlists and record racks, and for all the Corporation's much vaunted personal links to the black community in Detroit, which supplied artists, staff and even impromptu panels to audition material for possible release, his priorities were essentially those of a hard-nosed entrepreneurial capitalist who just happened to be black. Gordy simply hired the best help he could afford, regardless of colour or sentiment.

And this was probably critical, rather than incidental, to his phenomenal success in a world where myriad obstacles to successful black businesses persisted. It was, Harold Battiste admiringly conceded when he contemplated Gordy's successful pursuit of a decidedly slim main chance, "part of what it takes to do what he did, and a part of what I couldn't do".[70]

The birth of soul radio

One of the main consequences of the strong white presence among Motown's promotional and distribution staff was that the label enjoyed much better access to white-controlled retail outlets and radio playlists than most other black-owned companies. "Black radio was everything to people like me", Berry Gordy admitted, and Motown's success was inextricably bound up with developments in radio during the 1960s.[71]

Black-oriented radio had flourished in the decade after the Second World War by successfully filling a market niche which had been underexploited by established broadcasters. In the late 1950s, as the once rigid boundaries between the audiences for black-oriented and white pop radio dissolved, the former no longer held a monopoly in the programming of Rhythm and Blues music, while the latter conceded a portion of the young white audience to black-oriented stations. During the early-to-mid 1960s, however, black-oriented stations tended to become niche players once more, programming mainly black music for predominantly, if seldom exclusively, black audiences.

This trend was essentially a function of legislation, economics and changing musical predilections. Following the payola hearings, any publishing or recording company interests held by station owners, deejays or managers were ruled to constitute a conflict of interest and a source of public deception. The FCC demanded divestment of all such holdings and called for more rigorous accounting procedures to monitor the sources and disbursement of station revenue. In September 1960, Congress amended the Federal Communications Act of 1934 to include fines of up to $10,000 and possible imprisonment for payola offenders. Moreover, it placed responsibility for the observance of these new rules firmly with station management. Under this increased scrutiny, radio station owners drew even more power to themselves and their programme managers. This further curtailed the already limited independence of deejays, who were compelled to sign affidavits forswearing the acceptance of payola. These developments helped hasten the gradual demise of the broker deejays who had dominated r&b and early rock and roll radio. They also accelerated the national trend towards Top Forty pop radio, in which formats, playlists and petty cash flow were ever more closely controlled by station owners, managers and programme directors.[72]

In this new broadcast environment, black-oriented stations were frequently unable to secure or maintain a major share of the white youth audience in their catchment areas. Those youths were increasingly tuning into Top Forty stations which played all the latest hits, including the most successful black records. Consequently, in the early-to-mid 1960s, black-oriented stations refocused on a black audience which was moving steadily away from black and white pop towards the more racially discrete sounds of soul. Unlike many white pop fans who were happy to hear Sam Cooke next to Simon and Garfunkel, black listeners were less and less interested in sitting through dozens of white pop hits to hear the few black ones which made the playlist.

Because of the racial identification factor which had always given black broadcasters an edge in the battle for black listeners, soul deejays preserved a degree of personal intimacy with, and potential influence on, their black audiences which was rare among Top Forty deejays. The sounds of soul and the hip street patter and mild espousal of the Cause by black deejays like E. Rodney Jones at WVON-Chicago, Bobby Q-Day on WCHB-Detroit, George "Hound Dog" Lorenz at WUFO-Buffalo, and Nathaniel "Magnificent" Montegue at KGFJ-Los Angeles appealed to the black community's burgeoning sense of cultural identity and pride. Indeed, as sociologist Ulf Hannerz later noted, soul radio itself became a defining feature of contemporary black culture. "Black radio, its programming and its personnel . . . take their place among the things ghetto dwellers know they have in common, the things which serve to define their community".[73]

These stations and deejays also had a unique commercial potential which many record labels were keen to exploit. For record companies struggling to get their products onto the tightly regulated Top Forty airwaves, a concentrated effort to get good coverage for a disk on the nation's most important black-oriented stations could result in enough black sales – somewhere over 100,000 copies – to nudge it into the lower reaches of the pop charts. Once there, it could attract Top Forty airplay and reach a much wider white market. In the early 1970s, several major recording companies, led by CBS, would adopt this strategy extensively, using the breakout potential of black-oriented broadcasting and the black market to consolidate their domination of the national pop charts.[74]

In the 1960s, however, no company was more adept than Motown at courting black-oriented radio both as the conduit to a black community which had some $27,000 million of spending power by 1966, and as a stepping-stone to the even more lucrative white market. Initially without the financial resources or promotional and distribution networks to compete with even the bigger black-oriented Independents like Vee Jay or Atlantic, let alone with the resurgent Majors of the early 1960s, Berry Gordy made personal, race-based appeals to black deejays for preferential treatment, and sent out his promotional staff to badger those in key markets to play

Motown records. He even offered the free services of some of his acts when deejays put on live shows to persuade them to give Motown products a sympathetic hearing.[75]

The appointment of esteemed veteran "Jockey" Jack Gibson to the label's promotional department in 1962 strengthened the links with black deejays until, as Nelson George explained, "it got to the point that Motown began, not totally unreasonably, to take black radio for granted, since these deejays were committed to Motown's success by economics and by race". This strategy was a conspicuous success. Long before the Supremes enjoyed their first hit record, Mary Wilson recalled tours on which she heard the group's songs, and those of other Motown artists, already on black-oriented stations throughout the nation. Meanwhile, the presence of white executives in sales and distribution helped ease the path of Motown product onto black-oriented stations which still had white programme directors and owners, and did no harm at all when dealing with Top Forty stations either.[76]

Racial solidarity and Gordy's keen eye for the main chance apart, however, it was the quality of Motown's recordings that ultimately accounted for the company's extraordinary access to both the pop and soul airwaves. Until the late 1960s and the advent of stereo FM radio and improved hi-fi, Motown records were carefully geared to the audio limitations of the humble transistor radio, particularly the car radio, and the portable record player. Mike McClain, the technical wizard of the Motown studios, even rigged up a radio speaker in the label's quality control office so that Gordy and his advisors could hear newly recorded songs as the potential customer might over the airwaves. For much the same reason Gordy insisted on hearing cut disks, rather than pristine tapes or acetates, when selecting material for release.[77]

Not only did Gordy take exceptional care to ensure that his records were mixed just right for radio, he also catered for the mechanics of Top Forty playlist selection. Top Forty station manager Bill Drake reckoned he routinely reviewed a hundred records for possible airplay in a 30-minute session, rejecting those which did not immediately grab his attention. Thus, it was no accident that many Motown singles should have particularly startling or seductive intros: the gunshot which opened Jr Walker's "Shotgun", or the beguiling flute and galloping drum beat which launched the Four Tops' "Reach out, I'll be there". Motown records, with their riveting openings and customized sound, impressed programmers and frequently got onto Top Forty stations, where, because of the concern with balanced playlists, the number of soul records scheduled for any week was strictly limited.[78]

In stark contrast to Top Forty stations, by the mid 1960s, there was little besides soul music on most black-oriented radio outlets. This soulful diet was modified only by traditional gospel and religious slots on Sundays, and parsimonious helpings of jazz, talk shows, news, and current affairs programming. It was certainly ironic that the quantity and quality of news and public affairs broadcasting on most black-oriented stations probably declined during the decade or so after *Brown* just as the civil rights movement blossomed. With cautious and occasionally flagrantly hostile whites still exercising overwhelming financial and managerial control over black-oriented radio, the capacity of individual stations, deejays, or civil rights groups to use radio to encourage – or sometimes even to report accurately – the ongoing black struggle remained sorely limited.[79]

Nevertheless, by the early 1960s many black-oriented stations were at least willing to provide airtime to the mainstream civil rights organizations. In 1964, 95 per cent of the NAACP branches seeking airtime on local stations were successful. By the following summer 70 black-oriented stations, including southern facilities such as WOKJ-Jackson, WRMA-Montgomery and WYLD-New Orleans, carried the Urban League's weekly flagship shows, *The Leaders Speak* and *Civil Rights Roundup*, which provided a weekly digest of Movement activities. In December 1964, shortly after an SCLC executive retreat had recommended that the organization should "discontinue paying for weekly radio programs", Zenas Sears offered WAOK-Atlanta's free services to produce and syndicate a series of fundraising and informational announcements for the organization. The station also produced the 15-minute *Martin Luther King Speaks* show, which was aired every Sunday on WAOK and co-operating stations, eventually reaching a weekly audience of over two million.[80]

Individual black deejays also played their part in raising money and supporting particular campaigns. John Henry Faulks of WINS-New York could be relied upon to plug local civil rights benefits, like SNCC's 1962 "Salute to southern students" in Carnegie Hall. Martin Luther King noted how Purvis Spann of WVON-Chicago had raised crucial funds for the Freedom Summer of 1964, while at WDAS-Philadelphia, Georgie Woods raised money and organized on-air voter registration drives to harness the political potential of the city's black population.[81]

Events in Birmingham in 1963 offered an even more dramatic example of the way in which an engaged black-oriented station and activist deejays could occasionally assume a genuinely supportive role in the southern struggle. When the SCLC decided to employ Birmingham's black schoolchildren in the demonstrations of 2 and 3 May, the major black-oriented station in the city, WENN, was an ideal vehicle for getting word of the protests to the city's youth.

Shelley "The Playboy" Stewart had joined WENN from WEDR a few years earlier. Together with the charismatic newsman-turned-disk-spinner "Tall" Paul White, Stewart directed people to the mass meetings and demonstrations by broadcasting coded announcements concerning a "big party" to be held in the city's downtown Kelly Ingram Park, or at the 16th Street Baptist Church. "We good old Baptists knew there wasn't going to be any dance", recalled Larry Russell, a high school participant in the demonstrations who, like most black kids in Birmingham, knew precisely what the deejays meant. Rev. Abraham Woods, an activist minister who spent much of his time in and out of local schools trying to rally other people's children to join the protests, certainly appreciated how effective the medium was. By the time Woods returned home to talk to his own children, he found that Tall Paul had already done the job and his three oldest girls were in the park when Bull Connor unleashed the dogs and turned on the fire hoses.[82]

Clearly, WENN's broadcasts were of great practical, as well as inspirational, value to the Movement in Birmingham – not least, as Martin Luther King later acknowledged, in helping to keep the official campaign almost entirely nonviolent despite white provocation. Yet activists like Larry Russell appreciated that deejays at the station hardly had a free hand. They still had to air secret, coded messages out of fear of attracting the attention of hostile Birmingham whites, or offending sponsors, or running foul of the station's white owners. "You knew it was coded for the protection of their jobs", Russell recalled. Stewart would sometimes report the turnout at a mass meeting after the event, because "Then it's news, and he's covered himself. He might add something in a real quick and sly way – 'I wonder how many are going to be there Wednesday night?' and then he'd go into a rap". Certainly, without the complicity of WENN's sympathetic white station manager Joe Lackey, who did much to facilitate the station's on-air commitment to community affairs, WENN announcers might have had considerably less room for manoeuvre.[83]

WENN's sort of cautious but committed interventionism remained exceptional during the early civil rights era. Black-oriented radio was more concerned with raising black consciousness – and sometimes cash – through the airing of black cultural productions than about efforts to direct either consciousness or cash towards organized protest. Indeed, in 1963, even relatively engaged, policitized black-oriented stations like WENN and WDAS still only allocated 3.8 per cent and 4.4 per cent of their respective schedules to news broadcasting.[84]

Despite this tentativeness, however, the first half of the 1960s did witness the first stirrings of a campaign to attain more community control over, and better news and public affairs broadcasting from, black-oriented radio. One of the earliest initiatives in this area was the Negro Radio Association (NRA). Founded in 1960 with 37 affiliated stations, the NRA had a mission to "develop and improve Negro programming and to foster and develop public service programming for the benefit of Negro groups". Revealingly, the NRA was made up entirely of white owners and executives like Egmont Sonderling, John McClendon and Robert Rounsaville. Even the fact that this was a time of rising optimism about the possibilities for meaningful interracial co-operation could not disguise the stark reality that black-oriented radio was being run almost entirely by, and for the profit of, white men.[85]

Deejays like "Tall" Paul White on WENN played a significant role in the Birmingham civil rights campaign of 1963.

The NRA was chaired by Francis Fitzgerald, the president-treasurer-owner of WGIV-Charlotte. A former announcer and programme director for various South Carolina stations, Fitzgerald simply does not fit easily with any generalizations about southern liberals, or about the motives of white owners of black-oriented stations. At WGIV, which Fitzgerald started in 1947, black deejays like "Chattie" Hattie Leeper and "Genial" Gene Potts excelled, as usual, at the microphone, but were also given executive positions. Leeper was Women's Affairs Director; Potts was both Public Affairs Director and a member of the Board of Directors of the station's parent company, the Charlotte Radio and Television Corporation. With black technical staff almost as rare as black management, Fitzgerald also hired Uriah Gooding as one of the first black radio engineers in the country. A founder member of the Opportunity Foundation, a biracial group dedicated to improving race relations in Charlotte, Fitzgerald's reputation in the local black community soared when, in the midst of the desegregation crisis – a time when many avowed southern racial moderates were struck dumb by the forces of massive resistance – WGIV boldly adopted a black-white handshake as its logo. In 1965, Fitzgerald offered a modest personal contribution and special rates for ads on WGIV to Fred Alexander in his successful bid to become Charlotte's first black city councilman.[86]

Yet, if Fitzgerald was more racially sensitive and enlightened than many of his colleagues in the business of black radio, the bottom line on the WGIV account ledger was never too far from his mind. The black community in Charlotte understood this perfectly well. When the black St Paul's Baptist Church presented the white Catholic Fitzgerald with an award for his contribution to racial progress in the city, it commended him for his lack of personal prejudice, generosity and commitment to the black community's programming needs, but also commemorated WGIV's economic success and the black advertising, retail and employment opportunities created as a result. "In a material world", the citation stated, "nothing more tangibly expresses brotherhood than to extend respectable and lucrative employment to members of a minority group of people, and to share unselfishly the fruits and substance of your property with a brother without regard to race, color, or creed". It was this blend of altruism and acquisitiveness which made Fitzgerald a sensible choice to head the NRA, where a commitment to better public service for blacks fused and sometimes collided with commercial priorities to "bring to the attention of advertisers the potential of the Negro market".[87]

During the early-to-mid 1960s, several other groups were also concerned with improving black representation, power and remuneration in the industry. These were worthy goals in themselves, but they were also pursued in the belief that a greater black presence in the industry, particularly at an executive and proprietorial level, would lead naturally to a more politically engaged and responsive mass medium. In late 1963, a time when the NAACP was debating whether to adopt the sort of direct action protest tactics used so effectively by other civil rights organizations, the Philadelphia branch of the Association, inspired by Georgie Woods, gave local station WIBG an ultimatum to hire black deejays and newscasters or face a black boycott, not just of the station, but of the products it advertised.[88]

Because blacks were not a sufficiently large portion of the WIBG audience to make the boycott effective, the Philadelphia campaign was unsuccessful.

The following year, however, the picketing of KFWB-Los Angeles by the NAACP, CORE and other local black pressure groups resulted in the hiring of black deejay Larry McCormack.[89]

The KFWB campaign was discussed at the 1964 NATRA convention in Chicago. Originally a loose social association of Rhythm and Blues and jazz deejays organized by Jack Gibson in the mid 1950s, a decade later NATRA emerged as the most dynamic organization in the struggle for greater black control over the content and rewards of black-oriented broadcasting. In Chicago, NATRA announced that it would not "encourage picketing of any station unless all reasonable means of arbitration or negotiations have first been explored". Thus it sounded a conciliatory tone, hoping, though none too certainly, that its aims might be achieved by negotiation, but reserving the option of direct action should this fail. Already, however, NATRA, like the civil rights movement as a whole in the aftermath of Atlantic City, was beginning to split into broadly identifiable radical and moderate factions.[90]

Del Shields, then a colleague of Georgie Woods at WDAS, delivered the most portentous address at the Chicago meeting. He urged black deejays to demand better remuneration from white station owners and better service from record companies. But he also demanded much greater station involvement in local politics and black community affairs. He called for an increase in black ownership and senior management to break the exploitative grip of whites and ensure greater responsiveness to black needs. "How can a white man know what a black man needs?", Shields asked. Black power was what was required.[91]

The following year, at NATRA's Houston convention, a new breed of young, highly politicized black deejays and staff, lead by Shields, his WDAS colleague Jimmy Bishop, Ed Wright of Clevelend's WABQ, plus veteran all-round music business fixer, Clarence Avante, seized control of NATRA's executive. This takeover ushered in a more militant phase in the struggle for black power within the music and broadcasting industries, as both rhetoric and tactics changed to reflect the black nationalism of the period. In a deeper sense, however, the co-ordinates of that struggle remained remarkably fixed. It was still defined by the same complex mixture of economic self-interest, personal ambition, racial loyalty, and communal responsibility which had characterized efforts to secure black power in the world of Rhythm and Blues during the first half of the 1960s.[92]

CHAPTER EIGHT

"On the outside looking in": Rhythm and Blues, celebrity politics and the civil rights movement

It is not a given that because somebody is brilliant, or talented, or great, that they have consciousness and they care about the world they participate in. You will find in every category, and especially with entertainers, a huge capacity to be self-serving. (Bernice John-son Reagon)[1]

The making of a myth

In October 1966, the black writer Rolland Snellings published an article in *Liberator* which proclaimed Rhythm and Blues a potent weapon in the black freedom struggle and hailed its singers as "PRIEST-PHILOSOPHERS" of the Movement. With jazz "taken over by racketeers and moved downtown into the clubs and bars of the middle-class pleasure seekers, away from the roots, away from the Heart, the Womb, away from the home of the people: uptown ghetto", Rhythm and Blues had become the "people's music, THIS is the reflection of their rising aspirations, THESE are the Truths sung by their modern PRIESTS and PHILOSOPHERS: WE are on the move and our music is MOVING with us".[2]

Snellings' powerful polemic has remained remarkably close to the conventional wisdom in writings both scholarly and popular on the relationship between Rhythm and Blues, its practitioners and the Movement. Some commentators have been even more forthright, claiming for soul singers a major leadership role in the Movement. Musicologist Portia Maultsby, for example, has written that "through their texts, soul singers not only discussed depressing social and economic conditions for black communities but also offered solutions for improvement and change". For A.X. Nicholas, soul music was nothing less than the "poetry of the Black Revolution", while in a memorably shallow, if sadly typical, piece of mythmaking Robert Stephens claimed that soul performers "defined the expectations of black Americans" and even "directed" them, acting as "quasi-political representatives" who offered the black masses political "strategies which were the antithesis of acceptance and accommodation".[3]

Of course, Snellings, Maultsby and the rest were absolutely right to claim that the hopes and dreams, fears and frustrations, of ordinary blacks were expressed and embodied in the various forms of Rhythm and Blues. Black popular music and dance reflected, encoded and, through radio, records, dances and tours, helped to nationalize the new black pride and conscious-ness which was inextricably linked, cause and effect, to the emergence of a viable mass campaign for black civil and voting rights. And yet, the claims that Rhythm and Blues provided some sort of explicit running commentary on the Movement, with the men and women of soul emerging as notable participants, even leaders, tacticians and philosophers of the black struggle, have usually depended more on partisan assertion than hard evidence.

The tendency to simplify the complex relationship between Rhythm and Blues and the Movement has been encouraged and exemplified by two characteristics in most writings on the subject. The first has been a heavy reliance on song lyrics to locate and explain Rhythm and Blues' social and political relevance. Overt references to, and advocacy of, the civil rights struggle, or gritty depictions of the black social and economic predicament, or rousing calls for black pride and resistance, have routinely been presented as the principal site and source of the music's multiple meanings. This has certainly been true among Movement historians who, on the rare occasions when they have actually ventured beyond the freedom songs to mention the musical form most important to the mass of black Americans, have usually settled for a passing mention of, typically, James Brown's "Say it loud, I'm black and I'm proud" as proof of soul's political engagement and racial consciousness.[4]

This essentially logocentric approach has obscured the fact that the pol-itics, meaning and influence of Rhythm and Blues did not reside solely – or even primarily – in such obviously engaged "social" or "political" lyrics. This was just as well, since "Say it loud" was not even cut until 1968, by which time the Movement was more than a dozen years old. Indeed, although there were some conspicuous exceptions, soul – like r&b, rock and roll, and black pop before it – had become the premier musical expression of mass black consciousness in the early-to-mid 1960s while paying relatively little explicit attention to the ongoing freedom struggle.

The second major impediment to a clear understanding of Rhythm and Blues' relationship to the Movement has been the tendency to exaggerate the extent of personal involvement in, or tangible support for, organized black protest by the heroes and heroines of soul. Because by the late 1960s it was more than any self-respecting soul sister or brother could afford in terms of conscience, credibility or commerce not to be pledging very public allegiance to the struggle, doing benefit concerts, donating to worthy black causes, and often boldly speaking or singing out against racism in the entertainment industry and society at large, there has been an assumption that Rhythm and Blues artists and entrepreneurs had always been so forthright, committed and engaged; that they had always given generously of their prestige, income, time and talent to the Movement.

Indeed, many writers have found it extremely difficult to explain the significance of Rhythm and Blues in the black community at a time of widespread political mobilization and heightened racial consciousness without establishing some kind of direct linkage between its performers and organized black protest. This is even apparent in such sophisticated works as Daniel Wolff's biography of Sam Cooke, in which the author simply tries too hard to root Cooke's contemporary meaning in his personal activism and public support for the Movement and its goals.[5]

Certainly, Wolff sets much store by the claim of former Impression and Ice-Man of soul, Jerry Butler, that soul singers were "at the vanguard of the movement". In the early 1960s, Butler recalled that Cooke and other "entertainers would go in with the kids", joining student protests quietly, without fanfare. Butler subsequently became a bold and powerful voice for black rights within the industry, and later still a Commissioner of Cook County, Illinois. There is certainly no reason to think that Butler did not recognize political participation when he saw it in the early 1960s.[6]

Nevertheless, one must certainly marvel at the stealth with which a superstar like Cooke managed to join "the vanguard of the movement" – or else radically redefine what we mean by a vanguard. There appears to be nothing in the records of the major civil rights organizations to suggest any involvement by Cooke, no newspaper accounts of his presence on any picket lines, sit-ins or marches; no mention of Cooke as a participant in the scores of oral history interviews with Movement veterans; no membership dues, benefit concerts or donations – at least not until late 1964 when he gave his most overtly political song, the sublime soul-spiritual "A change is gonna come", to an obscure *The Stars Salute Dr Martin Luther King* album designed to raise funds for the SCLC.

It is clear that Cooke felt that this was the most appropriate place for such potentially controversial political material. Even in 1965, when the album version of "Change" was edited for single release, out went the verse with the most explicit, if still slightly coded, commentary on the indignities of Jim Crow: "I go to the movies,/ I go downtown./ Someone keeps telling me,/ not to hang around". Thus, Cooke continued to tiptoe around the sensibilities of his mainstream white audience, even as seven years into his secular career he was inspired by Bob Dylan's "Blowing in the wind" to address racial issues in his own songs for the first time.[7]

Perhaps the most subtle way in which Daniel Wolff seeks to close the distance between Cooke and the Movement is by the narrative ploy of juxtaposing key moments in Cooke's career with civil rights events in which he took no part, and on which he made no known comment. To give but one example, we learn of Cooke's momentous decision to insist on the desegregation of his concert with Jackie Wilson at the Norfolk Arena on 12 June 1959 amid discussions of contemporaneous events like Mack Charles Parker's lynching in Mississippi, Orval Faubus' latest enthusiasms for massive resistance, and a note about the volatile mood in Harlem that summer.[8]

Of course, at one level, this was quite appropriate. The Movement and the changing state of American race relations provided a crucial context for the development of Cooke's own career and political consciousness, and for the ways in which he and his music were interpreted by his peers. At another level, however, Wolff's approach is disingenuous and potentially misleading. Because there was apparently "no publicity" for Cooke's challenge to Virginia's segregation laws, the only cited source for the Norfolk incident is an interview with a local record store owner. This alone is certainly no reason to doubt its veracity, although it is puzzling that the *Norfolk Journal and Guide*, which usually advertised all forthcoming black attractions, offers no evidence that Cooke was even in Norfolk on 12 June 1959. Certainly, two days later when Cooke and Wilson played in Birmingham they were doing their regular segregated gigs once more.[9]

What really matters here, however, is less the accuracy of the Norfolk story – Cooke certainly did give up Jim Crow gigs earlier than most of his contemporaries – than that it illustrates how Wolff sometimes spreads the largely anecdotal evidence for Cooke's personal involvement in Movement-related activities exceedingly thin. It was as if he felt that Cooke's status in the black community at a time of great social struggle could only be understood and given the appropriate profundity by transforming him into a bold Movement warrior. That is to misrepresent the nature, rather than the extent, of Cooke's significance.

In fact, Wolff himself offers a fascinating account of the diverse factors which actually fused to create Cooke's special meaning and resonance in the black community, and upon which his real claim to some kind of spiritual and psychological, cultural and even economic leadership rested. Regardless of subject matter, the way in which Cooke had grafted gospel onto a pop and r&b base was always expressive of black consciousness and aspirations in an era which prized both integration and the growing affirmation of a distinctively black American heritage and identity. His entrepreneurial activities with KAGS, Sar and Derby had made him both rich and relatively independent of white artistic and financial controls, which prompted vicarious enjoyment and admiration in black America. Cooke had also set up a series of studios, called Soul Stations, which were dotted around Los Angeles in a bid to nurture local black talent which might otherwise never get a break. Coupled with his artistic and business successes, these studios helped to make Cooke a living exemplar of the black struggle to get into the system, with a sense of black pride and community responsibility intact. Similarly, although he never joined the sect, his growing interest in the Black Muslims and friendship with black boxing icon Muhammad Ali helped to mark Cooke as a proud race man.

In sum, Cooke's political significances and cultural meanings were derived from a wide range of personal and public, artistic and economic factors, acts and decisions, and from the ways in which these were interpreted by his contemporaries. His prestige and influence in the black community were certainly not reducible to, or even particularly dependent on, a minor association with the organized freedom struggle or a couple of explicitly engaged "political" songs which only appeared very late in his tragically short career.

Like most Rhythm and Blues singers, Sam Cooke was ultimately more inspirational than instrumental in the development of the civil rights movement. Indeed, while the cumulative effect of reading many Rhythm and Blues histories, autobiographies and interviews is to come away with a carefully cultivated sense of self-conscious engagement and political participation, until the second half of the 1960s there was often little more than sympathy and synchronicity. Certainly, the boasts and insinuations of some of these artists and their biographers contrast sharply with the memories of most civil rights workers "I don't think they made a helluva contribution", stated June Johnson bluntly.[10]

The SNCC Freedom Singers and the Southern Folk Cultural Revival Project

The relative anonymity of Rhythm and Blues artists in Movement-related activities before the late 1960s did not indicate that they were somehow indifferent to the progress of the racial struggle. It did, however, reflect the existence of very real economic, personal, ideological, and even terroristic constraints on their capacity to offer much public support until the later 1960s. It also reflected the fact that, although most civil rights workers appreciated the formidable power of black secular and sacred musics in the black community, few actually gave much consideration to whether, let alone precisely how, Rhythm and Blues might be used as, in Snellings' phrase, a "political weapon". Indeed, although SNCC's John O'Neal rightly claimed "It was a singing movement", the civil rights struggle actually spawned relatively few attempts to use music as an instrument of education, enlightenment and possibly even mobilization for those not already in, or close to, the struggle.

One institution which did make a concerted effort in this area was the Highlander Folk School and, in particular, its musical director Guy Carawan. Carawan had long been interested in using folk music as a vehicle and resource for the sort of progressive democratic social movements the school was dedicated to promoting. Indeed, while historians have tended to assume that the freedom songs, with their stylistic blend of spirituals, gospel and folk-blues influences, emerged naturally as the distinctive soundtrack of the Movement, it was in no small part due to Carawan's efforts that they did so.

Thanks to the popularity of both gospel and Rhythm and Blues, old style, spiritual-based communal singing was moribund in many southern black communities by the start of the 1960s. This was especially true in the urban South, and even more particularly so among the young students who formed the vanguard of the early Movement. Thus while an older generation of black adults, like those who attended Highlander's first wave of Citizenship Schools in the South Carolina Sea Islands in the early 1960s, related instantly to a traditional style of communal singing over which new political lyrics were laid, Carawan found that the Fisk University students engaged in the Nashville sit-ins "initially reacted with embarrassment to new freedom songs that were sung with handclapping and in a rural free swinging style". With prompting from Carawan and others, however, southern students began to refashion this basic form, adding new lyrics and stylistic flourishes of their own to create the first round of contemporary freedom songs – as heard on the *Nashville Sit-In* album – and establish this revitalized musical form at the heart of the Movement's musical culture in the early 1960s.[11]

The best known attempt to use these freedom songs to proselytize beyond the Movement itself involved the SNCC Freedom Singers, who emerged during the Albany campaign of 1962, featuring Cordell Reagon, Bernice Johnson Reagon, Charles Neblett, Rutha Mae Harris and, occasionally, Bertha Gober. This group, its successors and imitators, performed on the frontline in the South, singing in the halls and churches, streets and jails where Movement workers and their host communities congregated. But the Freedom Singers also ventured further afield, where, as Julian Bond remembered, they represented SNCC's "public face, at least as much as Chuck McDew, John Lewis, or later Stokely Carmichael". The Freedom Singers showed "an audience of our peers on white college campuses around the country who we are".[12]

Playing to those predominantly white, usually student audiences, the Freedom Singers combined an important fundraising function with an explicitly educational mission. "The Freedom Singers were a tremendous Movement force", recalled campus organizer Stanley Wise. "I guess they worked a group of about 150 to 200 campuses around the country . . . [They] pulled songs from Movement groups all over the South. And they would sing those songs to groups around the country telling them of instances in which that song was created, or why that song was sung then, or how it was used." With Cordell Reagon as narrator, the group used this blend of story and song "to engender a feeling in you that you were in fact there, participating with them".[13]

Bernice Johnson Reagon explained that the Freedom Singers "called ourselves a singing newspaper", and there was always an element of show, as well as tell, in their performances. While they urged their audiences to join or pledge monetary support to a particular organization dedicated to pursuing particular goals by particular methods, the songs themselves were often more demonstrative than didactic. At a time when Reagon and the Movement were still optimistic that "There was a thirst in the country outside of the South for people who wanted in some way to be part of dismantling segregation", the Freedom Singers sang songs and told tales about the racial situation in the South which promoted sympathy for the black struggle and passionately affirmed its moral rectitude. Then they waited confidently for their audience's consciences to lead them to support for the Movement.[14]

A second major attempt to use music as a formal component of Movement work was the Southern Folk Cultural Revival Project (SFCRP), co-founded by the ubiquitous Bernice Johnson Reagon and Anne Romaine. Romaine, who had joined SSOC while completing a master's thesis on the MFDP at the University of Virginia, was the strawberry-blonde folk-singing daughter of liberal North Carolina state senator Pat Cooke. Her own family history was inextricably bound to the cotton mill culture of North Carolina. In order to pay for law school, Pat Cooke had worked summers in the same Cramerton textile mills where his parents had once laboured. Before that, his grandfather had worked in the Earlanger Mills in Lexington. As a result, Anne Romaine's youthful world was full of the music and tales of mill factory workers and their families. These were people who, in order to preserve a deep sense of community and personal worth, had – much like their black neighbours – fashioned from meagre material resources a remarkably vibrant and resilient grassroots culture. This background profoundly influenced Romaine's ideas about the role music, and culture more generally, might play in progressive community politics.[15]

Appropriately, the idea for the SFCRP emerged during a conference Romaine attended at Highlander in the fall of 1965. At this meeting, SNCC staffers, including Bob Moses, suggested that the impecunious young SSOC might try to raise money by using sympathetic folk singers like Bob Dylan and Joan Baez for benefits, just as SNCC had done. After discussions with Bernice Johnson Reagon, however, the concept was modified. Instead of bringing in northern-based folk celebrities, the SFCRP would use local southern musicians of both races to dramatize and celebrate a common, essentially working-class heritage of struggle against poverty and injustice through the various indigenous musics of the region.[16]

The SFCRP's "Mission Statement" announced that it was "concerned with building a South in which black people and white people can live together in mutual respect. Our feeling is that this goal can be advanced by each recognizing the worth of his own grassroots tradition as well as the values of the underlying cultural exchange that [has] existed in the South for several centuries". Romaine and Reagon held that the traditional blues, folk and country musics of the southern states, with their wonderfully chaotic maelstrom of cross-racial influence and counter-influence, could be used to highlight the deep interpenetration and manifold similarities of black and white experiences in the region, while still preserving respect for the distinctiveness of each.[17]

Predicated on the belief, as Reagon put it, that "southern culture had ways in which [it] did not obey the race laws", the SFCRP was thus an attempt to render into song and performance the Movement ideal of the beloved community. Indeed, at its most radical, the project implied that the foundations for that community already existed in the South, usually hidden deep beneath layers of ignorance, poverty, and racial and class oppression, but periodically revealing themselves in southern musical culture.[18]

In the mid 1960s, at Stax, Fame, American, SS7 and many other southern studios, black and white southerners were engaged in precisely the sort of mutually respectful, biracial musical exchanges which the SFCRP extolled as a pathway to better racial understanding in the region. And yet, there was just no equivalent attempt by the Movement to use southern soul, or any other form of Rhythm and Blues music, as an educational or mobilizing tool, even though its audience, black and white, was much larger than for either freedom songs, or for grassroots southern musics. As we shall see, there were good reasons for this neglect. Nevertheless, it is important to stress that the Movement's own reluctance to use Rhythm and Blues and its artists in any systematic way partially accounted for their generally low profile in the civil rights activities of the early 1960s.

Making a statement, taking a stand

Perhaps inevitably, there were some Rhythm and Blues artists whose own consciences soon led them into the heart of the civil rights struggle, despite the general indifference of the Movement, or concerns about the possible effects of such activism upon their careers. In April 1963, the *Norfolk Journal and Guide* noted that Clyde McPhatter was "One of the first to take an active part in a public demonstration of anger and disgust with the status quo". McPhatter had joined the Atlanta lunch-counter sit-ins in early 1960, and subsequently appeared on picket lines and at benefit concerts for both SNCC and the NAACP, of which he was a life member.[19]

McPhatter was unusual in apparently giving considerable thought to the utilitarian value of his art and celebrity. He believed he could make a special contribution by convincing young people, not least his white fans, of the legitimacy of the protests against Jim Crow. In the spring of 1960, for example, he and organist Bill Doggett – another NAACP life member – staged a series of youth rallies at which McPhatter applauded "the young white students who, rejecting their heritage of racial prejudice, have stood shoulder-to-shoulder with Afro-American youth in this irresistable crusade", and urged more to do the same.[20]

If McPhatter was a consistent voice and presence in the early 1960s, even as his own career entered a terminal slump which ended with chronic alcoholism and his death from a heart attack in 1972, others flitted in and out of the Movement scene. Julian Bond remembered local star Gladys Knight doing some very early benefits for the Atlanta Student Movement, before even the birth of SNCC or Knight's first round of national celebrity with "Every beat of my heart" and "Letter full of tears" in 1961. Bunny Sigler was a smooth-toned balladeer who had a decent hit with "I won't cry" in the early 1960s, later cut some proto-Philly soul for Parkway ("Let the good times roll") and Neptune ("Great big liar"), and resurfaced in the mid 1970s as writer-producer of a light funk-disco-pop stew for the Trammps, Drells and himself. In the summer of 1963, however, he was marching with Greensboro students to protest segregation in downtown restaurants and theatres, and leading 500 of them off to temporary jails set up at the Central Carolina Hospital.[21]

The Birmingham campaign in the spring of 1963 produced one of the most inspiring examples of personal courage from a black singer, when the blind veteran Al Hibbler, whose major mid-1950s hits "Unchained melody" and "He" had smouldered somewhere between torch-song jazz and gospel-blues, joined the demonstrations. While Ray Charles later excused his own absence from civil rights protests partly on the grounds that he would not know when to duck if white racists started throwing rocks, Hibbler bravely faced up to Bull Connor's men, dogs and hoses. On 9 April, the singer was arrested while picketing outside Loveman's, a downtown department store which ran a segregated lunch counter. Birmingham's police department, not noted for its sensitivity to bad publicity, drew the line at imprisoning a blind man and Hibbler was released at the gates of the city's southside jail.[22]

"Though I'm blind, I can see the injustice here", Hibbler announced and the next day he was back on the picket line. "He tried his best to get arrested", recalled WENN's station manager Joe Lackey. "He'd go down there and march and Bull Connor would go down there and personally arrest him. Put him in a police car and take him back to the motel. He would not put him in jail". On one occasion, while the other demonstrators were being herded into police vans and Hibbler was being ushered towards a waiting police car, he broke free and tried to rejoin his fellow pickets. "The police are trying to segregate me from my own people", he complained. An incensed Connor intervened, forced Hibbler back against a wall and launched what was, even by his own craven standards, an astonishing verbal attack on the singer. "You can't work and anyone who goes to jail has to earn his food", Connor raged. "You can't do anything, even entertain". The national press reported the exchange, which only helped to reinforce in the public mind the link between Birmingham's vicious resistance to desegregation and a basic lack of human decency.[23]

While he was in Birmingham, Hibbler had also performed a benefit concert for the Movement. Four months later, a much bigger "Salute to freedom 1963" concert was held in Birmingham under the auspices of the American Guild of Variety Artists. The show, which raised around $9,000 for the CUCRL and the forthcoming March on Washington, featured an eclectic group of speakers and entertainers, including Ray Charles, Nina Simone, the Shirelles, Dick Gregory, and Martin Luther King. It was originally booked for Birmingham's Municipal Auditorium, scene of the Nat King Cole attack in 1956, but at the last moment the city authorities decided it was imperative to have the facility painted on the day scheduled for the concert. The show was moved to Miles College, where a hastily assembled stage even more hastily disassembled itself when a section collapsed beneath the silky-toned black pop balladeer Johnny Mathis. Earlier in the summer Mathis, who was just beginning to make a regular place on the lucrative white supper-club and cabaret circuit, had put that crossover audience at some risk by performing a couple of high-profile outdoor benefits in New York and Chicago, raising at least $20,000 for the NAACP and SCLC.[24]

Roy Hamilton performed benefits for most of the civil rights organizations in the early 1960s. Following his private attendance at the March on Washington in August 1963, however, he informed CORE's James Farmer, "I still feel that there is something more that I can personally contribute . . . whenever my services are needed, don't hesitate to call upon me". Like most other civil rights organizations, CORE had no idea of what exactly that "something more" might be. It never found a niche for the willing Hamilton beyond the fundraising shows which were the staple expressions of Movement support for most concerned black entertainers, unless, like Hibbler, McPhatter and Sigler, they chose to take to the streets.[25]

Another regular performer at Movement benefits was Jackie Wilson. In October 1963, Wilson was given an award by Philadelphia NAACP president Cecil Moore in appreciation for his efforts on behalf of the organization, which included raising $5,000 as headliner for a local "Freedom fund show" organized by deejay Georgie Woods. In March 1965, it was Woods who put together the massive "Freedom show" in support of the Selma campaign which attracted many Rhythm and Blues stars, including several Motown acts, and foreshadowed the much greater public profile for soul performers at Movement-related events in the second half of the decade.[26]

Among the acts at Woods' "Freedom show" were the Impressions. Curtis Mayfield, the group's chief inspiration, guitarist, singer and songwriter, was one of the most politically engaged lyricists of an era which actually produced very few soul songs explicitly about the struggle or racial injustice. In June 1964, just as the Civil Rights Act passed into law and the Freedom Summer gathered momentum, the Impressions' "Keep on pushing" perfectly captured the mood of the moment, oozing confidence that the harnessing of black pride to concerted action would result in victory over oppression.

> Look yonder,
> What's that I see?
> A great big stone wall,
> stands there ahead of me.
> But I've got my pride,
> and I'll move it all aside,
> and I'll keep on pushing.

Perhaps the most sublime Mayfield song of the mid 1960s was "People get ready". This gorgeous long-lined spiritual, delivered by the Impressions in exquisite close harmony style, used the Exodus motif to invoke a vision of black national unity and the dogged faith required to complete the journey into freedom.

> People get ready,
> for the train to Jordan,
> picking up passengers,
> coast to coast.
> Faith is the key,
> open the doors,
> unbar them,

Mayfield sang in his beautiful, delicate high tenor. Mayfield and the Impressions continued to produce these sorts of positive, uplifting rallying cries throughout the 1960s. Invariably wedded to gospel imagery, songs like "Amen", "Meeting up yonder", and "We're a winner" celebrated black pride and offered unmistakeable endorsements and encouragement for those involved in the black struggle. Mayfield "always seemed to be right on time", remembered Stanley Wise. "You could see [his records] on every Movement turntable".[27]

Mayfield was unusual among the soul stars of the early-to-mid 1960s in his willingness to tackle social and racial issues regularly. Yet, because Mayfield favoured beatific gospel imagery and rich allegory over simple documentary-style narratives, few of his early lyrics made explicit mention of race or the Movement at all. Instead, their racial politics were made manifest by their use of black religious and secular idioms, and their setting amid the soulful black harmonies of the Impressions. It was this combination of sound, sense and style which bound Mayfield's songs to the new black consciousness generated by the early Movement.

Most of the other "engaged" soul songs of the early-to-mid 1960s also used quasi-religious imagery and the sounds of soul, rather than direct invocations of race, Jim Crow or the Movement, to make their racial provenance and political relevance obvious. Sam Cooke's "A change is gonna come" was a good example. So was Joe Tex's intensely moving "The love you save may be your own", which owed much to "Change" – even if the spare organ and guitar sound was a little more "downhome" churchy than on Cooke's lush citified production.

Released in early 1965, "The love you save" described how racism and its psychological and economic consequences still accounted for much of the domestic instability in black America, and thereby impeded black unity and progress. Tex, testifying as ever, placed his own travails and observations at the centre of a song which evoked all too common experiences in black America:

> People, I been misled and I been afraid.
> I been hit in the head and left for dead.
> I been abused and been accused.
> I been refused a piece of bread.
>
> I been pushed around; I been lost and found,
> I been given to sundown to get out of town.
> I been taken outside and brutalized.
> And I had to always be the one,
> to smile and apologize . . .

Not until the late 1960s would such lyrics become commonplace in soul music and by that time the prevailing mood of the nation, black and white, was very different.

Prior to the politicization of soul in the second half of the decade, the most constantly engaged star from anywhere near that musical universe was Nina Simone. Born Eunice Waymon in North Carolina in the heart of the Depression, like many of her generation Simone was raised to cope with and endure, rather than struggle against, the ways of the Jim Crow South. Consequently, as she tried to build her musical career in New York in the mid-to-late 1950s she was initially slow to recognize the "connection between the fights I had and any wider struggle for justice" being waged by the civil rights movement.[28]

In the early 1960s, however, under the tutelage of the black playwright-activist Lorraine Hansberry, Simone began to reconsider her own position and struggle for acceptance "as a black person in a country run by white people and a woman in a world run by men". Meditations on these two themes – race and gender – would later inform her best songwriting.[29]

Simone's interest in the civil rights movement increased steadily but was not manifested in either personal participation or the lyrics of her songs until the summer and autumn of 1963. The murder of Medgar Evers and the horror of the Birmingham 16th Street Baptist Church bombing resulted in her own political "road to Damascus . . . it came as a rush of fury, hatred and determination. In church language, the Truth entered me and I 'came through'". Simone resisted the urge "to go out and kill someone", and instead channelled her anger into the composition of "Mississippi Goddam" – her first explicitly "political" song.[30]

"Mississippi Goddam" was the closest Rhythm and Blues got in the early 1960s to Martin Luther King's "Letter from Birmingham jail", the famous 1963 epistle in which the imprisoned civil rights leader confronted the criticisms of some white clergymen that he was irresponsibly seeking too much racial change too quickly. "'Wait' has almost always meant 'Never'", King wrote, insisting that blacks were tired of deferring their rights until such time as whites saw fit to bestow them.[31] With its bold gospel-jazz chording and stentorian vocals, Simone's song perfectly captured the same mood of mounting impatience with white prevarication and false promises:

Oh, this whole country's full of lies,
Y'all gonna die and die like flies,
I don't trust you anymore,
When you keep sayin',
"Go slow, go slow" . . .
Do things gradually and bring more tragedy.

Simone had "even stopped believin' in prayer", and instead trusted only to the mobilization of the black masses for deliverance.

For the next seven years, Simone's writings, recordings and performances were driven by her personal commitment to the struggle. She appeared at numerous marches and fundraising events, regularly heading south to perform for activists on the front line. In August 1963, for example, she was part of the Miles College benefit concert where one newspaper reported that her "ululating rendition of Oscar Brown Jr's 'Brown Baby' had thousands cheering to the skies". In April 1964, she performed a benefit for SNCC at Carnegie Hall, and in June headlined a SNCC "Freedom concert" in Westbury, New York to raise money for the Mississippi Summer Project. For many activists, "Mississippi Goddam" became an anthem that summer. "I mean everybody in the Movement just sort of took that as a tribute to the Mississippi Summer Project", remembered Stanley Wise. Although in the strictest sense it was no such thing, having been written the year before the Freedom Summer, this was a good example of the ways in which the meanings of a particular song could be amplified, manipulated or simply imposed thanks to acts of creative consumption by its listeners.[32]

In the spring of 1965, Simone played for the marchers making their way from Selma to Montgomery. The following summer she returned to Mississippi, joining those who continued James Meredith's solo "walk against fear", after he had been wounded by a sniper. "Unannounced she sort of came and played . . . did a concert for us right on stage", Wise recalled. In fact, when Simone had found out she was not on the original list of entertainers slated to join the Meredith March, she had virtually demanded to be involved. "They think we are always well organized in these things", confessed Stanley Levison, who as co-ordinator of many SCLC fundraising projects certainly knew better. Levison immediately made arrangements to fly the eager Simone south. Later the same year, CORE granted Simone a special award for her work on its behalf, which had included a series of east coast benefits in late 1965.[33]

By the end of the 1960s, Simone was singing "Revolution" and had joined many black militants in abandoning an always guarded faith in the efficacy of nonviolence and moral-suasion to secure black equality. One of those militants, and from the spring of 1967 SNCC's new chairman, H. Rap Brown, hailed her as "the singer of the black revolution because there is no other singer who sings real protest songs about the race situation". In 1970, black students gathered in the Student Union Grill at Ole Miss had played Simone's records before flambeauxing a confederate flag and marching on the chancellor's house to demand a black studies programme on campus.[34]

Nina Simone's conspicuous personal involvement in the struggle and willingness to discuss the black predicament in her lyrics was obviously a major factor in explaining her special status among Movement workers. Stanley Wise and Julius Lester, also of SNCC and himself a gifted folk singer, both named daughters in her honour. And yet, as Bernice Johnson Reagon explained, their respect depended on more than Simone's regular appearances at marches, fundraising and morale-raising concerts, and her lyrical beligerance at a time of great timidity among most black celebrities. The very sound of her music and the way in which she comported herself on stage and in her private and business life also helped to define her political and racial significance. "Simone helped people to survive", Reagon recalled. "When you heard her voice on a record it could get you up in the morning . . . She could sing anything, it was the sound she created. It was the sound of that voice and piano . . . Nina Simone's sound captured the warrior energy that was present in the people. The fighting people". There was a self-possessed assurance – critics would call it arrogance and bloody-mindedness – about Simone; an independence of mind, spirit and action which seemed both refreshing and inspirational. It was this combination of message, music and manner which made her such a potent figure for the Movement. She was, as MFDP chairman Lawrence Guyot neatly summarized, "an individualist, very strong, very committed, who talked about race in song like very few other people did".[35]

Simone's level of involvement was unmatched by any of the major figures of Rhythm and Blues in the early-to-mid 1960s, and it was probably not coincidental that she was actually outside the main run of soul artists. Simone was a classically trained singer-pianist; a Juillard graduate whose predilection for mixing Bach fugues, jazz, blues, folk and gospel frequently confounded attempts by critics, record label executives, producers, and nightclub owners to assign her to any of the stylistic slots routinely reserved for black artists. "I didn't fit into white ideas of what a black performer should be. It was a racist thing", she later wrote. Her distinctive hybrid stylings also meant that her principal black audience comprised mainly intellectuals and Movement workers who appreciated her candid lyrics and personal commitment. Her other fans were mostly white folk, jazz and blues aficionados, many of whom were northern college students or budding bohemians. They also tended to be racial liberals and as such were untroubled by Simone's politics.[36]

If Simone had less to lose in commercial terms than, for example, Diana Ross, in terms of giving public expression to her support for the black struggle, this should not detract from her courage, or impugn her motives. After all, it was Simone's life, not just her chart position, money and coiffure which she sometimes put at risk. Hard choices had to be made and, regardless of how much the peculiar composition of her audience gave her a certain room to manoeuvre, Simone chose to align herself publicly and proudly with an ongoing black freedom struggle with little regard for the personal or professional consequences.

Jazz, folk and the early civil rights movement

With the exception of Nina Simone and a few others, the low level of personal, financial or artistic support for the Movement from the Rhythm and Blues community during the decade after Montgomery contrasted with the contribution of many black, and some white, musicians and artists in other branches of showbusiness. Paradoxically, while the reputations of soul singers as Movement activists have generally been inflated over the subsequent decades, the important role of many from the worlds of jazz, folk and Hollywood have been consistently neglected or underplayed. While it may appear heresy to some, the fact remains that in certain respects Joan Baez was more important and conspicuously committed to the early Movement than James Brown, while Harry Belafonte did more to assist the struggle for black freedom in practical terms than all the soul icons of the 1960s combined.

In the summer of 1965, Betty Garman, who acted as a co-ordinator between SNCC's national office in Atlanta and support groups around the country, wrote to Dick Perez of the Cleveland Friends of SNCC, regarding the possibility of Perez staging some celebrity benefit concerts in the city. "Unfortunately, we don't have any quick, sure fire way of scheduling big time performers for concerts – for anything for that matter", Garman admitted. Nevertheless, she explained, "There are a certain few artists who do things for us consistently and with whom we have certain kinds of arrangements with respect to their time . . . The people we can reach [are] [Pete] Seeger, [Theo] Bikel, Belafonte, Sammy Davis, Jr, Peter Paul and Mary, or Baez or Dylan".[37]

This was hardly an exhaustive list of the performers who did benefits for SNCC or contributed to the Movement in other ways in the early 1960s. Nevertheless, while a case might be made for the inclusion of some jazz artists, Garman's emphasis on white folk singers and black stars from Hollywood and Broadway accurately reflected the areas within the entertainment industry from which the Movement had come to expect the most visible, valuable and voluble support.

The celebrity turnout at the March on Washington in August 1963 featured a similar array of black and white artists and entertainers. The roll-call for the era's most dramatic set-piece demonstration of Movement support included Sammy Davis, Jr, Harry Belafonte, Ossie Davis, Ruby Dee, Sidney Poitier, Diahann Carroll, James Garner, Pearl Bailey, Burt Lancaster, Marlon Brando, Paul Newman, Joanne Woodward, Kirk Douglas, Dick Gregory, Eartha Kitt, James Baldwin, Lorraine Hansberry, Bobby Darin and Lena Horne. The March's official programme featured black soprano Marian Anderson, gospel star Mahalia Jackson, black folk-blues singer Josh White, and white folk singers Joan Baez, Peter, Paul and Mary, and Bob Dylan.[38]

Many of these entertainers also signed a proclamation to the effect that "all forms of racial segregation are injurious to the arts of the nation". No Rhythm and Blues artists signed this proclamation and, although Roy Hamilton and Little Willie John attended in a private capacity, apparently none were invited – or for that matter requested – to join the official cultural contingent which marched and was introduced to the crowd. The indifference of the Movement towards these artists and the reluctance of soul men and women to become publicly associated with civil rights protest appeared to be well-matched.[39]

Rhythm and Blues was not the only strain of black popular music missing from the official entertainment or cultural contingent at the March. As hard-working jazz saxophonist John Handy angrily noted, "of the large number of the 'cream of the crop' Negro and white artists and entertainers present, there was not one jazz artist on the program". Handy found this sleight incredible, "because jazz, along with the spirituals, has played a major role in the Negro's struggle for freedom. After all, jazz has been the Negro's artistic means of self-expression and has opened many minds and hearts to the Negro". In fact, unknown to Handy, there had been one informal attempt to include jazz on the programme when Duke Ellington was approached. Although he had long performed benefit concerts for the NAACP, Ellington generally avoided both public participation in Movement activities and statements on the racial situation. Despite the efforts of Dick Gregory and Robert Kennedy, he could not be tempted to join the March, complaining rather lamely that "I'd love to go, but I've got sore feet. I can't walk that far".[40]

Handy's response to the absence of jazz at the March was revealing. A member of CORE's San Francisco chapter who had already been jailed for his civil rights activities, Handy rapidly convened an integrated Freedom Band to go out on the road. The Freedom Band, he announced, would act as the "musical troubleshooter for the Movement", with which it would identify "not only through its music, but also through its mode of dress, which is essentially the same as the uniform worn in the South by SNCC workers – i.e., work shirts, dark pants, denim jackets, etc.". CORE in particular supported the Freedom Band initiative, which included a benefit on its behalf with Dizzy Gillespie and Bill Cosby at the Masonic Auditorium in San Francisco in September 1964. There was no evidence of any similar response from the Rhythm and Blues artists who had also been ignored by the organizers of the March on Washington.[41]

More generally, the participation of jazz musicians like Handy in Movement-related activities was rather more impressive than that of their Rhythm and Blues counterparts – although Nat Hentoff suggested that in 1961 the much touted political consciousness and commitment of the black jazz avant-garde was still largely chimerical or, at a significant best, largely a matter of aesthetics. Hentoff doubted "If one in five hundred even belonged to the NAACP".[42]

Nevertheless, in the decade after Montgomery there were distinct signs of jazz's growing identification with the formal Movement and its goals. This was reflected most obviously in the titles of works like Charles Mingus' "Fables of Faubus", Sonny Rollins' *Freedom suite,* John Coltrane's breathtaking "Alabama", and Max Roach's *We Insist! The Freedom Now Suite* album, which at Roach's instigation Candid Records offered to civil rights organizations at a knockdown price so that they could re-sell them to raise funds. The sense of political engagement was further promoted by the liner notes of many jazz albums, especially the crackling prose Imamu Amiri Baraka contributed to Impulse releases by Coltrane.[43]

Support for the Movement was also encoded in the aesthetics of the New Jazz, especially in the quest for a structural, particularly harmonic and rhythmic, freedom in a music which many heard as a sonic analogue to the black drive for liberation. SNCC worker Fay Bellamy certainly recognized sympathy for the Movement "in how the rhythms changed in jazz", adding perceptively that "I think the kind of mind-set a jazz person might have, versus the mind-set a Rhythm and Blues person might have, might have been somewhat different in that period of time". Bellamy was surely right. Unlike

Rhythm and Blues men and women, modern jazz artists tended to emerge from, and work mostly within, a self-conscious cultural vanguard, where music and racial, personal and collective politics were expected to mix. This was one reason why many critics reified the jazz avant-garde as the true sound of the black revolution, even as they grappled with the bothersome fact that the black masses seemed frustratingly indifferent to the music of their own liberation.[44]

Throughout the late 1950s and early 1960s, jazz men and women gave hundreds of performances to raise vital funds for the Cause. In the summer of 1959, for example, the Chicago Urban League staged a major jazz festival in collaboration with *Playboy* magazine which featured Miles Davis, Count Basie, Dave Brubeck, Dizzy Gillespie, Dakota Staton and Kai Winding, and netted tens of thousands of dollars for the organization. Julian "Cannonball" Adderley, Charles Mingus and Thelonius Monk joined Nina Simone in sponsoring SNCC's "Salute to southern students" concert at Carnegie Hall in February 1963. In the fall of that year CORE staged the "Jazz salute for freedom" concert which gave rise to its loosely related, highly lucrative double-album. In February 1964, Miles Davis played a benefit for SNCC at the Lincoln Center, funds from which supported voter registration work in Mississippi. The following year, Max Roach and Abbey Lincoln took the *Freedom Now Suite* to the stage and raised around $900 for the Boston Friends of SNCC. In mid-decade Imamu Amiri Baraka invented the Jazz-mobile, a black educational and jazz initiative which toured the Harlem streets teaching black history and preaching black cultural pride and unity, funded mainly by money liberated from President Johnson's Great Society programmes.[45]

Meanwhile, there were a number of individual challenges to the racial structure and economy of the jazz industry itself. Ornette Coleman, musically one of the most radical of the New Jazz players in his deconstruction of conventional Western harmonic and melodic conventions, withdrew from public performances for three years because none of the predominantly white-owned nightclubs would pay him what he "knew" his music was worth. The fiery pianist Cecil Taylor denounced the basic racial configuration of power in the music business and called for "a boycott by Negro musicians of all jazz clubs in the United States. I also propose that there should be a boycott by Negro jazz musicians of all record companies. I also propose that all Negro jazz musicians boycott all trade papers and journals dealing with music . . . We're no longer reflecting or vibrating to the white-energy principle". Again, the white bohemian and black intellectual coteries who comprised the core audience for jazz were unlikely to withhold their custom because of these and similar expressions of black pride and assert-iveness. Indeed, they rather expected such displays of militancy as a sort of guarantee of their heroes' credentials as renegade critics of the existing social, economic, political and racial order.[46]

At a time when relatively few soul singers were conspicuous in Movement activities, folk singers like Joan Baez were more likely to be found on the front line. Here Baez accompanies author James Baldwin (left) and SNCC's Jim Forman on a march in Alabama.

While jazz furnished its share of early Movement supporters and a music which some found hugely inspirational, black folk singers like Josh White, Leon Bibb and Odetta Gordon, and gospel stars such as the Staple Singers and Mahalia Jackson, were equally conspicuous in fundraising efforts. In

Chicago, in May 1963, Jackson not only performed, but also arranged for free use of the auditorium and band to raise some $40,000 for the SCLC. A more modest New York benefit for CORE in August raised nearly $2,000, while another for SNCC the same year cleared nearly $6,500.[47]

White folk singers like Joan Baez, Bob Dylan, the Kingston Trio, Peter, Paul and Mary, the Chad Mitchell Trio, Theodore Bikel, Phil Ochs and the veteran Pete Seeger were also heavily involved in the early 1960s, doing innumerable benefit shows, joining marches and speaking out unequivocally on behalf of the Movement. "There was a significant array of white artists who were progressive politically . . . all of them came out of the folk movement", Harry Belafonte remembered.[48]

As Belafonte appreciated, these people initially came into the Movement because of their personal politics, not because the Movement had consciously sought them out. There was a selflessness and fierce moral commitment among some of these white folkies which mirrored that of the frontline Movement workers and sometimes had very tangible financial ramifications. In the summer of 1964, for example, a Seeger-Baez benefit concert for the New York SNCC office raised a respectable $1,350. Since neither artist would accept a fee or expenses, all but $27 of this was profit. By contrast, while the Nina Simone benefit at Westbury during the same summer had grossed over $2,800, after the support acts were paid, and publicity and expenses for Simone were deducted – she usually asked for $1,000, about one-third of her usual fee, for Movement shows – the organization grossed just over $577.[49]

Stanley Wise remembered seeing "Bob Dylan when I was a freshman at Howard. I remember him up there helping load trucks to take food to Mississippi. I mean he was right there on the frontline. I don't remember that from a lot of people". Julian Bond also recalled Movement workers who had seen and heard the young Dylan down in Mississippi, "saying . . . he didn't sound like anybody I'd ever heard before. But strangely engaging". Dylan's "Blowing in the wind" was quickly a fixture at civil rights rallies, while "Oxford Town" offered a stinging indictment of the response to James Meredith's 1962 efforts to desegregate Ole Miss.

> He went down to Oxford Town,
> guns and clubs followed him down,
> all because his face was brown.
> Better get away from Oxford Town.

> Oxford Town in the afternoon,
> everyone's singing a sorrowful tune,
> two men died beneath the Mississippi moon.
> Somebody better investigate soon.

Dylan's plea to "investigate soon" and his mocking question to the white community in another verse, "What do you think about that my friend?", gave encouragement to those who detected a growing impatience with American racism among young whites.[50]

Dylan was just one of the many white singer-songwriters who discussed racial protest and Movement matters with a candour seldom found in the Rhythm and Blues of the period. Pete Seeger's "Ballad of old Monroe", for example, celebrated the career of Robert Williams, the controversial NAACP secretary in Monroe, North Carolina, whose insistence on the black right to armed self-defence had seen him drummed out of the Association and hounded into exile in Cuba. If Nina Simone might have written something similar, it is difficult to imagine James Brown, let alone Holland-Dozier-Holland or Sam Cooke, tackling such subjects in the early 1960s.

Paul Simon's "He was my brother" was an earnest if maudlin paean to slain civil rights worker Andrew Goodman, who was a friend of Simon's from their days in acting class at Queen's College in New York. Tom Paxton's "Goodman, Schwerner and Chaney" mourned the same tragedy. Phil Ochs memorialized Medgar Evers in the "Ballad of Medgar Evers", while his "Ballad of William Worthy" celebrated the contribution of the black CORE worker who had participated in the Fellowship of Reconciliation's first Freedom Ride back in 1947 and later became a solon of the contemporary struggle. Others, in the mode of Dylan's "Blowing in the wind" or "Only a pawn in their game" ("the very first song that showed the poor white was as victimized by discrimination as the poor black", according to Bernice Johnson Reagon), sang out about injustice and intolerance as part of a broader critique of contemporary American society and its moral inadequacies. As Barry McGuire's pop chart topping "Eve of destruction" noted, Jim Crow and racism made a mockery of America's Cold War claims to moral superiority over the communist bloc. "Think of all the hate there is in Red China,/ Then take a look around at Selma, Alabama", McGuire rasped.[51]

While civil rights workers were deeply appreciative of the public and artistic stands people like Seeger, Baez and Dylan were taking, it was usually their politics and the money and public sympathy they generated for the Movement, rather than their music, which appealed to black activists. These preferences were even more evident beyond Movement circles, where few blacks gave a hootenanny about folk. CORE's Jimmy McDonald tried desperately to shift tickets for an October 1963 Dylan benefit in Syracuse, New York, but recognized that "most Negroes do not know that much about 'folk music', so that Bobby Dylan does not have that much appeal in the Negro community". A particularly ill-conceived Boston Friends of SNCC "folk concert" in the black Roxbury district raised a mere $89, of which nearly $67 was devoured by advertising and expenses. When Joan Baez played the all-black Morehouse College for SNCC in Atlanta in May 1963, the audience was 70 per cent white, just as it had been for an earlier concert at Miles College in Birmingham, and just as it would be when she played Tougaloo College chapel in Mississippi in April 1964. The dedicated Baez was so concerned that she should only play before integrated audiences that it was written into her contract. Promoters then "had to call up the local NAACP for volunteers to integrate an audience for someone they'd never heard of". It was ironic that while jazz and folk had the "right" progressive message and performers who often showed a clear and eager public commitment to the organized struggle, those musical forms had a relatively small black audience compared with Rhythm and Blues, which had far fewer formal links to the Movement.[52]

Hollywood on parade

More important than soul, folk or jazz performers, in terms of keeping the Movement just about solvent in the early 1960s, were a number of stars from Hollywood and Broadway. In addition to consistent white supporters like Burt Lancaster, Tony Bennett, Paul Newman, Joanne Woodward, Marlon Brando and Shelley Winters, regular black presences at marches and fundraising events included Sidney Poitier, Eartha Kitt, Dorothy Dandridge and the deeply committed husband and wife team of actors Ossie Davis and Ruby Dee, who offered steadfast personal, financial and moral support to all phases of the Movement. Indeed, when Stanley Levison was desperate to find suitable ghostwriters to work with Martin Luther King on his account of the Birmingham campaign, *Why we can't wait*, he considered Davis a possibility, because "he's highly dedicated . . . has integrity . . . and has talent and could contribute something". In 1964, Davis and Dee had helped to found the short-lived fundraising vehicle, the Association of Artists for Freedom, in collaboration with author John O. Killens. Even Malcolm X courted the couple, seeking their endorsement and financial help for his Organization of Afro-American Unity, the proposed vehicle for his post-Nation of Islam engagement with a civil rights struggle which increasingly bore his intellectual and rhetorical imprint. Davis read the eulogy at Malcolm's funeral in 1965.[53]

Even more crucial to the Movement was a glamorous showbiz quintet of Lena Horne, Diahann Carroll, Dick Gregory, Sammy Davis, Jr, and Harry Belafonte. With the partial exception of Gregory, the reputations of all these performers withered, or were systematically destroyed, by the peculiar demands of the black power era. In the late 1960s and early 1970s, black stars who managed to maintain both black and white celebrity and refused to trade a complex, essentially humanitarian progressivism informed by resolute racial pride, for the far simpler, more reactionary, racial sectarianism then in vogue, were routinely pilloried as "Uncle Toms" or "Aunt Jemimas". It only made matters worse that Belafonte, Davis and Horne all had white

310

spouses – a sure sign of self- and race-hatred among those who measured racial integrity by such exacting standards as a fondness for kente cloth and whose own contribution to black liberation sometimes extended no further than the end of a well-kempt afro. Unfortunately, historians of the black power era have readily accepted and repeated such characterizations as if they represented an accurate assessment of these artists' roles or reputations among Movement workers and the black masses.[54]

Actress-singer-dancer Lena Horne had the longest protest pedigree of this querulous quintet. In 1919, at the age of two, she was featured in a New York NAACP branch bulletin as the youngest member of the organization. Horne was outspoken about the racial politics of the entertainment industry for most of her career. In 1945, following a meeting with a then little-known Little Rock NAACP official called Daisy Bates, she quit a government-sponsored tour of southern army bases, publicly denouncing the discrimination against black troops she had found at Camp Joseph T. Robinson. In the Cold War environment such gestures sometimes made it difficult for her to find work as producers carefully avoided anyone tainted with a reputation for radicalism. "I don't know what things will be like for the next generation", she admitted in 1949, "I only know we're having a hell of a time".[55]

When that next generation emerged to take up the struggle for black liberation, Horne was an immediate supporter – even if nonviolent discipline was not something which came easily. In 1960, she earned considerable street credibility when she hit a white engineering executive, Harvey St Vincent, with an ashtray and lamp after he had racially abused her in a swanky Beverly Hills restaurant. An unrepentant Horne explained that St Vincent had used "a word for Negro people that I don't use . . . and then he made sure my sex was properly noted with a nasty five letter word". She promptly split his eye and earned herself sackloads of black fan mail from all over the country.[56]

Horne was heavily involved in raising funds and generating publicity for the Movement, especially CORE, NAACP, and SCLC. In September 1963, shortly after performing a major SCLC benefit in Atlanta, Horne gave a typically forthright account of why she was so committed to supporting the civil rights campaign. "No Negro, whatever his station in life, is able to ignore it", she insisted, invoking the deep sense of personal calling and service which characterized all those entertainers who came forward to make a substantial contribution of time, energy and resources to the Movement. "The struggle is becoming a revolution and I want to be part of it, in whatever role I can fill best", she explained.[57]

Actress-singer Diahann Carroll was another regular performer at fund-raising affairs like the May 1960 concert for the CDMLK organized by Harry Belafonte at the New York Regiment Armory. She was also a co-sponsor of the 1963 "Salute to southern students" show for SNCC. Two years later

A veteran of many struggles against discrimination within the entertainment industry, Lena Horne had become acquainted with the NAACP's Daisy Bates long before Bates became a national figure during the Little Rock school desegregation crisis in 1957. The inscription on this photograph, sent by Horne to Bates, reads: "Dear Daisy, my love and admiration, Lena".

her commitment was formally recognized when she and Julie Belafonte, Harry's second wife and a former dancer with the Kathleen Dunham dance troupe, were appointed co-chairs of SNCC's new Women's Division. Gloria Richardson, the fearless heroine of the Cambridge, Maryland, civil rights campaign, served as co-ordinator of the Division's steering committee, which was, Richardson wrote, "convened for the express purpose of providing funds for the southern workers and projects of SNCC on a continuing basis" through a range of social events and presentations. In the meantime, in 1963 Carroll had joined the board of directors of the Gandhi Society. This was essentially a fundraising heir to the CDMLK, conceived in part by Belafonte, and in turn succeeded by the American Foundation on Non-violence.[58]

From the late 1950s, black comedian Dick Gregory had ridiculed Jim Crow from the stage, in his books, and, when networks were feeling especially brave, on television. Gregory memorably characterized a southern liberal as "someone who'll lynch you from a low tree", and speculated on the new breed of long-limbed black supermen who would evolve if southern bus companies agreed to hire black drivers, but still required them to sit in the rear. It is unlikely that Gregory actually converted too many people to the black cause through his satire. Black fans hardly needed convincing of the cruel absurdities of Jim Crow, while his white fans were almost by definition broadly sympathetic and willing to have their collective consciences wittily pricked. Nonetheless, Movement workers certainly appreciated his refreshingly barbed take on American race relations and the way in which his acerbic commentaries helped to reinforce, for them and others, the righteousness of their fight.[59]

In the spring of 1963, Gregory joined voter registration efforts in LeFlore County, Mississippi and returned regularly to the state over the next few years. He brought with him not only his morale-boosting presence and valuable publicity, but also the funds he helped to raise in the supperclubs and concert halls of the North. A 23-state tour for SNCC in 1964 generated more than $35,000. He even brought in food – seven tons of it in 1963, and 15,000 Xmas turkeys in December 1965 – for poor local blacks who suffered dreadfully when state authorities cut off federal food aid in an attempt to undermine support for voter registration. "He played an indispensable role at a time that it was needed", MFDP chairman Lawrence Guyot acknowledged.[60]

Gregory was not just in Mississippi in the 1960s, he was all over the country, frequently putting his body as well as his time and talent on the line. "He was like a fireman; whenever it would break out, he'd turn up on the scene", recalled *Jet* editor Robert Johnson. "He felt he could turn the spotlight on it, hoping there was a streak of decency running either in the democratic system, the institutions of justice, or individuals themselves that would somehow justify the position of the civil rights people once the people looked in and saw what was happening".[61]

In the summer of 1964, Gregory regularly turned up to support Gloria Richardson and the volatile Cambridge Movement. "We usually asked him to come in when things were getting too much out of control", Richardson recalled, "because he could say the same things that everybody else was saying, but it kind of lessened the tension in terms of his performance and his political jokes". Just as germane, Richardson noted "he was available", which was more than could be said for most black stars.[62]

In early August 1965, Gregory was imprisoned for joining street protests against the reappointment of Chicago's notorious superintendent of schools, Benjamin Willis, whose policies had ensured that the city's public school system remained functionally segregated. By this time Gregory had already been to prison in Chicago (on a previous occasion), Greenwood, Birmingham, Selma and Pine Bluff, Arkansas in connection with various civil rights protests. He had also supported an unsuccessful campaign for black athletes to boycott the 1964 Tokyo Olympics, and quietly endowed a private fund to subsidize poor black students in Chicago who wanted to stay in school but were forced out to work because of financial problems. A few weeks after his August 1965 arrest, Gregory was shot in the leg during the Watts riots, which he subsequently endorsed as "urban renewal without the graft".[63]

Another black entertainer who could be expected to show public support for the early Movement was Sammy Davis Jr. The quintessential all-round Hollywood-Broadway star performed at countless benefit shows, served as an informal consultant to the NAACP on various fundraising ventures, and also acted as a recruitment agent for the Association. In one personal appeal to his showbiz colleagues Davis wrote, "We artists have set an inspiring example of tearing down race barriers in our own field. Now we must put our time, our money, our whole-hearted efforts on the line with our conscience". Entertainers should, he urged, "help the NAACP fight for freedom" by giving benefit concerts, taking out life memberships – Davis had three – making financial contributions and speaking out "on the importance of civil rights".[64]

With a lucrative adult, white, middle American crossover audience, as well as perennially cautious sponsors and producers, to lose if he appeared too radical, any public identification with the black struggle entailed some personal risk on Davis' part. Nevertheless, he worked diligently to lure fellow Hollywood rat-packers Frank Sinatra, Peter Lawford, Dean Martin and Joey Bishop to join him in major benefit concerts like the 27 January 1961 "Tribute to Martin Luther King" for the SCLC at Carnegie Hall which raised over $22,000. This was roughly 12 per cent of the SCLC's total income for the grim fiscal year 1960–61. Another show at the Westchester Auditorium in White Plains, New York in December 1962 was barely less successful.[65]

Davis also staged the "Broadway answers Selma" show at the Majestic Theater in New York in April 1965, which raised money for the families of slain civil rights activists James Reeb and Jimmie Lee Jackson. Each of the four major civil rights organizations also netted around $24,500 from the concert. In July 1965 he organized the "Stars for freedom" show which provided important seed-money for the SCLC's new Summer Community Organization for Political Education (SCOPE) project. These benefits were supplemented by regular out-of-pocket payments, including the earnings from a week of shows in May 1963 (estimated at $20,000) which Davis donated to the SCLC.[66]

Although cruelly baited as a "Black Caucasian" during the black power era, and largely ignored or marginalized by Movement historians ever since, Harry Belafonte played a major role in the development of the civil rights movement during the decade after Montgomery. "The respect for that guy runs as deep as for anybody", stated Bernice Johnson Reagon, who appreciated that Belafonte's personal commitment and contribution was unmatched by anyone, from any realm of either black or white entertainment.[67]

For Belafonte, that involvement began in earnest in early 1956, when Martin Luther King arranged a private meeting in New York to seek his advice about promoting national support for the Montgomery bus boycott. King was encouraged to seek out Belafonte because his progressive politics and outspokenness on racial issues were already well known. Born to poor West Indian parents in Harlem in 1927, after the Second World War Belafonte had become closely involved in the rump of left-wing politics in New York as it struggled to survive the onslaught of McCarthyism. He associated closely with labour organizers, joined the Young Progressives of America, and in 1948 worked for Henry Wallace's left-liberal Progressive Party in Wallace's doomed bid for the presidency.[68]

By the mid 1950s, Belafonte's stage, recording and film career had also taken off. Critically acclaimed screen performances in box-office smashes like *Carmen Jones* in 1954, coupled with his captivating live and recorded blend of African-American folk materials, labour songs, and tunes from the Caribbean islands, had made him one of the nation's best-known entertainers. His RCA albums outsold even Elvis in the late 1950s, with *Belafonte Sings of the Caribbean* the first record by a solo artist to sell a million copies. In 1955 his income was estimated at around $350,000; two years later he grossed over a million dollars.[69]

Caricatured visions of a bare-chested Belafonte, the classic island exotic, bellowing "The banana boat song" in his cut-off jeans, trademark big-buckled belt, open-toed sandals and floral shirts, still dominate popular memories of the singer. Yet there was a quiet subversiveness about much of his art in the 1950s. In retrospect, it is remarkable that this political radical and racial malcontent actually achieved enormous crossover success at all in the midst of anti-communist paranoia and the heightened racial sensitivities associated with the battle against Jim Crow and the rise of rock and roll. In a world where gradations of skin colour and physiognomy mattered, it no doubt helped that Belafonte, like Lena Horne, had a relatively light, coffee'n'cream complexion, and that his features were rather more Caucasian than African. Nevertheless, to have attained such celebrity with materials which juxtaposed tales of workers' toil and class struggle with songs of black pride and celebrations of a pan-African diasporic heritage was still astonishing. "When I sing 'John Henry' ", he explained in 1957, "I project myself into the roots of the song. I'm charged with pride in what John Henry means to all Negroes". In a world where miscegenation remained the ultimate white taboo, even his film roles were tinged with controversy. In *Island in the Sun* he played the love interest that dared not speak its name opposite white actress Joan Fontaine.[70]

With his art already making bold racial statements, and with his personal wealth and status at stake if he lost the large white portion of his audience, Belafonte might well have chosen to stay mute on matters of racial politics, or to distance himself from the Movement. Instead, he very deliberately sought to use his art and the public platform it provided, to denounce racial and economic injustices and support various struggles against them at home and abroad. This was testament to both his own integrity and to the lessons he had learned from Paul Robeson, who, alongside W.E.B. DuBois, profoundly influenced Belafonte's conception of the role that artists might play in progressive politics. "Robeson could not have embodied a more perfect model for me as to what to do with your life as an artist deeply immersed and sensitive to social issues and activism", he recalled. "Service is the purpose of art. What else is it in the service of? The fact that I can get off selfishly in an act of self-expression is itself wonderful. But what does that do?"[71]

At his first meeting with Martin Luther King, Belafonte was persuaded that nonviolent direct action, with its blend of pragmatism and moral vigour, was the perfect constructive outlet for the bitterness, anger and frustrations which he, like so many other blacks, keenly felt but had struggled to parlay into effective political action. After this initial encounter, Belafonte put himself and his art at King's disposal and quickly became a close friend, trusted advisor, effective recruiter and nonpareil fundraiser for the civil rights leader and the Movement more generally.[72]

Like most sympathetic artists, much of Belafonte's work for the Movement involved benefit shows, like the one in 1956 which raised money for the Montgomery protests and was one of literally dozens which he either participated in or helped to organize over the next decade. Yet Belafonte's role extended far beyond benefit concerts. In 1960, for example, he worked with Stanley Levison and Bayard Rustin to create the CDMLK. With labour leader A. Philip Randolph and New York minister Rev. Gardner Taylor as co-chairs, Belafonte served alongside Sidney Poitier on the CDMLK's cultural committee, while Nat King Cole acted as treasurer.[73]

The CDMLK quickly moved beyond its immediate goal of helping King fight spurious tax-evasion charges in Alabama. Correctly predicting that this would not be the last time southern authorities used quasi-legal means to harass King and the Movement, the CDMLK worked to establish "significant reserves of funds to be able to meet these onslaughts on Dr King's person", so that King would not be "forever tied up in jail". In addition, the CDMLK contributed to the SCLC's "Crusade for Citizenship" voter registration drive and nurtured the burgeoning student activism in the South by creating a "Revolving bail fund" for those jailed in sit-ins. The CDMLK also provided half of the $2,000 that the SCLC used to help fund a meeting of student leaders at Shaw University, Raleigh. It was from this meeting in mid April 1960 that SNCC emerged.[74]

These projects obviously required substantial sums of money and by the end of 1960 the CDMLK had raised around $86,000. After the deduction of publicity and administrative expenses it was able to contribute more than $51,000 to various aspects of the southern struggle. Most of this income came from corporate, union and private donations – including an unspecified amount from Belafonte himself. However, the largest single contribution was the $10,000 generated by the 17 May 1960 "Night of stars for freedom" concert Belafonte staged at New York's Regiment Armory, where Diahann Carroll had appeared alongside Poitier, Dorothy Dandridge, Shelley Winters and the embattled King. More than simply a concert, the event was preceded by a well-publicized gathering of many black artists and celebrities at the Statue of Liberty, where they laid a wreath in mourning for lost black civil rights. This, Belafonte noted, was a classic example of the ways in which celebrity involvement could work by making the affair both a "fund-raising event" and "an opportunity to interpret the message of our Committee to a huge segment of the community".[75]

Beyond raising funds and morale for King's civil rights work, Belafonte appreciated that at a more personal level, the mental and financial demands of leadership weighed heavily on King and his family. Since King had to be careful about accepting personal gifts because they might provide an opportunity for southern authorities to harass him on tax matters, or for his enemies to condemn him for profiteering from his position in the Movement, Belafonte quietly began to contribute money towards the running of the King family home. He helped to hire private secretaries and even nannies so that Martin and his wife Coretta could be seen together in public at important strategic moments and thus present the image of middle-class domestic respectability which might help endear them and their cause to middle white America. By 1961, Belafonte was even secretly paying the premiums for a life insurance policy which gave the virtually uninsurable King $50,000 of cover, payable to Coretta on her husband's death.[76]

Belafonte was also useful to King and the Movement as a conduit to the Kennedy brothers. In 1960, presidential nominee John Kennedy had sought a meeting with the star to discuss civil rights and secure Belafonte's influential endorsement. Belafonte told Kennedy that he would do better to stop courting black celebrities and enter into a meaningful dialogue with real black political leaders like King. After Kennedy's election victory, however, Belafonte, who later worked as an advisor to Kennedy's Peace Corps, emerged as a sort of mediator-cum-courier between the administration, SCLC and SNCC, who all appreciated his basic reasonableness and discretion.[77]

Those same qualities also enabled him to act as an effective mediator within the civil rights movement, where he helped to keep the often fractious relationship between SCLC and SNCC from undermining a common struggle. "I worked a long time trying to keep them from just completely tearing each other apart", he recalled. Fay Bellamy saw this aspect of Belafonte's contribution first-hand when she attended some particularly tense meetings at the White Horse Hotel in Selma in 1965. "He was present because he was trying to act as a mediator between SNCC and SCLC because we were always falling out", she remembered. By and large, Bellamy felt he succeeded because both groups "had a lot of respect for Belafonte's ability to try to be fair".[78]

While Belafonte was especially close to King and the SCLC, he actually worked with all the major civil rights organizations at one time or another, although his relationship with the NAACP was often rather fraught. While he admired individual NAACP branches and members, and respected the Association's quasi-autonomous Legal Defence and Educational Fund Inc., Belafonte mistrusted the organization's "fraudulent" and "elite" national leadership, which he saw as a self-serving conservative black clique. "I didn't think the organization should be killed", Belafonte later admitted. "I think the NAACP served a very important purpose. I just thought that the leadership should be swiftly annihilated. Nonviolently!"[79]

Conversely, although the NAACP recognized Belafonte's potential for generating publicity and funds, its leadership remained deeply worried about his adverse impact on their moderate image. Although Belafonte quipped that "My leftist background couldn't have been half as frightening to them as their rightist background was to me", NAACP executive secretary Roy Wilkins was extremely reluctant to court or accept Belafonte's help. This was apparent at the 1957 Prayer Pilgrimage in Washington, organized by a consortium of civil rights organizations and led by Martin Luther King. Ella Baker, another product of the Old Left and one of the great intellectual and organizational wellsprings of the modern Movement, recalled that "they had a press conference at the NAACP headquarters. I was told that they had banned [Belafonte] . . . They may have thought of him as 'Red'. I think it was an anti-communist reaction on the part of the NAACP".[80]

There were other issues involved too: not least the sense that Belafonte's "presence would only send a shudder through Eisenhower . . . because he did not look favourably on my political behavior". Ironically, some 18 months later, with Martin Luther King hospitalized following a near-fatal stabbing by a deranged Harlem woman, Belafonte accompanied Coretta Scott King, A. Philip Randolph and Jackie Robinson to deliver a petition to the White

House. The petition, which demanded the immediate desegregation of public schools, was the final act of the Youth March for Integrated Schools, from which, as David Garrow has noted with eloquent brevity, "notably absent were Roy Wilkins and other NAACP officials".[81]

If Belafonte's relationship with the NAACP was strained, it was rather better with CORE. In 1960, for example, Belafonte allowed the organization to use his signature on 200,000 letters appealing for funds and recruits. This initiative helped to swell CORE's membership by some 40 per cent during the year to a total of 20,000.[82]

Belafonte was even closer to SNCC, which accorded him a respect and deference it bestowed with great selectivity on older blacks. Julian Bond recalled that Belafonte "had a lot of moral authority because his politics were so decent and he had behaved in such a decent way all of his public life". He "was very much out in front", agreed June Johnson. Stanley Wise remembered that Belafonte's contributions came in all shapes and, except where his clothing was concerned, sizes. Whenever SNCC workers were in New York they would routinely stay in Belafonte's apartment where he would give out useful gifts to his impecunious young guests. "We used to get his clothes . . . Oh God, he had such rich clothes. But he had such long legs". Nothing would fit the diminutive Wise. "I hated him, because I loved his taste in clothes!", Wise joked. "Belafonte was just a key friend to the Movement . . . I mean, there is just no other way to describe him".[83]

In fact, as Jim Forman movingly noted in December 1963, there were times when Belafonte appeared to be personally bankrolling many of SNCC's activities.

> Not only did you pledge your support, but you gave the first grant to make the dream of an independent student movement equipped with a staff a reality. Since the summer of 1961 your commitment to our struggle has not faltered and you have on many occasions enthusiastically given your time, your money, and encouraged your friends to support us. We shall never forget this.[84]

Belafonte was more than simply a patron, fundraiser or clothier for SNCC – although these functions were all invaluable for an organization sometimes operating on little more than passion and a shoestring budget. Throughout the early 1960s he was regularly consulted regarding specific initiatives, like a book-buying campaign for the under-resourced Miles College, and a protest against police brutality in Americus, Georgia.[85]

Belafonte also advised on much broader strategic issues, most importantly SNCC's 1962 decision to undertake voter registration work in the Deep South under the auspices of the Voter Education Project (VEP). The VEP was, in part at least, a gambit by the Kennedy administration to get black protestors off the streets and highways and into the electoral arena after the domestic and international embarrassment of the bloody freedom rides. It offered tax-exempt status to contributions from wealthy philanthropic foundations who wished to support voter education work in the South. However, with SNCC getting much less than it had expected from the VEP – despite having the most ambitious projects – resources for its voter registration work depended heavily on fundraising efforts by Belafonte and others. Indeed, without the revenue yielded by events like the 1963 show Belafonte organized in Carnegie Hall, SNCC's painstaking work could not have continued on the scale it did. Fundraising events accounted for over $32,000, or more than 10 per cent, of SNCC's total income of around $307,000 in 1963. With record sales and the Freedom Singers' tours generating another $20,300, "entertainment" of one kind or another accounted for about 17 per cent of SNCC's income that year.[86]

Meanwhile, Belafonte contributed to SNCC's Deep South efforts in many other practical ways. When, in the summer of 1961, several SNCC workers were imprisoned in McComb, Mississippi for trying to register black voters, their colleague Charles Jones feared they might be lynched. Jones immediately called not only the Justice Department's civil rights attorney, John Doar, but also Belafonte, who frequently provided the bond money to free SNCC workers from southern jails, or else contacted attorney-general Bobby Kennedy who then pressurized recalcitrant southern officials to release, or at least protect, their prisoners.[87]

Belafonte was sometimes even to be found on the frontline in Mississippi. In the wake of the Freedom Summer and the Atlantic City challenge, he and Sidney Poitier dodged the Klan to smuggle $60,000 to workers in Greenwood; money which enabled the MFDP and SNCC to continue their registration work the following year and eventually take better advantage of the 1965 Voting Rights Act. When Belafonte arrived in Mississippi he was shocked to find many of the leading activists utterly spent from the physical, mental and emotional efforts of the previous two years. Suffering from "battle fatigue, they were really like in shock, just worn out", he recalled. "And just the fatigue ... alone was getting in the way of clear thinking". Belafonte promptly paid for ten leading SNCC workers, including Bob and Dona Moses, Ruby Doris Robinson, Julian Bond and Bob Zellner, plus the indomitable Fannie Lou Hamer, to go on a physically and spiritually rejuvenating trip to Africa.[88]

The Africa trip was just one more example of Belafonte's personal generosity. From the late 1950s, it was estimated that around 20 per cent of his annual income was diverted into the tax-exempt Harry Belafonte Foundation of Music and Arts, disbursed to various scholarship funds for needy children, as well as to educational and arts projects. In 1962, he assigned his appearance fees for television's *What's My Line* and the *Merv Griffin Show* to SNCC. He regularly underwrote benefits like the "Salute to southern students" and gave numerous, and ultimately incalculable, out-of-pocket donations, usually of around $500, but amounting to more than $8,000 to SNCC alone during the critical summer of 1964.[89]

Belafonte's humanitarian work continued into the black power era which saw the steady discrediting of his record for its alleged moderation. This was not without its ironies. While black power militants of various stripes frequently romanticized the ghetto as the untapped source of a black revolutionary vanguard, Belafonte was actually a product of that environment. He had precisely the ghetto background, the street-based radicalism and deep racial consciousness, which Huey Newton or Maulana Ron Karenga – doing their best to conceal their own college backgrounds and entrepreneurial ambitions beneath layers of carefully cultivated streetwise affectations and pseudo-Africanisms – would have sold their berets and dashikis to boast.

Moreover, Belafonte clearly saw much value in the more constructive, community-building and consciousness-raising aspects of the broad black power impulse. In the summer of 1966, just as Stokely Carmichael was emerging as one of black power's most eloquent spokesmen and the latest black bogeyman for white Americans, Belafonte announced on national television that he was "in great part committed to the humanist desires and aspirations of a Stokely Carmichael". The same year he publicly endorsed A Philip Randolph's ambitious but doomed Freedom Budget proposal – a slice of imaginative socialism which would have provided a sort of federally planned and administered Marshall Plan for black America.[90]

In many ways Belafonte's growing public attention to the economic co-ordinates of racial injustice and, as he came out strongly against the Vietnam war, global militarism and imperialism, simply signalled a reaffirmation of his own left-labour radical roots. Nevertheless, in April 1967 Belafonte's longstanding personal assistant Gloria Cantor was so alarmed by what she perceived as her employer's new militancy that she called to discuss the situation in confidence with Stanley Levison – and, of course, with the FBI agents who were tapping Levison's phone at the time. Deeply torn by competing loyalties and affections for Belafonte and Martin Luther King, Cantor told Levison that after a recent strategy meeting attended by Belafonte, Levison, King, Carmichael and Andrew Young, she was "very upset about Harry because I felt that he was pushing Dr King and he was siding with SNCC . . . He's pushing [Dr King] to side with SNCC". Cantor stressed that "Dr King sets a great deal of store by [Belafonte]", and feared that, since Belafonte was still secretly paying many of King's domestic bills, King was "dependent in an area which he doesn't have to be". This Cantor felt, made King very susceptible to Belafonte's influence.[91]

Levison was less convinced that King could do without Belafonte's financial support. "He has a struggle with expenses", he reminded Cantor. He did, however, agree that "Harry has been attracted emotionally" to the fiery rhetoric and theatrical presence of Carmichael and the Black Panthers. Nevertheless, Levison reassured Cantor that it would be impossible for

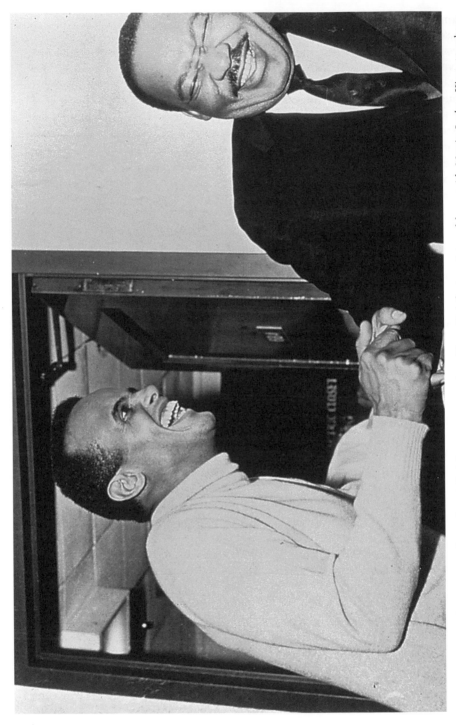

No celebrity played a greater role in the civil rights movement than Harry Belafonte, pictured here with Martin Luther King, to whom

anyone to persuade King to endorse programmes which often rested on notions of armed self-defence and sometimes advocated withdrawal from progressive biracial politics into racial separatism. Moreover, he and King were both confident that when it came "down to the harder points" of tactics, Belafonte would always reject ill-conceived shows of bravado over clearly defined programmes of constructive action.[92]

Certainly, the benefit concerts for the SCLC continued in 1967 as Belafonte and Joan Baez tried, with decidedly mixed results, to raise enthusiasm and funds for the Poor People's Campaign which eventually took place after Martin Luther King's death. In the aftermath of that assassination, Belafonte became one of the executors of the King estate, chaired the Martin Luther King Jr Memorial Fund, and eventually joined the board of directors of the SCLC, where he was one of several who tried to stop the woefully inept Ralph Abernathy from completely destroying an already devastated organization.

Although Belafonte remained a very wealthy man throughout this period of intense political involvement, his commitment took a certain toll on his health and career. His nerves were at times shredded by the contradictory demands of his career, concerns for his and his family's well-being, and the needs of his public activism. He faced his share of physical dangers: bomb threats, Klan pursuits, and a tear-gas assault through the air-conditioning system at a Houston benefit. He regularly had to cope with sneering editorial criticisms of his activism, and hurtful condemnations by conservatives and self-styled militants alike for his views. Hollywood studios ignored him and he did not appear on the big screen at all during the 1960s. Sponsors repeatedly threatened to withdraw support from television shows in which he was scheduled to appear. There are still few entertainers of his stature never to have been offered a product to endorse, or to have had a corporate sponsor for a show or tour.[93]

And yet, when Belafonte weighed "that evil of being blacklisted and denied opportunity against what we were achieving, and I weigh that loss of opportunity against what I was experiencing with Fannie Lou Hamer and Julian Bond, and Bob Moses and Ella Baker, and Dr King and all of that, the loss seems almost inconsequential". For Belafonte, the Movement was an irresistible moral crusade and joining it was simply not optional. "There was just no other choice. There was no other army to join. There was no other country to go to. There was no other head of state to appeal to. It was it. It was the day. I felt that there was no place else in the world to be other than here".[94]

Explaining an absence

Perhaps more than anything else, it was Harry Belafonte's sense of personal calling, what he described in 1957 as a "nerve-wracking sense of duty", coupled with his capacity for self-sacrifice, which distinguished him and a few others from their fellow entertainers and largely accounted for their highly conspicuous presence in Movement-related activities. As Bernice Johnson Reagon recalled, "There is a real difference between what people will say about, say a Belafonte, or a Pete Seeger. There did not seem to be anything self-serving. It was no fad, it was no 'I'll do a benefit today'. It was like, 'This is a part of my life. As this Movement goes, so will I go'". The Movement did not have to go looking for these people. They came to the Movement, offering to do whatever they could on its behalf because, as Reagon put it, their "biggest fear was that it would be over before they had a chance to participate".[95]

For all their appeals to soul brotherhood and potent musical expressions of black pride and consciousness, very few Rhythm and Blues singers and entrepreneurs felt or, perhaps more accurately, succumbed to the pull of the early Movement in quite this way. Reagon was frustrated, if not altogether surprised, that they did not contribute more to the early struggle. "We really thought those people should be sending money. They should be doing benefits". They were getting their money, in part at least, from black people, who were "on the move", and whose activism promised to improve the lives of all blacks, artists included. "We thought all of them should be there. But, you know, what you think and what they think are different things . . . Sometimes, I think, they couldn't quite see an interest".[96]

Harry Belafonte himself often found it "extremely difficult" to get his fellow entertainers to make any sort of public artistic, personal and financial commitment to the Movement. "Especially in black America, where I thought my task would be easier, I found enormous resistance", he lamented. "When the time came for show and tell, nobody showed, they had nothing to tell". Yet, even within this general pattern of celebrity diffidence, Belafonte felt that the leading Rhythm and Blues artists – James Brown, Sam Cooke, the Motown stable – were particularly cautious. "All of these people distanced themselves from the Movement; not only once removed from it, but sometimes twenty times removed from it, I think".[97]

There was no mystery about this abstentionism. Most successful or ambitious Rhythm and Blues artists and entrepreneurs were anxious to avoid potentially controversial gestures which might alienate, or permanently put beyond their reach, a highly lucrative white record-buying, concert-going and radio-listening public – this at a time when equal black access to the rewards of the mainstream consumer market was widely accepted as one of the Movement's legitimate goals. Yet it was also a time of widespread white support for legislation to protect basic black civil rights and Belafonte felt that many black performers exaggerated the extent to which support for the Movement would damage their careers. Pointing to his own continued success, in 1960 he argued that "it is false to think one's concern with political life and one's country is necessarily at the risk of one's career". Blasting his fellow artists for their lack of engagement, Belafonte complained "I see fear all around me and I have no respect for it".[98]

Grounded or groundless, these fears were nonetheless real enough. Even Belafonte acknowledged that they decisively shaped the responses of many aspiring or established soul artists to the early Movement. "I think most of them were in great, great fear of losing their platform", he suggested. They dreaded "losing their newly found moments of opportunity". Julian Bond also suspected that for many Rhythm and Blues artists, their expanded personal ambition – itself a correlate of the Movement's early promise – prompted a feeling that "this could be my big break. I could break out. I could go into the larger white market. I better tread lightly here".[99]

R&b and soul singers were hardly unusual in their reluctance to align themselves conspicuously with a Movement which was frequently dangerous to life, limb and livelihood. While the extent of mass black participation was remarkable given the perils involved, Bernice Johnson Reagon recognized that it "was always a minority" who took part in protest activities. Lawrence Guyot put it even more bluntly: "The reason more artists weren't involved was because a large segment of the black population wasn't involved – for the same reason, terror".[100]

Guyot actually had great sympathy for the dilemma of black musicians and entrepreneurs in this period, trapped between the narrow demands of economic self-interest and personal safety, and broader needs of a fight against the racial injustices which ultimately robbed all blacks of freedom, opportunity and security. "A musician before 1965 who said, 'Yes, I support voter registration' put everyone in his group in danger If he was to travel in the South", Guyot stated. "Now, if he was prepared to say that and not travel in the South and thereby lose that market he had to make that decision".[101]

Very few made any such decision and the problem was especially acute for local, frequently impoverished, southern performers. Regardless of their own feelings on the Movement, economic realities ensured that many had little choice but to remain silent on racial issues and provide entertainment in facilities which remained functionally segregated long after the 1964 Civil Rights Act had outlawed such arrangements. Indeed, while both the NAACP and SNCC ran successful campaigns to keep black and white entertainers, including classical musicians Gary Graffman and Birgit Nilsson, the Journeymen folk group, and the cast of television's *Bonanza*, from appearing at segregated Mississippi venues in 1964, a disarmingly honest Roscoe Shelton admitted that he and most of his southern contemporaries continued to play Jim Crow dates throughout the 1950s and 1960s.[102]

Shelton desperately wanted the Movement to succeed. Yet he played no benefits and took part in no demonstrations until 1965, when he joined the last 18 miles of the Selma to Montgomery March. As Lawrence Guyot had appreciated, for Shelton and many others, a simple but decisive blend of fear and finances accounted for his inaction. "Mostly the southern entertainers were a little reluctant to get involved", explained Shelton, "because they still had to live pretty much in that region and they were a little – I don't want to say frightened – reluctant".[103]

Worth Long, an SNCC worker heavily involved in the Greenwood movement, and one of those most interested in trying to use popular culture as an educational as well as a fundraising tool, found the same widespread caution among musicians in the region. "Now, very few of the musicians actually participated except by going to mass meetings", he admitted. "I don't know any musician who's gotten arrested, for instance, during the '60s for demonstrating ... And I've talked to a lot of them about that. They say, 'no, well, you know, I couldn't do that and play a set tonight too' ".[104]

While this sense of personal priorities goes a considerable way towards explaining the relatively meagre support Rhythm and Blues artists afforded the early Movement, the nature and extent of their participation was also circumscribed by the fact that few black singers had much control over the key decisions which affected their careers. Fay Bellamy recognized that "They were stars to the masses", but what, she asked, "was really going on in their lives? Did they own their music? ... Were they working for Berry Gordy, or some other company?" For the most part, Julian Bond felt that individual artists "had nothing to do with where they went; who they appeared before; what the circumstances were. They were just out there churning out the music, night after night, and leaving all the decisions to somebody else who, typically, is business-oriented and doesn't care about these things, and is frightened that if the artist gets involved in these things they will lose money".[105]

Bond was right. The configuration of economic and managerial power within the recording and broadcasting industries of the early-to-mid 1960s consistently worked against the likelihood that Rhythm and Blues would become a major source of artistic comment on American racism, or of public support for black insurgency. The whites and the handful of blacks in positions of real power within the music business usually proved more concerned with market penetration than political mobilization. As Stanley Wise recalled, "Marvin Gaye had attempted for a number of years to just do something with us ... And I know Stevie Wonder was just trying really hard. They were the two I remember specifically who indicated over and over again they wanted to do something with us. They wanted to help us somehow". Before Selma, however, despite repeated attempts to enlist their services, Motown's support was usually, at best, covert and fleeting. "I think it was primarily because ... they just weren't sure how the population would accept that. Because they were trying to get to their main market and ... they didn't want to be viewed as militants or belligerents, or that sort of stuff".[106]

If black singers, their managers and labels were cautious about getting visibly involved in Movement-related activities, it is important to recognize that there was a stultifying cycle of inactivity at work here. Because few Rhythm and Blues artists came forward, the Movement simply did not put much time or energy into trying to recruit from their ranks.

At CORE, this neglect was compounded by the fact that the key figures in its fundraising activities until the mid 1960s, Val Coleman and Marvin Rich, were middle-aged white men who, for all their many qualities, were just not very attuned to the world of soul. Although volunteer lawyer George Schiffer, who worked as Berry Gordy's copyright expert, provided CORE with a natural conduit to Motown, the inexperience in this field was indicated by the fact that Coleman's first three attempts to secure Stevie Wonder's services were directed to Milt Shaw's Shaw Artists Corporation, rather than Motown's ITMI. Rich's subsequent plea for Wonder, the Marvelettes and Contours to appear in a series of benefits was sent to one "Berry Gardy" of the "Motonen Record Company".[107]

If race and generation partially explained Rich and Coleman's initial lack of interest, and general lack of success, in courting Rhythm and Blues stars, it was much the same at SNCC. Because of its own student base and bira-cialism, one might have expected the young SNCC to try to do more with popular black singers whose audiences were also young and often biracial. Experience, however had quickly persuaded Julian Bond "that you can't appeal to . . . this class of entertainers. That if you are going to get help it's going to be the Belafontes, the Dick Gregorys, the folk people . . . but these other people are just not going to be there". As a result, Stanley Wise sum-marized that "there was never any real effort on our part unless the artists themselves pushed it. In other words, artists had to do something for us despite our hesitancy".[108]

In a sense, this neglect simply reflected the low priority which Rhythm and Blues, per se, was accorded as an educational tool or mobilizing vehicle in the early Movement. Sympathetic artists and entertainers were conceived of primarily as the fillers of tills and drawers of publicity, rather than as political leaders, strategists, or educators. Harry Belafonte was a partial excep-tion to this rule, yet around the time of the Meredith March Stanley Levison reminded Gloria Cantor that entertainers, including her boss, needed to know their place. They were sought, Levison said, "because they give you a cer-tain image and the press pays more attention when you have celebritics with you. That's all it is. They call attention to you".[109]

Levison's brusque assessment was not unusual and some black artists were deterred by the rather cavalier treatment they received from organiza-tions which only turned to them when they were deep in financial trouble. According to Coretta Scott King, a frustrated Mahalia Jackson once com-plained of the SCLC that "those niggers don't ever bother with me until they want something". Junius Griffin's work as the SCLC's director of public relations, and then in Motown's publicity department, gave him a unique dual perspective on these matters. He, too, felt that when Rhythm and Blues artists were brought in for fundraising dinners or rallies they were often treated insensitively and left disillusioned by the whole experience.[110]

According to Griffin, Esther Gordy had once explained to him that "Motown was reluctant to allow their artists to participate in Movement events and activities because they were used as mere addendums to programs and never as an integral part of the activities". Singers were invariably asked to perform in the aftermath of dozens of speeches so that, although these artists had often drawn the crowds to the benefit in the first place, they were made to feel like an afterthought. Often grappling with inadequate sound systems, these proud performers were served up to the audience as a light fluffy dessert, to be enjoyed only after the real main course – the hearty political messages of struggle and freedom – had been devoured. Moreover, Griffin recalled, while these singers "were always given a lively welcome . . . when they were ready to leave the following morning, no one was present to say goodbye. Artists and their management were highly offended by this practice. It was a classic battle of egos . . . of civil rights stars and the recording stars not understanding the needs of each other".[111]

This mishandling of notoriously fragile celebrity egos was related to the broader problem of the Movement's basic inexperience at organizing fundraising events or dealing with entertainers. In 1965 Betty Garman admitted that SNCC's use of celebrities was "kind of a hit and miss operation". Garman was nothing if not honest and the Movement's use of entertainers, whether for recruitment purposes, publicity, or fundraising, tended to be extremely haphazard. Certainly, Junius Griffin could recall "no concerted efforts to court soul artists during [his] years with SCLC". There may have been "individual efforts", where civil rights workers had personal contacts with performers. But even here, Griffin felt that there was little understanding of "how to convert these relationships into capital for the Movement".[112]

Poor Stanley Levison could never quite decide which alarmed him most: the amateurism and ineptitude with which the SCLC planned and executed some of its own fundraising events, or the exorbitant costs of hiring professional promoters to do the job properly and increase the chances of a good return. An early SNCC fundraising primer had also highlighted this dilemma, suggesting that while "benefit concerts and entertainers are probably the most lucrative field exploited by professional promoters", with those professionals at the helm "such affairs seldom net more than 10 per cent to the beneficiary".[113]

In an effort to cut costs and increase the rate of return from these benefits, civil rights groups – particularly at the local level – frequently trusted to the enthusiasm and ingenuity of Movement workers who rarely had any previous experience or contacts in the world of entertainment or concert promotion. There were some exceptions, like ex-singer Jimmy McDonald at CORE's New York office, and Richard Haley, who, before he became CORE's assistant to the national director and then director of its Southern Regional

Office in New Orleans, had accompanied the greats of black music in the Apollo house band.[114]

In the main, however, workers in Movement fundraising, communications and publicity departments were novices who learned how to do their jobs, with varying degrees of success, by actually trying to do them. While these resourceful pragmatists arranged many successful parties, events and shows, Betty Garman explained to Dick Perez of Cleveland's Friends of SNCC that such enterprises were fraught with dangers for the amateur organizer, especially when bigger stars and venues were involved. "Very often the Friends of SNCC group itself sets up its own contact and makes a date directly with the performers. The only problem with this is that sometimes the Friends can't pull off a concert and the big time performer sings to an empty house – which then sours him or her on ever doing another concert for SNCC". In these circumstances, as CORE's Marvin Rich noted, civil rights groups frequently found themselves trying to pass off ill-conceived, hastily planned, inadequately promoted, or poorly timed fundraising events, which actually raised little or no money, as "good publicity" for their organization.[115]

Regardless of who actually organized and promoted these benefits, they ran the gamut from disastrous to highly profitable. After advertising, accommodation and musicians' expenses were deducted, an entire week of concerts by Sammy Davis at the Apollo in 1958 netted the disappointed NAACP less than $4,000, of which $1,300 came in the form of a donation from sympathetic theatre owner Frank Schiffman. A major show at Nashville's Ryman Auditorium in September 1961, organized by the city's SCLC affiliate and featuring Harry Belafonte, the Chad Mitchell Trio and South African folk singer Miriam Makeba, cleared little more than $600. In May 1964, a much more modest benefit by black folk-blues singer Josh White grossed $577 for SNCC. Unfortunately, by the time White's fee of $300 was deducted and the show's promoter, Bill Powell, had fraudulently used the rest to have his car repaired, SNCC was left with nothing. Even worse, in 1965 CORE accepted author James Baldwin's offer to use the opening night of his play *Amen Corner* as a fundraising event, and then contrived to make a net loss on the evening of $29.[116]

At the other end of the spectrum, however, there were some very impressive returns. A 1964 New York jazz concert hosted by baseball star Jackie Robinson raised $25,000 for an outlay of just $500. The 1965 "Broadway answers Selma" promotion, headed and partly organized by Sammy Davis, generated nearly $100,000 in ticket sales, donations and merchandising, divided equally among NAACP, CORE, SCLC and SNCC. Above all, this was what the Movement sought from its celebrity contacts – the money with which to continue its work and the chance to publicize its efforts.[117]

These priorities help to explain not only the Movement's general lack of interest in courting Rhythm and Blues performers, but also the sorts of entertainers whose support it did covet. In the summer of 1965, an excited Constancia "Dinky" Romilly caught wind of a rumour that the Beatles were willing to do a benefit for SNCC. Even when Romilly, who like Betty Garman worked as a co-ordinator between SNCC's Atlanta headquarters and its nationwide support groups, had established that "there is not much basis to the rumours", she still wrote hopefully to Joan Baez and Bobby Dillon (sic) asking for their help in making contact with the group and stressing the severity of SNCC's latest financial crisis.[118]

Although Julian Bond remembered that he and "other people in SNCC were interested in [the Beatles'] music", there was an even greater interest in the group as a cultural phenomenon; as youthful symbols of a growing disdain for the established social order. "They were so fresh and irreverent. So close to a little bit of what we imagined ourselves to be – contemptuous of adult forms and not willing to conform to the standard way of dressing or thinking . . . They were irreverent and we were irreverent and I think there was a kind of identification there", Bond recalled.[119]

Notwithstanding such identification, however, Romilly's primary concern was the sheer pecuniary and propaganda value of having the most popular act on the planet perform for the organization. An SNCC guide to fundraising had already suggested that if the New York office really wanted to put on a spectacular benefit, "James Brown or the Beatles could be added" to the programme. If there was a touching naiveté about the assumption that either act could be induced to perform, it is clear that SNCC really saw little difference between the two in terms of their usefulness to the Movement.[120]

Like SNCC, CORE was also mired deep in financial crisis in the summer of 1965, with debts of more than $220,000. Val Coleman and James Farmer made a similar bid for celebrity salvation, trying unsuccessfully to persuade Frank Sinatra to do a huge outdoor benefit at Shea Stadium in the wake of the Beatles' triumph there. Coleman recognized that the key to raising major sums of money was enlisting a superstar like Sinatra. "Without Frank we should hang it up and go back to $150 tea parties", he argued. The following year, Martin Luther King discussed with Levison the possibilities of getting someone – anyone, it really did not matter who – to play for the SCLC at the newly built Madison Square Gardens, because curiosity alone would guarantee a sell-out.[121]

In all these cases, publicity and a high box-office return were what mattered most, irrespective of who performed, or whether they or their art had any real link to black America or the Movement. For the same reasons, it actually made perfect sense for the Movement to woo sympathetic, wealthy Hollywood and Broadway figures, not least because they could afford to be more personally generous. After a spring 1963 all-star rally in Los Angeles had raised over $35,000 for the SCLC, the mainly white celebrities involved retired to actor Burt Lancaster's house where they collected another $20,000 in loose change and pledges, with $5,000 and $1,000 respectively coming from stalwart supporters Marlon Brando and Paul Newman. When Diahann Carroll threw a modest private party for a few well-heeled friends in New York in 1964, it made a profit of nearly $4,000 for SNCC.[122]

At the top end of the Rhythm and Blues pay scale, a few individuals might have been able to match this sort of personal generosity. Fats Domino earned $700,000 in 1957; Ray Charles commanded between $3,500 and $4,500 per performance by 1961; Motown grossed $8 million in 1965, while in the same year James Brown earned more than $1 million from live shows alone. However, these were exceptions and very few Rhythm and Blues stars had anything like this sort of money to give, even if they were so inclined. Black musical celebrity did not always indicate financial well-being, let alone political consciousness.[123]

But it was not just the pocketbooks of the stars themselves which the Movement wanted to pick. The attention, hopefully hearts, and definitely money of their fans, friends and associates were targets too. However, the critical constituency here was again white not black. Since the earliest days of the Montgomery bus boycott and the fledgling SCLC, when black churches were a principal source of funding, white Americans had been the major sponsors of the civil rights movement which blacks largely created and populated. At least until 1966, about 95 per cent of CORE's funding came from whites, mostly from Jewish Americans who were disproportionately represented among the white benefactors of, and participants in, the organization. In 1966, whites provided about 70 per cent of SCLC's income.[124]

Movement fundraisers, keenly aware of the economic distress of many black communities, were naturally reluctant to try to grind any extra income from that meagre resource. Instead they concentrated on encouraging more whites to recognize the legitimacy of the struggle and make a contribution. Direct mailing campaigns were the most successful means of extracting this support and all the major organizations solicited "big names" precisely because they appreciated that, as an SNCC report put it, "Many contribute to organizations only because well-known persons are listed as sponsors, endorsers or board members".[125]

Again, these strategic and economic priorities militated against major efforts to recruit Rhythm and Blues artists. In fact, Harold Battiste reckoned that, in a broader sense, the early Movement's determination to project an image of unimpeachable middle-class respectability rendered most Rhythm and Blues artists unsuitable for its needs, and in turn made those artists uncomfortable about getting involved. There was a class dynamic within the early Movement which reflected both the nature of the white audience it was trying to reach, and its own heavy dependence on clerical and student leadership.[126]

In this environment, soul stars of humble origins and minimal education were often left on the outside looking in. Purely according to the Movement's own fiscal agenda, there was little use for performers whose black fans were often poor, and whose white audience was often smaller, younger and less affluent than that of major showbiz figures like Sammy Davis or Marlon Brando, or even black literati like author James Baldwin, who SNCC also used as a magnet for white liberal funds. If endorsements from Wilson Pickett or James Brown might have done much to raise black morale and even some black cash, they were unlikely to have been as effective among those whites whose consciences and cheque books the Movement desperately needed to reach.[127]

By presenting this broader context for the relative anonymity of Rhythm and Blues stars in the early Movement, it is possible to understand, rather than simply condemn on one hand, or excuse on the other, their widespread failure to participate in Movement-related activities. There clearly were opportunities to get involved at any number of financial, artistic or personal levels, yet for a variety of reasons few Rhythm and Blues singers chose, or were able, to take advantage of them in the decade after Montgomery. Conversely, however grateful they were when Nina Simone or Curtis Mayfield validated their struggle in song, or when Al Hibbler and Clyde McPhatter joined their protests on the street, civil rights leaders made no attempt to try to use Rhythm and Blues music in any systematic way, or to make its artists feel truly wanted and welcome among their ranks.

All of which begs that most perplexing of questions: so what? What, if anything, did the early Movement really lose as a result of its own indifference towards Rhythm and Blues music and its artists, and the general caution or inability of the artists themselves to get more involved? Would the course of the Movement have been significantly different if more soul men and women had become involved earlier? And if so, in what respects?

In monetary terms, it is clear that Rhythm and Blues represented an underexploited, if limited resource. Even relatively impecunious black artists were in a position to generate funds, if not by personal donations then by doing benefit shows – even on the chitlin' circuit – or by donating proceeds from some of their recordings. The Artists' Civil Rights Action Fund, founded in 1965, even offered the chance to contribute a day's earnings each year to the Movement in secret, thereby avoiding whatever risks there were in pledging public support. Apparently, no Rhythm and Blues artists took advantage of the scheme and the main benefactors were a familiar crew of Belafonte, Davis, folk singers Chad Mitchell and Mary Travers of Peter, Paul and Mary, white popster Bobby Darin, and authors James Baldwin and Joseph Heller.[128]

Furthermore, it was in the nature of the Movement and its oscillating fortunes that any and all contributions, however small, could be disproportionately important at the recurring moments of financial crisis. No sooner did civil rights organizations experience an upsurge in income, as happened to CORE after the Freedom Rides, to all the groups during the momentous summer of 1963, to SNCC in the freedom summer of 1964, and again to

SNCC and SCLC during the 1965 Selma campaign, than they expanded their staffs and operations, stretching human and fiscal resources dangerously thin. The very sense of urgency which motivated and characterized the early Movement meant that long-term financial planning and security were frequently sacrificed in order to pursue more immediate goals and establish much-needed new projects. Consequently, any additional income was potentially priceless, helping to keep operations ticking over by paying perpetually overdue staff salaries, covering phone and electricity bills, and keeping ageing cars refuelled and in working order until the next big windfall, benefit, or direct mailshot replenished the coffers.[129]

Irrespective of the extent to which a concerted fundraising effort involving Rhythm and Blues acts might have helped to alleviate a little of the Movement's financial hardships, there was also an important non-pecuniary dividend to be redeemed from such public expressions of solidarity in terms of their inspirational and educational value. While it is unlikely that any amount of personal or artistic engagement with the Movement would have produced extra legions of activists or donors from the ranks of the once hostile, indifferent, or even mildly sympathetic, it is nevertheless true that popular music and its heroes did help to shape the ways in which people – especially young people – perceived the world, sorted out its heroes from its villains, and evaluated the relationship between its rights and its wrongs.

There was undoubtedly a sense that those black and white artists who did volunteer some kind of public commitment to the Cause had a genuine impact upon the way their fans viewed the struggle. Even the congenitally cynical Stanley Levison recognized that Joan Baez offered important access to college students, "not only for the money but the educational value". Lawrence Guyot believed that the involvement of such artists "was tremendously important because it gave a legitimacy to protest at a time that that was a question, rather than an affirmation, not only in the South, but in the country . . . They did it and helped expand the range of those to whom the stand was not only acceptable but necessary". Their visible support for the struggle, whether at benefits, or on marches and at demonstrations, or even in their songs, brought the Movement and its goals "to a lot of people who wouldn't necessarily listen to a freedom song, or to a gospel song, that 'hey, this is legitimate . . . because Leon Bibb, who I respect, says its legitimate – or Nina Simone, or Lena Horne'. And we should never underestimate the importance of people . . . who had some of the cult groups saying to their groupies, 'this is good' ".[130]

There was certainly evidence that when black artists did speak out against racism, or for the Movement, the black community, activist or otherwise, greatly appreciated the gesture and wished that more would do the same. In late September 1957, for example, Louis Armstrong launched a scathing public attack on President Eisenhower's handling of the Little Rock crisis, to which Lena Horne and Eartha Kitt quickly added their own chorus. Accusing Ike of having "no guts", Armstrong claimed that the president was allowing Orval Faubus, an "uneducated plowboy", to make a mockery of the law and dictate to the government. Meanwhile, Armstrong protested, the president "smiles and goes out to play golf". Armstrong eventually pulled out of a government-sponsored goodwill tour of the Soviet Union because of "the way they are treating my people in the South".[131]

A vox-pop survey of black Virginians in the aftermath of Armstrong's remarks revealed that many took enormous heart from the way in which a few of their leading celebrities had put their heads above the parapet and spoken out for racial justice. Contrasting Armstrong, Horne and Kitt to the "gutless" Ike and their equally gutless silent showbiz contemporaries, Manchester Greene of Portsmouth expressed "great admiration for their intestinal fortitude. I wish we had more Armstrongs and Ertha (sic) Kitts in our group". George Perkins of Norfolk thought "Armstrong knew what he was doing and is ready to accept whatever the consequences. Wise or unwise I have only praises for him". The views of Rhythm and Blues singers on the Little Rock crisis were not made public.[132]

For those already in the Movement, this sort of encouragement and endorsement of the Cause and their work could only help to reinforce their sense of purpose and commitment, demonstrating that their sacrifices were appreciated by artists they often greatly admired. Certainly, Martin Luther King valued the psychological uplift public support from black celebrities could provide. In early 1961, in the wake of Sammy Davis' Carnegie Hall benefit for the CDMLK, King personally drafted a letter to the performer which amounted to his most extended meditation on the role black entertainers might play in the freedom struggle. King began by noting that "Not very long ago, it was customary for Negro artists to hold themselves aloof from the struggle for equality, in the belief that the example of this personal success was in itself a contribution, in that it helped to disprove the myth of Negro inferiority – which indeed it did".[133]

Yet King characterized this position, which was the one adopted by most Rhythm and Blues singers and entrepreneurs, as an "essentially defensive position which does not meet the needs of our time when the Negro people as a whole are vigorously striding toward freedom". He commended entertainment "giants like Harry Belafonte, Sidney Poitier, Mahalia Jackson" and Davis, who were not "content to merely identify with the struggle. They actively participate in it, as artists and as citizens, adding the weight of their enormous prestige and thus helping to move the struggle forward". Who, King asked rhetorically, "can measure the impact, the inspirational effect upon the millions of Negroes" of learning of such involvement by "one of their idols . . . ?"[134]

Inspiration was a difficult thing to quantify, yet the success of the early Movement was heavily dependent on the spirit and morale of its participants. To keep on keeping on in the face of persistent white racism, intimidation and violence, and federal prevarication, required a constant reaffirmation of the belief that the struggle was righteous, winnable and supported by all right-thinking Americans – but especially by a unified black community marching irresistibly towards freedom, justice and equal opportunity. The inability or unwillingness of most soul artists to associate publicly with the early Movement robbed civil rights workers of another potentially useful source of validation and inspiration for their efforts.

Ultimately, however, it should be remembered that the black community actually expected rather less of their singers and popular music in terms of political leadership or Movement-related activities than subsequent commentators have suggested. In the decade after Montgomery, singers and songs were not necessarily where the black community looked first when searching for political direction, or economic leadership, or personal role models. As Eldridge Cleaver observed, white America has an arrogant habit of trying to determine who are the real leaders and voices of the black community, invariably choosing them from the "apolitical world of sport and play". This, Cleaver argued, was a way to take the "'problem' out of a political and economic and philosophical context and [placing] it on the misty level of 'goodwill', 'charitable and harmonious race relations'". The many critics, black as well as white, who have routinely exaggerated, or misrepresented the political and leadership roles of Rhythm and Blues artists and their music in the early years of the Movement are in some ways the unwitting heirs to this tradition.[135]

Rhythm and blues artists were much admired, of course. But Georgia's feisty state representative, Billy McKinney – a community activist since before he became one of Atlanta's first black policemen in 1948 – felt that, in the main, "They were not leaders, just musicians. They were not role models   we just didn't expect them to put anything [back] in the community". McKinney linked this to the more general observation that personal economic and status considerations have always cut across racial solidarity in black America. "One of the fallacies of black society is that those who make it . . . put a whole lot back into it", he observed. On the rare occasions when an individual entertainer broke with this pattern to assume a more engaged stance, McKinney felt simply that "it put them above the average artist . . . Harry Belafonte would fit into a role-model-type person, but I can't think of a whole lot of musicians who were role models".[136]

On the face of it, Billy McKinney's dismissal of the notion that the black community had much expectation that its musicians would participate in, let alone lead, black protest seems too sweeping. It is certainly unsettling, since it appears to fly in the face of what we think we know about the enormous emotional investment black audiences have traditionally made in their music and celebrities. It seems to compromise our understanding of the ways in which popular black artists have served as cultural representatives of the black community and its changing consciousnesses. Moreover, it seems to ignore the fact that some blacks clearly did hope that their celebrities would become more active supporters of the Movement at various personal, economic and artistic levels.

And yet, hope and expectation are hardly synonyms. Black hopes that their favourite musicians might emerge in the vanguard of Movement-related activities, or as bold advocates and patrons of the freedom struggle, were seldom realized. As a result, there was a rather lower level of expectation about any such involvement. In any case, as Cleaver and McKinney agreed, in the 1950s and early 1960s, black America had a whole range of political organizers and labour leaders, philosophers of social change, and dedicated Movement workers, who seemed to be helping the mass of blacks take meaningful strides towards freedom and equality. Consequently, black entertainers were simply not so sorely needed, or expected, to fulfil anything resembling formal roles in the early years of the Movement. Any help with fundraising, recruiting, education or morale-boosting was welcome, but their main community responsibility was to do their damnedest to be hugely successful in America, while helping to sustain the spirits, identity and cohesion of the black community through their music.

This was no trifling contribution, of course, and in itself constituted one type of leadership. And, perhaps, in the final analysis, it is a definition of leadership which is at issue here. While political education and community mobilization were largely beyond the functional capacity of Rhythm and Blues, and any involvement in the formal struggle was low on the agenda of most of its artists, the music nonetheless performed a valuable function. They also served who watched, watusied and wailed. By dramatizing and celebrating the black community's refusal to succumb to the mental and spiritual ravages of racism and poverty, Rhythm and Blues did what black popular culture had always done best; it promoted and sustained the black pride, identity and self-respect upon which the Movement and its leaders were ultimately dependent.

In this respect, however, most Rhythm and Blues singers were not much like civil rights leaders and activists at all. Instead, they were more like those cautious black ministers who took no formal part in the early struggle, but whose churches, sermons and even musical offerings nonetheless helped to foster the emotional strength, the psychological resources, and even some of the money, which others transformed into a mass movement for black civil and voting rights. Soul singers and their songs did much the same, offering another example of the way in which various social, political and economic functions in black life had been largely transferred from the sacred to the secular sphere.

PART THREE

One nation (divisible) under a groove

CHAPTER NINE

"Tell it like it is": soul, funk and sexual politics in the black power era

If you're going to come away from a party singing the lyrics of a song, it is better that you sing of self-pride like "We're a winner" instead of "Do the boo-ga loo"! (Curtis Mayfield)[1]

An unfinished revolution

Having once largely skirted political issues, the Rhythm and Blues of the later 1960s and early 1970s was full of songs explicitly about the struggle, about the social, political and economic plight of black Americans, and about the state of American race relations. Soul singers who had previously avoided much artistic engagement with the Movement began to echo and give a distinctive public voice to the rising clamour for black power through their songs. As we shall see in later chapters, many artists and entrepreneurs also supported organized efforts to secure that power, both in America at large and within the narrower confines of the recording and broadcasting industries. Even the sound of soul seemed to darken audibly during this period of rising nationalist sentiment.

As always, the most important changes in the sound, sense, presentation, performance practices and economic structure of Rhythm and Blues were closely related to changes in the state of mass black consciousness. While the Civil Rights Act of 1964 and the Voting Rights Act of 1965 were momentous victories which promised much for an integrated, pluralistic America with opportunity and justice for all, by the turn of the decade they also seemed like markers on the road to a half-finished racial revolution. At the same historic moment, America's bloody south-east Asian misadventures intensified black bitterness and cynicism about the nation's commitment to racial equality. It was bad enough that blacks were disproportionately victims of the draft and tragically over-represented in the body bags. It was worse still that they were still being denied full access to the freedoms at home for which they were ostensibly fighting and dying abroad.

This is not, however, to deny that the struggles of the 1950s and 1960s yielded tangible economic and political gains for many blacks. Whereas black family income in 1954 was just 56 per cent of white median income, the differential had narrowed to around 62 per cent by the mid 1970s, with average earnings for black women running at 96 per cent those of white women. During the 1960s, the proportion of blacks in the middle class of American society virtually doubled, rising further to account for nearly 38 per cent of the black workforce by 1981. In the South, Jim Crow practices were largely dismantled and, despite a mixture of white legal and extra-legal obstructionism, the black political presence increased many-fold. In 1964 only 35.5 per cent of voting age southerners were registered to vote, but by 1969 that proportion had risen to about 65 per cent. Similarly, whereas there were only 100 black elected officials in the region in 1965, by 1969 there were 1,185, and by 1980 nearly 2,500.[2]

Yet behind these encouraging indicators were equally clear signs that the herculean efforts and pathbreaking legislation of the 1960s had moderated, but hardly ended, the pernicious effects of racism and systemic discrimination. Moreover, statutory equality itself did little to remedy the debilitating effects of centuries of abuses and disadvantage, or to prepare black Americans to compete on an equal footing with whites for their slice of the all-American dream pie. Inadequate housing, inferior educational provision and access, compromised political power, and high rates of poverty and unemployment continued to plague many sections of the black community, North and South.

In the early 1970s, the already sluggish narrowing of income differentials between the races slowed even further – and in any case, much of that improvement had reflected the spectacular expansion of the black middle class, rather than a more broadly based rise in income levels throughout black America. Around mid decade, the trend actually began to reverse and black-white income differentials widened once more. In fact, the earnings of blacks relative to whites actually improved more during the period 1940 to 1960 than in the period 1970 to 1990.[3]

Black unemployment also worsened in the 1970s, both in absolute terms and relative to rates among whites. Having fallen to a low of around 8 per cent in the boom years of the mid 1960s, black unemployment rose to nearly 15 per cent during the recession a decade later, and ran at between 14 and 20 per cent in the early 1980s. For black teenagers the rates were much higher, ranging between 35 and 70 per cent in the city, compared with an average black teenage unemployment rate of about 13 per cent in 1955. By the mid 1970s, even the initially impressive expansion of the black middle class had stalled, and was more than offset by the devastation of the black skilled and unskilled working class. Major economic and technological changes ravished the old heavy manufacturing and processing industries which had provided steady, if often dangerous and underpaid, employment for many blacks. With little attempt to create new opportunities or retrain these workers, and with many blacks lacking the education to move into the new high-tech industries, tens of thousands were consigned to a rapidly expanding underclass of permanently unemployed or underemployed black urbanites. By 1981 some 34 per cent of black families, as opposed to 11 per cent of white ones, lived in poverty, while the "feminization" of that poverty was reflected in the fact that over half of the 40 per cent of black families then headed by a woman lived below the official poverty level.[4]

Furthermore, while Thomas Blair may have exaggerated when he moaned that "Black elected officials are a mere token force within the white establishment", the hard-won new black political power did appear cruelly limited and uneven. By 1980, less than 1 per cent of elected officials in the United States were black, although the black population comprised over 11 per cent of the total. In the Deep South, especially, economic intimidation and the careful gerrymandering of electoral districts successfully contained much of the potential power of the black vote. The fragmentation of the Movement also contributed to the under-utilization of black political power, as apathy replaced action, and various forms of specious black nationalism supplanted, rather than sustained, the harder task of political organizing for real black power in America. In the late 1970s, about 35 per cent of Mississippi's population was black, yet blacks still only accounted for 5 per cent of the state's elected officials. By the mid-to-late 1970s, the annual rate of increase of elected black officials had actually begun to decline. In 1992, blacks still held only 2 per cent of the elected offices in the nation, many of them of relatively low significance. In the South, where blacks comprised 20 per cent of the population, they accounted for just 4 per cent of officeholders.[5]

Even when blacks did secure office, their capacity to do much to help their black constituents was often limited. In places like Jackson, Mississippi, a self-serving, conservative black leadership – most of whom had been conspicuously absent from the struggles to re-enfranchise blacks in the 1960s – used racial appeals to acquire political power, but then generally allowed the state to return to business as usual, addressing the needs of white business interests far more eagerly than the needs of those who had put them in power. Throughout the nation, the new breed of black mayors who emerged in the late 1960s and early 1970s – including Richard Hatcher in Gary, Carl Stokes in Cleveland, and Maynard Jackson in Atlanta – often found themselves presiding over ever-blacker cities, robbed of vital revenue by a mixture of white suburban flight, industrial decline and commercial relocation.[6]

If the black political caucus was by no means a negligible force in Washington politics, it was nonetheless powerless to halt the general trend towards disengagement from vigorous federal action on behalf of blacks. The interventionism and often bipartisan vigour of the late Kennedy and early Johnson administrations had first shown signs of disintegrating in 1966, when Republicans stymied Johnson's legislative efforts to secure greater federal protection for civil rights workers, and to tackle discrimination in housing. Although the fair housing provision eventually became part of the Civil Rights Act of 1968, it was a sign of the changing times that this legislation also incorporated anti-riot provisions directed against the activities of black agitators, supposedly roving the country inspiring urban uprisings. This was a concession to the white backlash to black protest which shifted into full gear around 1968, and found dramatic expression in George Wallace's strong showing far beyond his natural southern constituency during the 1968 presidential primaries. Richard Nixon and the Republican Party exploited and exacerbated this white reaction through a highly effective "southern strategy", whereby southern – and a good many northern – white fears of urban disorder, creeping black equality, and "reverse discrimination" were converted into votes.[7]

Those votes twice elected a president whose concern for law and order included support for the extension of the FBI's unconstitutional and murderous COINTELPRO operation directed against the Black Panther Party and other black militants. Nixon also opposed busing and pursued a policy of, at best, "benign neglect" on racial matters, and at worst resistance to any extension of government efforts to help ordinary blacks. Even the potentially promising Philadelphia Plan – an affirmative action initiative, whereby construction workers' unions engaged in government contracts had to recruit a certain number of minority workers – actually represented an effort to shift the burden of meeting equal opportunity requirements from government to labour. The hike in government aid for minority businesses from $200 million to $472 million during Nixon's presidency reflected a desire to promote black capitalism which left the problems of poor blacks unaddressed and helped to solidify growing class cleavages within the black community.[8]

In the early 1970s, the Supreme Court seemed to offer a partial counterbalance to Nixon's mixture of indifference and inaction. Under Chief-Justice Warren Burger, the Court initially continued its support for civil rights advances, most notably in the field of voting rights, where it interpreted the 1965 Act very broadly and helped to create the climate for its renewal and extension in 1970. The Burger court was also initially progressive in education, handing down pivotal decisions like *Alexander* vs *Holmes County*, which ordered an immediate end to that Mississippi county's dual education system, and offering steady support for busing as a means to remedy the continued *de facto* segregation of many of the nation's public schools. Thus the court helped to promote a good deal of school integration, especially in the South, where the proportion of blacks in mixed-race schools rose from just 2 per cent in 1964 to around 60 per cent in the early 1970s.

By mid decade, however, the Court's growing conservatism, bolstered by the arrival of new Nixon appointees, led to a disavowal of busing, which in turn encouraged a tendency towards resegregation. By 1980, less than 50 per cent of black students in the South attended integrated schools, and the proportion continued to decline, notwithstanding some variations in individual locales, thereafter. This was still better than in the urban North, where residential patterns and naked prejudice maintained the much higher level of functional segregation which busing had attempted, with mixed success and in the face of much hostility, to rectify. This change of attitude over the admittedly thorny and complex busing issue gave notice of the Court's steady retreat from its previous progressive position on legislative efforts to promote equality of minority opportunity in America.[9]

This retreat was sounded even more loudly with the Court's ambiguous ruling on affirmative action in the 1978 *Bakke* case. Alan Bakke, an unsuccessful white applicant to the University of California at Davis, sued the institution for having set aside 16 places for minority students, some of whom had lower grades and test scores than him. Although the Court accepted the principle that race had a legitimate role to play in designing affirmative action programmes, it rejected California-Davis' particular plan as discriminatory and ordered Bakke's admittance. In so doing, the Court offered a clear warning that in future fixed set aside quotas for minority candidates were likely to be ruled unconstitutional as a means to compensate for centuries of all pervasive discrimination. This abrogation of responsibility helped further undermine what little was left of black faith in the system, and in the federal commitment to doing what was necessary to create genuine equality of opportunity in America.[10]

These difficulties and disappointments were compounded by growing uncertainty within the black community concerning how best to confront its obdurate racial, social, political and economic problems. In response to this dilemma, the later 1960s saw the emergence of the diverse, overlapping creeds and programmes usually coralled together as black power. With Malcolm X casting a long posthumous shadow over black political thought and consciousness, various forms of black nationalism and sometimes separatism emerged as powerful strains in the ideologies of now racially exclusive black organizations like SNCC and CORE, and among a squadron of militant new groups, like the Black Panther Party and the Revolutionary Action Movement. These organizations broke most conspicuously with the old ethos and tactics of the Movement by rejecting the doctrine of nonviolence in favour of a belief in armed self-defence. Meanwhile, Maulana Ron Karenga's US organization pursued a cultural path to black liberation in America, contending that a return to putatively "African" value systems and cultural practices was the best way forward for blacks in America. For some, like CORE under the leadership of Floyd McKissick and later Roy Innis, black power was essentially expanded black economic power and the development of black capitalism. For others it was black political power, to be fought for, organized and exercised through the ballot box.

Ultimately, then, this was a confusing, almost schizophrenic phase in the black freedom struggle. The era was characterized by the dense, tense interplay of black insurgency and apathy, political action and creeping despair, dogmatism and pragmatism, all wrapped up with the revived black pride which was among the most positive and enduring legacies of the Movement. On one hand, the period gave rise to some of the most incisive critiques of American racism, some of the most creative, inspirational, and progressive attempts at black cultural, political and economic empowerment. And yet, on the other hand, it also saw some of the most craven, cynical, exploitative, sexist and reactionary impulses masquerade as black power politics. Paradoxically, the same groups and individuals were often responsible for both the best and worst manifestations of black power.

In several ways, the problems and confusions of the period were deepened by the murder of Martin Luther King in April 1968. In recent years, Movement historians have sought to correct the early over-emphasis on King's role in the struggle, in order to acknowledge the enormous contribution of many other local and national figures and institutions. Yet it is as well to remember that King was the single most important player in the Movement, and that his death robbed the diverse, often antagonistic, progressive elements in America, black and white, of their most effective and powerful centrifugal force.

Certainly, King had fully appreciated the psychological appeal of black power rhetoric at a time of raised black consciousness and acute frustration with the enduring barriers to black progress. Moreover, as he began to advocate a form of democratic socialism as the best solution to those problems, King shared with many black radicals the belief that American racism, capitalism and imperialism were inextricably linked in a global web of colour-coded oppression. Like many militants, King emphasized the need for radical economic and social reforms and groped for a strategy which might dramatize the systemic inequalities, racial and otherwise, which pervaded American society.

Nevertheless, by rejecting the separatist and violent undercurrents of black power, and some of its more reactionary racial chauvinism, King actually remained close to the heart of the black masses. For most of them, integration, racial pride, and cultural pluralism – not separation or assimilation – remained the touchstone of their dreams. While many blacks seriously questioned the nature and values of the society to which they had fought so hard to gain access, King appreciated that, in essence "The American racial revolution has been a revolution to 'get in' rather than to overthrow".

Consequently, he continued to press for coalitions with a dwindling band of white liberals and radicals who shared his vision of a reformed and redeemed, equalitarian America, guided by humanitarian principles.[11]

King's effort to forge a new biracial coalition of America's dispossessed, as witnessed by the Poor People's Campaign he was working on at the time of his death, was ironic in the sense that it took place just as the real limits of white support for black advance became all too clear. King's own experiences in Chicago in 1966 confirmed the depth of white racism beyond the South, while many of those whites who had endorsed civil rights reform and the re-enfranchisement of southern blacks simply felt that their racial agenda had been completed with the legislation of the mid 1960s. They were reformists who had hoped, sincerely enough, to open up the American Dream to everyone, but who could never countenance the wholesale restructuring of American society, government and economy necessary to make that a reality.

By the late 1960s, liberal faith in the efficacy of legislation, education and time to ensure that merit, not race, class or gender, would become the critical determinants of opportunity and success in America was shaken by the manifest persistence of racism, discrimination and inequality to which they had no real response. Moreover, as the widespread prosperity which had underpinned the Great Society's beneficence faltered, as Vietnam, the counter-culture, and native American, women's and gay rights partially displaced the black struggle as rallying points for national dissent, and as the frustrations of unfulfilled expectations and broken promises boiled over into the paramilitary fringes of black power and the violence of the urban riots, many white liberals cut their losses. They abandoned a half-finished revolution which, in Robert Weisbrot's phrase, had "abolished formal barriers to equality while leaving intact the basic features of a system in which blacks had played a subordinate, marginal role". This liberal retreat left the way open for a white conservative backlash which grew steadily in strength over the next two decades, until it not only stymied further efforts to help minorities but actually began to erode some of the advances and protections of black rights which the Movement had secured in the 1960s.[12]

"Thank you for talkin' to me Africa": an afrocentric interlude

The ways in which successive Rhythm and Blues styles arranged and manipulated nominally black and white musical techniques helped to fix those styles on a conventional spectrum between black and white American sensibilities. It also positioned those styles between the broadly nationalistic and integrationist sentiments which had always jostled with each other in mass black consciousness. The actual sound and texture of black popular music offered both a crude analogue of the state of black consciousness at a particular moment, and a way for black artists to avow racial pride and a general commitment to the black cause, regardless of any obvious lyrical content or personal participation in the organized struggle. Thus it was significant that the mid-to-late 1960s witnessed a number of musical attempts to further "darken" the sounds of a soul music which was already rooted deep in the rich, dark soil of black gospel.

As respect for the roots of the black experience rekindled interest in African languages, history and cultures, there was a minor vogue in black America for African musicians. These included the "Soul Makossa" man, saxophonist Manu Dibango from Cameroon, South African trumpeter Hugh Masekela – whose "Grazing in the grass" was a black number one in 1968 – his compatriots, jazz pianist Dollar Brand (Abdullah Ibrahim) and Miriam Makeba, who had her first national chart hit in 1967 with "Pata pata". Meanwhile, relentless jazz explorers like John Coltrane, Lonnie Smith, and Randy Weston took musical and spiritual inspiration from Africa, and fused it with a multitude of other influences in their work.

Real and imagined musical echoes both of Africa and of a more recent spiritual and physical black homeland, the American South, also became more prominent in the soul of the period. As many labels successfully turned to southern studios and musicians to produce an earthier, gutbucket soul sound, even Motown experimented with a more raw-boned approach to some of its recordings. This was most evident in the field-holler soul of Edwin Starr, who said it all in the hard-driving screech of "Funky music sho' nuff turns me on".

In the mid 1960s, Berry Gordy had reactivated an old gospel label, fortuitously entitled Soul, where songwriter-producer Norman Whitfield cut a number of highly successful tracks with Gladys Knight and the Pips. "Take me in your arms and love me" and the original version of "I heard it through the grapevine" glittered with as much southern grit as Detroit polish. When Whitfield took over writing and production duties for the Temptations from Smokey Robinson in 1966, he began experimenting with tom-toms and elaborate Africanesque cross-rhythms. For a while almost all Whitfield's productions for the group, including the classic soul ballad "Ain't too proud to beg" and the string-driven "You're my everything", were laced with these percussive "ethnic" trimmings. It was as if Whitfield was trying to sound an ever blacker note within the context of the basic Motown formula and Gordy's congenital caution about addressing racial matters in Motown lyrics. Only in 1968, however, did Whitfield begin to merge these Africanesque flourishes with psychedelic rock and solid r&b grooves on records which also had explicitly social messages, like the Temptations' "Ball of confusion" and Edwin Starr's "War".

This was a boom time for sales of bongos and wood-blocks as African rhythmic garnishes began to show up everywhere in soul. Yet, while some groups, like Mandrill, Earth, Wind and Fire, and Kool and the Gang – whose

In the black power era, many groups, including the Temptations, swapped their tuxedos for ghetto chic and began to incorporate much more social commentary in their songs.

Spirit of the boogie album included songs like "Ancestral ceremony" and featured African artwork on the sleeve – made a studied effort to explore these musical and cultural links, much of what passed for African influence had a pretty nebulous connection to any actual African music or techniques. Fortunately, this was largely irrelevant. These were musical gestures with a clearly understood racial provenance and a deep symbolic resonance. Functionally, they served to push soul further towards the black end of the black-white musical spectrum in American popular music and thereby reflected the appeal of a new nationalistic black consciousness.

In many ways, these sorts of musical Africanisms were much like the manufactured Africanisms promoted by some of the era's leading cultural nationalists. Maulana Ron Karenga's Kawaida, for example, was conceived as an attempt to slip the shackles of white cultural and psychological domination by reverting to a putatively African system of values. Kawaida's precise relationship to any known form of African philosophy or system of cultural practice was a matter of some debate. It was more a synthesis of certain cultural and philosophical essences which Karenga and others believed defined African, and therefore all truly black, consciousness throughout the diaspora and across the ages. Like most Afrocentrists, Karenga's identification was less with any real historical Africa than with a mythic, homogenized Africa of the mind, conveniently emptied of any of the national, tribal, linguistic, religious, gender, cultural and class divisions which have characterized the history of the continent, just as they have the history of the West.[13]

Nevertheless, Karenga's basic proposition that psychological liberation was a necessary prerequisite to an effective black freedom struggle was broadly shared by most civil rights leaders and black power groups. This emphasis on the need to cultivate collective cultural and psychological resistance to white power had intensified with the canonization of Malcolm X, who bequeathed to the struggle his insistence that blacks should embrace their blackness with pride not shame. The trend was also encouraged by the vogue for the ideas of Frantz Fanon, the black psychiatrist from Martinique who had theorized the structure of colonial uprisings from his own experiences in the Algerian revolt against French rule. Fanon urged the oppressed of the world to nurture their own unique sense of history and use it as the basis for an oppositional culture from whence would emerge, when the time was right, an army of bloody but glorious liberation.[14]

Black Americans were understandably quite selective in what they took from Fanon, whose ideas were not always particularly relevant to their situation – armed revolution, for example, was more suicidal than revolutionary. One of the nuances Ron Karenga initially chose to ignore was Fanon's injunction against embalming ancient cultural traditions as an end in itself. As many of his critics, led by the Black Panther Party, noted, Karenga and his acolytes appeared to be making an ego-gratifying fetish and healthy profit out of these pseudo-African trappings while doing little to convert the racial consciousness and solidarity they promoted into meaningful challenges to white power. Blacks were still being oppressed, it was just that now some endured that oppression while proudly wearing natural hair, dashikis, bubas, kente cloth, and tikis. Some even learned how to complain in Swahili.

While former SNCC chairman and black power icon Stokely Carmichael flirted with Karenga-style cultural nationalism as part of his rapid sifting and shifting of ideological and tactical positions during the late 1960s and early 1970s, most civil rights veterans were seasoned in the painstaking work of grassroots political organizing. Like the Panthers, most were deeply sceptical

of claims that the route to black liberation in America lay in romanticizations of Africa and cosmetic affectations. SNCC's Stanley Wise thought
that Karenga's cultural nationalism "was our worst hour". Wise felt that
the retreat to a mythic Africa was a grave mistake which was neglectful
and ultimately disrespectful of the heroic culture of survival and struggle
which peoples of African descent had carved out and continued to extend
in America:

> We were at a point then when we really needed a great infusion
> of what in fact our culture had been . . . We needed a historical
> perspective more than anything else . . . and I think rather than do
> that, to take the hard road, researching and all that sort of stuff, we
> took the easy road. Let's sell trinkets and see if they'll buy. Let's
> have kwanzaa – something that doesn't exist – and pretend it's a
> national holiday in Africa.
> They were mainly absolute capitalists. Capitalist pigs if you want
> to be precise. And their only program was they fantasized about
> what great royalty they had all been thousands of years ago in
> Africa . . . And they set up these little trinket shops and . . . started
> burning candles, reading tarots, nonsensical stuff . . . And they just
> sort of pushed that oil on our community.[15]

And yet, if there was considerable truth in Wise's criticisms and some
aspects of the cultural nationalist impulse did smack of escapism, faddism
and commercial opportunism, it was nonetheless psychologically important
for many in the black community. In the late 1960s, Angela Davis' marxism
had given her a clear insight into the interrelationship between economics,
colonialism and racism. Coupled with her personal experience of the misogyny which tainted Karenga's US organization, this perspective meant that
she could never accept racial and sexual chauvinism as the key to black
liberation. "But, at the same time", Davis admitted, "I needed to say 'Black is
beautiful' as much as any of the intransigent anti-white nationalists. I needed
to explore my African ancestry, to don African garb, and to wear my hair
natural as much as the blinder-wearing male supremacist cultural nationalists". These were, like changing tastes in the sound and sense of black
popular music, the outward symbols of inner changes within mass black
consciousness.[16]
Perhaps the crucial point here is that during the black power era, black
pride, the quest for a common black heritage, and the celebration of a distinctively black world view were simultaneously a genuine reflection of a new
black consciousness, and a lucrative commercial and marketing opportunity.
Even the most escapist rituals and crass exploitation of the search for roots
and cultural validation could be transformed by acts of creative individual

and collective consumption into thoroughly positive assertions of self and community.

"Grooveallegiance": the triumph of funk

James Brown succeeded more brilliantly than any other artist in "blackening" the sound of his soul in the mid-to-late 1960s. Building on the raw gospel-r&b synthesis of his early work, "Out of sight" in 1964, followed by "Papa's got a brand new bag" in 1965, and by "Cold sweat" two years later, were benchmarks in the development of a new black funk which in its mature form revitalized the Rhythm and Blues of the late 1960s and early 1970s. By 1974, James Brown had reinvented himself – the latest phase in an endless process of self-renewal and redefinition – as the Minister of the New Heavy Heavy Funk.

Utilizing a succession of remarkably talented musicians, Brown's funk pared down the harmonic and melodic elements of his soul to expose the sheer gut-wrenching, body-popping physicality of his music. He did not just make music where powerful rhythms carried the songs; his protean rhythms sometimes became master of his melody, harmony and lyrics. Again, this emphasis on rhythm was conventionally associated with the African end of the African-American musical spectrum.[17]

Like most musical qualities, funk was considerably easier to detect and dance to than to describe. The term itself had first been applied to the hardbop of jazzmen like Milt Jackson, Horace Silver, Art Blakey and Charles Mingus. In the 1950s, these men had rescued jazz from some of the more esoteric extremes of be-bop and West Coast cool by revisiting their gospel and blues roots. The word and the music reeked of earthiness, blood, sweat and semen, and proudly proclaimed its connection to the essential forces of human, but more particularly black, existence. Indeed, as funk creatively scrambled conventional linguistic meanings into hip blackspeak – "nasty" was nice, "baaaad" was good – critic Frank Kofsky argued that it reflected "a uniquely black idiom . . . To call a composition, a passage, or a player 'funky' was not only to offer praise in general, but a means of lauding the object of praise for its specifically black qualities". As in the broader soul phenomenon with which funk overlapped, the absence of a concrete definition of the term indicated that it was for the in-group, the cognoscenti; primarily black Americans who simply knew when they were in the presence of something truly funky.[18]

In Rhythm and Blues, funk followed Brown's lead and pushed the traditional rhythmic priorities of much black music even further to the fore. Melodic and harmonic instruments were often pressed into percussive service to create intricate latticeworks of heavily syncopated rhythms. Sometimes the reverse was true, however, with the electric bass supplementing its rhythmic duties by popping and chopping, cutting and chasing through the mix with snatches of bubbling melody. There were two major influences here. The first was the thumb-thwacking, talking-bass growl which Larry Graham developed with Sly and the Family Stone and later with his own Graham Central Station. The second was the elastic bass interventions – stretching out melodically, but always snapping back into rhythmic shape – which William "Bootsy" Collins made during his year with the James Brown band, then with George Clinton's P-Funk empire, and later in his own aptly-named Bootsy's Rubber Band.

By turns swampy, sensual and languid, tight, frantic and insistent, funk was not just a new dance-based idiom in its own right, but a new mode of rhythmic playing which could underpin a variety of soul sounds. From the lush, symphonic soul produced by the Philadelphia International label, through the percolating, vaguely latin-tinged, sounds of the solo Curtis Mayfield, to the fervid gospel-soul shouts of Stax's Johnnie Taylor, and the black rock'n'soul of the Bar-Kays, a funk sensibility was often at work, filling up the bottom ranges of the mix with molten mosaics of rhythm.

Funk, then, was in every sense a music of motion, with a lot of melodic, harmonic and rhythmic cross-currents scuttling around, yet all somehow locked into a common groove which variously drove or seduced fans onto the dance floor. The key to this locked-in groove was the magical "one" – the unifying downbeat at the start of each bar which funk's first major chronicler, Rickey Vincent, treats with almost religious veneration. The "one" served to organize the maelstrom of musical activity into a coherent, propulsive sound. It was the sound of rootedness, a rhythmic anchor at a time, and in a music, of great turbulence [19]

Vincent's long-overdue history, *Funk*, is a true labour of love. Rich in biographical and discographical detail and punctuated by passages of thoughtful analysis and interpretation, it jumps with the contagious joy of an enthusiast moved to the depths of his soul by the music he describes. Its exuberance reminds us that however much we prod and probe the music for its cultural, political and historical meanings, it was its capacity to bring pleasure, to entertain and excite, which determined much of its value and social significance.

Moreover, while he rides his African-retentions hobby-horse too hard and too far, one of the best things about Vincent's book is his recognition that it was what happened to those African practices and sensibilities during the course of several centuries in America which generated a distinctively African-American culture and the mighty funk he celebrates. Indeed, Vincent is careful to give due respect to sincere and gifted white funkateers, like Scotland's Average White Band ("Pick up the pieces") and, more equivocally, to the mixed-race K.C. and the Sunshine Band, whose bright dancing Miami horns and minimalist vocal chants ("Get on down", "That's the way (I like it)") topped both the black and white charts in the mid 1970s.

Frank Zappa, Elton John, Edgar Winter and David Bowie – whose *Young Americans* album was indeed a fine funk-glamrock hybrid – are among the other whites commended for delivering the funk. More puzzlingly, Vincent adds Eric Clapton and Eddie Money to his list, but then funk has always been to some degree in the ear of the beholder.[20]

None of this in any way compromises the essential black roots of funk style and sensibility. And neither does Vincent's single most important, if under-developed, insight, which is that while James Brown provided funk's major influence, the Beatles and the whole progressive rock scene which bloomed around 1966 and 1967 were the other great sources of inspiration, not just for funk, but for the whole of Rhythm and Blues in the late 1960s and early 1970s. The giants of funk and soul expanded their musical and lyrical vocabulary in tandem with mostly white rock artists (Jimi Hendrix and Arthur Lee of the group Love excepted) who were redefining the use of the studio and playing with the new technologies of sound production – notably synthesizers and a variety of distortion pedals for guitar and bass. These rock artists also established the album, not just the single, as the essential medium for their music. Moreover, they made political commentary commonplace in commercially successful rock music at a time when soul was still struggling to overcome its caution about recording such material.[21]

For the revitalized Isley Brothers, the relationship with rock was especially close. In 1964, they recorded a song called "Testify" for the T-Neck label they had recently formed in their hometown of Teaneck, New Jersey. The single bombed, but it did feature a volcanic – and not particularly well integrated – guitar eruption by then session-man Jimi Hendrix. After a temporary revival of their careers at Motown with "This old heart of mine", the Isleys revisited Hendrix territory at the end of the decade, wedding rock riffing to their gruff soul harmonies on hits like "It's your thing" and "Freedom", and even covering rock songs like Stephen Stills' "Love the one you're with" and Bob Dylan's "Lay lady lay". In the early 1970s, this musical bond was tightened further when brother Ernest moved from bass to lead guitar, discovered the fuzzbox and subsequently smeared beautiful, soaring, Hendrixesque solos all over sturdy r&b grooves on masterpieces like "That lady" and "Take me to the next phase".

The Isleys were just one of a whole raft of self-contained black ensembles who sailed forth on the funk scene during this period. Previously, Rhythm and Blues had generated relatively few such bands. Solo vocalists and individual record labels often had their own regular studio or road bands, and many vocal groups had a single guitarist in their ranks. But, with some notable exceptions, like the New Orleans-based Meters and the mixed-race Booker T. and the MGs, there were simply not many soul groups who played all their instruments, sang and often wrote their own songs, and got to see their names on the marquee or record label. While the Beatles, Byrds and Band had made the group the major, if by no means the only, vehicle for white rock and roll, Rhythm and Blues was still built around headline vocalists and their backing musicians.

In the late 1960s and early 1970s, this all changed. A diverse range of successful black instrumental-vocal groups appeared, many of them erasing neat divisions between rock, soul, funk and jazz styles. Among the most successful were the Bar-Kays, Ohio Players, Earth, Wind and Fire, Kool and the Gang, Tower of Power, Blackbyrds, Brass Construction, Fatback Band and B.T. Express. In a sense, this shift was necessitated by the musical demands of funk, the elusive blend of tight discipline, spontaneity and freedom to jam required an almost jazz-like level of musical trust, understanding and empathy among the players which only working together at length could produce.

The waxing, waning and weirdness of dreams: George Clinton and Sly Stone

The bright florescence of black funk-soul-rock ensemble talent in the late 1960s threw up two enormously influential bands who, together with James Brown, virtually defined the trajectory of the new funk stream in Rhythm and Blues as the decade turned. The long career of the various Parliament, Funkadelic and P-Funk combinations put together by George Clinton, and the briefer musical incandescence which was Sly and the Family Stone, revealed much about the state of black consciousness and race relations as the initial confidence and relative unity of the early civil rights movement disintegrated.

This contextualization of funk in the disenchantment and tactical disarray of the early 1970s reverses Rickey Vincent's view of its socio-historic origins. Vincent sees full-blown funk as a product of the "decade of integration", casting the 1970s as an era of optimism and expanded opportunity, when blacks were "no longer marginalized", but instead "turned the social fabric upside down" on their triumphant march into the mainstream of American society. This seems to misrepresent, or at least oversimplify, the experience of the black masses during this period. The 1970s was a decade of cantering, and then galloping disappointment and frustration for those blacks who were not able to scramble aboard the rapidly passing middle-class bandwagon. Many experienced what Thomas Blair called a "retreat to the ghetto", and this was not always a positive, voluntary embrace of black fellowship, culture and community. More often it was a necessary response to continued exclusion from the mainstream, and the encrustation of a permanent black urban underclass.[22]

Certainly, as Vincent recognized, while Clinton and early Sly both had broad church conceptions of their music and its potential audience, funk was at heart a black street music: the sound of "unassimilated blacklife", Vincent called it. Few of the legions of bold black funkateers with "pride in their stride, and a dip in their hip", as Parliament put it on "Chocolate City" in 1975, were exactly dancing for joy at the end of their marginalization in America. Increasingly trapped inside the ghetto and crucified by endemic racism, poverty and unemployment, they were grooving to survive the terrifying crash which followed the emotional highs and rich promise of the early 1960s. Funk and even early disco, with which it overlapped in the mid-to-late 1970s, put a premium on personal expressivity, embraced a sort of manic hedonism, and reified the cool arts of dressing up and getting down in distinctively black ways. This was both great fun and a cultural response to the absence of any viable mass struggle for integration into an equalitarian, pluralistic America. Once more, black Americans were dancing to keep from crying.[23]

Nobody encouraged Americans, black and white, to dance harder than George Clinton. Born in Kannapolis, North Carolina in 1941, Clinton moved to New Jersey in his mid teens. There he worked as a barber, formed his own doowop group called the Parliaments, and in 1959 recorded a couple of long-forgotten singles: "Poor boy" on Apt, and "You make me wanna cry" on Flipp. A group move to Detroit saw Clinton find work as a staff writer for Jobete, while the Parliaments cut some unreleased demos for Motown, and issued one single on Golden World. It was not until 1967, however, that the Parliaments hit paydirt, when Clinton merged his four-man vocal group with a five-man backing band to make a self-contained musical unit. "(I wanna) testify" on the local Revilot label was a top three black hit and even reached the pop top twenty. It heralded the arrival of Clinton's unique psychedelic funk-rock vision.

Various contractual snafus meant that Clinton lost his right to the name "Parliaments" to Revilot. Consequently, when the group moved to Westbound in 1970, it assumed the descriptive moniker Funkadelic. More contractual disputes led to the formation of another outfit, less radically renamed Parliament. This group signed with the Invictus label set up by disaffected Motown writers Holland-Dozier-Holland. In 1973, Parliament moved to the Casablanca label and three years later Funkadelic signed to the major Warner Brothers for whom it did its most consistent work. Throughout this period personnel in the two bands overlapped, with the classically trained keyboard wizard Bernie Worrell, guitarists Ernie Hazel and later Mike Hampton, and a succession of fine bassists, including Bootsy Collins, at the core. Overall, Funkadelic was a little more rock-oriented (one song was playfully entitled "Who says a funk band can't play rock?"), and Parliament was a bit more soulful, but these distinctions were far from absolute.

Both groups racked up their share of hit singles – especially in the extraordinarily creative period between 1976 and 1980, when Parliament had major crossover successes with the likes of "Flashlight" and "Aquaboogie", and Funkadelic hit with "Tear the roof off the sucker" and the anthemic "One nation under a groove". Nevertheless, albums and live shows were really their métier, since they allowed the bands to develop the long, sometimes over-extended, but often mesmerizing jams which were standard issue in funk's arsenal. They also enabled Clinton to touch bases with more of the diverse influences which he and his musicians/co-writers brought to the P-Funk collective.

Clinton's bands absorbed, played with, honoured and parodied an extraordinary range of musical styles, regurgitating them in a mess of freaky, but usually danceable, rock-soul-funk. Major points of reference were his old doowop idols Frankie Lymon and the Teenagers, Ray Charles, Motown soul and, of course, James Brown. Yet, he insisted, "The Beatles are my all time favorites", with his contemporary Sly Stone not far behind. He also had ties with the white Detroit trash'n'thrash rock underground of Iggy Pop and MC5, and was fascinated by the musical experimentation of Hendrix and white progressive rock acts, whose sonic sculpting and studio-craft he emulated.[24]

Often Clinton's manic eclecticism gave his albums a schizophrenic quality, which in turn became part of their design and appeal. Like the equally eccentric, gifted and ludic Frank Zappa – his nearest white counterpart – Clinton never let his listeners settle too long in one place before rocketing them off into another musical universe. Parliament's first album, *Osmium*, careened from country and western, through a sort of mutant folk-rock, to gospel-tinged rock and more straight-ahead soul. Funkadelic's early albums dripped with a druggy off-beat humour and musically careened from Motownish soul ("I bet you" from the eponymous first album was covered by the Jackson Five), avant-garde feedback-fests in the tradition of the Velvet Underground ("Free your mind and your ass will follow" from the 1971 album of the same name was an extreme example), and speed metal thrashes ("Super stupid" on *Maggot Brain*), to lush orchestral soul in the Isaac Hayes mode ("You hit the nail on the head" from *America Eats Its Young*), more or less straight vocal group r&b (half of 1973's *Cosmic Slop* was in this vein), and the sort of slightly decentred, psychedelic funk-rock jams at which the band excelled.

Not all of these syntheses and collisions worked especially well. Clinton and his cohorts could occasionally lose the plot and become as overblown and self-absorbed as some of the progressive rock behemoths like Yes and Emerson, Lake and Palmer with whom they were contemporaries. But at their best, as on Funkadelic's 1975 *Mothership Connection*, and *One Nation Under a Groove* two years later, their albums were freebasing tours de funk through the most popular music styles of the rock era.

Clinton's music represented the sounds of blackness in dialogue with contemporary American society and its most popular musics. The bottom of the mix was all rhythm and groove – liquid made solid, unshakeable but fluid, everything united by that miraculous "one". In concert Clinton would even get his audience to chant "On the one, everybody on the one". On the top of this molten rhythmic core, Clinton could sample or embrace any number of styles. Fearlessly and shamelessly treating the whole of the musical universe as his to use and traduce as he pleased, Clinton plundered from far beyond the conventional black musical tradition. Like all great black musicians, he simply used whatever it took to get the job done while staying proudly mired in black funk.[25]

Clinton wrote many explicit lyrical commentaries on black street life, poverty and American race relations. "Chocolate City", "Funky dollar bill", "You and your folks, me and my folks", a good portion of 1972's *America Eats Its Young* album, which included the stirring call to action of "Wake up", were all in this mode. Yet, although Clinton's vision was always primarily black, it was also extremely ecumenical, even intergalactic in its breadth and appeal. Whitey could certainly benefit from loosening up and getting a therapeutic shot of funk, but Clinton never stopped believing that his music could do the trick.

It was this belief in music's redemptive and rejuvenating power which underscored the alternative realities, the weird parallel universes which Clinton created and explored in his work; places peopled by heroes like the Phfunklords and villains like Sir Nose D'Void of Funk. Dressed in an ever-changing, futuristic, hokey-couture which seemed to mix'n'match discarded space suits, brightly spangled bathing attire, knee-length platform boots, diaphanous priestly robes and a smattering of Africana, the P-Funk crew certainly looked as if they had descended from another planet. Indeed, in the wake of Funkadelic's 1976 album, *Mothership Connection*, they embarked on an Earth Tour, spending $275,000 on a mind-boggling live show, complete with a full-size Mothership landing onstage.

The same irresistible march of Clinton and his all-conquering black funkateers was captured by Pedro Bell's cartoonish cover art and fantasy prose for many Funkadelic albums. P-Funk were depicted as black redeemers from a far funkier, funnier and more forgiving place where everybody could come together on the "one", just as Clinton believed they had in some distant, harmonious past. The earth, Clinton explained in his own account of the planet's (re)creation, had "languished in funklessness for centuries". Where once, "in the day of the Thumpasaurous Peoples and the Funkapus, Funk was a commonly accepted part of daily life. It was a gift from higher intelligences in the universe, but people misused it". The world was just "awaiting the day when it could return", and Clinton was there to provide the necessary *Mothership Connection*.[26]

This was a tribalistic, utopian vision of transcendent community which betrayed not only that Clinton had taken far too many drugs, but that he remained at heart an unreconstructed black hippy with a great sense of off-beat, sometimes scatological, humour and an absolute mastery of spectacle and showmanship. He made a big-hearted, generous music which was rooted deep in black consciousness and black musical traditions, but which, unlike much of what passed for black cultural nationalism, was also extraordinarily open and inclusive, both in terms of the influences he grafted onto his funk, and those who were invited to join the dance. This was the heir to Jimi Hendrix's Electric Sky Church, and not too far removed from the universalist mysticism of jazzman Sun Ra and his Arkestra, who also philosophized that music could be used to invoke positive cosmic energies and direct them towards humanistic goals. It was a secularized version of the sort of vision which gospel and the black church had traditionally offered, with their fortifying tales of a Promised Land and better world in the hereafter.

Clinton was hardly alone in his musical and visual embrace of otherworldliness. Funk-soul groups like the Sylvers, LaBelle, Isley Brothers, Commodores, and later Rick James all wore their futuristic rubberized shoulder pads and mirrored jump suits with pride, transmitting hugely flared funk signals from another, better place. Earth, Wind and Fire used illusionists Doug Henning and David Copperfield to develop a stage show which rivalled P-Funk's for sheer spectacle. On stage, the group conjured up links with Egyptology, African mysticism and interplanetary travel to show how their horn-led, and by mid decade hugely successful, brand of joyous jazz-funk-soul recognized no barriers of time or place. And if Earth, Wind and Fire were serious about their "Boogie wonderland", so were Aquarian Dream, whose eponymous first record – one of a handful of coherent and still listenable albums to come out of the disco craze – imagined a future age of love and tranquillity.

In a sense, this mixture of escapism and utopianism was all part of a cultural response to the crisis which had enveloped the black liberation movement. Historically, what was significant about these visions was that by the early 1970s it was only in outer space, or in a parallel world conjured up by religious mysticism, magic, drugs, or through some romanticized vision of a lost beatific, sometimes African, past, that it was really possible to site a coherent vision of interracial – or even black – harmony.

Certainly, in the here and now, as black protest and American racial liberalism entered their own twilight zones, things looked increasingly bleak for black America and the state of race relations. Timmy Thomas might have sung "Why can't we live together?", but that was, after all, a question. Veteran Wilbert Harrison could rework "Let's stick together" as "Let's work together", but that was a rallying cry, not an observation. The Temptations may have been doing fine up on a drug-induced "Cloud nine", but most blacks living the day-to-day reality of black life were not, and had little faith that music or anything on the political horizon was going to change their fortunes anytime soon. It was a paradox, to be sure, but just about the only

way Clinton and his contemporaries could articulate a vision which combined black pride with notions of interracial respect and harmony and still
be taken seriously by the mid 1970s was to remove them from the "real"
world and construct a weird, wonderful and wishful alternative where the
power of black music might still redeem the racial soul of America.

This was a significant departure from the time when the crossover
of r&b and the expansion of black-oriented radio programming had been
widely viewed as a symbol of, and even as a possible catalyst for, better
racial understanding. Indeed, Clinton and his spaced cadets were in some
respects an anachronism here, since in the black power era there remained
precious little sense that continued white enthusiasm for black music meant
anything other than an economic opportunity for a handful of talented
and fortunate blacks. Soul survivor Wilson Pickett's attitude was typical. He
described to Gerri Hirshey the trauma of discovering what he called "The
Big Lie", whereby it became apparent that acceptance in the mainstream
of American popular music culture did not indicate that the stars of soul,
any more than the black masses whose aspirations they embodied, were
really accepted as respected, permanent, equal participants in that culture.
Instead, they were promoted and consumed as the latest in a long line of
hip black fads. Once again, white racial prejudices proved more than flexible enough to accommodate notions of black talent, even genius, without
crumbling.[27]

Nowhere in Rhythm and Blues was this sense of disenchantment and
betrayal expressed more dramatically than in the career of Sly Stone. Born
Sylvester Stewart in Texas, but raised in San Francisco, Sly had worked as a
deejay on KSOL, where he reflected the integrationist ideals of the early-to-
mid 1960s by daringly introducing records by the Beatles and Bob Dylan
into a previously rigid soul format. Sly absorbed the heady west coast atmosphere and several of the more popular chemical concoctions which fuelled
the various "summers of love". He emerged in 1968 with a multi-racial band
– the Family Stone – and a fresh, unclassifiable, soul-pop-funk brew.[28]

Sly was a highly creative songwriter-arranger who audaciously fused
soulful vocals, latinate horns and psychedelic rock flourishes into rousing
invocations of both black pride and universal brotherhood on songs like
"Dance to the music", "Everyday people", and "Stand". As late as 1970, he
was still aligning himself with the silent mass of black Americans, whose
racial consciousness the civil rights struggle had done so much to stir but
who rejected or mistrusted the more extreme manifestations of black nationalism. These were the people who still hankered after inclusion in the American system, flawed though it surely was. As Sly put it:

> There are a lot of people who understand reality . . . but the ones
> who do all the talking are usually the people like Leslie Uggams,
> who seems like kind of a white/black person – or H. Rap Brown, a

black/black person – and all the people in between – you never hear about them.[29]

Sly and the Family Stone enjoyed huge pop and soul hits. They were fêted by the white rock press and adored by the progressive rock audience, particularly after their success as the only soul act at the Woodstock festival. With his proud afro and rainbow-hued band, Sly appeared to be the perfect musical and iconographical symbol of the compatibility of black pride, cultural pluralism and crossover commercial success.

In 1971 this all fell apart. Ironically, Sly was "liberated" from commercial considerations by his growing drug habit and its consequent personal eccentricities. His label, the CBS subsidiary Epic, even announced that he had been diagnosed with a split personality. Increasingly, Sly began to register his disillusionment with the unchanging racist core of white America. He systematically rejected the expectations of black crossover stars in a way which none of his more stable soul and funk counterparts dared. Amid rumours that the Black Panthers had pressured him into firing his white manager, David Kapralnick, Sly began to miss concert and recording dates and failed to show up for interviews. When he did make it onto the stage, he often gave surly, shambolic performances, only enlivened by ritualistic abuse of those who had paid good money to see him, and of himself for succumbing to the star-making machinery.

At the end of the year, having scrapped work on a projected album of upbeat, optimistic songs   a delay which breached his contract and prompted CBS to suspend his royalty payments – Sly released *There's a Riot Going On*. This was an uncompromising assault on America and its values. The cover featured an American flag in which the stars were replaced by flowers. The juxtaposition of these symbols of America and the so-called "love generation" with the bleak subject matter of the album mocked the political and racial complacency of the hippies who had worshipped Sly in San Francisco. Haight-Ashbury – the centre of the hippy universe – was "the first segregated Bohemia I've ever seen", according to one disillusioned journalist, and Sly picked up this theme on the track "Luv 'n' Haight". His old ode to personal empowerment, "Thank you for lettin' me be mice elf again", was reworked as the stark, troubled "Thank you for talkin' to me Africa", with its anguished cry, "I'm dying, I'm dying". "The poet" ridiculed the notion that artists had any meaningful role to play in improving a hopelessly corrupt, vindictive and grasping world. The album's title track summed up the disintegration of Sly's optimism about the future of America: it was blank.[30]

The album was brilliant but difficult, disturbing and haunted. Although it generated three hit singles, it ultimately alienated many of the white fans who had revered Sly as another funky black apostle of good times, but who, as Dave Marsh observed, were often not "prepared for such a harsh, direct look at black experience". Therein lay the basic disparity between white responses to black music, which could be extremely deep and passionate, and white understanding, sympathy and respect for the diverse realities of black culture and experience, which were rarely more than superficial. Black music was still enthusiastically admired when it fulfilled romanticized white expectations about black grace and ease with leisure, pleasure, sex and style. But this still required no real consideration of, or empathy with, the frequently unromantic circumstances from whence those qualities in black culture emerged. When Sly laid bare some of the anxieties, confusions and bitterness which riddled black consciousness as the Movement unravelled, many whites were less interested.[31]

Elsewhere within the rock and soul community, racial tensions also intensified amid the nationalism of the black power era. Peter Guralnick personally recalled the "cold stares and hostile words" which sometimes greeted white fans who attended black performances in the late 1960s. And while the nation's press celebrated and hyped the "love generation" and its "Aquarian" gathering at Woodstock in August 1969, few even bothered to report the tragedy which occurred at Altamont Speedway in California that December.[32]

At Altamont, Meredith Hunter, a black man with eclectic, multi-racial musical tastes, was stabbed to death by Hell's Angels as he and his white girlfriend, Patty Bredaloff, watched the Rolling Stones. This was a brutal killing with ugly racial overtones. "I don't know if their being a mixed couple had anything to do with it", said Hunter's sister, before breaking down and adding bitterly, "it may have quite a lot to do with it. The Hell's Angels are just white men with badges on their backs". For her, the message of the murder was that all white men were still capable of such acts against black men, especially those who broke white sexual codes. Altamont carried a terrible symbolic burden. Whereas blacks had once greeted the interracialism of early rock and roll dances and concerts as portents of a new era of race relations, the concert at Altamont had simply provided the occasion for another lynching.[33]

All things black and beautiful: soul sings of the struggle

In 1966, Imamu Amiri Baraka predicted that the music industry would soon respond to what he believed, judging from the creative political readings he and others were making of songs like Martha and the Vandellas' "Dancing in the street" and Little Milton's "We're gonna make it", was a growing black desire for more self-consciously political lyrics. "It is my thought that soon, with the same cycle of the general 'integrated' music bizness, the R&B songs will be more socially oriented", he wrote, noting that the "'integrated' music

Long before most soul singers began to sing openly of the freedom struggle many people had detected something "political" in the songs of Martha Reeves and the Vandellas, pictured here at the University of Virginia in November 1967.

bizness" – the white rock world – was already paying more explicit atten-tion to social and political issues than soul.[34]

Baraka was correct and in many ways the striking increase in the level of lyrical engagement with the freedom struggle by Rhythm and Blues artists from around 1967 was a function of the two agendas he had identified – communal and commercial – coming together. The demands of the black audience for more explicit racial and social commentary in soul lyrics coin-cided with the industry's recognition that not only was this a necessity in order to maintain credibility and sales among black consumers whose collective annual income topped $1,000 million in the early 1970s, but that such songs would not automatically alienate the white market. On the con-trary, this public blossoming of soul's social and racial conscience corres-ponded with a period of great crossover success for black acts. Although there was no longer much crossing the racial divide from the other direc-tion, in 1971 around a third of Top Forty hits were by black artists, as were 36 of *Billboard*'s top 100 records of 1973.[35]

Perhaps more than any other recording, it was Aretha Franklin's chart-topping version of Otis Redding's "Respect" in 1967 which swelled the trickle of overtly engaged, political soul songs into a flood. It was certainly an appropriate transitional record, since it too was in part politicized by an act of black creative consumption. While black journalist Phyl Garland was just one of many who heard "Respect" as a "new national anthem", a bold affirmation of what the black struggle was all about, Franklin herself stead-fastly denied that she had any such agenda when she sang it. Indeed, she appreciated that her songs could have very different meanings for her and for her listeners. "As an artist you're happy when people get *involved*", Franklin explained to Gerri Hirshey. "But what they hear and what I feel when I sing it can be very, very different. Sometimes, I wish I could make them understand that".[36]

For Franklin, "Respect" was primarily an appeal for domestic respect which had particular personal relevance in the midst of her tempestuous marriage to manager Ted White. Nevertheless, it was musically and lyrically ideal for appropriation as a black rallying cry. The unvanquished black spirit was enshrined in the sound of Franklin's gospel vocals as they soared above a sturdy southern soul groove provided by mostly white musicians. The device – not used in Redding's 1965 original – of spelling out "R-E-S-P-E-C-T" and adding the demand "find out what it means to me!" confirmed its chant potential and assured its unique place in black popular culture and consciousness.

In the wake of "Respect" and its artistic and commercial triumph, soul was awash with lyrical expressions of black pride and lionizations of black style. Songs like James Brown's "Say it loud, I'm black and I'm proud" and "Soul pride", Charles Wright and the Watts 103rd Street Rhythm Band's "Express yourself", the Impressions' "We're a winner", and the Staple Singers' "Respect yourself" were among the many which offered black listeners unequivocal assurances that they and their culture mattered.

Even the names of new black groups boldly proclaimed this black pride in race, place and culture. Black Ivory, Ebonys, Professor Funk and His Eighth Street Funk Band, Watts Prophets, and dozens of soulful variations like Soul Children, Soul Searchers, S.O.U.L., and Brothers of Soul, all re-flected the drive for black self-definition which was one of the unifying features of the amorphous black power impulse. Dyke and the Blazers, a group from Buffalo, New York, whose lead singer Arlester Christian was shot to death in Phoenix in 1971 at the height of the group's popularity, pulled the entire soul phenomenon together in one proud, defiant blast of sub-Brown funk.

> Tellin' the world,
> sisters and my brothers,
> we got more soul.
> When we walk,
> we got more soul, we got it.
> When we talk,

we got more soul, we got it.
When we sing, Lord have mercy,
we got more soul, we got it.
When we dance,
we got more soul.

Meanwhile, the iconography of Rhythm and Blues, whether on stage, television, or album covers, changed too. Many acts traded their tuxedos and processed pompadours for ghetto chic and natural hair, or intergalactic funk fashions, or African-derived cloth, which boldly announced their new racial consciousness. Together with the spate of blaxploitation movies which followed the success of *Sweet Sweetback's Baadasssss Song* in 1971, Don Cornelius' networked *Soul Train* television show ensured that new dances, images and fashions spread throughout black America at a prodigious rate, maintaining the sense of a national black popular culture built around music and dance which had survived all the vicissitudes of the Movement.

Alongside soul's many paeans to black pride and style appeared many more documentary-style descriptions of black poverty, disadvantage, and betrayal by the system than early soul had mustered, among them Syl Johnson's "Is it because I'm black?", Les McCann's "Compared to what", the Temptations' "Ball of confusion", War's "Slippin' into darkness", and the Whatnauts and Whatnauts Band's "Message from a blackman". There were still some songs which called for racial harmony and soul brotherhood – even on this planet, in the here and now. These included Sly and the Family Stone's "Everyday people", with its "different strokes for different folks" pluralism, Bill Withers' "Lean on me", the Isley Brothers' "Harvest for the world", O'Jays' "Love train", and Harold Melvin and the Bluenotes' "Wake up everybody". Yet these were offset by a new emphasis on the dangers of relying on others, as in the O'Jays' own tale of betrayal in love, "Back-stabbers", and Undisputed Truth's barely veiled barb against treacherous whites, "Smiling faces sometimes (tell lies)".

As faith in the power of collective black action to secure black freedom declined, songs like Jerry Butler's "Only the strong survive", Aaron Neville's "Hercules", and James Brown's "I don't want nobody to give me nothing" abandoned the communalism of gospel texts in favour of the intense, stoic individualism of the blues tradition. Instead of romanticizing soul brotherhood, these songs stressed the self-reliance and ruthlessness often required to survive in an urban environment which was increasingly depicted as a vicious, exploitative jungle. The Spinners' incongruously sweet "Ghetto child", James Brown's "Down and out in New York City", Kool and the Gang's "This is you, this is me", and Bobby Womack's magnificent "Across 110th Street" tried to preserve some kind of balance between describing the nitty-socio-economic-gritty of inner-city deprivation and celebrating the vital urban culture blacks had developed to try to survive it.

These new songs remained mostly descriptive. Only rarely – and in the most general sense – were they ever didactic, as in James Brown's exhortation to "Get up, get into it, get involved", Curtis Mayfield's "Move on up", and James Carr's "Freedom train" ("We gotta ride the freedom train,/ We ain't gonna live this way again"). A few songs were rather more shrill, however, chastising the black community for its timidity in the face of white power and oppression. The Last Poets, were a radical New York-based group of Black Muslim rhythmic rhymers who served as a sort of link between the performance beat poetry of Baraka and the rappers of the 1980s. They spouted a lot of nonsense about the coming armed struggle, "when . . . guns and rifles will be taking the place of poems and essays" ("When the revolution comes"), and berated their brothers for not joining the uprising in the title track of their 1970 album, *Niggers Are Scared of Revolution*. More lyrical and insightful were the songs of poet and creative writing instructor Gil Scott-Heron, whose most famous song announced that "The revolution will not be televised", and who later declared with chilling acuity that for minorities it was becoming a permanent "Winter in America".

At one level, it was hardly surprising that blacks in soul should seek to discuss the realities of the black situation more openly in the late 1960s and early 1970s, or that their black audience should increasingly require them to do so. After all, black performers, writers, arrangers, deejays and music business entrepreneurs were all members of the larger black community and shared the general sense of intense frustration as the optimism of the early 1960s dwindled. As black arranger René DeKnight explained in 1967, "The time of singing 'I love you, baby' is rapidly passing". Moreover, DeKnight recognized, as had Imamu Amiri Baraka a year earlier, that any widespread lyrical contemplation of political subjects by soul was actually linked to changes of attitude towards social commentary in popular music among white audiences, white rock artists, and the white-dominated music business. As rock acts like Buffalo Springfield ("For what it's worth"), Jefferson Airplane ("Volunteers"), and Creedence Clearwater Revival ("Fortunate son") began to record more songs about contemporary social problems and politics, "our songs are going to have to depict what's happening", insisted DeKnight.[37]

There was, of course, a certain irony in the fact that soul, so long venerated by black and white critics for its earthy social realism and intimate links to the essential circumstances of black life – not unreasonably, just indiscriminately – was actually under attack for failing to pay enough attention to the black predicament and struggle. The irony was compounded in this case by the fact that the Fifth Dimension, the group with whom René DeKnight was most closely associated in the late 1960s, actually offered a very slick, soft-psychedelic soul sound carefully aimed at a crossover market. Much of the group's repertoire was written by white songsmith Jim Webb, or, like the group's biggest hit "Stone soul picnic", by the brilliant white folk-soul songstress Laura Nyro.

As ever, some artists responded to the changing mood in black society, and the call of their own consciences, more conspicuously and more powerfully than others. For Stevie Wonder, the new political edge in his work at the turn of the decade was almost literally a function of growing up. The blind teenager who as Little Stevie Wonder had unleashed a maelstrom of gospelesque fervour with "Fingertips Part 2" in 1963, had, by the late 1960s, matured into a consummate singer-songwriter with songs like "Uptight" and "For once in my life". With the release of "Signed, sealed, delivered" in the summer of 1970, Wonder also assumed his own production duties. Having topped the black charts with his version of Bob Dylan's "Blowing in the wind" in 1966 – another illustration of the black community's growing hunger for some political beef amid all the "Mashed potato" and "Gravy" – Wonder returned to social commentary in the early 1970s. The turning point was his version of Ron Miller's contemporary hymn "Heaven help us all", which moved lyrically from the particulars of the black situation –

> Heaven help the black man,
> if he struggles one more day.
> Heaven help the white man
> if he turns his head away.
> Heaven help the man,
> who kicks the man who has to crawl.
> Heaven help us all.

– to a wider humanitarian plea for all the oppressed of the world:

> Now I lay me down,
> before I go to sleep.
> In a troubled world,
> I pray the Lord to keep;
> keep hatred from the mighty,
> and the mighty from the small.
> Heaven help us all.

On reaching the age of 21 in 1971, Wonder negotiated an unparalleled deal with Berry Gordy. This allowed him to set up his own Taurus Productions, which leased product to Motown for release, rather like Sam Cooke had used his Tracey company to supply RCA with recordings. Wonder also claimed higher royalties on disk sales than his peers and secured his own share of the publishing rights for his songs. Having won much greater artistic and economic freedom than most other Motown acts, Wonder's new political and social concerns, as heralded by "Heaven help us all", were brilliantly explored in the six albums released in the early-to-mid 1970s: *Where I'm Coming From, Music of My Mind, Talking Book, Innervisions,*

Fulfillingness First Finale and the double-album plus EP which comprised 1976's *Songs in the Key of Life*, and topped the national album charts for 14 weeks. "We as a people, are not interested in 'baby, baby' songs any more", Wonder declared after the release of *Talking Book* in 1973. "There's more to life than that!" As with many other progressive black artists of the era, the album became the primary medium for Wonder's expanding vision. "I think singles are very important", he conceded, "but they are only one page in the book. An album is a book".[38]

Wonder's albums sparkled with bright musical and lyrical ideas, traversing such an enormous range of moods, subjects and influences that by comparison George Clinton sounded almost like a one-trick pony. Among composers of American music, perhaps only Charles Ives and Duke Ellington (to whom, among other giants of black music, Wonder paid homage on the swinging "Sir Duke") have been able to wield such a variegated musical palette with such assurance. Apart from the remarkable music, these albums contained – in addition to the lush romantic ballads like "Blame it on the sun" and "Golden lady" at which Wonder was especially adept – some of the most incisive social commentary of the period.

"Superstition" and "He's misstra know it all" ("He's the man with a plan, got a counterfeit dollar in his hand"), were twin indictments of false ghetto messiahs and those who "put faith in things they don't understand" in their search for easy answers to difficult social questions. With its gutsy horns, funky synthesizer rumblings and wickedly flanged guitars, "Superstition" went to number one in both the black and white charts in 1974 and did much to endear Wonder to a progressive rock audience. "Village ghetto land" from *Songs in the Key of Life* isolated Wonder's deliberately cool, almost dispassionate, vocals and set them against a sumptuous classical string arrangement. The effect of juxtaposing this elegant music, the sounds of opulence, with lyrics that clinically described the wastefulness and tragedy of the ghetto was breathtaking. The sparse, vaguely be-bop, high-hat groove of "Too high" offered a sardonic take on efforts to escape the grim realities of that ghetto through the false deliverance of drugs.

The epic "Living for the city", which owed some musical debt to Donny Hathaway's extended black pride jam, "The ghetto", was one of the era's defining musical moments. The song, another major hit single in a truncated version, recounted the tale of a poor Mississippian who fled the South, where "To find a job is like a haystack needle,/ 'cause where he lives, they don't use colored people". The newcomer's arrival in New York was described in a dramatic playlet which saw him duped into drug running by a "brother", arrested and hauled off to jail. While the condemnation of the racist police was clear enough ("Get in the cell, nigger!"), the song was also an indictment of the ruthlessness and destructive brutality of the black streets. There was no redeeming sense of a vibrant black culture, community or fellowship here; just the sordid and highly exploitative urban jungle which racism and poverty had created.

There were dozens of other musically memorable and politically pointed tracks in Wonder's early 1970s work, but one of the most interesting was the country-tinged "Big brother". This song conjured up images of Orwellian state surveillance around the same time that the FBI's COINTELPRO operation against the Black Panther Party and other radical black groups was at its wretched peak. "Big brother" condemned politicians for paying lip service to strategically important black voters ("I live in the ghetto,/ you just come and see me 'round election time"), yet denying the legitimacy of further black demands for equitable opportunity: "You say that you are tired of me protesting,/ of children dying every day". The song ended on a note of deep disillusionment, as Wonder pondered the fate of his community and the country as a whole. "You've killed all our leaders./ I don't even have to do nothing to you,/ you've caused your own country to fall", he mourned.

This tone of resignation was rare in Wonder's work. As with Curtis Mayfield, Marvin Gaye and the grossly under-rated Lenny Williams – the Tower of Power lead singer, whose eponymous solo album was one of the most consistent and thoughtful of these black consciousness and commentary albums – either God or a more generalized, beatific "love" frequently served as an antidote to dissolution and despair. "When you feel your life's too hard,/ just go have a talk with God", Wonder advised in "Have a talk with God". In "I love everything about you", he tells his lover, "There's only one I place above ya,/ It's Him that I place above ya", knowing that there could be no higher praise.

Here Wonder presaged Al Green's song "Belle", where Green confessed to his lover, "It's you that I want,/ but it's Him that I need". However, while the younger, Michigan born northerner had no difficulty combining songs of deep personal faith with his often highly sensual secular music, in an echo of a bygone era the Arkansas-born, Memphis-based southerner Green, eventually found it impossible to reconcile the tension between his religious beliefs and the physical passions associated with his secular music. In the wake of a long string of smouldering soul and pop hits for Hi Records in the early-to-mid 1970s ("Tired of being alone", "Let's stay together", and "L-O-V-E"), the *Belle* album in 1977 signalled a halt to Green's career as the sexiest of all the latter-day soulmen. For more than a decade Green recorded only religious and inspirational music and, having been ordained in 1976, devoted most of his energies to pastoring the Full Gospel Tabernacle Church in Memphis.

Like Stevie Wonder, Motown stablemate Marvin Gaye simply could not resist the pull of contemporary affairs upon his music in the late 1960s and early 1970s. He was prompted by a combination of his brother's letters from

Vietnam and the ghetto riots to "re-evaluate [the] whole concept of what I wanted my music to say". Gaye wondered, "with the world exploding around me, how am I supposed to keep singing love songs?" Ultimately, the tenor of his troubled times found expression in *What's Going On*, a genuinely seminal album released in 1971. Synthesizing Gaye's deep, if idiosyncratic, spirituality with his increasingly public concern for the military, economic and ecological devastation of his planet, *What's Going On* also blended a gentle, intimate, jazzy ambience with the gospel flavourings of soul and some low-key, after-hours funk. Overlaying the whole mellow mixture was Gaye's deliciously smooth, multi-tracked voice. Irrespective of its subject matter, the album was a triumph of technology and musical vision. The title track set the scene with its catalogue of problems besetting the world. "Inner city blues (Makes me want to holler)" travelled to the heart of ghetto deprivation; "Save the children" circled outwards to confront the catastrophic possibilities of nuclear war. "Flyin' high (in the friendly sky)" offered a sympathetic, but nonetheless salutary warning to those who sought to escape their troubles through drugs. Written from the perspective of one who had been down that road, it was a portentous song. Gaye's last troubled years, before his shooting death at the hands of his own father in 1984, were blighted by his own drug dependency.[39]

Gaye followed up the innovations of *What's Going On* with "You're the man", a stridently militant single which failed to cross over into the white pop charts despite the fact that Gaye's stock with the progressive white rock audience had increased greatly as a result of *What's Going On*. Perhaps this failure also revealed something of the limitations of white liberal support for black demands. *What's Going On*'s essentially humanistic globalism was acceptable, but a song which in the election year of 1972 called for a candidate who would end inflation, cure chronic ghetto unemployment and support busing seemed too much. On the other hand, it was not one of Gaye's finest musical moments either and the road to good intentions has been paved with many a poor tune.

What was especially revealing, and highly typical, about Gaye's new-found political concerns was his continued unwillingness to jeopardize his hard-won commercial success in order to voice them. Pondering the turmoil of his troubled times, he had asked, "Why didn't our music have anything to do with this? Wasn't music supposed to express feelings? No, according to BG [Berry Gordy], music's supposed to sell. That's his trip. And it was mine". Gaye never stopped wanting to be the new American Sinatra. After the commercial failure of "You're the man", he generally eschewed overt political and social commentary until the apocalyptic, and unfinished, *Once in a Lifetime* album, released against his wishes by Motown in 1981. Instead, Gaye concentrated on erotic politics in albums like *Let's Get It On*, *I Want You* and *Midnight Lover*, embracing sex as salvation on boudoir ballads like "You sure love ball", "Sanctified lady" (originally "Sanctified pussy") and "Sexual healing". "Suffering and injustice are things which I've always felt deep in my soul", Gaye explained, "and I wondered what I was doing singing rock and roll in some dive instead of leading the marchers. I know that I had that ability, but that wasn't my role". Stanley Levison could not have said it better.[40]

What's Going On was clearly not the standard singles, showtunes, B-sides and outtakes fare of most previous Motown albums. It was a coherent suite of songs, daringly conceived and stunningly realized. Even those fellow artists who eschewed the politics of Gaye's work were captivated by its artistry. This included Smokey Robinson, who, as Berry Gordy's best friend and Motown vice-president, had endorsed the conservative black corporate policy towards racial politics in soul. Robinson himself stated that "there's a time and place for everything, I think. I'm proud of my blackness, sure, but I don't think the stage is a place to lecture about it". Nevertheless, Robinson was one of those who sided with Gaye against the perennially cautious Gordy and the Motown sales department to secure the release of *What's Going On*. Later Robinson declared it "the greatest album, in my opinion, ever made by anyone".[41]

Robinson, like scores of others, also used Gaye's album as a musical template for his own work. The introspective *A Quiet Storm* was an influential album in its own right, since it spawned a whole new style of mellow late-night black-oriented radio programming, beginning with Melvin Lindsay's *Quiet Storm* show on Howard University's WHUR. Meanwhile, in the wide wake of Gaye's record, Robinson eventually got around to addressing the black social matters he had generally ignored in his compositions since 1959's "Got a job" or, more obliquely, "First I look at the purse".[42]

On "Just my soul responding" Robinson employed a native American chant and repeated allusions to the decimation of the Indians as the musical and lyrical counterpoint to a Vietnam veteran's bitter condemnation of the domestic conditions facing minorities in America. "You may say I'm unpatriotic,/ but I deserve an explanation,/ for too many roaches,/ and not enough heat to keep my babies warm", Robinson sang, his delicate porcelain tones giving poignancy and quiet dignity to a song of seething rage. There was no sloganeering, no crude didacticism; just the terrible beauty of an utterly convincing evocation of black consciousness. It was one of the finest moments in 1970s soul.

"Soul superman": the sexual politics of black power and male soul

As the black community's belief in its own capacity – and America's commitment – to end racially based discrimination disintegrated, frustrations and energies which had once been tapped or assuaged by a mass insurgency were increasingly channelled back into the domestic arena. A vicious sexism and revived black macho were among the least progressive features of the black power era, colouring the rhetoric and actions of many male black power leaders. "We shall have our manhood", pledged self-confessed political rapist and Black Panther Minister of Information Eldridge Cleaver in a statement redolent of the new priorities of the black struggle for some self-proclaimed liberation warriors. "We shall have it or the earth will be levelled by our attempts to gain it", Cleaver vowed.[43]

Until his death during an alleged attempt to escape jail, George Jackson was the incarcerated idol of many black radicals. Jackson initially urged his black brothers to break the grip of matriarchy which, as Daniel Moynihan among others had conveniently explained, was really responsible for the lack of black progress and power. "How could I . . . or any of the men of our kind accomplish what we must as men if we think like bourgeois women, or let our women think for us?", Jackson asked. Echoing influential black psychologists William Grier and Price Cobbs, who in 1968 had written that black mothers wanted "systematically to drive our manliness from our sons", Jackson chastised them for securing the simple survival of their male children "at the cost of their manhood". He dismissed the idea of women's liberation as "*the* factor in the breakdown of the family unit", and condemned the black woman as hopelessly parasitic. "All the women I've had", Jackson announced with unabashed proprietorial candour, "tried to use me, tried to secure through me a soft spot in this cutthroat system for themselves. All they ever wanted was clothes and money to be taken out to flash these things". The ghosts of Wynonie Harris and Eddie "Cleanhead" Vinson were stirring – no doubt looking for that long-lost sense of self-deprecating humour which had partially ameliorated some of the shouters' sexism and braggadocio.[44]

Sexism and sexual violence seem to have been particularly rife within the Black Panther Party, which made Jackson an honorary field marshal. Indeed, in the many, often contradictory and invariably carping reminiscences by ex-Panthers, just about the only constant is the sense of an organization riddled with sexual tensions, latent, sometimes actual, sexual violence, and abusive, exploitative personal relationships. Hugh Pearson, author of a particularly lurid account of the life and death of the party's charismatic co-founder Huey Newton, is probably right that if Newton was a genius of sorts, he was also a petty criminal and sexual psychopath. Newton not only once forcibly raped Panther co-founder Bobby Seale, but preyed mercilessly upon some of the women in the party, and later murdered a prostitute for calling him "baby". As Pearson pointed out, while there were many sterling qualities about the Panthers which deserved to be celebrated, there was also an uglier, seamier side to many chapters where ego-gratification, cheap gangsterism, exploitation of the black community, and brutish sexual aggression masqueraded as revolutionary black nationalism.[45]

It was not only some of the male Black Panthers, with their phallocentric gun-toting revolutionary posturing, who began to erase the distinction between patriarchal assertion and political activity. Other male leaders also tried to gender black liberation and make it synonymous with the exercise of various forms of male power and control. In the late 1960s, this sort of misogyny and sexism had driven Angela Davis out of US, whose leader, Maulana Ron Karenga, would later serve time in jail for a sexual assault on one of the organization's female members. Davis later observed that "some black activists . . . confuse their political activity with an assertion of their maleness . . . These men view Black women as a threat to their attainment of manhood – especially those Black women who take initiative and work to become leaders in their own right". Even Martin Luther King, hardly free of sexist assumptions of his own, managed to sound suspiciously like the patriarchal Malcolm X when identifying one of the most positive aspects of black power as its "psychological call to manhood".[46]

For some black men, then, the initially radical struggle for black freedom and the redemption of American society narrowed into a compensatory exercise in interlocking racial and sexual chauvinism. Once again soul reflected these developments, confirming the basic congruity between the changing tenor of sexual politics in Rhythm and Blues and black perceptions of the potential for securing respect and equitable treatment in America.[47]

That said, neither the abruptness nor the extent of this transition should be exaggerated, any more than it should be suggested that all black men suddenly abandoned domestic responsibilities or political struggle to take refuge in a revived macho and misogyny. Male soul had always combined dreamy romance with raunchy desire; fidelity, understanding and respect, with infidelity, sexual objectification, bitter recrimination and poisonous suspicion. Ian Hoare has generalized that male soul consistently betrayed "a volatile mixture of self assertive, free-floating independence and an almost childlike vulnerability". For him, Wilson Pickett and Otis Redding represented the archetypes. Pickett was the super sexual athlete, the slick, confident, predatory "Midnight mover", the permanently available "A man and a half" (call him up on "634–5789"), who revelled in the physical delights of "Mini-skirt Minnie". Redding, by contrast, was "Mr Pitiful", tenderly offering up "My lover's prayer", and pledging timeless fidelity on "That's how strong my love is".[48]

There clearly was something to this distinction, but Pickett could also deliver tender love pleas like "I'm in love", while Redding could belt out storming macho struts like "Love man". In fact, as Hoare appreciated, there were not really two breeds of soulmen at all. Most male soul singers of the early-to-mid 1960s had just about managed to hold the macho and romantic elements in a dynamic, if often precarious, creative tension; certainly within their repertoires as a whole, but sometimes within a single performance.

Nowhere was this more apparent than in the country-soul of Joe Tex, whose dusty tenor and folksy, self-penned country-soul raps had rescued him from the poverty of a sharecropping youth in Baytown, Texas. Tex enjoyed a long run of Rhythm and Blues chart hits between 1964 and the start of his ministry for Elijah Muhammad and the Black Muslims in 1972. By the mid 1960s Tex's soul homiletics already ranged from the lascivious boast of "You got what it takes" ("To take what I got!"), to the self-recrimination of "I've got to do a little better". On 1965's "You better get it" Tex sounded a note of intense individualism which became increasingly common in the late 1960s, but at least accorded women equal rights in the pursuit of love and happiness, even respecting their equal right to satiate simple lusts.

Yet, even at his most generous and even-handed, Tex's mid-1960s songs were still circumscribed by traditional male assumptions about sexual roles and responsibilities. In "A woman can change a man" Tex conceded a woman's power and influence over her man ("She can make him weak,/ or she can make him strong./ Make him do right,/ or make him do wrong"), and insisted that "everything a man does/ he does it for a woman". However, the song also suggested that it was a woman's duty to try to tame a man whose "natural" inclination was to fulfil the macho stereotype: "A man can say,/ 'you can't tie me down',/ but if she really wants/ him to stay around/ a woman can change a man". Moreover, one of the strategies a woman could use was to give her man "children that look just like him". Thus, Tex fixed upon a woman's biological function as a mother and placed a premium on her sexual fidelity, while implying that the "natural" state from which the black man must be weaned was one of sexual adventurism.

Tex's songs, and those of many other soulmen who worked the borderlines between macho boasts and romantic idealism, reflected a continuing tension in black male culture, particularly, if not exclusively, lower-class black culture. On one hand was a venerable and enduring, if ultimately destructive and oppressive, macho tradition; on the other hand were the demands of a nuclear, patriarchal family modelled on mainstream ideals which required the man to offer not just generous helpings of great sex, but protection, fidelity, understanding, shelter and economic security. The preservation of this tension in soul required at least some faith that the mainstream ideal was actually attainable. When that faith began to decline in the late 1960s, it often left in its place a harsh, uncompromising battle for sexual power. Consequently, the balance which soul had struggled to preserve in the early-to-mid 1960s proved much more elusive in the very different political and psychological climate of the black power era.[49]

James Brown offered an influential example of the way in which much male soul lurched back towards a macho and objectifying agenda in the later 1960s and early 1970s. Brown's music had never been devoid of its raunchier side, with boasts of personal potency mingling with feverish demands for satisfaction and a fine eye for female form on tracks like "Good good lovin'" and "Fine old foxy self". Yet many of Brown's most successful recordings before 1967, both commercially and artistically, betrayed a raw sensitivity and an almost desperate romanticism. "I'll go crazy", "Bewildered", "Lost someone" and "Prisoner of love" were impassioned pleas for love and mutual affection. After 1967, however, the macho component in Brown's music was thrust ever more firmly to the fore. Brown massaged his own ego and those of his beleaguered black brothers by becoming a "Sex machine" who could cast a connoisseur's eye over the contents of "Hot pants".

Brown's reification of his own sexual potency and the increasingly curt treatment of women in his songs fused seamlessly with the new political engagement of his lyrics. On the defiant "I don't want nobody to give me nothing", Brown explicitly equated black pride and power with a Cleaveresque assertion of black manhood: "We don't want no sympathy,/ just wanna be a man". Like the despised "nigger" of old, the black woman in Brown's songs had to learn her place, and should she fail in her duties or stray from her man, there was no forgiveness. "The payback" – a marvellously sinister slab of funk, which opened with Brown's menacing cry "Revenge! I'm mad!" – appeared to work on two levels, conflating the threat of domestic male revenge on a faithless partner with wider black retribution for the racial abuses and injustices wrought by white America. "Papa don't take no mess" was a blunt declaration of sexual mastery aimed squarely at the potentially treacherous black woman, although the no-nonsense sentiment could again translate into the political arena. "It's a new day" was simply a list of instructions for the black woman to follow in order to keep her man satisfied. The black woman was told "Never get too confident", and instructed to "Take care of business", since the black man's sexual needs must be serviced. It seemed that Brown's "New day" would be characterized by the triumph of black patriarchal authority and sex on demand, not by the economic, social or political empowerment of the black community.

What made this all the more tragic was that Brown's behaviour towards the women in his private life seemed just as retrogressive. "When I'm on the road, I behave just like a teenager . . . Bang, Bang, Bang", he told a reporter in 1971. When, in December 1988, he was sentenced to six years' imprisonment (he was paroled in February 1991) for a reckless driving incident and an assault on his long-suffering third wife, Adrienne, tales surfaced of years of wife-beating, as well as financial extortion and drug abuse. In January 1996, Adrienne died after undergoing cosmetic surgery, reputedly in a last desperate bid to keep James' attentions from wandering.[50]

Brown was not the only male artist to chronicle and reinforce the vigorous revival of black macho, the deterioration of relationships between the sexes, and the eclipse of the romantic idealism of the early 1960s. In much of the male soul of the black power era, fear and suspicion of female infidelity constantly poisoned personal relationships. This was not just apparent between men and women, as in the Saints' heart-rending "Mirror mirror", where a man's unfounded accusations pushed his woman into the arms of another ("The lies you visualized, are now a reality"), but also between male friends. The O'Jays' majestic "Backstabbers" described the black man's fear that the sexually insatiable, shamelessly materialistic black woman of macho mythology was entertaining his so-called friends behind his back: "They smile in your face,/ but all they want to do is take your place – Backstabbers . . . Why do all your friends come to see your lady?/ Man, some of those friends they sure look shady". Howard Tate's "How come my bulldog don't bark" ("How come my bulldog don't bark,/ when Big Jim comes around/, when everyone knows/ I got the meanest bulldog in town?") explored the same theme of brotherly betrayal, again laying the blame squarely on the fast and loose black woman, rather than on "Big Jim", the "legitimately" predatory black man. The Unifics' melodramatic "Court of love" from 1968 vividly presented the black man's case against the unfaithful black woman to a jury of his peers. The woman was charged with deception and abusing a man's precious love – crimes which had stripped him "of all [his] manly pride". Not surprisingly, the court found the woman guilty and the man rejoiced, "I got justice in this courthouse". By the early 1970s, then, justice, a keynote of the black struggle for freedom and equality, was being defined in terms of saving male face and convicting the black woman for the sort of sexual adventurism which was once again becoming a badge of honour among black soulmen.

Clarence Carter, a blind, cavern-voiced Alabamian who recorded some magnificent deep country-soul for the Fame label, virtually made a career from tales of unbridled lust and illicit sex like "Slip away" and "I can't leave your love alone". Fittingly, Carter, like Stax's irrepressible veteran Rufus Thomas, even revived the Dominoes' "Sixty minute man". The return of Lovin' Dan was a neat symbol of the way in which the macho-misogynistic strain in black male popular culture had reasserted its primacy. In fairness, Carter's broad humour and distinctive satyrical chuckle saved much of his work from its darkest undertones, harking back to some of the more tongue-in-cheek boasts of the old shouters. His hilarious version of Roger Hatcher's adulterer's anthem "I got caught", perfectly captured his philosophy. Pondering the serious moral and medical implications of a recently discovered dalliance with his best friend's wife, Carter admitted, "Now I know what I did, was a shame and a sin./ But, I know if I had the chance – and wasn't in this hospital – I'd do it all again!"

Other soul and funk men were usually far less witty than Carter in their demands for sexual gratification and boasts of conquest and potency. Although Funkadelic's sprawling "Wars of Armageddon", with its mantra about "more power to the peter, more power to the pussy, more pussy to the peter", was a difficult one to categorize, songs like General Crook's "Gimme some" and "Do it for me" were devoid of any sense of humour or eroticism. Others, like Timmy Willis' "Mr Soul Satisfaction", the Hesitations'

"Soul superman", and most of Wilson Pickett's late 1960s repertoire, suggested that sexual conquest was not simply a means to personal prestige but, in the absence of a viable mass black Movement, could now conveniently be interpreted as "correct" black male politics.

Macho, misogyny and objectification were hardly absent from white cultural forms, of course, and they (mis)informed many of the puerile adolescent cock-rock fantasies of heavy-metal music. Nevertheless, after a period of relative remission, they seemed especially virulent in black male popular music once more. By almost any meaningful standard songs like Israel Tolbert's "Big leg woman (with a short short mini skirt on)", J.J. Jackson's "I dig girls", the O'Kaysions' "Girl watcher", Johnnie Taylor's "Love bones", Brothers Johnson's "Land of ladies", Intruders' "Me Tarzan, you Jane", 100 Percent Proof Aged In Soul's "One man's leftovers (is another man's feast)" and "Too many cooks (spoil the soup)", and even Joe Tex's "Skinny legs and all", tended to slip beyond honest sexual admiration to base objectification and voyeurism.

In some respects, part of what was going on here was simply a reflection of the greater frankness in discussing sexual matters which was a feature of American – indeed, Western – life in the late 1960s and early 1970s. Nonetheless, as David Caute has noted, "Male chauvinism was often decked out as 'sexual liberation', involving a gallop into pornography". Certainly, there was plenty in the soul of the period to reinforce Gerda Lerner's claim that throughout the long history of patriarchy and sexual inequality in Western culture, "It is not women who are reified and commodified, it is women's sexuality and reproductive capacity which is so treated".[51]

Indeed, many of the songs celebrating male sexual prowess, power and control exhibited a verbal violence against women which, in another context, Deborah Cameron has suggested "is, in fact, in itself a form of social control". Male soul increasingly resorted to what Cameron has called "pornoglossia" – a verbal equivalent of pornography which "reduces all women to men's sexual servants". There was even a visual correlate to this process of lyrical objectification, as album covers by groups like the Ohio Players began to feature black women in various states of undress and titillating S&M adventures. It was a perfect image for a group whose hottest singles – "Fire", "Pain", "Ecstasy" and "Sweet sticky thing" – merged an unctious jazz-funk with lyrics that fumbled for eroticism but usually wallowed in prurience.[52]

The wave of blaxploitation action movies also tended to reify images of cool black studs for whom sexual conquest of the bevy of black and, sometimes, white beauties draped around the set like so many props was a powerful means of self-affirmation. On the positive side, these films were part of the process of moving soul beyond the structural confines of the hit single, since the soundtracks were often composed by leading black artists. Isaac Hayes won an Oscar for *Shaft*; jazz-funksters Roy Ayers and Willie

Hutch did *Coffy* and *The Mack* respectively; Bobby Womack scored *Across 110th Street*; even Brother James got in on the act, contributing to the score of *Black Caesar* and *Slaughter's Big Rip-Off*, while Curtis Mayfield did the elegant, sinewy *Super Fly*, which was arguably the best of all the films and unarguably one of the best soundtracks.

On the negative side, these films rarely escaped clichés about black street life and hyper-sexuality in which black men were invariably gangsters, pimps, drug pushers, and drug addicts, or else heroic all-action sexmachines who were bent on ridding the neighbourhood of such strangely attractive, stylish and wealthy vermin. After decades of neglect by Hollywood, it may have been a thrill for black audiences to see so many black faces – and many other bits of black bodies – on the screen in identifiably black environments, but, as black film historian Donald Bogle has noted, most of these movies played shamelessly "on the legend of the blacks' highpowered sexuality. While the movies assiduously sought to avoid the stereotype of the asexual tom, they fell . . . into the trap of presenting the wildly sexual man". And so it was that the unambiguously named John Shaft was celebrated as "the private dick, who makes it with all the chicks"? "Damn right!", crowed Isaac Hayes.[53]

With women rarely more than sex objects in these resolutely masculine films, even the major black movie heroine of the era, Pam Grier (*Cleopatra Jones* and *Coffy*), was essentially a male fantasy figure – "as ready and anxious for sex and mayhem as any man", according to Bogle – with whom few black women identified. Ultimately, the Bucks and Vixens of these films offered about as accurate and comprehensive a vision of black America as had the black screen domestics and Pullman Porters who peopled the films of previous generations.[54]

Male soul was not completely swept up by the macho-sexist wave which broke across the black power era, any more than all black men succumbed to it. Tenderness, fidelity, vulnerability, respect, reciprocity and romantic idealism still struggled to contain the swell of priapism, misogyny and sexual paranoia. Some artists, among them Smokey Robinson, Percy Sledge, Tyrone Davis, Joe Simon, the Chi-lites, Delfonics and Stylistics rarely strayed far from themes of love and loss, despair and happiness, yet generally avoided the vindictiveness and cynicism which once more stalked much male Rhythm and Blues. Others, like Al Green, Marvin Gaye, Teddy Pendergrass (both as lead singer with Harold Melvin and the Bluenotes and as a soloist), and Barry White, unashamedly put sex to the fore, but usually strove for a more reciprocal, less exploitative erotic vision. That said, White, the gargantuan "walrus of love", whose deep baritone raps and satin-sheets orchestrations on hugely successful crossover hits like "Can't get enough of your love, babe" and "You're my first, my last, my everything", got things hopelessly wrong on the campy "Love serenade" when he foolishly hazarded the rhyming couplet, "take off your brassiere, mah dear". It was about as sexy as the Chipmunks on a bad fur day.

Expanding on the Impressions' 1965 celebration of colour and gender, "Woman's got soul", some soulmen actually delivered extremely sympathetic and appreciative homilies to the fortitude and beauty of black women, without necessarily degenerating into crude sexual objectification. In "Black woman", for example, Don Covay called for the black woman to "go stand beside your man" (a definite improvement on "behind your man") and looked forward to the time when she would reap the rewards for her long suffering: "Baby, you know you paid your dues,/ now take off your worried mind,/ put on your good life shoes".

Interestingly, while faithless and demanding lovers and wives tended to bear the brunt of male resentment in black-power-era soul, mothers were generally spared. The former were viewed by black men as both potential rivals for, and impediments to, their exercise of social, economic and sexual power; the latter were often accorded special status as the repository of black wisdom, culture and stability. And, of course, mothers could also be defined purely in terms of the primary role assigned to women in a patriarchal society, as the bearers and nurturers of children.

Certainly, some of male soul's more compassionate and thoughtful treatments of black women involved mother figures. The Intruders' cloying "I'll always love my mama" was typical in its depiction of the black mother as the rock of both family and communal life, while Funkadelic's first hit single, "Music for my mother", was dedicated to those who held the black world together. Syl Johnson's "Is it because I'm black?" and Joe Tex's "A mother's prayer" also recognized the sacrifices black mothers made to raise children amid the deprivations of both rural and urban poverty. By 1970, more than 34 per cent of all black households were headed by a woman – virtually double the figure in 1950.[55]

While the dread of ego-shattering female infidelity, indeed any expression of sexual freedom or power, permeated much male soul and funk, prostitutes, like mothers, were largely exempt from criticism. Again there was a psychological and social logic to this; Prostitutes exemplified conventional sex roles, enabling men to define, evaluate, and exploit women purely according to their sexual, if not reproductive, function. The prostitute was the quintessential embodiment of sex as a commodity, to be coveted, bought and owned by men. Yet, if there was little guilt about the sexist dimensions of prostitution, with successful pimps elevated to the status of ghetto heroes in blaxploitation films and songs, there was often a genuine sympathy and understanding of the economic imperatives which compelled black women to sell sex.

"Don't give it away", by Syl Johnson, for example, advised that "'Coz romance without finance won't get you nowhere ... don't give it away, make 'em all pay". The exact moral co-ordinates of Johnson's position are ambiguous here, yet there is little doubt that he had identified the key economic motivation for prostitutes. In "Who's gonna take the blame" Smokey Robinson went even further, actually accepting responsibility for a girl-friend's slide into prostitution as a result of his inability to provide a stable home for her. Funkadelic's *Cosmic Slop* album spawned two further medita-tions on this theme. "Trash a-go-go" described the trial of a man who had put his girlfriend on the streets to pay for his drug habit, while the title track was about a poor mother who sold her body to make money to raise her children.

Perhaps the most remarkable of all soul's depictions of prostitution actu-ally involved a mother-figure. O.C. Smith's 1968 country-soul "Son of Hickory Holler's tramp" described how a mother, abandoned by her drunken, wom-anizing husband, had pledged to raise her 14 children alone. It was told from the perspective of a son who only realized years later that she had kept her promise by "sacrific[ing] her pride" and turning to prostitution: "The path was deep and wide,/ from footsteps leading to our cabin,/ above the door there burned a scarlet lamp./ And late at night,/ a hand would knock,/ and there would stand a stranger,/ Yes, I'm the son of Hickory Holler's tramp". Rather than condemnation, the son is full of understanding and gratitude: "Let them gossip all they want,/ she loved us and she raised us,/ the proof is standing here a full grown man".

The use of the word "tramp" here was a good example of the way in which language was gendered in soul, reflecting and contributing to the construction of sexually differentiated roles and identities in the black com-munity. In Smith's song "tramp" had its usual connotations of sexual wan-tonness when applied to a woman. However, in the duet between Carla Thomas and Otis Redding, "Tramp", Redding revelled in the description, linking it to his pride in his southern, agrarian roots and his status as a demon lover. Similarly, in Joe Tex's "Papa was too", "tramp" became a term of approval: "Tramp! Alright, baby, you can call me that,/ my papa was too . . . Papa was a tramp, but he was a lover too./ So why can't I,/ do like papa do?"

It is revealing to compare father songs like "Papa was too" with soul's mother songs. While some, like the Chi-lites' "Let me be the man my daddy was", Joe Tex's "Papa's dream", and Clarence Carter's "Patches", depicted dutiful fathers who took care of their families as best they could, others like the Temptations' epic "Papa was a rolling stone" revealed the ravages wrought upon the black community by the interplay of racism, poverty and macho irresponsibility. The finest musical creation of Motown's psychedelic phase, the brooding "Papa was a rolling stone" told the cautionary tale of a family whose father "Spent all his time chasing women and drinking . . . And when he died, all he left us was alone".

"Papa was a rolling stone" was a good example of the way in which male soul did sometimes manage honest critiques, rather than blind celebrations, of black macho. Sam and Dave, for example, chastised their own macho alter-egos (as celebrated in "Soul man") in the brassy "Soul sister, brown sugar". "Girl, you're always out there with your man,/ now its time he took your hand", they sang. Indeed, while male soul rarely embraced the full-blown guilt about infidelity which has characterized much white country music, many songs did point out the perils of playing the errant black stud: a lifestyle which undermined the family unit, and thereby black solidarity, and also risked driving the good black woman into the arms of another. Stax's Johnnie Taylor ploughed the field of male infidelity and its consequences deeper than most. Not averse to a spot of sexual objectification ("Love bones"), or sexual cavalierism ("I got to love somebody's baby"), his hugely successful "Who's making love?" was a classic tale of the cuckolder cuckolded. "Who's making love to your old lady, while you're out making love?", Taylor asked, echoing Little Milton's 1965 hit "Who's cheating who?".

Just as Joe Tex had warned against the "Woman stealer", so Taylor, on songs like "Take care of your homework", helped to popularize a similar sexual opportunist, the anti-hero known as Jody, who eagerly took care of those women whose sexual and emotional needs were being neglected by their menfolk. Taylor's lesser-known labelmate, Jimmy Lewis, brilliantly explored the same theme in "You gotta stop half-loving these women". The Jody-esque protagonist made no apology for his own predatory opportunism, but blamed his black brothers for "causing me to have to work so much all of the time". "A lot of you men, you got first class women, but you only give them third class love", Lewis sang. In a refreshing departure from the common depiction of the black man as innocent victim or sexual beneficiary of the congenitally unfaithful black woman, he suggested that "there ain't no woman in the world,/ I don't believe,/ that would ever do no wrong/ if she was getting everything she need at home".

Clarence Reid's "Real woman" was an even more telling indictment of black male insensitivities and inadequacies in forging mutually respectful relationships. In the early 1970s, Reid recorded an ambitious "concept" album about black domestic life called *Running Water*. Cut for the Alston label at the Criteria Studios in Miami – very much an "in" location for soul production in the late 1960s and early 1970s, with Aretha Franklin, Wilson Pickett, and Betty Wright among its clientele – *Running Water* was itself a testament to soul's expanded musical vision.

"Real woman" began with Reid extolling the virtues of his "real woman" in classic sexist clichés: "She stays home alone when I'm gone (She's a real woman)/ She stays there with the kids and keeps her dislikes hid (She's a real woman)". As the song progressed, however, Reid acknowledged his mistake in taking her so for granted. "Sometimes I treat her bad, but she still don't seem mad,/ although her tears show she's hurt./ It makes me wonder what kind of man I am,/ to treat a woman like her like dirt". Yet he still cannot resist the lure of slipping around and in a marvellous dénouement gets his just deserts. "One night I came home and all her clothes were gone,/ and outside the door I saw her footprints in the sand./ Made me realize my real woman/ had gone to find herself a real man".

What made Reid's sensitivity and insight here even more intriguing was that shortly after *Running Water* had failed to set the charts alight, he reinvented himself as a carnal character called Blowfly and released a string of highly successful X-rated comedy funk albums. There were some genuinely funny ribald riffs on the black stud stereotype on these records, but their humour revolved almost exclusively around graphic tales of sexual hunts, conquests and the routine humiliation and degradation of women. It was as if Reid had simply given up on the struggle to maintain any balance between honest descriptions of powerful sexual needs, lusts and longings, and other aspects of black life and relationships. Instead, he created a crudely sexist alter-ego and gave the macho, voyeuristic, exploitative element of his soul full vent.

It certainly did not appear to matter much to Reid that Blowfly sacrificed a broader, more nuanced vision of black life and sexual politics for a reductionist set of stereotypes. The raised racial consciousness of the era did not seem to provoke the purveyors of this prurience to consider whether their music might be helping to perpetuate or legitimize destructive sexist attitudes within their communities. What mattered was that this stuff sold. Records by Blowfly, Rudy Ray Moore (also known as Dolomite), and the more gangster-oriented *Hustlers Convention* album by members of the Last Poets (renamed Lightnin' Rod for the occasion), bequeathed this sense of commercial priorities to many of the gangsta rappers of the 1980s and 1990s, along with their nascent rapping style, street subject matter and easy misogyny.

In sum, then, male Rhythm and Blues from the late 1960s to the mid 1970s continued to deal with every conceivable human emotion and activity relating to domestic and sexual relationships. Within that continued diversity, however, there was a marked revival of the sexism and sexual hostilities which had been so much a part of r&b before the birth of the modern civil rights movement, but which had been far less conspicuous between Montgomery and Selma. Sadly, as a progressive movement fuelled by radical equalitarian ideals splintered, a form of retrogressive entrenchment took place. Frustrated, angry and increasingly desperate and alienated, black men, particularly the masses who failed to escape into the black middle class, where they could practise a different, more mainstream, form of patriarchy and sexism, sometimes took refuge in a peculiarly intense form of racial and sexual chauvinism. The revival of black macho and the myth of matriarchy in soul were cultural manifestations of that phenomenon.

Fighting fire with fire: female soul in the black power era

The female soul of the 1960s and early 1970s described much the same arc as its male counterpart. In the main, as in the girl group repertoire of the black pop era, women soul singers were initially most concerned with celebrating romantic epiphanies and the triumph of true love in songs like Doris Troy's "Just one look", Theola Kilgore's "The love of my man", Carla Thomas' "B-A-B-Y", Barbara Lewis' "Baby, I'm yours", Mary Wells' "My guy" and the Supremes' "I hear a symphony"; or else they mourned the absence and demise of such idealized relationships, as in Irma Thomas' "I wish someone would care" and Baby Washington's "That's how heartaches are made".

Even by mid decade, however, there were already growing signs of domestic discontent and much greater assertiveness in female soul. Betty Everett's "Can't hear you no more" and "You're no good", with its curt disavowal of a departed lover's significance ("Feeling better, now that we're through"), were typical statements of female independence. Martha and the Vandellas refused to be devastated at the end of a relationship on "Come and get these memories", with its sting in the tail: "Come along and get 'em,/ 'Cause I've found me somebody new". Mitty Collier laid down her conditions and expectations in "I had a talk with my man", directed one of the great forgotten voices of mid 1960s soul to the subject of male infidelity on "I'm your part time love", and exposed the domestic damage which "slippin' around" could wreak on "No faith, no love". Irma Thomas' "Time is on my side", with its confident coda, "You'll come running back", was a mighty assertion of female sexual power, as, in its wry way, was her "(You can take my husband) Don't mess with my man".

In the late 1960s, while male soul and funk revived black macho and the myth of matriarchy, its female counterpart articulated the complex responses of black women to the changing tenor of black protest. Black women certainly recognized the reorientation of much black male militancy in the black power era. Margaret Wright, a Los Angeles mother of four who was active in the Women Against Repression organization, blamed the *Moynihan Report* ("some white man wrote this book about the black matriarchy, saying that black women ran the community. Which is bull") for placing patriarchy, rather than racial justice, at the heart of black power and thereby undermining the radical egalitarian impulse of the early Movement:

> The black man used to admire the black women for all they'd endured to keep the race going. Now the black man is saying he wants a family structure like the white man's. He's got to be head of the family and women have to be submissive and all that nonsense. Hell, the white woman is already oppressed in that setup.
> Black men have been been brainwashed into believing they've been emasculated. I tell them they're nuts. They've never been

emasculated. Emasculated men don't revolt . . . Black women ain't
oppressing them. We're helping them get their liberation. It's the
white man who's oppressing them, not us.[56]

As black male frustrations with the system were sometimes decanted into
a compensatory macho and misogyny, black women found themselves in
the invidious position of having to balance support for a racial struggle
which was now largely defined and led by black men according to increasingly sexist criteria with the particular needs of black womanhood. Finding little common ground with the essentially white, middle-class, careerist
agenda of the national women's movement, many chose to put racial allegiances first. Many subordinated their own gender-specific interests to the
"liberation" of the black community through the black man's pursuit of
patriarchal authority and power.

Some female black power activists encouraged black men to fulfil the
mainstream provider and protector ideal, while dutifully accepting the role
in the struggle assigned to them by its male leadership: that of bearing and
nurturing the progeny of the revolution. Some even rejected contraception
and abortion, reproductive technologies which actually offered all women
greater control over their lives, as "counter-revolutionary". The pill was
"deadly poison" and "The hidden meaning of the Trojan was to emasculate
the Black man". At the 1969 convention of the rapidly disintegrating Students for a Democratic Society, Chaka Walls of the Illinois Black Panther
Party announced that the role of women in the Movement was "for love
and all that . . . for pussy power . . . The way women contribute is by getting
laid".[57]

In a related impulse, some black women not only agreed to stand dutifully behind their menfolk, but elevated them to prodigious aesthetic and
sexual heights, boosting male self-esteem in an effort to spur them on to
greater economic, political, cultural and sexual achievements. Poetess Nikki
Giovanni immortalized the "Beautiful black men", including soul luminaries
Jerry Butler, Wilson Pickett, the Impressions and Sly Stone, as "beautiful
beautiful beautiful outasight/ black men/ with they afros". In 1968, Florence
Grier, an Oklahoman who had migrated to the west coast to work as a
domestic, was fully aware of her special – if hardly matriarchal – power as
a black woman within her own household and community, yet responded
to the ascendancy of black militants like Stokely Carmichael and H. Rap
Brown with great relief and pride. They fitted her image of what a real black
man should be like: proud and patriarchal, dominant and assertive. "This is
the kind of man we've been waiting for. All Negro girls, they're looking for
this kind of man", Grier explained.[58]

Most black women, however, remained deeply cynical of black power's
macho strain, particularly as it became clear that persistent racism, poverty
and unemployment meant that many black men were still unable to fulfil

their protector-provider side of the unequal patriarchal bargain. This failure was given added poignancy by the fact that black women had closed the income gap on white women much more successfully than black men had on their white counterparts and also experienced generally lower levels of unemployment. Certainly, female soul once more began to offer increasingly bitter, often darkly humorous, critiques of black male inadequacies, coupled with proud assertions of female rights to better treatment at home, at work, and in bed. Laura Lee, for example, boldly stated her claims for equal rights to sexual satisfaction in "Woman's love rights" and, like the philandering black man, had no compunction about getting them outside the marital bed in "Wedlock is a padlock". Millie Jackson probed the emotional and sexual politics of sequential and concurrent relationships throughout the 1970s, most notably on her album *Caught Up*, with its version of Luther Ingram's "If loving you is wrong (I don't want to be right)".

This theme of guiltless infidelity was further explored by the Soul Children on "I'll be the other woman". Honey Cone's "While you were out looking for sugar" reminded errant black men that black women were no longer willing to sit quietly at home, waiting and hoping for love and affection while their menfolk roamed: "How long I'll be faithful,/ I don't know./ But if I find myself in the arms of someone else,/ darling, it's all your fault", they warned.

The veteran Patti LaBelle, who with her Bluebelles had been happily walking "Down the aisle" back in 1963, re-emerged in 1975 with her latest space-age, aluminium-wrapped group LaBelle. LaBelle worked with the Meters to create the blistering funk-soul hit "Lady Marmalade", with its irresistible "Voulez-vous couchez avec moi, ce soir?" hook. This was about as coy as Rhythm and Blues got in the mid 1970s as Donna Summer began to fake her monumental orgasms over some neat Teutonic synthesizer disco-pop courtesy of Munich based producer Giorgio Moroder on hits like "Love to love you baby".

In this atmosphere of, at its most positive, a more confident, honest and expressive female sexuality, a sense of shared black sisterhood and experience emerged, culminating in the late 1970s in songs like Sister Sledge's "We are family". Male infidelity was usually dismissed as a simple, loathsome, but ineradicable fact of black life, as in Doris Duke's "To the other woman", Ann Peebles' "Part time love", and Mitty Collier's "Sharing you". Yet the women involved in such bizarre love triangles were usually slow to blame their rivals for any wrong-doings. An exception was Betty Wright's "Clean up woman", which cited the failure of black women to satiate the prodigious sexual appetites of black men as the cause of much male philandering.

More usual, however, were sisterly warnings not to trust black men, as in Mary Wells' tough valediction for shattered dreams, "Never give a man the world". Shirley Brown's "Woman to woman" warned "the other woman" that she had clothed, fed and supported her man, only to be repaid with deceit and heartache. Some women plotted vengeance against such unfaithful men, as in Candi Staton's chilling "Evidence" and Ann Peebles' "Tear your playhouse down". Others belittled the macho at the heart of much male soul by criticizing male sexual shortcomings. In Inez Foxx's electrifying "Circuits overloaded", the man's playing around left him unable to "take care of business" at home. Jean Knight's mocking "Mr Big Stuff" ("Take him,/ you can have my man"), Sweet Inspirations' sexually frustrated "(Gotta find) A brand new lover", and Veda Brown's graphic "Short stopping" ("I need your love every night,/ you give me a little bit . . . you ain't doing it right"), were in the same deflationary mode. Denise LaSalle insisted that satisfying her was a "Man sized job" and complained that, for all their boasting, none of her lovers measured up.

Bold and brazen though they were, these sorts of songs can hardly be said to have carved out a distinctively black feminist agenda in soul, since they were essentially reactive, not proactive. They were born of a proud, defiant urge to, as southern soul siren Shay Holliday put it in her own rousing account of retaliatory infidelity, "Fight fire with fire". The women of soul rejected the role of helpless victims, not by articulating a discernibly feminist programme, but by giving as good as they got in the male-defined sex wars of the late 1960s and early 1970s. Soul women earned respect by outdoing men on their own terms. It was the equivalent of women in the Panthers earning the respect of their male colleagues by picking up the gun – the ultimate symbol of phallocentric power – and behaving as much like men as possible.

As a consequence, there is a risk of applying a sort of inverted sexual double-standard to this raunchy and sexually assertive strain of female funk and soul. Male soul can certainly be criticized for too frequently, and too uncritically, celebrating images of irresponsible, predatory sexual adventurism; for reducing women to mere sex objects, even presenting them as the actual cause of black disadvantage; and for over-emphasizing exploitative and abusive personal relationships. These tendencies not only helped to make sexism, misogyny and domestic paranoia seem routine, but they presented an extremely jaundiced and narrow view of black society, in which most blacks continued to struggle to conduct decent, productive, responsible lives and relationships in spite of the distorting influences of racial and economic oppression.

The point is that the same criticisms could be levelled against some of the most powerful female soul and funk of the late 1960s and early 1970s. Many songs celebrated female sexual predation, infidelity, deceit and opportunism. Many more portrayed black men as inadequate, irresponsible, untrustworthy and profligate; as the root cause of the black woman's distress and the source of most black social and economic ills. Nevertheless, there has been a tendency to excuse these preoccupations in female soul as a legitimate response to flagrant displays of sexism and the eager pursuit of sexual and patriarchal power in male soul. It is not difficult to understand why, of course. There was something invigorating, inspiring and empowering about the simple refusal of these women to lay down, so to speak, before the onslaught of male sexism. Nevertheless, there remains a sense that the net result of fighting fire with fire may just have been that more people got burned.

Fortunately, as in male soul, the sheer breadth and diversity of the perspectives and attitudes on display in female soul and funk militated against too narrow and distortive a rendering of black life and loves. What is at issue here, again, is the revival of a highly combative, often cynical and vituperative strain of female Rhythm and Blues, which had been largely in remission during the decade after Montgomery. Certainly, Chaka Khan, the most important of the relatively few female performers to emerge from a funk band background, managed to range across the whole spectrum of female emotions, moods and attitudes. A veteran of the Black Panther Free Breakfast programmes in Chicago, Khan cut some excellent funk-rock with the multi-racial group Rufus and then as a solo artist. A powerful jazzy-gospel singer and fine songwriter, Khan could bump and grind with the best of them, but she also had a quieter, more contemplative side. By turns coy and uninhibited, vulnerable and aggressive, tortured and simply out to dance away the blues, Khan resisted entrapment by any stereotypes, in part by embracing them all and subordinating them to her proud, inviolable sense of self. "I'm a woman (And I'm a backbone)" from the 1975 Rufus album *Rufusized*, and her 1978 solo black number one, "I am every woman", were universalized assertions of her personal strength and every woman's right to complexity and respect.

Aretha Franklin was another self-professed "Natural woman", who also embraced just about every possible perspective on black sexual politics and domestic relationships from the late 1960s, while remaining unimpeachably "Lady Soul". "Respect" and "Think" ("you better think,/ what you're trying to do to me!"), were unequivocal demands for domestic respect. "Do right woman – Do right man" called for shared responsibility for, and commitment to, the success of a relationship. The gorgeous "Angel" rekindled the romantic visions of the early 1960s – a vision which survived elsewhere in songs like Martha and the Vandellas' "(We've got) honey love", and doe-eyed devotionals like Jackie Montre-el's "I worship the ground you walk upon", and Diana Ross' "Ain't no mountain high enough".

More ambiguous in Franklin's repertoire were songs like Don Covay's "Chain of fools", in which she acknowledged male infidelity, but posited female powerlessness, perhaps even reluctance, to escape an exploitative relationship in the face of the sexual satisfaction only a black man could provide ("your love is too strong"). Similarly, "Dr Feelgood" was simultaneously a bold claim to sexual fulfilment and a homage to the black man's unique

For many of her fans, Aretha Franklin came to embody the indomitable spirit of black America. She is pictured here with deejay Ed Castleberry at the Jamaica Club, Columbus, Ohio, in 1962.

ability to provide that fulfilment. Even on "Natural woman", it was a man's love which had led to that self-actualization. This was arguably soul's most potent depiction of the personal potential unleashed by a mutually respectful, sexually and emotionally fulfilling relationship.

"I never loved a man (The way I love you)" was an even more complex meditation on this theme. The song began with a fierce condemnation of male infidelity ("You're a no good heartbreaker"), but later revealed masochistic undertones in describing acquiescence to such mistreatment. Franklin actually made a virtue out of her capacity to suffer and respond to her lover's cruelty with a monumental, unshakeable love. This was a major subtext in much female soul. In 1964, Motown's Brenda Holloway had hinted at the same dogged loyalty to a feckless lover in "Every little bit hurts", a theme subsequently pursued in Denise LaSalle's "Trapped by a thing called love" and Mary Love's "The hurt is just beginning".

Franklin was rather like Ray Charles, sharing his umbilical ties to gospel and its imperative to tell the truth through her music. It was no matter that those truths were often complex and paradoxical. Aretha laid bare her soul in these songs, exposing the scars of a personal life which had always been stormy and sometimes abusive, but testifying to her capacity to endure and, ultimately, overcome. Not surprising, then, that Franklin should become such an icon in black America, where she seemed to embody the indomitable spirit of a people. Even as the white backlash set in and the latest phase in a centuries-old struggle for black freedom stalled and then shattered, Aretha Franklin stood unbowed and "Rock steady".

CHAPTER TEN

"Get up, get into it, get involved": black music, black protest and the black power movement

That's part of what's wrong with you. You do too much singing. Today it's time to stop singing and start swinging. (Malcolm X)[1]

Saying it loud: James Brown joins the Movement

The widespread politicization of the Rhythm and Blues scene of the late 1960s and early 1970s can be explained primarily by the decline of the three major impediments to any such engagement before the mid 1960s. Two of these changes have been noted already. First, whereas the recording and broadcasting industries had once been extremely wary of any public artistic or personal links between performers and the Movement, they came to recognize that social commentary, bold expressions of racial pride, and even righteous condemnations of American racism were not commercial suicide but a sound commercial strategy. Second, the fate of the Movement and the changing tenor of the times weighed heavily on both black audiences and on individual black artists and entrepreneurs, many of whom simply found it impossible to remain on the outside looking in and found a variety of ways to show support and solidarity.

The third key change involved much greater efforts by black activists to enlist the help of Rhythm and Blues performers. Whereas the early Movement had shown relatively little interest in seeking to use soul, the late 1960s and early 1970s saw a torrent of treatises seeking to isolate a unique "black aesthetic", and a mountain of manifestos postulating how distinctively black cultural productions might be used to fashion a revolutionary consciousness among the black masses. The new cultural politics of the black power era, coupled with a shift in the funding base of the struggle from whites towards blacks, meant that activists began to curry the support of soul stars and black music entrepreneurs in a far more systematic and sometimes highly aggressive manner.

In a related development, the recording and broadcasting industries themselves became fields where blacks fought, collectively and individually, for more economic and executive power, and for greater responsiveness to community needs. The ways in which successful black artists, executives and entrepreneurs tried to balance broad racial concerns with their own eager pursuit of expanded personal opportunity in America's culture industries reflected the dilemmas of black capitalists and the burgeoning black middle class in what historian Clayborne Carson has dubbed the "post-revolutionary era".[2]

The Movement's courting of soul singers really began in earnest around the mid 1960s. In January 1965, a meeting of CORE's special steering committee debated whether it should devote more attention to fundraising within the black community as a means to alleviate the organization's worsening debt. Traditionally, CORE had preferred to tap more bountiful white resources, but Eva Levy suggested that if the organization was serious about bidding for scarce black dollars, "rock and roll" entertainers might be one avenue to explore. Ten months later nothing much had been done to pursue Levy's idea and Alan Gartner admitted that "we have not done anywhere near as well as we hoped" at "fund-raising within the Negro community". Gartner had, however, "begun to make some contacts with entertainers in the R & R and R & B field" and he proudly announced that James Brown had agreed to do a benefit for the CORE chapter in Queens.[3]

The CORE initiative in late 1965 heralded Soul Brother Number One's belated public involvement in Movement-related activities and the following year Roy Wilkins virtually shamed him into endorsing the NAACP from the stage of the Apollo Theatre. Also instrumental in drawing Brown into the Movement's orbit was Donald Warden. In 1962, Warden, a former "Boy Preacher" with a radio ministry in Pittsburgh, established a pioneering Afro-American Association to promote race consciousness among black students at Berkeley, where he was a law student. Two years later, he met Brown and claimed he saw in the singer the potential to become a major positive influence on black youth. "I've always said that the only thing that unites our race is music", Warden explained. And although he "knew many musicians and entertainers who could be used to raise money", until he met Brown he had seen "none with the power and vision to be an Afro leader for young people".[4]

Warden felt that Brown could reach a generation that established civil rights leaders were struggling, or neglecting, to reach. "We said, 'you got to help us 'cause if you don't we can hang it up. We've never heard Martin Luther King come on television and talk to the race. Everytime he comes on television he's talking to white people'". Warden wanted Brown to "assume no white people exist", and talk to black kids about staying in school "as you talk to your family . . . you're just trying to encourage your own family".[5]

In 1966, apparently at Warden's suggestion, Brown made a tour of the ghetto areas of San Francisco counselling black kids to stay in school. Shortly thereafter he released his first explicit "message" song, "Don't be a drop out". It was a thoroughly conservative endorsement of the American system, which urged kids to get an education so that they could enjoy the opportunities which Brown and his political mentor, vice-president Hubert Humphrey, believed America now offered all its qualified citizens. According to Warden, this was "the first time someone had used the cultural music of our race, and big beat and hip language, to get through to the kids. And also to the parents. James has been successful in direction of the young and old in the pursuit of educational excellence".[6]

Brown's next foray into social commentary was the patriotic "America is my home". The song was released in June 1968, just before Brown went on a government-sponsored tour to entertain troops in Vietnam. If "Don't be a drop out" smacked of the establishment, this was even more conciliatory. It was certainly not quite the audacious political coming-out for which many black nationalists had hoped. Imamu Amiri Baraka dismissed "America is my home" for possessing only the surface texture of black culture and art, not its inner spirit. The song, Baraka claimed, "was an example of Afro-American culture, an R&B song for sure, but it did not have the consciousness of Black, so it could not be called Black. To sing lies about America is not beneficial to the Black Nation, therefore, it's not conscious of Blackness". Worse still followed in March 1968, when Brown dismissed the wearing of natural, unprocessed hair as an irrelevant symbol of racial pride. "Hair doesn't make the man", Brown insisted in response to criticisms of his own precious conk. "I know I'm blacker in my heart than any man", he insisted. And, of course, in a sense his songs had proudly worn a metaphorical musical afro for years before he finally succumbed to public pressure and allowed his artificially relaxed coiffure to coil into a natural.[7]

Around the same time, in August 1968, Brown recorded "Say it loud, I'm black and I'm proud". Although he later revealed that he had actually used mainly Asian and white children on the chorus, this was more what the militants had in mind: a song explicitly extolling black pride and geared to raising racial consciousness. Moreover, beyond his ever funkier and more forthright art, Brown was becoming more publicly supportive of a diverse range of Movement-related activities. In the summer of 1966, he had flown to James Meredith's bedside when the civil rights campaigner was felled by a sniper in Mississippi. The following year he joined Harry Belafonte and Joan Baez for some of the 1967 "Stars for freedom" shows on behalf of the SCLC. He also did some benefits for SNCC, and in the early 1970s turned out alongside Julian Bond and John Lewis to publicize various voter registration drives in the South.[8]

By the late 1960s and early 1970s black politicians and activists like Julian Bond (left) could expect much greater public support from black celebrities than had been the case a decade earlier. Here Bond is shown with James Brown promoting a voter registration drive.

At the end of 1968, Brown organized his own Operation Black Pride, dressed himself up as Santa Claus, and personally distributed certificates which entitled 3,000 New York ghetto residents to a free Christmas meal. While cynics might note that this well-publicized philanthropy conveniently coincided with the release of Brown's "Santa go straight to the ghetto" single, and *A Soulful Christmas* album, (God)Father Christmas did cancel an estimated $175,000 worth of shows to do Movement benefits during the year. "I may not do as much as some other individuals who have made it big", Brown admitted with impressive candour. "But you can bet your life that I'm doing the best I can . . . I owe it to the black community to help provide scholarships, to help children stay in school, to help equip playgrounds and recreation centers, and to keep kids off the street".[9]

Despite this greater artistic and personal involvement in the freedom struggle, however, Brown always remained something of a frustrating enigma to many black power activists. Larry Neal recalled meetings with other members of the flourishing Black Arts Movement where they would ponder, "Suppose James Brown had consciousness . . . It was like saying, 'Suppose James Brown read Fanon'". They were to be permanently disappointed.

Black activists coveted the power, prestige and influence of a man whose presence could apparently stop major riots in Boston and Atlanta in the wake of Martin Luther King's murder. Yet they rarely approved of his un-flinching patriotism and enduring faith in a capitalist system which, in his view, had enabled him to rise from the meanest rural poverty and racial oppression to boast earnings and assets worth millions of dollars by the early 1970s. What the radicals usually failed to appreciate was that it was this conspicuous material success, the Lear jets and limousines, the busi-nesses and bulging bank account, which combined with his music to fix Brown's unique place in black American consciousness. "I'm no leader of no black community", he later explained. "I'm a role model, but I don't lead".[10]

Brown had made his position on black capitalism and black power clear enough shortly after the release of "Say it loud". He announced that he was "totally committed to black power, the kind that is achieved not through the muzzle of a rifle but through education and economic leverage". Brown endorsed black capitalism as a means to inspire and rejuvenate black soci-ety, without ever seriously contemplating the possible relationship between capitalism and the operation of modern American race relations.[11]

Like many successful self-made men, Brown never lost that fierce inde-pendence and, at times, ruthlessness which had enabled him to succeed against all the odds in the first place. As trombonist Fred Wesley told Cynthia Rose, Brown's capricious and often bruising personality was forged in his early experiences of acute poverty, racism and struggle. "James was bossy and paranoid . . . I couldn't understand the way he treated his band, why he was so *evil* . . . It was ridiculous that somebody of his power and popularity could be so insecure. But later on, I got to understand. He had to have been like that just to stay alive".[12]

As a result of his own capacity not just to stay alive but to prosper, Brown had a "bootstrap" mentality which sat uneasily with his periodic insistence that blacks were still being denied equal opportunities, and brought him perilously close to the classic conservative position of blaming the victims of structural and habitual racism for their own distress. "Opportun-ities today are much better", Brown announced in 1971, "but opportun-ities are made. They just don't open up by themselves. A lot of black kids don't get anywhere because they never try". This belief that with hard work, thrift and proper application all things were now possible for blacks in America, made "America is my home" less the exercise in bad faith which Baraka claimed, and more a legitimate expression of one aspect of Brown's, and mass black, consciousness. During the 1972 presidential cam-paign, those same priorities also made Brown's support for Richard Nixon – that other great advocate of black capitalism as black deliverance – quite logical.[13]

Out of the shadows: Motown joins the Movement

What with CORE and the NAACP pushing hard for James Brown's support, and persistent rumours that a rather less subtle form of pressure from the Black Panthers had actually prompted him to begin writing songs like "Say it loud", Brown's new political engagement was symptomatic of an era in which civil rights and black power groups made a much more concerted effort to recruit soul stars. There were two major reasons for this change. The first had to do with finances; the second with new notions about the role black music and culture might play in the freedom movement.[14]

As white liberal support and financial help for an increasingly militant Movement dwindled, there was a growing dependency on black funding, which in turn encouraged a more vigorous courtship of black stars who could help tap that meagre resource. At the SCLC, Stanley Levison was already bemoaning the decline in white funding by late 1966. That summer's Chicago campaign had revealed continued northern resistance to real social equality for blacks, and widespread unwillingness on the part of whites to support a radical struggle to realize that goal. As a consequence, when Jesse Jackson and his SCLC-sponsored Operation Breadbasket sought to sustain the Chicago struggle after Martin Luther King's departure, Levison noted – with only slight exaggeration – that "This is the first time the negro community has been asked to support a civil rights movement".[15]

Constantly searching for new methods of generating funds, King and Levison even briefly considered a proposal by millionaire benefactor Dick Russell that the SCLC should join him as joint owners of a record and tape retail company. Certainly, crossover stars like Harry Belafonte, and white folkies like Joan Baez, who had for so many years spearheaded the SCLC's celebrity fundraising efforts, were simply no longer so effective. King and Levison were alarmed that the 1967 Belafonte-Baez "Stars for freedom" shows struggled to break even, except in Chicago. A Belafonte house party in March 1968 was similarly disappointing, raising nowhere near the projected $15,000 to $20,000.[16]

Soul, by contrast, appeared to offer a better conduit to black cash and publicity. Moreover, with political alignment clearly not sounding a commercial death-knell, many more soul stars and black music entrepreneurs seemed willing to donate time, energy and money to the Movement. "It was", Junius Griffin recalled wryly, "a match made for justice – both sides appreciated huge audiences".[17]

Griffin himself was partly responsible for the steady increase in Motown's level of public engagement in Movement-related activities during the decade after Selma. In the summer of 1966, while still the SCLC's director of publicity, Griffin had successfully pestered Motown into allowing Stevie Wonder to join B.B. King and the Red Sanders Orchestra for a benefit concert at Soldier Field in support of the Chicago movement. As a consequence of his work on this show, Griffin came to the attention of Esther Gordy, who eventually persuaded her brother to hire him in May 1967. Berry Gordy later described Griffin as "passionate, deeply committed to the civil rights movement. Junius was our link to the black community and theirs to us". According to Gordy, Griffin, lawyer George Schiffer and Ewart Abner, who joined Motown as director of ITMI after the demise of Vee Jay, were the "most outspoken at Motown when it came to social causes". Together, they helped to ease the label in the direction of more conspicuous Movement-related activities.[18]

Shortly after Martin Luther King's death, it was Griffin who, with Gordy's blessing, hastily arranged for leading Motown acts to play a major bene-fit for the SCLC and the Poor People's Campaign in Atlanta. Griffin also ensured that Motown outpaced the competition to be first in the stores with a posthumous compilation of King's greatest speeches, *Free At Last*. Griffin assured Levison that Gordy was "not concerned with how the proceeds should be handled", or with "the programmatical part of it but with SCLC getting as much money out of the thing" as possible. According to Griffin, Gordy had already assured Ralph Abernathy, King's successor as president of the SCLC, that "if he needs money a cheque will be forthcoming. He can advance him as much money as he wants to keep going". Griffin was even "getting some funds to be sure [Abernathy] has the right kind of clothes". Unfortunately, it would have taken more than a decent suit to convert Abernathy, a woefully inefficient administrator and thoroughly vainglorious man, into a credible leader of the bereaved SCLC.[19]

Even amid this genuine altruism and concern to preserve and extend King's legacy, Gordy's entrepreneurial instincts remained unimpaired. All he wanted out of the arrangement with the SCLC for *Free At Last* was an assurance that Motown had exclusive rights to produce the official mem-orial album. "One thing has to be made clear right away to the public and everyone else", Griffin explained to Levison: "that one recording company is going to handle this thing". In terms of enhancing Motown's reputation as an engaged, socially responsible black enterprise, there were obvious advant-ages in seeking this exclusive sanction from the SCLC and King's heirs, not least from Coretta Scott King, who was in the process of being canonized for her choice of husband. Yet the arrangement also suited Levison and others who were understandably concerned about controlling the rash of memorabilia which King's death generated, or, as Levison said, making sure that his widow and the SCLC got "at least something out of them".[20]

Motown songwriting and production stalwart Mickey Stevenson claimed that "Motown was a very strong backer of Martin Luther King's total pro-gram" and the King connection certainly endured after the civil rights leader's death. Having missed out on the 1963 March on Washington, in June 1968 Gordy joined other celebrities, including Sammy Davis, Sidney Poitier, Jerry

Butler, Marlon Brando and Paul Newman, for a Solidarity Day as part of the Poor People's Campaign in Washington. On the first anniversary of King's assassination, he had his acts play benefit concerts around the country and, perhaps even more astonishing given Gordy's notoriously strict business regimen, gave all other Motown employees a day's paid leave.[21]

In 1969, Gordy also allowed Diana Ross and the Supremes to join Sammy Davis, Nancy Wilson, Bill Cosby, Dick Gregory and Diahann Carroll in publicly endorsing a bill presented by black Michigan congressman John Conyers, calling for King's birthday to be made a public holiday. When the King holiday was finally secured in 1983, Motown – and especially Stevie Wonder – was again at the forefront of the campaign. By that time Gordy had also contributed funds to the founding of the Martin Luther King Jr Center for Non violent Social Change in Atlanta, while in the 1990s, Gordy has been one of the sponsors of the Martin Luther King papers project based at Stanford University.[22]

Throughout the late 1960s and early 1970s, Berry Gordy's personal ambitions and business priorities often danced an awkward sort of dance with his wider concerns for black justice, power and opportunity in America. For a while he devoted considerable energy to trying to keep the demands of capitalism, conscience and community in some kind of step, never letting the one tread all over the needs of the other. When push came to shove, however, there was seldom any doubt where his priorities lay.

Gordy, the most successful black entrepreneur of his generation and a living embodiment of black integrationist aspirations, was always reluctant to allow his artists to embrace potentially controversial subjects or publicly espouse causes which might jeopardize their white audience. This basic conservatism and caution persisted even in Motown's most activist phase during the black power era. When the Jackson Five emerged as the label's hottest property in the late 1960s and 1970s with massive crossover hits like "I want you back" and "ABC", Gordy was paranoid that the young group might somehow appear too black or too militant and alienate their white audience. After one interviewer asked the brothers if their impressive afro hairdos "had something to do with Black Power", Gordy promptly banned discussion of any political matters – and drugs – in all future press conferences.[23]

Typically, Gordy had accepted more social commentary in Motown recordings, alongside more progressive sounds and a new attitude towards making albums, only when he was convinced that they would increase sales and street credibility. Moreover, it is important to recognize that the musical and lyrical innovations of the Temptations, Stevie Wonder and Marvin Gaye were sanctioned at a time when the classic Motown sound was losing its pre-eminence in the market place to white rock, southern soul, and the new black funk-rock-soul fusions. In other words, Motown's politicization was always a commercial as well as a political and racial decision, with Gordy following, rather than leading, broader social and cultural trends.

Another vinyl initiative which bespoke Gordy's new, public social conscience was the creation of the Black Forum subsidiary, which opened in October 1970 with a collection of Martin Luther King's anti-Vietnam speeches, *Why I Oppose the War*. The label subsequently became an outlet for recordings by both black political nationalists, including the Black Panthers' Deputy Minister of Information and subsequent chair, Elaine Brown, and cultural nationalists like Larry Neal and Imamu Amiri Baraka. At a time when the Panthers and Ron Karenga's US were exchanging bullets as well as verbal insults on the west coast in their debates over the proper strategies for black liberation, at least political and cultural nationalists could co-exist peacefully on Black Forum, which survived a couple of years before poor sales prompted Gordy to close it.[24]

As part of the general expansion of Gordy's financial support for certain individuals, organizations and causes through corporate and private donations, benefit concerts and public endorsements, some of the proceeds from Black Forum releases went directly to the Martin Luther King Jr Memorial Fund Foundation and the SCLC. Given the distinctly ambivalent attitude to the nonviolent tactics and integrationist goals of the SCLC expressed by many of the contributors to the Black Forum releases, this disbursement of royalties was not without its irony. It did, however, suit Motown's purposes rather well, allowing the label to flirt with black radicalism and acquire a patina of militancy, while actually offering much more formal and tangible – which is to say financial – support to what were perceived as more moderate civil rights groups and black initiatives.

Certainly, Motown contributed to the mayoralty campaigns which ushered in a new era of black electoral politics in the North during the late 1960s and early 1970s. It supported Richard Hatcher in Gary, Indiana, the hometown of the Jackson Five, who performed with Gladys Knight and the Pips, Shorty Long and Motown's white Canadian soul band, Bobby Taylor and the Vancouvers, in a benefit concert at Gary's Gilroy Stadium. In Newark, Stevie Wonder, the Supremes and recent Motown acquisition Chuck Jackson, joined other black celebrities – and even some of the dwindling band of white celebrity activists, like Dustin Hoffman – in the campaign Imamu Amiri Baraka organized to raise money and support for Kenneth Gibson. After Gibson's triumph, the Supremes returned in December 1971 and performed another benefit concert, swaddled in African costumes and spouting the odd phrase of Swahili much to the delight of an audience rejoicing in its new Afrocentric identity.[25]

Apart from providing promotional and financial support for the SCLC and black politicians, other recipients of Gordy's largesse included the NAACP and its Legal Defense and Education Fund, the United Negro College Fund, the National Association for Sickle Cell Diseases, the Afro-American Heritage Association, the Urban League, Howard University, and boxer Sugar Ray Robinson's Youth Foundation. These grants were usually administered in amounts of less than $1,000 and rarely more than $10,000 through the Gordy Foundation Inc., although they were reputedly supplemented on occasions by much larger personal contributions. Again, it is striking that almost all of this money went to decidedly respectable, moderate groups and organizations. Gordy made no secret of his essential conservatism when it came to strategies for black protest. He even defended the unfashionable workhorse of the black struggle, the legalistic NAACP, from radicals who complained that it "had done too little". Gordy insisted that "if it hadn't been for them we wouldn't have come this far".[26]

As befitted a corporation suffused with an integrationist ethic, not all the recipients of Motown's generosity were black. Detroit's East Catholic High School, the National Jewish Hospital in Denver, the Detroit Symphony Orchestra and the Los Angeles International Film Exposition were among the beneficiaries. The label also supported liberal white Democratic Party candidates and endorsed coalition, rather than separatist, politics. As early as June 1965, the Supremes had contributed to a CBS television special promoting Lyndon Johnson and his War on Poverty. Again, this was a shrewd choice of political allegiance, since by endorsing a presidential social welfare programme which just happened to greatly benefit blacks, the label demonstrated its social concerns, but avoided rigid identification with exclusively black issues.[27]

A year later, the same group graced a presidential fundraiser in Las Vegas for Lyndon Johnson and Hubert Humphrey, who the label eventually endorsed for the presidency in 1968 after the murder of Robert Kennedy. The company also contributed to both the Humphrey Institute in St Paul, Minnesota and the Robert F. Kennedy Memorial in Washington, while proceeds from a $1,000-a-plate fundraising concert by Diana Ross and the Supremes in April 1969 were used to defray some of Kennedy's outstanding political debts. The Kennedy connection continued when Edward attended a June 1969 benefit concert by the Temptations on behalf of Michigan's white Democratic senator Philip Hart.[28]

This all amounted to a significant contribution to the financing and promotion of the mainstream civil rights movement and what remained of its liberal allies during the late 1960s and early 1970s. Yet Gordy never allowed these new racial and political concerns to compromise his spirited quest for an ever larger share of the white market. There was no retreat to the ghetto for Gordy; no real ideological connection with the growing parochialism and insularity of much black cultural, economic and political nationalism. Indeed, if at one level Gordy's mission was to promote an unmistakably black American music in the mainstream, on another level it was just to compete in that mainstream successfully, irrespective of the product – and that was a far more radical gesture within the context of America's continued racial compartmentalization. In the heart of the black pride and consciousness era, Motown signed and recorded a succession of white artists, including Kiki Dee, Chris Clark and Crystal Mansion. Gordy also established the rock-oriented Rare Earth and MoWest labels, and the highly successful country subsidiary, Melodyland, all of which were conceived initially to produce white acts for a primarily white audience.[29]

At the same time, Gordy continued to push his established stars away from the black theatres and clubs, towards the showbusiness mainstream. Between the Supremes' breakthrough appearance at the Las Vegas Copacabana Club in May 1965 and Stevie Wonder's date at the New York Copa in March 1970, eight Motown artists had headlined at these shrines of middle-American wealth and blue-rinse respectability. Motown acts also became more visible to a national audience via television. While many black artists struggled for exposure, there were regular spots for Motown performers on prestigious network shows hosted by Ed Sullivan, Dinah Shore and Mike Douglas. Gordy cultivated an especially close relationship with NBC. In January 1968, the network even broadcast an episode of *Tarzan* – the most watched in the series' history – in which the Supremes played three nuns. The following April, NBC provided Diana Ross with her first solo appearance on the *Dinah Shore Show*. Marvin Gaye's duet with Tammi Terrell on a July 1967 television commercial for Coke represented another breakthrough into a previously white-dominated field. That same month, Gordy signed a lucrative distribution deal with the mail-order Columbia Record Club, expressly for the purpose of reaching the white market even more efficiently.[30]

At a time when the relationship between corporate capitalism, racism and systemic inequalities in American society was the subject of intense scrutiny among many black power activists, the cosy relationship between Gordy, Motown and major white corporations like Coca-Cola and NBC was sometimes viewed suspiciously. When, in July 1967, the Four Tops and Supremes were scheduled to play Central Park under contract to the Schaefer Beer Company, death threats from black militants led to a major security operation. That same month, the worst of all the 1960s racial uprisings forced the temporary closure of Motown's offices on Detroit's West Grand Boulevard. Allegedly following an anonymous phone call threatening that "Motown will burn by Halloween", the company decided to move, first to a more salubrious part of Detroit and then, in 1972, to Los Angeles, where Gordy had spent increasingly long periods since the mid 1960s.[31]

The move westwards was perfectly justified in terms of Motown's new interest in film and television as manifested in the motion pictures *Lady Sings the Blues* and *Mahogany*, a succession of Motown television specials, and the Jackson Five's animated television series. Gordy was head of an ambitious, rapidly diversifying entertainment corporation and naturally wanted to be nearer the main levers of media power and showbusiness influence. Nevertheless, Motown's abandonment of its neighbourhood roots in pursuit of profit simply intensified black radical and white critical resentment of a company whose major sin was to pursue the American Dream with relentless enthusiasm, verve and extraordinary success.

Gordy was undaunted by accusations that he was selling out black America and traducing its culture. He took comfort from the fact that blacks continued to buy Motown records in huge numbers throughout the black power era. Indeed, they seemed considerably more impressed by his conspicuous material success and relative power in a white-controlled industry than bothered about his refusal to pay lip service to voguish ideas of racial, political, cultural or economic correctness. Like James Brown and most black capitalists and professionals, Gordy firmly believed that the creation of personal wealth and attainment of mainstream success *was* a form of progressive racial politics, and of black economic and cultural leadership. Paradoxically, however, this sometimes required a ruthless disregard, or subordination, of racial loyalties and ultimately helped to legitimize a socio-economic system in which racism flourished and exploitation was deeply embedded.

Certainly, Gordy did not hesitate to terminate his dealings with black booking agencies like Henry Wynne's Supersonic Attractions in favour of white tour operators like International Creative Management and the William Morris Agency who were better placed to book Motown artists into plush white venues. Moreover, at a time when NATRA and other black media and civil rights groups were campaigning for greater black managerial opportunities within the recording and related industries, he continued to hire white executives and professionals to key strategic positions, simply because they would help secure better access to the white market. By 1970 four of Motown's eight executive vice-presidents were white. When in 1974 another white, Rob Cohen, was appointed creative vice-president of the newly consolidated Motown Industries, his brief was to find "fresh new approaches with the broadest possible appeal to the largest potential audience".[52]

For Gordy, then, black power was a worthy goal, but one which he felt must necessarily be pursued pragmatically, within the context of superior white economic, political, legal and police power. Some of these beliefs brought him close to Jesse Jackson, who also had little time for fanciful notions of black economic and political separatism. Instead, Jackson sought better black opportunities and power within the established political and corporate structure, and more investment from existing corporations in the development of black-owned businesses and financial institutions. In October 1969, Motown supplied the Four Tops, Originals, Marvin Gaye, and Martha and the Vandellas to perform in support of the first Black Business and Cultural Exposition in Chicago, a celebration of black capitalism with a conscience organized under the auspices of Operation Breadbasket. Jackson warmly thanked Gordy, who also sent a "galaxy of Motown stars" to subsequent expositions, for his support. "Motown's presence here establishes beyond a doubt that you are personally committed to the struggle for social justice and that Motown, an economic corporate giant, also has a corporate social conscience", said Jackson.[33]

In September 1971, Gordy also supported the launch of Jackson's new organization, People United to Save Humanity (PUSH). As part of PUSH's inaugural sessions in Chicago, Gordy delivered an address to the annual National Businessmen's Breakfast which sounded the unmistakable note of self-interest at the heart of his brand of black capitalism. "I have been fortunate to be able to provide opportunities for young people", he explained. "Opportunities are supposed to knock once in a lifetime, but too often we have to knock for an opportunity. The first obligation we (as black businessmen) have is to ourselves and our own employees, the second is to create opportunities for others". It was a sense of priorities Gordy shared with most entrepreneurial capitalists.[34]

Aretha Franklin, Joe Tex and Wattstax

James Brown and the Motown acts were hardly the only soul performers to forge a closer relationship with various strands of organized black protest and community activism in the late 1960s and early 1970s. Indeed, what had once been exceptional became routine and occasionally perfunctory as labels and artists pledged various forms of artistic, moral and financial support to the black cause. Sometimes those contributions were far from negligible in monetary terms. In June 1968, for example, Atlantic Records sponsored a major benefit concert which – although Stanley Levison had to leave after ten minutes because he could not stand the noise – raised $110,000, the bulk of which was split between the Martin Luther King Jr Memorial Fund ($65,000) and the increasingly radical NATRA ($35,000).[35]

The headliner at the Atlantic benefit was Aretha Franklin and her visible presence in and around the Movement increased dramatically in the late 1960s. Franklin's father, C.L. Franklin, was pastor of Detroit's New Bethel Baptist Church and himself something of a radio and recording celebrity. He was also a good friend of Martin Luther King and the civil rights leader used that personal connection to draw Franklin into Movement work. The exact nature and extent of her contribution remains unclear since, as Jerry Wexler recalled, "She wouldn't talk about it – this was private". According to Wexler, however, "She devoted an enormous piece of her life to Martin Luther King, yet she never became merely a sloganeer or polemicist. She acted out of the purest wellsprings of faith and belief".[36]

Stanley Wise certainly remembered Aretha, like Ray Charles, boosting the morale of SNCC workers by arranging for them to attend her concerts for free. "And she'd always have everybody stand up and she'd sing something to us . . . Just very, very personal things". In late 1967 she appeared on some of the "Stars for freedom" dates for the SCLC, and joined Sidney Poitier as the guest performer at the organization's tenth anniversary celebrations in Atlanta. In February 1968, in her hometown of Detroit, Martin Luther King presented Franklin with a special award for her Movement work. It was an expression of genuine gratitude which also did nothing to harm the SCLC's credentials among her legions of fans. Two months later Franklin sang a transcendent version of Thomas Dorsey's gospel classic "Precious Lord, take my hand" at King's funeral.[37]

In the early 1970s, Joe Tex embarked on a rather different form of public activism. In 1972, in the wake of his biggest ever crossover success with "I gotcha", Joe Tex changed his name to Joseph Hazziez and began touring the country on behalf of Elijah Muhammad's Black Muslims. Tex preached a message of black separatism born of profound disillusionment with white America. "Boss is not going to do anything for us", he warned students at Greensboro A&T; blacks were going to have to do it for themselves. The first step, Tex explained, was to stop all fraternization with whites and make sure blacks only bred with other blacks. Racial purity was the first step to racial liberation.[38]

According to the student newspaper, Tex's appearance at A&T was "greeted with what appeared to be little genuine interest". It was, the paper suggested, indicative of an era of "Revolutionary consciousness", coupled with "regressive apathy" when it came to actual participation in any organized struggle. Earlier visits to the home of the Greensboro sit-ins by John Lewis and Julian Bond had also failed to stimulate much enthusiasm for the hard graft of voter registration work. Meanwhile, the paper noted, at a talent show on the evening of the Tex visit "the school auditorium was jam-packed with a capacity crowd of students, screaming, stamping, clapping, and completely devoid of any apathy whatsoever". There was a sense, the paper suggested, that black popular culture was becoming a surrogate, rather than the soundtrack, for a coherent mass movement of liberation.[39]

One of A&T's most famous alumni was Jesse Jackson, who acted as a sort of lightning rod for many of soul's most interesting political initiatives in early 1970s. For a while Jackson's Operation Breadbasket even had its own house band in Chicago. In a sign of those macho times, the group – which featured Sam and Dave's old horn section and the molasses vocals of future solo star Jeffrey Osborne – was originally called Love Men Limited. They changed this to Love Ltd., and eventually became quite successful as L.T.D., enjoying a run of light jazz-funk crossover hits in the mid 1970s, most notably "(Everytime I turn around) Back in love again". In 1970, Operation Breadbasket had also benefited from the SCLC's collaboration with the Stax subsidiary Pride, in its "Right on" campaign. Sympathetic black deejays were solicited to play and promote Kim Weston's soulful version of James Weldon Johnson's venerable "black national anthem", "Lift ev'ry voice and sing", with the proceeds from sales channelled to Operation Breadbasket.[40]

Unable to work with Ralph Abernathy, and fired with equal intensity by fierce personal ambition and a deep sense of mission, Jackson left Operation Breadbasket to launch PUSH in mid 1971. There his rare gift for – and obvious delight in – courting celebrities and publicity ensured that the organization received considerable support from the world of soul. In addition to Motown's initial endorsement, PUSH was especially aided by its public association with the August 1972 Wattstax Festival in Los Angeles. On a number of levels, the politics, economics, iconography, artistry and almost sacramental ritualism of that festival vividly illustrated the relationship between Rhythm and Blues, black consciousness, corporate commerce and the freedom struggle in the heart of the black power era.

The racial economics of Wattstax were complex. The artists performing were all black. All were from Stax or its subsidiaries. All performed free of charge. The Schlitz Brewery Co. meanwhile underwrote the hire of the Memorial Coliseum venue and helped to subsidize tickets so that they cost the 90,000 or more people who attended just one dollar. A predominantly black crew filmed the event for general distribution by Columbia Pictures. Eventually, about $100,000 was collected from the proceeds of the concert itself, the motion picture, and two double-album record sets which Stax released with the quasi-religious subtitle, *The Living Word*. This money was divided between PUSH, the Watts Summer Festival Fund, the Martin Luther King Jr Hospital in Watts, and the Sickle Cell Anemia Foundation.[41]

Nelson George, doggedly searching for examples of a time when black economic power was effectively harnessed to an activist mentality and a deep sense of communal responsibility, has celebrated Wattstax as "a symbol of black self-sufficiency". In fact, Wattstax was a conspicuous example of continued black economic dependency, even as it affirmed the capacity of black popular culture to transcend the strict economics and politics of its production and realize a valuable and sustaining social role. At Wattstax, fundraising for black community projects and the celebration of what Jesse Jackson, who gave the benediction at the festival, termed black "Somebodiness", depended on funding from white corporations (Columbia Pictures and Schlitz), and a white-owned record company (Stax) which was at the time largely bankrolled by white loans from the Union Planters National Bank, Deutsche Grammophon and Columbia (CBS).[42]

The main players – Stax, Schlitz and Jackson – all became involved from some measure of self-interest. "This sort of all-star benefit is not so humanitarian as to be entirely without profit", admitted Stax vice-president Larry Shaw. "And it's a rare opportunity that lets you do something corporately valuable without being guilty of exploitation". This was the crux of enlightened black capitalism: it meant doing something for the community, as long as it did not jeopardize, and would ideally improve, economic prospects. Wattstax, as concert, movie and album, offered Stax wide exposure for its artists and, just as importantly in an era of heightened black consciousness, the prestige of having conspicuously aided a number of worthy black projects.[43]

For Jackson, who a couple of years before Wattstax had actually recorded several albums for Pride, billed as The Country Preacher, Wattstax provided both funds for PUSH and a conspicuous public occasion on which to press his claims to national black leadership. For Schlitz president Robert Urhlein, it provided a convenient opportunity to publicize the company's reconciliation with Jackson, who had previously organized a boycott of the company's products in an effort to secure more black jobs and greater patronage of black financial and manufacturing companies. On 20 August 1972, the opening day of the festival, Jackson publicly accepted an undertaking from the brewing giant to provide 286 new black jobs, ranging from unskilled to management level, and to redirect $37 million in contracts, insurance and investments to black firms and financial institutions. In the context of this breakthrough, Schlitz's involvement in Wattstax reflected its concern to recapture and extend its share of the black market.[44]

The interplay of these economic and racial, personal and corporate, selfish and altruistic agendas critically shaped the staging and marketing of Wattstax. Yet appreciating the complex politics of its production does not exhaust its historical significance or contemporary meaning. In the Coliseum, or in the theatres where the movie played, or wherever the records were heard, the power of the performances and the creative engagement of these multiple audiences enabled Wattstax to succeed in its avowed intention of commemorating the seventh anniversary of the Watts uprising in a positive celebration of black unity and cultural pride.

The Reverend Jackson, resplendent in a brightly coloured striped dashiki and proudly sporting a formidable afro, opened the proceedings and set the tone of the Festival:

This is a beautiful day. It is a new day. It is a day of black awareness. It is a day of black people taking care of black people's business. It is beautiful that the Stax record company has come out [of the] South to talk about liberation through music and lyrics. Stax record company is located in Memphis, Tennessee, on the banks of the Mississippi River and it has come to Los Angeles on the banks of the Pacific river (sic) still talking about liberation.

Today on this programme you gonna hear gospel and rhythm and blues music, and jazz. All those are just labels. We all know all our people got soul. Our experience determines the texture, the taste and the sound of our soul. So whether it's Jimmy Jones singing "Somebody bigger than you and I", or the Staple Singers singing "Uncloudy day", or Black Moses singing "I stand accused", all of us are one people – singing our music, popping our fingers and doing our thing. . . .[45]

As Jackson pointed out, the musical programme at Wattstax ran the gamut of black styles from jazz, through blues, to gospel and soul. Consequently, there were some peculiar hybrids and juxtapositions of nominally sacred and secular artists and materials. Indeed, Wattstax offered further evidence that the old distinctions between the sacred and secular spheres in black American culture had largely disappeared. Carla Thomas opened her set with an unabashed celebration of the pleasures of the flesh in "I like what you're doing (to me)", but concluded it with her own testimony to the centrality of God in her life, "I have a God who loves me", apparently seeing no contradiction. Secular Stax soulmen like William Bell, Eddie Floyd, Frederick Knight and the Temprees joined gospel singer Jimmy Jones for a spirited, if shambolic, rendition of "Old time religion". The Emotions, a female vocal group who alternately purred like the Supremes and roared like the Ward Sisters, came closest to breaking up the house with an intensely moving performance of "Peace be still".

Apart from the gospel songs and spirituals which referred explicitly to God or Jesus, inspirational or message songs abounded on the programme, bridging the sacred and secular divide with a blend of pride, optimism, determination and righteous indignation which had become fairly ubiquitous in soul lyrics of the period. The Staple Singers, stalwarts of a swampy rural gospel tradition from the mid 1950s until they crossed over to the secular world of Stax in 1967, summed up the whole spirit of the Festival, indeed a central impulse of soul and the black liberation movement, with "Respect yourself" and "I like the things about me (That I once despised)". On the latter, Pops Staple brought down the volume and engaged in a little downhome sermonizing on the subjects of equality, dignity and unity which have also been the traditional keynotes of black religion. "We are somebody!", he insisted, echoing Jackson's Black Litany. "No nationality could go through what we been through and survive like the black people".

At Wattstax, the presence of Isaac Hayes, the Black Moses, dominated proceedings. When, during his sermonette, Pops Staple ran through his list of great black men in history, Hayes was there right next to George Washington Carver. Jesse Jackson, who like all good preacher-performers knew how to work his audience, was also careful to mention Hayes in his opening remarks. When he did, a huge roar rose from the crowd.

Hayes had originally been a writer, producer and session musician at Stax. In partnership with David Porter he wrote and produced some of the most memorable no-nonsense soul of the 1960s, co-authoring songs like "Soul man" and "Hold on, I'm coming" for Sam and Dave, and "B-A-B-Y" for Carla Thomas. After a moderate success with *Presenting Isaac Hayes*, Hayes emerged as a star in his own right in 1969 with the album *Hot Buttered Soul*, a project undertaken to fulfil one of Al Bell's more extravagant publicity campaigns whereby Stax was to release an album by every artist on its roster during the month of May. Hayes' album slipped out on

Isaac Hayes (left) and Jesse Jackson shared the stage at the 1972 Wattstax Festival in Los Angeles.

the Enterprise subsidiary alongside the other 26. It featured just four tracks, the shortest of which was well over five minutes, the longest some eighteen minutes. This should have been the kiss of death for any commercial aspirations Hayes or Stax may have harboured. Black-oriented radio had yet to develop a counterpart to those progressive FM rock stations which regularly played lengthy album tracks, while the black record market was still heavily singles-based. Again, the black audience proved itself no respecter of easy commercial categorizations as the album went triple platinum, topping both the soul and jazz charts.

Hayes' writing and production for other artists had furnished quintessential southern soul, characterized by sharp, punchy rhythm tracks, with clipped guitar figures, percussive piano and driving horns, all topped with the call and response vocal strategies of gospel. His solo work was very different. On *Hot Buttered Soul* and the albums which followed, Hayes developed a style of lush, symphonic soul which incorporated expansive and expensive string orchestrations courtesy of the Memphis Symphony Orchestra. "In high school music appreciation, I'd heard Bach, Beethoven, Greig, Debussy and, damn, they were really doing some wonderful things", Hayes recalled. He combined these soaring strings with the more traditional instruments of southern soul and an interest in the latest technological innovations, like the wah-wah pedal which percolated the guitar sound of his biggest hit, "Shaft".[46]

Above this richly textured sound Hayes' deep, resonant, ultra-cool voice was smeared sensuously across the production like vocal honey. His singing rarely meandered far from his speaking tones and he never engaged in the testifying, full-throated emotionalism of the other Stax performers. Nevertheless, as with the most fervent exhorters of gospel and soul, part of his appeal depended on the projection of honesty and truth. His voice was so highly miked that you could actually hear the sound of his breathing, and like the greatest of soul's deep balladeers Hayes transmitted conviction and emotion by the sheer immanent presence of his voice. There was something profoundly confessional about it all. On record he was unhurried when the funk began to fly, unbowed as he unravelled his personal tales of love and deceit, and unabashed as he sought some kind of spiritual rejuvenation through immersion in the pleasures of the flesh and the existential possibilities of the body.

Aside from his music, religious symbolism, commerce, politics, spectacle and music merged in the construction of Hayes' public persona. At Wattstax, he appeared with his head shaven, eyes hidden behind a pair of perfectly impenetrable dark glasses, and sporting a Malcolm X beard. He wore a vest of gold chains, thereby converting the marks of slavery into, on the one hand, a reminder of a distinctive black heritage and the long struggle against oppression, and on the other hand a proud symbol of triumph and material success. He was escorted onto the stage by two huge Harley-Davidson motor cycles, a sort of hip sweet-chariot in which he was no doubt supposed to be carried off to some promised land. Indeed, on the cover of his 1972 album, *Black Moses*, Hayes appeared in biblical robes by the side of what presumably is meant to represent the River Jordan – an image which reappeared in the shot of Stevie Wonder on the sleeve of *Talking Book*. Getting across, making it to the promised land, and the thrill of blacks in motion were still important symbolic touchstones in black popular culture and consciousness.

The image of Hayes as Black Moses, the deliverer from oppression, was reinforced by his own activist credentials. After he had appeared at, and then agreed to appear in, a black drama presentation at Memphis State University in May 1972, a local reporter observed that he seemed to have "a deeper and warmer sense of identity with community goals and endeavours than we usually find in our celebrities". In February 1972, the *Memphis Press-Scimitar* had noted that "it hasn't been merely through his driving music that Hayes has been a driving force in the community. He has served his city well as a civic leader". The paper noted that Hayes was vice-chairman of the Black Knights, an organization formed in the wake of Martin Luther King's assassination to address problems of police brutality, job discrimination and inadequate housing for blacks in Memphis. Through the Knights, the paper reported, Hayes "was instrumental in organizing youth programs and providing Christmas baskets for the needy in the black community", while proceeds from his annual Christmas concert at the Malaco Theater benefited poor black families.[47]

Hayes got involved in many other major and minor examples of community activism and political advocacy. On the grand scale, the Isaac Hayes Foundation was an ambitious project on the lines of the Harry Belafonte Foundation, whose major effort was to help fund an old people's home. At a more personal level, a low-key benefit concert in New Jersey for a local women's organization, coupled with a personal donation, had, in the *Press-Scimitar*'s rather unfortunate phrase, "helped give a leg up to a 6-year-old double amputee" by providing funds to pay for her artificial limbs. Proudly black and righteously angry at the treatment of his people, there was an aura of steely assertion and incipient insurgency about Hayes which made for an interesting combination with his essentially integrationist social vision. On the one hand, Hayes appeared at Hunter College in New York in a benefit for the Soledad Brothers, insisting that "This is where I'm at. I'm not the turn-the-other-cheek kind of person", and aligning himself with the militant wing of black political nationalism. Yet, on the other hand, Hayes was a winner of the NAACP Image Award who often paused to celebrate the interracialism of his audience – "this is beautiful . . . black and white together", he announced from the stage of the Mid-South Coliseum in Memphis.[48]

Hayes' heyday was brief. He was adversely affected by Stax's mid-1970s collapse and had to sue his way out of a contract with the label in September 1974. Unfortunately his own Hot Buttered Soul label did little business and in September 1976 the IRS issued the first of several suits against Hayes demanding payment of overdue taxes. By the end of the year he had filed for bankruptcy, and during 1977 and 1978 all his personal property was auctioned off to pay creditors. A career comprised mostly of bit-parts in television and movies in the late 1970s and 1980s was partially resuscitated with his rediscovery by a generation of hip-hoppers who were fascinated by anything to do with the black power era and blaxploitation movies like *Shaft*.[49]

Ultimately, it is still difficult to get to the heart of Hayes' extraordinary popularity at the start of the 1970s. Partly it had to do with the fact that he helped to provide a new direction for black soul. If lyrically Hayes teetered on the erotic/exploitative precipice when it came to matters of the flesh, his soulful musings complimented the musical and lyrical progressivism of Sly Stone, Donny Hathaway, Marvin Gaye and Stevie Wonder, and encouraged the eclecticism of young black deejays like Frankie Crocker on WBLS-New York who sought to break the stranglehold of three-minute soul songs on black-oriented radio. Hayes' appeal, however, clearly transcended his music. His popularity also derived from the powerful image he projected to a people who have always invested an enormous amount of emotional and creative capital in the construction and veneration of their heroes. Hayes came across as a sort of divinely ordained, unflappably cool, unvanquishable Bad Nigger. In Nixon's America, with the advances of the civil rights era looking decidedly fragile and tragically circumscribed, that was a potent combination.

Class and race, soul and jazz, the Black Panthers
and cultural nationalism

In 1968, Larry Neal described the Black Arts Movement – an eclectic group of black writers, artists and performers dedicated to defining and celebrating a uniquely "black aesthetic" – as the "spiritual sister" of the black power movement. In *New day in Babylon*, historian William Van DeBurg examined this relationship between black culture and other forms of black power politics more closely. Rightly refusing to draw overly rigid distinctions between black cultural nationalists and political or revolutionary nationalists, Van DeBurg demonstrated that black culture often provided much of the common ground for a disparate, and often desperate and fractious, drive for black empowerment. "Ideological enemies may have been opposed to the cultural nationalists' ordering of priorities, but they were not against incorporating cultural elements into their own definitions of black power", Van DeBurg explained. Nobody was going to object to the development of black art forms which stressed the "distinctiveness of African-American culture", extolled the "virtues of black life-styles and values", and promoted "race consciousness, pride, and unity".[50]

This self-conscious embrace of a vibrant black cultural heritage in America was probably the most important achievement and legacy of the black power years – especially if one includes the rapid expansion of black studies programmes designed to explore the historical and cultural co-ordinates of the black American experience. As Clayborne Carson has commented, since the black power movement conspicuously failed in its efforts to "produce greater power for black people", and may even have "led to a decline in the ability of African-Americans to affect the course of American politics", its "lasting contributions . . . were more significant in the intellectual and cultural rather than the political arena".[51]

The point is that all black power groups were, at some level at least, engaged in a cultural enterprise. They were battling to rescue black minds from any lingering sense of inferiority, or deference to an imposed white value system, or obeisance to jaundiced, self-serving white versions of black and American history. Certainly, most activists appreciated that, as Harold Cruse stated in his influential 1967 treatise, *The crisis of the Negro intellectual*, "no social movement of a protest nature . . . can be successful or have any positive meaning unless it is at one and the same time *a political, economic and cultural movement*". Culture was to be used simultaneously as an instrument of self- and communal affirmation, and as a catalyst for political action which would lead to fundamental changes in the black predicament. The problems came over exactly which forms of black art were to be considered "authentic" expressions of black consciousness and culture; which ones were best suited to the political and ideological needs of particular groups; and precisely how these revivifying cultural initiatives were to be integrated effectively into a broader programme of black protest and struggle.[52]

These were difficult questions which generated numerous responses and revealed much about the nature and priorities of the particular groups involved. And as various black organizations and individuals considered how best to harness distinctively black cultural forms, including soul music, to genuinely progressive political and educational ends, they boldly confronted some of the theoretical and practical issues which the early Movement had largely ignored. It was ironic, however, that the mixed results of black power's earnest attempts to develop and deploy black culture for overtly political, sometimes even revolutionary, ends suggested that the early Movement may actually have been rather prudent not to try to force the issue.

It was also ironic that while Maulana Ron Karenga, prophet of a cultural path to black liberation, insisted "Black art must be for the people, by the people and from the people", his relentless recourse to Africa for validation of authentic African-American cultural forms meant that he had little time for the popular music and dance which were actually among the most vibrant expressions of the black experience in America. Karenga contemptuously complained that "The 'Negro' has more records than books and is dancing his life away"[53]

In fairness, Karenga was not the only black activist to have doubts about the efficacy of soul in the liberation struggle. Many cultural nationalists, unsettled both by soul's obvious popularity with whites and its relationship with a white-dominated recording and radio industry, preferred to put their faith in modern black jazzmen like Archie Shepp, Ornette Coleman, Albert Ayler, Pharaoh Sanders, Eric Dolphy and the ghost of Charlie Parker. One such figure was black playwright-activist, Ronald Milner. In 1967 Milner had discovered a culturalist manifesto in the form of an advertisement for a New York poetry reading. The advertisement read: "BLACK MAGIC, BLACK ART, WILL TOPPLE THE CITADEL OF RACIST AMERICA!" Prompted by the discovery of this bold credo, but chastened by the insistence of a political nationalist friend – subsequently dismissed by Milner as "one of those who believes we black artists should beat our saxophones and typewriters into spears and daggers" – that art would have little part in the forthcoming black revolution, he began to reconsider the political potential of black culture. Milner's conclusion was that "Black art can do a lot to topple white, racist America, if it is *black* enough". Consequently, he turned to the jazz avant-garde, which he held was "the blackest of the arts", with practitioners who were "furthest along in self-assertion and unrestrained, unaccommodating self-expression". Milner hailed John Coltrane as "a man who through his saxophone before your eyes and ears, completely annihilates every single western influence".[54]

In *Black fire*, an important culturalist anthology edited by Imamu Amiri Baraka and Larry Neal, James T. Stewart provided a further theoretical justification for this reification of modern jazz. Echoing Baraka's contention that "what's needed now for 'the arts' is to get them away from white people", Stewart called for a "Black Revolutionary Artist" who would completely reject white critical standards and assumptions in the quest for a "pure" expression of the black experience in America. Conveniently disregarding the American context in which African-American identity and values have historically been forged, Stewart urged black artists to construct an autonomous black aesthetic, which "means that he can not be 'successful' in any sense that has meaning in white critical evaluations. Nor can his work ever be called 'good' in any context of meaning that could make sense to that traditional critique".[55]

For James Stewart, as for Baraka, Milner and many others, the strength and political potential of the jazz avant-garde resided in its apparent racial exclusivity. The more these restless experimenters challenged Western conceptions of harmony, rhythm, melody and tone to create a music which was by turns dense and austere, powerfully primitive and dazzlingly complex, the more their supporters felt they projected an image of uncompromising and uncompromised black identity.

In fact, although the jazz avant-garde appealed to the cultural nationalists as an example of black cultural autonomy, and as more immune from the distorting influences of the white market and the white-controlled industry than soul music, this supposed independence and insularity was largely chimerical. White-owned recording companies – Blue Note, Prestige, Impulse, Fantasy, Atlantic – recorded most of the New Music; whites owned most of the clubs in which it was performed, and most of the journals which helped to create a hip mystique around the new jazzmen. Meanwhile, as cultural nationalists drooled over Coltrane's *Africa Brass* album as a sign of his return to roots, few noted that he was at least as interested in and influenced by Indian music, and had more than a passing acquaintance with modern classical experiments in serialism and atonality.

Even more disturbing for the claims of the cultural nationalists was the fact that whites continued to constitute the major audience for modern black jazz. The black public remained supremely indifferent to the intense, earnest, but sometimes highly esoteric, playing of these modern jazz giants. Sympathetic black critics like Lawrence Nahs recognized the practical problems in claiming revolutionary potential for a music which was not even reaching the people whose racial consciousness it was supposed to be raising. In a review of A.B. Spellman's *Black music: four lives in the be-bop business*, Nahs accepted the New Jazz's artistry, but questioned its ultimate claims to social relevance. "Currently, the only things revolutionary about the 'new music' are its technological innovations. And those are not enough". To be truly revolutionary, Nahs wrote, the music "must extend itself into the black community in a manner which, heretofore, it has failed to do. It must mean to the community what the Supremes, the Impressions, and James Brown now mean".[56]

Even Spellman had to admit that the jazz avant-garde could not match the influence and prestige of soul performers among blacks.

> The reality is that it was Greenwich Village which heard the evolution of the New, not Harlem. The man standing in line for the Otis Redding show at the Apollo almost certainly never heard of tenor saxophonist Albert Ayler, and wouldn't have the fuzziest idea of what he was doing if he did hear him.[57]

Unlike the music itself, which was usually born of a more subtle and complex mix of spiritual and artistic, as well as commercial, racial and political imperatives, the cultural nationalist deification of Coltrane, Coleman and the rest was in part an elitist, intellectual project. It had much more in common with romantic Western bourgeois ideals of the suffering, soul-searching artist than most of its well-educated, increasingly Afrocentric advocates could either recognize or easily admit. The modern jazzman's self-conscious pursuit of a meaningful "art", the embrace of social alienation as a performance technique, and the use of inaccessibility as a political statement, actually had little to do with an African tradition, preserved and endlessly re-created in the most popular African-American musics, which invariably sought to collapse the distance between performer and audience, and between art and social function.

In their enthusiasm for an art which seemed to slip the yoke of Western cultural imperialism, the cultural nationalists had made a virtue of the jazz avant garde's tendency to disregard the necessary snatch of "America" and the West which actually defined African-American culture and made it coherent and meaningful to the black masses. This iconoclasm merely helped render the jazz avant-garde alien and largely irrelevant to the vast majority of blacks, for whom social and political messages in music – not to mention joy and emotional solace – were most frequently borne by the sturdy, compelling rhythms of dance music, or atop the crest of an irresistible vocal wave.

The New Jazz was not too difficult for those masses, it was merely not as redolent of their experience as soul, nor, ultimately, as responsive to changes in black consciousness. Paradoxically, the same commercial co-ordinates which made Rhythm and Blues so problematic for some activists ensured that the music had to retain its relevancy for a mass black audience, and regularly reinvented itself in order to retain or recapture that market. By contrast, jazz survived with support from a much smaller, mainly white, coterie of dedicated musical vanguardists. In fairness, some musicians and activists did work hard to try to broaden jazz's appeal to the black masses

411

through locally rooted, community initiatives like Baraka's Jazzmobile in New York, Muhal Richard Abrams' even older Association for the Advancement of Creative Musicians in Chicago, and its many offshoots and imitators, like the Art Ensemble of Chicago and BAG in St Louis. Nevertheless, the fact is that many jazz fans not-so-secretly revelled in the music's professed indifference to broader commercial considerations and the vagaries of mass taste, as if this were some kind of guarantee of artistic quality and racial integrity.

The black masses were largely unmoved by the claims of artistic, ideological and racial virtue made on behalf of the jazz avant-garde. Indeed, even within the rarified world of jazz in the early 1970s, the New Jazz was eclipsed in popularity by the fusion style, pioneered by Herbie Hancock, veteran Miles Davis, Billy Cobham and the group Weather Report. Cultural nationalists might have noted that fusion's unusual commercial success for a contemporary jazz idiom – with both races – was built on a marriage of modern jazz, soul and rock influences. There was nothing "pure" about fusion. Musically it could be ponderous and gauche, commercially it could be opportunistic and crass, but at its best it was vital and engaging and added another chapter to the long history of cross-fertilization between adjacent musical traditions. Much the same could be said of the dance-oriented jazz-funk-disco hybrids with which erstwhile jazzmen like the Crusaders, Donald Byrd, Roy Ayers, Stanley Turrentine, and Ronnie Laws had success in the late 1970s.

Like the cultural nationalists, the Black Panther Party was also critical of soul's lack of lyrical attention to black protest, and deeply suspicious of the capitalist mode of its production and marketing. Emory Douglas, the party's Minister of Culture, revolutionary artist and chief theoretician on the political uses of art, even denounced the sainted first lady of soul, Aretha Franklin, and blues legend B.B. King, for "singing about cultural nationalism" and love, without advancing ideas or information which might concretely lead to revolution. James Brown was even worse, using his special status within the black community to make money for himself and the capitalist system by which, in the Panthers' class-first analysis, blacks were principally oppressed. "You hear James Brown talking about Black and Proud, then you hear him on the radio saying, 'Why don't you buy this beer?'", Emory complained. This situation was unlikely to change, he suggested, while black artists like the Godfather were signing contracts with the "Mafia-controlled record industry".[58]

Unlike the cultural nationalists, however, the Black Panthers never really embraced the jazz avant-garde as an example of a self-consciously engaged, economically independent, politically useful black art form. The Panthers' street-orientation and their powerful identification with the "lumpen" – the urban underclass and dispossessed among whom they believed genuine revolutionary potential lurked – meant that soul was the most acceptable, if by no means perfect, vehicle for their few musical forays into cultural politics. For the class-conscious Panthers, popular and populist soul music had little of the intellectual pretension or elite cliquishness of the jazz scene.

This is not to suggest that the Panthers initially put much faith in the political efficacy of soul at all, even when they were producing it themselves. The original advertisement for *Seize the Time*, an album by Elaine Brown released in early 1969, carried a reminder of the limited role the Panthers believed music could play in the struggle. "Songs, like all art forms, are an expression of the feelings and thoughts, the desires and hopes, and so forth, of a people. They are no more than that. A song cannot change a situation, because a song does not live and breathe. People do".[59]

Nevertheless, less than a year after the release of Brown's album – an interval which witnessed an impressive outpouring of "politicized" commercial soul – at least one branch of the Panther-National Committee to Combat Fascism (NCCF) coalition had begun to re-evaluate the revolutionary potential of black popular music. A report from New Jersey described how five members of the NCCF had been arrested for singing " 'There's a pig up on the hill, if the people don't get them the Panthers will' while they walked through the black community selling papers". This incident, the correspondent explained, symbolized the popularity of a new crop of "revolutionary" songs in the black community, songs which he argued could act as a form of education and a spur to black rebellion.

> The singing of revolutionary songs has spread throughout the Black Panther Party and NCCFs all across the country. Children have replaced their traditional meaningless songs with revolutionary songs that are full of the realities of the black community . . . The singing of revolutionary songs is a very effective form of education for Black people, because they relate very heavily to music. Revolutionary songs not only tell the people that revolution has come and that it's time to pick up the gun but they also tell the people if they want things like, no more pigs in our community, they must seize the time and off the pig.[60]

Two weeks after this letter was published, the Panthers announced the release of a single by their very own soul emissaries, the Lumpen, on the Seize The Time label. Boasting music and lyrics by Bill Calhoun, this "Black Panther Party production" featured "No more" and "Free Bobby now" – a song dedicated to the Panthers' co-founder and chairman, Bobby Seale, who was at the time awaiting trial for his part in riots in New Haven. The lyrics to "No more" were suitably militant, describing black determination to rise up and seize freedom: "we'll get guns to defend our communities . . . we'll control our destiny".[61]

As the Lumpen joined first Elaine Brown, then white progressive rock bands like the Grateful Dead, in a series of fundraising concerts, the Panthers' Ministry of Information felt obliged to clarify the latest party line on the Lumpen and soul more generally. "The Lumpen is a revolutionary singing group, that has taken the ideology of the Black Panther Party and put it to musical form. Singing the ideology does not discredit it in any way". The Ministry then revealed its own misunderstanding of the ways in which popular music works and its meanings are constructed, by locating its politics entirely in the worthy intentions of its creators and sponsors.[62]

"The Lumpen sing not to make profit or stimulate emotions, but to make revolution and stimulate action", the Ministry assured the Panther faithful, warning against the perils of succumbing to the emotional and physical joy provided by artists who did not share the Lumpen's selfless commitment to profitless, emotionless, revolutionary music.

> Music today is tied up in stimulations, the blues makes you sad while rhythm makes you happy and you end up dancing to keep from crying, dancing while pigs are ripping off brothers and sisters in the streets of Babylon, and across the globe. We know music plays an important role in our culture, and we don't mean to stop singing or changing the sound at all. We dig singing and we dig the sound, but the words are what we're changing to fit our situation today.
>
> We like the beat of James Brown, we say the Temptations sound great, but if we try to relate what they are saying to our conditions we'd end up in a ball of confusion. If we run around saying, "It's my thing and I can do what I want to do," we would never be free or singing "Cloud 9" to help the Mafia launch a new era of drugs, ain't no way . . .
>
> So now when we hear the Temptations song, "Old Man River", tell them to keep the sound, but to borrow the words from the Lumpen and sing "Old Pig Nixon".

In all these polemics, the Panthers tended to underestimate the politics of pleasure. They neglected the sensual gratification which crucially shapes an audience's potential receptivity to any message in popular music and makes it difficult for any artist to "educate", let alone "mobilize", without first entertaining. This was a relationship which sophisticated, politically engaged soulmen like Curtis Mayfield recognized only too well. "Our purpose is to educate as well as to entertain. Painless preaching is as good a term as any for what we do", Mayfield explained.[63]

In fact, there was no reason to believe that the black community would have responded favourably to an unrelieved diet of politically correct songs about racial oppression and the coming revolution. Such a narrow range of subject matter would have ignored vast areas of the black experience which were not wholly, at all times, in all places, dominated by questions of race, poverty and struggle. Moreover, a relentlessly didactic approach was unlikely to yield much reward because of the way in which popular music works. The folk singers who had proselytized on behalf of the Communist Party as part of the People's Songsters between the 1930s and 1950s had recognized this. Woody Guthrie and the young Pete Seeger found that crude agit-prop sloganeering quickly became wearing for an audience and creatively unrewarding for the artists. It was far more effective to describe a situation which illustrated an injustice; or to celebrate an act of resistance; or simply tell a tale of beauty, love and decency achieved against the odds of poverty and oppression.[64]

What was needed, then, was a mixture of exhortation, explication and illustration designed to promote a more radical world view among blacks and encourage a predisposition towards taking collective action to secure and protect their rights. Anne Romaine and Bernice Johnson Reagon had attempted something along these lines with the SFCRP. The Panthers, however, tried unsuccessfully to use an unrelenting barrage of strident soul propaganda to bludgeon black people into adopting their politics and joining their revolution.

Far less self consciously radical than the Panthers, by the end of the 1960s the SCLC had a much better understanding of the potential of music in black politics and its role in black lives. In 1968, it renamed its newsletter *Soul force* in dual deference to Gandhian notions of satyagraha and Gordyan notions of soul power. Two years later, the SCLC announced that it was working with soul in much the same way that it had once used freedom songs, "in the belief that music is one way of unifying black people". After more than a dozen years of civil rights struggle, the SCLC was certainly not naive enough to believe that the mere hearing of politically correct black protest songs was likely to persuade politically apathetic blacks to become activists, let alone provide an effective medium through which to direct their activism. Yet it rightly felt that the music could promote a general sense of collective black identity and encourage the pride and positivity which was a vital prerequisite for any engagement in political struggle. The problem in the 1970s was that even the theatrical militancy of black power and the bright florescence of black creativity could neither conceal, nor reverse, the steady demise of mass black activism. Nor could they prevent the erosion of the once robust faith that racism and discrimination in America would soon be vanquished.[65]

The Black Panther's "revolutionary singing group", The Lumpen, put the party's ideology into musical form in an attempt to reach the black masses.

CHAPTER ELEVEN

"Take that to the bank": corporate soul, black capitalism and disco fever

It is the goal of the Black Panther Party to negate capitalism in our communities . . . However, we recognize that people in the Black community have no general dislike for the concept of Black Capitalism. (Huey Newton)[1]

Philadelphia International Records, CBS and the corporatization of soul

Although the racial structure of the recording industry remained fundamentally unaltered during the black power era, there was nonetheless a steady, if slow and equivocal, expansion of black executive and managerial power within it. A handful of important new black-owned labels also emerged, including Holland-Dozier-Holland's Hot Wax and Invictus, Willie Mitchell's Hi, Dick Griffey's Solar, and Sylvia and Joe Robinson's All Platinum. The most important of these newcomers was Philadelphia International Records (PIR), whose fate was typical of many putatively independent black and white labels at a time when giant corporations were tightening their grip on the American, indeed the global, entertainment industry.

PIR's founders, Kenny Gamble and Leon Huff, were stalwarts of a moderately vibrant mid-1960s Philadelphia soul scene which had coalesced around the Cameo-Parkway label and the efforts of a notoriously hardnosed independent black record producer called – with some aptness given his business methods – Jesse James. James hired local talent and studio time at Virtual Studios to record a string of groove-based dance hits like Johnny C's "Boogaloo down Broadway" and Cliff Nobles' "The horse". When James' cavalier mistreatment of his musicians got too much to bear, key players deserted to Gamble and Huff at their Gamble and later Neptune labels, and

417

on the sessions they supervised for other companies at the Sigma Sound Studio.[2]

Pianist-arranger Bobby Martin, bassist Ronnie Baker, guitarists Norman Harris, Ronald Chambers and Bobby Eli, drummer Earl Young, and arranger Don Renaldo, together with writer-arranger Thom Bell and white lyricist Linda Creed, were crucial to the creation of the Philly Sound: a sort of velvet-cased soul-funk amalgam which was characterized by rich string and horn arrangements, taut rhythm tracks, and dramatic gospel vocals delivering thoughtful, storyline lyrics. This was the Rhythm and Blues rock upon which Gamble and Huff built their economic empire.

The Neptune label had been distributed by Chess Records, but following the death of Leonard Chess in July 1970 Gamble and Huff regrouped as PIR. The following year, the label released its first record, the Ebonys' "You're the reason why", and immediately secured a distribution deal with CBS to market its product to the widest possible audience. "We've never thought along the lines of a black music thing", Kenny Gamble told journalist Tony Cummings. "We'd said to them, 'here's a new kind of music, something which has all the ingredients to appeal to all audiences, black and white'". And they were right. The O'Jays' "Backstabbers" started a run of massive crossover hits, including Harold Melvin and the Bluenotes' "If you don't know me by now", Billy Paul's "Me and Mrs Jones", the Spinners' "I'll be around", and the Three Degrees' "When will I see you again".[3]

By 1975, PIR was the second biggest black-owned corporation in the country – Motown was still the biggest – with gross revenue of more than $25 million. Even beyond PIR, the Philly Sound was a powerful presence in both the black and white charts. Thom Bell, who had worked with Gamble and Huff for years, joined forces with them in the Mighty Three Music publishing enterprise, and emerged as a very successful writer-producer. Bell achieved a somewhat mellower variant on the basic Philly Sound with the sopranic Stylistics ("Betcha by golly wow", "You make me feel brand new"), and the luscious Delfonics ("La-la means I love you"). Variations on the same sound reverberated in the satin-sheet soul of Barry White and later in the silken strings which dressed disco and its strictly regimented dance beats in a cloak of sophistication.[4]

PIR's enormous success both typified and exacerbated a number of important generational and structural changes taking place within the world of Rhythm and Blues during the early 1970s. Unlike Berry Gordy at Motown, whose crossover dreams they shared, it never occurred to Gamble and Huff that social messages and robust expressions of black pride and unity might be commercially disabling. Songs like the O'Jays' "Ship ahoy", an evocative narrative of the slave journey from Africa, and the anti-materialistic "For the love of money" were common fare. All the label's albums bore the legend "Message in the Music", and most lived up to the tag. As Nelson George put it, Kenny Gamble increasingly saw PIR as a "platform from which to proselytize, espousing a world view that obliquely revealed his private beliefs in the tenets of Islam. Gamble developed a tough, male-dominated, anti-materialist perspective . . .".[5]

As George also noted, the irony of this situation was that Gamble's "preaching reached its apex while under the protection of CBS records". Indeed, while PIR was black-owned and instrumental in developing the careers of several important black music industry professionals and executives – including Tony Bell, Phil Hurtt, and future CBS vice-president, LeBaron Taylor – the label was heavily dependent on the promotional muscle and carefully placed cash of CBS for its success and crossover opportunities. Indeed, while PIR was the biggest "independent" black enterprise to emerge during the black power era, it was also deeply implicated in the steady corporatization of black – and white – popular music during the period. By the start of the 1970s, the apparent diversity of American music and the plethora of putatively independent labels actually concealed a concentration of power unknown since the early 1950s. CBS, ABC, RCA, Capitol-EMI, Polydor, MCA, and WEA (a conglomerate of Warner Brothers, Elektra and Atlantic) increasingly dominated the recording industry, controlled most record distribution, sales, music publishing and concert promotion, and heavily influenced the structure and content of American music television and radio.[6]

In the world within a world of Rhythm and Blues, this general trend towards the concentration of capital and control was hastened by a report prepared for CBS by the Harvard University Graduate School of Business. This 1971 report revealed that some 30 per cent of the nation's pop Top Forty singles broke out from a base in soul radio stations and solid sales in the black market. Thus, it recommended that CBS should make a concerted effort to develop its meagre black music catalogue – which, with the Okeh subsidiary moribund, consisted of little more than Sly Stone on its Epic imprint – as a means to access the white market more effectively. The report also chastised CBS for its historic neglect, bordering on contempt, for the black market, and urged much greater recruitment of black executives. There was even a suggestion that CBS might invest in record shops in the black community and franchise them out to local residents. The bottom line, however, was that with the right sort of crossover material and access to black radio and the black retail market, Rhythm and Blues could provide CBS with a springboard to the much greater riches of the mainstream market. This was something which Berry Gordy had figured out without the aid of Harvard nearly a decade earlier.[7]

Responding to the Harvard study, CBS president Clive Davis set up a black music division headed by a young black executive called Logan Westbrooks. He also negotiated a series of complex distribution deals with powerful soul labels, most notably PIR, Brunswick/Dakar, and Stax, which had been distributed through the Gulf + Western corporation since the collapse of its relationship with Atlantic in 1968. Although Davis was replaced in 1973, accused of tax evasion and irregularities relating to his expense account, CBS's bid for soul power continued. By the end of 1973, CBS had secured a 15 per cent share of the black music business. By the end of the decade it had 125 black acts on its books and had hired a whole slew of energetic black executives and representatives, like Westbrooks, LeBaron Taylor and Vernon Slaughter, all of whom were committed to breaking CBS's black products as widely as possible. By 1979, black music accounted for about a quarter of all CBS record sales.[8]

One reason for CBS's extraordinary success was the fact that in 1973 the CBS-TV network acquired the nationwide syndication rights for Don Cornelius' increasingly popular *Soul Train* show. *Soul Train* was a sort of funky *American Bandstand*, which started on a local Chicago station in 1970 and survived long past its heyday amid the flares, tank tops and platform shoes of the 1970s. MFSB's Gamble and Huff-produced instrumental hit, "The sound of Philadelphia", was the show's opening theme, and records with CBS links did about as well in terms of exposure on *Soul Train* as those with a Dick Clark connection had once done on *American Bandstand*.[9]

Another way of securing good access to the broadcast media for CBS-related recordings was to grease the wheels of commerce with liberal applications of payola. In the early 1970s, *Variety* carried several reports that payola, hash as well as cash, was on the increase again, noting that the relatively low salaries of black deejays made them particularly easy marks for this practice. Rumours of such activities continued to circulate in the industry and sometimes in the music press until February 1973, when CBS A&R director David Wynshaw revealed to a Newark hearing of the Federal Strike Force Against Organized Crime that his company had an annual payola fund of some $250,000 secreted within its promotion department's official budget. Most of this money was dedicated to easing the passage of recordings by CBS's newly assembled black roster onto the black-oriented airwaves.[10]

CBS initially denied Wynshaw's claims, fired him, and shortly afterwards dismissed his boss, Clive Davis – the man most closely associated with the corporation's black music initiatives. However, once Wynshaw had opened the floodgates, other informants appearing before the Strike Force suggested that his estimate of how much CBS was spending on payola was actually rather conservative. As press interest in the scandal mounted, New York Republican James L. Buckley led the campaign for a senate investigation. As in the early 1960s, the FCC, Justice Department and senate, in the form of Arkansas Democrat John McClellan's Sub-committee on Copyright, eventually launched overlapping investigations into payola in the music industry.

The racial co-ordinates of these investigations were far from clear. At the time, Lucky Cordell, the black general manager of WVON-Chicago and executive director of NATRA, complained that "Whenever there's talk about payola, the finger's always pointed at the black man". It was certainly true that these probes had set out to find evidence that payola was integral to the relationship between companies making, or distributing, black music and black-oriented radio stations. They had, however, generally ignored – or investigated less vigorously – other areas of the industry where abuses may have been just as rampant.[11]

It was particularly unfortunate that the racial focus of the investigations cast a shadow over many black-oriented labels where there was no evidence of malpractice. At Motown, for example, in the wake of the 1970s payola investigations and Elaine Jesmer's thinly fictionalized account of life and alleged mafia involvement at the label, *Number one with a bullet*, rumours resurfaced that Gordy had established Motown's excellent links with broadcasters by lavish payola payments. Some even suggested that one reason why Gordy had founded such a multitude of separate labels was to foil FCC efforts to detect the influence of payola, which was often revealed by the tell-tale over-representation of a single label on radio station playlists. Rumour and innuendo aside, however, no real evidence of malpractice was ever presented against Motown.[12]

And yet, there was no smoke without reefer and the corporate intervention into Rhythm and Blues was accompanied by widespread corruption. On 14 June 1975, the Justice Department issued indictments against 19 individuals and 6 corporations on a total of 86 counts derived from its payola investigations. Among these was Clive Davis, by then president at Arista, who was eventually only found guilty of a single charge of tax evasion and fined $10,000. Also indicted were Nat Tarnopol, president of Brunswick/Dakar, and six other executives from that company. Tarnopol and three others were initially fined and sentenced to jail in April 1976, although the sentences were reversed by an appellate court the following year. Kenneth Gamble and Leon Huff were also indicted. Although the case against Huff was subsequently dropped, Gamble pleaded *nolo contendere* to the charge that PIR had spent thousands of dollars on payola of one sort or another to radio stations and their personnel. He was fined $2,500.[13]

Unlike in 1960, record companies and their distributors, rather than the deejays themselves, were the principal target for the 1970s payola probes. Deejays generally proved very co-operative in the Justice Department's investigation and most were granted immunity from prosecution in return for information. The only station employee included in the mass indictments of June 1975 was Paul Burke, programme director of WAOK-Atlanta, who had lied about receiving payola from Kenny Gamble. The following year, however, WBLS-New York's deejay-programme director, Frankie Crocker, was indicted by the Newark grand jury. Crocker's trial revealed a list of secret benefactors which included PIR and James Brown's manager Charles Bobbit. Crocker denied taking payola to play certain disks, but was convicted of perjury, fined $1,000, and sentenced to a year in jail. Again, this sentence was overturned on appeal, suggesting that the evidence against at least some of these alleged Rhythm and Blues rogues was less than secure. Nevertheless, of the 60 people indicted on payola charges by the Newark grand jury, 25 actually pleaded guilty.[14]

Roy Innis, the latest national director of a rapidly disintegrating CORE, was in no doubt that if payola did exist in the black music industry, big business, the corporate mentality and its monopolistic tendencies were to blame. Twelve corporations, out of the 3,000 companies making records, "influence or outrightly control every record spun on the turntable", Innis claimed. The FCC and Federal Trade Commission, meanwhile, did nothing to curtail this near monopoly of the entertainment industry, making it impossible for black businessmen to compete legitimately against this corporate might. Black record companies and radio station personnel thus had to make the invidious decision of whether to stake out the moral high ground and risk perpetual marginalization and ruin, or to throw in their lot with the major corporations and accept their dubious business ethics.[15]

If Innis had a rather simplistic view of the saints and sinners here – implying that black record and radio personnel had never dreamed of payola until corrupted by the major corporations – he was nonetheless right that it was becoming virtually impossible for any independent label to prosper without the financial or structural assistance of these giant entertainment corporations. Even the strongest Independent of them all, Motown, began to haemorrhage key acts to Major labels in the 1970s and early 1980s, simply because they could reach places in the market and offer rewards which Motown could not match. The Jacksons (as the Jackson Five became known – Gordy owned the name), the solo Michael Jackson, Marvin Gaye and Gladys Knight, all fled to CBS, while Diana Ross moved to RCA. In 1983 Gordy conceded the changing structure of the business and signed a distribution deal with MCA, ending the label's more than two decades of relative autonomy. Five years later he finally sold his record company and its fabulously lucrative back catalogue to the international entertainment conglomerate Sony for $61 million.[16]

The story of Curtis Mayfield's Curtom label illustrated how new labels also struggled to accommodate themselves to the new era of corporate power in black music while still retaining some capacity for independent action. Mayfield had established Curtom in 1968 as a vehicle for his own songwriting and production talents, and those of others like Ed Townsend and Marv Stewart. In the late 1960s and early 1970s Curtom put out some marvellous Chicago soul by Mayfield, the Impressions, Notations, Major Lance, Billy Butler and Gene Chandler. Curtom's soul was a creamy mix of smooth vocals, cresting horns, rippling blues-flecked guitars, and sinewy bass lines. Initially distributed by Buddah, by 1975 the label was a big enough player to cut a distribution deal with Warner Brothers. It seemed a shrewd move. The corporation had just established its own black music division, headed by black vice-president Tom Draper, and already boasted a raft of black talent like Ashford and Simpson, Graham Central Station, George Benson and Al Jarreau. Under the new arrangement, Curtom initially prospered, with gross sales in excess of $10 million in 1976.[17]

Unfortunately, however, the label chose to assert its independent spirit at this time by investing heavily in the black film industry just as the vogue for blaxploitation movies was fading. Moreover, despite some success with the superior disco diva Linda Clifford, the label's funk-lite soul sound slipped out of favour around 1977. Not dense enough for the heavy funk crowd; too old-school soulful and introspective for the disco crowd in a razzle-dazzle world of mirror-balls and 125-beat-per-minute dance cuts, Curtom's sales began to dwindle. Within a year or so, the label's relationship with Warners was over. By 1979 Curtom was little more than a logo on the RSO company lists. When Mayfield relocated self and studio to Atlanta in 1980, it was effectively dead.

Without many major, self-contained acts, Curtom was always vulnerable to periodic losses of touch and form by its key producers and writers. More crucially, however, Warners had clearly lost interest in the company the instant that Mayfield's hit-making power appeared to falter. This was a frequent problem for black acts signed to the Majors, and for small labels locked into distribution deals with major corporations. Although the Majors all signed their share of established veterans like Johnnie Taylor at CBS, or James Brown at Polydor, or the Staple Singers at Warners, they were usually more concerned with marketing crossover hit singles than with long-term career development. Certainly, they were extremely impatient with any fallow periods away from the pop charts and tended to offload black acts and labels as soon as they went cold in the white market place. Even PIR felt this pinch in the early 1980s as Gamble and Huff ran out of hit-making steam and CBS turned its attention to promoting its own roster of black acts. By the end of the decade Gamble and Huff were out of the corporate loop and doing their own distribution for a scaled-down Gamble and Huff Records.

This corporate ruthlessness towards black acts and soul labels was only partially offset by the much better financial deals they were able to offer. Nelson George estimated that in addition to a signing on fee of some $350,000, the Jacksons received from the CBS subsidary Epic a royalty rate which was about 500 per cent greater than they had enjoyed at Motown. However, these huge advances and fat returns also intensified the pressure to achieve crossover success. In the process, they subtly reshaped the artistic and commercial priorities of many acts and their managers and producers. It was not that blacks in the record business had not always wanted cross-over hits, and sometimes gone to great musical and promotional lengths to try to attain them. It was more that under the new corporate regimes, with so much money at stake and so little scope for genuinely independent action by black-oriented labels, a purely black hit was often no longer considered an unqualified success. Once the bread-and-butter of most soul labels and many soul acts for most of their careers, a black hit was no longer something to be striven for as an end in itself; it was now conceived more like a consolation prize, somewhat awkwardly accepted if the bid for the crossover market failed. Such hits rarely satisfied the ambitions of corporate paymasters.[18]

Of course, on one hand this seemed a positive sign, in that black artists were being encouraged to bid for a biracial American market which 20 years earlier would have been unthinkable. On the other hand, industry pressure on black popular music to conform and assimilate to perceived white tastes and expectations had never been greater. Since the mid 1950s, the sounds and social significances of Rhythm and Blues had always been squeezed out from the intersecting, sometimes antithetical, needs and agendas of the artists, the industry, and its black and white audiences. At various times, with various artists, labels and songs, one or more of these forces might have exerted greater influence than the others, but there was usually some kind of negotiation and balance between them. In the mid-to-late 1970s, that balance was increasingly upset as the growing corporate imperative to sell white began to threaten even the fierce integrity of much Rhythm and Blues.

Disco: dancing to keep from crying – again

The most obvious musical manifestation of the intensified industry pressure to cross over was the triumph of disco. A couple of upstart, white-owned, independent labels – Neil Bogart's Casablanca (which released Donna Summer's beat erotica) and Harry Stone's T.K. Records (which hit big with the nascent disco of George McCrae's "Rock your baby") – were among the earliest to move records out of a burgeoning nightclub dance scene onto black-oriented radio playlists, and from there into the black and white charts. In 1975, CBS sold 2.5 million copies of veteran Johnny Taylor's "Disco lady" and from that point on the muscle of the Majors transformed a trend towards functional dance music into a disco tidal wave which all but swamped black and white popular music for several years.

Disco, as it swept America between roughly 1976 and 1980, was a simplified, sanitized and straightened version of a genuinely exciting and innovative dance and style-based phenomenon which had flourished first – and continued to do so throughout disco's commercial apotheosis – in gay black clubs. As such, it provided a forum for creative expression and communal identity for a section of black America which was doubly oppressed by virtue of race and sexual orientation. According to Walter Hughes, in an era before AIDS awareness, the sheer corporeal demands of disco caught the

424

mood of an emboldened, post-Stonewall gay scene which was revelling in its new openness, sexual licence and eager explorations of the gay body and its erotic possibilities. While there were some gay male disco stars, most notably Sylvester – whose "You make me feel mighty real" was an exhilarating anthem of affirmation, pride and identity – and the clownish Village People ("YMCA", "In the navy"), disco divas like Donna Summer, Gloria Gaynor ("I will survive"), Grace Jones ("I need a man"), Miquel Brown ("So many men, so little time"), and even the repackaged Diana Ross ("Upside down") were especially popular among gay men. The urgent eroticism of these singers, their lack of apology for obeying the needs of their bodies, and the way in which they often portrayed themselves as victims of sensual desire, degraded and exploited for following their loves and lusts, mirrored the thrill of sexual liberation for some gays, as well as reminding them of their likely abuse and mistreatment by an uncomprehending and intolerant mainstream.[19]

At its often elusive and critically unappreciated best, disco was the latest in a long line of high energy black dance styles, albeit with more regimented beats than those associated with the gospel swing of soul, or the molten swagger of funk. Some of the singles by groups like Rose Royce, Gap Band, Shalimar, Whispers, Crown Heights Affair, Sister Sledge, and soloists like Evelyn "Champagne" King, Cheryl Lynn, and Stephanie Mills, together with the handful of listenable "disco" albums like Michael Jackson's brilliant *Off the Wall* and the eponymous Aquarian Dream set, stand comparison with the best dance-floor funk and soul of the early 1970s. Moreover, as the club scene, gay and straight, black and white, flourished, it was initially a highly democratic and responsive form of popular culture. Instant dance floor approval from feverish Saturday night masses, desperate to escape the day-to-day routine of the repression-hit Carter years, was the main arbiter of what got played, and for how long, by deejays who were the real stars of the street-level disco scene. As Bernie Edwards, whose collaboration with Nile Rodgers in Chic produced some of disco's more enduring grooves ("Good times") explained he just wanted to "provide care-free music for those who work hard five days a week and go out on the weekend to dance and have fun".[20]

Disco was also rather democratic in another sense, in that it drew on musical influences and boasted practitioners from far beyond the world of black Rhythm and Blues. For example, many erstwhile jazzmen cut disco singles, hoping at long last to wring some decent money from their musical talents. Although ultimately constrained by the formulaic structure of much disco, their extended workouts over taut hi-energy beats and perfunctory vocal chants provided some of the style's more dramatic and interesting musical moments. Records like Donald Byrd's "Dominoes", Charles Earland's "Let the music play", Eddie Henderson's "Prance on", and the Crusaders' "Street life" – where Randy Crawford's vocals were anything but perfunctory

– were great club fodder, but were listenable at home too. Many of these jazzy disco-experimenters, who included Roy Ayers, Stanley Clarke, Ronnie Laws, Lonnie Liston Smith, Stanley Turrentine, Grover Washington, and the hugely successful guitarist-cum-balladeer George Benson, made albums which slipped a few straight-ahead jazz pieces among the disco tracks in an attempt to stimulate wider interest in the form.

Beyond the jazz community, the Hispanic input into the dance and disco scene, especially in New York, Los Angeles and Miami, was also highly significant, as acknowledged in Van McCoy's "Latin hustle". There were also important European links, with Donna Summer, Silver Convention ("Fly robin fly") and the kitsch Boney M. ("Ma Baker") emerging from Munich, Cerrone ("Supernature") and Gino Soccio ("Dancer") based in Italy, and Hot Chocolate ("Disco queen" and "Everyone's a winner") hailing from Britain's Afro-Caribbean community. And, of course, disco could also appear in the white-face guise of the Bee Gees ("Stayin' alive", "Jive talkin'"), Leo Sayer ("You make me feel like dancing"), Rod Stewart ("Do ya think I'm sexy"), and Blondie ("Heart of glass").

The fact that just about anyone seemed capable of piecing together a passable disco-by-numbers record probably explains why black records, many of which were disco-oriented in the late 1970s, actually failed to cross over quite as successfully to the pop charts as in earlier years. Whereas previously if you wanted to buy soul and funk then you invariably had to buy black, if you wanted disco you could get it in many shades. In 1973, 36 black records featured in *Billboard*'s top 100 records of the year, but in 1977 that number was down to just 23. Moreover, while the average peak position of a black chart-topper in the pop charts was 15 in 1974, it was only 22 in 1978, the apogee of disco fever.[21]

For a while disco – good, bad and indifferent, black, Latino and white, American and European – sold by the crateload to a biracial adolescent and young adult audience which could not escape it on the radio, and which had been targeted by a shrewd marketing campaign that concentrated on the clubs where youth reigned sweaty, style-conscious and supreme. At its worst, however, disco was a banal and vacuous caricature of black music's more corporeal and sensual drives. The rhythmic complexity of black dance music was reduced to a brisk procession of dehumanized beats, swathed in syrupy synthesizers or sub-Philly strings to give it a sheen of pseudo-sophistication, and then topped with a few cursory chanted phrases. It could hold its own in the sexism and objectification stakes, too, as songs like Instant Funk's "Got my mind made up" urged, "Push it to me, baby/ slide it to me, baby./ If you want my money,/ you gotta make it good as honey".

Disco forsook the narrative themes of much soul and some funk for tireless exhortations to "Dance, dance, dance" (Chic), "Get down on it" (Kool and the Gang), and "Boogie-oogie-oogie" (A Taste of Honey). As a result, older black artists, or those with more complex lyrical visions and messages, were often neglected, or ill-served, by their record companies. Some, like Tyrone Davis ("Get on up, disco"), Gene Chandler ("Get down"), the Isley Brothers ("It's a disco night"), and Edwin Starr ("Contact"), found themselves aping the disco sound for Major labels who showed little understanding, and even less concern, for what these artists really did best. Indeed, Nelson George, who has rather melodramatically dated "the death of rhythm and blues" to the disco era and the consolidation of corporate control of black music in the mid 1970s, has argued more persuasively that the whole process of "incorporation" encouraged the fragmentation of a once relatively unified black music market "by class, and for the first time since the swing-bebop break, by age".[22]

Of course, this fragmentation was real enough and not simply the invention of corporate marketing strategies. Nevertheless, George was right that the industry did begin to exploit, and thereby accentuate and help give musical expression to, the deepening fissures in black society in the post revolutionary era. The simultaneous growth of a strong, better-educated, black professional and middle class with greater access to mainstream opportunities, and the encrustation of a massive poor, undereducated black working and non-working class, gave rise to markedly different lifestyles, expectations and perspectives even within the shared experience of being black in America. While race and racism continued to shape all black lives, regardless of whether one was a corporate executive or a welfare mother, these forces were increasingly experienced in different ways by different sectors of the black community in their day-to-day lives.

As ever, these different experiences generated different world views and musical tastes among black Americans. Rhythm and Blues was capacious enough to cater to them all. Although distinctions were never rigid, by the late 1970s and early 1980s many black middle-class adults had joined their white classmates in a fondness for smooth crossover acts like Lionel Richie, Teddy Pendergrass and later Anita Baker and Whitney Houston, and for stylish soulful vocalists like Frankie Beverly of the group Maze, Luther Vandross, Alexander O'Neal, and Freddie Jackson. These elegant artists were not diluting some black essence with their lush productions and uptown image of glitzy sophistication: they were merely expressing a particular aspect of the increasingly diverse black experience. Lower-class black adults, meanwhile, tended to go for darker funk tones, deep soul classics, and later for the rap stylings which spoke more directly to their still functionally segregated and disadvantaged black lives.

Cutting across these class lines were broadly discernible generational distinctions. Youngsters coming of age in the 1970s and early 1980s were less aware than their parents of the distance travelled by black Americans during the previous two decades of titanic struggle, but were only too conscious of the fact that it had not been nearly far enough to ensure

427

genuine equality of opportunity, let alone condition, for them. This sense of generational resentment and frustration against the system again manifested itself differently according to education, status and visible horizons. Many young middle-class blacks took up the personal challenge to try to make it in the mainstream through higher education and professional training, hoping to defy the enduring effects of racism and discrimination by going hell-for-leather after the American Dream. Some of these college graduates and young professionals ended up in the music industry where they tended to act primarily in accordance with their class allegiances and corporate responsibilities, and only thereafter with any discernible racial agenda.

Inner-city black kids, however, were usually without the education or opportunity to pursue such integrationist options and so had to make the ghetto their primary field of action, emotional succour, employment and entertainment. Not only were integration and opportunity seldom part of their experience, but unlike the generation which came of age amid the hopes and optimism of the early 1960s, they rarely allowed themselves the luxury of letting such far-fetched dreams interfere with their day-to-day struggle for money, shelter, self-respect and community. They functioned within an increasingly isolated and alienated black spatial and cultural enclave.

Disco had something to offer both these emerging young black cohorts in the mid-to-late 1970s. For the first generation of post-Movement, upwardly mobile, young middle-class blacks, gamely testing the extent to which traditional barriers to black advance really had been erased in the new meritocracy, disco's crossover success (white to black, as well as black to white) immediately gave it a certain cachet, while its glitzy sheen and plush nightclubs smacked of some sort of urbane, raceless modernity and sophistication.

In the inner cities, disco music was played at rather less grand neighbourhood clubs and house parties. Nonetheless, disco, with its subordination of mind and body to the discipline of the beat – fans were all "Slave to the rhythm", as Grace Jones put it – and its obsession with the most conspicuous consumerism and gaudiest styles, enabled poor young blacks to escape the ghetto temporarily into a world of frenetic dance steps and avid sartorial style wars.

Disco, then, was more than just a danceable form of music. It was a time and place of leisure where an alternative, exciting, exotic and passionate lifestyle could be imagined, lived and enjoyed in the paradoxical peace of a high volume, high energy, rhythmfest. Disco was more individualistic than the old vocal group, gang and dance scenes, yet it was nonetheless part of the same tradition of psychological survival. Jeff Lane, who managed and co-produced B.T. Express ("Do it 'til you're satisfied") and Brass Construction ("Movin'") – two fine bands who demonstrated that disco was often just streamlined funk – believed that "There's nothing in it that could help a person mentally. It's just dance, dance, dance. Blacks aren't accomplishing much by dancing". At one level Lane was right: disco was pretty much bereft of any political messages for blacks. Chic's Bernie Edwards was glad that other groups were "Laying down the heavy messages" because for him, too, disco was about dance and escapism.[23]

Yet, at another level, Lane and Edwards were missing the point; imagining too much, or rather the wrong sort of, power and politics in black popular music. On its own Rhythm and Blues had never *made* mass political or social action possible, or even likely, in any direct or simple way. It had always navigated the territory between being a cultural expression of a black insurgency which was organized by other means and essentially shaped by other intellectual, political and socio-economic forces, and being a surrogate for such action. In the late 1970s, in the absence of a viable Movement dedicated to opening up meaningful economic, social, political and educational opportunities for the black masses, music, dance and style once again became more of a surrogate, offering a vital cultural mechanism for personal expression and mental survival.

The intense energy, creativity and passion which many young inner-city blacks lavished on a disco phenomenon which, at the point of record production at least, had quickly lost much of its artistic integrity, reflected the need to escape, however temporarily, the grim realities and mounting frustrations of black urban life. In the process, these dancing and preening young blacks and their deejays appropriated disco and reinscribed it as a potent cultural, rather than simply a profitable commercial, phenomenon. As dazzlingly dexterous black club deejays worked the twin turntables of their huge sound systems, they transformed the stark electronic hardware into a flexible musical instrument in its own right, cutting and mixing together the best sections of the best 12-inch disco singles. These swollen singles were not only easier for deejays to manipulate than 7-inch disks, but the broader spacing of the grooves meant that they could be played at much greater volumes without too much distortion. In particular, deejays worked with the obligatory extended rhythm breaks featured on most disco 12-inchers. Using the second turntable to overlay snippets of old and fresh funk, lost-found soul classics, and even splashes of reggae, rock and rhetoric, they created seamless collages of new danceable black noise. Sometimes the deejays or their aides even took to chanting rhymes, boasts and encouragements to dancers over the mix; sometimes they rotated the disks backwards and forwards, making a rhythmic scratching sound which added to the percussive complexity of the mix. These early helter-skelter rides on the wheels of steel by the likes of DJ Hollywood and the Jamaican-born Kool DJ Herc in the Bronx, and the fearsome dance-offs they inspired among their fans, sowed the seeds of the rap music and hip-hop culture which flowered in the 1980s.

"On your radio": NATRA and black-oriented radio
in the black power era

As payola investigators discovered, the success of disco and the growing corporate presence in Rhythm and Blues depended crucially on securing access to black-oriented radio. At the same time, the relative racial integration of the popular music market in this new corporate discofied age also encouraged many black-oriented broadcasters to reorient their programming towards a more general market audience. In the mid-to-late 1970s, many putatively soul stations began to re-designate themselves "urban" or "contemporary hits" stations. These offered much more eclectic, racially mixed playlists where, for a while, disco of various hues dominated, and where later Michael Jackson, Anita Baker and Prince nestled comfortably next to Elton John, Madonna and George Michael.

Back in 1966, an earnest white civil rights activist called Dave Berkman had suggested in the *Columbia Journalism Review* that this sort of multi-racial programming should be encouraged as in keeping with the avowed integrationist goals of the civil rights movement. Blacks, Berkman argued, ought not to support racially distinct broadcasting services, particularly not soul radio which encouraged stereotyped pastiches of black speech and lifestyles while promoting the crudest, least elevating of black musical styles. Soul radio, Berkman maintained, was a cynical commercial ploy by white station owners and managers who cared nothing about the quality of the music they played, or the black community's struggle for equality, beyond its marketability.[24]

Michael Lottman, the black editor of *The Southern Courier*, based in Montgomery, responded indignantly to Berkman's article, defending the role of black-oriented broadcasting in promoting a sense of communal identity and pride. "Here in Montgomery", he explained, "the Negro stations are the only ones that take the slightest interest in the Negro community". He also chastised Berkman for his elitist dismissal of black popular culture. "Mr Berkman may prefer cultured white tones to what he calls the 'Negro speech pattern', and he may prefer 'quality' Negro jazz to 'soul' music", Lottman railed, but the mass of blacks did not.[25]

As the decade wore on, although black activists never joined Berkman's call for an end to specifically black-oriented programming, they did increasingly echo his core criticisms of the medium rather than Lottman's praises. In 1970, Bernard Garnett published a report for the Race Relations Information Center in Nashville in which he asked, "Is the broadcasting industry's budding sense of 'blackness' much more than the recognition of black power as a new commercial commodity? . . . Is 'soul', black radio style, the acceptance of the black man's quest for self-determination or is it a superficial sales slogan?"[26]

In an era when *Ebony* shamelessly ran advertisements for "Soul brothers blended scotch whiskey", and promoted Brut aftershave with the crass slogan, "There's a little bit of Brut in every soul. There's a little bit of soul in every Brut", there was a fear that the sort of cultural pride and solidarity promoted by soul music and soul radio might atrophy and become a dead end in itself; that the black community's new capacity to feel good about itself might degenerate into a sort of souled-out complacency rather than act as the catalyst for effective challenges to the black predicament. "Do we need 24 hours of James Brown?", asked William Wright of the Unity House project in Washington, D.C., and founder of the black media pressure group Best Efforts for Soul in Television (BEST). "We need to talk about drug addiction, about slum landlords, about jobs, about education. But the white man gives us 24 hours of 'soul' because it pads his already stuffed pockets and keeps black people ignorant".[27]

It was this lack of attention to black community affairs and the paucity of reliable news coverage which motivated organizations like NATRA, BEST, the National Black Media Coalition (NBMC), the Citizens' Communications Center, the United Church of Christ, as well as SCLC, SNCC and NAACP, to intensify the campaign for greater coverage of black social, political and economic matters on air. These campaigners also sought to increase the numbers of black station owners (which had crawled up to about a dozen at the turn of the decade), executives and senior management in the industry, believing that this was the key to unlocking black oriented radio's latent political and communal potential. "For blacks to gain control of a significant portion of the electronic media", insisted Charles Hamilton, Stokely Carmichael's collaborator on the influential *Black power* manifesto, "would be the most important single breakthrough in the black struggle, and would justify every bit of time, talent and resources expended towards its achievement".[28]

In the late 1960s and early 1970s, this campaign for black media control and accountability became an important part of the quest for black power, uniting many diverse and often hostile elements within that notoriously loose coalition. Harold Cruse, for example, advocated a sort of black power as ethnic politics and called for black control of the apparatus of black cultural production and dissemination as an important step towards realizing the political and economic potential of the black masses. SNCC's James Forman argued that it was the absence of black "control of the means of communication" which had enabled opponents of black power to redefine that term for their own ends. As a result "black power" had too easily become equated with "anti-white", rather than "pro-black", sentiment. Even the Congress of Afrikan Peoples, at a 1970 Atlanta conference which was in many respects the apogee of the cultural nationalist impulse, temporarily emerged from its preoccupation with Maulana Ron Karenga's Africanisms to address the logistical problems of securing black control of the black communications media in America.[29]

The concern about harnessing the political potential of black-oriented radio was not just restricted to manifestos and theoretical position papers. One of the most intriguing attempts to put ideas into action came from Robert Williams, the idiosyncratic civil rights leader from Monroe, North Carolina, who had been drummed out of the NAACP in 1959 for publicly endorsing the black right to armed self-defence. In exile in Cuba, Fidel Castro allowed Williams to set up his *Radio Free Dixie* show, which from July 1962 to March 1966 beamed thrice-weekly condemnations of Yankee imperialism, reports of black protests, and critiques of the capitalist roots of racial oppression into the American South. "*Radio Free Dixie* was meant to be a voice of agitation and prophesy", Williams explained. "It played the music, the bitter protest songs, and spoke a biting truth that no other station dared program". Williams recognized that there were few things more likely to have his listeners scrambling for the dial than hour after hour of unrelieved propaganda and so segued his political messages into a mix of "Afro-American jazz, the blues and good soul music".[30]

Mainstream civil rights groups also continued their attempts to weld the elusive political, educational and economic potential of black-oriented radio to progressive ends. Activists from the Urban League and NAACP in Washington were among those who formed the Washington Community Broadcast Company (WCBC) in 1966. The WCBC appealed to the FCC against the re-licensing of WOOK, charging that the station's all-soul format was "far beneath [the] dignity and educational standards" of the black audience. After a protracted campaign, in which the SCLC also took part, the station's licence was finally revoked in 1975.[31]

Around the turn of the decade, there was also a spate of direct action protests designed to challenge discriminatory employment practices and inadequate service to the black community at a number of other soul stations, including WOIC-Columbia, South Carolina and WVOL-Nashville. In Richmond a coalition of black organizations grouped around the city's NAACP chapter to lobby the FCC about 17 local radio and television stations which it was claimed discriminated against blacks in hiring and promotion practices.[32]

The FCC was a particular source of anger and resentment. Not only did this body lack a single black member until Ben Hooks was appointed in 1972, but it was argued that the Commission consistently failed to use its powers to enforce compliance with fair employment laws on behalf of blacks, or to honour its own "public interest" criteria when renewing licences for stations serving the black community. As Del Shields had complained at NATRA's 1967 convention, too often, white-owned, black-oriented stations secured their licences from the FCC with a proposal to serve the black audience, but then sought to "change R & B stations to general market stations at the expense of the Negro community". The FCC's inaction in such cases merely served to highlight the yawning gap between the statutory equality won by the early civil rights movement and genuine equality of opportunity and condition.[33]

Following the emergence of a more radical executive committee in the mid 1960s, NATRA stood at the forefront of the campaign for greater black power within the recording and radio business. The growing black militancy and escalating racial tensions within these interdependent industries eventually culminated at NATRA's 1968 Miami Convention, when violence, real and imagined, pervaded the proceedings. For several months before the August meeting Shields was the victim of anonymous warnings and one physical assault urging him to tone down NATRA's increasingly shrill condemnations of whites and demands for black power. Other members of NATRA were similarly harassed and tensions mounted between black broadcasters and the whites who still occupied the major positions of power and influence in radio, and in the recording industry which furnished it with product.

The assassination of Martin Luther King in April 1968 had greatly increased those tensions, dramatizing the question of what constituted "responsible" broadcasting to the black community in the midst of urban unrest. Interestingly, the response of black-oriented radio to the King riots, as to earlier ones in Harlem, Watts and Detroit, was generally to downplay events, offering highly selective news coverage and generally emphasizing the "legitimate", nonviolent, channels for airing black grievances. Nighthawk, on WOL-Washington DC, for example, urged everyone to restrain from violence and go home out of respect for King. As Shields himself recalled, "everybody who was on the air at that time, including myself, told people to cool it. We tried to do everything possible to keep the black people from just exploding even more than they were".[34]

These responsible actions earned approval from various establishment bodies. City Hall representatives in Cleveland thanked WABQ and WJMO for helping to calm the situation. Similar commendations came from the Los Angeles police department for KGFJ and from Denver police chief George Seaton for KDKO. Other stations, including WSM and WMCT in Memphis, earned commendations from local police and state officials for their pacifying roles. At WMCT, the news director, Norm Brewer, was "extremely careful. I ordered everyone on my staff to report only what he had seen, not what someone had told him". In fact, many stations regularly censored news of rioting, hoping to avoid copycat incidents.[35]

In the midst of the destruction and violence of April 1968, the moderating response of black-oriented stations and their deejays was understandable. But it is important to locate this specific response under exceptional circumstances within the broader context of a consistently conservative attitude by most black-oriented stations towards the goals and tactics of the black struggle. In 1967, even NATRA radicals Clyde Otis, Del Shields and Clarence Avante had established the Take A Look Foundation to coordinate efforts to use black-oriented radio to defuse the tensions which had boiled over into violence during the "long hot summers" of the 1960s.

WILA-Danville had a tape of moderating messages from civil rights leaders and black celebrities especially prepared for broadcast in the event of summer rioting. At KCOH-Houston, white president Robert Meeker explained the station's policy towards the coverage of urban rioting: "Our news is screened so that when an individual with treasonous motives says 'go out in the street and kill and burn' we do not report this".[36]

Apart from such manipulation of news information, militants felt that soul radio discouraged black protest and insurgency and reinforced the racial and economic status quo in more subtle ways. Corporate giants, Lever Brothers, for instance, sponsored an uplifting show called *Spotlight on Your Future*, which stressed the basic openness of the American system and what young blacks could achieve with just "proper education and training". Somewhat more responsive to the needs of the community were a new breed of radio "phone-ins" like *The People Speak* on WNJ-Union, New Jersey, and *Family Line* on WAOK-Atlanta, which appeared, often in response to organized community pressure, towards the end of the decade. These shows provided the black community with both a valuable arena for peer discussion and, through the use of guest experts, a free source of information and advice on a variety of legal, medical, economic and political matters. But these shows were seldom the vehicles for any sort of mass community mobilization. As Leon Lewis, the host of WLIB-New York's award-winning *Community Opinion*, admitted, his intention was to defuse black anger, not to channel it into militant politics or revolutionary action. "I'm just trying to keep the lid on", he explained. It was this basic conservatism, the way in which black-oriented radio was routinely used as a social palliative rather than a stimulus to mass action against continuing racism and its effects, which NATRA and its allies hoped to rectify by securing greater black ownership and executive power in the broadcasting industry.[37]

At NATRA's Miami meeting in August 1968, a sinister group of armed black New Yorkers calling themselves the Fair Play Committee (FPC) and led by Dino "Boom Boom" Woodward and writer-producer Johnnie Baylor stalked the Convention. The FPC demanded money with menaces from the white record company and radio executives present and insisted on the immediate black takeover of black cultural and media resources. There were rumours of kidnappings, guns were brandished, fists flew and insults were exchanged. Some of the whites at the hub of the soul industry, like record producer and label owner Marshall Sehorn, were attacked. Otis Redding's manager Phil Walden was threatened and verbally abused. Jerry Wexler was hung in effigy and, like most of the white executives present, left speedily.[38]

As black Stax songwriter Homer Banks explained to Peter Guralnick, there was a certain inevitability to this confrontation after years of white exploitation of black musical talent and under the pervasive influence of black power rhetoric. "I really think a lot of hostilities surfaced . . . It was heavy, but it was destined to come, if not at Miami then somewhere else . . . Blacks made the music, Blacks made the audience, but the ownership was white". Del Shields said much the same during his Miami address. "The black man sings, records, arranges, produces, sells and exposes the records. However . . . he does not enjoy positions and responsibility in management where decisions are made which affect his future".[39]

Yet, if the NATRA conventions in Miami and the following year in Washington exemplified black militancy within the broadcasting and recording industries, closer examination revealed the ambiguous nature of that militancy. It is clear that many blacks felt alienated by the wave of black nationalism which swept the conventions. The radicalism of powerful contingents within NATRA, though dynamic and highly conspicuous, actually concealed a core of more moderate blacks who continued to work for gains within the established framework of the radio and recording industries.

The tension between these different groupings and strategies within NATRA was apparent in Shields' own rhetoric and represented a microcosm of the broader tactical and ideological schisms of the black power era. Shields' angry demands for black ownership and community accountability were tempered by more pragmatic pleas for fairness from the white executives and owners who still dominated the industry. Shields even invoked recent memories of black-oriented radio's moderating response to the riots which followed Martin Luther King's assassination to urge station owners to provide greater rewards and opportunities for responsible black broadcasters: "You called on us during the dark hours after the death of Dr King and we responded well", Shields reminded them.[40]

Here was realism intruding on the radical posturing and doomed separatism of black power; a recognition that the distribution of resources and power in the industry, as in the larger American context, was such that demands for black power, however dramatically expressed or psychologically potent, were unlikely to force the redistribution of economic and political power along new racial lines. The same pragmatism was evident when, at the height of the Miami convention, a group of southern black deejays complained that NATRA's executive officers should spend less time politicking and concentrate instead on securing pay rises.

It was only when the militants abandoned NATRA in 1969 – Shields and Avante went west to buy station KACE-Los Angeles – that the true centre of political gravity among black broadcasters became clearer. Under the control of a more representative executive NATRA rapidly returned to its original function as a social club which quietly sought patronage for black-oriented radio and expanded black opportunities within the existing structure of the industry. This new-found moderation was reflected in the fact that even Motown felt it safe to renew its links with the organization. In August 1970, after the radical exodus, Gordy generously donated $25,000 to NATRA. This was five years after the Supremes had recorded a theme song, "Things are changing", for the organization and, no doubt coincidentally, a matter of months after Gordy was named the first recipient of NATRA's Martin Luther King Jr Leadership Award. In 1972, Alvin Dixon, president of NATRA from 1969 to 1971, left to set up a southern-based alternative, Broadcast and Music Arts, complaining bitterly that NATRA had abandoned the struggle for better black opportunities and community service in black radio to become "nothing but a social fraternity".[41]

By mid-decade, NATRA was dead and a number of new organizations emerged to fill the void. In 1974, one of the dogged heroes of the ongoing battle for better, more responsible black-oriented broadcasting, Pluria Marshall, founded the National Black Media Coalition. By 1987, the NBMC had secured $3 million in scholarships and $6 million in grants and equipment for black-oriented broadcasting, as well as facilitating the sale of 82 radio and television outlets to black buyers. The late 1970s also saw the emergence of the National Association of Black-owned Broadcasters, the Young Black Programmers Coalition, and the Minority and Special Services Division of the National Assocation of Broadcasters. All of these groups worked to stop discrimination and open up black opportunities in the broadcasting industry.[42]

The real successor to NATRA, however, was the Black Music Association (BMA), which had a similar vision but a broader brief to protect black interests in the overlapping worlds of recording, radio, concert promotions and music publishing. BMA, however, was heavily dependent on sponsorship to the tune of $500,000 a year from major companies like CBS, A&M, RCA and Motown. It was soon dominated by a new breed of ambitious black executives working for, or closely with, those same corporations. Personally and financially enmeshed in the corporate structure of the recording and radio industry, BMA ultimately proved to be an even more conservative organization than the latter-day NATRA.[43]

Despite these diverse initiatives by NATRA, its allies and heirs, Rhythm and Blues remained the staple diet of black-oriented radio. By the early 1970s, typical stations like WVON-Chicago, WWRL-New York, WCHB-Detroit, KDIA-San Francisco, and WYLD-New Orleans devoted more than 90 per cent of their airtime to music and most others programmed over 70 per cent. SCLC advisor and Washington, D.C. representative Walter Fauntroy might make the legitimate observation that while "[t]he great appeal is the rhythm and blues music[, p]eople tune in to listen to the music . . . then they hear about employment and slums and action", in reality there was still relatively little of that sort of programming on commercial black-oriented radio. Nationally, less than 5 per cent of black-oriented airtime was allocated to news and public affairs in the 1970s – considerably less than stations like WDIA and WERD had provided 20 years earlier.[44]

Stax and the end of a dream

Relationships between blacks and whites within the music and broadcasting industry deteriorated rapidly after the Miami uprising of 1968. For a while the FPC functioned like the armed wing of NATRA. Darkening the door-ways of black-oriented record companies, distributors and radio stations, members of the groups collected payola and protection monies at gunpoint from executives, black and white, who wished both to stay healthy and keep their products on the air and in the shops. Many of those who had initially sympathized with the drive to secure better rewards and opportunities for blacks within the industry realized that, not unlike many chapters of the Black Panther Party, the FPC had degenerated into little more than an extortion racket cum street gang, which masqueraded as a black political organiza-tion and did much to poison already ailing race relations in the business.[45]

Even Harold Battiste, ever a champion of black power in the industry, was disillusioned with the new turn of events. Once he and the AFO Exec-utives had admired NATRA for its efforts at black empowerment. "We really thought they were on a similar mission, trying to own some radio stations, trying to get into ownership". By 1968, however, NATRA – or powerful elements associated with it – had long since traded that original idea to indulge in a rather sordid form of self-serving gangsterism. NATRA, com-plained Battiste, had become all about money. It was "the sort of place where they could get money and put the pressure on record companies to get money and do all that stuff".[46]

Joe Lackey at WENN recalled the FPC coming into his Birmingham sta-tion with their "dashikis and sawn-off shotguns", demanding a share of the station's profits in return for protection. Lackey had also once been a sup-porter of NATRA, sponsoring a regional meeting of the Association in 1964, and hiring an agent to run "Tall" Paul White's unsuccessful candidacy for the presidency of the organization the same year. But this invasion was a bit too much for the placid white station manager who called the FBI. Although the FBI did not appear to be particularly interested, according to Lackey shortly afterwards Sheriff Mel Bailey and his men cornered the FPC mem-bers in a house they were using and riddled it with warning gunfire. Within hours "the Fair Play Committee hit the road", but the atmosphere at the station remained tense. Even WENN's foremost gospel deejay, the Reverend Erskine Faush, started coming to work packing a pistol. It was a tragic indictment of a worsening situation that, whereas in 1963 WENN's black staff had worked in fear of white racist attacks – and done so willingly in the service of a great progressive cause – in the early 1970s they sought protection from renegade elements in the black community who used the mask of radical racial politics to hide their cynical profiteering.[47]

Dickie Kline was a promotion man at Atlantic, which did pay protection money to the FPC to avoid boycotts of its records. Kline felt that this sort of black militancy actually led to the partial re-segregation of the music business. Record companies, anxious to appear sensitive to black demands for more control over the production and dissemination of black music, began to organize separate black subsidiaries, and separate black promotional and distribution departments to supply black products to black retail and broadcasting outlets. Ironically, while this undoubtedly opened up positions for those blacks lucky enough to make it through the rapidly revolving door of corporate opportunity, this sort of re-segregation also reversed the tentative trends and bolder dreams of the previous two decades.[48]

These developments were particularly destructive at Stax, where the key figure was Al Bell. By 1970, Bell, an Arkansas-born political science graduate, ex-deejay and songwriter, had risen to become a vice-president

Veteran deejay and singer Rufus Thomas had been with Stax virtually from the beginning, and hung on until the bitter end. Here he is shown with Jondelle Johnson, herself a veteran of the Atlanta student movement and subsequently a stalwart of the NAACP in the city.

and partner in the company. As one might expect of a veteran of an SCLC leadership training summer school, Bell remained basically proud of the racial integration which had given Stax its distinctive character and sound: "when you look at Booker T. and the MGs, you see four guys, two black and two white, who have been integrated for the past seven years", Bell enthused.[49]

The FPC and other black power radicals, however, had a different perspective on Stax's biracialism and saw it as just another example of white exploitation and expropriation of black creativity. Although the circumstances remain obscure, the FPC had somehow got to Al Bell at the Miami NATRA convention, when he mysteriously disappeared for several days. Joe Lackey, who knew Bell from his short spell as a deejay at WENN, heard that the FPC had actually broken Bell's legs in order to state their case for a stake in Stax more forcefully. Certainly, after Miami, FPC leaders "Boom Boom" Woodward and Johnnie Baylor were suddenly invited to join the label's staff. Immediately, they tried to make the company a bastion of black power, driving a wedge between the black and white artists, writers and producers who had made it great. Booker T. Jones was advised not to play with his white colleagues in the MGs, while guitarist Steve Cropper was accused of taking unfair royalty payments for his numerous production credits on Stax records. The atmosphere at the label became unbearable, particularly in the wake of the King riots which raged in the neighbourhood where Stax was located. Memphis street gangs began to demand protection money and guns became almost as common in the studio as guitars.[50]

By late 1972, the label's white founder Jim Stewart had had enough. In October 1972, a couple of months after Wattstax, Al Bell completed arrangements to buy out Stewart's remaining 50 per cent share of Stax. For this Bell used part of the $6 million advance he had secured from CBS's Clive Davis for expansion – money which was really the sweetener that allowed the corporation to take over the distribution of Stax products. Not surprisingly, when Davis was ousted the relationship between Stax and CBS – sealed by a handshake, rather than a contract – was less close and increasingly contentious, with each side claiming the other was failing to meet its responsibilities.[51]

Bell's inability to work amicably with CBS only partially explains why, between 1972 and 1975, Stax disintegrated in a confused jumble of financial irregularities, mismanagement, and internal friction. In November 1972, Johnnie Baylor was arrested after flying from Memphis to Birmingham with a suitcase stuffed with $140,000 in cash. Although Baylor was subsequently released on a technicality relating to the circumstances of the seizure in Birmingham, the discovery precipitated an IRS investigation into his affairs. In June 1973, his own KoKo label – distributed by Stax – was served with a $1.8 million lien. The following year a bank audit revealed that Stax had been renting an extravagant $250,000-a-year apartment for Baylor in New

York. Eventually, in October 1978, Baylor was found guilty of fraudulently obtaining some $2.54 million from Stax during the years 1972 and 1973.[52]

In the midst of the national concern with payola, the Baylor bag snatch and trial also prompted investigations into Stax's financial affairs by the IRS and a New York grand jury. In August 1973, these probes revealed a kickback scheme worth over $406,000 run by two Stax executives, Ewell Roussell and Herbert Kolsesky, and involving the strategic placement of thousands of free records and tapes around the country in return for a cut of the profits from subsequent sales. In September 1974, Isaac Hayes sued the company for $5.3 million for non-payment of his own salary and royalties. A month later CBS sued Stax for reneging on its agreement to produce product for distribution, while in February and April 1975 respectively RCA and Viewlex also sued Stax for non-payment of various bills. Worse was to follow. In July 1975, Bell and an official of the Union Planters National Bank in Memphis, Joseph Harwell, were indicted for securing fraudulent bank loans totalling some $18 million. In April 1976, Bell was cleared of these and related tax evasion charges, although Harwell – already serving a five-year sentence for embezzlement – was found guilty on two of the eleven counts in his indictment. By this time Stax, the great hope of southern biracialism, was doomed. In December 1975, Stax's creditors successfully filed a bankruptcy petition, and seven months later, after several counter-suits, stays of executions and rescue attempts, the company was declared finally and irredeemably bankrupt.[53]

According to Bell this was premature. He felt that Stax had fallen victim to the white Memphis business community's desire to save the troubled Union Planters National Bank by immediately recouping around $10.5 million in loans to Stax – loans which had initially been arranged on a long-term basis. He also felt that there was pressure from those same white interests to destroy the powerful, increasingly militant black-owned business which had emerged in their midst. Bell was not alone in this assessment of the racial co-ordinates of the various suits and investigations visited upon Stax. During his own fraud trial, a defence witness testified that a business consultant hired by the Union Planters Bank to help run Stax's publishing arm, East Memphis Music Corp., had boasted that he would get "all the niggers out of Stax". Ralph Abernathy, who with Walter Fauntroy attended part of Bell's trial, saw a legal echo of Martin Luther King's assassination in the "false and untrue" charges levelled against Bell, describing them as "another attempt to destroy" a black leader in Memphis. Rev. Billy Kyles of PUSH, which had itself received some $100,000 from Stax, publicly condemned the bank for "making some obvious moves to destroy a black giant".[54]

While these suspicions were probably not without foundation, it really did not need a racially motivated conspiracy to send Stax to the wall once the FPC entered the picture. There was more than enough internal incompetence, confusion and avarice to account for its demise. The problems were certainly not at the creative end, since throughout its tribulations Stax continued to make and sell some excellent records by the likes of the Staple Singers, Johnnie Taylor, Isaac Hayes and Luther Ingram. In 1972, revenue of some $10 million made the newly black-owned (if still largely white-funded) Stax the twelfth biggest "black" enterprise in America. As numerous legal and fiscal crises raged in and around it, Stax's relative financial position actually improved. By mid 1974, it was the fifth biggest black-owned business in America. Remarkably, in the midst of the black power era it was even dabbling quite successfully in country music with the "black speck" O.B. McClinton ("Don't let the green grass fool you"), and the white Cliff Cochran.[55]

In fact, the problem was not revenue, which was over $13 million in 1974, nor persecution, but improper accounting procedures, lax management, and a criminal element which undermined the label's financial stability and integrity from within. This combination produced a spate of cripplingly high salaries and unsecured loans for company employees and the sundry other hangers-on who haunted Stax in its last years. It also allowed for virtually limitless, and generally unmonitored, expense accounts for most of its executives. This created the ample opportunities for fraud and deception which Baylor and others were quick to exploit.[56]

By the time O.B. McClinton (right) emerged as one of Stax's foremost black country talents in the early 1970s, tensions at the label were nearing breaking point, and armed guards were a regular presence in the studio.

Black-oriented radio and the dilemmas of black capitalism

Al Bell spent more than a decade clearing himself of any charges of wrong-doing relating to Stax. During the label's grim collapse and its aftermath he maintained a degree of quiet integrity and community conscience which contrasted with the bolder and brassier, but frequently hollow posturing and rhetoric of many avowed militants. Indeed, the actions of Baylor and other blacks in the industry suggested that they saw black power chiefly as a means to, maybe even a synonym for, personal gain. They could talk the talk of revolution and castigate whitey – always an easy, if understandably popular, option for wannabe black militants. Yet these people often had little sense of communal responsibility, let alone a programme for using their power to advance anyone's interests but their own.[57]

This was rather a blow to those militants who had assumed that the latent political, social and economic potential of black-oriented radio, and of the music which constituted its main fare, would be realized once blacks acquired more labels and stations, and enjoyed greater representation at managerial and executive levels. In fact, while both black-oriented radio and the recording industry were classic examples of continuing black economic underdevelopment and restricted opportunity, the belief that a simple increase of black ownership and senior management would inevitably herald a new era of racial responsibility and political leadership was deeply flawed.

Some, like the Black Panthers, were under few illusions that black capitalists would necessarily prove to be much better for the black masses than their white counterparts. Many militants, however, routinely misjudged the dominant impulses of entrepreneurial capitalism in general and, in particular, the motivations, priorities and freedom of action of those few blacks who did rise to positions of executive responsibility or proprietorial power within the recording and broadcasting industries.

The dilemmas of these successful black entrepreneurs, artists and professionals could be clearly seen in the story of black-oriented radio during the black power era. Radio stations were expensive to build, buy and operate and thus any extension of black ownership was severely hampered by a basic lack of the necessary finance capital. Consequently, when black individuals or consortiums did secure station ownership, they could often afford only small, underpowered facilities, unable to reach the most lucrative metropolitan audiences. Somewhere near the bottom of the price scale was WORV-Hattiesburg, the first black-owned radio station in Mississippi, which cost Reuben C. Hughes and brothers, Vernon C. and Robert L. Floyd $60,000 to put into service in 1969. At the top end of the scale were prime urban stations like WBLS/WLIB-New York, which in 1971 cost the Inner City Broadcasting group between $1.7 million and $1.9 million.[58]

Given the cost of entry into the radio business, those blacks who did acquire stations, either as individuals or as members of cartels like Sheridan

Broadcasting and Inner City Broadcasting, had usually made fortunes else-where already. They were highly successful businessmen, professionals and entertainers, like restaurateur Charles J. Prickard (WMPP-Chicago Heights), dentists Haley Bell and Wendell Cox (WCHB-Detroit), gynaecologist William V. Banks (WGPR-Detroit), engineer Earl Clark (WWWS:FM-Saginaw), mil-lionaire publishers Clarence Jones of the *Amsterdam News* (WBLS/WLIB-New York) and John H. Johnson of Johnson Publishing (WVON-Chicago), and singer James Brown (WEBB-Baltimore, WJBE-Knoxville and WRDW-Augusta).

Nevertheless, few were in a position to buy their stations outright and most black-owned stations were actually purchased through private, often white, investment companies, government-sponsored Minority Enterprise Small Business Investment Companies (MESBICs), or a combination of both. Between 1969 and 1983, MESBICs financially assisted some 4,000 small com-panies, including 90 per cent of all black-owned communications firms. Inner City Broadcasting's purchase of WBLS/WLIB, for instance, was achieved with the assistance of a MESBIC and the Chemical Bank corporation. This dependency of nominally "black" enterprises on corporate and state finan-cial apparatus, coupled with the need for FCC licence accreditation and revenue from corporate advertising, exposed the myth of black economic self sufficiency so dear to some proponents of black capitalism as black power.[59]

By the early 1970s, the tiny group of wealthy black station owners had been joined in the business by a slightly larger corps of black college gradu-ates, many of whom were alumni of Howard University where there was a prestigious communications course. Ambitious, talented black professionals like Vernon Slaughter, Gwen Franklin, Paris Eley, Shiela Eldridge, Milton Allen, Tom Draper, and Logan Westbrooks emerged from this college back-ground to take up important and lucrative positions throughout the black-oriented broadcasting and recording industries. There they found positions as programme directors and station managers, as well as deejays and news reporters, and, with the partial re-segregation of many recording compan-ies, as heads of black A&R, promotion and marketing departments.[60]

This professional and entrepreneurial elite constituted an unlikely stra-tum of black society from which to expect support for radical black politics, since their racial loyalties were often tempered by personal economic and status considerations. Their entry into positions of some power and influ-ence within the corporate entertainment industry, no matter how circum-scribed that power, represented a triumph of sorts and they were cautious about jeopardizing it for the sake of racial militancy.

Indeed, it ultimately proved difficult for any black organization to be-grudge individual blacks, or black cartels, their economic success and secur-ity in the midst of continuing racial discrimination. Sometimes against their better judgement, and always against the lessons of history, many militants continued to invest at least tentative hopes for the future of the black masses in expanded black capitalism and the entrenchment of a strong black middle and upper class. Even the Black Panthers tried to make a tricky distinction between those black capitalists who simply pursued their narrow self-interest, and the more enlightened "black capitalist who has the interest of the community at heart" and "responds to the needs of the people", by putting back something – jobs, housing, social facilities, money – into that community. Huey Newton appreciated that for the black masses such capitalists represented positive examples of "black control of local institutions".[61]

Harry Belafonte, whose own radicalism sometimes left him perplexed as to whether successful blacks like himself were doomed to be a permanent part of the wider problem of racial and economic exploitation, rather than instrumental in its solution, recognized that here was a real double-bind. "In all its naivety, I don't know what the options were", he admitted. "If you are talking about integrating into America", economic success, wealth and power "is everyone's dream in America . . . The integration movement held that as a part of the implicit rewards for that effort. The hope was that enough people would get into that place of power and be astute enough, morally driven enough, to turn around and make a significant difference where it counted most. And that has not happened".[62]

Certainly, the principal concern of most of those involved in the business of black-oriented radio was to deliver the largest possible audience to sponsors and advertisers, just as most of those involved in the business of recording Rhythm and Blues sought to sell as many of those recordings as possible. As with James Brown, Berry Gordy and most other successful black entrepreneurs in the recording industry, specifically racial agendas and community commitments were routinely subordinated to, if rarely eradicated by, the pursuit of maximum economic rewards.

This complex layering of personal and communal priorities was apparent in the 20-year broadcasting career of Jesse Blayton, the Oklahoma-born black Georgia accountant, businessman and educator, who in 1949 had bought WERD-Atlanta: the first black-owned radio station in the country. Blayton was an admirer and protégé of Heman E. Perry, one of the most prominent black businessmen in Atlanta in the early twentieth century and a living exemplar of Booker T. Washington's self-help ethic. In 1932, three years after Perry's death, Blayton and two black partners purchased Perry's flagship banking operation, Citizens Trust Bank, as the first step in an impressive empire-building career. In 1948, Citizens Trust became the first black bank to be included in the Federal Reserve System, while BLAMIYA – the holding company Blayton set up with his partners, Lorimer Milton and Clayton Yates – controlled a substantial share of the thriving segregated business of black Atlanta.[63]

Blayton's expertise was in finance and accountancy and in 1949, when he ploughed his entire estate into WERD, he was the only black certified public accountant in the state of Georgia. He was a prominent, if rather self-effacing, member of black Atlanta's professional, business and social elite. This was a relatively large, but tightly-knit, almost incestuous, cadre of prominent black men. For example, Martin Luther King Jr's father, Daddy King, was a trustee of Citizens Trust, of which Blayton was president. Blayton himself was a trustee of the Ebenezer Baptist Church, where both Kings held pastorates.[64]

It would be a gross misrepresentation to suggest that men like Daddy King or Jesse Blayton accepted the legitimacy of segregation in the South: indeed, there is ample evidence that they loathed the system and resisted it, publicly and privately, at every opportunity. Yet there is also no doubt that they had found a pragmatic *modus vivendi* with Jim Crow and had become men of considerable wealth and influence within their racial enclave. This relative comfort resulted in an understandable caution on matters of civil rights activism on the part of the black professional and entrepreneurial elite. While generally sympathetic to the call of race advancement, they feared that untoward agitation would bring down the wrath of the white South and destroy their hard-won, if segregated, social and business positions.

Mrs Mack Saddler, Blayton's longtime assistant and wife of WERD's station manager, Al Saddler, insisted that Blayton desperately "wanted the civil rights movement to succeed. He gave it all he could in the way of money, and more than he should have in the way of free time". Yet even the loyal Saddler admitted that Blayton mostly offered a behind-the-scenes sort of assistance which avoided any dangerous public association with black insurgency. Indeed, so covert was Blayton's personal involvement that it largely escaped the notice of most blacks engaged in either the Movement or black broadcasting in Atlanta. WERD's news broadcaster and *Atlanta World* journalist William Fowlkes believed Blayton was actually rather more conservative on matters of racial protest than other black Atlanta entrepreneurs at this time. "He lent support, but didn't speak out . . . he wasn't very active politically", Fowlkes recalled. Gospel deejay Esmond Patterson, who got his start on WERD, agreed with Fowlkes. "Blayton wasn't that type of man. He was a businessman. He was no civil rights worker . . . that wasn't his bag . . . Blayton just was not involved in civil rights. He let those that were involved in it be on his station . . . but he was never involved in that".[65]

In Blayton's case, the relationship between economic interests and the broader needs of the Movement was dramatized by his ambiguous role in the affairs of Martin Luther King Jr following King's indictment by an Alabama grand jury on tax evasion charges in February 1960. As a family friend, business associate and, in his capacity as a trustee of Ebenezer, one of King's bosses, it was not surprising that Blayton should put his accounting skills at the service of the civil rights leader. He undertook a detailed analysis of King's financial records with a view to producing a defensible case in court. Yet Blayton clearly viewed these services as a commercial transaction and in June billed the embattled King $4,000 for two weeks' work. Disillusioned and disappointed, King wrote archly to Morehouse president Benjamin Mays, complaining that "I never felt that lawyers and accountants would charge such exorbitant fees". "Before he was through", Taylor Branch has noted, Blayton "had charged King nearly as much to audit two tax returns as King earned from Ebenezer in an entire year". If this "milking King's predicament", as Branch called it, was hardly evidence of a burning commitment to the Movement, it was entirely in keeping with Blayton's hardnosed, unflappable, commercial agenda.[66]

As with his work for Martin Luther King, Jesse Blayton's motives for financing WERD were at root economic. Indeed, for Blayton, as for Berry Gordy and James Brown, black entrepreneurial success was a form of progressive community politics. "He was always thinking capital, capital, capital", explained Mack Saddler, who often heard Blayton arguing that "the reason we can't do anything is that we don't have the capital to invest" in black business enterprises. Throughout his career, Blayton let very little sway him from his goal of accumulating that capital and using it to expand black economic and employment opportunities. For example, he had always run the station in part to provide jobs for graduates from the black Midway Radio and Television Institute of Georgia, of which he was a patron and where he occasionally served as an instructor.[67]

Blayton was not, then, unaware of the broader social and possibly political potential of his station, nor immune to the pull of racial solidarity and responsibility. It was more that he saw his own success as an instrument of black advance and judged WERD's value according to how much it helped him attain that wealth and power. "I saw it as a medium for bringing together black people – as it *did*. But I thought it might bring them together *economically* as well as socially. It didn't!", he complained. In 1969, having run the station on a slender, sometimes non-existent profit margin for a couple of years, Blayton simply decided to sell WERD to the highest bidder, the white-owned Radiad Inc. In so doing he rejected an offer from a black syndicate headed by his friends and colleagues, Al and Mack Saddler. He also disregarded the pleas of Chuck Stone, president of the National Conference on Black Power, that he wait until a way could be found for it to be retained under the control of Atlanta's black community.[68]

Blayton's agenda had not suddenly changed. He had always been calculating and conservative. Indeed, in the 1960s, WERD was one of the many black-oriented stations which had routinely censored news of black urban unrest for fear of inciting further disturbances. WERD's manipulation of news information made it especially ironic when, in 1967, SNCC attacked the hiring of a white programme director at the neighbouring, white-owned WAOK as a "clear example of whites controlling the orientation of news and radio programming supposedly geared to the black community". A picket and boycott of the station went largely unsupported by black Atlantans who recognized that while SNCC – like many groups in the black power era – could no longer see past the race of WAOK's owners and managers, the station had actually been the most consistently responsive and responsible broadcasting service for blacks in the city. "WAOK was the big station", recalled James Bond. Most civil rights workers in Atlanta shared his sense that it had always been rather more publicly committed to the Movement and the needs of the local black community than WERD.[69]

A few years later at WENN-Birmingham there was a rather different example of the way in which this sort of racial tunnel vision could undermine genuinely progressive forces. In 1976, black millionaire A.G. Gaston bought WENN and summarily fired white station manager Joe Lackey, who ironically had helped Gaston negotiate the buy-out. The next day "Tall" Paul White announced on air that WENN's black deejays were walking off the job in protest because, as his colleague Shelley Stewart put it, after two decades of struggle for human, as well as black, rights, "we would not take an injustice given by a black man, which was A.G. Gaston, against a white man". Under Gaston's ownership and the leadership of a black management team headed by Kirkland Balston, WENN became a timorous shadow of its former feisty self. Riding the rhythms of disco and adopting an "urban contemporary" programming format, WENN increasingly sought to attract a general market audience. In the process, it lost something of its black audience and community credibility to the revitalized veteran WJLD, and to WATV, the new enterprise which Stewart, Erskine Faush and Joe Lackey launched in March 1976. Within months WATV was the market leader in the Birmingham area.[70]

The crucial point in all of this is that throughout the history of black-oriented broadcasting most leading black, as well as white, owners and managers have shared Jesse Blayton's commercial priorities. In 1953, Leonard Evans established Negro Network News to provide a co-ordinated news service for black-oriented radio stations. "This is not a crusade for the intermingling of the races", Evans assured prospective advertisers and affiliates. "We're out to move tonnage, to sell merchandise. If we do help race relations it's incidental". Two decades later, in the heart of the black power era, Eugene Jackson launched the National Black Network, funded by means of a 50 per cent loan from the Bank of America, with a similar pledge, assuring 119 affiliated soul stations that "No other network can give you our kind of service and profits".[71]

Black broadcasting owners and executives, like their record company counterparts, rarely made any secret of their ambitions to break into the mainstream market. In Long Beach, wealthy black mortician John Lamar Hill directed his KJLH station – staffed by two blacks and five whites – to play white middle-of-the-road music simply because he found it to be a more lucrative commercial niche in his catchment area than black programming. When Inner City Broadcasting bought WBLS/WLIB-New York, the black consortium immediately switched the station to an integrated music format, hoping to attract a multi-racial audience. The station hired Frankie Crocker, at the time the nation's foremost crossover black deejay, and moved to offices in downtown Manhattan, away from the Harlem community which radicals mistakenly assumed it would be content to serve. "We're not an ethnic station", Manhattan Borough President and Inner City Broadcasting executive Percy Sutton insisted, "we're a people station. We want to be in the mainstream of radio".[72]

In the mid 1970s, around the time of his entanglements with the payola investigations, Frankie Crocker changed the tag-line for his show from *The Total Black Experience in Sound* to *The Total Experience in Sound*. In the late 1970s, Crocker happily programmed the biggest white disco hits of the day, went on Polydor's payroll as a consultant, and along with deejays like Sonny Joe White at KISS-FM in Boston helped to spearhead the shift away from unmistakeably black-oriented programming to the more racially ambiguous "urban" and subsequently "contemporary hits" format. White, Crocker and Sutton were no different from the majority of black owners, managers and deejays. Indeed, they were no different from the mass of black Americans, whose dream, as expressed most powerfully in the civil rights movement, was always to succeed and be respected, black and proud, within the American mainstream, not marginalized and restricted to success in a racial enclave.[73]

A conclusion of sorts

In the black power era black militants fought a diverse, often spirited and principled, sometimes craven and self-serving, battle to secure greater black control over the production and dissemination of black popular music. But not only did they meet with limited success in purely economic and structural terms, but their plans to use black popular music and soul radio for political purposes rested on a basic misunderstanding of the nature, rather than the extent, of their function and influence in the black community.

It has always proved difficult for the few engaged black activists, moderate or radical, conservative or revolutionary, in positions of real power and influence within the broadcasting and recording industries to impose their ideas of politically "relevant" radio and recordings on black audiences who listen primarily for "entertainment" – although the special place "entertainment" has occupied in black life as a focus for communal identity and as a vehicle for resistance to white cultural domination must be fully acknowledged. Thus, while at various times militants demanded a more politicized form of Rhythm and Blues, or more attention to black social and economic issues on the black-oriented airwaves, or simply more stylistically diverse, although usually black, station playlists, the owners and managers of black-oriented record labels and radio outlets have pointed to continued black patronage as an endorsement of their policies.

"As broadcasters, we don't dictate taste; our listeners do", argued Alan Henry, vice-president of the Sonderling chain of stations in 1970. " 'Soul' music is what our listeners have shown they prefer, by and large, to other types. The reformists can like what they want, but the listeners dictate the programming". Nearly a decade later, KDAY-Los Angeles' black programme director Steve Woods concurred. "If 500 people call me on radio . . . and say, 'Hey, man, would you play the Bee Gees or 'Saturday night fever?', I'll be damned if I'm going to turn my cheek. I'm going to play it". In 1987, James Hutchinson, president of the black InterUrban group of broadcasters, noted that its WYLD-New Orleans outlet lost ground to its white-owned, all-music rival WQUE when it tried to increase the amount of news and public affairs programming on the station at the expense of an urban contemporary music format.[74]

The real strength of black-oriented radio and Rhythm and Blues music was its ability to dramatize and celebrate shared aspects of the black experience and, at its best, to give shape and form to barely apprehended hopes, dreams and aspirations. Thanks largely to the manner of their consumption by the black masses, black-oriented radio and Rhythm and Blues frequently transcended the racial politics and economics of their production to help promote a revived sense of black identity, pride, solidarity and common consciousness

This was no small matter and should be neither undervalued, nor divorced from our understanding of how the Movement was generated and sustained. As Stokely Carmichael and Charles Hamilton explained, "only when black people fully develop this sense of community, of themselves, can they begin to deal effectively with the problems of racism". Every black leader, from Martin Luther King to Malcolm X and Jesse Jackson, recognized that some form of collective and individual psychological empowerment, some renewed sense of black self-respect, must undergird a viable black freedom struggle. This was not just a prerequisite, but one of the goals and lasting consequences of participation in political action.[75]

Music and radio, records and concerts, helped to spread that sense of pride, empowerment, and cultural unity far beyond the ranks of the front-line activists who were transformed by their personal experience of protest and struggle. It was certainly no coincidence that "R-E-S-P-E-C-T" became the critical word in the lexicon of soul. It was, however, simply beyond the functional capacity of Rhythm and Blues to transform black solidarity and racial pride into effective, organized protest and political action. That responsibility lay elsewhere and for more than a decade after Montgomery it appeared as if direct action campaigns, voter registration drives, and other political and legal activities offered a means to channel black positivity into a dynamic movement for freedom and equality.

By the end of the 1960s, that moment had already passed. The black power movement achieved much in psychological, intellectual and artistic terms, but in the face of widespread, if by no means uniform, white apathy and indifference to continued racial inequality and injustice, it failed to produce much in the way of economic or political power for the black masses. Indeed, it often neglected the hard chores of political education, mass mobilization and coalition-building in favour of the sort of racial scapegoating, and sexual and racial chauvinism, which white America had been practising for centuries. Whatever its shortcomings, Rhythm and Blues could not be blamed for that.

Coda

When Jesse Jackson concluded his opening remarks at the Wattstax Festival in August 1972, he called upon the crowd to rise and join him in the Black Litany. "I am somebody", he insisted, and the audience echoed his words. "I may be poor, but I am somebody. I may be on welfare, but I am somebody. I may be unskilled, but I am somebody". The crowd bellowed back its approval after each phrase. Johnnie Taylor, who also performed at Wattstax, had recently enjoyed a big hit with a song entitled "I am somebody", employing much the same cadences, many of the same lines, and precisely the same sentiments as Jackson's litany. "I am black, beautiful and proud", Jackson continued in an ever more impassioned voice. The audience shouted back even more enthusiastically. "I must be respected", he roared, eloquently voicing black America's core demand and invoking the spiritual heartbeat of Rhythm and Blues music.[76]

Epilogue

God bless your soul and keep livin'. (Public Enemy, "Welcome to the terrordome")

During the 1980s and 1990s, the struggle for black freedom and power has continued at any number of local and national, political and cultural, economic and educational levels. However, it is readily apparent that this struggle has at best yielded fitful progress and uneven rewards for many African-Americans. Intolerance, resentment, ignorance and misunderstanding between the races continue to rend the fabric of American society. Despite the steady expansion of the black middle class and black political power, literally millions of African-Americans are still engaged in a daily struggle against poverty, unemployment or underemployment, inferior housing, inadequate medical provision, meagre educational opportunities, and sometimes chronic levels of crime in and around their still functionally segregated communities.

Despite these circumstances, most blacks continue to forge constructive, meaningful and responsible lives, and to protect their families and communities from multiple internal and external threats as best they can. In this ongoing struggle for survival and power, black popular music has continued to express the complexities and paradoxes, as well as the essences and certainties, of the diverse black experience in America. From Michael Jackson, Whitney Houston, DeBarge and Prince, through Bobby Brown, Boyz II Men, TLC and R. Kelly, to Run DMC, Public Enemy, Snoop Doggy Dogg and the Fugees, the most popular contemporary black music has acted as a bulwark against the psychological ravages of racism, frustration, often poverty, and sometimes despair in the black community. Whether as musical creators and entrepreneurs, or as creatively participating listeners and dancers, African-Americans have continued to find in their music a vital means to express

451

individual and collective identities, earn respect, and, in some cases, secure considerable material rewards. Certainly, when Grandmaster Flash and the Furious Five's lead vocalist Melle Mel rapped "Its like a jungle sometimes, it makes me wonder, how I keep from going under" on "The message", he was actually providing one answer to his own rhetorical question by the very act of asking it. As for previous generations of African-Americans, making and consuming popular music remains a crucial way to "keep from going under".[1]

Notes

Introduction

1. V. Harding, *Hope and history: why we must share the story of the movement* (New York: Orbis, 1990), pp. 126–7.
2. See S. Propes, "The Chords", *Goldmine*, 19 June 1987, p. 6.
3. L. Levine, *Black culture and black consciousness: Afro-American folk thought from slavery to freedom* (New York: Oxford University Press, 1977), p. x.
4. See J.C. Scott, *Domination and the arts of resistance* (New Haven: Yale University Press, 1991). For the Frankfurt School theories see T.W. Adorno, *Introduction to the sociology of music* (New York: Continuum, 1988).
5. My theoretical understanding of the politics and semiology of black popular music, and mass culture more generally, derive mainly from S. Chapple & R. Garafalo, *Rock 'n' roll is here to pay: the history and politics of the music industry* (Chicago: Nelson Hall, 1977); G. Dent (ed.), *Black popular culture: a project by Michele Wallace* (Seattle: Bay, 1992); S. Frith, *Sound effects: youth, leisure and the politics of rock and roll* (London: Constable, 1984); C. Geertz, *The interpretation of cultures* (New York: Basic, 1973); P. Gilroy, *The black Atlantic: modernity and double consciousness* (Cambridge, Mass.: Harvard University Press, 1993), pp. 72–110; M. Haralambos, *Right on: from blues to soul in black America* (New York: Drake, 1975); D. Harker, *One for the money: politics and popular song* (London: Hutchinson, 1980); D. Hatch & S. Millward, *From blues to rock: an analytical history of pop music* (Manchester: Manchester University Press, 1987); D. Hebdige, *Subculture: the meaning of style* (London: Methuen, 1979); C. McGregor, *Pop goes the culture* (London: Pluto, 1984); R. Peterson, "Cycles in symbol production: the case of popular music", *American Sociological Review* **40**, 1972, pp. 158–73; C. Small, *Music of the common tongue* (London: J. Calder, 1987); J.M. Spencer, *Re-searching black music* (Knoxville: University of Tennessee Press, 1996); J. Street, *Rebel rock: the politics of popular music* (Oxford: Blackwell, 1986).
6. P. Tagg, "Open letter: 'Black music', 'Afro-American music' and 'European music'", *Popular Music* **8**(3), 1989, pp. 285–98.

7. For accessible discussions of black and white musical conceptions and exchanges, see Small, *Music of the common tongue*, pp. 201–4, 271–2; J.L. Collier, *The making of jazz* (New York: Macmillan, 1981), pp. 438–9; C. Joyner, "African and European roots of southern culture: the 'central theme' revisited", in *Dixie Debates: perspectives on southern cultures*, R.H. King & H. Taylor (eds) (London: Pluto, 1996), pp. 12–30; B. Sidran, *Black talk* (New York: Da Capo, 1981), pp. 59–62, 72–3, 101–8; H. Courlander, *Negro folk music of the USA* (New York: Columbia University Press, 1963), pp. 13–23; J.S. Roberts, *Music of two worlds* (New York: Praeger, 1972).

8. I have been influenced here by Lisabeth Cohen's exploration of the unifying function of mass black popular culture in inter-war Chicago. L. Cohen, *Making a new deal: industrial workers in Chicago, 1919–1939* (Cambridge: Cambridge University Press, 1990), pp. 99–158.

9. For a cautionary overview of the ways in the which the black charts are compiled, see G. Ortizano, *On your radio: a descriptive history of rhythm-and-blues radio during the 1950s* (PhD thesis, Ohio University, 1993), pp. 44–54.

10. A. Shaw, *Honkers and shouters* (New York: Macmillan, 1978); G. Hirshey, *Nowhere to run* (New York: Macmillan, 1984); P. Guralnick, *Sweet soul music: rhythm and blues and the southern dream of freedom* (London: Virgin, 1986); B. Hoskyns, *Say it one time for the broken hearted* (Glasgow: Fontana, 1987).

11. *Billboard*, 4 April 1970, pp. 8/11. At the lower end of the income scale, by the mid-to-late 1960s 84 per cent of blacks owned phonographs and listened to them on average for about an hour and a half each day. Both these figures were appreciably higher than for low-income whites. By the late 1950s, around 90 per cent of American blacks already owned radios and 75 per cent of them tuned in on four or more days a week, usually to black-oriented stations. See B.S. Greenberg & B. Dervin, *Uses of the mass media by the urban poor* (New York: Praeger Special Studies in US Economic & Social Development, 1970), pp. 10–27; Radio Advertising Bureau, *Radio and the Negro market* (New York: Radio Advertising Bureau, 1957), p. 5; P. Garland, *The sound of soul* (Chicago: Regnery, 1969), pp. 19, 129.

12. L.P. Nahs, "Black musician in white America", *Negro Digest* (March 1967), pp. 56–7.

13. T. Vincent, *Keep cool: the black activists who built the jazz age* (London: Pluto, 1995). See also L. Portis, "The cultural dialectic of the blues", *Canadian Journal of Political and Social Theory* **9**(3), Fall 1985, pp. 23–36.

14. F. Marshall Davis (ed., with an introduction, by J.E. Tidwell), *Livin' the blues: memoirs of a black journalist and poet* (Madison: University of Wisconsin Press, 1993), p. 290.

15. A. Murray, *Omni-Americans: some alternatives to the folklore of white supremacy* (New York: Vintage, 1983), p. 22. L. Jones (I.A. Baraka), *Black music* (New York: Wm Morrow, 1967), pp. 180–211.

16. Revealingly, Harris "did not travel across Africa to find my roots. I travelled the South to find them. For the South, not Africa, is home to Blackamericans, and Blackamericans as a race are essentially southerners". E.L. Harris, *South of haunted dreams: a ride through slavery's old backyard* (New York: Simon & Schuster, 1993), pp. 88, 36. H.L. Gates, Jr, *Loose canons: notes on the culture wars* (New York: Oxford University Press, 1992), p. xvi.

17. *Our World* (November 1955), p. 40.

18. For Bob Moses and Frankie Lymon, see E. Burner, *And gently he shall lead them: Robert Parris Moses and civil rights in Mississippi* (New York: New York University Press, 1994), p. 16; N. Lemann, *The promised land: the great black migration and how it changed America* (London: Papermac, 1992), p. 99. R.S. Denisoff, "Protest songs: those on the top forty and those on the street", *American Quarterly* **22**, Winter 1970, p. 807; R.S. Denisoff and R.A. Peterson (eds), *The sounds of social change* (Chicago: Rand McNally, 1972), p. x. For exaggerated claims that soul singers were political leaders see P. Maultsby, "Soul music: its sociological and political significance in American popular culture", *Journal of Popular Culture* **17**(2), 1984, pp. 51–60; R. Stephens, "Soul: a historical reconstruction of continuity and change in black popular music", *Black Perspectives in Music* **12**(1), Spring 1984, pp. 21–43.
19. S. Frith, "Towards an aesthetics of popular music", in *Music and society: the politics of composition, performance and reception*, R. Leppert & S. McClary (eds) (Cambridge: Cambridge University Press, 1987), p. 149.

Chapter One

1. Ruth Brown, quoted in C. Deffaa, *Blue rhythms: six lives in rhythm and blues* (Champaign, Ill.: University of Illinois Press, 1996), p. 24.
2. L. Jones (I.A. Baraka), *Blues people* (New York: Wm Morrow, 1963), p. 169; P.H. Ennis, *The seventh stream: the emergence of rock 'n' roll in American popular music* (Hanover, N.H · Wesleyan, 1992), pp. 201, 210.
3. *Billboard*, 29 January 1955, p. 56.
4. *Ibid.*, 22 December 1956, p. 49; 13 January 1958, p. 15; Ennis, *Seventh stream*, p. 241.
5. C. Hamm, *Yesterdays: popular song in America* (New York: Norton, 1979), p. 391.
6. C. Gillett, *The sound of the city*, revd edn (London: Souvenir, 1983). See also N. George, *The death of rhythm and blues* (New York: Omnibus, 1988), pp. 23–39; Jones, *Blues people*, pp. 170–1; L. Redd, *Rock is rhythm and blues* (Detroit: Michigan State University Press, 1974); C. Small, *Music of the common tongue* (London: J. Calder, 1987), pp. 369–73; R.A. Peterson, "Why 1955? explaining the advent of rock music", *Popular Music* **9**, 1990, pp. 97–116.
7. See K. Hammill, "The record business – it's murder", *Fortune* (May 1961), pp. 148–50; S. Chapple & R. Garafalo, *Rock 'n' roll is here to pay: the history and politics of the music industry* (Chicago: Nelson-Hall, 1977), p. 173. For an introduction to the rise of the Independents, see C. Escott & M. Hawkins, *Catalyst: the Sun Records story* (London: Aquarius, 1975); Ennis, *Seventh stream*, pp. 176–82; Gillett, *Sound of the city*, pp. 67–118; C. Gillett, *Making tracks: the story of Atlantic Records*, 2nd edn (London: W.H. Allen, 1988); A. Shaw, *Honkers and shouters* (New York: Macmillan, 1978); Donald Mabry, "The rise and fall of Ace Records: a case study in the independent record business", *Business History Review* **64**, Autumn 1990, pp. 411–50.
8. See Gillett, *Making tracks*, pp. 19–27; J. Picardie & D. Wade, *Atlantic and the godfathers of rock and roll*, revd edn (London: Fourth Estate, 1993), pp. 1–38; J. Wexler (with D. Ritz), *The rhythm and the blues* (New York: A. Knopf, 1993), pp. 75–83.

9. On the importance of jukeboxes see Ennis, *Seventh stream*, pp. 164, 177; A. Shaw, *Honkers*, p. 182.

10. Art Rupe, quoted in *ibid.*, p. 182.

11. Several writers have erroneously claimed that many of these Independents were black-owned. Samuel Charters, for example, suggested "There were hundreds of companies recording blues, many of them Negro-owned, and many of them in the South", before discussing Chess, Savoy and Atlantic, none of which were black-owned or southern. S. Charters, *The country blues* (New York: Rinehart, 1959), p. 234. Also, J. Kamin ("small, independent, often Negro-owned record companies"), in "Taking the roll out of rock 'n' roll: reverse acculturation", *Popular Music and Society* **2**, 1972, p. 5. Black-owned record labels established before 1959 included: Angeltone/Atlas (New York: Thomas Robinson); Apogee (Chicago: Norman Spaulding); Anna (Detroit: Anna Gordy and Harvey Fuqua); Big Town/Irma/Plaid/Art-Tone/Cavatone/DownTown/Rhythm (Oakland: Bob Geddins); Bronze (Los Angeles: LeRoy Hurte); Cash/Money (Los Angeles: John Dolphin); Chicago (Chicago: Howard Bednoe); Class (Los Angeles: Leon René); DC (Washington: Lillian Claiborne); Dootone (Los Angeles: Dootsie Williams); Earl (New York: Tommy Smalls); Flash (Los Angeles: Charlie Reynolds); Flick/Lu Pine (Detroit: Robert West); Fortune (Detroit: Jack and Devora Brown); Gem (Chicago: Paul King); Great Lakes (Detroit: Ken Campbell); Job (Chicago: Joe Brown); Junior (Philadelphia: Kae Williams); JVB (Detroit: Joseph Von Battle); KRC (New Orleans: Lloyd Price); Nu-Kat (Petersburg, Va.: Benjamin Allen); Peacock (Houston: Don Robey); Red Robin/Whirlin'Disc/Fire/Everlast/Fling/Enjoy/Fury (New York: Bobby Robinson); Sunbeam (Chicago: Marl Young); Swingtime (Los Angeles: Jack Lauderdale); Tamla (Detroit: Berry Gordy); Vee Jay/Falcon (Chicago: Vivian Carter and James Bracken); Winley/Cyclone (New York: Paul Winley). Because of their transient nature, accurate figures on the numbers of Independents are difficult to find. Philip Ennis suggests, with understandable imprecision, that there were between 400 and 600 labels with a commitment to r&b in the immediate post-war era (Ennis, *Seventh stream*, p. 176). Andre Millard reckons that there were about 3,000 Independent labels by 1960: A. Millard, *America on record: a history of recorded sound* (Cambridge: Cambridge University Press, 1995), pp. 229–30.

12. Marshall Chess, later a vice-president at the Chess label founded in Chicago by his father Leonard and his uncle Phil, believed that Ahmet Ertegun and his brother Nesuhi, who joined Atlantic in 1955, were very different from his own family and most of the others who controlled the r&b industry in their passion for the music. While Chess admitted that most owners were simply interested in making money, "Ahmet and Nesuhi were different – the only ones I'd ever met who were different because they were rich – it was their hobby, it was their fun". Marshall Chess, quoted in Picardie & Wade, *Godfathers of rock and roll*, pp. 60–1.

13. Ahmet Ertegun quoted in *Billboard*, 13 January 1958, pp. 24/39. At King, Ralph Bass and Henry Glover held similarly influential positions as staff writers-arrangers-producers, while Sonny Thompson's sassy band and his own robustly melodic blues piano were a distinctive feature of many of the company's recordings. At Vee Jay in Chicago, arrangers Von Freeman and Riley Hampton usually worked closely with studio bandleader Al Simpson and his regulars of Lefty Bates (guitar), Quinn Wilson (bass), Paul Gusman or Al Duncan (drums) and

Horace Palm (piano) and brassmen Harlan Floyd, Red Holloway, Lucius Washington, Vernel Fournier and McKinley Easton.

14. D. Fileti, liner notes, *The Best of Onyx Records*, Relic 5005 (n.d.).
15. In 1953 it was reckoned that an r&b record could be classified a hit with around
    40,000 sales, and that major black hits rarely sold more than 300,000 copies. See
    Ennis, *Seventh stream*, p. 176. For the Mellows, see D. Fileti, liner notes, *The
    Best of Celeste*, Relic 5014 (n.d.). For the Jayhawks, see D. Fileti, liner notes, *The
    Best of Flash*, Relic 5049 (n.d.).
16. Al Silver, quoted in F. Bailin, "Herald-Ember", *Bim Bam Boom* **1**(6), 1972, p. 25.
17. Shaw, *Honkers*, pp. 154–5, 195, 248. R. Sanjek, *American popular music and its
    business* (New York: Oxford University Press, 1988), vol. 3, p. 340.
18. See Picardie & Wade, *Godfathers of rock and roll*, pp. 39–88.
19. *Billboard*, 4 September 1954, p. 12.
20. George, *Death of rhythm and blues*, p. 26.
21. Figures drawn from *Billboard*, 1947 to 1959, and Big Al Pavlow, *The r & b book:
    a disc-history of rhythm and blues* (Providence: Music House, 1983), pp. 78–9,
    81. For the post-war country scene see Ennis, *Seventh stream*, pp. 168–71.
22. Figures and trends drawn from *Norfolk Journal and Guide*, 23 November 1957,
    p. 1; "Air media and the US market", *Sponsor*, 17 August 1964, p. 32; US Bur-
    eau of the Census, *Statistical abstract of the United States: 1965* (Washington,
    D.C.: Government Printing Office, 1965), pp. 342, 346, V. Perlo, *Economics of
    racism, USA: roots of black inequality* (New York: International Publishers,
    1975), pp. 82–3.
23. For the Four Fellows, see J. McGowan, *Hear today! hear to stay!* (St Petersburg,
    Fla.: Sixth House, 1983), p. 74.
24. See H. Weinger, "The Platters' glory days", *Goldmine*, 21 February 1992, pp. 10–
    15, 104.
25. See A. Shaw, *The rockin' 50s* (New York. Hawthorn, 1974), pp. 49–56.
26. P. Chaney, "The Cardinals", *Yesterday's Memories* **1**(4), 1975, pp. 18–22.
27. Jerry Wexler quoted in T. Fox, *In the groove: the people behind the music* (New
    York: St Martin's, 1986), p. 127; Jerry Wexler quoted in *Billboard*, 13 January
    1958, p. 24. Wexler was referring to Stick McGhee's 1949 Atlantic hit, "Drinkin'
    wine spo-dee-o-dee".
28. Niki Sullivan quoted in J. Goldrosen & J. Beecher, *Remembering Buddy* (Lon-
    don: Pavilion, 1987), pp. 47–8. For a solid narrative account of r&b radio, see
    G.L. Ortizano, *On your radio: a descriptive history of rhythm-and-blues radio dur-
    ing the 1950s* (PhD thesis, Ohio University, 1993); R. Kloosterman & C. Quispel,
    "Not just the same old show on my radio: an analysis of the role of radio in the
    diffusion of black music among whites in the south of the United States, 1920 to
    1960", *Popular Music* **9**, 1990, pp. 151–64.
29. See for example, B. Hoskyns, *Say it one time for the broken hearted* (Glasgow:
    Fontana, 1987), pp. 60–2; Gillett, *Sound of the city*, pp. 38–9; George, *Death of
    rhythm and blues*, pp. 39–57.
30. Al Benson, in *Jack Gibson and Al Benson: excerpts*, 1971, Museum of Television
    and Radio (hereinafter, MT&R). For the history of WERD, see G. Blackwell,
    *Black-controlled media in Atlanta, 1960–1970: the burden of the message and
    the struggle for survival* (PhD thesis, Emory University, 1973), pp. 121–62. For
    black ownership figures, see Cloyte Murdoch, *Negro radio broadcasting in the
    US* (MA Thesis, University of Wisconsin, 1970), p. 97; S. Surlin, "Ascertainment

of community needs by black-oriented radio stations", *Journal of Broadcasting* **16**, Fall 1972, p. 421; J.F. MacDonald, *Don't touch that dial!* (Chicago: Nelson-Hall), p. 366.

31. P.K. Eberly, *Music in the air: America's changing taste in popular music, 1920–1980* (New York: Communication Arts, 1982), pp. 171, 166.

32. J. Goodrich, "The mayor of melody", *Tan* (February 1950), p. 70. For the growth of television, see US Bureau of the Census, *Statistical abstract of the United States* (Washington, D.C.: Government Printing Office, 1960), p. 518.

33. Figures drawn from "The Negro market: $15 billion annually", *Sponsor*, 24 August 1953, p. 66; "How to use Negro radio successfully", *ibid.*, 20 September 1954, pp. 54–5; "Air media"; R. Kahlenberg, "Negro radio", *Negro History Bulletin*, March 1966, p. 128; Radio Advertising Bureau, *Radio and the Negro market* (New York: Radio Advertising Bureau, 1957), p. 5; M. Newman, *Entrepreneurs of profit and pride: from black appeal to soul radio* (New York: Praeger, 1988), p. 80; F. Ferretti, "The white captivity of black radio", *Columbia Journalism Review*, Summer 1970, p. 35.

34. For accounts of WDIA's development, see L. Cantor, *Wheelin' on Beale: how WDIA-Memphis became the nation's first all-black radio station and created the sound that changed America* (New York, Pharos, 1992); Newman, *Entrepreneurs of profit and pride*, pp. 105–22; *Our World* (February 1950), pp. 37–8; "Tan town disc jester", *Tan* (March 1955), pp. 68–71; A. Abarbanel & A. Haley, "New audience for radio", *Harper's Magazine* (February 1956), pp. 57–9; "Biggest Negro radio station, WDIA", *Time*, 11 November 1957, pp. 85–6; George, *Death of rhythm and blues*, pp. 48–52; C. Sawyer, *B.B. King: the authorized biography* (Poole, Dorset: Blandford, 1981), pp. 59–63.

35. *Variety*, 25 February 1953, p. 39.

36. Abarbanel & Haley, "New audience", p. 57.

37. *Broadcasting Yearbook* (February 1957), pp. 342–4.

38. Nat Williams quoted in M. McKee & F. Chisenhall, *Beale black and blue* (Baton Rouge: Louisiana State Press, 1981), p. 93. Bert Ferguson quoted in "Negro radio: 200-plus special stations", *Sponsor*, 24 August 1953, p. 79.

39. Mort Silverman quoted in Abarbanel & Haley, "New audience", p. 57.

40. J. Edward Reynolds quoted in "Dream radio station", *Negro Digest* **8**(3), January 1950, pp. 23–4. Shelley Stewart, interview with Brian Ward, 26 October 1995, University of Newcastle upon Tyne Oral History Collection (hereinafter UNOHC).

41. *Ibid.*

42. George, *Death of rhythm and blues*, p. 36; also, pp. 39–57.

43. "Broadcasters' creed" in *Broadcasting Yearbook*, 19 January 1953, pp. 31–3. On Hooks and the FCC see *Jet*, 27 April 1972, p. 5.

44. For "Sixty minute man", see S. Dennison, *Scandalize my name: black imagery in American popular music* (New York: Garland, 1982), pp. 481–2. As Mark Zucker has pointed out, "Three thirty three" made knowing reference to the Dominoes' song: "You can get a little bit of everything; wine, women and song./ You can stay there for sixty minutes; or lay there all night long." M. Zucker, "The saga of Lovin' Dan: a study in the iconography of rhythm & blues music of the 1950s", *Journal of Popular Culture* **16**(2), Fall 1982, pp. 43–51.

45. George, *Death of rhythm and blues*, p. 43. *Amsterdam News*, 28 April 1956, p. 16. Vernon Winslow, interview with Jane D. Julian, 13 April 1972, subject file: racism, Hogan Jazz Archive. "Dr Daddy-O!", *Tan* (May 1955), p. 76.

46. "WWRL-New York: Promotional Booklet" (n.d.), III-A-265, Papers of the NAACP.

47. "Program for 'Genial Gene Day', Charlotte Armory Auditorium, 22 November 1953", p. 5. Copy in possession of the author.
48. Radio's role in the formation of a new black consciousness and its subsequent contributions to the civil rights and black power movements have been largely ignored by historians of the black freedom struggle. For recent attempts to link the development of black-oriented radio to black resistance and protest, see J.L. Dates and W. Barlow, *Split image: African-Americans in the mass media* (Washington, D.C.: Howard University Press, 1990), pp. 175–209; Newman, *Entrepreneurs of profit and pride;* Ortizano, *On your radio,* pp. 246–57; B. Ward, *Race relations, civil rights and the transformation from rhythm and blues to soul, 1954–1965* (PhD thesis, University of Cambridge, 1995), pp. 83–120, 265–71, 363–7; B. Ward & J. Walker, "'Bringing the races closer'?: black-oriented radio in the South and the civil rights movement", in *Dixie debates: perspectives on southern cultures,* R.H. King & H. Taylor (eds) (London: Pluto, 1996), pp. 130–49.
49. *Broadcasting Yearbook* (1957), pp. 342–4. See also J.D. Cruz, *The politics of popular culture: black popular music as "public sphere"* (PhD thesis, University of California, Berkeley, 1986), pp. 2–4, 13–15.
50. For one of the few serious studies of this subject, see J. Kamin, "The white r&b audience and the music industry, 1952–1956", *Popular Music and Society* **6,** 1978, pp. 150–67. See also Ennis, *Seventh stream,* pp. 246–52.
51. Pavlow, *The r & b book,* p. 3. Kamin, "The white r&b audience", pp. 152–3.
52. M. Bayles, *Hole in our soul: the loss of beauty and meaning in American popular music* (Chicago: University of Chicago Press, 1994), pp. 140–1.
53. Ibid., p. 141.
54. Jerry Wexler quoted in Shaw, *Honkers,* p. 79. See also Kamin, "The white r&b audience", p. 161; "Under the boardwalk", *New Musical Express,* 29 August 1987, pp. 12–15; J.S. Coleman et al., *The adolescent society: the social life of the teenager and its impact on education* (New York: Macmillan/Free Press, 1961), pp. 205–6.
55. Although he rather underestimates the importance of white college student support for early r&b and early rock and roll, George Lipsitz has argued convincingly that white working-class passion for these musics often expressed a desire to escape the mental and physical bonds of workplace discipline into a more sensual and expressive world of leisure. See G. Lipsitz, *Rainbow at midnight: labor and culture in the 1940s* (Urbana: University of Illinois Press, 1994), p. 327.
56. Gillett, *Making tracks,* pp. 50–1, 91–9. Nick Tosches, *Unsung heroes of rock and roll* (New York: Scribner, 1984), pp. 11–19.
57. *Billboard,* 13 January 1958, pp. 24/39.
58. US Bureau of the Census, *County and city data book, 1962: a statistical supplement* (Washington, D.C.: Government Printing Office, 1963), pp. 476–575. *Statistical abstract of the United States: 1965,* p. 34.
59. Isaac Hayes quoted in G. Hirshey, *Nowhere to run* (New York: Macmillan, 1984), p. 5. The declining popularity of the blues among black Americans is discussed in M. Haralambos, *Right on: from blues to soul in black America* (New York: Drake, 1975). See also W. Barlow, *Looking up at down: the emergence of blues culture* (Philadelphia: Temple University Press, 1989), p. 341; G. Oakley, *The devil's music,* revd edn (London: Ariel, 1983), pp. 216–33.
60. W. King, Jr, "Searching for the brothers kindred: rhythm and blues of the 1950s", *Black Scholar* (November 1974), p. 26.

61. Jay Butler quoted in Haralambos, *Right on*, p. 66.
62. A welcome exception to the general silence on white pop's popularity and influence on black r&b is Ortizano, *On your radio*, pp. 58–60. For Roy Brown, see Tosches, *Unsung heroes*, p. 57; A. Shaw, *Black popular music in America* (New York: Schirmer, 1986), p. 179. Chuck Berry quoted in *Rock and Roll: Renegades*, episode 1, PBS-TV documentary, 1995. On B.B. King's show, see Newman, *Entrepreneurs of profit and pride*, p. 134. L. Jones (I.A. Baraka), *The autobiography of LeRoi Jones/Amiri Baraka* (New York: Freundlich, 1984), p. 49. For Ruth Brown, see Deffaa, *Blue rhythms*, p. 25. Billy Williams, interview with Dick Clark, *American Bandstand*, WFIL-TV, Philadelphia, 17 December 1957, MT&R.
63. Bernice Johnson Reagon, interview with Brian Ward, 24 January 1996, UNOHC. T. Turner (with K. Loder), *I, Tina* (London: Penguin, 1987), pp. 60, 45. Bobby Bland quoted in *The Tennessean*, 3 August 1978, in "Blacks in country music", Country Music Hall of Fame Clippings File.
64. Ahmet Ertegun quoted in *Billboard*, 13 January 1958, p. 24.
65. Hugo Peretti and Luigi Creatore quoted in *Billboard*, 12 March 1955, p. 13. These sales figures were subsequently revised upwards to 219 million for 1953 and 213 million for 1954. See Sanjek, *American popular music*, vol. 3, p. 355; L. Feist, *An introduction to popular music publishing in America* (New York: National Music Publishers Association, 1980), pp. 105–6. Thanks largely to the r&b/rock and roll boom, the value of record sales by 1959 had soared to $603 million. See Gillett, *Sound of the city*, p. 472.
66. McGowan, *Hear today*, p. 66. Tommy Smalls quoted in *Amsterdam News*, 28 April 1956, p. 16. See also *Our World* (November 1955), p. 43.
67. *Variety*, 9 February 1955, p. 51.
68. George, *Death of rhythm and blues*, p. 67.
69. *Variety*, 29 December 1954, pp. 1/55.
70. See *Ebony* (December 1953), pp. 40–1.
71. L. Jones (I.A. Baraka), *Black music* (New York: Wm Morrow, 1967), p. 207. P. Maultsby, "Beginnings of a black music industry", in *Who's who in black music*, R.E. Rosenthal & P. Maultsby (eds) (New Orleans: Edwards Printing, 1985), p. xi.
72. Winfield Scott quoted in *Good rockin' tonight: the history of black music, part one, 1947–55*, WKRS-FM, New York, 9 June 1991, MT&R.
73. Otis Blackwell quoted in *Philadelphia Daily News*, 20 October 1983, p. 18b. See G. Giddins, *Riding on a blue note: jazz and American pop* (New York: Oxford University Press, 1981), p. 28. The best account of Presley's early life is P. Guralnick, *Last train to Memphis: the rise of Elvis Presley* (Boston: Little, Brown, 1994).
74. M.M. Cole (president of the Chicago-based publishing firm, Cole Corporation), letter to the *Hearing before the subcommittee on communications of the committee on interstate and foreign commerce: Amendment to the Communications Act of 1934 (prohibiting radio and television stations from engaging in music publishing or recording business)*, 7 March 1957, US Senate, 85th Congress (Washington, D.C.: Government Printing Office, 1958), p. 972. The importance of these new publishing firms is discussed in *Variety*, 9 February 1954, pp. 51/4.
75. For Jay & Cee Music, see J.W. Rumble, "Roots of rock & roll: Henry Glover at King Records", *Journal of Country Music* **14**(2), 1992, pp. 30–42.
76. See H.F. Mooney, "Just before rock: pop music 1950–1953 reconsidered", *Popular Music and Society* **3**, 1974, pp. 65–108. Even Jonathan Kamin, generally the

most convincing writer on the cover phenomenon and its racial agenda, failed to note the sheer extent of the practice. See Kamin, "Taking the roll out of rock 'n' roll"; Kamin, "The white r&b audience", and J. Kamin, "Musical culture and perceptual learning in the popularization of black music", *Journal of Jazz Studies* **3**, 1975, pp. 54–65.

77. Carl Belz is one of the few writers to acknowledge the sheer pervasiveness of the cover syndrome. C. Belz, *The story of rock* (New York: Oxford University Press, 1972), pp. 25–30.

78. When "Sh-boom" was switched to the A-side the record was reissued with "Little mermaid" as the flip. Pavlow, *The r & b book*, p. 48; S. Propes, "The Chords", *Goldmine*, 19 June 1987, p. 6.

79. See Rumble, "Roots of rock & roll", pp. 30, 37–9.

80. Ruth Brown quoted in Deffaa, *Blue rhythms*, p. 45.

81. Interestingly, however, Begle found little real evidence that these exploitative practices were uniquely visited on black artists. Certainly, the courtroom victories won by the Rhythm and Blues Foundation – which became the institutional vehicle for this campaign for compensation – hinged less on the legality or morality of the 1950s contracts *per se* than on the fact that most companies had made no, or grossly inadequate, provision to reward artists for the subsequent reissues of their original recordings over the years. Beginning with Atlantic, which reimbursed Ruth Brown to the tune of some $21,000, since the late 1980s, the Foundation has pressurized a number of recording companies into revising their practices regarding reissues, and to make retrospective payments to aggrieved and often needy artists. *Ibid.*, pp. xv–xvii, 56–8.

82. Kamin, "Taking the roll", p. 8; Kamin, "Musical culture", p. 60.

83. *Billboard*, 5 May 1956, p. 18. *Ibid.*, 12 November 1955, p. 34. Bob DeBardelaben quoted in *Richmond Times-Dispatch*, 15 March 1958, pp. 1-A, 16-A.

84. See Kamin, "Musical culture"; Kamin, "Taking the roll".

85. Harold Battiste, interview with Brian Ward, 8 November 1995, UNOHC.

86. *Ibid.*

87. Little Richard quoted in *Good rockin' tonight, part 2: 1956–67*, 16 June 1991, MT&R.

88. *Billboard*, 15 October 1955, pp. 1/16.

89. Ahmet Ertegun quoted in *ibid.*, 13 January 1958, p. 39.

90. The use of strings did not *per se* make a record bad or trite. (See, for example, the plaintive pop-blues of Fats Domino's "Walking to New Orleans".) It was the manner of that usage which mattered and sentimental string arrangements were often tastelessly draped over unsuitable songs in a crude bid for a crossover hit.

91. Some have argued that this "sweetening" or "softening" of r&b represented the "feminization" of what had been essentially a highly masculine form of music. Not only does this underestimate the softer side of male r&b, even prior to the crossover of the mid 1950s, and neglect the importance of women in that music, but it reflects the association of "feminization" with the dilution and decline of the music, implying that all creativity and innovation is somehow "masculine". See S. Frith & A. McRobbie, "Rock and sexuality", in *On the record*, S. Frith & A. Goodwin (eds) (London: Routledge), 1990, pp. 371–89.

92. The a cappella and final versions of these songs by Lillian Leach and the Mellows can be found on *The Best of Celeste* and *Presenting Lillian Leach and the Mellows*, Relic 5039, n.d., which features their earlier work for Jay Dee and Candlelight as well as Celeste.

Chapter Two

1. In their monumental study of vocal group music, Anthony Gribin and Matthew Schiff neatly summarized the general trend in lyrics during the 1940s and 1950s. Between 1945 and 1951 vocal group lyrics were "often lascivious"; between 1952 and 1954 they were "still lascivious, but innocent love themes begin to take over"; between 1955 and 1959, the subject was "almost exclusively innocent young love", with "almost no politicizing or social commentary". Given the inherent problems of over-generalization in such a schematic approach, this seems right on the mark. See A.J. Gribin & M.M. Schiff, *Doo-wop: the forgotten third of rock 'n' roll* (Iola, Wis.: Krause, 1992), p. 46. Although the main focus here is on male vocal groups, there was a rich tradition of female black vocal groups dating back at least to the 1940s which is discussed in Chapter 4.

2. B. Millar, *The Drifters: the rise and fall of the black vocal group* (New York: Macmillan, 1971), p. 9. C. Gillett, *The sound of the city,* 2nd revd edn (London: Souvenir, 1983), p. 161. Christopher Small uses the term "musicking" to characterize the participatory ritual of music-making, in which the creative process has been more important than any resulting musical artefact. C. Small, *Music of the common tongue* (London: J. Calder, 1987), pp. 50–2.

3. See, for example, R.D. Abrahams, *Deep down in the jungle,* revd edn (Chicago: Aldine, 1970), and *Positively black* (Englewood Cliffs: Prentice-Hall, 1970); J. Borchet, *Alley life in Washington* (Urbana: University of Illinois Press, 1980); K. Clark, *Dark ghetto* (New York: Harper & Row, 1965); D.C. Dance, *Shuckin' and jivin'* (Bloomington: Indiana University Press, 1978); S.C. Drake & H.R. Cayton, *Black metropolis: a study of Negro life in a northern city* (London: J. Cape, 1946); U. Hannerz, *Soulside* (New York: Columbia University Press, 1969); C. Keil, *Urban blues* (Chicago: University of Chicago Press, 1966); E. Liebow, *Tally's corner* (Boston: Little, Brown, 1967); J.H. Rohrer & M.S. Edmondson, *The eighth generation grows up* (New York: Harper Torchbooks, 1964); D.C. Thompson, *Sociology of the black experience* (Westport, Conn.: Greenwood Press, 1974). For a deeply critical review of much of this literature and its tendency to homogenize the black urban experience by focusing only on the black poor and under-class, see Mitchel Duneier, *Slim's table: race, respectability, and masculinity* (Chicago: University of Chicago Press, 1992).

4. W.E.B. Du Bois, *The souls of black folk,* 8th edn (Chicago: A.C. McClurg, 1909), pp. 3–5.

5. The "pathological model" of ghetto culture is advanced in Clark, *Dark ghetto,* pp. 81–110, and W.H. Grier & P.M. Cobbs, *Black rage* (New York: Basic, 1968). The classic theoretical statement on creative social "deviancy" is R.K. Merton, "Social structure and anomie", *American Sociological Review* **3**, October 1938, pp. 672–82.

6. The sociologist, Hortense Powdermaker, pointed out this dynamic link between changes in black consciousness and cultural production in the 1940s. H. Powdermaker, "The Channeling of Negro aggression by the cultural process", *American Journal of Sociology* **48**, 1943, pp. 750–8.

7. W. King, Jr, "Searching for the brothers kindred: rhythm & blues of the 1950s", *Black Scholar* **6**(3), November 1974, p. 23. C. Brown, *Manchild in the promised land* (New York: Signet, 1965), p. 103. See also S.L. Goosman, *The social and cultural organization of black group vocal harmony in Washington, D.C. and Baltimore, Maryland, 1945–1960* (PhD thesis, University of Washington, 1992),

pp. 82–3. It should be noted that neither gang activity nor street-corner singing were unique to black urban youth culture. Both were evident in most lower-class urban communities. See W.B. Miller, "Lower class culture as a generating milieu of gang delinquency", *Journal of Social Issues* **14**(3), 1958, pp. 5–19.

8. Other school-based groups included the Spaniels (Roosevelt High School in Gary, Indiana), Cleftones (Jamaica High School in Queens, New York), Four Buddies (Frederick Douglass High School in Baltimore), Clovers (Armstrong High School in Washington, D.C.), Five Blue Notes (Francis Jnr. High School in Georgetown, Maryland) and Diablos (Central High School in Detroit). And it was not only students who were involved in this schoolhouse harmonizing. Four custodians working for the Los Angeles Board of Education formed a group called the Nuggets and secured a contract with Capitol. Their moment of dubious glory came in 1955 when they backed Frank Sinatra on his none-too-shabby cover of the Charms' "Two hearts". *Variety*, 29 December 1954, p. 42.

9. Goosman, *Black group vocal harmony*, pp. 11–12. See also P. Groia, *They all sang on the corner*, 2nd edn (New York: Phillie Dee, 1983).

10. Goosman, *Black group vocal harmony*, p. 98. J. Dawson, "Jesse Belvin", *Goldmine*, 5 December 1986, pp. 12, 16–17.

11. J. Picardie & D. Wade, *Atlantic and the godfathers of rock and roll*, revd edn (London: Fourth Estate, 1993), pp. 10, 46, 301.

12. Gaynel Hodge quoted in Dawson, "Jesse Belvin", p. 12.

13. Paul Winley, quoted in P. Winley (with P. Groia), "The Paul Winley story", *Bim Bam Boom* **3**(9), 1973, pp. 30–1, 52. Groia, *They all sang on the corner*, p. 118.

14. Arlene Smith quoted in C. Greig, *Will you still love me tomorrow?* (London: Virago, 1989), p. 14. Paul Willis uses the term "homology" to describe the way in which the core values and means of cultural expression of a sub-cultural group are vitally linked at the level of symbolic representation. Dick Hebdige also stresses the internal coherence of sub-cultures, they function according to rules and codes which remain a mystery to the mainstream. P. Willis, *Profane culture* (London: Routledge, 1978); D. Hebdige, *Subculture: the meaning of style* (London: Methuen, 1979).

15. Keil, *Urban Blues*, p. 15.

16. L. Jones (LA Baraka), *The autobiography of LeRoi Jones/Amiri Baraka* (New York: Freundlich, 1984), p. 44.

17. M. Goldberg, "The Plants", *Yesterday's Memories* **4**(8), 1976, p. 17.

18. P. Groia & M. Goldberg, liner notes, *The Best of The Valentines*, Murray Hill 000202 (1986). H. Cox & S. West, "The heart and soul of the Cleftones", *Goldmine*, 21 February 1992, p. 16.

19. M. Goldberg & M. Redmond, "The Swallows", *Yesterday's Memories* **4**(4), 1975, pp. 10–14. P. Chaney, "The Cardinals", *ibid.*, pp. 18–22. P. Chaney, "The Honey Boys", *ibid.*, **4**(8), 1976, p. 13. M. Goldberg & M. Redmond, "The Five Blue Notes", *ibid.*, **4**(4), 1975, pp. 15–16.

20. A. Shaw, *The rockin' 50s* (New York: Hawthorn, 1974), p. 118. S. Flam, "The Vee Jay story", *Bim Bam Boom* **1**(4), 1972, p. 18. B. Robinson, "Bobby Robinson: king of the New York sound", *Record Exchanger* **2**(5), 1972, pp. 5–6/8–10. Ben E. King, quoted in G. Hirshey *Nowhere to run* (New York: Macmillan, 1984), p. 33.

21. *Yesterday's Memories* **4**(8), 1976, p. 24. See also F.L. Gonzales, *Disco-file: the discographical catalog of American rock and roll and rhythm and blues vocal harmony groups, 1902 to 1976*, 2nd edn (Flushing, N.Y.: Gonzales, 1977). Richard Berry quoted in Dawson, "Jesse Belvin", p. 16.

22. M. Stearns & J. Stearns, *Jazz dance* (New York: Macmillan, 1968), pp. 315–26. D. Burley, "The truth about rock and roll", *Tan* (July 1956), p. 82.

23. Goosman, *Black vocal group harmony*. See also *Yesterday's Memories* **4**(4), 1975; *ibid.* **4**(8), 1976. Phil Groia's idiosyncratic blend of fact and demi-fact also reveals something of the distribution of New York street-corner groups. Groups from Washington Heights, popularly known as Sugar Hill, included the Solitaires, Savoys, Dubs, Valentines, Velvets and Frankie Lymon and the Teenagers. Further downtown, along West 115th and 119th Streets, between 5th and 8th Avenues, another group scene, including the Willows, Channels, Charts, Ladders, Desires and Matadors, coalesced around Raoul Cita of the Harptones, who rehearsed many acts in the basement of a 119th Street house. Beyond Manhattan, in the Morrisania district of the Bronx, the Chords, Lillian Leach and the Mellows, Jupiters and Wrens grew up. In Brooklyn, groups included the Jesters, Velours, Duponts, Paragons, Montereys and Collegians. See Groia, *They all sang*.

24. Nolan Strong and the Diablos cut 15 singles for Fortune between 1954 and 1962. The *Billboard* territorial listings show that most of these were hits in Detroit and some beyond – most notably "The wind". Goldberg & Redmond, "The Five Blue Notes", pp. 15–16.

25. M. Goode, liner notes, *The Paragons Meet The Jesters*, Jubilee JGM 1098 (1957). This commodification of competition was not restricted to vocal groups. King released two *Battle of the Blues* albums, and two 45-rpm EPs, featuring the shouters Wynonie Harris and Roy Brown.

26. The importance of the channel at the Apollo is noted in Groia, *They all sang*, p. 108. A useful analogy here is with the dozens, where the best practitioners manipulated the language of insult within strict conventions to secure communal respect. One of the main informants for Roger Abrahams' study of the dozens, toasts and tales of the Philadelphia ghetto, *Deep down in the jungle*, was Charles Williams, himself a member of the Turbans vocal group. See also A. Bergesen, "Spirituals, jazz, blues and soul music: the role of elaborated and restricted codes in the maintenance of social solidarity", in *The religious dimension: new directions in quantitative research*, R.Wuthnow (ed.) (New York: Academic, 1979), pp. 333–50.

27. Ben E. King, quoted in Hirshey, *Nowhere to run*, p. 34. D. Henderson, "Boston Road blues", in *Black fire*, L. Jones & L. Neal (eds) (New York: Wm Morrow, 1968), pp. 233–8.

28. The Squires' "S'Cadillac" was never officially released and this exchange can be found on *The Best of Vita Records*, Relic 5007 (n.d.). Anthony Gourdine quoted in J. Smith, *Off the record: an oral history of popular music* (New York: Warner, 1988), p. 133. Millar, *The Drifters*, p. 40.

29. Lillian Leach and the Mellows' rehearsals can be found on *The Best of Celeste*, Relic 5014 (n.d.) and *Presenting Lillian Leach and the Mellows*, Relic 5039 (n.d.).

30. Wexler's views changed little over the years. His liner notes to a 1987 compilation still put a premium on the tightness of vocal group harmonies. He praised the Delta Rhythm Boys' "Dry bones" for its "perfect, in tune rendition", but memorably, if affectionately, slated the Robins' "All night long" because the "harmony is as raggedy as a bowl of yat ga mein". J. Wexler, liner notes, *The RCA-Victor Blues and Rhythm Revue*, RCA PL86279(2) (1987).

31. S. Propes, "The Chords", *Goldmine*, 19 June 1987, p. 6; Groia, *They all sang*, p. 132. Jesse Stone quoted in C. Gillett, *Making tracks: the story of Atlantic Records*, 2nd edn (London: W.H. Allen, 1988), pp. 53–4.

32. Winley, "Paul Winley Story", p. 30.
33. Cox & West, "The heart and soul of the Cleftones", p. 16. J. McGowan, *Hear today! hear to stay!* (St Petersburg, Fla.: Sixth House, 1983), pp. 4, 9.
34. See, for example, Bill Millar's statement that "many were formed overnight, which bears testimony to the rhythmic sense of those who complemented the lead singer". Millar, *The Drifters*, p. 62. For the Mellows rehearsals, see *Best of Celeste*.
35. See T. Fox, *Showtime at the Apollo* (New York: Holt, Rinehart & Winston, 1983), pp. 109–10.
36. Cox & West, "The heart and soul of the Cleftones", pp. 18/20. Small, *Common tongue*, p. 81.
37. The Fortune statistics include the Hi-Q subsidiary. See *Bim Bam Boom* 1(5), 1972, pp. 20–2. The Red Robin discography appears in "Bobby Robinson", pp. 11–12.
38. The Atlantic figures include subsidiaries, Atco, East-West and Cat, but exclude the 600 and 700 jazz series. Gospel quartets – a stylistic, not strictly numerical, designation – have been counted with secular groups, but larger gospel choirs excluded. For Atlantic, see M. Ruppli, *Atlantic records: a discography*, 4 vols (Westport, Conn.: Greenwood Press, 1979). For Vee-Jay, *Bim Bam Boom* 1(4), 1972, pp. 19–21. For Herald-Ember, *ibid.*, 1(6), 1972, pp. 26–7.
39. W. King, "Brothers kindred", p. 21. Ben E. King quoted in Hirshey, *Nowhere to run*, p. 36.
40. Ben E. King quoted in Hirshey, *Nowhere to run*, p. 36.
41. Henderson, "Boston Road blues", p. 234. D. Hilliard & L. Cole, *This side of glory: the autobiography of David Hilliard and the story of the Black Panther Party* (Boston. Little, Brown, 1993), pp. 74–5.
42. In the absence of an adequate collective term for songs about predatory sex, infidelity, gambling, drinking, terminal bad luck, poverty, pestilence, natural disaster, personal humiliation and sudden violence, they are referred to here as "adult". Jones/Baraka, *Autobiography*, p. 50. Panther David Hilliard's first sexual experiments also took place to the sound of Hank Ballard and the Midnighters' "Annie" records. Hilliard & Cole, *This side of glory*, p. 83.
43. E.F. Frazier, *The Negro family in the United States*, revd abr. edn (Chicago: University of Chicago Press, 1966). D.P. Moynihan, *The Negro family: the case for national action* (Washington, D.C.: Government Printing Office, 1965).
44. E. Genovese, *Roll Jordan roll: the world the slaves made*, 2nd edn (New York: Vintage, 1976). L. Levine, *Black culture and black consciousness: Afro-American folk thought from slavery to freedom* (New York: Oxford University Press, 1977). H. Gutman, *The black family in slavery and freedom* (New York: Pantheon, 1976). E.L. Ayers, *The promise of the New South: life after Reconstruction* (New York: Oxford University Press, 1992), p. 69. *The Negro almanac: a reference work on the Afro-American*, H.A. Ploski & J. Williams (eds), 4th edn (New York: J. Wiley, 1983), p. 476. A. Hacker, *Two nations: black and white, separate, hostile, unequal*, revd edn (New York: Ballantine, 1995), p. 74.
45. J. Ladner, *Tomorrow's tomorrow: the black woman* (Garden City, N.J.: Anchor, 1972), pp. 30–5. D. White, *Ar'n't I a woman* (New York: Norton, 1985). Brenda Stevenson's study of slave and free black life in antebellum Virginia offers a partial rebuttal to Gutman and others by insisting that most of the state's slave children were born into single-, usually female, headed households and that slavery did significantly undermine black male self-esteem, domestic power and social authority. Nevertheless, even Stevenson resists the urge to cast black slave

society as a matriarchy and instead stresses the flexibility and diversity of black family and social arrangements under slavery and beyond in which matrifocality was but one possible, if pronounced, tendency. B. Stevenson, *Life in black and white: family and community in the slave South* (New York: Oxford University Press, 1996), pp. 206–25, 286–319. See also G. Lerner, "Placing women in history: definitions and challenges", *Feminist Studies* **3**(1/2), Fall 1975, p. 9.

46. See b. hooks, *Ain't I a woman?* (Boston: South End, 1981), pp. 71–86.
47. *Ibid.*
48. Dance, *Shuckin' and jivin'*, pp. 110–11. Similarly, Roger Abrahams interpreted the dozens, the ritualistic trading of personal insults in which the mother figure is both the primary vehicle and object of the insults, as a means to exorcise matriarchal influence and establish an independent masculine identity. Abrahams, *Deep down in the jungle*, pp. 46–58.
49. Dance, *Shuckin' and jivin'*, pp. 224, 225–46. See also Levine, *Black culture*, pp. 367, 407–40.
50. M.B. White, " 'The blues ain't nothin' but a woman want to be a man': male control in early twentieth century blues music", *Canadian Review of American Studies* **24**, Winter 1994, p. 25.
51. For Robert Johnson, see P. Guralnick, *Searching for Robert Johnson* (New York: Dutton, 1989).
52. For a discussion of sexual objectification, violence and machismo in the blues, see White, "The blues ain't nothin' "; P. Oliver, *Blues fell this morning: meaning in the blues* (Cambridge: Cambridge University Press, 1990), esp. pp. 95–116; Levine, *Black culture*, pp. 276–9; J.T. Titon, *Downhome blues lyrics: an anthology from the post-World War II era* (Boston: Twayne, 1981).
53. Elliot Liebow commented on this alternative value system in Washington: "Conceding that to be head of a family and to support it is a principal measure of a man, he [the black male] claims he was too much of a man to be a man. He says his marriage did not fail because he failed as a breadwinner and head of the family but because his wife refused to put up with his manly appetite for whiskey and other women, appetites which rank high in the scale of shadow values on the street corner." Liebow, *Tally's corner*, pp. 214–15, 116–26.
54. Wynonie Harris quoted in *Tan* (October 1954), p. 76. See also pp. 28–31, 76–77.
55. In a different context, bell hooks makes a related point that, "As the crudest and most brutal expression of sexism, misogynistic attitudes tend to be portrayed by the dominant culture as always an expression of male deviance. In reality, they are part of a sexist continuum, necessary for the maintenance of patriarchal social order": b. hooks, *Outlaw culture: resisting representations* (New York: Routledge, 1994), p. 116.
56. E. Vinson, "I spent $100,000 on women", *Tan* (August 1954), pp. 28–9, 68–70.
57. For an excellent review of the sexual politics of the female blues singers of the 1920s, see H. Carby, "It jus be's dat way sometime: the sexual politics of women's blues", *Radical America* **20**(4), 1987, pp. 9–22. See also Levine, *Black culture*, pp. 275–8, 281–2.
58. For an analysis of black satire and humour directed at whites, see Levine, *Black culture*, pp. 300–20; Dance, *Shuckin' and jivin'*, pp. 165–223.
59. Chris Strachowitz quoted in A. Shaw, *Honkers and shouters* (New York: Macmillan, 1978), p. 259. See also Millar, *The Drifters*, pp. 52–67; L. McCutcheon, *Rhythm and blues: an experience and adventure in its origins and development* (Arlington, Va.: Beatty, 1971), p. 53.

60. Frankie Lymon quoted in Millar, *The Drifters*, p. 76.
61. The Lymon-Russell pictures were reprinted in *Ebony* (February 1967), p. 42. For the Lymon incident on Freed's show, see J.A. Jackson, *Big beat heat: Alan Freed and the early years of rock & roll* (New York: Schirmer, 1991), p. 168. For Till's murder, see S.J. Whitfield, *A death in the Delta: the story of Emmett Till* (New York, Free Press, 1988); A.S. Rubin, "Reflections on the death of Emmett Till", *Southern Cultures* **2**(1), Fall 1995, pp. 45–66.
62. For white doowop, see E.R. Engel, *White and still all right* (New York: Crackerjack, 1977). For Chicano rock and roll in east Los Angeles, see G. Lipsitz, "Land of a thousand dances", in *Recasting America: culture and politics in the age of the cold war*, Larry May (ed.) (Chicago: University of Chicago Press, 1989), pp. 267–84.
63. M. Bane, *White boy singin' the blues* (London: Penguin, 1982), p. 98.
64. For the various John Henry sagas, ballads and blues, see Levine, *Black culture*, pp. 420–7; Oliver, *Blues fell this morning*, pp. 26, 274.
65. For varieties of overt and covert black working-class resistance to Jim Crow, see R.D. Kelley, "'We are not what we seem': rethinking black working-class opposition in the Jim Crow South", *Journal of American History* **80**, 1993, pp. 75–112; A. Gilmore, "The Black southerners' response to the southern system of race relations: 1900 to post-World War II", in *The age of segregation: race relations in the South, 1890–1945*, R. Haws (ed.) (Jackson: University of Mississippi Press, 1987), pp. 67–88.
66. The vinyl career of Lovin' Dan on disks like the Dominoes' "Pedal Pushing Papa", Du Droppers' "Can't do sixty no more", Charms' "Fifty-five seconds", Checkers' "Don't Stop Dan", is described in M. Zucker, "The saga of Lovin' Dan: a study in the iconography of rhythm and blues music of the 1950s", *Journal of Popular Culture* **16**(2), Fall 1982, pp. 43–51.
67. Gribin & Schiff, *Doo-wop*, p. 27.
68. M. Ellison, *Extensions of the blues* (London: Cape, 1989), pp. 1, 15. A. Murray, *Stomping the blues*, 2nd edn (New York: Vintage, 1982), p. 45.
69. U. Hannerz, "Lower-class black culture", in *Soul*, Lee Rainwater (ed.) (n.p.: Transaction, 1970), p. 177.
70. Liebow, *Tally's corner*, pp. 154–6.
71. D. Horton, "The dialogue of courtship in popular songs", *American Journal of Sociology* **62**, May 1957, p. 569.

Chapter Three

1. Congressman D.R. "Billy" Matthews, "Talk on states' rights", (Gainesville, Florida, September 1957), box 198: Speeches, D.R. Matthews papers.
2. For white "musical acculturation" and "perceptual learning", see J. Kamin, "Taking the roll out of rock 'n' roll: reverse acculturation", *Popular Music and Society* **2**, 1972, pp. 1–17; J. Kamin, "Musical culture and perceptual learning in the popularization of black music", *Journal of Jazz Studies* **3**, pp. 54–65.
3. See, for example, C. Belz, *The story of rock* (New York: Oxford University Press, 1972), pp. 56–9; J. Kamin, "Parallels in the social reaction to jazz and rock", *Journal of Jazz Studies* **2**, 1974, pp. 95–125; J.R. Oakley, *God's country: America in the fifties* (New York: Dembner, 1986), pp. 273–86. Even the best

book on the subject, L. Martin & K. Segrave, *Anti-rock: the opposition to rock 'n' roll* (Hamden, Conn.: Archon, 1988), devotes only 3 pages of the 100 dealing with the period 1953–60 to analyzing the racial co-ordinates of the attack on rock and roll. See pp. 41–3.

4. Peter Potter quoted in *Billboard*, 11 September 1954, p. 19, and in *ibid.*, 26 March 1956, p. 20. *Variety*, 29 December 1954, p. 21. Potter's salary was estimated at $60,000 a year, exclusive of various extras like appearance money and endorsements. The only r&b deejay to warrant a listing was the white Al (Jazzbo) Collins, then on WRCA-New York. Charlie Gillett mistakenly includes Potter in his list of early supporters of r&b, C. Gillett, *The sound of the city*, 2nd revd edn (London: Souvenir, 1983), p. 38.

5. *Variety*, 8 December 1954, p. 46. *Rolling Stone rock almanac* (London: Macmillan, 1984), p. 8. C. Hamm, *Yesterdays: popular song in America* (New York: Norton, 1979), p. 399. O.J. Dodds quoted in *Richmond Times-Dispatch*, 11 July 1956, p. 16.

6. *Billboard*, 25 September 1954, p. 33; 2 October 1954, p. 19; 28 February 1953, p. 57; 27 February 1954, p. 22.

7. *Variety*, 23 February 1955, p. 19.

8. See Martin & Segrave, *Anti-rock*, pp. 27–39; G.L. Ortizano, *On your radio: a descriptive history of rhythm-and-blues radio during the 1950s* (PhD thesis, Ohio State University, 1993), pp. 311–19.

9. Ralph Bass quoted in M. Lydon & E. Mandel, *Boogie lightning*, repr. edn (New York: Da Capo, 1980), pp. 83–4.

10. *Billboard*, 30 October 1954, p. 16.

11. John Broven, *Rhythm and blues in New Orleans* (Gretna, La.: Pelican, 1974), p. 116; Ortizano, *On your radio*, p. 319.

12. J.B. Gilbert, *A cycle of outrage: America's reaction to the juvenile delinquent in the 1950s* (New York: Oxford University Press, 1986), p. 76. See also Oakley, *God's country*, pp. 268–71. See also T. Jackson Lears, "A matter of taste: corporate cultural hegemony in a mass consumption society", in *Recasting America: culture and politics in the age of the cold war*, L. May (ed.) (Chicago: University of Chicago Press, 1989), pp. 38–57.

13. Gilbert, *Cycle of outrage*, p. 15.

14. *Billboard*, 29 January 1955, p. 56.

15. *Birmingham News*, 11 April 1956, p. 2. This account of the Cole attack and its aftermath has been drawn primarily from the following sources: *Baltimore Afro-American*, 11–21 April 1956; *Birmingham News*, 11–21 April 1956; *Birmingham World*, 13–24 April 1956; *New Orleans Times-Picayune*, 11–21 April 1956; *The American Negro* 1(7), June 1956, pp. 5–8; and Schomburg Center Clippings File: "Cole" (hereinafter, SC-File: "Cole"). See also M. Cole (with L. Robinson), *Nat King Cole: an intimate biography* (London: Star/W.H. Allen, 1982), pp. 122–9; J. Haskins (with K. Benson), *Nat King Cole: the man and his music* (London: Robson, 1991), pp. 137–143. An earlier account of the Cole incident and its significance appeared as B. Ward, "Racial politics, culture and the Cole incident of 1956", in *Race and class in the American South since 1890*, M. Stokes and R. Halpern (eds) (Oxford: Berg, 1994), pp. 181–208.

16. *Birmingham News*, 12 April 1956, pp. 1/9; *Baltimore Afro-American*, 21 April 1956, p. 6; *Atlanta Journal*, 12 April 1956; SC-File: "Cole"; *Atlanta Inquirer*, 1 June 1963, p. 1; Cole, *Nat King Cole*, p. 123.

17. After the Anniston bus bombing, Adams was also convicted of firing shotgun blasts into various black homes and churches on Mother's Day 1963. *Atlanta Inquirer*, 1 June 1963, p. 1.
18. *Birmingham News*, 16 April 1956, p. 23. The appearance bonds for Mabry (case nos. 65376/65377/65378), Clevenger (case nos. 65398/65399), and E.L. Vinson (case nos. 65359/65360/65361) can be found in the Birmingham Recorder's Court Records, Birmingham Public Library Archives. Fox's appearance bond could not be located, but according to the Recorder's Court docket his charges were consolidated as case no. 65368.
19. Sam Englehardt quoted in *Birmingham News*, 12 April 1956, p. 9.
20. D. Cater, "Civil war in Alabama's citizens' councils", *The Reporter*, 17 May 1956, p. 20.
21. Charles Block, memo to Governor H.E. Talmadge, 23 December 1952, series B, subject: Press and Public Statements, box 13, folder 15, H.E. Talmadge Governor's papers. For the background to the NAACP's legal campaign against segregation, see M. Tushnet, *The NAACP's campaign against segregated education, 1925–1950* (Chapel Hill: University of North Carolina, 1987). For the history of massive resistance, see N. Bartley, *The rise of massive resistance* (Baton Rouge: Louisiana State University Press, 1969); N. McMillen, *The citizens' council: organized resistance to the second reconstruction* (Urbana: University of Illinois Press, 1971); F.M. Wilhoit, *The politics of massive resistance* (New York: G. Braziller, 1973).
22. A. Morris, *The origins of the civil rights movement: black communities organizing for change* (New York: Free Press, 1984), p. 29. Wilhoit, *Politics of massive resistance*, p. 45.
23. Sam Englehardt quoted in *Birmingham News*, 17 May 1954, p. 1, City Commissioners' statement, quoted in *ibid.*, 18 May 1954, p. 1; editorial in *ibid.*, 24 May 1954, p. 2. For Alabama's initially measured response to the *Brown* decisions, see J.T. Harris, *Alabama's response to the Brown decision, 1954–56: a study in early massive resistance* (Doctor of Arts thesis, Middle Tennessee State University, 1978), R. Corley, *The quest for racial harmony: race relations in Birmingham, Alabama, 1947–1963* (PhD thesis, University of Virginia, 1979), pp. 79–114; McMillen, *Citizens' council*, pp. 41–2; Bartley, *Massive resistance*, p. 77.
24. For the eclipse of Alabama's moderates and the intensification of massive resistance, see Harris, *Alabama's response to the Brown decision*; Corley, *Quest for racial harmony*; McMillen, *Citizens' council*, pp. 41–58; Bartley, *Massive resistance*, pp. 87–90, 131–5, 201–6, 279–86; Wilhoit, *Politics of massive resistance*, pp. 46, 105–7, 111–12, 171–4, 196–8.
25. Events at the University of Alabama in 1956 and their wider significance are vividly described in E. Culpepper Clark, *The schoolhouse door: segregation's last stand at the University of Alabama* (New York: Oxford University Press, 1993), pp. 3–133. W.C. Wade, *The fiery cross: the Ku Klux Klan in America* (New York: Touchstone, 1988), pp. 301–3; Bartley, *Massive resistance*, pp. 201–6.
26. J. Bartlow Martin, *The deep south says never* (New York: Ballantine, 1957), p. 7; *Birmingham News*, 19 February 1956, p. 1; McMillen, *Citizens' council*, pp. 43–4.
27. Cater, "Civil war in Alabama councils", pp. 19–21; *Birmingham News*, 4 March 1956, p. A-26; 7 March 1956, pp. 1/2; McMillen, *Citizens' council*, pp. 50–8.
28. *Ibid.*, pp. 53–4; Harris, *Alabama's reaction to the Brown decision*, pp. 290–4.

29. See *The Southerner* (March 1956), p. 5. For coverage of these early r&b shows, see *Birmingham News*, 15 January 1956, p. E-3; 15 March 1956, p. E-3.
30. *Ibid.*, 11 April 1956, p. 2. *The Southerner* (May 1956), p. 6.
31. Asa Carter quoted in *Birmingham News*, 12 April 1956, p. 9.
32. Wilhoit, *Politics of massive resistance*, p. 122.
33. *Birmingham News*, 11 March 1956, p. A-22. Such assumptions about blacks and their promiscuity were commonplace at all levels of southern white society. In Tuscaloosa, as the University of Alabama's Board of Trustees groped for non-racial criteria by which to reject Autherine Lucy's application, Edward Lord, president of Alabama College, "joked" that a requirement to pass the Wasserman syphilis test might prove a good way to exclude black candidates without obvious reference to race. See Clark, *Schoolhouse door*, p. 46.
34. J. Melancon, letter, *Birmingham News*, 7 March 1956, p. 14.
35. L. Crick, letter, *ibid.*, 5 March 1956, p. 12.
36. Walter Givhan quoted in *ibid.*, 17 January 1956, p. 3.
37. *The Southerner* (May 1956), pp. 2–3, 8; (August 1956), p. 8; (March 1956), p. 5.
38. *Ibid.* (August 1956), p. 16.
39. *Ibid.* (March 1956), p. 5.
40. Roy Wilkins quoted in *New York Times*, 30 March 1956, p. 39.
41. Asa Carter quoted in *Down Beat*, 2 May 1956, p. 7. Dave Bartholomew quoted in *ibid.*, p. 7.
42. Asa Carter quoted in *Newsweek*, 23 April 1956, p. 32.
43. *Birmingham News*, 21 May 1956, pp. 1/6, 30. See also *The Southerner* (August 1956), p. 3.
44. *Birmingham News*, 9 April 1956, p. 9. Ralph Edwards and Asa Carter, letter to James Morgan, 8 May 1956, folder 3.27, James W. Morgan, Mayoral papers (hereinafter, JWM).
45. Mrs Mary B. Anderson et al., letter to Mr James W. Morgan, 7 May 1956; Fred McCallum, letter to Jack House, 4 December 1956, both folder 3.27, JWM. *Birmingham News*, 21 May 1956, p. 2.
46. The dilemma of southern liberals is discussed in T. Badger, "Fatalism not gradualism: the crisis of southern liberalism, 1945–1965", in *The making of Martin Luther King and the civil rights movement*, B. Ward & T. Badger (eds) (New York: New York University Press, 1996), pp. 67–95.
47. *Louisiana revised statutes annotated* 4:451–55 (Supp. 1956), Act 579. See also C. Reynaud, "Legislation affecting segregation", *Louisiana Law Review* **17**, December 1956–June 1957, pp. 101–22.
48. See J. Record & W. Record, *Little Rock, USA: materials for analysis* (San Francisco: Chandler, 1960), p. 32.
49. *Norfolk Journal and Guide*, 19 October 1957, p. 15. That same month there was further evidence that Norfolk authorities were tightening Jim Crow enforcement at concerts in line with massive resistance. Virginia State College, which had been using the downtown Center Theater venue for its bigger events for two years on a non-segregated basis, chose to relocate a concert by jazz pianist Teddy Wilson to its own campus auditorium, rather than accept the Center's new insistence on segregated seating. *Ibid.*, 26 October 1957, p. 14.
50. See *Jacksonville Journal*, 10 August 1956, p. 2; 11 August 1956, p. 1; J.B. Leviton & G.J. Rijff, *Elvis close-up* (London: Century Hutchinson, 1989). On San Antonio, see *Variety*, 18 July 1956, p. 31. On Houston, see Martin & Segrave,

Anti-rock, pp. 23–4; A. Shaw, *Honkers and shouters* (New York: Macmillan, 1978), pp. xxiv–xxv.

51. J.A. Jackson, *Big beat heat: Alan Freed and the early years of rock & roll* (New York: Schirmer, 1991), p. 78. *Carolina Times* (Afro Magazine Section), 16 November 1957, p. 10.

52. *Tan* (February 1957), pp. 16–19, 51–6.

53. *American Nationalist*, n.d., box 255.39 (Interposition and Segregation, 1951–1956), Folder: Segregation, General, Nell Battle Lewis papers.

54. *New York Times*, 9 July 1956, p. 26; 12 July 1956, p. 25; *Variety*, 18 July 1956. Dr Francis J. Braceland quoted in *New York Times*, 28 March 1956, p. 33. The Very Reverend John Carroll quoted in *Variety*, 23 April 1956, p. 32.

55. Robert T. Convey quoted in *Rolling Stone rock almanac*, p. 36.

56. *Billboard*, 17 March 1956, p. 18; *Michigan Chronicle*, 9 June 1956, p. 13. *Rolling Stone rock almanac*, p. 39. In 1955, some seven years after WDIA and WOOK exposed the vast potential of black-oriented broadcasting, ABC became the first major network to really explore that market by initiating a series called *Rhythm and Blues on Parade*, hosted by Harlem favourite Willie Bryant. J.F. MacDonald, *Don't touch that dial!* (Chicago: Nelson-Hall, 1979), pp. 364–6.

57. *Billboard*, 7 April 1958, p. 4.

58. Shelley Stewart, interview with Brian Ward, 26 October 1995. University of Newcastle upon Tyne Oral History Collection.

59. *Ibid.*; *Birmingham News*, 29 May 1958, p. 66.

60. For the Chicago agreement, see "Memo: from the City Desk and Radio-Television Desk, City Bureau of Chicago", 9 August 1966, "Minutes of Radio-Television Meeting", 12 August 1966; "Minutes of WGN-Continental Broadcasting Co.", 12 August 1966, all references Ed Marciniak File. See also J. Ralph, *Northern protest: Martin Luther King, Jr, Chicago and the civil rights movement* (Cambridge, Mass.: Harvard University Press, 1993), p. 144. Bert Ferguson quoted in L. Cantor, *Wheelin' on Beale: how WDIA-Memphis became the nation's first all-black radio station and created the sound that changed America* (New York: Pharos, 1992), p. 3. Eddie Phelan quoted in *Arkansas Gazette*, 14 June 1964.

61. Ralph Bass quoted in Lydon & Mandel, *Boogie lightning*, pp. 83–4.

62. *New York Times*, 16 September 1956, Sec. 2, p. 13. *Look*, 7 August 1956, p. 84. *Life*, 18 April 1955, pp. 166–8; 24 August 1956, pp. 101–9.

63. *Birmingham News*, 13 January 1956, p. E-5; 2 January 1956, p. 18; 4 March 1956, p. 18.

64. *Ibid.*, 6 May 1956, p. E-5; 4 March 1956, p. 35; 25 September 1956, p. E-5.

65. Cited in Gilbert, *Cycle of outrage*, p. 18.

66. *Raleigh News and Observer*, 28 April 1956, p. 8. Bill Randle quoted in *Variety*, 2 March 1958, p. 49.

67. Lewis' colourful career is brilliantly described in N. Tosches, *Hellfire: the Jerry Lee Lewis story* (London: Plexus, 1982); see also M. Lewis (with M. Silver), *Great balls of fire! the true story of Jerry Lee Lewis* (London: Virgin, 1982). For Woods' arrest, see *Michigan Chronicle*, 19 May 1956, p. 6. The Flamingos' bust is described in *Chicago Defender*, 22 August 1959, p. 1. For the Platters' arrest and trial, see *Amsterdam News*, 15 August 1959, p. 15; *Pittsburgh Courier*, 29 August 1959, p. 4; *Baltimore Afro-American*, 19 December 1959, p. 1; *Norfolk Journal and Guide*, 19 December 1959, p. 2.

68. *Amsterdam News*, 19 March 1960, pp. 1/31; *Atlanta Daily World*, 9 June 1960, p. 3; *Chicago Defender*, 11 June 1960, p. 17; *Baltimore Afro-American*, 1 April 1961, p. 15. See also C. Berry, *The autobiography of Chuck Berry* (London: Faber & Faber, 1988), pp. 195–209.

69. For the Martin and Escalanti cases, see D.J. Langum, *Crossing over the line: legislation, morality and the Mann Act* (Chicago: University of Chicago Press, 1994), pp. 186–8. *Baltimore Afro-American*, 1 April 1961, p. 15. For Berry's belated admission that he had actually served time in prison, see Berry, *Auto-biography of Chuck Berry*, pp. 195–209. Berry long maintained that he had been acquitted – see his 1972 interview with Patrick William Salvo, in *The Rolling Stone interviews, 1967–80*, B. Fong-Torres (ed.) (New York: St Martin's, 1981), pp. 224–35. For the Meridian incident, see *New York Times*, 29 August 1959, p. 38. *Baltimore Afro-American*, 5 September 1959, p. 1; 12 September 1959, p. 7.

70. See H. Smead, *Blood justice: the lynching of Mack Charles Parker* (New York: Oxford University Press, 1986).

71. See J. Silver, *Mississippi: the closed society* (New York: Harcourt Brace, 1964). For more recent scholarly accounts of racial oppression and resistance in Mississippi before the 1960s, see J. Dittmer, *Local people: the struggle for civil rights in Mississippi* (Urbana: University of Illinois Press, 1994), pp. 1–89; Neil McMillen, *Dark journey: black Mississippians in the age of Jim Crow* (Urbana: University of Illinois Press, 1989).

72. The information on and from Tommy Ridgley comes from Tommy Ridgley, interviews with Tad Jones, 2 March 1986 and 23 April 1986, both Hogan Jazz Archive. See also J. Berry, J. Foote & T. Jones, *Up from the cradle of jazz* (Athens: University of Georgia Press, 1986), p. 172.

73. For the New York incident, see *Amsterdam News*, 12 November 1955. For Washington and Richmond, see *Richmond Times-Dispatch*, 9 June 1956, p. 8; 26 March 1958, pp. 1/4; 27 March 1958, p. 16; 8 May 1958, p. 18.

74. *Amsterdam News*, 18 February 1956, p. 2.

75. This account of the Roanoke incident is drawn from *New York Times*, 6 May 1956, p. 78; *Norfolk Journal and Guide*, 12 May 1956, p. 1; *Roanoke World News*, 4 May 1956, p. B-12; 5 May 1956, p. 1; 7 May 1956, p. 1; 8 May 1956, pp. 1, 6.

76. Anonymous police officer quoted in *Roanoke World News*, 7 May 1956, p. 1.

77. For the anonymous black and white statements on Roanoke's lack of racial tensions, see *Norfolk Journal and Guide*, 12 May 1956, p. 2. For the city council discussions and Legion decision, see *Roanoke World News*, 7 May 1956, p. 1; Ran Whittle quoted in *ibid.*, 8 May 1956, p. 1.

78. For the Newport "riot", see *Richmond Times-Dispatch*, 19 September 1956, p. 28; 28 September 1956, p. 16. For the Fayetteville "riot", see *Fayetteville Observer*, 2 November 1956, pp. 1/14; 3 November 1956, pp. 1/10; *Raleigh News and Observer*, 3 November 1956, pp. 1/3. Not all of the racial violence associated with rock and roll in 1956 took place in and around the concert hall. In May there was a bizarre and tragic coda to the Nat King Cole incident in Royal Oaks, Michigan, when Cecil Edgil, a 31-year-old white Alabama migrant, was charged with the baseball bat murder of Lenver Norris, a black barbershop employee, following an argument over the assault. In a further twist, Edgil's son-in-law was then killed in a car crash as he travelled back to Alabama to tell Edgil's mother of her son's arrest. *Birmingham World*, 1 May 1956, p. 3.

79. *Boston Globe*, 15 April 1957, p. 13; *New York Times*, 15 April 1957, p. 23; *ibid.*, 17 July 1957, p. 23.

80. P. Groia, *They all sang on the corner*, 2nd edn (New York: Phillie Dee, 1983), p. 136.

81. Buddy Holly quoted in J. Goldrosen & J. Beecher, *Remembering Buddy* (London: Pavilion, 1987), p. 75. See also *ibid.*, pp. 70–5, which despite the error about the Crickets' mistaken identity offers a useful discussion of the 1957 tour. Better still is E. Amburn, *Buddy Holly: a biography* (New York: St Martin's, 1995), pp. 85–9, 99. See also B. Floyd, "Crickets appearance at the Apollo", *Reminiscing Magazine* (Fall 1983), p. 18.

82. *Tan* (February 1957), p. 73. Reather Turner and Emma Patron quoted in D. Garvey, "The Bobbettes", *Goldmine*, 21 February 1992, pp. 24/30.

83. Groia, *They all sang*, p. 100.

84. Mayor Hynes and Alan Freed are both quoted in *Boston Globe*, 6 May 1958, pp. 1/7. See also *ibid.*, 5 May 1958, p. 4; 7 May 1958, pp. 1/35; 8 May 1958, pp. 1/11; 9 May 1958 pp. 1/37; *New York Times*, 5 May 1958, p. 48; 9 May 1958, p. 49; 15 May 1958, p. 59; *Richmond Times-Dispatch*, 5 May 1958, p. 1. See also Jackson, *Big beat heat*, pp. 192–210, 225, 247.

85. For Freed's first encounter with anti-rock and roll sentiment in Boston, see *ibid.*, pp. 96–8.

86. John F. Kennedy/*Newsday*, *Congressional record: appendix*, 85th Congress, 1st Session, 15 August 1957 (Washington, D.C.: Government Printing Office, 1957), p. A6688. *Congressional record*, 85th Congress, 1st Session, 21 August 1957 (Washington, D.C.: Government Printing Office, 1957), pp. 15499–15501.

87. Kennedy's support for Smathers' bill was also related to his own 1956 proposal to amend the 1934 Communications Act so as to encourage the FCC to grant more licences to applicants who already owned stations and had therefore proved themselves competent and responsible programmers. See J.F. Kennedy, Statement: amendment to Sec. 308 of 1934 Communications Act (1956), Box 666, Folder: Federal Communications Commission, John F. Kennedy Pre-Presidential Papers (hereinafter, JFK). For Kennedy's and Goldwater's Senate support for Smathers, see *Congressional record*, 21 August 1957, p. 15500.

88. For the founding of BMI and the roots of ASCAP's campaign against it, see P.H. Ennis, *The seventh stream: the emergence of rock'n'roll in American popular music* (Hanover, N.H.: Wesleyan, 1992), pp. 4–6, 11–12, 105–9, 165–7; R. Sanjek, *American popular music and its business*, (New York: Oxford University Press, 1988), vol. 3, pp. 175–82, 396–438; "ASCAP's war on BMI", *Broadcasting Telecasting*, 9 September 1957, pp. 4–6, 60–1.

89. New writers tended to join BMI because it admitted them on submission of their first composition and administered royalties on a simple set fee per performance basis. By contrast, ASCAP maintained what country star Gene Autry described to the Hearings as a "closed-door policy towards any new writers and publishers of music", refusing to admit songwriters until the publication of their fifth song, and operating a payment gauge which unequally divided rights payments among members according to criteria such as "their contribution to American music, their seniority in the society, their 'availability' over the years and the number and popularity of their hits". Gene Autry to *Smathers bill hearings*, p. 449. See also H. Meyer, *The gold in Tin Pan Alley*, repr. edn (Westport, Conn.: Greenwood, 1977), p. 98. *Variety*, 16 February 1955, p. 39.

90. Arthur Schwartz, letter and memorandum to Senator George Smathers (n.d.: received, Washington, D.C., 4 November 1957), box 13 (466), folder 70: Music

S.2834, George A. Smathers papers (hereinafter, GAS). Arthur Schwartz, letter to Senator John F. Kennedy, 16 September 1957, box 525, folder 3, JFK.

91. See *House committee on judiciary: sub-committee on anti-trust monopoly problems in regulated industries*, U.S. House of Representatives, 84th Congress, 2 vols (Washington, D.C.: Government Printing Office, 1956/57) (hereinafter, *Celler committee*). Russell Sanjek has claimed that this apparent evenhandedness towards both major publishing associations concealed a distinct bias in the chairman's attitude towards BMI, since he had initially called only for BMI to be investigated. Sanjek, *American popular music*, vol. 3, pp. 404–7, 422–3. See also Ennis, *Seventh stream*, pp. 165–7.

92. The best contemporary critiques of ASCAP's case are "ASCAP's war on BMI", and Bruce Barrington (President of Missouri Broadcasters Association), letter to Senator Stuart Symington, 30 December 1957, box 13 (466), folder 71, GAS. See also Sanjek, *American popular music*, vol. 3, pp. 396–438.

93. "ASCAP's war on BMI", pp. 5–6; *Smathers bill hearings*, p. 1235; *Variety*, 23 April 1958, p. 47; Sanjek, *American popular music*, vol. 3, pp. 333–64; A. Shaw, *The rockin' 50s* (New York: Hawthorn, 1974), p. 157. On Jesse Stone, see N. Tosches, *Unsung heroes of rock and roll* (New York: C. Scribner, 1984), pp. 11–19. Lew Chudd, the owner of Imperial, had one ASCAP company (Post Music) and several registered with BMI (Travis, Commodore, and Reeve). See Lew Chudd to *Smathers bill hearings*, p. 565.

94. *House select committee on small business: House sub-committee No. 5: policies of American Society of Composers, Authors and Publishers*, US House of Representatives, 85th Congress (Washington, D.C.: Government Printing Office, 1958).

95. Stanley Adams to *Celler committee*, **2**, p. 4142.

96. Frank Sinatra, telegram to Senator George Smathers, 27 August 1957, box 13 (466), folder 70: Music S.2834, GAS.

97. Arlan Coolidge to *Smathers bill hearings*, p. 25.

98. V. Packard, *Hidden persuaders* (New York: D. McKay, 1957).

99. Vance Packard to *Smathers bill hearings*, pp. 109, 136. See also *ibid.*, pp. 106–41.

100. *Ibid.*, pp. 108, 119, 134–6.

101. Senator Albert Gore to *Smathers bill hearings*, pp. 141–2. Governor Frank Clement, telegram to Albert Gore, 12 March 1958, Albert Gore Papers, folder: LEGIS (Interstate and Foreign Commerce, Interstate Broadcasting, 1958) (hereinafter, AG).

102. Smathers received far more letters opposing his bill and defending BMI than supporting his position. As well as correspondence from individuals, these included a number of resolutions passed by state broadcasters' associations in Arizona, Missouri, North Carolina, Tennessee and Virginia. See box 13 (466), 1957, folder 71: Music, S.2834, GAS. Frank Clement, Albert Gore, and his fellow Tennessee senator, Estes Kefauver, were also inundated with letters from country singers and songwriters (including Roy Acuff, Ernest Tubb, Jim Reeves and Hank Snow), song publishers (Jimmy Denny, Hubert Long and Joseph Csida), broadcasters (John DeWitt, Jack Stapp and F.C. Sowell), and record company owners – some of whom, like Sam Phillips of Sun Records, recorded black artists as well as white. All denied a BMI conspiracy, denounced Smathers' proposed bill, and asked for the opportunity to testify before the hearings. See folder: LEGIS (Interstate and Foreign Commerce, Interstate Broadcasting, 1958), AG.

103. Senator John Pastore to *Smathers bill hearings*, pp. 10–11.

Chapter Four

1. H. Weinger, "The Platters' glory days", *Goldmine*, 21 February 1992, p. 11.
2. The Drifters were refashioned after Clyde McPhatter's departure by manager George Treadwell and featured several lead singers, most notably Ben E. King, Rudy Lewis and Johnny Moore.
3. *Greensboro A&T College Register*, 6 March 1964, p. 2.
4. Black pop has, however, been given far more attention in general histories of rock and pop. See C. Gillett, *The sound of the city*, revd edn (London: Souvenir, 1983), pp. 189–223, and C. Belz, *The story of rock*, 2nd edn (New York: Oxford University Press, 1972), pp. 60–117. There have also been two fine studies of girl groups – in many respects the quintessential expression of the biracial pop era. A. Betrock, *Girl groups: the story of a sound* (London: Putnam, 1983) and C. Greig, *Will you still love me tomorrow?* (London: Virago, 1989).
5. Diane Nash quoted in J. Williams, *Eyes on the prize* (New York: Viking, 1987), p. 131.
6. C. Denby, *Indignant heart: a black worker's journal* (Detroit, Wayne State University Press, 1989), p. 196. Ivanhoe Donaldson quoted in H. Hampton & S. Fayer, *Voices of freedom: an oral history of the civil rights movement from the 1950s through the 1980s* (New York: Bantam, 1990), p. 168.
7. Poll (27 February 1956), in *The Gallup poll: public opinion, 1935–1971* (New York: Random House, 1972), vol. 2, pp. 1401–2, Poll (12 February 1961), in *ibid.*, vol. 3, pp. 1705–6.
8. See D. Chappell, *Inside agitators: southern whites and the civil rights movement* (Baltimore: Johns Hopkins University Press, 1994), pp. 59–145. Also, J. Cobb, *The selling of the South: the southern crusade for industrial development, 1936–1980* (Baton Rouge: Louisiana State University Press, 1982); E. Jacoway & D.R. Colburn (eds), *Southern businessmen and desegregation* (Baton Rouge: Louisiana State University Press, 1982); T. Badger, "Segregation and the southern business elite", *Journal of American Studies* **18**, 1984, pp. 105–9.
9. J. Meredith, *Three years in Mississippi* (Bloomington: Indiana University Press, 1966), p. 52.
10. J. Farmer, *Freedom – when?* (New York: Random House, 1965), p. 91.
11. J. Blassingame, "The revolution that never was: the civil rights movement, 1950–1980", *Perspectives: U.S. commission on civil rights* **14**(2), Summer 1982, p. 3. John Lewis quoted in H. Raines, *My soul is rested: movement days in the Deep South remembered* (New York: Putnam, 1977), pp. 98–9.
12. M.L. King, *Stride toward freedom: the Montgomery story* (New York: Harper, 1958), p. 217.
13. *Baltimore Afro-American*, 31 October 1954, p. 7.
14. *Down Beat*, 30 May 1956, p. 14. Harry Weinger quoted in "The Platters' glory days", p. 11. C. Johnson quoted in "Under the boardwalk", *New Musical Express*, 29 August 1987, p. 13. Herbie Cox quoted in P. Groia, *They all sang on the corner*, 2nd edn (New York: Phillie Dee, 1983), p. 128.
15. Shelley Stewart, interview with Brian Ward, 26 October 1995, UNOHC.
16. Ibid.; *Birmingham World*, 23 July 1960, p. 2.
17. Shelley Stewart quoted in *ibid.*, p. 2; Stewart interview.
18. Ralph Bass quoted in M. Lydon & E. Mandel, *Boogie lightning*, repr. edn (New York: Da Capo, 1980), p. 92; see also *Newsweek*, 18 June 1956, p. 42.

19. *Louisiana Weekly*, 28 September 1963, p. 22. The segregation Act was declared unconstitutional following a class action suit brought by the NAACP's Horace Bynum against the Mayor of New Orleans, Victor Schiro (Bynum vs Schiro, Civ. A. No.12439, 1 July 1963, 168 *Federal Supplement* 149). See also A. Fairclough, *Race and democracy: the civil rights struggle in Louisiana, 1915–1972* (Athens, Ga.: University of Georgia Press, 1995), pp. 335–6.
20. Nat King Cole quoted in *Baltimore Afro-American*, 21 April 1956, p. 1.
21. Nat King Cole quoted in *Christian Science Monitor*, 12 April 1956, in Schomburg Center Clippings File: "Cole" (hereinafter, SC-file: "Cole"). Nat King Cole quoted in *Birmingham News*, 14 April 1956, p. 2.
22. Judge Ralph E. Parker, "Statement prior to sentencing defendants in Cole case", 18 April 1956, 23.17: Recorder's Court, James W. Morgan Mayoral Papers.
23. *Chicago Defender*, 21 April 1956, p. 10. *Daily Worker*, 29 April 1956, SC-file: "Cole".
24. Marshall's jibe is reported in M. Cole (with L. Robinson), *Nat King Cole: an intimate biography* (London: Star/W.H. Allen, 1982), pp. 122–9. Roy Wilkins, telegram to Nat King Cole, 13 April 1956, III-A-272, Papers of the NAACP (hereinafter, NAACP).
25. Nat King Cole, telegram to Roy Wilkins, 14 April 1956; "Statement by Nat King Cole", Detroit, 22 April 1956, both III-A-272, NAACP; Nat King Cole, letter to *Down Beat*, 30 May 1956, p. 4. Cole's move to Hancock Park provided an early opportunity to test the efficacy of the 1948 *Shelley versus Kramer* Supreme Court decision which forbade federal and state courts to enforce restrictive covenants in the housing market.
26. *Daily Worker*, 29 April 1956, SC-file: "Cole"; *Amsterdam News*, 21 April 1956, p. 1; *American Negro* (June 1956), pp. 5–8.
27. Harry Belafonte, interview with Brian Ward, 12 March 1996, UNOHC. Nat King Cole quoted in *Pittsburgh Courier*, 25 January 1958, p. 23.
28. *Michigan Chronicle*, 28 April 1956, pp. 1/4, 1/16. For the officers of the Committee to Defend Martin Luther King Jr, see Tom Kahn, letter to Maude Ballou, 27 April 1960; and "Statement on the indictment of Martin Luther King, Jr", 3 March 1960, both box 4, I, folder 22, Martin Luther King papers (hereinafter MLK). See also *Amsterdam News*, 12 March 1960, pp. 1/35.
29. Nat King Cole, letter to Martin Luther King, 25 June 1963; Nat King Cole, telegram to Martin Luther King, 16 July 1963, both box 37A, folder 54, MLK. Nat King Cole, letter to James Forman, 26 June 1963, A-VII-1, Student Nonviolent Coordinating Committee Papers (hereinafter SNCC). Nat King Cole, letter to Roy Wilkins, 26 June 1963; Leo Branton Jr, letter to Dr Christopher L. Taylor, 30 September 1963, both III-A-44, NAACP.
30. *Carolina Times*, 21 April 1956, p. 1.
31. *Billboard*, 14 April 1956, p. 63.
32. Belz, *Story of rock*, p. 23.
33. *Our World* (November 1955), p. 42. See also *ibid.* (February 1955), pp. 64–6.
34. Little Richard quoted in *Rolling Stone interviews*, Ben Fong-Torres (ed.) (New York: Paperback Library, 1971), p. 371. Screaming Jay Hawkins quoted in G. Hirshey, *Nowhere to run* (New York: Macmillan, 1984), p. 11.
35. D. Burley, "The truth about rock 'n' roll", *Tan* (July 1956), p. 82.
36. L. Cantor, *Wheelin' on Beale: how WDIA-Memphis became the nation's first all-black radio station and created the sound that changed America* (New York: Pharos, 1992), pp. 193–6.

37. N.D. Williams, "Down on Beale", *Pittsburgh Courier*, 22 December 1956, p. 24.
38. L. Robinson, "'The Pelvis' gives his views on vicious anti-Negro slur," *Jet*, 1 August 1957, pp. 58–61; "What you don't know about Elvis Presley", *Tan* (November 1957), pp. 30–1, 75.
39. *Birmingham World*, 20 January 1956, p. 6; *Chicago Defender*, 17 November 1956, p. 15. Bill Haley quoted in *Down Beat*, 30 May 1956, p. 10. See also Alan Freed quoted in *ibid.*, 20 April 1955, p. 41, and *Look*, 26 June 1956, p. 48.
40. M. Wilson (with P. Romanowski & A. Juillard), *Dreamgirl: my life as a Supreme* (London: Sidgwick & Jackson, 1987), p. 24.
41. James Bond, interview with Brian Ward, 18 October 1995, UNOHC.
42. *Ibid.*; Julian Bond, interview with Brian Ward, 20 March 1996, UNOHC.
43. *Ibid.*
44. *Ibid.*
45. Nelson George, *The death of rhythm and blues* (New York: Omnibus, 1988), pp. 66–8.
46. Stewart interview. J.L. Dates & W. Barlow, *Split image: African-Americans in the mass media* (Washington, D.C.: Howard University Press, 1990), p. 218.
47. *Memphis Commercial Appeal*, 9 June 1950, 29 September 1968; 26 September 1993; *Memphis Press-Scimitar*, 22 October 1956. All references from the Memphis & Shelby County Room Clippings Files: "WHBQ". WDIA's hours were extended to midnight in 1954, when it was upgraded to 50,000 watts. Cantor, *Wheelin' on Beale*, p. 107.
48. Esmond Patterson, interview with Brian Ward & Jenny Walker, 19 October 1995, UNOHC. Julian Bond interview.
49. Tommy Ridgley, interview with Tad Jones, 22 March 1986, Hogan Jazz Archive. Stanley Wise, interview with Brian Ward & Jenny Walker, 19 October 1995, UNOHC. J. Brown (with B. Tucker), *James Brown: the godfather of soul* (Glasgow: Fontana, 1988), p. 53. J. Egerton, *Speak now against the day: the generation before the civil rights movement in the South* (New York: A. Knopf, 1994), p. 538. See also B. Hoskyns, *Say it one time for the broken hearted* (Glasgow: Fontana, 1987), pp. 60–2, 130–9.
50. M. Ochs, *Rock archives* (Poole, Dorset: Blandford, 1985), pp. 38–9; *Billboard*, 5 June 1954, p. 4; *Our World* (August 1954), pp. 33–5; see also Jackson, *Big beat heat*, pp. 95–6. *Amsterdam News*, 6 February 1960, p. 15. Even when, in September 1954, veteran black deejay Willie Bryant complained that the syndication of Freed's *Moondog Show* on WINS-New York was putting black deejays out of work, or when, the following February, *Our World* argued that Freed's success with black teenagers was undermining support for black jocks, it confirmed that Freed was a personality of some importance in the black community, even as it highlighted the continued lack of black opportunity in the industry. See *Billboard*, 18 September 1954, p. 11; *Our World* (February 1955), pp. 64–6.
51. *Billboard*, 7 January 1956, p. 21.
52. Tommy Smalls quoted in *Chicago Defender*, 14 April 1956, p. 13.
53. Stewart interview. Jack Gibson, "Excerpts from a 1959 WCIN-Cincinnati broadcast", in *Jack Gibson and Al Benson*, Museum of Television and Radio (hereinafter MT&R).
54. Harold Battiste, interview with Brian Ward, 8 November 1995, UNOHC.
55. George, *Death of rhythm and blues*, pp. 67–8. Charlie Gillett has pointed out that formerly black-oriented radio stations began playing a substantial amount

of white rock and roll in the mid 1950s, hoping to attract white listeners and advertisers, and that, consequently, "black audiences may have known fewer black records and so bought those they heard on their radios". However, even this insight misses the fact that black-oriented radio programming was, in part at least, a response to emerging black consumer preferences. Gillett, *Sound of the city*, p. 189.

56. N. Spaulding, *The history of black-oriented radio in Chicago, 1923–1963* (PhD thesis, University of Illinois at Urbana-Champaign, 1981), p. 114.

57. Wise interview.

58. *Amsterdam News*, 12 November 1955, p. 33. D. Gillespie (with A. Fraser), *To be or not to bop* (London: Quartet, 1982), p. 230. J. Wexler & D. Ritz, *Rhythm and the blues: a life in American music* (New York: A. Knopf, 1993), p. 78. David Rosenthal argues for the continued popularity of jazz in the ghettos until the 1970s, but concedes that "very little jazz reached the r & b charts between 1953 and 1960". Thereafter, when "jazz" singles by Nat Adderley, Jimmy McGriff and Roy Harris did begin to appear regularly, they were invariably gospel-tinged, r&b groove numbers which reflected the rising popularity of soul, not a renewed mass black interest in modern jazz. D. Rosenthal, "Jazz in the ghetto: 1950–1970", *Popular Music* 7, January 1988, pp. 51–6.

59. C. Sawyer, *B.B. King: the authorized biography* (Poole, Dorset: Blandford, 1981), p. 86.

60. B.B. King quoted in L. Redd, *Rock is rhythm and blues* (Detroit: Michigan State University Press, 1974), p. 104. See also Brownee McGhee's interview in *ibid.*, p. 115 ("I've been through five changes, and it's been for commercial purposes").

61. Bill Doggett quoted in *Billboard*, 24 March 1958, pp. 11/66.

62. Little Richard quoted in C. White, *The life and times of Little Richard* (London: Pan, 1985), p. 161.

63. C. Berry, *The autobiography of Chuck Berry* (London: Faber & Faber, 1988), pp. 200–9.

64. Brown, *Godfather of soul*, p. 82.

65. Battiste interview.

66. For the best assessment of Cooke's career see D. Wolff et al., *You send me: the life and times of Sam Cooke* (New York: Wm Morrow, 1995). Bernice Johnson Reagon, interview with Brian Ward, 24 January 1996, UNOHC.

67. George, *Death of rhythm and blues*, pp. 81, 79. J. McEwen, *Sam Cooke: the man who invented soul* (New York: Sire, 1977), p. 19; Wolff et al., *You send me*, esp. pp. 209–13.

68. Hugo Peretti quoted in Hirshey, *Nowhere to run*, p. 112.

69. *Ibid.*, pp. 170–4, 300–7.

70. Sid Feller quoted in M. Lydon & E. Mandel, *Boogie lightning*, repr. edn (New York: Da Capo, 1980), p. 211.

71. George, *Death of rhythm and blues*, pp. 77–9. G. Giddins, *Rhythm-a-ning: jazz tradition and innovation in the '80s* (New York: Oxford University Press, 1985), pp. 146–52.

72. S. Robinson (with D. Ritz), *Smokey: inside my life* (London: Headline, 1989), pp. 49, 101–2.

73. June Johnson, interview with Brian Ward, 22 January 1996, UNOHC. Johnson and her remarkable family are discussed in C. Payne, *I've got the light of freedom: the organizing tradition and the Mississippi freedom struggle* (Berkeley:

University of California Press, 1995), pp. 225–33. The Winona beatings are discussed in K. Mills, *This little light of mine: the life of Fannie Lou Hamer* (New York: Dutton, 1993), pp. 56–77. Lena Horne quoted in *Birmingham World*, 14 September 1963, p. 5.

74. Unfortunately, there are no reliable statistics regarding the levels of black domestic violence during the peak years of civil rights activity, let alone comparisons with earlier periods. Nevertheless, the anecdotal evidence that black domestic violence – and internecine black violence more generally – declined wherever Movement activities flourished is quite compelling. Bernice Johnson Reagon, for example, recalled that in Albany there was a black business and entertainment district dubbed Harlem, "where things could get rough and people could get cut, shot, or even killed, except during the Civil Rights Movement, when the violence level almost disappeared". B. Johnson Reagon et al., *We who believe in freedom* (New York: Anchor, 1993), pp. 155–6. In a similar vein, Gloria Richardson of the Cambridge Non-Violent Action Committee reckoned that "during the whole time we were demonstrating actively there were almost no fights in this ward and almost no crime". When the Cambridge movement disintegrated, the gangs went "back to fighting each other again". Gloria Richardson quoted in M. Kempton, "Gloria, Gloria", *New Republic*, 16 November 1963, p. 17.

75. J.A. Gibson Robinson, *The Montgomery bus boycott and the women who started it* (Knoxville: University of Tennessee Press, 1987), pp. 36–7.

76. While there is still little scholarship on the role of white women in the Movement, historians have begun to acknowledge the contribution of black women, particularly at the local level. See, for example, the collection, *Women in the civil rights movement*, V. Crawford, J. Rouse & B. Woods (eds) (New York: Carlson, 1990); C. Curry, *Silver rights* (Athens, Ga : University of Georgia Press, 1995); Payne, *I've got the light of freedom*; Mills, *This little light*.

77. Carmichael's fellow SNCC worker, Mary King, insisted that his private, mildly intoxicated, comment was meant and interpreted at the time as a joke. M. King, *Freedom song* (New York: Wm Morrow, 1987), p. 452. Julian Bond, however, maintains that Carmichael's comments were not taken so lightly and caused some offence at the time. J. Bond, "The Politics of civil rights history", in *New directions in civil rights studies*, A.L. Robinson & P. Sullivan (eds) (Charlottesville: University Press of Virginia, 1991), p. 10. See also S. Evans, *Personal politics: the roots of women's liberation in the civil rights movement and the new left* (New York: A. Knopf, 1979), p. 87; C. Carson, *In struggle: SNCC and the black awakening of the 1960s* (Cambridge, Mass.: Harvard University Press, 1981), p. 148. John Lewis quoted in H.S. Jaffe & T. Sherwood, *Dream city: race, power, and the decline of Washington DC* (New York: Simon & Schuster, 1994), p. 41 (see also pp. 48–9).

78. J. Street, *Rebel rock: the politics of popular music* (Oxford: Blackwell, 1986), p. 166.

79. E. Brooks Higginbotham, "Beyond the sound of silence: Afro-American women in history", *Gender and History* **1**, Spring 1989, p. 56.

80. *Tan* (May 1960), p. 12. See also *ibid.* (May 1954), p. 10; J.A. Hutchinson, "Black culture and consciousness as revealed in a contents analysis of *Tan*, 1953–1962", unpublished Masters paper (Department of History, University of Newcastle upon Tyne, 1996). Copy in possession of author. Reagon interview.

81. See C. Stack, *All our kin: strategies for survival in a black community* (New York: Harper & Row, 1974).

82. See J. Ladner, *Tomorrow's tomorrow: the black woman* (Garden City, N.Y.: Anchor, 1972), p. 247. Higginbotham, "Beyond the sound of silence", p. 56. Figures in H.A. Ploski & J. Williams, *The Negro almanac: a reference work on the Afro-American*, 4th edn (New York: J. Wiley, 1983), p. 486. The persistence of this ideal of conventional domesticity in black America is also noted in L. Rainwater, *Behind ghetto walls: black families in ghetto slums* (London: Allen Lane, 1971), p. 62, and Stack, *All our kin*, pp. 113, 125–6.

83. bell hooks, *Ain't I a woman?: black women and feminism* (Boston: South End, 1981), p. 178.

84. *Tan* (January 1954), pp. 6/71.

85. Early all-girl groups included the Enchanters, Devaurs, Deltairs, Originals, Dreamers, Four Chickadees, Miller Sisters, Jackson Sisters, Hampton Sisters, Ruth McFadden and the Supremes, Bobbettes, Queens and Joyettes. Male groups with a female lead included Lillian Leach and the Mellows, Ann Nichols and the Bluebirds, Patti Anne and the Flames, Sweet Georgia Brown and Her Whipporwills, Wini Brown and her Boyfriends, Carmen Taylor and the Boleros, Goldie Boots and the Falcons, the Chestnuts (Ruby Whitaker), Capris (Rena Hinton), Minors (Yvonne Lee) and Dovers (Miriam Grate). Occasional mixed-sex collaborations included Savannah Churchill with the Four Tunes, Dinah Washington with the Ravens, and Little Esther with the Ravens, Robins and Dominoes. Permanent mixed-sex combinations included the Sugartones (three female, one male), Tuneweavers (two of each sex), and the Platters with Zola Taylor.

86. Betrock, *Girl groups*.

87. For a sensationalist account of Spector's career, see M. Ribovsky, *He's a rebel: the truth about Phil Spector – rock and roll's legendary madman* (New York: E.P. Dutton, 1989).

88. Betrock, *Girl groups*, p. 8.

89. Greig, *Will you still love me?*, p. 33. See also B. Bradby, "Do talk and don't talk: the division of the subject in girl group music" (1988), in *On the record*, S. Frith & A. Goodwin (eds) (London: Routledge, 1990), pp. 341–68.

90. P. Gilroy, *The Black Atlantic: modernity and double consciousness* (Cambridge, Mass.: Harvard University Press, 1993), p. 85.

91. See Gillett, *Sound of the city*, pp. 190, 472; L. Feist, *An introduction to popular music publishing in America* (New York: National Music Publishers Association, 1980), pp. 105–6; R.A. Peterson, "Cycles in symbol production: the case of popular music", *American Sociological Review* **40**, 1975, p. 165.

92. See R. Sanjek, *American popular music and its business* (New York: Oxford University Press, 1988), vol. 3, pp. 333–64.

93. *Billboard*, 7 April 1958, p. 1.

94. Paul Ackerman to *Hearings before a subcommittee of the committee on interstate and foreign commerce: second session on payola and other deceptive practices in the broadcasting field*, parts 1 & 2, US House of Representatives, 86th Congress (Washington, D.C.: Government Printing Office, 1960), p. 900 (hereinafter, *Harris hearings*). According to showbiz legend, it was the Willis Woodward Company which began the practice of paying vaudeville performers to include certain material in their acts. See C. Hamm, *Yesterdays: popular song in America* (New York: Norton, 1979), pp. 284–90.

95. *Variety*, 16 February 1955, p. 39.

96. For an excellent account of payola practices and the congressional hearings, see K. Segrave, *Payola in the music industry, 1880–1991* (Jefferson, N.C.: McFarland, 1994). Also, Sanjek, *American popular music*, vol. 3, pp. 438–49; R. Serge Denisoff, *Solid gold: the popular record industry* (New Brunswick, N.J.: Transaction, 1975), pp. 223–33; J. Picardie & D. Wade, *Atlantic and the godfathers of rock and roll*, revd edn (London: Fourth Estate, 1993), pp. 71–88.

97. Morty Craft quoted in *ibid.*, p. 55.

98. Greg Harris quoted in *Chicago Defender*, 5 December 1959, pp. 1–2.

99. George Goldner to *Harris hearings*, p. 1099. See also *New York Times*, 20 February 1960, pp. 1/2. Norman Prescott to *Harris hearings*, p. 7.

100. Syd Nathan to *Harris hearings*; also, *New York Daily News*, 21 November 1959, p. 4.

101. For Goldner's testimony, see *Harris hearings*, pp. 1095–1112.

102. Details of Clark's business interests and methods appear in *ibid.*, pp. 1171–5, 1191–4. For Clark's testimony see *ibid.*, pp. 1168–1233, 1245–1368. *Billboard* carried extensive reports of the Harris hearings: of particular interest concerning Dick Clark's testimony are the issues of 2 May 1960, pp. 1, 1/30, 3/16, 4/11, 4/12, 4/14, 11; and 9 May 1960, pp. 1, 1/27, 3/15, 8, 8/18.

103. Clark's version as to why the cheque was not made out in his name was as follows: "At the time Mr Lowe brought me this information that he had $7000, I fortunately was in a position not to need it. I said to him, 'Bernie, there is one way I would like to be able to forward to my mother-in-law such moneys as she needs for the education and the operation she needs...'", Hence the cheque was made payable to Mrs Margaret Mallery. Clark to *Harris hearings*, p. 1188.

104. *Amsterdam News*, 29 May 1960, pp. 1/39. Freed's treatment is dealt with in Jackson, *Big beat heat*, pp. 243–303.

105. M. Shore & D. Clark, *The history of American Bandstand* (New York: Ballantine, 1985).

106. D. Clark, *Your happiest years* (New York: Rosho, 1959), pp. 61–4, 82–98.

107. Black twist singles and albums included Sam Cooke, "Twistin' the night away"; Jimmy Soul, "Twistin' Matilda"; Gary "US" Bonds, "Dear Lady Twist"; Isley Brothers, "Twist and shout"; Marvelettes, "Twistin' postman"; Bobby Freeman, *Twist With*; Jimmy McCracklin, *Twist With*; Fats Domino, *Twistin' The Stomp*; Etta James, *Twist With*; Crystals, *Twist Uptown* (which also included the track "Frankenstein twist"). White twisters included Joey Dee and the Starlighters, "Peppermint twist"; Danny and the Juniors, "Twistin' USA"; Bill Black Combo "Twist-her".

108. E. Cleaver, *Soul on ice* (New York: Dell, 1968), pp. 173–83.

109. Vera Brooks (1968 interview), quoted in B. Blauner, *Black lives, white lives* (Berkeley: University of California Press, 1990), p. 76.

110. J. Otis, "Let's talk", *Los Angeles Sentinel*, 28 January 1960, p. 4A. For Otis' career, see J. Otis, *Listen to the lambs* (New York: W.W. Norton, 1968).

111. See, for example, J. Otis, "Let's talk", *Los Angeles Sentinel*, 7 January 1960, p. 4A; *ibid.*, 14 January 1960, p. 4A.

112. *Ibid.*, 28 January 1960, p. 4A.

113. Shore & Clark, *History of American Bandstand*, p. 7. Julian Bond interview.

114. The story of *The Buddy Deane Show*, cunningly disguised as *The Corny Collins Show*, is lovingly evoked in John Waters' film, *Hairspray*, and his book, *Crackpot:*

the obsessions of John Waters (New York: Macmillan, 1986), pp. 88–100. For *Saturday Hop*, see J. Berry, J. Foose & T. Jones, *Up from the cradle of jazz: New Orleans music since World War II* (Athens, Ga.: University of Georgia Press, 1986), p. 108.

115. D. Bell, "Interpretations of American politics" (1955), in *The radical right*, D. Bell (ed.) (New York: Anchor, 1964), pp. 63–4.

116. *Norfolk Journal and Guide*, 9 November 1957, p. 12. E. Barnouw, *The image empire* (New York: Oxford University Press, 1970), p. 68; B. Schwartz, *The professor and the commissions* (New York: A. Knopf, 1959), p. 96.

117. Bell, "Interpretations of American politics", p. 61.

Chapter Five

1. M.L. King, "Advice for living", *Ebony* (April 1958), p. 104.

2. *Shindig*, 16 September 1964, ABC-TV. Museum of Television and Radio.

3. M. King, *Freedom song* (New York: Wm Morrow, 1987), p. 3. B.J. Reagon et al., *We who believe in freedom* (New York: Anchor, 1993), p. 154.

4. *Billboard*, 30 January 1965, p. 88.

5. L. Jones (I.A. Baraka), *Black music* (New York: Wm Morrow, 1967), pp. 205–6. *Billboard*, 16 August 1968, p. S-6. The Beatles, for example, recorded the Cookies' "Chains", Isley Brothers' "Twist and shout", Miracles' "She's really got a hold on me", Arthur Alexander's "Anna", Chuck Berry's "Rock and roll music", and Larry Williams' "Dizzy Miss Lizzy". The Rolling Stones, who lifted their name from a Muddy Waters song, favoured the blues end of r&b and cut Slim Harpo's "I'm a king bee", Irma Thomas' "Time is on my side", Benny Spellman's "Fortune teller", and Bobby Womack's "It's all over now".

6. Nina Simone quoted in *Evening News and Star*, Schomburg Center Clippings File: "Nina Simone". James Bond, interview with Brian Ward, 16 October 1995, University of Newcastle upon Tyne Oral History Collection (hereinafter UNOHC). Julian Bond, interview with Brian Ward, 20 March 1996, UNOHC. M. Bayles, *Hole in our soul: the loss of beauty and meaning in American popular music* (Chicago: University of Chicago Press, 1994), pp. 186–7.

7. See C. Sawyer, *B.B. King: the authorized biography* (Poole, Dorset: Blandford, 1981), pp. 91–117; *Newsweek*, 26 May 1969, p. 23; M. Haralambos, *Right on: from blues to soul in black America* (New York: Drake, 1975), p. 84.

8. *Time*, 1 April 1966, p. 75.

9. J. Farmer, "The march on Washington: the zenith of the southern movement", in *New directions in civil rights studies*, A.L. Robinson & P. Sullivan (eds) (Charlottesville: University Press of Virginia, 1991), pp. 30–7. Southern Regional Council (SRC), "Civil rights: year-end summary", 31 December 1963, XI-127-14, SCLC papers. The responses of the Kennedy and Johnson administration to the civil rights movement are discussed in M. Stern, *Calculating visions: Kennedy, Johnson and civil rights* (New Brunswick, N.J.: Rutgers University Press, 1992).

10. See D. Nieman, *Promises to keep: African-Americans and the constitutional order* (New York: Oxford University Press, 1991), p. ix.

11. SRC, "Civil rights: year-end summary".

12. The struggle for black voting rights is best told in S.F. Lawson, *Black ballots: voting rights in the South, 1944–1969* (New York: Columbia University Press,

1976). See also D. Garrow, *Protest at Selma* (New Haven, Conn.: Yale University Press, 1978), esp. figs. on pp. 7, 11, 19.

13. For a sociological dissection of community organizing in Mississippi, see C.M. Payne, *I've got the light of freedom: the organizing tradition and the Mississippi freedom struggle* (Berkeley: University of California Press, 1995). The Freedom Summer and the Atlantic City challenge are vividly portrayed in J. Dittmer, *Local people: the struggle for civil rights in Mississippi* (Urbana: University of Illinois Press, 1994), esp. pp. 215–302.

14. H.R. Brown, *Die nigger die!* (London: Allison & Busby, 1970), p. 54. Moses' disillusionment is discussed in E. Burner, *And gently he shall lead them: Robert Parris Moses and civil rights in Mississippi* (New York: New York University Press, 1994), pp. 200–23. See also J. Forman, *The making of black revolutionaries* (New York: Macmillan, 1972); C. Sellers (with R. Terrell), *The river of no return: the autobiography of a black militant and the life and death of SNCC*, 2nd edn (Jackson: University of Mississippi Press, 1990).

15. See Garrow, *Protest at Selma.* For the immediate impact of the 1965 Act see Lawson, *Black ballots*, p. 331. S.F. Lawson, *Running for freedom: civil rights and black politics in America since 1941* (New York: McGraw-Hill, 1991), pp. 116, 122.

16. Southern school integration figures from H. Sitkoff, *The struggle for black equality, 1954–1992*, revd edn (New York: Hill & Wang, 1993), p. 224. Unemployment figures in A. Hacker, *Two nations: black and white, separate, hostile, unequal*, 2nd revd edn (New York: Ballantine Books, 1995), p. 109. Income statistics in Lawson, *Running for freedom*, p. 262.

17. For Watts see G. Horne, *Fire this time: the Watts uprising and the 1960s* (Charlottesville: University Press of Virginia, 1995); J. Otis, *Listen to the lambs* (New York: W.W. Norton, 1968), p. 87. For a provocative, but persuasive, overview of the 1960s riots as a purposeful effort to "gain control of the central city black community, and to assert its importance vis-a-vis other metropolitan area communities", see K. Fox, *Metropolitan America: urban life and urban policy in the United States, 1940–1980* (New York: Macmillan, 1985), pp. 137–62.

18. S. Lubell, *White and black: test of a nation* (New York: Harper & Row, 1964), pp. 108, 134.

19. D. McAdam, *Political process and the development of black insurgency, 1930–1970* (Chicago: University of Chicago Press, 1982), pp. 48–51. R.H. King, "Citizenship and self-respect: the experience of politics in the civil rights movement", *Journal of American Studies* 22, April 1988, p. 8. King's ideas are explored in greater detail in R.H. King, *Civil rights and the idea of freedom* (Oxford: Oxford University Press, 1992).

20. Franklin McCain quoted in H. Raines, *My soul is rested: movement days in the Deep South remembered* (New York: Putnam, 1977), p. 78.

21. J. Farmer, *Freedom – when?* (New York: Random House, 1965), p. 36. For Chicago, see J.R. Ralph, *Northern protest: Martin Luther King, Jr, Chicago and the civil rights movement* (Cambridge, Mass.: Harvard University Press, 1993).

22. Franklin McCain quoted in Raines, *My soul is rested*, p. 78.

23. A. Moody, *Coming of age in Mississippi* (New York: Dell, 1968), p. 384.

24. U. Hannerz, "Lower-class black culture", in *Soul*, L. Rainwater (ed.) (n.p.: Transaction Books, 1970), p. 22. See also J. Riedel, *Soul music – black and white: the influence of black music on the churches* (Minneapolis: Ausburg Publishing House, 1975), p. 21. For the broader soul phenomenon, see also U. Hannerz,

Soulside (New York: Columbia University Press, 1969); T. Kochman, *Rappin' in and stylin' out* (Chicago: University of Chicago Press, 1977); W.L. Van DeBurg, *New day in Babylon: the black power movement and American culture, 1965–1975* (Chicago: University of Chicago Press, 1992).

25. For the idea of black pride being manifested in the assertion of differences, see King, *Civil rights*, p. 71. J. Szwed, "Musical style and racial conflict", *Phylon* **27**, Winter 1966, pp. 358–66.

26. Booker T. Jones quoted in A. Shaw, *The world of soul* (New York: Cowles, 1970), p. 181; Mike McGill quoted in L.E. McCutcheon, *Rhythm and blues: an experience and adventure in its origins and development* (Arlington, Va.: Beatty, 1971), p. 22.

27. Don Covay quoted in G. Hirshey, *Nowhere to run* (New York: Macmillan, 1984), p. 51.

28. R. Charles & D. Ritz, *Brother Ray* (London: Futura, 1980), p. 151.

29. J. Bond, "Ray Charles — the bishop of Atlanta", in *Sweet soul music: rhythm and blues and the southern dream of freedom*, P. Guralnick (ed.) (London: Virgin, 1986), p. 50. H.J. Bond, "I, too, hear America singing", in *Student Voice*, June 1960, p. 4. Bernice Johnson Reagon, interview with Brian Ward, 24 January 1996, UNOHC.

30. A. Moody, *Coming of age in Mississippi*, p. 320.

31. *Muhammad Speaks*, 15 July 1962, p. 2. See also Charles & Ritz, *Brother Ray*, pp. 164–6.

32. Stanley Wise, interview with Brian Ward & Jenny Walker, 19 October 1996, UNOHC.

33. For an extended disquisition on the African roots and social function of the ring-shout in African-American culture, see S. Stuckey, *Slave culture: nationalist theory and the foundations of black America* (New York: Oxford University Press, 1987), pp. 3–97. Also, E. Genovese, *Roll, Jordan, roll: the world the slaves made*, 2nd edn (New York: Vintage, 1976), p. 239.

34. L. Levine, *Black culture and black consciousness: Afro-American folk thought from slavery to freedom*, (New York: Oxford University Press, 1977), p. 178; also, pp. 136–89. Similar reservations were evident in Dude Botley's apocalyptic account of the secular-sacred fusions of Buddy Bolden, an influential turn of the century New Orleans cornet player: "He is *mixing* up the blues with the hymns . . . That is the first time I had ever heard hymns and blues cooked up together. Strange cold feeling comes over me. I get sort of scared because I know the Lord don't like that mixing the devil's music with his music." Dude Botley quoted in L. Neal, "The ethos of the blues", *Black Scholar* **3**(10), Summer 1972, p. 43.

35. W. Broonzy (as told to Y. Bruynoghe), *Big Bill's blues* (London: Cassell, 1955), p. 9. Big Bill Broonzy quoted in P. Guralnick, *Sweet soul music: rhythm and blues and the southern dream of freedom* (New York: Harper & Row, 1986), p. 27. Other bluesmen working around the Mississippi Delta often felt obliged to use pseudonyms when they cut sacred material. Charlie Patton adopted the guise of Elder J.J. Hadley, while Blind Lemon Jefferson's *nom de dieu* was Deacon L.J. Bates. See P. Oliver, *Songsters and saints: vocal traditions on race records* (Cambridge: Cambridge University Press, 1984); F. Hay, "The sacred-profane dialectic in delta blues: the life and lyrics of Sonny Boy Williamson", *Phylon* **48**, Winter 1987, pp. 317–27.

36. Jones, *Black music*, p. 204. Reagon interview. Reagon et al., *We who believe in freedom*, pp. 133–50.
37. Yasmeen Williams, in *ibid.*, pp. 85, 77. Alleasie Titus, letter to Martin Luther King, 21 June 1958, box 24, folder 28, Martin Luther King papers. M.L. King, "Advice for living", *Ebony* (April 1958), p. 104.
38. Cooke's crossover dilemma is admirably described in D. Wolff et al., *You send me: the life and times of Sam Cooke* (New York: Wm Morrow, 1995), pp. 129–42.
39. Roscoe Shelton, interview with Brian Ward, 30 October 1995, UNOHC. Little Richard quoted in *Norfolk Journal and Guide*, 2 November 1957, p. 14.
40. Harold Battiste, interview with Brian Ward, 8 November 1995, UNOHC.
41. Wolff et al., *You send me*, pp. 143–60. Battiste interview.
42. For Cooke's rejection by gospel fans, see V. Broughton, *Black gospel: an illustrated history of the gospel sound* (Poole, Dorset: Blandford, 1985), p. 96; A. Heilbut, *The gospel sound: good news and bad times*, revd edn (New York: Limelight International, 1985), p. 90. Shelton interview.
43. Esmond Patterson, interview with Brian Ward & Jenny Walker, 19 October 1995, UNOHC.
44. Nina Simone quoted in P. Garland, *The sound of soul* (Chicago: Regnery, 1969), p. 186.
45. George Lewis has theorized just such a process of secularization, suggesting that, "If the cultural shift in contemporary industrial society from the sacred to the secular . . . has produced a de-emphasis in the strength of religious institutions, this should not be interpreted as a *loss*, but as a *transfer* of function to secular institutions. Thus, the solidarity once produced in the sacred sphere is now a function of . . . [popular] culture." G. Lewis, "Between consciousness and existence: popular culture and the sociological imagination", *Journal of Popular Culture* **15**, 1982, p. 86. See also P. Berger, *The sacred canopy* (New York: Doubleday, 1967), pp. 107–8.
46. D.C. Thompson, *Sociology of the black experience* (Westport, Conn.: Greenwood Press, 1974), pp. 158–9. W.E. Buck, "The decline of the Negro clergy", *Phylon* **29**, Spring 1968, p. 57.
47. Yancey Martin quoted in Raines, *My soul is rested*, p. 61. A. Fairclough, "The Southern Christian Leadership Conference and the second reconstruction", *South Atlantic Quarterly* **80**, Spring 1981, p. 178. J. Dittmer, *Local people*. A. Fairclough, *Race and Democracy: the civil rights struggle in Louisiana, 1915–1972* (Athens, Ga.: University of Georgia Press, 1995). For a more positive assessment of the black church's role in the southern civil rights movement, see A. Morris, *The origins of the civil rights movement: black communities organizing for change* (New York: Free Press, 1984). The ambiguous political role of the black church is neatly captured in Gayraud Wilmore's assertion that "it is at once the most reactionary and the most radical of black institutions, the most imbued with the mythology and values of white America, and yet the most proud, the most independent and indigenous collectivity in the black community". G.S. Wilmore, *Black religion and black radicalism* (New York: Doubleday, 1973), p. xiii.
48. The prevailing ethos of the early SNCC, for example, was partly shaped by the influence of Nashville seminarians like James Lawson, John Lewis and James Bevel. By 1963, however, SNCC had already lost much of its religious character and, as Clayborne Carson puts it, Lewis' speech at the March on Washington

"expressed the militancy of SNCC, but its religious imagery and emphasis on non-violent protest were out of step with SNCC's dominant orientation by the summer of 1963". When Stokely Carmichael ousted Lewis as chairman in May 1966, its religious roots were just about severed. See C. Carson, *In struggle: SNCC and the black awakening of the 1960s* (Cambridge, Mass.: Harvard University Press, 1981), p. 95; also pp. 29, 199–204.

49. C. McKay, *Harlem: Negro metropolis*, repr. edn (New York: Harvest, 1968), pp. 82, 49.

50. S.C. Drake & H.R. Cayton, *Black metropolis: a study of Negro life in a northern city* (London: J. Cape, 1946), pp. 417, 423.

51. C. Brown, *Manchild in the promised land* (New York: Signet, 1965), pp. 208–9, 69, 27–8.

52. Thomas A. Dorsey quoted in V. Broughton, *Black gospel*, p. 46. See also M. Harris, *The rise of gospel blues: the music of T.A. Dorsey in the urban church* (New York: Oxford University Press, 1992); Levine, *Black consciousness*, pp. 174–89. For Nix, see Oliver, *Songsters and saints*, p. 151.

53. E.F. Frazier, *The Negro church in America* (New York: Knopf, 1964), pp. 56, 53. A. Fauset, *Black gods of the metropolis* (Philadelphia: University of Pennsylvania Press, 1944), p. 85.

54. See D. Crawford, "Gospel songs in court: from rural music to urban industry in the 1950s", *Journal of Popular Culture* 11, 1977, pp. 551–67. Clara Ward quoted in *Amsterdam News*, 12 December 1959, p. 1; *Chicago Defender*, 12 December 1959, p. 1.

55. Reagon interview.

56. See T. Fox, *Showtime at the Apollo* (New York: Holt, Rinehart & Winston, 1983), p. 227.

57. Cissy Houston quoted in Hirshey, *Nowhere to run*, p. 26.

58. Broughton, *Black gospel*, p. 85.

59. Charles Hobson, "The gospel truth", *Down Beat*, 30 May 1968, pp. 17–20. The same tendency to contrast the "real", "authentic" sounds of gospel with the more "artificial" and "commercial" music of soul also haunts Anthony Heilbut's *The gospel sound*.

60. J.R. Washington, Jr, *Black religion*, repr. edn (Lanham, Md.: University Press of America, 1984), p. 44. Many theologians and historians have located the same central theme in black religion: an emphasis on what Cornel West has called the "radical egalitarian ideal . . . The Christian principle of the self-realization of individuality within community". C. West, *Prophesy and deliverance: an Afro-American revolutionary Christianity* (Philadelphia: Westminster, 1982), p. 16.

61. Washington, *Black religion*, pp. 51–2.

62. C. West, *Prophetic fragments* (Grand Rapids, Mich.: Wm Eerdmans, 1988), p. 161. Eugene Genovese has also written of the equalitarian and communalizing imperatives of the highly emotional public conversion experiences of black slaves, which "equalized the status of all before God, thereby giving the slaves a special self-identity and self-esteem in contrast with the inferior roles imposed upon them in American society". The argument here is that, even with God out of the picture, the communal and ecstatic core of the ritual preserved its main social and psychological functions. Genovese, *Roll, Jordan, roll*, pp. 264–5.

63. West, *Prophetic fragments*, p. 163. Jones, *Black music*, p. 191.

64. Solomon Burke quoted in C. White, Liner notes, Solomon Burke, *Cry To Me*, Charly CRB 1075 (1984). For more on Burke, see B. Dahl, "Solomon Burke: the

bishop of soul", *Goldmine*, 16 September 1994, pp. 42/44/46/48/50/51/194; Guralnick, *Sweet soul music*, pp. 76–96; Hirshey, *Nowhere to run*, pp. 80–98.

65. Solomon Burke quoted in, Guralnick *Sweet soul music*, pp. 79.
66. See Dahl, "Bishop of soul", p. 50.
67. See Hirshey, *Nowhere to run*, pp. 80–92.
68. *Billboard* did not even have a black album chart until 1965 and Brown's previous album, *JB & His Famous Flames Tour the USA*, had run to just 3,500 pressings. In 1963, *Live at the Apollo* was the 32nd best selling album in America; in the pop field only the Beach Boys' *Surfin'* sold more. Accounts of the recording and subsequent success of *Live at the Apollo* include J. Brown (with B. Tucker), *James Brown: the godfather of soul* (Glasgow: Fontana, 1988), pp. 130–42; C. White, "Roots of a revolution", pamphlet accompanying *Roots of a Revolution*, Polydor, REVO 1 (1986), pp. 12–13; Fox, *Showtime*, pp. 239–43; Guralnick, *Sweet soul music*, pp. 235–8.
69. *Ibid.* M. Jackson, *Moonwalk* (New York: Doubleday, 1988), p. 37. Reginald Defour quoted in *Greensboro A&T College Register*, 9 October 1970, p. 5.
70. The distinction here is between Roland Barthes' concepts of *plaisir* and *jouissance*. In *plaisir*, pleasure is linked to the satisfactory working out, or resolution, of a performance within a known cultural framework, giving rise to feelings of both completion and community. The more ecstatic *jouissance* requires the rupture of known codes, the novel departure from familiar and expected patterns to produce a feeling of exhilaration. R. Barthes, *Image – music – text* (London: Fontana, 1977), p. 9. For a musicological analysis of the communalizing function of ostinati and repetition, see R. Middleton, *Pop music and the blues: a study of the relationship and its significance* (London: Gollancz, 1972), esp. pp. 40–51, 212–22; B. Sidran, *Black talk*, revd edn (New York: Da Capo, 1981), pp. 8–9.
71. K.P. Taylor, *The death and resurrection show* (London: A. Blond, 1985), p. 15.
72. Reagon interview. B. Johnson Reagon, *Songs of the civil rights movement, 1955–65* (PhD thesis, Howard University, 1975), pp. 105–20.
73. *Ibid.*
74. J. Van Matre, "Report from plaquemine", 13 July 1964, repr. in *Louisiana – Summer, 1964*, J. Peck (ed.) (New York: CORE, 1964), E-III-92, CORE papers addendum.
75. Little Milton quoted in M. Haralambos, *Right on: from blues to soul in black America* (New York: Drake, 1975), p. 73. James Bond interview.
76. Marvin Gaye quoted in D. Ritz, *Divided soul: the life of Marvin Gaye* (New York: McGraw-Hill, 1986), p. 110. Jones, *Black music*, pp. 180–211.
77. Figures and trends taken from B. Rustin, *Strategies for freedom: the changing patterns of black protest* (New York: Columbia University Press, 1976), p. 33; S.A. Levitan, W.B. Johnson & R. Taggert, *Still a dream: the changing status of blacks since 1960* (Cambridge, Mass.: Harvard University Press, 1975), pp. 15–17, 32, 41. J. Blackwell, *The black community: diversity and unity* (New York: Harper & Row, 1985), pp. 60–3.
78. For southern white weekends, see, W.J. Cash, *The mind of the South* (New York: A. Knopf), pp. 295–7; S.A. Smith & J.N. Rogers, "Saturday night in country music: the gospel according to Juke", *Southern Cultures* **1**, Winter 1995, pp. 229–40.
79. C. Berry, *The autobiography of Chuck Berry* (London: Faber & Faber, 1988), p. 157.
80. *Ibid.*, p. 158.

81. Ian Hoare offers an excellent analysis of the use of these phrases in soul in "Mighty, mighty spade and whitey: black lyrics and soul's interaction with white culture", in *The soul book*, I. Hoare (ed.) (London: Eyre Methuen, 1975), pp. 124–7. See also G. Smitherman, *Black language and culture: sounds of soul* (New York: Harper & Row, 1975).

82. *Baltimore Afro-American* (magazine section), 26 March 1960, p. 12.

83. Stokely Carmichael quoted in *Ebony* (September 1966), p. 30.

84. L. Neal, "Black art and black liberation", in *The black revolution: an Ebony special issue* (Chicago: Johnson, 1970), p. 42.

85. K. Miller, *Voice of deliverance: the language of Martin Luther King and its sources* (New York: Free Press, 1992), p. 19. Paul Oliver has described a blues lyrical tradition which was full of tales of literal and, like gospel, spiritual journeys, usually north to freedom, and of celebrations of the cars and locomotives which made them possible. Paul Oliver, *Blues fell this morning: meaning in the blues* (Cambridge: Cambridge University Press, 1990), pp. 12–68.

86. Miller, *Voice of deliverance*, pp. 13–28.

87. James Farmer quoted in Raines, *My soul is rested*, p. 110.

88. See C.A. Barnes, *Journey from Jim Crow: the desegregation of southern transportation* (New York: Columbia University Press, 1988); T. Branch, *Parting the waters: America in the King years, 1954–1963* (New York: Simon & Schuster, 1988), pp. 412–91.

Chapter Six

1. D.R. Roediger, *The wages of whiteness: race and the making of the American working class* (New York: Verso, 1991), p. 4.

2. Until recently, the subject of black-white interaction in southern soul has been poorly served in the literature. For example, P. Maultsby, "Soul music: its sociological and political significance in American popular culture", *Journal of Popular Culture* **17**, 1984, pp. 51–60, and R. Stephens, "Soul: a historical reconstruction of continuity and change in black popular music", *Black Perspectives in Music* **12**, Spring 1984, pp. 21–43, both ignore the contribution of southern whites completely, while Imamu Amiri Baraka, in *Blues people* (New York: Wm Morrow, 1963), and *Black music* (New York: Wm Morrow, 1967), and Nelson George in *The death of rhythm and blues* (New York: Omnibus, 1988), greatly underestimate white input, except where denouncing it as an entirely negative, diluting influence. For many years, Phyl Garland's *The sound of soul* (Chicago: Regnery, 1969), written in the midst of the black power era, was the best account of the contribution of southern whites, at least at Stax. More recently, P. Guralnick, *Sweet soul music: rhythm and blues and the southern dream of freedom* (London: Virgin, 1986), B. Hoskyns, *Say it one time for the broken hearted* (Glasgow: Fontana, 1987), and R. Gordon, *It came from Memphis* (Boston: Faber & Faber, 1995) have greatly extended our understanding of this phenomenon.

3. Rick Hall's work and the Fame studios are discussed in Hoskyns, *Say it one time* (esp. pp. 99–127), and Guralnick, *Sweet soul music* (esp. pp. 181–219, 339–44).

4. Chips Moman and his American operation are described in Gordon, *It came from Memphis*, pp. 99, 157–8, 166–72; Guralnick, *Sweet soul music*, pp. 99–101,

126–8, 216–9, 291–7, 339–41; Hoskyns, *Say it one time*, pp. 74–9, 85–94, 207–12.

5. Roscoe Shelton, interview with Brian Ward, 30 October 1995, University of Newcastle upon Tyne Oral History Collection (hereinafter UNOHC). Hoskyns, *Say it one time*, pp. 131–8.

6. Shelton interview. Hoskyns, *Say it one time*, p. 132.

7. For the history of Stax, see Garland, *The sound of soul*, pp. 123–52; Gordon, *It came from Memphis*, pp. 47, 52–3, 58, 66–70, 150, 167, 194, 237–9, 256–7; Guralnick, *Sweet soul music*, pp. 120–8, 152–76, 354–73; G. Hirshey, *Nowhere to run* (New York: Macmillan, 1984), pp. 295–309, 333–58; Hoskyns, *Say it one time*, pp. 77–81.

8. Dan Penn quoted in *ibid.*, p. 108; Joe Tex quoted in Hirshey, *Nowhere to run*, p. 328; David Porter quoted in A. Shaw, *The world of soul* (New York: Cowles, 1970), p. 189.

9. T. Russell, *Blacks, whites and blues* (London: Stein & Day, 1970), p. 26. See also "Profiles in black and white", in *Journal of Country Music* **14**(2), 1992, pp. 8–42. For two excellently researched and commendably balanced accounts of the interconnections between African and American-European elements in southern music, see R. Cantwell, *Bluegrass breakdown: the making of the old southern sound* (Urbana, Ill.: University of Illinois Press, 1984), and C. Conway, *African banjo echoes in Appalachia* (Knoxville: University of Tennessee Press, 1995).

10. P. Gilroy, *The black Atlantic: modernity and double consciousness* (Cambridge, Mass.: Harvard University Press, 1993), p. 100.

11. *Ibid.*, p. 101.

12. Al Bell quoted in Garland, *The sound of soul*, p. 134; Solomon Burke quoted in Hirshey, *Nowhere to run*, p. 94. For the Klan show, see *ibid.*, p. 51.

13. Rev. D.A. Noebel, *Rhythm, riots and revolution: an analysis of the communist uses of music* (Tulsa: Christian Crusade Publications, 1966), p. 78.

14. Gladys Knight quoted in J.R. Taraborelli, *Motown: hot wax, city cool and solid gold* (New York: Doubleday, 1986), p. 83. Marvin Gaye quoted in D. Ritz, *Divided soul: the life of Marvin Gaye* (New York: McGraw-Hill, 1986), p. 51.

15. Shelton interview. M. Wilson (with P. Romanowski & A. Juillard), *Dreamgirl: my life as a Supreme* (London: Sidgwick & Jackson, 1987), pp. 123, 125. See also M. Reeves & M. Bego, *Dancing in the street: confessions of a Motown diva* (New York: Hyperion, 1994), pp. 71–2; B. Gordy, *To be loved: the music, the magic, the memories of Motown: an autobiography* (New York: Warner, 1994), pp. 165–6. The Shreveport incident is described in Hirshey, *Nowhere to run*, pp. 97–8.

16. For a history of desegregation at Tuscaloosa, see E. Culpepper Clark, *The schoolhouse door: segregation's last stand at the University of Alabama* (New York: Oxford University Press, 1993).

17. *Crimson-White*, 3 May 1962, pp. 1–3.

18. *Ibid.*, 17 May 1962, p. 1; 20 September 1962, p. 1.

19. Minutes of Meeting of Executive Committee of the Board of the University of Alabama, 16 August 1962. J. Jefferson Bennett, letter to Frank Rose, 30 August 1962, box 22, folder: Bennett, Frank A. Rose Papers. Seymore Trammell quoted in D.T. Carter, *The politics of rage: George Wallace, the origins of the new conservatism, and the transformation of American politics* (New York: Simon & Schuster, 1995), p. 98. For Trammell's background and the Tuscaloosa crisis, see *ibid.*, pp. 97–9, 122–3, 142–51.

20. John Blackburn quoted in *Crimson-White*, 3 December 1964, p. 1.
21. *The Corolla* (1955), p. 366; *Crimson-White*, 3 December 1964, pp. 1/3.
22. See, for example, the student opinion poll on integration, in *ibid.*, 17 May 1962, pp. 1/3. G. Guerrero, *SSOC newsletter* **3**(3), April 1965, p. 6; *Crimson-White*, 25 February 1965, p. 1. *The Corolla* (1965), p. 107; *ibid.* (1966), pp. 175–7.
23. *Cavalier Daily*, 13 April 1956, p. 2.
24. Palmer Weber's activities in Charlottesville are described in P. Sullivan, *Days of hope: race and democracy in the New Deal era* (Chapel Hill: University of North Carolina Press, 1996), pp. 72–3, 80–3, 104.
25. *Cavalier Daily*, 3 October 1958, p. 1. The Georgia ban is noted in *Vanderbilt Hustler*, 13 March 1959, p. 4. For Tulane, see *Louisiana Weekly*, 14 October 1961.
26. See *Cavalier Daily*, 4 May 1954, p. 1 (Gillespie); 7 December 1954, p. 2 (Garner); 2 November 1955, p. 1 (Basie); 23 November 1955, p. 2 (Powell); 22 November 1961, pp. 1/4 (White); 11 April 1962 (Odetta); 30 April 1963, p. 1 (Makeba); 6 November 1964, p. 1 (Charles); 13 November 1964 (Diddley); 9 April 1965 (Berry); 1 October 1965, p. 1 (Ellis and the Vandellas); 30 October 1965, p. 1 (Reed). The pro-Selma march is reported in *ibid.*, 18 March 1965, p. 1.
27. *Vanderbilt Hustler*, 7 February 1958, p. 5. *Ibid.*, 13 March 1959, p. 4. For the Nashville sit-ins, see F. Powledge, *Free at last?: the civil rights movement and the people who made it* (New York: HarperCollins, 1991), pp. 203–10.
28. R.H. King, "Politics and fictional representation: the case of the civil rights movement", in *The making of Martin Luther King and the civil rights movement*, B. Ward & T. Badger (eds) (New York: New York University Press, 1996), p. 162.
29. D. Marsh, *Fortunate son* (New York: Random House, 1985), p. xxv.
30. M.L. King, "Transforming a neighborhood into a brotherhood", Address to NATRA, 11 August 1967, *Jack the Rapper* **13**(666), January 1989, p. 1.
31. Wolf Stephenson, quoted in Hoskyns, *Say it one time*, p. 166.
32. Shelton interview.
33. Important recent studies which discuss the historical importance of the presence of blacks in the creation of American (especially working-class) perceptions of "whiteness" include Roediger, *Wages of whiteness*; A. Saxton, *The rise and fall of the white republic: class politics and mass culture in nineteenth-century America* (London: Verso, 1990). See also S.F. Fishkin, "Interrogating 'whiteness', complicating 'blackness': remapping American culture", *American Quarterly* **47**(3), September 1995, pp. 428–66, and J.E. Phillips, "The African heritage of white America", in *Africanisms in American culture*, J. Holloway (ed.) (Bloomington: University of Indiana Press, 1990), pp. 225–39.
34. See W.D. Jordan, *The white man's burden* (New York: Oxford University Press, 1974).
35. Roediger, *Wages of whiteness*, pp. 19–36.
36. R. Horsman, *Race and manifest destiny: the origins of American racial anglo-saxonism* (Cambridge, Mass.: Harvard University Press, 1981); Roediger, *Wages of whiteness*; Saxton, *Rise and fall of the white republic*.
37. Roediger, *Wages of whiteness*, p. 14.
38. J. Jacobi, "Symbols in an individual analysis", in *Man and his symbols*, C.G. Jung & M.L. von Franz (eds) (London: Aldus, 1974), p. 300.
39. For the racial politics of the minstrel shows see Roediger, *Wages of whiteness*, pp. 115–31; R.C. Toll, *Blacking-up: the minstrel show in nineteenth-century America* (New York: Oxford University Press, 1974).

40. See L.A. Erenberg, *Steppin' out: New York nightlife and the transformation of American culture, 1890–1930* (Chicago: University of Chicago Press, 1981), p. 73; E.L. Ayers, *The promise of the New South: life after Reconstruction* (New York: Oxford University Press, 1992), pp. 376–7.

41. *Ibid.* For the Cole and Johnson songs, see Russell, *Blacks, whites and blues*, p. 16. M.P. Ely, *The adventures of Amos'n'Andy: a social history of an American phenomenon* (New York: Free Press, 1991).

42. *Ibid.*, pp. 115–29, 160–244.

43. For the rise of eugenics, social darwinism, and the related triumph of radical racism in the late nineteenth century – and for much else germane to this chapter – see G.M. Fredrickson, *The black image in the white mind* (Hanover, N.H.: Wesleyan University Press, 1987), esp. pp. 228–319; and J. Williamson, *A rage for order: black-white relations in the American South since emancipation* (New York: Oxford University Press, 1986), esp. pp. 70–205.

44. See A. Gramsci, *Selections from the prison notebooks*, ed. Q. Hoare & G.N. Smith (New York: International Publishers, 1971).

45. M. Bayles, *Hole in our soul: the loss of beauty and meaning in American popular music* (Chicago: University of Chicago Press, 1994), p. 11. Fenton Bott quoted in N. Leonard, *Jazz and the white Americans*, 2nd edn (Chicago: University of Chicago Press, 1972), p. 34.

46. In this context, it is revealing that when F. Scott Fitzgerald retrospectively dubbed the 1920s "The jazz age", music came only third in his list of definitions of the word, after sex and dancing. F. Scott Fitzgerald, "Echoes of the jazz age" (1931), in *The crack up*, repr. edn (London: Penguin, 1983), pp. 9–19. See also F. Hoffman, *The twenties* (New York: Free Press, 1965), p. 307.

47. See N. Mailer, "The white Negro" (1957), in N. Mailer, *Advertisements for myself*, repr. edn (New York: Putnam, 1959), pp. 337–58.

48. N. Hentoff, *The new equality*, 2nd edn (New York: Viking Compass, 1965), p. 64 (see also pp. 62–72); L. Hansberry quoted in *ibid.*, p. 64. R. Wright, *Black boy* (1945) (New York: Harper & Row, 1966), p. 46.

49. Shelton interview. Bob Montgomery quoted in J. Goldrosen & J. Beecher, *Remembering Buddy* (London: Pavilion, 1987), p. 16.

50. P. Oliver, "Crossroads blues", *Jazz Beat* (February 1965), pp. 20–1. R. Palmer, *Deep blues* (New York: Penguin, 1981), pp. 256, 258. See also R. Middleton, *Pop music and the blues a study of the relationship and its significance* (London: Gallancz, 1972), p. 127; Bayles, *Hole in our soul*, pp. 162–6, 187–91.

51. N. Podhoretz, "My Negro problem – and ours", *Commentary* (February 1963), p. 99. Hentoff, *New equality*, p. 65.

52. J. Bond, "How to be SNCCY", n.d., Memphis Civil Rights Museum.

53. Tad Richards quoted in K. Reese, *Chuck Berry* (London: Proteus, 1982), pp. 36, 40. *Cavalier Daily*, 17 April 1956, p. 2.

54. Bonnie Bramlett quoted in T. Turner (with K. Loder), *I, Tina* (London: Penguin, 1987), p. 79. Martha Bayles also makes much of this distinction between eroticism and obscenity in popular music, arguing that "Afro-American music is sometimes erotic, but it is never obscene, because there is always a larger whole – whether spiritual ecstacy, physical exuberance, or emotional catharsis – to which erotic qualities are joined". For Bayles, the two greatest tragedies in post-war popular music have been the steady dehumanization of sex and the way in which genuine black eroticism has been torn from its social context in lived black lives, principally by white performers and consumers who

have pruriently viewed and reworked that eroticism as a disembodied, in her terms "obscene", commercial product. Like much of Bayles' book, this is a provocative argument, which blends keen insight with simple wrong-headedness. The idea that the older black musical forms she romanticizes had "never" been obscene is clearly suspect. There was a very virulent, commercially lucrative strain of sexual objectification, violence and dehumanization within the multi-faceted blues and Rhythm and Blues traditions long before rap music, which for Bayles marks the nadir of sexual obscenity in popular music; long before even the emergence of the Rolling Stones, who she especially demonizes for dehumanizing the erotic impulses in the r&b they copied. Bayles, *Hole in our soul*, pp. 198–9.

55. S. McClary, "Same as it ever was: youth culture and music", in *Microphone fiends: youth and youth culture*, A. Ross & T. Rose (eds) (New York: Routledge, 1994), pp. 34–6.

56. *Ibid.*; E. Cleaver, *Soul on ice* (New York: Dell, 1968), pp. 185–7.

57. The white creation and black manipulation of the sambo stereotype are discussed in J. Boskin, *Sambo: the rise and demise of an American jester* (New York: Oxford University Press, 1986); Roediger, *Wages of whiteness*, pp. 115–32. Harold Battiste, interview with Brian Ward, 8 November 1995, UNOHC. G. Giddins, *Rhythm-a-ning: jazz traditions and innovation in the '80s* (New York: Oxford University Press, 1985), pp. 146–152. Johnny Otis quoted in *Rolling Stone interviews 2*, B. Fong-Torres (ed.) (New York: Paperback Library, 1973), pp. 314–15.

58. George, *Death of rhythm and blues*, p. 109.

59. *Ibid.*; R. Vincent, *Funk: the music, the people, and the rhythm of the one* (New York: St Martin's, 1996), pp. 105–11.

60. Eric Clapton quoted in *Rolling Stone*, 11 May 1968, p. 12. See also C.S. Murray, *Crosstown traffic: Jimi Hendrix and the post-war rock 'n' roll revolution* (New York: St Martin's, 1989), pp. 58–77; Gilroy, *Black Atlantic*, pp. 93–4.

61. See D. Henderson, *'Scuse me while I kiss the sky: the life of Jimi Hendrix* (New York: Bantam, 1981), p. 133.

62. H. Shapiro & C. Glebbeek, *Jimi Hendrix: electric gypsy* (New York: St Martin's, 1995), p. 369 (see also pp. 368–71, 391–3). *Rolling Stone*, 9 March 1968, p. 13.

63. There are no entirely convincing biographies of Joplin, but the best is D. Dalton, *Piece of my heart: the life, times and legend of Janis Joplin* (New York: St Martin's, 1985).

64. Hot Lips Page quoted in J. Chiltern, liner notes, Roy Eldridge, *Roy Eldridge: The Early Years*, CBS 88585 (1982).

65. Alan M. Wells, letter to Martin Luther King, Jr, 20 August 1965, box 17, folder 3, SCLC.

66. *Ibid.*

67. *Ibid.*

68. Thomas Jefferson, for example, conceded that his slaves were musically "more generally gifted than the whites with accurate ears for tune and time", without feeling the need to free them. T. Jefferson (ed. W. Peden), *Notes on the state of Virginia*, (Chapel Hill: University of North Carolina Press, 1955), p. 143.

69. *Carolina-Israelite*, January–February 1961, in Subject Files: "Race prejudice", Hogan Jazz Archive.

70. Roediger, *Wages of whiteness*, pp. 4–5.

Chapter Seven

1. Harold Battiste, interview with Brian Ward, 8 November 1995, University of Newcastle upon Tyne Oral History Collection (hereinafter UNOHC).
2. This account of Harold Battiste's career draws on AFO Notes File, Harold Battiste papers (hereinafter HB). H. Battiste, *Hal who: selections from the scriptures of Harold who?* (Los Angeles: At Last, 1989); J. Broven, "Harold Battiste: all for one", *Blues Unlimited* **46**, 1984, pp. 4–15; J. Berry, J. Foose & T. Jones, *Up from the cradle of jazz: New Orleans music since World War II* (Athens, Ga.: University of Georgia Press, 1986), pp. 143–53; Battiste interview.
3. *Ibid.*
4. Harold Battiste, quoted in Broven, "All for one", p. 10; Battiste interview.
5. *Ibid.*
6. H. Battiste, "Statement: Musicians Cooperative Records Inc.", 19 November 1959, AFO Notes File, HB.
7. Battiste interview. Battiste, "Diary: 29 May 1961", *Hal who?*. The executives at AFO were Mel Lastie (executive secretary and cornet); Alvin Tyler (treasurer and sax); Roy Montrell (A&R and guitar); Peter Badie (bass); John Boudreaux (drums); Battiste (president, piano and sax). See H. Battiste, "Letter to whom it may concern", n.d., box 1, folder: Outgoing Mail, AFO, HB.
8. Battiste interview. W.B. Gould, *Black workers in white unions: job discrimination in the United States* (Ithaca, N.Y.: Cornell University Press, 1977), pp. 126–7, 416–19.
9. Tommy Ridgley, interviews with Tad Jones, 23 April 1986 and 20 June 1986, Hogan Jazz Archive. Battiste interview.
10. *Ibid.* Battiste quoted in Broven, "All for one", p. 12.
11. Battiste interview. "AFO diary notes. 27 March 1962 and 29 March 1962", in Battiste, *Hal who?*. Broven, "All for one", pp. 12–13.
12. Battiste interview. "Diary. August–September 1967", in Battiste, *Hal who?*. For Hal Mel holdings, see Harold Battiste, letter to L. Grundeis, 1 December 1969, in *ibid.*
13. Battiste interview.
14. B. Gordy, *To be loved: the music, the magic, the memories of Motown: an autobiography* (New York: Warner, 1994), p. 169. Battiste interview.
15. This account of Motown draws from the following sources: P. Benjaminson, *The story of Motown* (New York: Grove, 1978); D. Bianco, *Heatwave: the Motown fact book* (Ann Arbor: Pierian, 1988); G. Early, *One nation under a groove: Motown and American culture* (New York: Ecco, 1995); S. Frith, "You can make it if you try", in *The soul book*, I. Hoare (ed.) (London: Eyre Methuen, 1975), pp. 32–59; N. George, *Where did our love go?* (New York: St Martin's, 1986); Gordy, *To be loved*; G. Hirshey, *Nowhere to run* (New York: Macmillan, 1984), pp. 184–92; D. Morse, *Motown and the arrival of black music* (London: November, 1971); J. Ryan, *Recollections – the Detroit years: the Motown sound by the people who made it* (Detroit: the author, 1982); J.R. Taraborelli, *Motown: hot wax, city soul and solid gold* (New York: Doubleday, 1986).
16. George, *Where did our love go?*, p. 25.
17. For the economics of Motown, see *ibid.*, esp. pp. 25–86, 139–54; Taraborelli, *Motown*, pp. 9–12.

18. See O. Williams (with P. Romanowski), *Temptations* (New York: G.P. Putnam, 1988), pp. 136–7. M. Reeves & M. Bego, *Dancing in the street: confessions of a Motown diva* (New York: Hyperion, 1994), p. 8.

19. James Jamerson quoted in I. Stambler, *Encyclopaedia of pop, rock and soul* (New York: St Martin's, 1974), p. 149. See also George, *Where did our love go?*, pp. 86, 107; Hirshey, *Nowhere to run*, pp. 186–9. For Gordy's own account of these matters, see *To be loved*, pp. 267–72.

20. The most accessible and sensible musicological analysis of the Motown Sound is J. Fitzgerald, "Motown crossover hits 1963–1966 and the creative process", *Popular music* **14**, 1995, pp. 1–11.

21. *Detroit Free Press*, cited by George, *Where did our love go?*, p. 49.

22. Berry Gordy quoted in *Rolling Stone*, 23 August 1990, p. 71.

23. See Fitzgerald, "Motown crossover hits", pp. 4, 9, on the creativity of Motown, even at its most "formulaic".

24. A. Shaw, *The world of soul* (New York: Cowles, 1970), p. 169. M. Jahn, *The story of rock from Elvis to the Rolling Stones* (New York: Quadrangle, 1975), p. 11. T. Cummings, "An English way to Marvin Gaye", *Black Music* (December 1976), p. 14. Michael Bane reduced Motown to "white music produced by blacks". M. Bane, *White boy singing the blues* (London: Penguin, 1982), p. 170. For the sign metaphor see, for example, A. Shaw, *Black popular music in America* (New York: Schirmer, 1986), p. 218; Hirshey, *Nowhere to run*, p. 304.

25. Otis Redding quoted in *Rolling Stone*, 20 January 1968, p. 13. For a good contemporary description of a Stax session, see P. Garland, *The sound of soul* (Chicago: Regnery, 1969), pp. 147–52.

26. For "Hold what you got", see B. Hoskyns, *Say it one time for the broken hearted* (Glasgow: Fontana, 1987), pp. 113–14.

27. See C. White & H. Weinger, "Are you ready for star time?", in *Star time*, C. White et al. (n.p.: Poly Gram Records, 1991), p. 27.

28. R. Vincent, *Funk: the music, the people, and the rhythm of the one* (New York: St Martin's, 1996), p. 84.

29. James Jamerson quoted in N. George, *Buppies, b-boys, baps & bohos* (New York: HarperPerennial, 1994), p. 171. See also Fitzgerald, "Motown crossover hits", p. 9; Jerry Wexler quoted in Hirshey, *Nowhere to run*, p. 299.

30. Cholly Atkins quoted in George, *Where did our love go?*; Mary Wilson quoted in *Melody Maker*, 19 September 1964, p. 7.

31. R. Gleason, "Like a rolling stone" (1967), repr. in *The age of rock: sounds of the American cultural revolution*, J. Eisen (ed.) (New York: Random House, 1969), p. 67. Frith, "You can make it", p. 59.

32. Kim Weston quoted in Ryan, *Recollections*, profile 40.

33. For statistics, see George, *Where did our love go?*, p. 139; Shaw, *Black popular music*, p. 224; Bianco, *Heatwave*; and Taraborelli, *Motown*, pp. i–ii.

34. "Deposits", 25 April 1966, part III, box 2, folder 16, CORE papers (hereinafter, CORE). "Contributors giving largest amounts, fiscal year, 1965–66", n.d., part III, box 5, folder 12, CORE. Frank M. Seymour, letter to James Farmer, 30 July 1965; "Americans in harmony – statement of income and expenses", 28 July 1965, both E-II-3, CORE papers Addendum (hereinafter CORE-Add). See also Frank M. Seymour, letter to John Lewis, 30 July 1965, A-IV-70, SNCC papers (hereinafter, SNCC).

35. Junius Griffin, interview with Brian Ward, 22 July 1996, UNOHC.

36. *Amsterdam News*, 27 July 1963, pp. 1/2; 17 August 1963, p. 15; 24 August 1963, p. 4; 31 August 1963, p. 13. Maele Daniele Dufty, letter to Dr John Morsell, 27 September 1963, reel 9, folder: March on Washington – album, Bayard T. Rustin Papers (hereinafter, BTR).

37. Liner notes to the *Nashville Sit-in Story* (Folkways FH5590, 1960) can be found in Fiskiana file: Fisk Student Sit-ins, 1960, Fisk University Library Collection.

38. Bernard LaFayette, letter to Folkways, 22 June 1962; Moses Asch, letter to Bernard LaFayette, 2 July 1962, both A-IV-128, SNCC.

39. James Forman, letter to Mr Asch, 10 July 1962; M. Asch, letter to Mr Forman, 19 July 1962; James Forman, letter to Mr Asch, 20 August 1962; Moses Asch, letter to Mr Forman, 19 September 1962, all A-IV-128, SNCC.

40. James Forman, letter to Mr Asch, 5 December 1962; James Forman, letter to Mr Asch, 14 December 1962, all A-IV-128, SNCC. *Atlanta Inquirer*, 1 September 1962, p. 4; *ibid.*, 6 October 1962, p. 3. The details of the Vanguard-SNCC arrangements for the *Freedom In The Air* recording, including the decision to insert an electronic beep over the name of the Sheriff of Terrell County rather than risk possible libel action, can be found in Maynard Solomon, letter to SNCC, 23 April 1962; Maynard Solomon, letter to James Forman, 18 May 1962; James Forman, letter to Maynard Solomon, 16 June 1962, and sundry other correspondence, all A-IV-384, SNCC.

41. "SNCC Income, January 1, 1963 to December 31, 1963", "SNCC cash receipts", 1965, both A-VI-6, SNCC. The SNCC Freedom Singers also recorded two albums for Mercury in 1964 (*We Shall Overcome* and *Sing of Freedom Now*).

42. For the Dauntless (a subsidiary of Audio Fidelity) album, see Marvin Rich, letter to Sidney Frey, 23 August 1962; Audio Fidelity to Marvin Rich, 5 September 1962, both E-II-39, CORE-Add. Val Coleman, memo to CORE group leaders, 12 September 1963, V:213, CORE papers, 1941–1967 (hereinafter CORE: 1941–67).

43. *Atlanta Inquirer*, 6 October 1962, p. 3. Val Coleman, letter to Morris Levy, 10 July 1963, E-II-32, CORE-Add.

44. Val Coleman, letter to Morris Levy, n.d. (October 1963?), E-II-32, CORE-Add. "Financial statement: June 1, 1963 thru Jan. 31, 1964", B-I-3, CORE-Add. James Farmer, letter to Claude Robarge, (Patrick Cudahy Inc.), 11 November 1963. Claude Robarge, letter to James Farmer, 13 November 1963, V:213, CORE: 1941–67.

45. Val Coleman, memo to CORE group leaders, 12 September 1963, V:213, CORE: 1941–67, Marvin Rich quoted in A. Meier & E.P. Rudwick, *CORE: a study in the civil rights movement, 1942–1968* (New York: Oxford University Press, 1973), p. 149. See also pp. 148–50, 225, 335–6, for CORE's finances to 1965.

46. King filed for copyright protection of "I have a dream" on 30 September 1963 and it was granted on 9 October. See also "*King* v *Mr Maestro, inc.*", *Virginia Law Review*, **50**, 1964, p. 940.

47. Alfred Duckett, letter to Maude Ballou, n.d.; Maude L. Ballou, letter to Mr Duckett, 20 April 1960, both box 23a, folder 20 (3a of 3), Martin Luther King Jr Papers (hereinafter, MLK).

48. Wyatt Tee Walker quoted in "Press release", n.d., box 122, folder 15, SCLC papers (hereinafter, SCLC).

49. Martin Luther King and Wyatt Tee Walker, both quoted in *ibid.*

50. Wyatt Tee Walker quoted in *ibid.* Henry Murray, letters to Mr Lewis, 28 January and 10 February 1965; Rick Willard, letter to Mr Lewis, 23 March 1965; Johanan

Vigoda, letter to Mr Lewis, 5 April 1965, "Contract: Sue Records and John Lewis", 28 January 1965, all A-I-43, SNCC.

51. "Profit and loss of M.L. King records to September 30 1962", box 121, folder 27, MLK.

52. Esther G. Edwards, letter to Rev. Martin Luther King, Jr, 27 September 1962, box 1, folder 11, SCLC. Gordy, *To be loved*, p. 249.

53. Martin Luther King, "'Deposition", 29 November 1963, *Martin Luther King vs Mr Maestro Inc., et al.*, F. Supp. 101, 103 (SDNY, 1963), all in box 122, folder 32, MLK.

54. *"King* v *Mr Maestro"*, pp. 939–45; King, "Deposition".

55. Morgan C. Robinson, letter to Bayard Rustin, 14 September 1963, reel 20, folder: general correspondence, November–December 1963, BTR. Samuel B. Lansky, "Dear Sir letter", 19 September 1963, reel 9, folder: March on Washington – album, BTR. Dufty, letter to Morsell. B. Holiday (with W. Dufty), *Lady sings the blues* (New York: Penguin, 1985).

56. *Washington Afro-American*, 8 October 1963, pp. 1–2; *ibid.*, 15 October 1963, p. 10. Like many aspects of Motown's dealings with King and the SCLC, it is difficult to resolve some of these matters completely. There are several relevant files among the personal papers of Martin Luther King, Jr, currently housed at the woefully mismanaged and under-resourced archives of the King Center in Atlanta. Unfortunately, the King family have generally denied researchers access to this collection in recent years.

57. L. Joseph Overton, letter to A. Philip Randolph, 31 October 1963, box 31, folder 6, Bayard T. Rustin papers, Manuscript Division, Library of Congress, Washington, D.C. For some reason this document was omitted from the microfilmed collection held at the University of Virginia, but was found among the originals in the Library of Congress.

58. Martin Luther King, letter to 20th Century Fox, 7 January 1964; Lloyd K. Garrison, letter to 20th Century Fox, 31 January 1964, both box 122, XVI, folder 32, MLK.

59. Morris Theorgood, letter to Marvin Rich, 20 March 1964; Marvin Rich, letter to Morris Theorgood, 27 March 1964, both V:213, CORE: 1941–67.

60. For the Chicago independent black soul labels, see R. Pruter, *Chicago soul* (Urbana: University of Illinois Press, 1991), esp. pp. 24–71, 142–5, 211–13, 304–25.

61. *Ibid.*, pp. 142–4.

62. George, *Where did our love go?*, p. 150.

63. M. Wilson (with P. Romanowski & A. Juillard), *Dreamgirl: my life as a Supreme* (London: Sidgwick & Jackson, 1987), pp. 68–70; D. Fileti, liner notes, *The Detroit Girl Groups*, Relic 8004 (n.d.).

64. *Billboard*, 4 March 1967, p. 4; Pruter, *Chicago soul*, pp. 42–5; Shaw, *Black popular music*, p. 191; George, *Where did our love go?*, p. 53; S. Flam, "The Vee Jay story", *Bim Bam Boom* **1** (1972), pp. 18–19.

65. See Pruter, *Chicago soul*, pp. 43–5; *Billboard*, 27 February 1965, p. 3; 19 June 1965, p. 10; 14 May 1966, p. 4; 11 February 1967, p. 10.

66. Al Bell quoted in Garland, *The sound of soul*, pp. 127–8.

67. S. Cooke, "Sam Cooke . . . man with a goal", *Pittsburgh Courier*, 8 October 1960, p. 24.

68. Cooke's business dealings and Allen Klein's role in them are recounted in Wolff et al., *You send me*, pp. 269–71, 282–3, 299–300, 315–16.

69. George, *Where did our love go?*, pp. 55, 154; Gordy, *To be loved*, esp. pp. 81–3, 141–2, 257, 263. Bane, *White boy singing the blues*, p. 165.

70. Battiste interview.

71. Gordy, *To be loved*, p. 133.
72. *Billboard*, 16 May 1960, pp. 1/14. R.S. Denisoff, *Solid gold: the popular record industry* (New Brunswick, N.J.: Transaction, 1975), pp. 232–3.
73. U. Hannerz, *Soulside* (New York: Columbia University Press, 1969), p. 156.
74. See George, *Death of rhythm and blues*, pp. 135–8, 144–58.
75. For the growth of the black consumer market, see "Advertisers' interest in Negroes zoom", *Broadcasting*, 7 November 1966, pp. 76–82.
76. George, *Death of rhythm and blues*, p. 88; Wilson, *Dreamgirl*, pp. 139–40.
77. See Frith, "You can make it", p. 39; George, *Where did our love go?*, pp. 113–14.
78. As station owner Bill Drake explained, Top Forty radio had strict limits on the airspace available for particular styles. "There would never be a week that we could put on Wilson Pickett and the Temptations and Otis Redding no matter if all three had made their greatest record." Although the effects of this policy may appear racist, the motivations were not specifically so as it also restricted opportunities for white country singers, progressive rock groups and other artists from specialist fields. Bill Drake quoted in R.S. Denisoff, *Solid gold*, p. 240.
79. See M. Haralambos, *Right on: from blues to soul in black America* (New York: Drake, 1975), p. 93; J.L. Dates and W. Barlow, *Split image: African-Americans in the mass media* (Washington, D.C.: Howard University Press, 1990), p. 221.
80. "Publicity handbook", III-A-311, Papers of the NAACP (hereinafter, NAACP). Sherwood Ross, Memorandum, 30 June 1965, 2–5–15, National Urban League Papers. "Minutes of SCLC Executive Committee Retreat", 10–12 November 1964, p. 4. Zenas Sears, letter to Randolph Blackwell, 24 December 1964, both references, box 141, folder 4, SCLC. Tom Offenburger, Memorandum, 2 February 1968, box 47, folder 24, SCLC.
81. See "List of sponsors for 'Salute to southern students'", (n.d.), A-IV-69, 3NCC. M.L. King, Jr, "Transforming a neighborhood into a brotherhood" (address to the National Association of Television and Radio Announcers, Atlanta, 11 August 1967), *Jack the Rapper*, 13(666), January 1989, p. 1.
82. Larry Russell quoted in *Freedom's children: young civil rights activists tell their own stories*, E. Levine (ed.) (New York: Avon, 1993), p. 101. Abraham Woods, interview with Brian Ward and Jenny Walker, 25 October 1995. See also Shelley Stewart, interview with Brian Ward, 26 October 1995; Joseph Lackey, interview with Brian Ward, 26 October 1995, all UNOHC. T. Branch, *Parting the waters: America in the King years, 1954–1963* (New York: Simon & Schuster, 1988), p. 755.
83. King, "Transforming a neighborhood". Larry Russell quoted in Levine, *Freedom's children*, p. 101. Stewart interview. Lackey interview. Woods interview.
84. WENN, "Application for renewal of broadcast station license", 11 December 1963, Box 180, FCC License Renewal Files, Federal Communications Commission Papers (hereinafter, FCC). WDAS, "Application for renewal of broadcast station license", 16 April 1963, Box 167, FCC. For a more positive assessment of black-oriented radio's contribution to the Movement, see S. Walsh, "Black-oriented radio and the southern civil rights movement, 1955–1972", unpublished paper (Southern Historical Association Conference, New Orleans, November 1995). See also B. Ward & J. Walker, " 'Bringing the races closer?': black-oriented radio in the South and the civil rights movement", in *Dixie debates: perspectives on southern cultures*, R. King & H. Taylor (eds) (London: Pluto, 1996), pp. 130–49.
85. Francis Fitzgerald quoted in *New York Times*, 5 August 1960, p. 33. "The new Negro Radio Association", *Sponsor*, 26 September 1960, pp. 14/52; "NRA: it's straining to profile its audience", *ibid.*, 9 October 1961, pp. 15/25.

86. For biographical information on Francis Fitzgerald, see *Who's who in the south-west, 1965–66* (Chicago: Marquis, 1965). See also "Staff of WGIV", August 1963 (exhibit XVIII, folder 4A), in WGIV, "Application for renewal of broadcast station license", box 196, FCC; A. Abarbanel & A. Haley, "New audience for radio", *Harper's Magazine* (February 1956), p. 59. For Fitzgerald's support of Fred Alexander, see "Receipt no. 36", 8 April 1965; "WGIV invoice to Fred Alexander", 19 April 1965, both references, folder 31, box 1, Fred D. Alexander papers.

87. "Citation for award to Francis M. Fitzgerald, from St Paul's Baptist Church, Charlotte'" (signed by J.C. Clemmons and Rev. James F. Wertz), July 1953, reprinted in "Program for 'Genial Gene Day'", Charlotte Armory Auditorium, 22 November 1953, p. 15. Francis Fitzgerald quoted in *New York Times*, 5 August 1960, p. 33.

88. Press release, 6 December 1963; "Report of direct action: Philadelphia branch NAACP for year 1963", p. 15, both III-C-137, NAACP. See also *Billboard*, 30 November 1963, pp. 3, 37; *ibid.*, 7 December 1963, p. 4.

89. "Los Angeles membership bulletin", 31 March 1964; "Why we are demonstrating", both F-II-10, CORE-Add.

90. "The Negro dj and civil rights", *Broadcasting*, 31 August 1964, p. 61. NATRA was originally NARA – the National Association of Radio Announcers – but became NATRA in 1965, when black television announcers were included. I have used NATRA throughout.

91. Del Shields quoted in Broadcasting, 31 August 1964, p. 60.

92. George, *Death of rhythm and blues*, pp. 111–13.

Chapter Eight

1. Bernice Johnson Reagon, interview with Brian Ward, 24 January 1996, University of Newcastle upon Tyne Oral History Collection (hereinafter, UNOHC).

2. R. Snellings, "Keep on pushin': rhythm & blues as a weapon", *Liberator* **5**, October 1966, pp. 6–8.

3. P.K. Maultsby, "Soul music: its sociological and political significance in American popular culture", *Journal of Popular Culture* **17**(2), 1984, p. 51. A.X. Nicholas (ed.), *The poetry of soul* (New York: Bantam, 1971), p. xiii. R. Stephens, "Soul: a historical reconstruction of continuity and change", *Black Perspectives in Music* **12**, Spring 1984, pp. 21–43.

4. See, for example, H. Sitkoff, *The struggle for black equality, 1954–1992*, revd edn (New York: Hill & Wang, 1993), p. 202. For a classic logocentric approach, see B.L. Cooper, "Popular music: an untapped resource for teaching contemporary black history", *Journal of Negro Education* **48**, Winter 1979, pp. 20–36.

5. D. Wolff et al., *You send me: the life and times of Sam Cooke* (New York: Wm Morrow, 1995).

6. Jerry Butler quoted in *ibid.*, pp. 238–9.

7. *Ibid.*, pp. 290–2, 314.

8. *Ibid.*, pp. 201–2.

9. See "Auditorium parking concession – car parking: June 1959", 1 July 1959, 3.28: Municipal Auditorium, James W. Morgan Mayoral Papers; *Birmingham News*, 14 June 1956, p. A-27.

10. June Johnson, interview with Brian Ward, 22 January 1996, UNOHC.

11. Guy Carawan, memo to Myles [Horton] and Connie [Conrad], n.d., reel 7, frame 347–353, Highlander Folk School Papers.
12. John O'Neal, interview 2 with Thomas Dent, 25 September 1983, Thomas Dent Holdings (hereinafter TDH). Julian Bond, interview with Brian Ward, 20 March 1996, UNOHC. Reagon interview. B.J. Reagon et al., *We who believe in freedom* (New York: Anchor, 1993), pp. 159–62.
13. Bond interview. Stanley Wise, interview with Brian Ward & Jenny Walker, 19 October 1995, UNOHC.
14. Reagon interview.
15. Biographical details about Anne Romaine are drawn from various unrecorded private conversations and clippings from the *Charlotte Observer*, 19 March 1994 and 3 September 1995; *Gaston Gazette*, 3 June 1994, p. 5, all in Anne Romaine press file, n.d. See also Anne Romaine, "Curriculum vitae", 1995; *Cavalier Daily*, 10 February 1983, pp. 4/6. For mill-town culture, see J. Dowd Hall et al., *Like a family: the making of a southern cotton mill world* (Chapel Hill: University of North Carolina Press, 1987).
16. This account of the origins of the SFCRP is drawn from A. Romaine, "Southern folk cultural revival project", box 2, folder: Anne Romaine narrative (SFCRP History), SFCRP papers (hereinafter SFCRP). Reagon interview.
17. "Draft mission statement", n.d.; "Proposal for SFCRP", n.d., both box 3, folder: correspondence with foundations, 1967 proposal, SFCRP.
18. Reagon interview.
19. *Norfolk Journal and Guide*, 20 April 1963, p. 23. Bond interview.
20. Clyde McPhatter quoted in *Amsterdam News*, 9 July 1960, p. 15. *Los Angeles Sentinel*, 25 February 1960, p. C-3. See also Marion Barry, letter to James Forman, 6 July 1962, A-IV-47, SNCC papers (hereinafter SNCC).
21. Bond interview. *Norfolk Journal and Guide*, 22 June 1963, p. 14.
22. *New York Times*, 10 April 1963, p. 29. R. Charles & D. Ritz, *Brother Ray* (London: Futura, 1980), pp. 272–6.
23. Al Hibbler quoted in *Norfolk Journal and Guide*, 20 April 1963, p. 23. Joseph Lackey, interview with Brian Ward, 26 June 1996, UNOHC. Al Hibbler and Bull Connor, both quoted in *New York Times*, 11 April 1963, p. 21.
24. *Ibid.*, 12 April 1963, p. 1. *Amsterdam News*, 27 July 1963, p. 15; 3 August 1963, p. 20; 10 August 1963, p. 1/42.
25. Bond interview. Roy Hamilton, letter to James Farmer, 20 September 1963; Val Coleman, letter to Roy Hamilton, 6 February 1964, both V:179, CORE papers, 1941–1967 (hereinafter CORE: 1941–67).
26. "The Philadelphia fund story" (n.d.), III-C-37, Papers of the NAACP (hereinafter NAACP). *Washington Afro-American*, 15 October 1963, p. 17. "Programme for Selma freedom show", box 3, Lawrence Henry collection.
27. Wise interview.
28. N. Simone (with S. Cleary), *I put a spell on you: the autobiography of Nina Simone* (London: Ebury, 1991), pp. 86–7.
29. *Ibid.*
30. *Ibid.*, pp. 88–9. For Simone's own account of her political education and activism, see *ibid.*, pp. 86–104, 108–10, 113–18. See also P. Garland, *The sound of soul* (Chicago: Regnery, 1969), pp. 169–90.
31. M.L. King, Jr, "Letter from Birmingham city jail", in *A testament of hope: the essential writings and speeches of Martin Luther King, Jr*, ed. James M. Washington (San Francisco: Harper & Row, 1986), p. 292.

32. *Amsterdam News*, 10 August 1963, p. 42. For details of Simone's SNCC work, see Julia Prettyman, letter to Nina Simone, 5 May 1964, B-I-12, SNCC; "Freedom Concert programme", B-I-1, SNCC. Johnson interview. Wise interview.

33. *Ibid.* Stanley Levison, to Billy [Rowe?], 22 June 1966, Martin Luther King, Jr, FBI Files, II: The King-Levison Files (hereinafter FBI:K-L). For Simone's CORE shows, see, for example, Andrew B. Stroud, letter to Jim McDonald, 16 August 1965; Alan Gartner, letter to Andrew Stroud, 20 August 1965, both E-II-44, CORE papers Addendum (hereinafter CORE-Add). Alan Gartner, "Memo re: Fund Raising Department Report", n.d., B-I-13, CORE-Add.

34. See Garland, *Sound of soul*, p. 183. *Newsweek*, 30 March 1970, p. 83.

35. Reagon interview. Wise interview. Lawrence Guyot, interview with Brian Ward & Jenny Walker, 16 December 1995, UNOHC.

36. Simone, *I put a spell on you*, p. 69.

37. Betty Garman, letter to Dick Perez, 14 July 1965, A-IV-70, SNCC.

38. See S. Davis Jnr. (sic), *Hollywood in a suitcase* (London: W.H. Allen, 1981), p. 207. Harry Belafonte, interview with Brian Ward, 12 March 1996, UNOHC. For the full list of participants in the cultural contingent to the March, see Clarence B. Jones, circular to Cleveland Robinson, Bayard Rustin and Ossie Davis, 21 August 1963, reel 8, folder: Ossie Davis, Bayard T. Rustin papers (hereinafter BTR).

39. *Billboard*, 12 October 1963, p. 1. For Little Willie John's attendance see Roscoe Shelton, interview with Brian Ward, 30 October 1995, UNOHC.

40. John Handy, "The Freedom Band", 14 September 1964, part I, box 7, folder 1, CORE papers (hereinafter CORE). Duke Ellington, quoted in D. George, *The real Duke Ellington* (London: Robson, 1982), pp. 113–14.

41. Handy, "The Freedom Band"; "Jazz at the Masonic – Program", 14 September 1964, part I, box 3, folder 7, CORE.

42. N. Hentoff, "Jazz and reverse Jim Crow", *Negro Digest* (June 1961), pp. 70–4.

43. For arrangements concerning *We Insist! The Freedom Now Suite*, see St Clair Clement, letter and enclosures to John Lewis, 7 August 1963, A-I-31, SNCC.

44. Fay Bellamy, interview with Brian Ward, 18 October 1995, UNOHC.

45. "Chicago Urban League Newsletter", July 1959; Bettye Jayne Everett, letter to William Sims, 25 July 1959, both in 8:5:Playboy Jazz Festival, National Urban League papers. "List of sponsors for 'Salute to southern students'", n.d.; James Forman, letter to Diahann Carroll, 13 February 1963, both A-IV-69, SNCC. For the "Jazz salute to freedom" concert, see Val Coleman, letter to Symphony Sid, 3 September 1963, II:6, CORE: 1941–67. For Miles Davis' benefit, see Jim Mansonis, letter to Miles Davis, 6 March 1964, B-I-12, SNCC. For the Roach-Lincoln concert, see "Boston Friends of SNCC: financial summary – first quarter, 1965", and "Boston Friends of SNCC: financial statement", April 1965, both A-VI-6, SNCC. The jazzmobile is discussed in L. Jones (I.A. Baraka), *The autobiography of LeRoi Jones/Imamu Amiri Baraka* (New York: Freundlich, 1984), pp. 211–12.

46. For Coleman see B. Sidran, *Black talk* (New York: Da Capo, 1981), p. 143. Cecil Taylor quoted in *Down Beat Yearbook – 1966*, pp. 19, 31.

47. The $40,000 figure is mentioned in Martin Luther King, telephone conversation with Stanley Levison, 28 May 1996, FBI:K-L. "Financial report – Mahalia Jackson concert", 7 August 1963, part II, box 11, folder 15, CORE. "SNCC: New York Branch – statement of receipts and disbursements from concerts and benefits, from Jan. 1, 1963 – Dec. 31, 1963", A-VI-6, SNCC.

48. Belafonte interview.
49. "New York Friends of SNCC: balance sheet (May 1 – Sept. 30, 1964)", A-VI-6, SNCC. For Simone's fees, see Andrew B. Stroud, letter to Jim McDonald, 16 August 1965, E-II-44, CORE-Add.
50. Wise interview. Bond interview.
51. For Paul Simon's friendship with Andrew Goodman, see P. Humphries, *The boy in the bubble: a biography of Paul Simon* (London: Hodder & Stoughton, 1990), p. 24. Bernice Johnson (Reagon) quoted in R. Shelton, *No direction home: the life and music of Bob Dylan* (New York: Beech Tree, 1986), p. 179.
52. Jimmy McDonald, letter to Marvin Rich, 23 October 1963, V:179, CORE: 1941–67. "Boston Friends of SNCC: financial statement, May 1965", A-VI-6, SNCC. *Atlanta Inquirer*, 25 May 1963, p. 7. J. Dittmer, *Local people: the struggle for civil rights in Mississippi* (Urbana: University of Illinois Press, 1994), pp. 228, 478–9, n. 31. J. Baez, *And a voice to sing with: a memoir* (New York: Summit, 1987), p. 103.
53. See John O. Killens & Ossie Davis, recruitment letter, 21 May 1964, Schomburg Center Clippings File: "Association of Artists for Freedom". Stanley Levison, telephone call with Martin Luther King, 21 May 1963, FBI:K-L. W.W. Sales, Jr, *From civil rights to black liberation: Malcolm X and the Organization of Afro-American Unity* (Boston: South End, 1994), p. 107.
54. See, for example, W. Van DeBurg's *New day in Babylon: the black power movement and American culture* (Chicago: University of Chicago Press, 1992), pp. 265–72.
55. See *New York Post Magazine*, 27 March 1945; Lena Horne quoted in *St Louis Post-Dispatch*, 27 September 1949, both in Schomburg Center Clippings File: "Lena Horne" (hereinafter, SC-File: "Horne"). L. Horne & R. Shickel, *Lena*, 2nd edn (Garden City, N.Y.: Limelight, 1986), pp. 173–7. In the early 1940s, Horne had complained how, on one hand, she was not allowed to talk to whites on screen because southern distributors objected to such interracial exchanges, while, on the other hand, her light complexion and aquiline features meant that she was not "considered" coloured enough for roles opposite black actors, lest audiences mistake her for a white woman. When Max Factor concocted a darkening make-up to help her out of this dilemma, she refused to use it, just as she refused to sing blues and spirituals simply because that was what white Hollywood expected all blacks to sing, preferring instead a smooth, vaguely jazzy pop style. *New York Post*, 30 June 1941; *New York Post Magazine*, 29 September 1963, both SC-File: "Horne".
56. Lena Horne quoted in *Amsterdam News*, 20 February 1960, pp. 1/10, 1/35; *Los Angeles Sentinel*, 18 February 1960, pp. 1-A/3-A; *New York Times*, 17 February 1960, p. 30. *New York Post*, 17 February 1960, p. 1.
57. For the Atlanta benefit, see *Atlanta Inquirer*, 3 August 1963, p. 8; *Amsterdam News*, 10 August 1963, p. 20. Lena Horne quoted in *New York Post*, 29 September 1963, p. 4. Horne's own refreshingly self-effacing account of her Movement work appears in Horne & Shickel, *Lena*, pp. 275–91.
58. *Amsterdam News*, 14 May 1960, p. 3. Carroll's support for SNCC is acknowledged in a letter from James Forman to Diahann Carroll, 13 February 1963, A-IV-69, SNCC. Gloria (Richardson) Dandridge, "Women's division report", 1 December 1965; Julie Belafonte & Diahann Carroll, "Dear friend letter", 8 December 1965, both A-IV-123, SNCC. See also Gloria Richardson Dandridge, interview with Jenny Walker, 11 March 1996, UNOHC. Stanley Levison acknowledged

Belafonte's influence in the Gandhi Society in a telephone conversation with Toni Hamilton and Clarence Jones, 17 April 1962, FBI:K-L.

59. Biographical details drawn from Schomburg Center Clippings File: "Dick Gregory" (hereinafter, SC-File: "Gregory"). D. Gregory, *Nigger: an autobiography* (New York: Dutton, 1964). See also D. Gregory, *From the back of the bus* (New York: Dutton, 1962).

60. *New York Post*, 2 April 1963; *ibid.*, 3 April 1963. *Jet*, 14 January 1965, SC-File: "Gregory". *New York Times*, 3 April 1963, p. 1/40. Guyot interview. Johnson interview. Dittmer, *Local people*, pp. 145, 152, 155, 174.

61. Robert E. Johnson, interview with John Britton, 6 September 1967, Ralph J. Bunche Oral History Collection.

62. Richardson interview.

63. *New York Times*, 26 February 1964; *New York Post*, 3 October 1963; 3 August 1965; 13 August 1965; 22 December 1965; 16 February 1966; 1 December 1966; 3 September 1968, all SC-File: "Gregory". *Ebony*, March 1964, p. 95. R. Johnson interview. Dick Gregory quoted in G. Horne, *Fire this time: the Watts uprising and the 1960s* (Charlottesville: University Press of Virginia, 1995), p. 184, p. 376 n. 81. Gregory's activism continued into the Black Power era. In 1966, he ran an unsuccessful write-in campaign for the mayoralty of Chicago and was jailed for a "fish-in" in support of Native American land rights in Washington State. In July 1968 he served yet more time for another illegal fishing expedition to the Nisqually River – by which point he had already fasted against the Vietnam war and announced his intention to run for the presidency on the Freedom and Peace Party ticket. See *New York Post*, 16 February 1966; 1 December 1966; 3 September 1968, all SC-File: "Gregory".

64. Sammy Davis Jr, "Letter to the entertainment field" (n.d.), III-A-44, NAACP.

65. For the Carnegie Hall show, see S. Levison, letter to Martin Luther King, 5 December 1960; Martin Luther King, letter to Sammy Davis Jr, 20 December 1960, both box 23, folder 20, Martin Luther King papers (hereinafter MLK). Ralph D. Abernathy, "Treasurer's report: fiscal year: September 1, 1960 – August 31, 1961", box 129, folder 15, SCLC papers (hereinafter SCLC). D.J. Garrow, *Bearing the cross: Martin Luther King, Jr, and the Southern Christian Leadership Conference* (New York: Vintage, 1988), pp. 155, 168. For Westchester, see Al Duckett, memo to Wyatt Tee Walker et al., 24 November 1962; "Westchester salute to Martin Luther King, Jr, benefit program", both box 45a, folder 78, MLK.

66. For the "Broadway answers Selma" show accounts and line-up see "Deposits", 4 June 1965, part III, box 2, folder 15, CORE; Marvin Rich, letter to Mr Albert Lee Lesser, 28 June 1965, part III, box 1, folder 6, CORE; "Deposits", 23 July 1965 and "Deposits", 31 August 1965, both part III, box 2, folder 15, CORE; "Deposits", 2 December 1965, part III, box 2, folder 16, CORE. See also "Broadway answers Selma – programme", and James Farmer, letter to Eli Wallach, 6 April 1965, both E-II-19, CORE-Add. For "Stars for freedom", see Martin Luther King, "Dear friend letter", 1 July 1965, box 128, folder 13, SCLC. SCOPE was an ambitious attempt to emulate the Freedom Summer's registration and educational efforts in Mississippi throughout the Deep South. See Garrow, *Bearing the cross*, pp. 415–16, 428–9, 438, 440–2, 446, 454. For Davis' personal donation to the SCLC in May 1963, see Stanley Levison, telephone conversation with Martin Luther King, 28 May 1963, FBI:K-L.

67. Reagon interview. For a largely uncritical account of the abuse heaped upon Belafonte and others, see Van DeBurg, *New day in Babylon*, p. 267. See also E. Cleaver, *Soul on ice* (New York: Dell, 1968), p. 89. The only Movement historian who has given Belafonte anything like his due is Taylor Branch. See T. Branch, *Parting the waters: America in the King years* (Simon & Schuster, 1989), pp. 275, 288–9, 388–9, 481, 485, 513–14, 877. See also Henry Louis Gates' sympathetic profile, H.L. Gates, Jr, "Belafonte's balancing act", *New Yorker*, 26 August/2 September 1996, pp. 132–43.

68. For Belafonte's first meeting with King, see Harry Belafonte, Martin Luther King & Merv Griffin, "*The Merv Griffin Show*, 6 July 1967: transcript", 3:1, Martin Luther King papers, printed matter. Also, Belafonte interview. For biographical information, see A. Shaw, *Belafonte: an unauthorized biography* (Philadelphia: Chilton, 1960); G. Fogelson, *Belafonte* (Los Angeles: Holloway House, 1980); Schomburg Center Clippings File: "Belafonte" (hereinafter SC-File: "Belafonte").

69. *Sunday News*, 1 May 1955, in SC-File: "Belafonte". *Look*, 25 June 1957, p. 142. *Time*, 2 March 1959, p. 40.

70. Harry Belafonte quoted in *Saturday Evening Post*, 29 April 1957, pp. 28, 69. See also *Look*, 25 June 1957, p. 142.

71. Belafonte interview.

72. *Ibid*. Belafonte et al., "*Merv Griffin Show* transcript".

73. Belafonte interview. For the Montgomery benefit, see *Amsterdam News*, 1 December 1956, p. 3.

74. Belafonte interview. CDMLK, "The revolving bail fund", n.d.; Stanley D. Levison, "Minutes of board meeting", 7 March 1960; Nat King Cole et al., "Dear friend letter", n.d., all box 23, Papers of A. Philip Randolph (hereinafter, APR).

75. CDMLK, "Statement of income and expenditure for the period ended July 31, 1960,"; Stanley Levison, "Minutes of board meeting", 7 March 1960; Martin Luther King, "Dear friend letter", 6 October 1960, all box 23, APR. *Amsterdam News*, 16 April 1960, p. 3; *ibid.*, 14 May 1960, p. 3.

76. Belafonte interview. Warren Ling, letter to Martin Luther King, 28 February 1961, David Adelman, letter to Martin Luther King, 1 March 1961; David Adelman, letter to Martin Luther King, 13 June 1961, all box 56, II, folder 36, MLK.

77. Belafonte interview. *The Reporter*, 2 March 1995, p. 1.

78. Belafonte interview. Bellamy interview.

79. Belafonte interview.

80. *Ibid*. Ella Baker, interview with Eugene Walker, 4 September 1974, Southern Oral History Program.

81. Garrow, *Bearing the cross*, p. 112.

82. A. Meier & E.P. Rudwick, *CORE: a study in the civil rights movement, 1942–1968* (New York: Oxford University Press, 1973), p. 127.

83. Johnson interview. Wise interview. Bond interview.

84. James Forman, letter to Harry Belafonte, 4 December 1963, A-IV-48, SNCC.

85. For the "Books for Miles College" programme, see (Horace) Julian Bond, letter to Harry Belafonte, 10 May 1962. For the Americus initiative, see James Forman, letter to Harry Belafonte, 5 September 1963, both A-IV-48, SNCC.

86. For Belafonte's material and tactical support of SNCC's voter registration campaigns, see C. Carson, *In struggle: SNCC and the black awakening of the 1960s* (Cambridge, Mass.: Harvard University Press, 1981), p. 70; Dittmer, *Local people*, p. 145; E. Burner, *And gently he shall lead them: Robert Parris Moses and civil*

rights in Mississippi (New York: New York University Press, 1994), pp. 38, 43, 61, 86. For Belafonte's role in the Carnegie Hall concert see James Forman, letter to Harry Belafonte, 4 December 1963, A-IV-48, SNCC. "SNCC Income, January 1, 1963 to December 31, 1963", A-IV-27, SNCC.

87. See Branch, *Parting the waters*, pp. 513–14.
88. For the Greenwood adventure, see Johnson interview, and June Johnson, interview with Thomas Dent, II, 22 July 1979, TDH; Belafonte interview. For the Africa visit see K. Mills, *This little light of mine: the life of Fannie Lou Hamer* (New York: Dutton, 1993), pp. 134–44. See also Belafonte interview; Carson, *In struggle*, pp. 134–6.
89. *Time*, 2 March 1959, p. 44. The assignment of television appearance fees is noted in (Horace) Julian Bond, letter to Harry Belafonte, 8 November 1962, A-IV-48, SNCC. SNCC's financial records rarely break down personal and general contributions by individuals, but some of Belafonte's donations can be traced through the related correspondence. See Gloria Cantor, letter to Charles McDew, 11 December 1962; James Forman, letter to Gloria Cantor, 18 December 1962; James Forman, letter to Gloria Cantor, 23 September 1963, all A-IV-48, SNCC; "List of sponsors for 'Salute to southern students'", (n.d), A-IV-69, SNCC; "Financial Report – Washington Office, Summer 1964", A-VI-6, SNCC.
90. Belafonte et al., *"Merv Griffin Show* transcript". Bayard Rustin, letter to Harry Belafonte, 8 September 1966; "Endorsees of Freedom Budget", both reel 13, folder: Freedom Budget (correspondence, requests for endorsement), BTR.
91. Gloria Cantor, telephone conversation with Stanley Levison, 17 April 1967, FBI:K-L.
92. *Ibid.*
93. Belafonte interview.
94. *Ibid.*
95. *Ibid.* Harry Belafonte quoted in *Look*, 25 June 1957, p. 142. Reagon interview.
96. *Ibid.*
97. Belafonte interview.
98. Harry Belafonte quoted in *Pittsburgh Courier*, 30 August 1960, p. 23.
99. Belafonte interview. Bond interview.
100. Reagon interview. Guyot interview.
101. *Ibid.*
102. For the NAACP and SNCC campaigns to keep artists out of Mississippi – a precursor of the 1980s Artists and Athletes against Apartheid campaign directed against South Africa by Harry Belafonte and tennis star Arthur Ashe – see *Musical America* (July 1964), pp. 9/55; *Student Voice*, 25 February 1964, p. 3. *New York Times*, 27 February 1964, 29 March 1964, 3 April 1964, 4 April 1964, 6 April 1964, 10 April 1964. Bond interview. "Press release, No. 36", n.d., B-I-127, SNCC. Mary King, "Cancellations: Oxford, Mississippi"; John Lewis, letter to the Journeymen, 25 March 1964, all A-I-31, SNCC.
103. Shelton interview.
104. Worth Long, interview with Thomas Dent, 29 July 1979, TDH.
105. Bellamy interview. Bond interview.
106. Wise interview. For an early attempt to secure the services of Motown acts, see Marvin Rich to Berry Gardy (sic), 4 May 1964, V:179, CORE: 1941–67.
107. Val Coleman, letters to Milt Shaw, 2 January 1964, 20 January 1964, 10 February 1964; Marvin Rich, letter to Berry Gardy (sic), 4 May 1964, all V:179, CORE: 1941–67.

108. Bond interview. Wise interview.
109. Stanley Levison, telephone conversation with Gloria Cantor (summary), 16 June 1966, FBI:K-L.
110. Coretta Scott King, telephone conversation with Stanley Levison, 24 May 1969, FBI:K-L. Junius Griffin, interview with Brian Ward, 22 July 1996, UNOHC.
111. *Ibid.*
112. Dick Perez, letter to Bobbi Jones, 8 July 1965; Betty Garman, letter to Dick Perez, 14 July 1965, both A-IV-70, SNCC. Griffin interview.
113. For example, Stanley Levison could not believe that the SCLC was paying Al Duckett $100 a day, possibly amounting to a total of around $4,000, to help organize a 1962 benefit in Westchester, New York. See Stanley Levison, telephone conversation with Jack (probably O'Dell), 9 October 1962, FBI:K-L. "Unwise or questionable fund raising methods", n.d., A-IV-13, SNCC.
114. For a brief biography of Jimmy McDonald, see "Betty Frank Radio Show", n.d., F-I-37, CORE-Add. For Richard Haley's musical background, see Meier & Rudwick, *CORE*, p. 113, and Richard Tinsley, letter to Richard Jewett, 16 February 1965, B-I-13, CORE-Add.
115. Garman to Perez. Marvin Rich, "Memo re: fundraising", 2 October 1964, E II-4, CORE-Add.
116. For the Sammy Davis Apollo shows, see Richard W. McLain, memo to Herbert Hill, 27 May 1958, John Morsell, letter to V. Jean Fleming, 18 August 1958; "Statement of receipts and expenditures for the Apollo Benefit, April 11–17, 1958", all references III-A-44, NAACP. For the Belafonte show in Nashville, see "Belafonte Concert: Financial Report", box 74, folder 10, Kelly Miller Smith Papers. "Pertaining to Bill Powell and the fraudulent misuse of funds raised for SNCC", n.d., A-IV-70, SNCC. For the Amen Corner benefit, see Jimmy McDonald, memorandum to Mrs Newman Levy, 20 April 1965, E-II-2, CORE-Add.
117. For the Robinson jazz concert, see Rich, "Memo re: fundraising". For the Broadway answers Selma show, see "Deposits", 4 June 1965, part III, box 2, folder 15, CORE, Marvin Rich, letter to Mr Albert Lee Lesser, 28 June 1965, part III, box 1, folder 6, CORE; "Deposits", 23 July 1965 and "Deposits", 31 August 1965, both part III, box 2, folder 15, CORE; "Deposits", 2 December 1965, part III, box 2, folder 16, CORE.
118. Dinky Romilly, letters to Joan Baez and Bobby Dillon (sic), 9 July 1965; Dinky Romilly, letter to Manuel Greenhill, 21 July 1965, all B-I-52, SNCC.
119. Bond interview.
120. "SNCC guide to fundraising", n.d., C-I-151, SNCC.
121. "Report of the Convention Fundraising Committee: statement of income and expenditures for year ending May 31, 1965", E:II:4, CORE-Add. Val Coleman, memo to James Farmer et al., 26 July 1965; James Farmer, letter to Frank Sinatra, n.d., both E:III:4, CORE-Add. Stanley Levison, telephone conversation with Martin Luther King, 30 November 1966, FBI:K-L.
122. Stanley Levison, telephone conversation with Martin Luther King, 28 May 1963, FBI:K-L. SNCC New York Office, "Special gifts – parties", A-VI-6, SNCC.
123. *Tan* (November 1957), pp. 30–1, 75. *New York Post*, 4 January 1962, in Schomburg Center Clippings File: "Ray Charles". N. George, *Where did our love go?* (New York: St Martin's, 1986), p. 139. *Time*, 1 April 1966, p. 75.
124. For CORE's white funding base see Meier & Rudwick, *CORE*, p. 336; I. Powell Bell, *CORE and the strategy of nonviolence* (New York: Random House, 1968), pp. 65–71. For SCLC's white funding base, see Martin Luther King, telephone

conversation with Stanley Levison (summary), 26 July 1966; Bill Stein, telephone conversation with Stanley Levison (summary), 19 October 1966, FBI:K-L. See also R. Cleghorn, "The angels are white: who pays the bills for civil rights", *New Republic*, 17 August 1963, pp. 12–14.
125. "Unwise or questionable fundraising methods".
126. Harold Battiste, interview with Brian Ward, 8 November 1995, UNOHC.
127. For the Baldwin mailing, see "SNCC New York Office, December 1964 – accounts", A-VI-6, SNCC.
128. See "Artists contribute to civil rights: press release", 25 January 1965; "Confidential Memorandum re: ACRAF", 3 August 1965, A-IV-51, SNCC.
129. To give but one example of this perennial financial hardship, in November 1964 CORE's Richard Haley announced that the Southern Project's Thanksgiving Retreat was to be cancelled for lack of funds. Acknowledging that already "many of the southern staff . . . have given up part of their tiny subsistence to help keep the project going", in the absence of any financial "angel", Haley had to call for "still more belt-tightening". Richard Haley, "Memorandum to southern staff", 18 November 1964, part II, box 11, folder 15, CORE.
130. Stanley Levison, telephone conversation with Martin Luther King (summary), 29 September 1966, FBI:K-L. Guyot interview.
131. Louis Armstrong quoted in *Norfolk Journal & Guide*, 28 September 1957, pp. 1/2.
132. Manchester Greene and George Perkins quoted in *ibid.*, p. 9.
133. Martin Luther King, draft letter to Sammy Davis, n.d., box 52a, folder 7a (2 of 3), MLK.
134. *Ibid.*
135. E. Cleaver, *Soul on ice*, p. 89.
136. Billy McKinney, interview with Brian Ward & Jenny Walker, 19 October 1995, UNOHC.

Chapter Nine

1. Curtis Mayfield quoted in *Soul*, 22 September 1969, p. 16.
2. Statistics on black economic and political trends are drawn from S.A. Levitan, W.B. Johnston and R. Taggert, *Still a dream: the changing status of blacks since 1960* (Cambridge, Mass.: Harvard University Press, 1975), pp. 15–17, 32, 36, 41. J. Blackwell, *The black community: diversity and unity* (New York: Harper & Row, 1985), pp. 52–74, 243–76; S.F. Lawson, *Black ballots: voting rights in the South, 1944–1969* (New York: Columbia University Press, 1976), p. 331; S.F. Lawson, *Running for freedom: civil rights and black politics in America since 1941* (New York: McGraw-Hill, 1991), p. 203.
3. A. Hacker, *Two nations: black and white, separate, hostile, unequal* (New York, Ballantine, 1995), pp. 107–9.
4. Useful critiques of the continuing black economic predicament are A. Pinkney, *The myth of black progress* (Cambridge: Cambridge University Press, 1986), and B. Landry, *The new black middle class* (Berkeley: University of California Press, 1987). See also Blackwell, *The black community*, esp. pp. 31–80, 117–49.
5. T. Blair, *Retreat to the ghetto* (New York: Hill & Wang, 1977), p. 242. Lawson, *Running for freedom*, p. 203. H. Sitkoff, *The struggle for black equality, 1954–1992*, revd edn (New York: Hill & Wang, 1993), p. 221. See also R. Weisbrot,

Freedom bound: a history of America's civil rights movement (New York: Plume, 1990), pp. 288–318.

6. For the triumph of conservatism in Mississippi, see J. Dittmer, *Local people: the struggle for civil rights in Mississippi* (Urbana: University of Illinois Press, 1994). For black mayors, see Lawson, *Running for freedom*, pp. 164–82.

7. For the Nixon-Ford administrations and race, see Lawson, *Running for freedom*, pp. 136–40, 183–9; Sitkoff, *Struggle for black equality*, pp. 212–14.

8. Lawson, *Running for freedom*, p. 140.

9. See Hacker, *Two nations*, pp. 166–71; Sitkoff, *Struggle for black equality*, p. 224. See also G. Orfield, *Must we bus?: segregated schools and national policy* (Washington, D.C.: Brookings Institution, 1978).

10. A.P. Sindler, *Bakke, DeFunis, and minority admissions: the quest for equal opportunity* (New York: Longman, 1978).

11. M.L. King, *Where do we go from here: chaos or community?* (New York: Bantam, 1967), p. 153.

12. Weisbrot, *Freedom bound*, p. xiii.

13. For a generally balanced overview of Karenga and cultural nationalism, see W. Van DeBurg, *New day in Babylon: the black power movement and American culture* (Chicago: University of Chicago Press, 1992), pp. 170–91.

14. See F. Fanon, *The wretched of the earth* (New York: Grove, 1968); F. Fanon, *Black skins, white masks* (New York: Grove, 1968).

15. Stanley Wise, interview with Brian Ward & Jenny Walker, 19 October 1995, University of Newcastle Oral History Collection (hereinafter, UNOHC).

16. A.Y. Davis, "Black nationalism: the cartoon and the minstrels", in *Black popular culture: a project by Michele Wallace*, G. Dent (ed.) (Seattle: Bay, 1992), p. 320.

17. For a while Brown even used two drummers, John "Jabo" Starks and Clyde Stubblefield. According to Brown, Stubblefield's meeting with the Nigerian musician Fela Kuti in Lagos was an influence on the rhythmic conceptions at the heart of the new funk. But then again, so were jazz drummers like Kenny Clark and Elvin Jones who "dropped bombs" in explosive rhythmic clusters, while Fela Kuti's own high-life music was already heavily indebted to Western rock and r&b influences, not least Brown's own brand of soul. J. Brown (with B. Tucker), *James Brown: the godfather of soul* (Glasgow: Fontana, 1988), p. 221.

18. F. Kofsky, *Black nationalism and the revolution in music* (New York: Pathfinder, 1970), p. 43.

19. R. Vincent, *Funk: the music, the people, and the rhythm of the one* (New York: St Martin's, 1996), pp. 37–8.

20. *Ibid.*, pp. 188–90.

21. *Ibid.*, pp. 57–8.

22. *Ibid.*, pp. 19, 6. In truth, historical accuracy is not among Vincent's many virtues: his civil rights movement starts with "the Desegregation Act of 1954" (there was no such "Act"), picks up momentum with the Greensboro, South Carolina sit-ins (Greensboro is in North Carolina), and ends with the decade's final piece of major legislation – the 1969 civil rights act against housing discrimination (it was actually passed in 1968). *Ibid.*, pp. 47–8.

23. Vincent, *Funk*, p. 4.

24. George Clinton quoted in G. Tate, *Flyboy in the buttermilk* (New York: Fireside, 1992), p. 39.

25. See Vincent, *Funk*, p. 37.

26. George Clinton quoted in *Amsterdam News*, 10 September 1977, p. 10.

27. Wilson Pickett quoted in G. Hirshey, *Nowhere to run* (New York: Macmillan, 1984), p. 314.
28. This account of Sly Stone's career draws on B. Fong-Torres, "Everybody is a star: the travels of Sylvester Stewart", *Rolling Stone*, 19 March 1970, pp. 28–34; G. Marcus, *Mystery train: images of America in rock 'n' roll music* (New York: Omnibus, 1977), pp. 75–111; D. Marsh, "Sly and the Family Stone" (1980), in *Fortunate son* (New York: Random House, 1985), pp. 55–60; T. Cruse, "Sly Stone: the struggle for his soul" (1971), in *What's that sound?: the contemporary music scene from the pages of Rolling Stone*, B. Fong-Torres (ed.) (New York: Anchor, 1976), pp. 289–303.
29. Sly Stone (Sylvester Stewart) quoted in Fong-Torres, "Everybody is a star", p. 29.
30. *San Francisco Oracle*, 9 February 1967, cited in C. Perry, *The Haight-Ashbury* (New York: Vintage, 1985), p. 138.
31. Marsh, "Sly and the Family Stone", p. 59.
32. P. Guralnick, *Feel like going home* (London: Omnibus, 1979), p. 31.
33. See *Rolling Stone*, 30 January 1970, pp. 14–30.
34. L. Jones (I.A. Baraka), *Black music* (New York: Wm Morrow, 1967), pp. 207–8.
35. See N. George, *The death of rhythm and blues* (New York: Omnibus, 1988), pp. 121, 136. *New York Times*, 7 January 1978, p. D-13.
36. See P. Garland, *The sound of soul* (Chicago: Regnery, 1969), p. 194; *Ebony*, October 1967, p. 47. Aretha Franklin quoted in Hirshey, *Nowhere to run*, p. 242. See also M. Bego *Aretha Franklin: the queen of soul* (London: Hale, 1989), pp. 87–9, 102–3.
37. René DeKnight quoted in *Ebony*, October 1967, p. 153.
38. Stevie Wonder, interview with Chris Welch (1972), in *Melody Maker file*, R. Coleman (ed.) (London: IPC, 1974), p. 12.
39. Marvin Gaye quoted in J. Ryan, *Recollections – the Detroit years: the Motown sound by the people who made it* (Detroit: the author, 1982), profile 8; Marvin Gaye quoted in D. Ritz, *Divided soul: the life of Marvin Gaye* (New York: McGraw-Hill, 1986), p. 110.
40. Marvin Gaye quoted in *ibid.*, pp. 110, 51.
41. Smokey Robinson quoted in M. Bane, *White boy singing the blues* (London: Penguin, 1982), p. 163. S. Robinson (with D. Ritz), *Smokey: inside my life* (London: Headline, 1989), p. 179.
42. For WHUR and the *Quiet Storm* programming, see George, *Death of rhythm and blues*, pp. 131–5.
43. E. Cleaver, *Soul on ice* (New York: Dell, 1968), p. 61.
44. G. Jackson, *Soledad brother* (New York: Coward McCann, 1971), pp. 62–4, 118, 220. Under the influence of Angela Davis and others, Jackson would later retract some of these misogynistic rants. W.H. Grier & P.M. Cobbs, *Black rage* (New York: Basic, 1968), p. 62.
45. See E. Brown, *A taste of power: a black woman's story* (New York: Pantheon, 1992); D. Hilliard (with L. Cole), *This side of glory: the autobiography of David Hilliard and the story of the Black Panthers* (Boston: Little, Brown, 1993). H. Pearson, *The shadow of the panther: Huey Newton and the price of black power in America* (Reading, Mass.: Addison-Wesley, 1994).
46. A. Davis, *Angela Davis: an autobiography* (London: Hutchinson, 1975), p. 161. King, *Where do we go from here*, pp. 44–5.
47. The idea that progressive black protest politics was subsumed by macho posturing in the black power era is discussed in Michele Wallace's controversial diatribe,

Black macho and the myth of the superwoman (London: J. Calder/Platform, 1979). For critical assessments of Wallace's work, see b. hooks, *Ain't I a woman?: black women and feminism* (Boston: South End Press, 1981); M. Marable, *How capitalism underdeveloped black America* (Boston: Pluto, 1983), esp. pp. 69–103. Clayborne Carson offers a broader critique of black power's counterfeit radicalism and chauvinism, contrasting it with the genuinely radical idealism and mass activism of the early civil rights era, in C. Carson, "Black political thought in the post-revolutionary era", in *The making of Martin Luther King and the civil rights movement*, B. Ward & T. Badger (eds) (New York: New York University Press, 1996), pp. 115–27.

48. I. Hoare, "Mighty, mighty spade and whitey: black lyrics and soul's interaction with white culture", in *The soul book*, I. Hoare (ed.) (London: Eyre Methuen, 1975), p. 137.

49. For the importance of what he calls a "ghetto-specific" black male archetype, see U. Hannerz, *Soulside* (New York: Columbia University Press, 1969), p. 74; also pp. 70–117. The sexual politics of soul in the late 1960s and 1970s are discussed in P. Freudiger & E.M. Almquist, "Male and female roles in the lyrics of three genres of contemporary music", *Sex Roles* **41**, 1978, pp. 51–65; N. Kimberley, "Paranoid Sex in 60s soul", *Collusion* **2**, February-April 1982, pp. 9–11; J.B. Stewart, "Relationships between black males and females in rhythm and blues music of the 1960s and 1970s", in *More than dancing: essays on Afro-American music and musicians*, I.V. Jackson (ed.) (Westport: Greenwood, 1985), pp. 169–86; Hoare, "Mighty, mighty", pp. 117–68.

50. James Brown quoted in *London Times*, 11 March 1971, p. 13. C. Rose, *Living in America: the soul saga of James Brown* (London: Serpent's Tail, 1990), p. 21. *Los Angeles Times*, 9 January 1996, p. B 3.

51. D. Caute, *Sixty-eight* (London: Hamish Hamilton, 1988), p. 235. G. Lerner, *The creation of patriarchy* (New York: Oxford University Press, 1986), p. 213.

52. D. Cameron, *Feminism and linguistic theory* (London: Macmillan, 1987), p. 77.

53. D. Bogle, *Toms, coons, mulattos, mammies & bucks: an interpretive history of blacks in American films*, 3rd edn (Oxford: Roundhouse, 1994), p. 240.

54. *Ibid.*, pp. 240, 251, 242 (see generally pp. 231–52).

55. Hacker, *Two nations*, p. 74.

56. Margaret Wright quoted in G. Lerner (ed.), *Black women in white America: a documentary history* (New York: Vintage, 1973), pp. 606–7.

57. Chaka Walls quoted in Caute, *Sixty-eight*, p. 238. See also Brown, *A taste of power*, p. 137; Marable, *How capitalism underdeveloped black America*, pp. 86–103.

58. N. Giovanni, "Beautiful black men" (1968), in *The black poets*, D. Randall (ed.) (New York: Bantam, 1981), pp. 320–1. Florence Grier quoted in B. Blauner, *Black lives, white lives* (Berkeley: University of California Press, 1989), pp. 28–9.

Chapter Ten

1. Malcolm X, "The ballot or the bullet" (1964), Malcolm X, *The Ballot or the Bullet* (Paul Winley Records LP135, n.d.).

2. C. Carson, "Black political thought in the post-revolutionary era", in *The making of Martin Luther King and the civil rights movement*, B. Ward & T. Badger (eds) (New York: New York University Press, 1996), pp. 115–27.

3. "Minutes of CORE special steering committee meeting", 15 January 1965, box 27, folder: CORE, 1961–1965, Harry G. Boyte papers. Alan Gartner, Memo to N[ational] A[dvisory] C[ommittee], n.d. [October 1965], B-I-13, CORE papers Addendum (hereinafter, CORE-Add).

4. See J. Brown (with B. Tucker), *James Brown: the godfather of soul* (Glasgow: Fontana, 1988), pp. 166–9; C. Rose, *Living in America: the soul saga of James Brown* (London: Serpent's Tail, 1990), p. 55. Donald Warden, interview with Robert Martin, 25 July 1969, Ralph J. Bunche Oral History Collection.

5. *Ibid.*

6. *Ibid.*

7. L. Jones (I.A. Baraka), *Raise, race, rays, raze: essays since 1965* (New York: Vintage, 1972), pp. 125–32. James Brown quoted in *Baltimore Afro-American*, 23 March 1968, in Press Clippings: 1965–68, James Brown Collection.

8. Rose, *Living in America*, p. 67. See also James Bond, interview with Brian Ward, 18 October 1995, University of Newcastle Oral History Collection (hereinafter, UNOHC).

9. James Brown quoted in *Jet*, 26 December 1968, pp. 55/56.

10. L. Neal, "The social background to the black arts movement", *Black Scholar* **18**(1), 1987, p. 19. James Brown quoted in D. Ehrlich, "James Brown interview", *Details* (July 1991), p. 56. At the end of the 1960s, Brown earned $4.5 million annually, owned his own publishing company (Try Me Music), production company (James Brown Productions), recording company (Fair Deal Recordings), and three radio stations. Beyond the entertainment world he owned a chain of soul food and chicken restaurants called Gold Platter, had shares in a number of securities operations and apartment block developments, and had his own beloved Lear Jet. See P. Garland, *The sound of soul* (Chicago: Regnery, 1969), p. 36.

11. See Brown, *The godfather of soul*, p. 203.

12. Fred Wesley quoted in Rose, *Living in America*, pp. 21–2.

13. James Brown quoted in P.T. Drotning, *Up from the ghetto* (New York: Regnery, 1970), p. 83.

14. See Rose, *Living in America*, p. 67; R. Vincent, *Funk: the music, the people, and the rhythm of the one* (New York: St Martin's, 1996), p. 78.

15. Stanley Levison, telephone conversation with Bill Stein, 19 October 1966, The Martin Luther King, Jr FBI File, part II: the King-Levison File (hereinafter, FBI:K-L).

16. "Stars for freedom programme, 1967", box 123, folder 27, SCLC papers (hereinafter SCLC). Stanley Levison, telephone conversation with Martin Luther King, 29 October 1966. Bill Stein, telephone conversation with Stanley Levison, 24 October 1967; Stanley Levison, telephone conversations with Chauncey Eskridge, 30 October 1967; Dora McDonald and Bill Rutherford, 18 March 1968; Adele Kanter, 25 March 1968, all references FBI:K-L.

17. Junius Griffin, interview with Brian Ward, 22 July 1996, UNOHC.

18. B. Gordy, *To be loved: the music, the magic, the memories of Motown: an autobiography* (New York: Warner, 1994), pp. 250–1; Griffin interview.

19. Coretta Scott King, telephone conversation with Stanley Levison, 15 May 1968; Junius Griffin, telephone conversation with Stanley Levison, 13 April 1968, both FBI:K-L.

20. *Ibid.* Stanley Levison, telephone conversation with Tom Ossenburger, 19 April 1968, FBI:K-L.

21. Mickey Stevenson quoted in J.R. Taraborelli, *Motown: hot wax, city soul and solid gold* (New York: Doubleday, 1986), p. 11. Gordy, *To be loved*, pp. 250–1, photo 48; R.D. Abernathy, *And the walls came tumbling down* (New York: HarperPerennial, 1990), pp. 522–8; B.W. Gilbert et al., *Ten blocks from the White House* (New York: Praeger, 1968), pp. 200–1; Taraborelli, *Motown*, pp. 59, 62. P. Benjaminson, *The story of Motown* (New York: Grove, 1978), p. 105.

22. John Conyers, "News release", 25 February 1969, box 47, folder 24, SCLC. C. Carson et al. (eds), *The papers of Martin Luther King, Jr. vol. 2: rediscovering precious values, July 1951–November 1955* (Berkeley: University of California Press, 1994).

23. J.R. Taraborelli, *Michael Jackson: the magic and the madness* (New York: Birch Lane, 1991), p. 79. This account of Gordy and Motown's politics in the black power era draws heavily on N. George, *Where did our love go?* (New York: St Martin's, 1986); Gordy, *To be loved*; Benjaminson, *The story of Motown*; D. Morse, *Motown and the arrival of black music* (London: November, 1971); J. Ryan, *Recollections – the Detroit years: the Motown sound by the people who made it* (Detroit: the author, 1982); J.R. Taraborelli, *Motown*; G. Hirshey, *Nowhere to run* (New York: Macmillan, 1984), pp. 184–92.

24. See Benjaminson, *The story of Motown*, p. 75. Black Forum featured *Writers of the Revolution* by Langston Hughes and Margaret Danner; *Black Spirits* – an album of new black poetry recorded live at the Apollo by the likes of Baraka, David Henderson, Larry Neal and Stanley Crouch; *It's Nation Time*, again featuring the poetry of Baraka, with the "African visionary music" of James Mtume, Idris Muhammed and Lonnie Tison Smith. In addition to these examples of black cultural nationalism, the label released *Free Huey* by Stokely Carmichael, and *Guess Who's Coming Home* by the Black Fighting Men – an album of interviews with black soldiers in Vietnam. Black Forum's only single release was "No time" by Elaine Brown, who also recorded an eponymous album for the label.

25. Taraborelli, *Michael Jackson*, p. 40; Taraborelli, *Motown*, p. 116; L. Jones (I.A. Baraka), *The autobiography of LeRoi Jones/Amiri Baraka* (New York: Freundlich, 1984), p. 283.

26. See Benjaminson, *The story of Motown*, p. 105. Gordy, *To be loved*, pp. 248–9.

27. Benjaminson, *The story of Motown*, p. 105; Taraborelli, *Motown*, pp. 68–9.

28. Benjaminson, *The story of Motown*, p. 105; Taraborelli, *Motown*, pp. 68–9.

29. Rare Earth was originally an outlet for recordings by the group of the same name, but later featured other white acts like R. Dean Taylor, Toe Fat and Sounds Nice. MoWest was founded in 1971, again with an avowedly pop-rock orientation, although the Commodores, Syreeta and Thelma Houston also made their first Motown recordings for this Los Angeles-based subsidiary. The country-oriented Melodyland label (later renamed Hitsville) maintained Motown's remarkable hit-making rate by claiming 12 country hits with its first 16 releases.

30. Taraborelli, *Motown*, p. 58.

31. *Amsterdam News*, 29 July 1967, p. 18; Benjaminson, *The story of Motown*, p. 114; Taraborelli, *Motown*, p. 57.

32. George, *Where did our love go?*, p. 55. See also *ibid.*, pp. 46–64, 86, 139.

33. Jesse Jackson quoted in Taraborelli, *Motown*, p. 71; see also *Chicago Defender*, 6 October 1969, pp. 1, 3/20; *ibid.*, 29 September 1971, p. 13.

34. Berry Gordy quoted in Taraborelli, *Motown*, p. 119; see also *Chicago Defender*, 29 September 1971, p. 13.

35. Stanley Levison, telephone conversations with unidentified, 2 June 1968; unidentified, 29 June 1968; Coretta Scott King, 29 June 1969, all references FBI:K-L.

36. Jerry Wexler quoted in M. Bego, *Aretha Franklin: the queen of soul* (London: Robert Hale, 1990), pp. 108–9; J. Wexler & D. Ritz, *Rhythm and the blues: a life in American music* (New York: A. Knopf, 1993), p. 215. See also Griffin interview.

37. Stanley Wise, interview with Brian Ward & Jenny Walker, 19 October 1995. Gloria Fraction, Memo to Martin Luther King Jr, 26 October 1966, box 128, folder 9; "SCLC banquet", 2 August 1967, box 133, folder 9, both references SCLC. Bego, *Aretha Franklin*, pp. 107–8.

38. Joseph X (Tex) quoted in *Greensboro A&T College Register*, 22 September 1972, p. 1.

39. *Ibid.*, 6 October 1972, p. 7.

40. See L. Hilderbrand, *Stars of soul and rhythm and blues* (New York: Billboard, 1994), pp. 169–70. Osborne became a major solo star in the 1980s, when, ironically, he smoothed off much of L.T.D.'s r&b edge in favour of a poppier soul balladry aimed at the crossover market, but then found only modest white success, compared with his succession of black hit singles, like "I really don't need no light" and "She's on the left". *Billboard*, 25 April 1970, p. 78.

41. For Wattstax, see *Jet* (September 1972), pp. 52–7; *Billboard*, 19 August 1972, pp. 3/8; *ibid.*, 2 September 1972, p. 66. See also P. Guralnick, *Sweet soul music: rhythm and blues and the southern dream of freedom* (London: Virgin, 1986), pp. 387–8.

42. See George, *Death of rhythm and blues*, p. 140.

43. Larry Shaw quoted in *Billboard*, 19 August 1972, p. 3.

44. *Los Angeles Sentinel*, 27 July 1972, p. B-3A; *ibid.*, 17 August 1972, p. B-1; *Chicago Defender*, 21 August 1972, pp. 4/20.

45. J. Jackson, "Introduction", on *Wattstax: The Living Word*, Stax STS-2–3010 (1972).

46. Isaac Hayes quoted in *Washington Post*, 24 September 1995, p. G-6.

47. *Memphis Press-Scimitar*, 9 May 1972; *ibid.*, 1 February 1972, both references from Memphis and Shelby County Room Clippings File: "Isaac Hayes" (hereinafter, M&SC-File: Hayes).

48. *Rolling Stone*, 17 February 1972, pp. 14–16. *Memphis Press-Scimitar*, 1 February 1972, M&SC-File: Hayes.

49. *Memphis Commercial Appeal*, 19 September 1974; 20 September 1974; 11 September 1976; 21 January 1977; *Memphis Press-Scimitar*, 11 November 1976; 6 May 1977; 1 February 1978. All references M&SC-File: Hayes.

50. L. Neal, "The Black Arts movement", *Drama Review* **12** (Summer 1968), pp. 29–40. W. Van DeBurg, *New day in Babylon: the black power movement and American culture* (Chicago: University of Chicago Press, 1992), pp. 175, 181. See also J. Runcie, "The black culture movement and the black community", *Journal of American Studies* **10** (1976), pp. 185–214.

51. Carson, "Black political thought", p. 122.

52. H. Cruse, *The crisis of the Negro intellectual* (New York: Wm Morrow, 1967), p. 86.

53. Maulana Ron Karenga quoted in *The quotable Karenga*, C. Halisi (ed.) (Los Angeles: US Organization, 1967), pp. 29, 10.

54. R. Milner, "Black magic, black art", *Negro Digest* **16** (1967), pp. 9–12.

55. Jones, *Raise, race, rays, raze*, p. 33; J.T. Stewart, "The development of the revolutionary black artist" in *Black fire: an anthology of Afro-American writing*, L. Jones (I.A. Baraka) and L. Neal (eds) (New York: Wm Morrow, 1968), pp. 3–9.

56. L.P. Nahs, "Black musician in white America", *Negro Digest* **16** (March 1967), pp. 56–7. For the importance of the white jazz audience, see also B. Sidran, *Black talk* (New York: Da Capo, 1981), p. 145.
57. A.B. Spellman, "Not just whistling Dixie", in Jones & Neal (eds), *Black fire*, p. 167.
58. Emory Douglas quoted in *Black Panther*, 22 November 1969, p. 6.
59. Elaine Brown quoted in *ibid.*, p. 17.
60. *Ibid.*, 12 September 1970, p. 8.
61. See *ibid.*, 26 September 1970, p. 18.
62. *Ibid.*, 7 November 1970, p. 12.
63. *Ibid.*, Curtis Mayfield quoted in *Soul*, 22 September 1969, p. 16. For the politics of pleasure in pop, see S. Frith, *Sound effects: youth, leisure, and the politics of rock 'n' roll* (London: Constable, 1984), pp. 164–5.
64. For the People's Songsters' responses to the political demands upon their music, see R. Lieberman, *"My song is my weapon": people's songs, American communism, and the politics of culture* (Urbana: University of Illinois Press, 1995), esp. pp. 59, 89–94.
65. *Billboard*, 25 April 1970, p. 78.

Chapter Eleven

1. Huey Newton, "Black capitalism re-analyzed", *Black Panther*, 5 June 1971, p. B.
2. The best account of Philly Soul is T. Cummings, *The sound of Philadelphia* (London: Methuen, 1975), esp. pp. 86–120. See also N. George, *The death of rhythm and blues* (New York: Omnibus, 1988), pp. 142–6; T. McGrath, "Soul survivors", *Seven Arts* (October 1995), pp. 41–2.
3. Kenneth Gamble quoted in Cummings, *Sound of Philadelphia*, pp. 108, 107.
4. McGrath, "Soul survivors", p. 41.
5. George, *Death of rhythm and blues*, p. 145.
6. *Ibid.*, p. 145 (and generally pp. 121–9); A. Millard, *America on record: a history of recorded sound* (Cambridge: Cambridge University Press, 1995), pp. 333–5.
7. George, *Death of rhythm and blues*, pp. 135–8; R. Sanjek, *American popular music and its business*, vol. 3 (New York: Oxford University Press, 1988), p. 555.
8. George, *Death of rhythm and blues*, p. 168; Sanjek, *American popular music*, pp. 555–6.
9. *Soul Train* is discussed in R. Vincent, *Funk: the music, the people, and the rhythm of the one* (New York: St Martin's, 1996), pp. 169–70.
10. *Variety*, 3 March 1971, pp. 1/70; *ibid.*, 26 April 1972, pp. 1/70. *New York Times*, 6 June 1973, pp. 1/51. For the 1970s payola investigations see K. Segrave, *Payola in the music industry: a history, 1880–1991* (Jefferson, N.C.: McFarland, 1994), pp. 166–94; Sanjek, *American popular music*, pp. 553–8.
11. Lucky Cordell quoted in *New York Times*, 9 June 1973, p. 3.
12. E. Jesmer, *Number one with a bullet* (New York: Farrar, Straus & Giroux, 1974). The rumours against Motown are discussed in P. Benjaminson, *The story of Motown* (New York: Grove, 1978), pp. 49–51, 95.
13. *Broadcasting*, 30 June 1975, pp. 27–9; *ibid.*, 29 August 1977, pp. 42–3; *New York Times*, 5 June 1975, pp. 1/40; *Rolling Stone*, 31 July 1975, p. 13; *ibid.*, 13 April

1976, p. 66; *Variety*, 2 July 1975, pp. 1/40. Segrave, *Payola*, pp. 184–7; Sanjek, *American popular music*, pp. 556–7.

14. *New York Times*, 23 July 1976, p. D-13; *Rolling Stone*, 21 April 1977, pp. 19–20. Segrave, *Payola*, pp. 187–8.

15. Roy Innis quoted in *New York Times*, 15 August 1973, p. 75.

16. B. Gordy, *To be loved: the music, the magic, the memories of Motown: an autobiography* (New York: Warner, 1994), pp. 389–98.

17. *Billboard*, 8 May 1971, p. 74; *ibid.*, 19 April 1975, p. C-6. See also R. Pruter, *Chicago soul* (Urbana: University of Illinois Press, 1991).

18. George, *Death of rhythm and blues*, p. 149.

19. W. Hughes, "In the empire of the beat: discipline and disco", in *Microphone fiends: youth music and youth culture*, A. Ross and T. Rose (eds) (New York: Routledge, 1994), pp. 147–57. See also R. Dyer, "In defense of disco", in *On the record*, S. Frith & A. Goodwin (eds) (London: Routledge, 1990), pp. 410–18.

20. Bernie Edwards quoted in *Amsterdam News*, 22 April 1978, p. D-6.

21. *New York Times*, 28 January 1978, pp. D2–3. George, *Death of rhythm and blues*, p. 157.

22. *Ibid.*, p. 153.

23. Jeff Lane quoted in *Amsterdam News*, 28 January 1978, p. 3. Bernard Edwards quoted in *ibid.*, 22 April 1978, p. D-6.

24. D. Berkman, "The segregated medium", *Columbia Journalism Review*, **5**(30), Fall 1966, pp. 29–32.

25. Letter from M.S. Lottman, *ibid.*, **5**(31), Winter 1966/67, pp. 54–5.

26. B. Garnett, *How soulful is "soul" radio?* (Nashville: Race Relations Information Center, 1970), p. 2.

27. *Ebony*, November 1967, p. 76; *ibid.*, August 1970, p. 30; William Wright quoted in Garnett, *How soulful*, p. 14. See also A. Meyer, *Black voices and format regulations: a study in black-oriented radio* (Stanford: ERIC Clearinghouse on Media and Technology, 1971).

28. For black radio ownership figures, see U. Gupta, "Integrating the airwaves", *Black Enterprise* (June 1982), pp. 125–7; S. Surlin, "Ascertainment of community needs by black-oriented radio stations", *Journal of Broadcasting* **16**(4), Fall 1972, p. 421. C. Hamilton, "Blacks and mass media", *Columbia Forum*, Winter 1971. (rpt) in *Issues and trends in Afro-America Journalism*, J.S. Tinney & J. Rector (eds) (Lanham, Md.: University Press of America, 1980), p. 226.

29. H. Cruse, *The crisis of the Negro intellectual* (New York: Wm Morrow, 1967). J. Forman, *The making of black revolutionaries* (New York: Macmillan, 1972), p. 459. L. Jones (I.A. Baraka) (ed.), *African congress: a documentary history of the first modern pan-African congress* (New York: Wm Morrow, 1972), pp. 451–7.

30. R.F. Williams, "Forward", in "*Radio Free Dixie*", unpublished manuscript, box 1, folder: Oct–Nov 1966, Robert F. Williams papers. Robert Williams quoted in R.C. Cohen, *Black crusader: a biography of Robert Franklin Williams* (Secaucus, N.J.: Lyle Stuart, 1972), pp. 210–11. See also T. Tyson, *Radio Free Dixie: Robert F. Williams and the roots of black power* (PhD thesis, Duke University, 1994).

31. *Washington Post*, 1 September 1966, p. B-1; *Jet*, 28 September 1972, p. 16.

32. *New York Times*, 6 December 1969, p. 75; *Jet*, 31 December 1970, p. 18; *ibid.*, 28 September 1972, p. 16.

33. Del Shields quoted in *ibid.*, 10 August 1967, p. 56.

34. U. Hannerz, *Soulside* (New York: Columbia University Press, 1969), p. 172. Del Shields quoted in George, *Death of rhythm and blues*, p. 111.

35. See Meyer, *Black voices*, p. 3. *New York Times*, 11 November 1968, p. 17. Norm Brewer quoted in *Billboard*, 20 April 1968, p. 74.

36. *Ibid.*, 12 August 1967, p. 3. *Ibid.*, 29 June 1968, pp. 18/30. Robert Meeker quoted in *New York Times*, 11 November 1968, p. 17.

37. Leon Lewis quoted in *Newsweek*, 8 May 1967. See also *Time*, 4 September 1966, p. 23; *New York Times*, 1 December 1968, p. 79.

38. The NATRA "uprising" is discussed in P. Guralnick, *Sweet soul music: rhythm and blues and the southern dream of freedom* (London: Virgin, 1986), pp. 381–5; J. Wexler & D. Ritz, *Rhythm and the blues: a life in American music* (New York: A. Knopf, 1993), pp. 227–9; George, *Death of rhythm and blues*, pp. 111–15; J. Picardie & D. Wade, *Atlantic and the godfathers of rock and roll*, revd edn (London: Fourth Estate, 1993), pp. 161–5; "Where the Negro DJ stands", *Broadcasting*, 19 August 1968, p. 36; "Swing to Negro activism", *ibid.*, 26 August 1968, pp. 30–1.

39. Homer Banks quoted in Guralnick, *Sweet soul music*, pp. 383–4; Del Shields quoted in *Billboard*, 24 August 1968, pp. 1/66.

40. *Ibid.*, p. 66.

41. Benjaminson, *The story of Motown*, p. 105. Alvin Dixon quoted in *Jet*, 5 October 1972, pp. 21–2.

42. For NBMC, see D. Ellis, "Communications at the crossroads: parity and perceptions of minority participation", unpublished paper (Washington, D.C.: National Association of Broadcasters, 1987), p. 14.

43. For BMA, see George, *Death of rhythm and blues*, pp. 165–7; *Amsterdam News*, 5 July 1980, p. 46.

44. Walter Fauntroy quoted in *Washington Post*, 7 May 1967, pp. 26–7. See M. Haralambos, *Right on: from blues to soul in black America* (New York: Drake, 1975), p. 93; Meyer, *Black voices*, p. 5; J. L. Dates & W. Barlow, *Split image: African-Americans in the mass media* (Washington, D.C.: Howard University Press, 1990), p. 221.

45. The corruption of the Black Panthers' initial progressive promise is described in H. Pearson, *The shadow of the panther: Huey Newton and the price of black power in America* (Reading, Mass.: Addison-Wesley, 1994).

46. Harold Battiste, interview with Brian Ward, 8 November 1995, University of Newcastle upon Tyne Oral History Collection (hereinafter UNOHC).

47. Joseph Lackey, interview with Brian Ward, 26 October 1995, UNOHC.

48. Picardie and Wade, *Godfathers of rock and roll*, p. 174 (and generally pp. 161–89).

49. Al Bell quoted in P. Garland, *The sound of soul* (Chicago: Regnery, 1969), p. 134. For accounts of Stax's demise, see Guralnick, *Sweet soul music*, pp. 353–74, 385–94; Picardie and Wade, *Godfathers of rock and roll*, pp. 161–89. See also Clippings File: Stax Records, M&SC.

50. Lackey interview.

51. For the Stax-CBS deal, see Guralnick, *Sweet soul music*, pp. 385–92; C. Davis (with J. Willwerth), *Clive: inside the record business* (New York: Ballantine, 1974), pp. 168–9. Picardie and Wade, *Godfathers of rock and roll*, pp. 187–9.

52. See *Memphis Press-Scimitar*, 20 June 1973; *ibid.*, 28 July 1973; *Memphis Commercial Appeal*, 7 February 1976; *ibid.*, 26 October 1978, all references, Clippings File: Stax Records, M&SC.

53. *Ibid.*, 10 April 1975, 9 February 1976, 3 August 1976; *Memphis Press-Scimitar*, 17 February 1975, 22 July 1976, 3 August 1976, all references, Clippings File: Stax Records, M&SC.

54. Picardie & Wade, *Godfathers of rock and roll*, pp. 187-9. Ralph Abernathy quoted in *Memphis Press-Scimitar*, 24 September 1975. Billy Kyles quoted in *ibid.*, 27 December 1975, both references, Clippings File: Stax Records, M&SC.

55. *Memphis Commercial Appeal*, 22 July 1973; *Memphis Press-Scimitar*, 20 May 1974, all references, Clippings File: Stax Records, M&SC.

56. *Memphis Commercial Appeal*, 9 February 1976, Clippings File: Stax Records, M&SC.

57. *Memphis Press-Scimitar*, 5 June 1982, Clippings File: Stax Records, M&SC.

58. *Jet*, 31 July 1969, p. 47. Figures concerning the cost of WLIB vary from $1.9 million (*Amsterdam News*, 17 July 1971, pp. 1/D11), to "an estimated 1.7 million dollars" (*Jet*, 13 July 1972, p. 98).

59. See *Amsterdam News*, 17 July, pp. 1/D11; L. Lewis, "Harlem's biggest business", *Sepia* (August 1978), pp. 33-5. Meyer, *Black voices*; R. Alston, "Black-owned radio: taking to the airwaves in a hurry", *Black Enterprise* (July 1978), pp. 20-5; L. Bogart, "Black is often white", *Mediascope* 3(11), November 1978, pp. 53-60. J. Blackwell, *The black community: diversity and change*, 2nd edn (New York: Harper & Row, 1985), pp. 233-5.

60. George, *Death of rhythm and blues*, pp. 132-5.

61. Newton, "Black capitalism re-analyzed", pp. A-D.

62. Harry Belafonte, interview with Brian Ward, 12 March 1996, UNOHC.

63. For Blayton's early career under the mentorship of Perry, see A.B. Henderson, "Heman E. Perry and black enterprise in Atlanta, 1908-1925", *Business History Review* Summer 1987, pp. 216-42. Mack Saddler, interview with Brian Ward, 19 October 1995, UNOHC.

64. For the history of WERD, see G. Blackwell, *Black-controlled media in Atlanta, 1960-70: the burden of the message and the struggle for survival* (PhD thesis, Emory University, 1973); *Chicago Defender*, 24 September 1949, p. 1; *ibid.*, 17 December 1949, p. 13; *Pittsburgh Courier*, 15 October 1949; *ibid.*, 17 December 1949, p. 30; *Jet*, 24 June 1954, p. 60; *ibid.*, 22 October 1959, p. 58; "WERD: the first black-owned radio station in the USA", *Black Radio Exclusive*, 15 June 1979, pp. 12-13.

65. Saddler interview. William Fowlkes, interview with Brian Ward, 18 October 1995; Esmond Patterson, interview with Brian Ward & Jenny Walker, 19 October 1995, all UNOHC.

66. Martin Luther King, letter to Benjamin Mays, 4 May 1960, box 31, folder 18a (2a of 3), Martin Luther King papers (hereinafter MLK). See also Jesse Blayton, "Statement" to Judge Hubert Delany, 29 April 1960, box 4, folder 24; Jesse Blayton letter (incl. "Statement", 8 June 1960) to Martin Luther King, 10 June 1960, box 4, folder 24; Jesse Blayton, letter to W.B. McNeil, 6 July 1960, box 20, folder 10, all references MLK. T. Branch, *Parting the waters: America in the King years, 1954-63* (New York: Simon & Schuster, 1988), pp. 269, 275, 287, 309. Mack Saddler denies that Blayton would have exploited King in this way, but there is little doubt King himself felt disappointed with Blayton's response to his predicament.

67. Saddler interview.

68. Jesse Blayton quoted in Blackwell, *Black-controlled media*, p. 157. *New York Times*, 1 November 1968, p. 17; Saddler interview.

69. *Billboard*, 29 June 1968, pp. 18/30. "SNCC news release", 24 May 1967, C-I-143, SNCC papers. James Bond, interview with Brian Ward, 16 October 1995, UNOHC. See also S. Walsh, "Black-oriented radio and the southern civil rights movement,

1955–1972", unpublished paper (Southern Historical Association Conference, New Orleans, November 1995), copy in possession of the author.

70. Lackey interview. Shelley Stewart, interview with Brian Ward, 26 October 1995, UNOHC.

71. Leonard Evans quoted in *Newsweek*, 18 January 1954, p. 51. Eugene Jackson quoted in *New York Times*, 19 March 1972, p. 12. "National Black Network Press Release", 20 March 1972, Clippings File: "Radio", Schomburg Center for Research in Black Culture. See also *Jet*, 18 May 1972, p. 46.

72. R. Famighetti et al., "Black radio: on a high wire with no net", *Broadcasting*, 31 August 1970, p. 45. Percy Sutton quoted in Alston, "Black-owned radio", p. 21. See also "Black-owned WBLS-FM finds right chemistry for success in US", *Broadcasting*, 5 March 1973, p. 52; "Black progressive WBLS-FM mixes up a magic formula", ibid., p. 54; "Power politics: New York style", *Ebony* (November 1972), p. 172.

73. On Crocker, see George, *Death of rhythm and blues*, pp. 127–31; Segrave, *Payola*, p. 188.

74. Alan Henry quoted in Garnett, *How soulful*, p. 15. Steve Woods quoted in *Sepia* (January 1979), p. 58. For WYLD-New Orleans, see *Wall Street Journal*, 23 September 1987, p. 16.

75. S. Carmichael and C.V. Hamilton, *Black power* (New York: Vintage, 1967), p. 39.

76. J. Jackson, "Introduction", *Wattstax: The Living Word* (Stax STS-2–3010, 1972).

Epilogue

1. While it is beyond the brief of this book to discuss the black popular music of the 1980s and 1990s in any detail, interested readers are directed to the following: H.A. Baker, *Black studies, rap and the academy* (Chicago: University of Chicago Press, 1993); M. Costello & D.F. Wallace, *Signifying rappers: rap and race in the urban present* (New York: Ecco, 1990); M.E. Blair, "Commercialization of the rap music youth subculture", *Journal of Popular Culture* **27**(3), Winter 1993, pp. 21–34; B. Cross, *It's not about a salary: rap, race and resistance in Los Angeles* (London: Verso, 1994); M.E. Dyson, *Between God and gangsta rap: bearing witness to black culture* (New York: Oxford University Press, 1996); J. Farr, *Moguls and madmen: the pursuit of power in popular music* (New York: Simon & Schuster, 1994); S. Hager, *Hip hop: the illustrated history of break dancing, rap music and graffiti* (New York: St Martin's, 1984); N. George, *The death of rhythm and blues* (New York: Omnibus, 1988); N. George, *Stop the violence: overcoming self-destruction* (New York: Pantheon, 1990); N. George, *Buppies, b-boys, baps & bohos* (New York: HarperPerennial, 1994); E.A. Henderson, "Black nationalism and rap music", *Journal of Black Studies* **26**(3), January 1996, pp. 308–39; R. Kelley, *Race Rebels: culture, politics and the black working class* (New York: Free Press, 1996), pp. 183–227; H. Nelson & M.A. Gonzales, *Bring the noise: a guide to rap music and hip-hop culture* (New York: Harmony, 1991); T. Rose, *Black noise: rap music and black culture in contemporary America* (Hanover: Wesleyan University Press, 1994) – the best book on rap yet written; G. Tate, *Flyboy in the buttermilk* (New York: Fireside, 1992); A. White, *The resistance: ten years of pop culture that shook the world* (New York: Overlook, 1995); D. Toop, *The rap attack: African jive to New York hip-hop* (London: Pluto, 1984).

Sources

Primary sources

Manuscript and oral history collections

Fred D. Alexander Papers, Special Collections, J. Murray Atkins Library, University of North Carolina at Charlotte. (FDA)

American Federation of Musicians Papers (Locals 174 and 496), Hogan Jazz Archive, Howard-Tilton Library, Tulane University, New Orleans. (AFM)

Daisy Bates Papers, Special Collections Division, University of Arkansas Libraries, Fayetteville. (DB)

Harold Battiste Papers, Amistad Research Center, Tulane University, New Orleans. (HB)

Birmingham Recorder's Court Records, Birmingham Public Library Archives, Birmingham. (BRCR)

Harry G. Boyte Papers, Manuscript Division, William R. Perkins Library, Duke University, Durham. (HGB)

James Brown Collection, Amistad Research Center, Tulane University, New Orleans. (JBC)

Ralph J. Bunche Oral History Collection, Manuscript Division, Moorland-Springarn Research Center, Howard University, Washington D.C. (RJBOHC)

Congress of Racial Equality Papers, Alderman Library, University of Virginia, Charlottesville. (CORE)

Congress of Racial Equality Papers, 1941–1967, Manuscript Division, Library of Congress, Washington D.C. (CORE: 1941–67)

Congress of Racial Equality Papers, addendum, 1944–1968, Manuscript Division, Library of Congress, Washington D.C. (CORE-Add)

Country Music Clippings File, Country Music, Hall of Fame Archives, Nashville. (CM-File)

Thomas Dent Holdings, Mississippi Oral History Collection, Amistad Research Center, Tulane University, New Orleans. (TDH)

Federal Communications Commission License Renewal Files, FCC Papers, National Archives II, Suitland, Maryland. (FCC)

Fiskiana Collection, Special Collections, Fisk University Library, Fisk University, Nashville. (FC)

Albert Gore Papers, Albert Gore Collection, University of Middle Tennessee, Murfreesboro. (AG)

Lawrence Henry Collection, Division of Photographs and Prints, Schomburg Center for Research in Black Culture, New York. (LH)

Highlander Folk School Papers, Social Action Collection, State Historical Society of Wisconsin. (HFS)

Hogan Jazz Archive Subject Files, Howard-Tilton Library, Tulane University, New Orleans. (HJA-File)

John F. Kennedy Pre-Presidential Papers, John F. Kennedy Library, Boston. (JFK)

The Martin Luther King, Jr FBI File, part II: The King-Levison File, Alderman Library, University of Virginia, Charlottesville. (FBI:K-L)

Martin Luther King Jr Papers, Mugar Memorial Library, Boston University, Boston. (MLK)

Martin Luther King Jr Papers, Printed Matter, Martin Luther King Jr Center for Nonviolent Social Change, Atlanta. (MLK-Atl)

Nell Battle Lewis Papers, North Carolina State Archives, Raleigh. (NBL)

D.R. Matthews Papers, P.K. Yonge Library of Florida History, University of Florida, Gainesville. (DRM)

Memphis Civil Rights Museum, Memphis. (MCRM)

Memphis & Shelby County Room Clippings File, Memphis & Shelby County Library, Memphis. (M&SC-File)

James W. Morgan Mayoral Papers, Birmingham Public Library Archives, Birmingham. (JWM)

Museum of Television and Radio Archive, New York. (MT&R)

National Association for the Advancement of Colored People Papers, Manuscript Division, Library of Congress, Washington D.C. (NAACP)

National Urban League Papers, Manuscript Division, Library of Congress, Washington D.C. (NUL)

Papers of A. Philip Randolph, Manuscript Division, Library of Congress, Washington D.C. (APR)

Frank A. Rose Papers, Special Collections, W.S. Hoole Library, University of Alabama, Tuscaloosa. (FAR)

Bayard T. Rustin Papers, Alderman Library, University of Virginia, Charlottesville. (BTR)

Schomburg Center Clippings File, Schomburg Center for Research in Black Culture, New York. (SC-File)

George A. Smathers Papers, P.K. Yonge Library of Florida History, University of Florida, Gainesville. (GAS)

Kelly Miller Smith Papers, Special Collections, Jean & Alexander Heard Library, Vanderbilt University, Nashville. (KMS)

Southern Christian Leadership Conference Papers, Martin Luther King Jr Center For Nonviolent Social Change, Atlanta. (SCLC)

Southern Folk Cultural Revival Project Papers, Southern Historical Collection, University of North Carolina, Chapel Hill. (SFCRP)

Southern Oral History Program, Southern Historical Collection, University of North Carolina, Chapel Hill. (SOHP)

Student Nonviolent Coordinating Committee Papers, Manuscript Division, Library of Congress, Washington D.C. (SNCC)

Herman E. Talmadge Governor's Papers, Series B, Richard Russell Library, University of Georgia, Athens. (HET)

University of Newcastle upon Tyne Oral History Collection, Department of History, University of Newcastle upon Tyne. (UNOHC)

Robert Franklin Williams Papers, Bentley Historical Library, University of Michigan, Ann Arbor. (RFW)

Printed primary sources

Official government publications

Congressional record, 85th Congress (Washington, D.C.: Government Printing Office, 1957).

Congressional record: appendix, 85th Congress (Washington, D.C.: Government Printing Office, 1957).

County and city data book, 1962: a statistical abstract supplement (US Bureau of Census, Washington, D.C.: Government Printing Office, 1963).

House committee on judiciary: sub-committee on anti-trust monopoly problems in regulated industries, U.S. House of Representatives, 84th Congress, 2 vols (Washington, D.C.: Government Printing Office, 1956/57).

Hearing before the subcommittee on communications of the committee on interstate and foreign commerce: Amendment to the Communications Act of 1934 (prohibiting radio and television stations from engaging in music publishing or record ing business), US Senate, 85th Congress (Washington, D.C.: Government Printing Office, 1958).

House select committee on small business. House sub-committee No. 5: policies of American Society of Composers, Authors and Publishers, US House of Representatives, 85th Congress (Washington, D.C.: Government Printing Office, 1958).

Hearings before a subcommittee of the committee on interstate and foreign commerce: second session on payola and other deceptive practices in the broadcasting field, parts 1 & 2, US House of Representatives, 86th Congress (Washington, D.C.: Government Printing Office, 1960).

Louisiana revised statutes annotated 4:451–55 (Supp. 1956), Act 579.

Martin Luther King vs Mr Maestro Inc. et al., F. Supp. 101, 103, (SDNY, 1963).

Statistical abstract of the United States (Washington, D.C.: Government Printing Office, 1960).

Statistical abstract of the United States (Washington, D.C.: Government Printing Office, 1965).

Statistical abstract of the United States (Washington, D.C.: Government Printing Office, 1970).

Newspapers, magazines and periodicals

American Negro
Amsterdam News
Arkansas Gazette
Atlanta Constitution
Atlanta Inquirer
Atlanta World
Baltimore Afro-American

Billboard
Birmingham News
Birmingham World
Black Enterprise
Black Panther
Black Stars (see also *Tan*)
Black World (see also *Negro Digest*)
Broadcasting
Broadcast Yearbook
Carolina Times
Cashbox
Cavalier Daily (University of Virginia)
Charlotte Observer
Chicago Defender
Corks & Curls (University of Virginia)
Corolla (University of Alabama, Tuscaloosa)
Crimson-White (University of Alabama, Tuscaloosa)
Down Beat
Ebony
Fayetteville Observer
Greensboro A&T College Register
Jacksonville Journal
Jet
Life
Look
London Times
Los Angeles Sentinel
Louisiana Weekly
Melody Maker
Michigan Chronicle
Montgomery Advertiser and Alabama Journal
Muhammad Speaks
Musical America
Negro Digest (see also *Black World*)
New Musical Express
New Orleans Times-Picayune
Newsweek
New York Daily News
New York Post
New York Times
Norfolk Journal and Guide
Our World
Philadelphia Daily News
Pittsburgh Courier
Raleigh News and Observer
Reporter
Richmond Times-Dispatch
Roanoke World News
Rolling Stone
Sepia

Soul
Southerner
Sponsor
Southern Student Organizing Committee Newsletter
Student Voice
Tan (see also *Black Stars*)
Time
Vanderbilt Hustler
Variety
Wall Street Journal
Washington Afro-American

Miscellaneous primary sources

Ed Marciniak Files, selected documents provided by James Ralph.
"A Celebration of Life for Mr Eugene S. 'Genial Gene' Potts: Memorial Service Programme, Little Rock, AME Zion Church, Charlotte, 16 April 1988" (copy provided by Tom Hanchett, in possession of the author).
"Program for 'Genial Gene Day', Charlotte Armory Auditorium, 22 November 1953" (copy provided by Tom Hanchett, in possession of the author).
Rock and Roll: Renegades, Episode 1, PBS-TV documentary, 1995.
Anne Romaine, "Curriculum Vitae", 1995 and press file (n.d.) (copy provided by Anne Romaine, in possession of the author).

Secondary sources

Books

Abernathy, R.D. *And the walls came tumbling down* (New York: HarperPerennial, 1990).
Abrahams, R.D. *Deep down in the jungle*, rev'd edn (Chicago: Aldine, 1970).
Abrahams, R.D. *Positively black* (Englewood Cliffs: Prentice-Hall, 1970).
Adorno, T.W. *Introduction to the sociology of music* (New York: Continuum, 1988).
Allen, R.L. *Black awakening in capitalist America* (Garden City, N.Y.: Doubleday, 1969).
Allport, G. *The nature of prejudice* (New York: Andover, 1968).
Amburn, E. *Buddy Holly: a biography* (New York: St Martin's, 1995).
Asante, M. *The Afrocentric idea* (Philadelphia: Temple University Press, 1987).
Ayers, E.L. *The promise of the New South: life after Reconstruction* (New York: Oxford University Press, 1992).
Bachman, R.D. *Dynamics of black radio: a research report* (Washington, D.C.: Creative Universal Products, 1977).
Baez, J. *And a voice to sing with: a memoir* (New York: Summit, 1987).
Baker, H.A. *Black studies, rap and the academy* (Chicago: University of Chicago Press, 1993).
Bane, M. *White boy singing the blues* (London: Penguin, 1982).
Barlow, W. *Looking up at down: the emergence of blues culture* (Philadelphia: Temple University Press, 1989).

Barnes, C.A. *Journey from Jim Crow: the desegregation of southern transportation* (New York: Columbia University Press, 1988).

Barnouw, E. *The image empire* (New York: Oxford University Press, 1970).

Barthes, R. *Image-music-text* (London: Fontana, 1977).

Bartley, N.V. *The rise of massive resistance* (Baton Rouge: Louisiana State University Press, 1969).

Bartley, N.V. & H.D. Graham. *Southern politics and the second reconstruction* (Baltimore: Johns Hopkins University Press, 1975).

Bass, J. *Unlikely heroes* (New York: Simon & Schuster, 1981).

Battiste, H. *Hal who: selections from the scriptures of Harold who?* (Los Angeles: At Last, 1989).

Bayles, M. *Hole in our soul: the loss of beauty and meaning in American popular music* (Chicago: University of Chicago Press, 1994).

Bego, M. *Aretha Franklin: the queen of soul* (London: Hale, 1989).

Bell, D. (ed.). *The radical right* (New York: Anchor, 1964).

Bell, I.P. *CORE and the strategy of nonviolence* (New York: Random House, 1968).

Belz, C. *The story of rock* (New York: Oxford University Press, 1972).

Benjaminson, P. *The story of Motown* (New York: Grove, 1978).

Berendt, J.E. *The jazz book*, revd edn (London: Paladin, 1984).

Berger, P.L. *The sacred canopy* (New York: Doubleday, 1967).

Berry, C. *The autobiography of Chuck Berry* (London: Faber & Faber, 1988).

Berry, J., J. Foote, T. Jones. *Up from the cradle of jazz: New Orleans music since World War II* (Athens, Ga.: University of Georgia Press, 1986).

Berry, M.F. & J.W. Blassingame. *Long memory: the black experience in America* (New York: Oxford University Press, 1982).

Betrock, A. *Girl groups: the story of a sound* (London: Putnam, 1983).

Bianco, D. *Heatwave: the Motown fact book* (Ann Arbor: Pierian, 1988).

Billingsley, A. *Black families in white America* (Englewood Cliffs: Prentice Hall, 1968).

Black, J. *Elvis: on the road to stardom* (London: W.H. Allen, 1988).

Blackwell, J. *The black community: diversity and unity*, 2nd edn (New York: Harper & Row, 1985).

Blair, T.L. *Retreat to the ghetto* (New York: Hill & Wang, 1977).

Blauner, B. *Black lives, white lives* (Berkeley: University of California Press, 1989).

Blauner, R. *Racial oppression in America* (New York: Harper & Row, 1972).

Bloom, J. *Class, race and the civil rights movement* (Bloomington: Indiana University Press, 1987).

Bogle, D. *Toms, coons, mulattos, mammies and bucks: an interpretive history of blacks in American films*, 3rd edn (Oxford: Roundhouse, 1994).

Borchet, J. *Alley life in Washington* (Urbana: University of Illinois Press, 1980).

Boskin, J. *Sambo: the rise and demise of an American jester* (New York: Oxford University Press, 1986).

Bracey, J.H., A. Meier, E.P. Rudwick (eds). *Black matriarchy: myth or reality* (Belmont, Calif.: Wadsworth, 1971).

Branch, T. *Parting the waters: America in the King years, 1954–63* (New York: Simon & Schuster, 1988).

Broonzy, W. (with Y. Bruynoghe). *Big Bill's blues* (London: Cassell, 1955).

Broughton, V. *Black gospel: an illustrated history of the gospel sound* (Poole, Dorset: Blandford, 1985).

Broven, J. *Rhythm and blues in New Orleans* (Gretna, La.: Pelican, 1974).

Broven, J. *Walking to New Orleans* (Bexhill: Blues Unlimited, 1974).

Brown, A. & M. Heatley (eds). *The Motown story* (London: Orbis, 1985).

Brown, C. *Manchild in the promised land* (New York: Signet, 1965).

Brown, E. *A taste of power: a black woman's story* (New York: Pantheon, 1992).

Brown, H.R. *Die nigger die!* (London: Allison & Busby, 1970).

Brown, J. (with B. Tucker). *James Brown: the godfather of soul* (Glasgow: Fontana, 1988).

Burner, E. *And gently he shall lead them: Robert Parris Moses and civil rights in Mississippi* (New York: New York University Press, 1994).

Cameron, D. *Feminism and linguistic theory* (London: Macmillan, 1987).

Cantor, L. *Wheelin' on Beale: how WDIA-Memphis became the nation's first all-black radio station and created the sound that changed America* (New York: Pharos, 1992).

Cantwell, R. *Bluegrass breakdown: the making of the old southern sound* (Urbana, Ill.: University of Illinois Press, 1984).

Carmichael, S. & C.V. Hamilton. *Black power* (New York: Vintage, 1967).

Carson, C. *In struggle: SNCC and the black awakening of the 1960s* (Cambridge, Mass.: Harvard University Press, 1981).

Carson, C. et al. (eds). *The eyes on the prize civil rights reader: documents, speeches, and firsthand accounts from the black freedom struggle, 1954–1990* (New York: Viking, 1991).

Carson, C. et al. (eds). *The papers of Martin Luther King, Jr: vol. 2: rediscovering precious values, July 1951–November 1955* (Berkeley: University of California Press, 1994).

Carter, H. III. *The South strikes back* (Westport: Negro Universities Press, 1959).

Cash, W.J. *The mind of the South* (New York: A. Knopf, 1941).

Caute, D. *Sixty-eight* (London: Hamish Hamilton, 1988).

Center for Research Marketing, Inc. *A study of the dynamics of purchase behavior in the Negro market. Negro radio stations* (New York: Center for Research Marketing, 1962).

Chafe, W. *Civilities and civil rights: Greensboro, North Carolina, and the black struggle for freedom* (New York: Oxford University Press, 1980).

Chambers, I. *Urban rhythms: pop music and popular culture* (London: Macmillan, 1985).

Chambers, L.A. (ed.). *America's tenth man* (New York: Twayne, 1957).

Chappell, D. *Inside agitators: southern whites and the civil rights movement* (Baltimore: Johns Hopkins University Press, 1994).

Chapple, S. & R. Garafalo. *Rock 'n' roll is here to pay: the history and politics of the music industry* (Chicago: Nelson-Hall, 1977).

Charles, R. & D. Ritz. *Brother Ray* (London: Futura, 1980).

Charters, S. *The country blues* (New York: Rinehart, 1959).

Clark, D. *Your happiest years* (New York: Rosho, 1959).

Clark, E.C. *The schoolhouse door: segregation's last stand at the University of Alabama* (New York: Oxford University Press, 1993).

Clark, K. *Dark ghetto* (New York: Harper & Row, 1965).

Cleaver, E. *Soul on ice* (New York: Dell, 1968).

Cobb, J. *The selling of the South: the southern crusade for industrial development, 1936–1980* (Baton Rouge: Louisiana State University Press, 1982).

Cohen, L. *Making a new deal: industrial workers in Chicago, 1919–1939* (Cambridge: Cambridge University Press, 1990).

Cohen, R.C. *Black crusader: a biography of Robert Franklin Williams* (Secaucus, N.J.: Lyle Stuart, 1972).

Cole, M. (with L. Robinson). *Nat King Cole: an intimate biography* (London: Star/ W.H. Allen, 1982).

Coleman, J.S. et al. *The adolescent society: the social life of the teenager and its impact on education* (New York: Macmillan/Free Press, 1961).

Coleman, R. (ed.). *Melody Maker file* (London: IPC, 1974).

Collier, J.L. *The making of jazz* (New York: Macmillan, 1981).

Compaine, B.M. (ed.). *Who owns the media?: concentration of ownership in the mass communications industry* (New York: Knowledge Industry, 1979).

Cone, J.H. *The spirituals and the blues: an interpretation* (New York: Greenwood, 1980).

Connor, M.K. *What is cool: understanding black manhood in America* (New York: Crown, 1995).

Conway, C. *African banjo echoes in Appalachia* (Knoxville: University of Tennessee Press, 1995).

Costello, M. & D.F. Wallace. *Signifying rappers: rap and race in the urban present* (New York: Ecco, 1990).

Courlander, H. *Negro folk music of the U.S.A.* (New York: Columbia University Press, 1963).

Crawford, V., J. Rouse, B. Woods (eds). *Women in the civil rights movement* (New York: Carlson, 1990).

Cross, B. *It's not about a salary: rap, race and resistance in Los Angeles* (London: Verso, 1994).

Cruse, H. *The crisis of the Negro intellectual* (New York: Wm Morrow, 1967).

Cummings, T. *The sound of Philadelphia* (London: Methuen, 1975).

Curry, C. *Silver rights* (Athens, Ga.: University of Georgia Press, 1995).

Cutler, C. *File under popular: theoretical and critical writings on music* (London: November, 1985).

Dalton, D. *Piece of my heart: the life, times and legend of Janis Joplin* (New York: St Martin's, 1985).

Dance, D. Cumber. *Shuckin' and jivin': folklore from contemporary black Americans* (Bloomington: Indiana University Press, 1978).

Daniel, P. *Standing at the crossroads: southern life in the twentieth century* (New York: Hill & Wang, 1986).

Dates, J.L. & W. Barlow. *Split image: African-Americans in the mass media* (Washington, D.C.: Howard University Press, 1990).

Davis, A. *Angela Davis: an autobiography* (London: Hutchinson, 1975).

Davis, C. (with J. Willwerth). *Clive: inside the record business* (New York: Ballantine, 1974).

Davis, F. Marshall (ed., with an introduction, by J.E. Tidwell). *Livin' the blues: memoirs of a black journalist and poet* (Madison: University of Wisconsin Press, 1993).

Davis, J.P. (ed.). *The American Negro reference book* (New York: Prentice Hall, 1966).

Davis, S. Jnr. *Hollywood in a suitcase* (London: W.H. Allen, 1981).

Deffaa, C. *Blue rhythms: six lives in rhythm and blues* (Champaign, Ill.: University of Illinois Press, 1996).

Denby, C. *Indignant heart: a black worker's journal* (Detroit: Wayne University Press, 1989).

Denisoff, R.S. *Solid gold: the popular record industry* (New Brunswick, N.J.: Transaction, 1975).

Denisoff, R.S. & R.A. Peterson (eds). *The sounds of social change* (Chicago: Rand McNally, 1972).

Denisoff, R.S. (with W.L. Schurk). *Tarnished gold: the record industry revisited* (New Brunswick, N.J.: Transaction, 1986).

Dennison, S. *Scandalize my name: black imagery in American popular music* (New York: Garland, 1982).

Dent, G. (ed.). *Black popular culture: a project by Michele Wallace* (Seattle: Bay, 1992).

Dittmer, J. *Local people: the struggle for civil rights in Mississippi* (Urbana: University of Illinois Press, 1994).

Drake, S.C. & H.R. Cayton. *Black metropolis: a study of Negro life in a northern city* (London: J. Cape, 1946).

Drotning, P.T. *Up from the ghetto* (New York: H. Regnery, 1970).

Duberman, M.B. *Paul Robeson* (London: Pan, 1991).

Du Bois, W.E.B. *The souls of black folk* (Chicago: A.C. McClurg, 1909).

Duneier, M. *Slim's table: race, respectability, and masculinity* (Chicago: University of Chicago Press, 1992).

Dyson, M.E. *Between God and gangsta rap: bearing witness to black culture* (New York: Oxford University Press, 1996).

Early, G. *One nation under a groove: Motown and American culture* (New York: Ecco, 1995).

Eberly, P.K. *Music in the air: America's changing tastes in popular music 1920–1980* (New York: Communication Arts, 1982).

Ebony. The black revolution: an Ebony special issue (Chicago: Johnson, 1970).

Egerton, J. *Speak now against the day: the generation before the civil rights movement in the South* (New York: A. Knopf, 1994).

Ehrenstein, D. & B. Reed. *Rock on film* (New York: Delilah Communications, 1982).

Eisen, J. (ed.). *The age of rock: sounds of the American cultural revolution* (New York: Random House, 1969).

Ellison, M. *Extension of the blues* (London: J. Cape, 1989).

Ellison, R. *Shadow and act* (New York: Random House, 1964).

Ely, M.P. *The adventures of Amos 'n' Andy: a social history of an American phenomenon* (New York: Free Press, 1991).

Engel, E.R. *White and still all right* (New York: Crackerjack, 1977).

Ennis, P.H. *The seventh stream: the emergence of rock 'n' roll in American popular music* (Hanover, N.H.: Wesleyan, 1992).

Erenberg, L.A. *Steppin' out: New York nightlife and the transformation of American culture, 1890–1930* (Chicago: University of Chicago Press, 1981).

Escott, C. & M. Hawkins. *Catalyst: the Sun Records story* (London: Aquarius, 1975).

Essien-Udom, E.U. *Black nationalism: a search for identity in America* (Chicago: University of Chicago Press, 1962).

Evans, S. *Personal politics: the roots of women's liberation in the civil rights movement and the new left* (New York: Knopf, 1979).

Ewen, D. *All the years of American popular music* (Englewood Cliffs, N.J.: Prentice Hall, 1977).

Fairclough, A. *To redeem the soul of America: the Southern Christian Leadership Conference and Martin Luther King* (Athens, Ga.: University of Georgia Press, 1988).

Fairclough, A. *Race and democracy: the civil rights struggle in Louisiana, 1915–1972* (Athens, Ga.: University of Georgia Press, 1995).

Fanon, F. *Black skins, white masks* (New York, Grove, 1968).

Fanon, F. *The wretched of the earth* (New York, Grove, 1968).

Farmer, J. *Freedom – when?* (New York: Random House, 1965).

Farr, J. *Moguls and madmen: the pursuit of power in popular music* (New York: Simon & Schuster, 1994).

Fauset, A. *Black gods of the metropolis* (Philadelphia: University of Pennsylvania Press, 1944).

Feist, L. *An introduction to popular music publishing in America* (New York: National Music Publishers' Association, 1980).

Fitzgerald, F.S. *The crack-up* (London: Penguin, 1983).

Fogelson, G. *Belafonte* (Los Angeles: Holloway House, 1980).

Fong-Torres, B. (ed.). *The Rolling Stone interviews*, vol. 2 (New York: Warner, 1973).

Fong-Torres, B. (ed.). *What's that sound?: the contemporary music scene from the pages of Rolling Stone* (New York: Anchor, 1976).

Forman, J. *The making of black revolutionaries* (New York: Macmillan, 1972).

Foster, R.N. *Innovation: the attacker's advantage* (New York: Summit, 1986).

Foucault, M. *Power/knowledge: selected interviews and other writings, 1972–1977* (New York: Pantheon, 1980).

Fox, K. *Metropolitan America: urban life and urban policy in the United States, 1940–1980* (New York: Macmillan, 1985).

Fox, T. *Showtime at the Apollo* (New York: Holt, Rinehart & Winston, 1983).

Fox, T. *In the groove: the people behind the music* (New York: St Martin's, 1986).

Frazier, E.F. *Black bourgeoisie* (Glencoe, Ill.: Free Press, 1957).

Frazier, E.F. *The Negro church in America* (New York: Knopf, 1964).

Frazier, E.F. *The Negro family in the United States*, revd abr. edn (Chicago: University of Chicago Press, 1966).

Fredrickson, G. *The black image in the white mind* (Hanover, N.H.: Wesleyan University Press, 1987).

Frith, S. *Sound effects: youth, leisure and the politics of rock 'n' roll* (London: Constable, 1984).

Frith, S. & A. Goodwin. *On the record* (London: Routledge, 1990).

Gallup Poll. *The Gallup poll: public opinion, 1935–1971*, 3 vols (New York: Random House, 1972).

Garland, P. *The sound of soul* (Chicago: Regnery, 1969).

Garnett, B. *How soulful is "soul" radio?* (Nashville: Race Relations Information Center, 1970).

Garon, P. *Blues and the poetic spirit* (New York: Eddison, 1978).

Garrow, D.J. *Protest at Selma: Martin Luther King, Jr and the Voting Rights Act of 1965* (New Haven: Yale University Press, 1978).

Garrow, D.J. *Bearing the cross: Martin Luther King, Jr, and the Southern Christian Leadership Conference* (New York: Vintage, 1988).

Garrow, D.J. (ed.). *We shall overcome: the civil rights movement in the United States in the 1950s and 1960s*, 3 vols (New York: Carlson, 1989).

Gart, G., R.C. Ames et al. *Duke/Peacock Records: an illustrated history with discography* (Milford, N.H.: Big Nickel, 1990).

Gates, H.L. *Loose canons: notes on the culture wars* (New York: Oxford University Press, 1992).

Geertz, C. *The interpretation of cultures* (New York: Basic, 1973).

Gelatt, R. *The fabulous phonograph, 1877–1977*, 2nd revd edn (New York: Macmillan, 1977).

Genovese, E. *Roll 'Jordan' roll: the world the slaves made*, 2nd edn (New York: Vintage, 1976).

George, D. *The real Duke Ellington* (London: Robson, 1982).

George, N. *Where did our love go?* (New York: St Martin's, 1986).

George, N. *The death of rhythm and blues* (New York: Omnibus, 1988).

George, N. *Stop the violence: overcoming self-destruction* (New York, Pantheon, 1990).

George, N. *Buppies, b-boys, baps & bohos* (New York: HarperPerennial, 1994).

Giddings, P. *When and where I enter: the impact of black women on race and sex in America* (New York: Wm Morrow, 1984).

Giddins, G. *Riding on a blue note: jazz and American pop* (New York: Oxford University Press, 1981).

Giddins, G. *Rhythm-a-ning: jazz tradition and innovation in the '80s* (New York: Oxford University Press, 1985).

Gilbert, B.W. et al. *Ten blocks from the White House* (New York: Praeger, 1968).

Gilbert, J.B. *A cycle of outrage: America's reaction to the juvenile delinquent in the 1950s* (New York: Oxford University Press, 1986).

Gillespie, D. (with A. Fraser). *To be or not to bop* (London: Quartet, 1982).

Gillett, C. *The sound of the city*, 2nd revd edn (London: Souvenir, 1983).

Gillett, C. *Making tracks: the story of Atlantic Records* (London: W H Allen, 1988).

Gilroy, P. *The black Atlantic: modernity and double consciousness* (Cambridge, Mass.: Harvard University Press, 1993).

Goldfield, D. *Black, white and southern: race relations and southern culture, 1940 to the present* (Baton Rouge: Louisiana State University Press, 1990).

Goldrosen, J. & J. Beecher. *Remembering Buddy* (London: Pavilion, 1987).

Gonzales, F.L. *Disco-file: the discographical catalog of American rock and roll and rhythm and blues vocal harmony groups, 1902 to 1976*, 2nd edn (Flushing, N.Y.: Gonzales, 1977).

Gordon, R. *It came from Memphis* (Boston: Faber & Faber, 1995).

Gordy, B. *To be loved: the music, the magic, the memories of Motown: an autobiography* (New York: Warner, 1994).

Gould, W.B. *Black workers in white unions: job discrimination in the United States* (Ithaca, N.Y.: Cornell University Press, 1977).

Gramsci, A. (ed. Q. Hoare & G.N. Smith). *Selections from the prison notebooks* (New York: International Publishers, 1971).

Grant, G.G. *The best kind of loving: a black woman's guide to finding intimacy* (New York: HarperCollins, 1995).

Greenberg, B.S. & B. Dervin. *Uses of the mass media by the urban poor* (New York: Praeger Special Studies in US Economic & Social Development, 1970).

Gregory, D. *From the back of the bus* (New York: Dutton, 1962).

Gregory, D. *Nigger: an autobiography* (New York: Dutton, 1964).

Greig, C. *Will you still love me tomorrow?* (London: Virago, 1989).

Gribin, A.J. & M.M. Schiff. *Doo-wop: the forgotten third of rock 'n' roll* (Iola, Wis.: Krause, 1992).

Grier, W.H. & P.M. Cobbs. *Black rage* (New York: Basic, 1968).

Groia, P. *They all sang on the corner* (New York: Phillie Dee, 1983).

Guralnick, P. *Feel like going home* (London: Omnibus, 1979).

Guralnick, P. *Sweet soul music: rhythm and blues and the southern dream of freedom* (London: Virgin, 1986).

Guralnick, P. *Searching for Robert Johnson* (New York: Dutton, 1989).

Guralnick, P. *Last train to Memphis: the rise of Elvis Presley* (Boston: Little, Brown, 1994).

Gutman, H. *The black family in slavery and freedom* (New York: Pantheon, 1976).

Hacker, A. *Two nations: black and white, separate, hostile, unequal*, 2nd edn (New York: Ballantine, 1995).

Hager, S. *Hip hop: the illustrated history of break dancing, rap music and graffiti* (New York: St Martin's, 1984).

Halisi, C. (ed.). *The quotable Karenga* (Los Angeles: US Organization, 1967).

Hall, J. Dowd et al. *Like a family: the making of a southern cotton mill world* (Chapel Hill: University of North Carolina Press, 1987).

Hamm, C. *Yesterdays: popular song in America* (New York: Norton, 1979).

Hampton, H. & S. Fayer (eds). *Voices of freedom: an oral history of the civil rights movement from the 1950s through the 1980s* (New York: Bantam, 1990).

Handy, D.A. *Black music: opinions and reviews* (Ettrick, Va.: B.M. & M., 1974).

Hannerz, U. *Soulside* (New York: Columbia University Press, 1969).

Haralambos, M. *Right on: from blues to soul in black America* (New York: Drake, 1975).

Harding, V. *Hope and history: why we must share the story of the movement* (New York: Orbis, 1990).

Harker, D. *One for the money: politics and popular song* (London: Hutchinson, 1980).

Harper, P.B. *Are we not men?: masculine anxiety and the problem of African-American Identity* (New York: Oxford University Press, 1996).

Harris, E.L. *South of haunted dreams: a ride through slavery's old backyard* (New York: Simon & Schuster, 1993).

Harris, M. *The rise of gospel blues: the music of Thomas A. Dorsey in the urban church* (New York: Oxford University Press, 1992).

Haskins, J. (with K. Benson). *Nat King Cole: the man and his music* (London: Robson, 1991).

Hatch, D. & S. Millward. *From blues to rock: an analytical history of pop music* (Manchester: Manchester University Press, 1987).

Haws, R. (ed.). *The age of segregation: race relations in the South, 1890–1945* (Jackson: University of Mississippi Press, 1987).

Haydon, G. & D. Marks (eds). *Repercussions* (London: Century, 1985).

Hebdige, D. *Subculture: the meaning of style* (London: Methuen, 1979).

Heilbut, A. *The gospel sound: good news and bad times*, revd edn (New York: Limelight International, 1985).

Henderson, D. *'Scuse me while I kiss the sky* (New York: Bantam, 1981).

Henry, C. *Culture and African American politics* (Bloomington: Indiana University Press, 1992).

Hentoff, N. *The new equality*, 2nd edn (New York: Viking Compass, 1965).

Herbst, P. (ed.). *The Rolling Stone interviews, 1967–80* (New York: St Martin's, 1981).

Hernton, C. *Sex and race in America* (New York: Grove, 1966).

Hilderbrand, L. *Stars of soul and rhythm and blues* (New York: Billboard, 1994).

Hill, R. *The strengths of black families* (New York: Emerson Hall, 1972).

Hilliard, D. & L. Cole. *This side of glory: the autobiography of David Hilliard and the story of the Black Panther Party* (Boston: Little, Brown, 1993).

Hillsman, J. *The progress of gospel music* (New York: Vantage, 1983).

Hirshey, G. *Nowhere to run* (New York: Macmillan, 1984).

Hoare, I. (ed.). *The soul book* (London: Eyre Methuen, 1975).

Hodgson, G. *America in our time* (New York: Random House, 1976).

Hoffman, F. *The twenties* (New York: Free Press, 1965).

Holiday, B. (with W. Dufty). *Lady sings the blues* (New York: Penguin, 1985).

Holloway, J. (ed.). *Africanisms* (Bloomington: University of Indiana Press, 1990).

hooks, b. *Ain't I a woman?: black women and feminism* (Boston: South End, 1981).

hooks, b. *Outlaw culture: resisting representations* (New York: Routledge, 1994).

Hopkins, J. *Hit and run* (New York: Perigee, 1983).

Horne, G. *Fire this time: the Watts uprising and the 1960s* (Charlottesville: University Press of Virginia, 1995).

Horne, L. & R. Schickel. *Lena*, 2nd edn (Garden City, N.Y.: Limelight, 1986).

Horsman, R. *Race and manifest destiny: the origins of American racial anglo-saxonism* (Cambridge, Mass.: Harvard University Press, 1981).

Hoskyns, B. *Say it one time for the broken hearted* (Glasgow: Fontana, 1987).

Hounsome, T. *New rock record guide* (Poole, Dorset: Blandford, 1987).

Humphries, P. *The boy in the bubble: a biography of Paul Simon* (London: Hodder & Stoughton, 1990).

Huntingdon, S.P. *American politics: the promise of disharmony* (Cambridge, Mass.: Harvard University Press, 1981).

Jackson, G. *Soledad brother* (New York: Coward McCann, 1971).

Jackson, I.V., (ed.). *More than dancing: essays on Afro-American music and musicians* (Westport: Greenwood, 1985).

Jackson, J.A. *Big beat heat: Alan Freed and the early years of rock & roll* (New York: Schirmer, 1991).

Jackson, M. *Moonwalk* (New York: Doubleday, 1988).

Jackson, M. (with E.M. Wylie). *Movin' on up* (New York: Hawthorne, 1966).

Jacoway, E. & D.R. Colburn (eds). *Southern businessmen and desegregation* (Baton Rouge: Louisiana State University Press, 1982).

Jaffe, H.S. & T. Sherwood. *Dream city: race, power, and the decline of Washington, DC* (New York: Simon & Schuster, 1994).

Jahn, M. *The story of rock from Elvis to the Rolling Stones* (New York: Quadrangle, 1975).

James, E. (with D. Ritz). *Rage to survive* (New York: Villard, 1995).

Jefferson, T. (ed. W. Peden). *Notes on the state of Virginia* (Chapel Hill: University of North Carolina Press, 1955).

Jesmer, E. *Number one with a bullet* (New York: Farrar, Straus & Giroux, 1974).

Jones, J. *Labor of love, labor of sorrow: black women, work and the family, from slavery to present* (New York: Basic, 1985).

Jones, L. (I.A. Baraka). *Blues people* (New York: Wm Morrow, 1963).

Jones, L. (I.A. Baraka). *Black music* (New York: Wm Morrow, 1967).

Jones, L. (I.A. Baraka) (ed.). *African congress: a documentary history of the first modern pan-African congress* (New York: Wm Morrow, 1972).

Jones, L. (I.A. Baraka). *Raise, race, rays, raze: essays since 1965* (New York: Vintage, 1972).

Jones, L. (I.A. Baraka). *The autobiography of LeRoi Jones/Imamu Amiri Baraka* (New York: Freundlich, 1984).

Jones, L. (I.A. Baraka) & L. Neal (eds). *Black fire* (New York: Wm Morrow, 1968).

Jordan, W.D. *The white man's burden* (New York: Oxford University Press, 1974).

Jung, C.G. & M.L. von Franz (eds). *Man and his symbols* (London: Aldus, 1964).

Keil, C. *Urban blues* (Chicago: University of Chicago Press, 1966).

Keiser, R.L. *The vice-lords: warriors of the street* (New York: Holt, Rinehart & Winston, 1979).

Kelley, R.D.G. *Race rebels: culture, politics and the black working class* (New York: Free Press, 1996).

Kilpatrick, J.J. *The southern case for school segregation* (New York: Cromwell-Collier, 1962).

King, Martin Luther. *Stride toward freedom: the Montgomery story* (New York: Harper, 1958).

King, Martin Luther. *Where do we go from here: chaos or community?* (New York: Bantam, 1967).

King, Mary. *Freedom song* (New York: Wm Morrow, 1987).

King, R.H. *Civil rights and the idea of freedom* (New York: Oxford University Press, 1992).

King, R.H. & H. Taylor (eds). *Dixie debates: perspectives on southern cultures* (London: Pluto, 1996).

Kochman, T. *Rappin' in and stylin' out* (Chicago: University of Chicago Press, 1977).

Kofsky, F. *Black nationalism and the revolution in music* (New York: Pathfinder, 1970).

Ladner, J. *Tomorrow's tomorrow: the black woman* (Garden City, N.Y.: Anchor, 1972).

Lamis, A.P. *The two-party South* (New York: Oxford University Press, 1984).

Landry, B. *The new black middle class* (Berkeley: University of California Press, 1987).

Langum, D.J. *Crossing over the line: legislation, morality and the Mann Act* (Chicago: University of Chicago Press, 1994).

Lawson, S.F. *Black ballots: voting rights in the South, 1944–1969* (New York: Columbia University Press, 1976).

Lawson, S.F. *Running for freedom: civil rights and black politics in America since 1941* (New York: McGraw-Hill, 1991).

Lemann, N. *The promised land: the great black migration and how it changed America* (London: Papermac, 1992).

Leonard, N. *Jazz and the white Americans* (Chicago: University of Chicago Press, 1972).

Leppert, R. & S. McClary (eds). *Music and society: the politics of composition, performance and reception* (Cambridge: Cambridge University Press, 1987).

Lerner, G. (ed.). *Black women in white America: a documentary history* (New York: Vintage, 1973).

Lerner, G. *The creation of patriarchy* (New York: Oxford University Press, 1986).

Lester, J. *Look out whitey! black power's gonna get your Mama* (New York: Allison & Busby, 1968).

Levine, E. (ed.). *Freedom's children: young civil rights activists tell their own stories* (New York: Avon, 1993).

Levine, L. *Black culture and black consciousness: Afro-American folk thought from slavery to freedom* (New York: Oxford University Press, 1977).

Levitan, S.A., W.B. Johnson, R. Taggert. *Still a dream: the changing status of blacks since 1960* (Cambridge, Mass.: Harvard University Press, 1975).

Leviton, J.B. & G.J. Rijff. *Elvis close-up* (London: Century Hutchinson, 1989).

Lewis, M. (with M. Silver). *Great balls of fire! the true story of Jerry Lee Lewis* (London: Virgin, 1982).

Lieberman, R. *"My song is my weapon": people's songs, American communism, and the politics of culture, 1930–50* (Urbana: University of Illinois Press, 1995).

Liebow, E. *Tally's corner* (Boston: Little, Brown, 1967).

Lincoln, C.E. *The black muslims in America* (Boston: Beacon, 1962).

Lincoln, C.E. *Race, religion and the continuing American dilemma* (New York: Hill & Wang, 1986).

Lipsitz, G. *Rainbow at midnight: labor and culture in the 1940s* (Urbana: University of Illinois Press, 1994).

Lomax, L. *The Negro revolt* (New York: Harper, 1962).

Long, C. *Love awaits: African-American women talk about sex, love and life* (New York: Bantam, 1995).

Lornell, K. *Happy in the service of the Lord: Afro-American gospel quartets in Memphis* (Urbana: University of Illinois Press, 1988).

Lubell, S. *White and black: test of a nation* (New York: Harper & Row, 1964).

Lydon, M. & E. Mandel. *Boogie lightning*, repr. edn (New York: Da Capo, 1980).

MacDonald, J.F. *Don't touch that dial!* (Chicago. Nelson-Hall, 1979).

Mahwhinny, P.C. *Music master: the 45 rpm record directory. 35 years of recorded music listed by artist, 1947 to 1982* (Pittsburgh: Music Master, 1983).

Mailer, N. *Advertisements for myself* (New York: Putnam, 1959).

Malcolm X (with A. Haley). *The autobiography of Malcolm X* (New York: Penguin, 1983 edn).

Malcolm X. *Malcolm X Speaks* (New York: Pathfinder, 1989).

Marable, M. *How capitalism underdeveloped black America* (Boston: Pluto, 1983).

Marable, M. *Race, reform and rebellion: the second reconstruction in black America, 1945–1982* (London: Macmillan, 1984).

Marable, M. *Black American politics: from the Washington marches to Jesse Jackson* (London: Verso, 1985).

Marcus, G. *Mystery train: images of America in rock 'n' roll music* (New York: Omnibus, 1977).

Marcus, G. (ed.). *Stranded* (New York: A. Knopf, 1979).

Marsh, D. *Fortunate son* (New York: Random House, 1985).

Marsh, D. & J. Swenson (eds.). *The Rolling Stone record guide* (London: Virgin, 1980).

Martin, J.B. *The Deep South says never* (New York: Ballantine, 1957).

Martin, L. & K. Segrave. *Anti-rock: the opposition to rock 'n' roll* (Hambden, Conn.: Archon, 1988).

Marx, G.T. *Protest and prejudice: a study of belief in the black community* (New York: Harper & Row, 1967).

May, L. (ed.). *Recasting America: culture and politics in the age of the cold war* (Chicago: University of Chicago Press, 1989).

McAdam, D. *Political process and the development of black insurgency, 1930–1970* (Chicago: University of Chicago Press, 1982).

McAdoo, H.P. *Black families*, 2nd edn (Newbury Park, Calif.: Sage, 1988).

McCutcheon, L.E. *Rhythm and blues: an experience and adventure in its origins and development* (Arlington, Va.: Beatty, 1971).

McEwen, J. *Sam Cooke: the man who invented soul* (New York: Sire, 1977).

McGowan, J. *Hear today! hear to stay!* (St Petersburg, Fla.: Sixth House, 1983).

McGregor, C. *Pop goes the culture*, revd edn (London: Pluto, 1984).

McKay, C. *Harlem: Negro metropolis* (New York: Harvest, 1968).

McKee, M. & F. Chisenhall. *Beale black and blue* (Baton Rouge: Louisiana State University Press, 1981).

McMillen, N. *The citizens' council: organized resistance to the second reconstruction* (Urbana: University of Illinois Press, 1971).

McMillen, N. *Dark journey: black Mississippians in the age of Jim Crow* (Urbana: University of Illinois Press, 1989).

Meier, A. & E.P. Rudwick. *CORE: a study in the civil rights movement, 1942–1968* (New York: Oxford University Press, 1973).

Meredith, J. *Three years in Mississippi* (Bloomington: Indiana University Press, 1966).

Merton, R.K. *Social theory and social structure* (Glencoe, Ill.: Free Press, 1957).

Meyer, A. *Black voices and format regulations: a study in black-oriented radio* (Stanford: ERIC Clearinghouse on Media and Technology, 1971).

Meyer, H. *The gold in Tin Pan Alley* (Westport, Conn.: Greenwood, 1977).

Middleton, R. *Pop music and the blues: a study of the relationship and its significance* (London: Gollancz, 1972).

Middleton, R. *"Reading" popular music* (London: Open University Press, 1981).

Millar, B. *The Drifters: the rise and fall of the black vocal group* (New York: Macmillan, 1971).

Millard, A. *America on record: a history of recorded sound* (Cambridge: Cambridge University Press, 1995).

Miller, K. *Voice of deliverance: the language of Martin Luther King and its sources* (New York: Free Press, 1992).

Mills, K. *This little light of mine: the life of Fannie Lou Hamer* (New York: Dutton, 1993).

Moody, A. *Coming of age in Mississippi* (New York: Dell, 1968).

Morris, A. *The origins of the civil rights movement: black communities organizing for change* (New York: Free Press, 1984).

Morse, D. *Motown and the arrival of black music* (London: November, 1971).

Moses, W.J. *Black messiahs and Uncle Toms: social and literary manipulations of a religious myth* (Philadelphia: Pennsylvania State University Press, 1982).

Moynihan, D.P. *The Negro family: the case for national action* (Washington, D.C.: Government Printing Office, 1965).

Murray, A. *Stomping the blues*, 2nd edn (New York: Vintage, 1982).

Murray, A. *Omni-Americans: some alternatives to the folklore of white supremacy* (New York: Vintage, 1983).

Murray, C.S. *Crosstown traffic: Jimi Hendrix and the post-war rock 'n' roll revolution* (New York: St Martin's, 1989).

Murrells, J. *Million selling records from the 1900s to the 1980s* (London: Batsford, 1984).

Muse, B. *Ten years of prelude* (New York: Viking, 1964).

Myrdal, Gunnar. *An American dilemma* (New York: Harper & Brothers, 1964).

Namorato, M.V. (ed.). *Have we overcome?: race relations since Brown* (Jackson: University of Mississippi Press, 1979).

Nelson, H. & M.A. Gonzales. *Bring the noise: a guide to rap music and hip-hop culture* (New York: Harmony, 1991).

Newman, M. *Entrepreneurs of profit and pride: from black appeal to soul radio* (New York: Praeger, 1988).

Newton, H. *Revolutionary suicide* (New York: Harcourt Brace Jovanovich, 1973).

Nicholas, A.X. (ed.). *The poetry of soul* (New York: Bantam, 1971).

Noebel, D.A. *Rhythm, riots and revolution: an analysis of the communist use of music – the communist master plan* (Tulsa: Christian Crusade, 1966).

Norman, P. *The road goes on forever* (London: Elm Tree, 1982).

Norrell, R.J. *Reaping the whirlwind: the civil rights movement in Tuskegee* (New York: Vintage, 1985).

Oakley, G. *The devil's music*, revd edn (London: Ariel, 1983).

Oakley, J.R. *God's country: America in the fifties* (New York: Dembner, 1986).

Ochs, M. *Rock archives* (Poole, Dorset: Blandford, 1985).

Ofari, E. *The myth of black capitalism* (New York: Monthly Review Press, 1970).

Oliver, P. *The story of the blues* (London: Penguin, 1972).

Oliver, P. *Songsters and saints: vocal traditions on race records* (Cambridge: Cambridge University Press, 1984).

Oliver, P. *Screening the blues: aspects of the blues* (New York: Da Capo, 1989).

Oliver, P. *Blues fell this morning: meaning in the blues* (Cambridge: Cambridge University Press, 1990).

Orfield, G. *Must we bus?: segregated schools and national policy* (Washington, D.C.: Brookings Institution, 1978).

Otis, J. *Listen to the lambs* (New York: W.W. Norton, 1968).

Packard, V. *Hidden persuaders* (New York: D. McKay, 1957).

Palmer, R. *Deep blues* (New York: Penguin, 1981).

Passman, A. *The deejays* (New York: Macmillan, 1971).

Pavlow, A. *The r & b book: a disc-history of rhythm and blues* (Providence: Music House, 1983).

Payne, C. *I've got the light of freedom: the organizing tradition and the Mississippi freedom struggle* (Berkeley: University of California Press, 1995).

Pearson, H. *The shadow of the panther: Huey Newton and the price of black power in America* (Reading, Mass.: Addison-Wesley, 1994).

Perlo, V. *Economics of racism, USA: roots of black inequality* (New York: International, 1975).

Perry, C. *The Haight Ashbury* (New York: Vintage, 1985).

Picardie, J. & D. Wade. *Atlantic: and the godfathers of rock and roll*, revd edn (London: Fourth Estate, 1993).

Pielke, R.C. *You say you want a revolution: rock music in American culture* (New York: Nelson-Hall, 1986).

Pinkney, A. *The myth of black progress* (Cambridge: Cambridge University Press, 1986).

Ploski, H.A. & J. Williams (eds). *The Negro almanac: a reference work on the Afro-American*, 4th edn (New York: J. Wiley & Sons, 1983).

Poitier, S. *This life: an autobiography* (London: Hodder & Stoughton, 1980).

Powledge, F. *Free at last?: the civil rights movement and the people who made it* (New York: HarperCollins, 1991).

Pruter, R. *Chicago soul* (Urbana: University of Illinois Press, 1991).

Radio Advertising Bureau. *Radio and the Negro market* (New York: Radio Advertising Bureau, 1957).

Raines, H. *My soul is rested: movement days in the Deep South remembered* (New York: Putnam, 1977).

Rainwater, L. (ed.). *Soul* (n.p.: Transaction, 1970).

Rainwater, L. *Behind ghetto walls: black families in ghetto slums* (London: Allen Lane, 1971).

Ralph, J.R. *Northern protest: Martin Luther King, Jr, Chicago and the civil rights movement* (Cambridge, Mass.: Harvard University Press, 1993).

Ramazanoglu, C. *Feminism and the contradictions of oppression* (London: Routledge, 1989).

Randall, D. (ed.). *Black poets* (New York: Bantam, 1981).

Reagon, B. Johnson et al. *We who believe in freedom* (New York: Anchor, 1993).

Record, J. & W. Record. *Little Rock, USA: materials for analysis* (San Francisco: Chandler, 1960).

Redd, L. *Rock is rhythm and blues* (Detroit: Michigan State University Press, 1974).

Reese, K. *Chuck Berry* (London: Proteus, 1982).

Reeves, M. & M. Bego. *Dancing in the street: confessions of a Motown diva* (New York: Hyperion, 1994).

Ribovsky, M. *He's a rebel: the truth about Phil Spector – rock and roll's legendary madman* (New York: Dutton, 1989).

Riedel, J. *Soul music – black and white: the influence of black music on the churches* (Minneapolis: Ausburg, 1975).

Ritz, D. *Divided soul: the life of Marvin Gaye* (New York: McGraw-Hill, 1986).

Roberts, J.S. *Black music of two worlds* (New York: Praeger, 1972).

Robinson, A.L. & P. Sullivan (eds). *New directions in civil rights studies* (Charlottesville: University Press of Virginia, 1991).

Robinson, J.A. Gibson. *The Montgomery bus boycott and the women who started it* (Knoxville: University of Tennessee Press, 1987).

Robinson, S. (with D. Ritz). *Smokey: inside my life* (London: Headline, 1989).

Roediger, D.R. *The wages of whiteness: race and the making of the American working class*, 2nd edn (New York: Verso, 1991).

Rohrer, J.H. & M.S. Edmondson. *The eighth generation grows up* (New York: Harper Torchbooks, 1964).

Rolling Stone. Rolling Stone rock almanac (London: Macmillan, 1984).

Rose, C. *Living in America: the soul saga of James Brown* (London: Serpent's Tail, 1990).

Rose, T. *Black noise: rap music and black culture in contemporary America* (Hanover: Wesleyan University Press, 1994).

Rosenthal, R.E. & P. Maultsby. *Who's who in black music* (New Orleans: Edwards Print, 1985).

Ross, A. & T. Rose (eds). *Microphone fiends: youth and youth culture* (New York: Routledge, 1994).

Ross, D. *Secrets of a sparrow: memoirs* (New York: Villard, 1993).

Ruppli, M. *Atlantic Records: a discography*, 4 vols (Westport: Greenwood, 1979).

Ruppli, M. *The Savoy label: a discography* (Westport: Greenwood, 1980).

Ruppli, M. *The Chess labels: a discography*, 2 vols (Westport: Greenwood, 1983).

Ruppli, M. *The Aladdin/Imperial labels: a discography* (New York: Greenwood, 1991).

Ruppli, M. (with B. Daniels). *The King labels: a discography*, 2 vols (Westport: Greenwood, 1985).

Russell, T. *Blacks, whites and blues* (London: Stein & Day, 1970).

Rustin, B. *Strategies for freedom: the changing patterns of black protest* (New York: Columbia University Press, 1976).

Ryan, J. *Recollections – the Detroit years: the Motown sound by the people who made it* (Detroit: the author, 1982).

Said, E. *Orientalism* (London: Peregrine, 1987).

Sales, W.W. Jr. *From civil rights to black liberation: Malcolm X and the Organization of Afro-American Unity* (Boston: South End, 1994).

Sanjek, R. *American popular music and its business*, vol. 3 (New York: Oxford University Press, 1988).

Sawyer, C. *B.B. King: the authorized biography* (Poole, Dorset: Blandford, 1981).

Saxton, A. *The rise and fall of the white republic: class politics and mass culture in nineteenth-century America* (London: Verso, 1990).

Schuman, H., C. Steeh, L. Bobo. *Racial attitudes in America: trends and interpretations* (Cambridge, Mass.: Harvard University Press, 1985).

Schwartz, B. *The professor and the commissions* (New York: A. Knopf, 1959).

Scott, J.C. *Domination and the arts of resistance* (New Haven: Yale University Press, 1991).

Seale, B. *Seize the time* (London: Arrow, 1970).

Seay, D. & M. Neely. *Stairway to heaven: religion in rock* (New York: Ballantine/ Epiphany, 1986).

Segrave, K. *Payola in the music industry, 1880–1991* (Jefferson, N.C.: McFarland, 1994).

Sellers, C. (with R. Terrell). *The river of no return: the autobiography of a black militant and the life and death of SNCC*, 2nd edn (Jackson: University of Mississippi Press, 1990).

Shapiro, H. & C. Glebbeek. *Jimi Hendrix: electric gypsy* (New York: St Martin's, 1995).

Shapiro, N. & N. Hentoff (eds), *Hear me talkin' to ya* (London: Reynhart, 1955).

Shaw, A. *Belafonte: an unauthorized biography* (Philadelphia: Chilton, 1960)

Shaw, A. *The world of soul* (New York: Cowles, 1970)

Shaw, A. *The rockin' 50s* (New York: Hawthorn, 1974).

Shaw, A. *Honkers and shouters* (New York: Macmillan, 1978).

Shaw, A. *Black popular music in America* (New York: Schirmer, 1986).

Shelton, R. *No direction home: the life and music of Bob Dylan* (New York: Beech Tree, 1986).

Shore, M. & D. Clark. *The history of American Bandstand* (New York: Ballantine, 1985).

Sidran, B. *Black talk* (New York: Da Capo, 1981).

Silver, J. *Mississippi: the closed society* (New York: Harcourt Brace, 1964).

Simone, N. (with S. Cleary). *I put a spell on you: the autobiography of Nina Simone* (London: Ebury, 1991).

Sindler, A.P. *Bakke, DeFunis, and minority admissions: the quest for equal opportunity* (New York: Longman, 1978).

Sitkoff, H. *The struggle for black equality, 1954–1992*, revd edn (New York: Hill & Wang, 1993).

Small, C. *Music of the common tongue* (London: J. Calder, 1987).

Smead, H. *Blood justice: the lynching of Mack Charles Parker* (New York: Oxford University Press, 1986).

Smith, J. *Off the record: an oral history of popular music* (New York: Warner, 1988).

Smith, W. *The pied pipers of rock 'n' roll: radio deejays of the 50s and 60s* (Marietta, Ga.: Longstreet, 1989).

Smitherman, G. *Black language and culture: sounds of soul* (New York: Harper & Row, 1975).

Sosna, M. *In search of the silent South: southern liberals and the race issue* (New York: Columbia University Press, 1977).

Spencer, J.M. *Re-searching black music* (Knoxville: University of Tennessee Press, 1996).

Spitz, R. *The making of superstars* (Garden City, N.Y.: Anchor, 1978).

Stack, C. *All our kin: strategies for survival in a black community* (New York: Harper & Row, 1974).

Stambler, I. *Encyclopaedia of pop, rock and soul* (New York: St Martin's, 1974).

Stearns, M. & J. Stearns. *Jazz dance* (New York: Macmillan, 1968).

Stern, M. *Calculating visions: Kennedy, Johnson and civil rights* (New Brunswick, N.J.: Rutgers University Press, 1992).

Stevenson, B. *Life in black and white: family and community in the slave South* (New York: Oxford University Press, 1996).

Stokes, M. & R. Halpern (eds). *Race and class in the American South since 1890* (Oxford: Berg, 1994).

Street, J. *Rebel rock: the politics of popular music* (Oxford: Blackwell, 1986).

Stuckey, S. *Slave culture: nationalist theory and the foundations of black America* (New York: Oxford University Press, 1987).

Sullivan, P. *Days of hope: race and democracy in the New Deal era* (Chapel Hill: University of North Carolina Press, 1996).

Taggert, R. *Still a dream: the changing status of blacks* (Cambridge, Mass.: Harvard University Press, 1975).

Taraborelli, J.R. *Motown: hot wax, city soul and solid gold* (New York: Doubleday, 1986).

Taraborelli, J.R. *Michael Jackson: the magic and the madness* (New York: Birch Lane, 1991).

Tate, G. *Fly boy in the buttermilk* (New York: Fireside, 1992).

Taylor, R.P. *The death and resurrection show* (London: A. Blond, 1985).

Thompson, D.C. *Sociology of the black experience* (Westport, Conn.: Greenwood, 1974).

Tinney, J.S. & J. Rector (eds). *Issues and trends in Afro-American journalism* (Lanham, Md.: University Press of America, 1980).

Titon, J.T. *Downhome blues lyrics: an anthology from the post-World War II era* (Boston: Twayne, 1981).

Toll, R.C. *Blacking-up: the minstrel show in nineteenth-century America* (New York: Oxford University Press, 1974).

Toop, D. *The rap attack: African jive to New York hip-hop* (London: Pluto, 1984).

Tosches, N. *Hellfire: the Jerry Lee Lewis story* (London: Plexus, 1982).

Tosches, N. *Unsung heroes of rock and roll* (New York: C. Scribner, 1984).

Tucker, D.M. *Memphis since Crump* (Knoxville: University of Tennessee Press, 1980).

Turner, T. (with K. Loder). *I, Tina* (London: Penguin, 1987).

Tushnet, M. *The NAACP's campaign against segregated education, 1925–1950* (Chapel Hill: University of North Carolina Press, 1987).

Van DeBurg, W. *New day in Babylon: the black power movement and American culture* (Chicago: University of Chicago Press, 1992).

Vincent, R. *Funk: the music, the people, and the rhythm of the one* (New York: St Martin's, 1996).

Vincent, T. *Keep cool: the black activists who built the jazz age* (London: Pluto, 1995).

Wade, W.C. *The fiery cross: the Ku Klux Klan in America* (New York: Touchstone, 1988).

Wallace, M. *Black macho and the myth of the superwoman* (London: J. Calder/Platform, 1979).

Ward, B. & T. Badger (eds). *The making of Martin Luther King and the civil rights movement* (New York: New York University Press, 1996).

Washington, J.M. (ed.). *A testament of hope: the essential writings and speeches of Martin Luther King, Jr* (San Francisco: Harper & Row, 1986).

Washington, J.R. Jr, *Black religion* (Lanham, Md.: University Press of America, 1984).

Waters, J. *Crackpot: the obsessions of John Waters* (New York: Macmillan, 1986).

Weisbrot, R. *Freedom bound: a history of America's civil rights movement* (New York: Plume, 1990).

West, C. *Prophesy and deliverance: an Afro-American revolutionary Christianity* (Philadelphia: Westminster, 1982).

West, C. *Prophetic fragments* (Grand Rapids, Mich.: Wm Eerdmans, 1988).

West, C. *Race matters* (New York: Vintage, 1994).

Wexler, J. & D. Ritz. *The rhythm and the blues: a life in American music* (New York: A. Knopf, 1993).

Whitburn, J. *Top rhythm and blues records, 1949–1971* (Menomonee Falls: Record Research, 1973).

Whitburn, J. *Billboard book of US top forty hits, 1955 to present* (New York: Billboard, 1983).

White, A. *The resistance: ten years of pop culture that shook the world* (New York: Overlook, 1995).

White, C. *The life and times of Little Richard* (London: Pan, 1985).

White, C. et al. *Star time* (n.p.: Poly Gram Records, 1991).

White, D. *Ar'n't I a woman* (New York: Norton, 1985).

Whitfield, S.J. *A death in the Delta: the story of Emmett Till* (New York: Free Press, 1988).

Who's who in the southwest, 1965–66 (Chicago: Marquis, 1965).

Whyte, W.F. *Street corner society* (Chicago: Chicago University Press, 1943).

Willhoit, F.M. *The politics of massive resistance* (New York: G. Braziller, 1973).

Wilkins, R. (with T. Matthews). *Standing fast* (New York: Viking, 1982).

Williams, J. (ed.). *Eyes on the prize: America's civil rights years, 1954–1965* (New York: Viking, 1987).

Williams, O. (with P. Romanowski). *Temptations* (New York: Putnam, 1988).

Williamson, J. *A rage for order: black-white relations in the American South since emancipation* (New York: Oxford University Press, 1986).

Willis, P. *Profane culture* (London: Routledge, 1978).

Wilmore, G.S. *Black religion and black radicalism* (New York: Doubleday, 1973).

Wilson, M. (with P. Romanowski & A. Juillard). *Dreamgirl: my life as a Supreme* (London: Sidgwick & Jackson, 1987).

Wolff, D. et al. *You send me: the life and times of Sam Cooke* (New York: Wm Morrow, 1995).

Woodward, C.Vann. *The strange career of Jim Crow* (Oxford: Galaxy, 1957).

Wright, R. *Black boy* (New York: Harper & Row, 1966).

Wuthnow, R. (ed.). *The religious dimension: new directions in quantative research* (New York: Academic, 1979).

Zinn, H. *The southern mystique* (New York: A. Knopf, 1964).

Articles

Abarbanel, A. & A. Haley. New audience for radio. *Harper's Magazine* (February 1956), pp. 57–9.

Alexis, M. Patterns of black consumption, 1935–1960. *Journal of Black Studies* 1(1), pp. 55–67, September 1970.

Badger, T. Segregation and the southern business elite. *Journal of American Studies* 18, pp. 105–9, 1984.

Badger, T. Fatalism not gradualism: the crisis of southern liberalism, 1945–1965. In *The making of Martin Luther King and the civil rights movement*, B. Ward & T. Badger (eds) (New York: New York University Press, 1996), pp. 67–95.

Bailin, F. Herald-Ember. *Bim Bam Boom* 1(6), pp. 24–7, 1972.

Bell, D. Interpretations of American politics. In *The radical right*, D. Bell (ed.) (New York: Anchor, 1964), pp. 63–4.

Bergesen, A. Spirituals, jazz, blues and soul music: the role of elaborated and restricted codes in the maintenance of social solidarity. In *The religious dimension: new directions in quantative research*, R. Wuthnow (ed.) (New York: Academic, 1979), pp. 333–50.

Berkman, D. The segregated medium. *Columbia Journalism Review* 5(30), pp. 29–32, Fall 1966.

Bim Bam Boom. The Fortune story. 1(5), pp. 20–2, 1972.

Black Radio Exclusive. WERD: the first black-owned radio station in the USA. 15 June 1979, pp. 12–13.

Blair, M.E. Commercialization of the rap music youth subculture. *Journal of Popular Culture* 27(3), pp. 21–34, Winter 1993.

Blassingame, J.W. The revolution that never was: the civil rights movement, 1950–1980. *Perspectives: U.S. commission on civil rights* 14(2), pp. 3–15, Summer 1982.

Bock, W.E. The decline of the negro clergy. *Phylon* 29, pp. 48–64, Spring 1968.

Bogart, L. Negro and white media exposure: new evidence. *Journalism Quarterly* 49, pp. 15–21, Spring 1972.

Bogart, L. Black is often white. *Mediascope* 3(11), pp. 53–60, November 1978.

Bond, J. Ray Charles – the bishop of Atlanta. In *Sweet soul music: rhythm and blues and the southern dream of freedom*, P. Guralnick (London: Virgin, 1986), p. 50.

Bond, J. The politics of civil rights history. In *New directions in civil rights studies*, A.L. Robinson & P. Sullivan (eds) (Charlottesville: University Press of Virginia, 1991), pp. 8–16.

Bradby, B. Do talk and don't talk: the division of the subject in girl group music. In *On the record*, S. Frith & A. Goodwin (eds) (London: Routledge, 1990), pp. 341–68.

Broadcasting Telecasting. ASCAP's war on BMI. 9 September 1957, pp. 4–6/60–1.

Broven, J. Harold Battiste: All for One. *Blues Unlimited* 46, pp. 4–15, 1984.

Carby, H. It jus be's dat way sometime: the sexual politics of women's blues. *Radical America* 20(4), pp. 9–22, 1987.

Carson, C. Black political thought in the post-revolutionary era. In *The making of Martin Luther King and the civil rights movement*, B. Ward & T. Badger (eds) (New York: New York University Press, 1996), pp. 115–27.

Cater, D. Civil war in Alabama's citizens' councils. *The Reporter*, 17 May 1956, pp. 19–21.

Chaney, P. The Cardinals. *Yesterday's Memories* 4(4), pp. 18–22, 1975.

Chaney, P. The Honey Boys. *Yesterday's Memories* 4(8), p. 13, 1976.

Chester, A. For a rock aesthetic. *New Left Review* 59, pp. 87–94, 1970.

Chiltern, J. Liner notes. *Roy Eldridge: The Early Years*, CBS 88585 (1982).

Cleghorn, R. The angels are white: who pays the bills for civil rights. *New Republic*, 17 August 1963, pp. 12–14.

Collins, L. Black radio conference. *Sepia* (January 1979), pp. 58–62.

Cooper, B.L. Popular music: an untapped resource for teaching contemporary black history. *Journal of Negro Education* **48**, pp. 20–36, Winter 1979.

Cox, H. & S. West. The heart and soul of the Cleftones. *Goldmine*, 21 February 1992, p. 16/18/20/150.

Crawford, D. Gospel songs in court: from rural music to urban industry in the 1950s. *Journal of Popular Culture* **11**, pp. 551–67, 1977.

Cruse, T. Sly Stone: the struggle for his soul. In *What's that sound?: the contemporary music scene from the pages of Rolling Stone*, B. Fong-Torres (ed.) (New York: Anchor, 1976), pp. 289–303.

Cummings, T. An English way to Marvin Gaye. *Black Music* (December 1976), pp. 10–16, 52–3.

Dahl, B. Solomon Burke: the bishop of soul. *Goldmine*, 16 September 1994, pp. 42/44/46/48/50/51/194.

Davis, A.Y. Black nationalism: the sixties and the nineties. In *Black popular culture: a project by Michele Wallace*, G. Dent (ed.) (Seattle: Bay, 1992), pp. 317–24.

Dawson, J. Liner notes. *Jesse Belvin Memorial Album*, Ace CH90 (1984).

Dawson, J. Jesse Belvin. *Goldmine*, 5 December 1986, pp. 12, 16–17.

Dawson, J. & S. Brigati. Liner notes. *Lost Dreams: the New Orleans vocal groups*, Stateside 6042 (1987).

Denisoff, R.S. Protest songs: those on the top forty and those on the street. *American Quarterly* **22**, pp. 807–23, Winter 1970.

Denisoff, R.S. The vinyl crap game: the pop record industry. *Journal of Jazz Studies* **1**(2), pp. 3–26, June 1974.

Denizen, N.K. Problems in analyzing elements of mass culture: notes on the popular songs and other artistic productions. *American Journal of Sociology* **75**, pp. 1035–40, 1970.

DeSiWa, E.E. The theology of black power and black song: James Brown. *Black Sacred Music: a Journal of Theomusicology* **3**(2), pp. 57–67, Fall 1989.

Dill, B.T. The dialectics of womanhood. *Signs* **4**(3), pp. 543–55, 1979.

Dyer, R. In defense of disco. In *On the record*, S. Frith & A. Goodwin (eds) (London: Routledge, 1990), pp. 410–18.

Edet, E.M. One hundred years of black protest music. *Black Scholar* (July 1976), pp. 38–48.

Erlich, D. James Brown interview. *Details* (July 1991), p. 56.

Fairclough, A. The Southern Christian Leadership Conference and the second reconstruction. *South Atlantic Quarterly* **80**, pp. 177–94, Spring 1981.

Fairclough, A. The preachers and the people: the origins and early years of the Southern Christian Leadership Conference, 1955–1959. *Journal of Southern History* **52**, pp. 403–40, August 1986.

Farley, R. The urbanization of Negroes in the United States. *Journal of Social History* **1**, pp. 241–58, 1968.

Farmer, J. The march on Washington: the zenith of the southern movement. *New directions in civil rights studies*, A.L. Robinson & P. Sullivan (eds) (Charlottesville: University Press of Virginia, 1991), pp. 30–7.

Ferretti, F. The white captivity of black radio. *Columbia Journalism Review*, pp. 35–9, Summer 1970.

Fileti, D. Liner notes. *The Best of Celeste*, Relic 5014 (n.d.).

Fileti, D. Liner notes. *The Best of Flash*, Relic 5049 (n.d.).

Fileti, D. Liner notes. *The Best of Onyx Records*, Relic 5005 (n.d.).

Fileti, D. Liner notes. *The Detroit Girl Groups*, Relic 8004 (n.d.).

Fishkin, S.F. Interrogating "whiteness", complicating "blackness": remapping American culture. *American Quarterly* **47**(3), pp. 428–66, September 1995.

Fitzgerald, F.S. Echoes of the jazz age. In *The Crack-up* (London: Penguin, 1983), pp. 9–19.

Fitzgerald, J. Motown crossover hits 1963–1966 and the creative process. *Popular Music* **14**, pp. 1–11, 1995.

Flam, S. The Vee Jay story. *Bim Bam Boom* **1**(4), pp. 18–19, 1972.

Floyd, B. Crickets appearance at the Apollo. *Reminiscing Magazine* (Fall 1983), p. 18.

Freudiger, P. & E.M. Almquist. Male and female roles in the lyrics of three genres of contemporary music. *Sex Roles* **41**, pp. 51–65, 1978.

Frith, S. You can make it if you try. In *The soul book*, I. Hoare (ed.) (London: Eyre Methuen, 1975), pp. 32–59.

Frith, S. Introduction. In *Pop goes the culture*, C. McGregor (London: Pluto, 1984), pp. 1–8.

Frith, S. Towards an aesthetics of popular music. In *Music and society: the politics of composition, performance and reception*, R. Leppert & S. McClary (eds) (Cambridge: Cambridge University Press, 1987).

Frith, S. & A. McRobbie. Rock and sexuality. In *On the record*, S. Frith & A. Goodwin (eds) (London: Routledge, 1990), pp. 371–89.

Funk, R. Liner notes. *Atlanta Gospel*, Gospel Heritage HT312 (1986).

Gates, H.L. Jr. Belafonte's balancing act. *New Yorker*, pp. 132–43, 26 August/2 September 1996.

Garvey, D. The Bobbettes. *Goldmine*, 21 February 1992, pp. 22, 24, 30, 106.

Gilmore, A.T. The black southerners' response to the southern system of race relations: 1900 to post-World War II. In *The age of segregation: race relations in the South, 1890–1945*, R. Haws (ed.) (Jackson: University of Mississippi Press, 1987), pp. 67–88.

Giovanni, N. Beautiful black men. In *Black poets*, D. Randall (ed.) (New York: Bantam, 1981), pp. 320–1.

Glasser, G.J. & G.D. Metzger. Radio usage by blacks. *Journal of Advertising Research*, pp. 39–45, October 1975.

Gleason, R. Like a Rolling Stone. In *The age of rock: sounds of the American cultural revolution*, J. Eisen (ed.) (New York: Random House, 1969), pp. 61–76.

Glenn, N.D. and E. Gotard. The religion of blacks in the United States: some recent trends and current characteristics. *American Journal of Sociology* **83**, pp. 433–51, 1977.

Goldberg, M. The Plants. *Yesterday's Memories* **4**(8), p. 17, 1976.

Goldberg, M. & M. Redmond. The Drifters. *Record Exchanger* **4**(2), pp. 4–25, 1974.

Goldberg, M. and M. Redmond. The Five Blue Notes. *Yesterday's Memories* **4**(4), pp. 15–16, 1975.

Goldberg, M. & M. Redmond. The Swallows. *Yesterday's Memories*, **4**(4), pp. 10–14, 1975.

Goode, M. Liner notes. *The Cadillacs meet the Orioles*, Jubilee 1117 (n.d.).

Goode, M. Liner notes. *The Paragons meet the Jesters*, Jubilee JGM 1098 (1957).

Graves, C. The right to be served: Oklahoma's lunch counter sit-ins, 1958–1964. In *We shall overcome: the civil rights movement in the US in the 1950s and 1960s*, vol. 1, D.J. Garrow (ed.) (New York: Carlson, 1989), pp. 283–98.

Groia, P. & M. Goldberg. Liner notes. *The Best of the Valentines*, Murray Hill 000202 (1986).

Guralnick, P. Liner notes. *Solomon Burke, Soul Alive!*, Demon 38 (1983).

Hammill, K. The record business – it's murder. *Fortune* (May 1961), pp. 148–50.

Hamilton, C. Blacks and mass media. *Columbia Forum*, (Winter 1971). In *Issues and trends in Afro-American Journalism*. J.S. Tinney & J. Rector (eds) (Lanham, Md.: University Press of America, 1980), pp. 225–31.

Hannerz, U. Lower-class black culture. In *Soul*, L. Rainwater (ed.) (n.p.: Transaction, 1970), pp. 15–30.

Harries, J. Negro teenage culture. *Annals of the American Academy of Political and Social Science* **338**, pp. 91–101, November 1961.

Hay, F. The sacred profane dialect in delta blues: the life and lyrics of Sonny Boy Williamson. *Phylon* **48**, pp. 317–27, Winter 1987.

Henderson, A.B. Heman E. Perry and black enterprise in Atlanta, 1908–1925. *Business History Review*, pp. 216–42, Summer 1987.

Henderson, D. Boston road blues. In *Black fire*, L. Jones & L. Neal (eds) (New York: Wm Morrow, 1968), pp. 233–38.

Henderson, E.A. Black nationalism and rap music. *Journal of Black Studies* **26**(3), pp. 308–39, January 1996.

Hey, K. "I'll give it a 95": an approach to the study of early rock 'n' roll. *Popular Music and Society* **3**, pp. 315–23, 1974.

Higginbotham, E.B. Beyond the sound of silence: Afro-American women in history. *Gender and History* **1**(1), pp. 50–67, Spring 1989.

Hoare, I. Mighty, mighty spade and whitey: black lyrics and soul's interaction with white culture. In *The soul book*, I. Hoare (ed.) (London: Eyre Methuen, 1975), pp. 117–68.

Horton, D. The dialogue of courtship in popular songs. *American Journal of Sociology* **62**, pp. 569–78, May 1957.

Hughes, W. In the empire of the beat: discipline and disco. In *Microphone fiends: youth music and youth culture*, A. Ross & T. Rose (eds) (New York: Routledge, 1994), pp. 147–58.

Jackson, J. Introduction. *Wattstax: The Living Word*, Stax STS-2-3010, 1972.

Jacobi, J. Symbols in an individual analysis. In *Man and his symbols*, C.G. Jung & M.L. von Franz (eds) (London: Aldus, 1964), pp. 272–303.

Jones, F.C. External crosscurrents and internal diversity: an assessment of black progress, 1960–1980. *Daedalus*, pp. 71–101, Spring 1981.

Joyner, C. African and European roots of southern culture: the "central theme" revisited. In *Dixie debates: perspectives on southern cultures*, R.H. King & H. Taylor (eds) (London: Pluto, 1996), pp. 12–30.

Kahlenberg, R.S. Negro radio. *Negro History Bulletin* (March 1966), pp. 127–8/142–3.

Kamin, J. Taking the roll out of rock 'n' roll: reverse acculturation. *Popular Music and Society* **2**, pp. 1–17, 1972.

Kamin, J. Parallels in the social reaction to jazz and rock. *Journal of Jazz Studies* **2**, pp. 95–125, 1974.

Kamin, J. Musical culture and perceptual learning in the popularization of black music. *Journal of Jazz Studies* **3**, pp. 54–65, 1975.

Kamin, J. The white r&b audience and the music industry, 1952–1956. *Popular Music and Society* **6**, pp. 150–67, 1978.

Kelley, R.D.G. "We are not what we seem": rethinking black working-class opposition in the Jim Crow South. *Journal of American History* **80**, pp. 75–112, 1993.

Kelly, P. Papa takes some mess. *Crawdaddy* (December 1975), pp. 44–52.

Kempton, M. Gloria, Gloria. *New Republic*, 16 November 1963, pp. 15–17.

Kimberley, N. Paranoid sex in 60s soul. *Collusion* **2**, pp. 9–11, February–April 1982.

King, M.L. Jr. Letter from Birmingham city jail. In *A testament of hope: the essential writings and speeches of Martin Luther King, Jr*, J.M. Washington (ed.) (San Francisco: Harper & Row, 1986), pp. 289–302.

King, M.L. Jr. Transforming a neighborhood into a brotherhood. *Jack the Rapper* **13**(666), p. 1, January 1989.

King, R.H. Citizenship and self-respect: the experience of politics in the civil rights movement. *Journal of American Studies* **22**, pp. 7–24, April 1988.

King, R.H. Politics and fictional representation: the case of the civil rights movement. In *The making of Martin Luther King and the civil rights movement*, B. Ward & T. Badger (eds) (New York: New York University Press, 1996), pp. 162–78.

King W. Jr. Searching for the brothers kindred: rhythm and blues of the 1950s. *Black Scholar* (November 1974), pp. 19–30.

Kloosterman, R. & C. Quispel. Not just the same old show on my radio: an analysis of the role of radio in the diffusion of black music among whites in the south of the United States, 1920 to 1960. *Popular Music* **9**, pp. 151–64, 1990.

Kofsky, F. The jazz tradition: black music and its white critics. *Journal of Black Studies* **1**, pp. 403–33, 1971.

Landau, J. A whiter shade of black. In *The age of rock*, J. Eisen (ed.) (New York: Random House, 1969), pp. 298–306.

Lash, J.S. The Negro and radio. *Opportunity* (October 1943), repr. in *Issues and trends in Afro-American Journalism*, J.S. Tinney & J. Rector (eds) (Lanham, Md.: University Press of America, 1980), pp. 167–82.

Lears, T.J. A matter of taste: corporate cultural hegemony in a mass consumption society. In *Recasting America*, L. May (ed.) (Chicago: University of Chicago Press, 1989), pp. 38–57.

Lerner, G. Placing women in history: definitions and challenges. *Feminist Studies* **3**(1/2), pp. 5–14, Fall 1975.

Lewis, D.K. A response to inequality: black women, racism and sexism. *Signs* **3**, pp. 339–61, 1977.

Lewis, G. Social protest and self-awareness in black popular music. *Popular Music and Society* **2**, pp. 327–33, 1973.

Lewis, G. Between consciousness and existence: popular culture and the sociological imagination. *Journal of Popular Culture* **15**(4), pp. 81–92, 1982.

Lewis, L. Harlem's biggest business. *Sepia* (August 1978), pp. 33–5.

Lipsitz, G. Land of a thousand dances. In *Recasting America*, L. May (ed.) (Chicago: University of Chicago Press, 1989), pp. 267–84.

Mabry, D. The rise and fall of Ace Records: a case study in the independent record business. *Business History Review* **64**, pp. 411–50, Autumn 1990.

Mailer, N. The white Negro. In *Advertisements for myself* (New York: Putnam, 1959), pp. 337–58.

Malcolm X. The ballot or the bullet. *The ballot or the bullet*, Paul Winley Records LP135, n.d.

Marx, G.T. Religion: opiate or inspiration of civil rights militancy among negroes? *American Sociological Review* **32**, pp. 64–72, 1967.

Maultsby, P. Soul music: its sociological and political significance in American popular culture. *Journal of Popular Culture* **17**(2), pp. 51–60, 1984.

Maultsby, P. Beginnings of a black music industry. In *Who's who in black music*, R.E. Rosenthal & P. Maultsby (eds) (New Orleans: Edwards Printing, 1985), pp. vii–xv.

McClary, S. Same as it ever was: youth, culture and music. In *Microphone fiends: youth and youth culture*, A. Ross & T. Rose (eds) (New York: Routledge, 1994), pp. 29–40.

McGrath, T. Soul Survivors. *Seven Arts*, pp. 41–2, October 1995.

Means, R.L. and B. Dolema. Notes on Negro jazz, 1920–1950. *Sociological Quarterly* **9**, pp. 332–42, Summer 1968.

Merton, R.K. Social structure and anomie. *American Sociological Review* **3**, pp. 672–82, 1938.

Miller, K.D. & E.M. Lewis. Touchstones, authorities and Marian Anderson: the making of "I have a dream". In *The making of Martin Luther King and the civil rights movement*, B. Ward & T. Badger (eds) (New York: New York University Press, 1996), pp. 147–61.

Miller, W.B. Lower class culture as a generating milieu of gang delinquency. *Journal of Social Issues* **14**(3), pp. 5–19, 1958.

Miner, R. Black magic, black art, *Negro Digest* **16**, pp. 9–12, 1967.

Mooney, H.F. Popular music since the 1920s: the significance of shifting taste. *American Quarterly* **20**, pp. 67–84, Spring 1968.

Mooney, H.F. Just before rock: pop music 1950–1955 reconsidered. *Popular Music and Society* **3**, pp. 65–108, 1974.

Moonogian, G. Oh that Annie, *Record Exchanger* **1**, pp. 20–1, 1977.

Myrick-Harris, C. Behind the scenes: Doris Derby, Denise Nicholas and the free southern theater. In *Women in the civil rights movement*, V.L. Crawford et al. (eds) (New York: Carlson, 1990), pp. 219–32.

Neal, L. The black arts movement. *Drama Review* **12**, pp. 29–40, Summer 1968.

Neal, L. Black art and black liberation. In *The black revolution: an Ebony special issue* (Chicago: Johnson, 1970), pp. 31–53.

Neal, L. The ethos of the blues. *Black Scholar*, pp. 42–8, Summer 1972.

Neal, L. The social background to the black arts movement. *Black Scholar* **18**(1), p. 19, 1987.

Nelsen, H.M., T.W. Raytha & M. Yokley. Black religion's Promethean motif: orthodox and militancy. *American Journal of Sociology* **81**, pp. 139–48, 1975.

Obatala, J.K. Soul music in Africa: has Charlie got a brand new bag? *Black Scholar* **2**(6), pp. 8–12, 1971.

O'Connor, D. & G. Cook. Black radio: the "soul" sellout. In *Issues and trends in Afro-American Journalism*, J.S. Tinney & J. Rector (eds) (Lanham, Md.: University Press of America, 1980), pp. 233–46.

Oliver, P. Crossroads blues. *Jazz Beat* (February 1965), pp. 20–1.

Peterson, R.A. Cycles in symbol production: the case of popular music. *American Sociological Review* **40**, pp. 158–73, 1975.

Peterson, R.A. Why 1955?: explaining the advent of rock music. *Popular Music* **9**, pp. 97–116, 1990.

Phillips, J.E. The African heritage of white America. In *Africanisms*, J. Holloway (ed.) (Bloomington: University of Indiana Press, 1990), pp. 225–39.

Podhoretz, N. My Negro problem – and ours. *Commentary* (February 1963), pp. 93–101.

Portis, L. The cultural dialectics of the blues. *Canadian Journal of Political and Social Theory* **9**(3), pp. 23–36, Fall 1985.

Powdermaker, H. The channeling of Negro aggression by the cultural process. *American Journal of Sociology* **48**, pp. 750–8, 1943.

Propes, S. The Chords. *Goldmine*, 19 June 1987, p. 6.

Reilly, A. The impact of technology on rhythm and blues. *Black Perspectives in Music* **6**, pp. 138–46, 1973.

Reynaud, C. Legislation affecting segregation. *Louisiana Law Review* **17**, pp. 101–22, December 1956–June 1957.

Robinson, B. Bobby Robinson: king of the New York sound. *Record Exchanger* **2**(5), pp. 5–6/8–10, 1972.

Rosenthal, D. Jazz in the ghetto: 1950–1970. *Popular Music* **7**(1), pp. 51–6, January 1988.

Rubin, A.S. Reflections on the death of Emmett Till. *Southern Cultures* **2**(1), pp. 45–66, Fall 1995.

Rumble, J.W. Roots of rock & roll: Henry Glover at King records. *Journal of Country Music* **14**(2), pp. 30–42, 1992.

Runcie, J. The black culture movement and the black community. *Journal of American Studies* **10**, pp. 185–214, 1976.

Smith, S.A. & J.N. Rogers. Saturday night in country music: the gospel according to juke. *Southern Cultures* **1**, pp. 229–44, Winter 1995.

Snellings, R. Keep on pushin'. *Liberator* **5**, pp. 6–8, October 1966.

Soley, L. & G. Hough. Black ownership of commercial radio stations: an economic evaluation. *Journal of Broadcasting* **22**, pp. 455–67, Fall 1978.

Spellman, A.B. Not just whistling Dixie. In *Black fire*, L. Jones (I.A. Baraka) & L. Neal (eds) (New York: Wm Morrow, 1968), pp. 27–32.

Stephens, R. Soul: a historical reconstruction of continuity and change in black popular music. *Black Perspectives in Music* **12**(1), pp. 21–43, Spring 1984.

Stewart, J.B. Perspectives on black families from contemporary soul music: the case of Millie Jackson. *Phylon* **41**, pp. 55–7, 1980.

Stewart, J.B. Relationships between black males and females in rhythm and blues music of the 1960s and 1970s. In *More than dancing: essays on Afro-American music and musicians*, I.V. Jackson (ed.) (Westport, Conn.: Greenwood, 1985), pp. 169–86.

Stewart, J.T. The development of the revolutionary black artist. In *Black fire*, L. Jones (I.A. Baraka) and L. Neal (eds) (New York: Wm Morrow, 1968), pp. 3–9.

Surlin, S. Black-oriented radio: programming to a perceived audience. *Journal of Broadcasting* **16**, pp. 289–98, Summer 1972.

Surlin, S. Ascertainment of community needs by black-oriented radio stations. *Journal of Broadcasting* **16**, pp. 421–9, Fall 1972.

Surlin, S. Broadcasters' misconceptions of black community needs. *Journal of Black Studies* **4**, p. 185, December 1973.

Szwed, J.F. Musical style and racial conflict. *Phylon* **27**, pp. 358–66, Winter 1966.

Tagg, P. Open letter: 'black music', 'Afro-American music' and 'European music'. *Popular Music* **8**, pp. 285–98, October 1989.

Taylor, J.E. Somethin' on my mind: a cultural and historical interpretation of spiritual texts. *Ethnomusicology* **29**(3), pp. 387–99, September 1975.

Tucker, B. Living metaphors: recent black music biography. *Black Music Research Journal* **43**, pp. 58–69, 1983.

Virginia Law Review. King v Mr Maestro, inc. **50**, p. 940, 1964.

Ward, B. Racial politics, culture and the Cole incident of 1956. In *Race and class in the American South since 1890*, M. Stokes & R. Halpern (eds) (Oxford: Berg, 1994), pp. 181–208.

Ward, B. & J. Walker. "Bringing the races closer"?: black-oriented radio in the South and the civil rights movement. In *Dixie debates: perspectives on southern cultures*, R.H. King & H. Taylor (eds) (London: Pluto, 1996), pp. 130–49.

Watkins, M. The lyrics of James Brown. *Amistad* **2**, pp. 22–8, 1971.

Weinger, H. The Platters' glory days. *Goldmine*, 21 February 1992, pp. 10–15, 104.

West, C. The dilemma of the black intellectual. *Cultural Critique* **1**, pp. 109–24, 1985.

West, C. On Manning Marable's "How black capitalism underdeveloped black America". In *Prophetic fragments* (Grand Rapids, Mich.: Wm Eerdmans, 1988), pp. 65–6.

Wexler, J. Liner notes. *The RCA-Victor Blues and Rhythm Revue*, RCA PL86279(2) (1987).

White, C. Liner notes. Solomon Burke, *Cry To Me*, Charly CRB 1075 (1984).

White, C. Liner notes. *Roots of a Revolution*, Polydor, REVO 1 (1986).

White, C. & H. Weinger. Are you ready for star time? In *Star time*, C. White et al. (eds) (n.p.: Poly Gram Records, 1991), pp. 14–45.

White, J. Veiled testimony: negro spirituals and the slave experience. *Journal of American Studies* **17**, pp. 251–63, 1984.

White, M.B. "The blues ain't nothin' but a woman want to be a man": male control in early twentieth century blues music. *Canadian Review of American Studies* **24**, pp. 19–40, Winter 1994.

Wills, G. The phallic pulput. *New York Review of Books*, 21 December 1989, p. 20.

Wilson, O. The association of movement and music as a manifestation of a black conceptual approach to music making. In *More than dancing: essays on Afro-American music and musicians*, I.V. Jackson (ed.) (Westport, Conn.: Greenwood, 1985), pp. 9–17.

Winley, P. (with P. Groia). The Paul Winley story. *Bim Bam Boom* **3**(9), pp. 30–1/52, 1973.

Yesterday's Memories. Baltimore/Washington, D.C. special. **4**(4), 1975.

Yesterday's Memories. Baltimore/Washington, D.C. special. **4**(8), 1976.

Zucker, M. The saga of Lovin' Dan: a study in the iconography of rhythm & blues music of the 1950s. *Journal of Popular Culture* **16**(2), pp. 43–51, Fall 1982.

Unpublished papers and dissertations

Blackwell, G. *Black-controlled media in Atlanta, 1960–70: the burden of the message and the struggle for survival* (PhD thesis, Emory University, 1973).

Boyd, T.E. *It's a black thang: the articulation of African-American cultural discourse* (PhD thesis, University of Iowa, 1991).

Corley, R. *The quest for racial harmony: race relations in Birmingham, Alabama, 1947–1963* (PhD thesis, University of Virginia, 1979).

Cruz, J.D. *The politics of popular culture: black popular music as "public sphere"* (PhD thesis, University of California, Berkeley, 1986).

Edmerson, E. *A descriptive history of the American Negro in United States professional radio, 1922–1953* (Masters thesis, University of California, Los Angeles, 1954).

Ellis, D.M. "Communications at the crossroads: parity and perceptions of minority participation". Unpublished paper (Washington, D.C.: National Association of Broadcasters, 1987).

Goosman, S.L. *The social and cultural organization of black group vocal harmony in Washington, D.C. and Baltimore, Maryland, 1945–1960* (PhD thesis, University of Washington, 1992).

Harris, J.T. *Alabama's response to the Brown decision, 1954–56: a study in early massive resistance* (Doctor of Arts thesis, Middle Tennessee State University, 1978).

Hutchinson, J.A. "Black culture and consciousness as revealed in a contents analysis of *Tan*, 1953–1962" (Masters essay, Department of History, University of Newcastle upon Tyne, 1996).

Labowitz, A. *Negro-orientated radio in Michigan, 1969–70* (PhD thesis, Michigan State University, 1970).

Murdoch, C. *Negro radio broadcasting in the United States* (Masters thesis, University of Wisconsin, 1970).

National Association of Broadcasters. "Minority broadcasting facts". Unpublished paper (Washington D.C., 1986).

Ortizano, G.L. *On your radio: a descriptive history of rhythm-and-blues radio during the 1950s* (PhD thesis, Ohio State University, 1993).

Reagon, B. Johnson. *Songs of the civil rights movement, 1955–1965: a study in culture history* (PhD thesis, Howard University, 1975).

Spaulding, N. *The history of black-oriented radio in Chicago, 1923–1963* (PhD thesis, University of Illinois at Urbana-Champaign, 1981).

Tyson, T. *Radio Free Dixie: Robert F. Williams and the roots of black power* (PhD thesis, Duke University, 1994).

Walsh, S. "Black-oriented radio and the southern civil rights movement, 1955–1972". Unpublished paper presented at Southern Historical Association Conference, New Orleans, November 1995.

Ward, B. *Race Relations, Civil rights and the transformation from rhythm and blues to soul, 1954–1965* (PhD thesis, University of Cambridge, 1995).

Permissions

Every effort has been made to locate current copyright holders of material either reproduced or quoted in this book. Please send any information regarding copyrighted material to the publisher.

Song permissions

"Wise man blues", John "Shifty" Henry. © Paul Reiner Music.

"Furry's Blues", Furry Lewis.

"Adam, come and get your rib", Weismantel and Henry Glover. © Jay & Cee Music.

"Lovin' machine", Merritt and Lambert. © Rockaway Music

"Money honey" words and music by Jesse Stone. © 1997 Walden/Mijac Music (50% USA/Canada) Warner/Chappell Music Ltd. London W1Y 3FA. Reproduced by permission of International Music Publications Ltd.

"Get a job", The Silhouettes. © Ulysses & Bagby Music/Wildcat Music.

"Cotton picking hands", R. Durand. © SBK United Partnership.

"I'm telling you", Jerry Butler and Curtis Mayfield. © Conrad Music.

"Gotta get a job", Allen Toussaint. © Marsaint Music, Inc.

"Working in a coalmine", Allen Toussaint. © Marsaint Music, Inc.

"Rip it up", Otis Blackwell and John S. Marscalco. © Sony/ATV Music Publishing.

"Another Saturday night", Sam Cooke. © ABKCO Music Inc.

"School days", Chuck Berry. © Jewel Music.

"Star revue", Warren Lee & Allen Toussaint. © Marsaint Music, Inc.

"Temptation was too strong", Don Covay. © Warner Bros. Music Ltd.

"All around the world", Little Willie John (original lyrics by Titus Turner).

"Kansas City", Jerry Leiber and Mike Stoller. © Carlin Music.

"Promised land", Chuck Berry. © Tristan Music.

"Uptown", Cynthia Weil and Barry Mann. © Screen Gems-EMI Music Inc.

"On Broadway", words and music by Mike Stoller/Jerry Leiber/Cynthia Weil/Barry Mann. © 1963 Screen Gems-EMI Music Inc. USA Screen Gems-EMI Music Ltd, London WC2H 0EA. Reproduced by permission of IMP Ltd.

"Back street", R. Hatcher and W. Sharpley. © Jobete Music Co Inc.

"A quiet place", Bell and Meade. © Rittenhouse Music Inc.

"Deep in the heart of Harlem", Jimmy Radcliffe and Carl Spencer. Copyright © 1963 (Renewed) by Embassy Music Corporation (BMI) and Warner Bros. Publications International Copyright Secured. All Rights Reserved. Reprinted by Permission.

"Ubangi stomp", Warren Smith.

"Keep on pushing", Curtis Mayfield. © Warner-Tamerlane Publishing.

"People get ready", Curtis Mayfield. © Warner-Tamerlane Publishing.

"The love you save may be your own", Joe Tex. © Sony/ATV Music Publishing.

"Mississippi Goddam", Nina Simone.

"Oxford town", Bob Dylan. © Kinney Music.

"We got more soul", Arlester Christian. © Drive-In-Music Co Inc.

"Heaven help us all", Ronald N. Miller. © Jobete Music Co Inc.

"Big brother", Stevie Wonder. © Jobete and Black Bull Music Inc.

"Just my soul responding", William Robinson Jr. and Marvin Tarplin. © Jobete Music Co Inc/EMI Music Publishing Ltd.

"A woman can change a man", Joe Tex. © Song/ATV Songs Tree.

"Backstabbers", Leon Huff, G. McFadden and J. Whitehead. © Mighty Three Music/ Carlin Music.

"How come my bulldog don't bark?", Ellison & Bell. © Rittenhouse Music.

"I got caught", Roger Hatcher and Clarence Carter. © CBS Songs.

"Black woman", Don Covay and Spooner Oldham.

"Son of Hickory Holler's tramp", D. Frazier. © Burlington Music.

"Papa was too", Joe Tex. © EMI Music Publishing Ltd.

"Stop half-loving these women", Jimmy Lewis. © Longitude Music Co.

"Real woman", Clarence Henry Reid. © Longitude Music Co.

"Got my mind made up", Instant Funk.

"Blue Monday", words and music by Antonie Domino and David Bartholomew. © 1957 Comodore Music/Warner Chappell Music Ltd, London W6 8BS and © 1957 (Renewed 1985) EMI Unart Catalog Inc. All Rights Reserved. Used by Permission. WARNER BROS. PUBLICATIONS U.S. INC., Miami, FL. 33014.

"Got a job", William Robinson Jr., Berry Gordy, and Tyran Carlo © 1958 Renewed 1986 JOBETE MUSIC CO., INC., TAJ MAHAL MUSIC, and THIRD ABOVE MUSIC All Rights on behalf of JOBETE MUSIC CO., INC. and TAJ MAHAL MUSIC Controlled and Administered by EMI APRIL MUSIC INC. (ASCAP) All Rights Reserved. International Copyright Secured. Used by Permission.

Photograph permissions

The Platters (courtesy of the Michael Ochs Archives/Venice, CA) p. 51.

Little Anthony and the Imperials, c.1958 (courtesy of the Michael Ochs Archives/ Venice, CA) p. 66.

Bo Diddley, November 1964 (courtesy of Ed Roseberry) p. 84.

The Drifters (courtesy of the Michael Ochs Archives/Venice, CA) p. 92.

Sam Cooke (photograph of unknown origin) p. 144.

The Shirelles (courtesy of the Michael Ochs Archives/Venice, CA) p. 156.

Bobby Freeman (courtesy of the Michael Ochs Archives/Venice, CA) p. 166.

Ray Charles (courtesy of the Michael Ochs Archives/Venice, CA) p. 186.

Solomon Burke (© Don Paulsen/Michael Ochs Archives/Venice, CA) p. 200.

Joe Tex and Buddy Killen (courtesy of the Country Music Hall of Fame) p. 223.

Ike Turner (courtesy of Ed Roseberry) p. 230.

Roscoe Shelton (courtesy of Brian Ward) p. 252.

All for One executives (courtesy of Harold Battiste/Tulane University) p. 256.

Elaine Brown album advertisement (from *The Black Panther*, Saturday, November 22, 1969 p. 17) p. 279.

"Tall" Paul White (photograph of unknown origin) p. 286.

James Baldwin, Joan Baez and James Forman (courtesy of the Schomburg Centre for Research in Black Culture/Laurence Henry) p. 307.

Lena Horne (taken from the Daisy Bates Papers, courtesy of the University of Arkansas) p. 312.

Harry Belafonte and Martin Luther King (courtesy of Harry Belafonte) p. 322.

The Temptations (photograph of unknown origin) p. 347.

Martha and the Vandellas, November 1967 (courtesy of Ed Roseberry) p. 361.

Aretha Franklin and Ed Castleberry (from the "photographic collection" at Indiana University Archives of African American Music and Culture/Ed Castleberry) p. 386.

James Brown and Julian Bond (courtesy of James Bond) p. 391.

Isaac Hayes and Jesse Jackson (courtesy of the Michael Ochs Archives/Venice, CA) p. 405.

The Lumpen (from *The Black Panther*, Saturday, December 26, 1970 p. 18) p. 416.

Rufus Thomas and Jondelle Johnson (courtesy of James Bond) p. 438.

O.B. McClinton (courtesy of the Country Music Hall of Fame) p. 441.

Index